W9-ATB-936

The **Rough Guide** to

Hong Kong
& Macau

written and researched by

Jules Brown and David Leffman

NEW YORK • LONDON • DELHI

www.roughguides.com

Contents

◄◄ Incense coils, Nam Mo Temple, Sheung Wan ◄ Boxes on display, Cheung Chau Island

Introduction to Hong Kong & Macau

Set 60km apart from each other across the Pearl River estuary, Hong Kong and Macau offer the visitor an exciting yet easy entry into the Chinese world. Colonies of Britain and Portugal respectively until they were returned to mainland China in the 1990s, today they are seeking to establish fresh identities for themselves under new administrations. While evidence of their colonial eras lingers in buildings, languages and high-tech infrastructure, the essentially Chinese heritage underpinning it all is becoming increasingly apparent.

In **Hong Kong**, the architecture is an engaging mix of styles, from the soaring towers of Central to the ramshackle town-housing and centuries-old Chinese temples; the markets and streetlife are compelling; while the shopping – if no longer the bargain it once was – is eclectic, ranging from open-air stalls to hi-tech malls. Hong Kong is also one of the best places in the world to eat **Chinese food** (and a good many other cuisines besides), while the territory's Western influence has left it a plentiful selection of bars and nightspots. Surprisingly, Hong Kong also boasts some beautiful **countryside**, featuring beaches, rugged hills and wild coastline. If there's a downside to the place, it's that commercialism and consumption tend to dominate life, making it hard to engage with the underlying Chinese culture – though there's a range of well-presented museums and the usual run of cultural events you'd expect to find in any big city.

Smaller and more immediately attractive than its neighbour, **Macau** is one of Asia's most enjoyable spots for a short visit. Chinese life here is tempered by an almost Mediterranean influence, manifest in the ageing Catholic churches, hilltop fortresses and a grand seafront promenade. Like Hong Kong, Macau is ethnically Chinese; but while all the temples and festivals of southern China are reproduced here, they're not the main reason for a visit. Instead, Macau offers alternative attractions, especially **gambling**: this is the only place in the region where casinos are legalized, pulling in swarms of punters from Hong Kong and mainland China. Eating is another highlight: **Macanese food** is an exciting combination of Portuguese colonial cooking, with dishes and ingredients taken from Portugal itself, Goa, Brazil, Africa and China, washed down with cheap, imported Portuguese wine, port and brandy.

▲ Yuen Post Bird Garden, Mongkok

Fact file

- The Special Administrative Region (SAR) of Hong Kong comprises a mainland peninsula and more than 260 islands on the southeastern tip of China, occupying a total **land area** of just under 1100 square kilometres. The region's **population** is approaching seven million, 95 percent of whom are Chinese in origin. Macau, 60km west of Hong Kong, consists of a peninsula and two islands, covering just over 25 square kilometres. Its population is roughly half a million, 96 percent of whom are of Chinese origin.
- Hong Kong's two official **languages** are Cantonese and English: Cantonese is the dominant everyday language, and English is the main business language. Macau's two official languages are Cantonese and Portuguese, although Portuguese is little used.
- The principal **religions** in Hong Kong are Taoism and Buddhism, with Confucianism also having a strong influence. Of the minority religions, 5 percent of the population are Protestant, 4 percent Catholic and 1 percent Muslim.
- Formerly European colonies, Hong Kong and Macau were both returned to Chinese sovereignty during the 1990s and are now **Special Administrative Regions** of China, headed by locally selected chief executives, themselves approved by the mainland Chinese government.

▲ São Domingos, Macau

What to see

Although Hong Kong is fairly compact – it's just 40km from the Chinese border in the north to the south coast of Hong Kong Island – and could be whizzed round in a few days, this small region packs in enough geographical and cultural diversity to fill weeks of exploration. **Hong Kong Island** itself is the heart of the territory, and houses the main business centre, known as **Central** – approaching here by Star Ferry across the harbour is one of the most thrilling city rides in the world. Central is where you'll find some of Hong Kong's most stunning contemporary landmarks, such as the Bank of China, the HSBC building and the IFC2 tower, which dominates the harbourfont skyline. However, traditional Chinese life is never very far away and the neighbouring district of Sheung Wan is thick with Chinese herbalists, raucous markets, smoky temples and narrow lanes, all largely unchanged since colonial times. Everyone should make the effort to visit the 550-metre-high **Victoria Peak**, whose summit gives unsurpassed views – the precipitous tram ride up is another Hong Kong institution. East of Central, the districts of **Wan Chai** and **Causeway Bay** are well known for their shops, restaurants, bars and nightlife. The island's south side is characterized by its bays and beaches, with settlements such as **Aberdeen** and its floating restaurants, **Shek O**, with its white-sand beach, and **Stanley**, with its market, being popular weekend destinations for locals and visitors alike.

Everyone should make the effort to visit the 550-metre-high Victoria Peak, whose summit gives unsurpassed views

Across the harbour is the **Kowloon** peninsula and the districts of **Tsim Sha Tsui** and **Tsim Sha Tsui East**, home to some of Hong Kong's major museums and the vast shopping horizons along **Nathan Road**. Here, on

Street addresses

Finding your way around Hong Kong isn't particularly difficult, though there are local peculiarities to be aware of. Addresses make great use of building names – often designated "Mansions" or "Plazas" – as well as street names and numbers, and usually specify whether the address is in Hong Kong (ie on Hong Kong Island) or Kowloon. Abbreviations to note are HK (Hong Kong Island), Kow (Kowloon) and NT (New Territories).

The shop or office numbering system follows this format: no. 803 means no. 3 on the 8th floor; 815 is no. 15 on the 8th floor; and so on. When written in English, floors are numbered in the British fashion (ie the bottom floor is the ground floor), but in Chinese they are numbered according to Chinese rules (ie the bottom floor is the first floor). Most abbreviations are straightforward: G/F is the ground floor; B indicates a basement level; M (mezzanine) and L (lobby) are also used.

In Macau, addresses are written in the Portuguese style: street name followed by number. Abbreviations you may come across are Av. or Avda. (Avenida), Est. (Estrada), Calç. (Calçada) and Pr. (Praça).

Hong Kong's "Golden Mile", every consumer durable under the sun is traded, while the further north you head, the less recognizably Western and more Asian the crowded grid of streets becomes. Noisy residential and shopping centres – in particular, **Yau Ma Tei** and **Mongkok**, the latter one of the world's most densely populated areas – host atmospheric markets devoted solely to items as diverse as goldfish, birds and jade.

When you tire of the city, the obvious escape is to one of the **outlying islands**, many of which are less than an hour away from Central by ferry. The southwestern group especially – **Lamma**, **Lantau** (home of the vast bronze Big Buddha), **Cheung Chau** and **Peng Chau** – is popular with beach-goers and seafood connoisseurs, though isolated temples, traditional villages, colonial forts and ornamental gardens all provide other reasons to visit.

But it's the **New Territories** – the mainland beyond Kowloon as far as the Chinese border – that give the best insight into the real Hong Kong. New Towns such as **Sha Tin**, home of the SAR's largest museum, **Tsuen Wan**, **Tuen Mun** and **Yuen**

▲ Serving up *won tons*, Macau

▲ Goldfish Market, Mongkok

Long help feed the colony and provide it with housing, labour and enterprise. The towns are all easily reached by public transport, and provide access to some unexpected countryside, such as the **Sai Kung Peninsula**, a glorious region of country parks, islands, bays and beaches.

Given the attractions of Hong Kong, many visitors wonder if it's worth making the side-trip to **Macau**. The answer, emphatically, is yes: not only for its mixture of Portuguese colonial architecture, Chinese culture and futuristic land-reclamation projects, but also for the very different pace of life. There's a more relaxed, historic atmosphere here than in frenetic, contemporary Hong Kong – tellingly, its most famous landmark is the ruin of the seventeenth-century church of **São Paulo** rather than any bank. Other **colonial relics**, too, set the tone – the solid walls of Portuguese fortresses, the cracked facades of Catholic churches, dusty squares, old cemeteries and formal gardens. But change is afoot in Macau, typified by the dramatic construction work taking place around the **Praia Grande** bay. The bay is also the location of Macau's most-visited attraction, the garish **Hotel Lisboa**, one of a dozen **casinos** and gambling operations that entice hundreds of thousands across the water every year. It costs nothing just to look, though if you prefer less mercenary diversions, Macau has its own offshore islands to visit – **Taipa** and **Coloane** – with some fine restaurants, beaches and colonial mansions.

▲ Tai Long Wan Beach, New Territories

When to go

Hong Kong and Macau's **subtropical climates** are broadly similar. Apart from a couple of months a year during which the weather is reliably good, for most of the time it's generally unpredictable, and often downright stormy. The heat is always made more oppressive by the **humidity**: you'll find your strength sapped if you try to do too much walking, and you'll need air-conditioning in your hotel room or – at the very least – a fan. Macau does have the bonus of the cool breeze off the sea in summer, which makes nursing a beer on the waterfront a pleasant experience.

The best time is undoubtedly **autumn** (mid-September to mid-December), when the humidity is at its lowest and days are bright and warm. In **winter** (mid-December to February), things get noticeably cooler (you'll need a jacket), and though the skies often stay clear, there will be periods of wind and low cloud – don't expect reliable, clear views from The Peak at this time. Temperatures and humidity rise during **spring** (March–May), and while there can be beautiful warm blue days towards April, earlier in the season the skies usually stay grey and there are frequent showers and heavier rain. The **summer** (June to mid-September) is dramatically different: it's terribly hot and humid, and best avoided, if possible. If you do visit, you'll need an umbrella to keep off both the rain and the sun; raincoats are hot and aren't much use in heavy downpours.

The summer also sees the **typhoon season**, which lasts roughly from July to September. The word comes from the Chinese *tai fung*, or "big wind", an Asian hurricane, and over the years typhoons whistling through Hong Kong have had a devastating effect – scores of people dead and millions of dollars' worth of damage. A typhoon signal 3 means you should tie things down on balconies and rooftops, and some public facilities, such as swimming

▲ *Aqua* restaurant, Tsim Sha Tsui

▲ Traditional bamboo scaffolding, Sheung Wan

pools, will close. Once a typhoon is in full swing (after the no. 8 signal has been announced), planes will start to be diverted, local transport such as buses and cross-harbour ferries will stop running, and you should stay indoors and away from exposed windows. Typhoon signal 10, known melodramatically as a "direct hit", is the strongest typhoon warning and means hurricanes of 118km/hr and upwards, with gusts of wind up to and above 220km/hr. Heavy rainstorms – which are not accompanied by the winds that characterize typhoons – can also be extremely disruptive, and businesses and transport links may close. Listen to the radio or TV to find out what's happening: weather signals for both typhoons and rainstorms are displayed as an icon on top of the pictures on local TV channels.

The other factor to consider in deciding when to visit is the region's many **festivals**. If you can, try and coincide with the picturesque Mid-Autumn Festival in September/October when lanterns are lit and fireworks colour the sky, or June's Tuen Ng Festival to watch the dragon-boat races. Hong Kong's most important festival, however, Chinese New Year, is best avoided, since many shops and businesses shut, locals stay at home so there's little to see, and travel is very expensive.

Average temperatures and humidity

Note that the figures below are averages. In summer, the temperature is regularly above 30°C, and the humidity over 90 percent. The winter is comparatively chilly, but the temperature rarely drops below 15°C.

	Spring	Summer	Autumn	Winter
°C (°F)	18 (70)	28 (82)	23 (73)	16 (60)
Humidity	84%	83%	73%	75%
Rainfall (mm)	137	394	43	33

things not to miss

It's not possible to see everything that Hong Kong and Macau have to offer in one trip – and we don't suggest you try. What follows is a selective taste of the regions' highlights: outstanding buildings, atmospheric markets, unforgettable views, glittering entertainment – as well as good things to eat and drink. All highlights have a page reference to take you straight into the guide, where you can find out more.

01 A dim sum lunch • Page **200** Knuckle down with the locals in one of Hong Kong's many noisy *dim sum* restaurants, such as *Lin Heung Tea House* in Sheung Wan, and fill up on snack-sized portions of steamed dumplings, vegetables and barbecued meats.

02 Climbing at Lion Rock • Page **125** Tremendous views over the New Town of Sha Tin reward climbers who conquer these dramatic rock faces.

03 Ten Thousand Buddhas Monastery • Page **129** This peaceful hilltop monastery near Sha Tin houses more than 13,000 black and gold Buddha statuettes, a crumbling pagoda with a spiral staircase, and giant statues of crudely painted deities and holy animals.

04 A tram ride up The Peak • Page **72** Since 1888, The Peak tram has inched up the 550m of Victoria Peak to give visitors some of the most spectacular views in the region.

05 Tea at the Peninsula Hotel • Page **107** High tea has been served in the lobby of the *Peninsula Hotel* in Tsim Sha Tsui to the strains of a string quartet since the 1920s; doilies and crumpets are still included.

06 Waterfront restaurants on Cheung Chau Island • Page **163** Cheung Chau is best known for its seafood restaurants along the harbourfront. Sit by the water's edge and enjoy garlic-fried prawns, steamed scallops and fresh fish.

07 The Star Ferry ride from Tsim Sha Tsui to Central

• Page **56** This cheap and evocative ferry ride across Victoria Harbour provides classic water-level views of Central's stunning skyline.

08 Pink Dolphins

• Page **171** Spend a half-day on the sea off Lantau Island, tracking down these rare and endangered creatures, which are unique to Hong Kong.

09 Watching tai chi in Kowloon Park

• Page **109** You'll have to get up early to catch the dawn *tai chi* artists run through their graceful slow-motion martial art.

10 A night at the Cantonese opera

• Page **232** Cantonese opera is Hong Kong's cultural trademark. Even if you can't understand the performance, you have to admire the choreography, costumes and musicianship.

11 The Hong Kong Central skyline • Page **53** Central's futuristic towers create one of Hong Kong's most memorable vistas, especially at night.

12 Temple Street Night Market • Page **113** As well as stalls selling clothing, tack and tat, the night market is renowned for its street restaurants.

13 Hiking on the Sai Kung Peninsula • Page **149** Explore the best of Hong Kong's outdoor scenery, with dozens of beautiful coastal headlands, seascapes, beaches and hills.

14 Wong Tai Sin Temple • Page **117** Every year, three million devotees flock to this colourful Kowloon complex of Taoist temples, shrines and gardens.

15 The ruins of São Paulo

• Page **282** All that's left of this magnificent Jesuit church built in Macau in 1602 is a flight of stone steps, and a facade carved with Christian symbols and Chinese characters.

16 Lord Stowe's Bakery, Coloane

• Page **297** The highlight of a visit to the quiet Macanese village of Coloane is sampling this bakery's superb *natas*, Portuguese custard tartlets.

17 Mongkok Bird Market

• Page **115** Admire elaborate bamboo cages amid the deafening chatter and song of the birds.

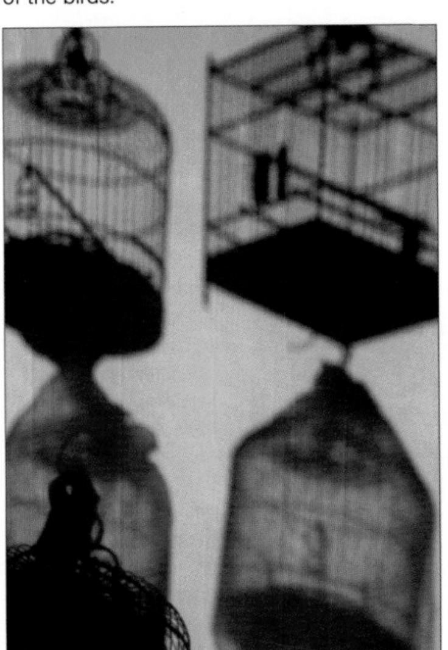

18 Po Lin Monastery and the Big Buddha

• Page **173** The serene Tian Tin Buddha (or Big Buddha) on Lantau Island is the world's tallest outdoor, seated bronze Buddha, and weighs as much as a Jumbo Jet.

19 Bird nest wholesale shops, Sheung Wan • Page **66** Sheung Wan's traditional stores offer rare medicinal ingredients such as ginseng, crushed pearls, dried sea slugs and birds' nests.

22 Largo do Senado • Page **279** This beautifully cobbled square at the heart of old Macau is surrounded by antique Portuguese Baroque churches and government buildings.

20 Tram ride from Central to Causeway Bay • Page **85** Ride a rattling old-fashioned tram between the modern high-rises lining Hong Kong Island's north shore.

21 The casino of the Hotel Lisboa • Page **315** *Hotel Lisboa*'s four-storey casino is the largest in Macau, packed with punters and prostitutes, and featuring scores of games where the stakes are high.

23 Horseracing at Happy Valley • Page **85** More than 23,000 race-goers pack the stands at each meeting to indulge in the only form of legal gambling in Hong Kong.

Basics

Basics

Getting there

Assuming you're not simply crossing from the Chinese mainland, the region's main entry point is Hong Kong International Airport, one of the busiest in the world; Macau's smaller airport handles flights from a few cities in China and a limited number of Southeast Asian countries. You can also reach Hong Kong overland by train from Europe via Russia, Central Asia and China, a classic trip that takes at least fourteen days and requires making the necessary travel and visa arrangements well in advance. Once in the region, high-speed ferries shuttle the 60km between Hong Kong and Macau, in around an hour.

Airfares to Hong Kong are at their highest during the fortnight before Christmas, the fortnight before Chinese New Year (see p.237) and from mid-June to early October. The cheapest time to fly is in February (after Chinese New Year), May and November. Note that flying at weekends can sometimes add up to US$100/£70 to the round-trip fare; price ranges quoted below assume midweek travel.

If Hong Kong and Macau are only stops on a longer journey, you might want to consider buying a **Round-the-World** (RTW) ticket: these generally come as 'off-the-shelf' varieties covering half a dozen cities (Hong Kong is on many itineraries), though agents can tailor individual RTW tickets at a higher price. Figure on £900/US$1450/AUS$2000/NZ$2800 upwards for an RTW ticket including Hong Kong.

You'll get the best deals on air fares by **booking online**, even if you prefer to actually buy your ticket through a high-street **discount agent** or **specialist operator**. Wherever you shop, you might also look out for **package tours** including accommodation and flights, either for Hong Kong alone or as part of a trip to China and other regions of Asia – something that can be very good value out of season.

Booking flights online

Many airlines and discount travel websites offer you the opportunity to book your tickets, hotels and holiday packages online, cutting out the costs of agents and middlemen; these are worth going for, as long as you don't mind the inflexibility of non-refundable, non-changeable deals. Almost all airlines have their own websites, offering flight tickets that can sometimes be just as cheap, and are often more flexible.

Online booking agents and general travel sites

ⓦ **www.cheapflights.com** Flight deals, travel agents, plus links to other travel sites.
ⓦ **www.cheaptickets.com** US discount flight specialists; also has deals on hotels and car hire.
ⓦ **www.ebookers.com** Efficient, easy-to-use flight finder, with competitive fares.
ⓦ **www.expedia.com** Discount air fares, all-airline search engine and daily deals.
ⓦ **www.flynow.com** Simple-to-use independent travel site offering good-value fares.
ⓦ **www.hotwire.com** US website with lots of last-minute deals, saving up to forty percent on regular published fares.
ⓦ **www.lastminute.com** Offers good last-minute holiday package and flight-only deals.
ⓦ **www.skyauction.com** Bookings from the US only. Auctions tickets and travel packages using a system similar to eBay.
ⓦ **www.ticketplanet.com** California-based site that claims to be the first to sell consolidator fares over the web. Especially good for round-the-world fares.
ⓦ **www.travelocity.com**, ⓦ **www.travelocity.co.uk** Good web fares and deals on car rental, accommodation and lodging.
ⓦ **www.travelshop.com.au** Australian website offering discounted flights, packages, insurance, and online bookings.

Flights from the UK and Ireland

The only direct flights to Hong Kong **from the UK** depart London Heathrow with British

Package tours

Packages to Hong Kong are fairly standardized, typically lasting from three to five days, with local tours and extra nights available. Some airlines also offer discounted accommodation if you book it along with your ticket as a **package**, which can work out not much more than the airfare alone. For a week (two nights on a plane and five nights in Hong Kong) expect to pay from around £700/US$1000/AUS$1200 per person. You should also check with specialist operators for accommodation deals in Hong Kong if you're planning a wider tour of the region, such as a trip through Southeast Asia or China, or the train journey from Europe to Hong Kong – see the box on p.24 for the latter.

Airways (3 daily), Cathay Pacific (3 daily), Qantas (3 weekly), and Virgin (1 daily). All charge between £525 low season and £725 in high season and take thirteen hours or so. Alternatively, many European and Southeast Asian airlines fly from London to Hong Kong **via their home hubs** (sometimes with a couple of other stops too). These flights can be cheaper than the nonstop services but take sixteen to thirty hours. Depending on the time of year, they cost around £380–900 return, though you'll need to book well in advance for seats at Christmas or Chinese New Year. Currently, Aeroflot (via Moscow) are offering the cheapest tickets at £380 (low season).

From **Ireland** your best bet is to connect at Heathrow or fly via another European hub with direct flights to Hong Kong such as Paris (Air France) or Amsterdam (Cathay Pacific).

Airlines

Aeroflot ⓣ020/7355 2233, in Republic of Ireland ⓣ01/844 6166, ⓦwww.aeroflot.com. Cheap flights three times a week from London Heathrow to Hong Kong via Moscow.

Air China ⓣ020/7630 0919, ⓦwww.air-china.co.uk. Good deals on fights to Beijing, where you can change for Hong Kong, or continue overland.

Air France UK ⓣ0845/359 1000, Republic of Ireland ⓣ01/605 0383, ⓦwww.airfrance.com. Daily flights to Hong Kong, via Paris with connections from UK and Irish airports.

British Airways ⓣ0870/850 9850, in Republic of Ireland ⓣ1800/626747, ⓦwww.ba.com. Nonstop thrice-daily flights from London Heathrow.

Cathay Pacific ⓣ020/8834 8888, ⓦwww.cathaypacific.com/uk. Hong Kong's flag carrier with direct flights daily between London Heathrow and Hong Kong (also flies direct from Amsterdam).

Emirates ⓣ0870/243 2222, ⓦwww.emirates.com. Daily flights from London Heathrow to Hong Kong via Dubai.

Gulf Air UK ⓣ0870/777 1717, ⓦwww.gulfairco.com. Daily from London Heathrow to Hong Kong via Dubai.

Lufthansa ⓣ0845/773 7747, in Republic of Ireland ⓣ01/844 5544, ⓦwww.lufthansa.com. Daily flights to Hong Kong via Frankfurt, with connections from UK and Irish airports.

Malaysia Airlines (MAS) ⓣ0870/607 9090, in Republic of Ireland ⓣ01/676 2131, ⓦwww.malaysia-airlines.com. Stopovers in Kuala Lumpur; at the lower end of the market.

Qantas UK ⓣ0845/774 7767, Republic of Ireland ⓣ01/407 3278, ⓦwww.qantas.co.uk. Same base rates as British Airways and Virgin, with daily flights to Hong Kong.

Singapore Airlines UK ⓣ0870/608 8886, Republic of Ireland ⓣ01/671 0722, ⓦwww.singaporeair.com. To Hong Kong via Singapore from London Heathrow and Manchester.

Swiss UK ⓣ0845/601 0956, Republic of Ireland ⓣ1890/200 515, ⓦwww.swiss.com. Daily flights to Hong Kong via Zürich with connections from London, Birmingham, Manchester, Edinburgh and Dublin.

Thai ⓣ0870/606 0911, ⓦwww.thaiair.com. Hong Kong via a Bangkok stopover.

Virgin Atlantic ⓣ01293/747747, in Republic of Ireland ⓣ01/873 3388, ⓦwww.virgin.com/atlantic. Direct flights from London to Hong Kong.

Travel agents

Aran Travel International Republic of Ireland ⓣ091/562 595, ⓦhomepages.iol.ie/~arantvl/aranmain.htm.

Bridge the World UK ⓣ0870/814 4400, ⓦwww.bridgetheworld.com.

Co-op Travel Care UK ⓣ0870/112 0085, ⓦwww.travelcareonline.com.

Flightcentre UK ⓣ0870/890 8099, ⓦwww.flightcentre.co.uk.

North South Travel UK ⓣ01245/608 291, ⓦwww.northsouthtravel.co.uk.

STA Travel UK ⓣ0870/1600 599, ⓦwww.statravel.co.uk.

Trailfinders UK ⓣ0845/0585 858, ⓦwww.trailfinders.co.uk; Republic of Ireland ⓣ01/677 7888, ⓦwww.trailfinders.ie.
Travel Bag UK ⓣ01/602 1904, ⓦwww.travelbag.co.uk.
usit NOW Republic of Ireland ⓣ01/602 1600, Northern Ireland ⓣ028/9032 7111; ⓦwww.usitnow.ie.

Specialist operators

Abercrombie and Kent ⓣ0845/070 0610, ⓦwww.abercrombiekent.co.uk. Upmarket sightseeing tours of Hong Kong, with knowledgeable guides; also experienced in the overland rail routes to Hong Kong from Europe.
Bales Worldwide ⓣ0870/241 3208, tailor-mades ⓣ0870/241 3212, ⓦwww.balesworldwide.com. High-quality escorted tours to China with a few days In Hong Kong, as well as tailor-made itineraries.
CTS Horizons ⓣ020/7836 9911, ⓦwww.ctshorizons.com. Chinese government-run tour operator offering umpteen China and Hong Kong tours.
Destinations Republic of Ireland ⓣ01/855 6641, ⓦwww.destinations.ie. Undemanding two-week tours that include Hong Kong.
Exodus ⓣ020/8675 5550, ⓦwww.exodus.co.uk. Adventure tour operators taking small groups on tours to China which finish up in Hong Kong.
Hayes & Jarvis ⓣ0870/898 9890, ⓦwww.hayes-jarvis.com. Specialists in upmarket long-haul holidays, including cruises and hotel packages around Southeast Asia taking in Hong Kong and southern China.
Jade Travel ⓣ0870 898 8928, ⓦwww.jadetravel.co.uk. Hong Kong company specializing in flights, hotels and sightseeing tours.
Kuoni Travel ⓣ01306/742 002, ⓦwww.kuoni.co.uk. Flexible package holidays combining a few nights in Hong Kong with multiple destinations in Southeast Asia, the Far East and Australia; good deals for families.
Magic Of The Orient ⓣ01293/537700, ⓦwww.magic-of-the-orient.com. Offers good-value Hong Kong accommodation deals.
Regent Holidays ⓣ0117/921 1711, ⓦwww.regent-holidays.co.uk. Specialist agent for trans-Siberian and trans-Mongolian train tickets.
Thomas Cook ⓣ0870/750 0512, ⓦwww.thomascook.co.uk. Long established agent for package holidays, tours and cruises taking in Hong Kong as well as China and Southeast Asia.
Twohigs Dublin ⓣ01/677 2666 or ⓣ01/670 9750. Far East specialists.
Viator ⓦwww.viator.com. Offers local half-day tours in Hong Kong.
World Travel Centre Dublin ⓣ01/416 7007, ⓦwww.worldtravel.ie. Specialists in flights and packages to the Far East.

Flights from the US and Canada

Airlines flying direct daily from the North American continent's **west coast** to Hong Kong include Cathay Pacific (from LA and Vancouver), Singapore Airlines (San Francisco), Thai (LA), Air Canada (Vancouver), and United Airlines (LA). Flying time is approximately fourteen hours; fares range from US$765 in low season to US$1100 or more in high. Non-direct carriers from the above cities and Honolulu include Japan Airlines, Korean Air, Air China and EVA (via Taipei) and Thai Airways: costs can be lower at around US$650–950, but the journey can take upwards of eighteen hours.

From the **east coast**, direct daily flights are with Cathay Pacific (from New York), United (New York and Chicago) and Air Canada (Toronto); flying time is about twenty hours and costs range between US$950 and US$1500 depending on season. Options involving a stopover include Thai (via Bangkok), Northwest (via Tokyo), Korea (Seoul), and Singapore (via Singapore); expect to spend twenty-four hours or more on the journey, and pay around US$800.

Airlines

Air Canada ⓣ1-888/247-2262, ⓦwww.aircanada.ca. Nonstop flights from Vancouver and Toronto, plus connections from most other major Canadian cities.
Cathay Pacific ⓣ1-800/233-2742, ⓦwww.cathay-usa.com. Nonstop flights daily from New York, LA, and Vancouver.
China Airlines ⓣ917/368-2000, ⓦwww.china-airlines.com. Flights from New York, LA and San Francisco via Taipei.
EVA Airways ⓣ1-800/695-1188, ⓦwww.evaair.com. Daily flights to Hong Kong or Macau from New York, LA, San Francisco, Seattle, Vancouver and Honolulu via Taipei.
Japan Airlines ⓣ1-800/525-3663, ⓦwww.japanair.com. Daily to Hong Kong via Tokyo from New York, LA, San Francisco, Chicago and Vancouver.
Korean Air ⓣ1-800/438-5000, ⓦwww.koreanair.com. Daily to Hong Kong via Seoul from New York, LA, Chicago, Dallas, Washington, San Francisco and Atlanta.
Northwest/KLM Airlines ⓣ1-800/447-4747, ⓦwww.nwa.com, ⓦww.klm.com. Daily flights to Hong Kong via Tokyo from Honolulu, Seattle, San Francisco, LA, Minneapolis, Detroit and New York.
Philippine Airlines ⓣ1-800/I-FLY-PAL, ⓦwww.philippineair.com. Flies daily from San Francisco, LA and Vancouver via Manila.
Singapore Airlines US ⓣ1-800/742-3333, Canada ⓣ1-800/387-8039, ⓦwww.singaporeair.com. Daily to Hong Kong from San Francisco (direct), and Toronto and New York (via Singapore).
Thai Airways US ⓣ1-800/426-5204, Canada ⓣ1-800/668-8103, ⓦwww.thaiair.com. LA, Toronto and New York to Hong Kong daily via Bangkok.
United Airlines ⓣ1-800/538-2929, ⓦwww.united.com. Nonstop daily to Hong Kong from New York, Chicago and LA.

Travel agents

Air Brokers International ⓣ1-800/883-3273, ⓦwww.airbrokers.com.
Airtech ⓣ212/219-7000, ⓦwww.airtech.com.
Airtreks ⓣ1-877/AIRTREKS, ⓦwww.airtreks.com.
Educational Travel Center ⓣ1-800/747-5551 or 608/256-5551, ⓦwww.edtrav.com.
Flightcentre US ⓣ1-866/WORLD-51, ⓦwww.flightcentre.us Canada ⓣ1-888/WORLD-55, ⓦwww.flightcentre.ca.
STA Travel US ⓣ1-800/329-9537, Canada ⓣ1-888/427-5639, ⓦwww.statravel.com.
Travel Avenue ⓣ1-800/333-3335, ⓦwww.travelavenue.com.
Travel Cuts US ⓣ1-800/592-CUTS, Canada ⓣ1-888/246-9762, ⓦwww.travelcuts.com.
Travelosophy US ⓣ1-800/332-2687, ⓦwww.itravelosophy.com.
Worldtek Travel ⓣ1-800/243-1723, ⓦwww.worldtek.com.

Specialist operators

Abercrombie & Kent ⓣ1-800/323-7308 or ⓣ630/954-2944, ⓦwww.abercrombiekent.com. Inventive themed tours to sites in China and Southeast Asia, with a day or two in Hong Kong. Also bookings for the overland train routes to or from Hong Kong.
Absolute Asia ⓣ1-800/736-8187 or ⓣ212/627-1950, ⓦwww.absoluteasia.com. Luxurious, in-depth tours of the SAR, including trips out to the New Territories and Macau.
Adventure Center ⓣ1-800/228-8747 or ⓣ510/654-1879, ⓦwww.adventurecenter.com. Hiking and adventure specialists with good-priced tours of Southeast Asia, China and Hong Kong.
CTS (China Travel Service) ⓣ1-800/899-8618, ⓦwww.chinatravelservice.com. Air tickets, visas, hotel bookings and tours by this major China-based tourist corporation.
Europe Train Tours ⓣ1-800/551-2085 or ⓣ704/876-9081, ⓦwww.etttours.com. Rail specialist which can organize travel on the Trans-Mongolian and Trans-Siberian expresses.
Globus and Cosmos ⓣ1-866/755-8581, ⓦwww.globusjourneys.com. City tours of Hong Kong, Singapore and Bangkok.
Goway Travel ⓣ1-800/387-8850 or 416/322-1034, ⓦwww.goway.com. Hong Kong coach tours. Options to pair with onward tours to Macau or China.
International Gay & Lesbian Travel Association ⓣ1-800/448-8550, ⓦwww.iglta.org. Trade group with lists of gay-owned or gay-friendly travel agents and accommodation in Hong Kong.
Journeyworld International ⓣ1-800/255-8735, ⓦwww.journeys-intl.com. Specializes in expeditions to China with the option of a few days in Hong Kong.
Maupintour ⓣ1-800/255-4266 or ⓣ913/843-1211, ⓦwww.maupintour.com. Lavish upmarket tours of the SAR, staying in the *Peninsula Hotel* and including cruises, beach trips and a concert.
Pacific Delight Tours ⓣ1-800/221-7179, ⓦwww.pacificdelighttours.com. Offers a wide range of Hong Kong tours and packages, which can be combined with river cruises in mainland China.

Travel Bound ⓣ1-800/456-8656, ⓦwww.booktravelbound.com. Good range of short-stay packages including air fare and accommodation, plus some local tours; most are extremely good value.
Vantage Travel ⓣ1-800/322-6677, ⓦwww.vantagetravel.com. Specializes in group travel for seniors worldwide.

Flights from Australia and New Zealand

Direct flights from Australia are covered by Cathay Pacific, who fly daily to Hong Kong from Sydney, Brisbane, Cairns and Perth; while Qantas fly from Sydney daily, and several times a week from Melbourne, Brisbane, Cairns, and Perth. Fares range from AUS$1050 low-season to AUS$1500 in high; the journey takes 8–10 hours. **Indirect flights** are offered by just about every Southeast Asian carrier, but are not always cheaper than a low-season fare with Cathay Pacific. At the time of writing good-value fares (AUS$750–900) were offered by Cathay Pacific, China Airlines, EVA airlines, and Singapore Airlines. All prices quoted above are about AUS$100 cheaper from Perth

Flights **from New Zealand** are limited and therefore expensive: about the best deal is on Air New Zealand or Singapore from Auckland to Hong Kong (NZ$1850–2200; 11hr). Malaysia, Singapore and other carriers also fly via hub cities to Hong Kong, though not for substantially less.

Airlines

Air New Zealand Australia ⓣ13 2476, New Zealand ⓣ0800/247 764, ⓦwww.airnewzealand.com. Five nonstop flights a week from Auckland.
Asiana ⓦwww.au.flyasiana.com. Korean-based airlines with pricey fares from Australia to Hong Kong via Seoul.
Cathay Pacific Australia ⓣ13 1747, New Zealand ⓣ09/379 0861, ⓦwww.cathaypacific.com. Daily flights from Sydney, Brisbane, Cairns, and Perth.
China Airlines Australia ⓣ02/9244 2121, New Zealand ⓣ09/308 3371, ⓦwww.china-airlines.com. Twice-weekly flights from Sydney via Taipei.
EVA Air Australia ⓣ02/8338 0419, New Zealand ⓣ09/358 8300, ⓦwww.evaair.com. Eastern Australia and New Zealand to Hong Kong via Taipei.
Malaysia Airlines Australia ⓣ13 2627, New Zealand ⓣ649/379 3743, ⓦwww.malaysiaairlines.com. Daily flights from Sydney and Brisbane via Kuala Lumpur.
Philippine Airlines Australia ⓣ02/9279 2020, ⓦwww.philippineair.com. Flights from Sydney via Manila, three times a week.
Qantas Australia ⓣ13/13 13, New Zealand ⓣ09/357 8900, ⓦwww.qantas.com. Sydney, Melbourne, Brisbane, Cairns and Perth to Hong Kong.
Singapore Airlines Australia ⓣ13/10 11 or ⓣ02/9350 0262, New Zealand ⓣ09/379 3209, ⓦwww.singaporeair.com. Daily flights from Sydney, Brisbane, Melbourne, Perth and Auckland via Singapore.
Thai Airways Australia ⓣ1300/651 960, New Zealand ⓣ09/377 3886, ⓦwww.thaiair.com. Daily flights from Sydney and Brisbane via Bangkok.

Travel agents

Flight Centre Australia ⓣ13 31 33 or 02/9235 3522, ⓦwww.flightcentre.com.au; New Zealand ⓣ0800 243 544 or 09/358 4310, ⓦwww.flightcentre.co.nz.
Holiday Shoppe New Zealand ⓣ0800/808 480, ⓦwww.holidayshoppe.co.nz.
OTC Australia ⓣ1300/855 118, ⓦwww.otctravel.com.au.
Plan It Holidays Australia ⓣ03/9245 0747, ⓦwww.planit.com.au.
STA Travel Australia ⓣ1300/733 035 or 02/9212 1255, ⓦwww.statravel.com.au; New Zealand ⓣ0508/782 872 or 09/309 9273, ⓦwww.statravel.co.nz.
Student Uni Travel Australia ⓣ02/9232 8444, ⓦwww.sut.com.au, New Zealand ⓣ09/379 4224, ⓦwww.sut.co.nz.
Trailfinders Australia ⓣ/9247 7666 or ⓣ1300/780 212, ⓦwww.trailfinders.com.au.
travel.com.au and travel.co.nz Australia ⓣ1300/130 482 or 02/9249 5444, ⓦwww.travel.com.au, New Zealand ⓣ0800/468 332, ⓦwww.travel.co.nz.

Specialist operators

Abercrombie and Kent Australia ⓣ02/9241 3213, New Zealand ⓣ0800/441 638; ⓦwww.abercrombiekent.com.au. Upmarket tours and packages; especially good for booking overland train travel if the Hong Kong–Europe trip appeals.
China Travel Service Australia ⓣ02/9211 2633, New Zealand ⓣ09/309 6458, ⓦwww.chinatravel.com.au. Package tours to all the main sites in China and Hong Kong.
Passport Travel Australia ⓣ03/9867 3888, ⓦwww.travelcentre.com.au. Experienced Trans-Siberia booking agents; also tours and packages in

China and Hong Kong.
Peregrine Adventures Australia ⓣ03/9662 2700, ⓦwww.peregrine.net.au. Specialists in adventure tours in China with a few days in Hong Kong at the end.
Sundowners Australia ⓣ03/9672 5300 or ⓣ1800/337 089, ⓦwww.sundownerstravel.com. Specialists in overland rail travel, including the Trans-Siberian Express and the Silk Road.
Travel Indochina Australia ⓣ1300 362 777 or ⓣ02/9244 2133, ⓦwww.travelindochina.com.au. Arranges tours to the less obvious sights and can arrange cross-border visas for Thailand, Laos, Vietnam, China and Cambodia.

Flying via Southeast Asia or China

If you are already in Southeast Asia, you'll find that the concept of no-frills **budget airlines** is just taking off in the region, with a couple of operators advertising seriously cheap tickets to both Hong Kong and Macau. The best deals are currently **from Bangkok** with Air Asia to Macau (single fares from £40/US$70/AUS$90), or Orient Thai Airlines to Hong Kong (return fares from £40/US$70/AUS$90); and **from Kuala Lumpur** with Air Asia to Macau, at just £16/US$30/AUS$40. Otherwise, Southeast Asia's major carriers all fly to Hong Kong at a reasonable cost from national capitals; expect to pay upwards of £170/US$310/AUS$400 for a return ticket.

Flying from China, it's considerably cheaper to aim for nearby airports at Guangzhou, Zhuhai or Shenzhen and make your way overland from there. For example, air fares from Beijing to Guangzhou with China Southern are around £75/US$130/AUS$170, instead of £130/US$230/AUS$300 to Hong Kong. Once in Guangzhou, a **train** to Hong Kong costs HK$200 and takes 2hr; or you can catch a **bus** for around half this. From Shenzhen or Zhuhai you can cross the borders on foot, or catch a ferry.

Airlines

Air Asia ⓦwww.airasia.com. Direct flights several times a week from Thailand and Kuala Lumpur to Macau.
Air China ⓦwww.airchina.com.cn/en/index.jsp. Direct daily flights from several Chinese cities including Beijing, Guangzhou and Shanghai to Hong Kong and Macau.
China Southern ⓦwww.cs-air.com/en. Direct daily flights from Chinese cities including Beijing, Guangzhou and Shanghai to Hong Kong.
Malaysia Airlines ⓦwww.malaysiaairlines.com. Five direct daily flights from Kuala Lumpur to Hong Kong.
Orient Thai ⓦwww.orient-thai.com. Daily direct flights from Bangkok to Hong Kong.
Philippine Airlines ⓦwww.philippineair.com. Three direct daily flights from Manila to Hong Kong, and around four times a week from Manila to Macau.
Singapore Airlines ⓦwww.singaporeair.com. Daily flights direct from Singapore to Hong Kong.
Thai Airways ⓦwww.thaiair.com. Daily flights direct from Bangkok to Hong Kong.

Overland by train

The **overland train route from London** passes through Eastern Europe, Russia and Mongolia to China and Beijing, from where trains run south to the end of the line in Hong Kong. It's a satisfying – though exacting – journey (the route follows the **Trans-Siberian**, one of the world's classic train journeys, for much of its length), but it doesn't save you any money compared with flying. Prices for the Moscow–Beijing/Hong Kong journey start at around £500/US$750/AUS$1600 one-way for a bed in an intolerably uncomfortable four-berth "hard-sleeper" compartment – with fares at their highest (£550) between May and October – but for an extra £100/US$150/AUS$320 you can upgrade to a two-berth cabin and improve the chances of a comfortable night's sleep for the duration. Prepare for a very long haul: from London to Moscow takes two days, Moscow to Beijing five or six days depending on the route, and it's another 24hr from there to Hong Kong.

If this doesn't put you off, you'll have to decide upon the route and train you want to take – services are operated by both the Russians and the Chinese, either passing through, or bypassing, Mongolia (for which you need a separate visa). To sort it all out, talk to an experienced agent (see "Specialist operators" for your home country listed above), who can organize all tickets, visas and stopovers and can arrange a cheap flight back to London – you'll need to plan at least six weeks ahead.

Red tape and visas

Citizens of the UK, Ireland, US, Canada, Australia, New Zealand and most European countries do not require a visa before arrival and can stay in Hong Kong for up to three months, and Macau for up to twenty days. Everyone else should consult the relevant Chinese Embassy, Consulate or High Commission in their country of origin for visa requirements. Passports for all visitors must be valid for at least six months from the date of entry. Note too that though Hong Kong and Macau are technically part of China, you still need a separate visa to enter the Chinese mainland – see the "Into mainland China" box, p.41.

Hong Kong

There shouldn't be any trouble with the **immigration officers** on arrival, all of whom speak English. You may be asked how long you intend to stay and, if it's a fairly lengthy period, for referees in Hong Kong and proof that you can support yourself without working, unless you have an employment visa (see p.48).

Given the length of time most people are allowed to stay in Hong Kong, you are unlikely to need to **extend your stay**. If you do, the simplest solution is to go to Macau for the weekend and come back, and nine times out of ten you'll just get another period stamped in your passport. If you want to ensure a longer stay, though, you'll need to apply for a visa in advance of your visit from the Immigration Department, as you will if you're intending to work in the territory. Allow at least six weeks for most visa applications.

If you're in trouble or lose your passport, or you want details of the visas necessary for travel on to neighbouring countries, consult the relevant **foreign consulate in Hong Kong** – there's a list on p.269.

Customs

You're allowed to bring the following **duty-free** goods into Hong Kong: 200 cigarettes (or 50 cigars or 250g of tobacco) and 1 litre of alcoholic beverages. You can take most other things into Hong Kong with little difficulty. Prohibited items include all firearms and fireworks, and if you're caught carrying any kind of illegal drugs you can expect very tough treatment.

Macau

You'll barely notice the **customs officials** as you arrive in Macau, though there might be the odd spot check (and the same penalties apply for drugs or firearms as in Hong Kong). Otherwise, the only thing to watch for is when returning to Hong Kong: there's no export duty on goods taken out of Macau, but the Hong Kong authorities will only allow you to bring in 1 litre of wine (or spirits) sold in Macau, and 200 cigarettes or 50 cigars.

Chinese embassies and consulates abroad

Australia

Embassy 15 Coronation Drive, Yarralumla, ACT 2600 ⓣ02/6273 4780, ⓦwww.chinaembassy.org.au.
Consular Offices 539 Elizabeth St, Surry Hills, Sydney ⓣ02/9698 7929, and 77 Irving Rd, Toorak (visa & passport enquiries ⓣ03/9804 3683).

Canada

Embassy 515 St Patrick's St, Ottawa, ON K1N 5H3 ⓣ613/789 3434, ⓦwww.chinaembassycanada.org.
Consular Offices 240 St George St, Toronto, ON M5R 2P4 ⓣ416/964 7260; 3380 Granville St, Vancouver, BC V6H 3K3 ⓣ604/736 3910; 1011 6th Ave SW, #100 Calgary, Alberta T2P 0W1 ⓣ403/264 3322.

Ireland

Embassy 40 Ailesbury Rd, Dublin 4 ⓣ053/12691707, ⓦwww.chinaembassy.ie.

New Zealand

Embassy 2–6 Glenmore St, Wellington ⓣ04/474 9631, ⓦwww.chinaembassy.org.nz.
Consulate-General 588 Great South Rd, Greenland, Auckland ⓣ09/525 1588, ⓦwww.chinaconsulate.org.nz.

UK

Visa Section 49–51 Portland Place, London W1B 1JL ⓣ020/72994049, ⓦwww.chinese-embassy.org.uk.
Consulate Denison House, Denison Rd, Victoria Pk, Manchester M14 5RX ⓣ0161/224 7480.

US

Embassy 2300 Connecticut Ave NW, Washington DC 20008 ⓣ202/338 2500 ⓦwww.chineseembassy.org
Consulates 520 12th Ave, New York, NY 10036 ⓣ212/330 7410; 100 W Erie St, Chicago, IL 60610 ⓣ312/803 0095; 3417 Montrose Blvd, Houston, TX 77006 ⓣ713/524 4311; 443 Shatto Place, Los Angeles, CA 90020 ⓣ213/807 8018.

Insurance

Though Hong Kong is essentially a safe place to travel, the cost of medical care alone makes taking out a travel-insurance policy worthwhile. Policies typically provide cover for loss of baggage, tickets and – up to a certain limit – cash or cheques, as well as cancellation or curtailment of your journey. Many policies can be chopped and changed to exclude coverage you don't need – for example, sickness and accident benefits can often be excluded or included at will. With medical coverage, ascertain whether benefits will be paid as treatment proceeds or only after return home, and whether there is a 24-hour medical emergency number. When securing baggage cover, make sure that the per-article limit – typically under £500/US$750 – will cover your most valuable possession. If you need to make a claim, you should keep receipts for medicines and medical treatment, and in the event you have anything stolen, you must obtain an official statement from the police.

Rough Guides travel insurance

Rough Guides has teamed up with Columbus Direct to offer you travel insurance that can be tailored to suit your needs. Readers can choose from many different travel-insurance products, including a **low-cost backpacker** option for long stays; a **short break** option for city getaways; a typical **holiday package** option, and many others. There are also **annual multi-trip** policies for those who travel regularly, with variable levels of cover available. Different sports and activities (trekking, skiing, etc) can be covered if required on most policies.

Rough Guides travel insurance is available to the residents of 36 different countries with different language options to choose from via our website – ⓦwww.roughguidesinsurance.com – where you can also purchase the insurance.

Alternatively call direct: UK residents ⓣ0800 083 9507; US citizens ⓣ1-800 749-4922; Australian citizens ⓣ1 300 669 999; all other nationalities ⓣ+44 870 890 2843.

Before paying for a new policy, however, check whether you are already covered: some all-risks **home insurance policies** may include your possessions when overseas, and items purchased with a credit card might enjoy limited protection against loss or damage. Private medical schemes sometimes include partial overseas coverage, as do Canadian provincial health plans, while holders of official student/teacher/youth cards in Canada and the US are entitled to limited accident coverage and hospital in-patient benefits. **Students** will often find that their student health coverage extends during the vacations and for one term beyond the date of last enrolment.

Health

You don't need to have any vaccinations to enter Hong Kong or Macau. The only stipulation is that if you've been in an area infected with cholera or typhoid during the fourteen days before your arrival, you'll need certificates of vaccination against the two diseases. These requirements might change, so ask your doctor if you're unsure about what constitutes an infected area. If you're travelling elsewhere in Asia or China, before or after Hong Kong and Macau, it's a good idea to make sure that all your inoculations (against typhoid, cholera, tetanus, polio and hepatitis) are up to date.

Health problems

The region's population density, along with steamy summers and high levels of airborne pollution, mean that both Hong Kong and Macau suffer regular occurrences of **respiratory infections**. Generally, this is nothing more serious than you'll encounter at home, though the 2002 outbreak of pneumonia-like **SARS** (Severe Acute Respiratory Syndrome), which originated in southern China, killed 300 people in Hong Kong. The outbreak was short-lived – Hong Kong has currently been SARS-free since June 2003 – but the lessons have been taken seriously; you'll often see locals wearing surgical face-masks in the streets. Another worry is that bird **flu**, which frequently occurs in poultry farms across Southeast Asia, might cross into humans with fatal results, and recent outbreaks have seen the mass slaughter of ducks and chickens in Hong Kong. None of this is reason for paranoia, however, and Hong Kong and Macau remain safe places to visit for a short stay – see the "Medical Contacts" websites on p.29 for up-to-date information.

General **hygiene standards** are reasonable, though don't expect surgical cleanliness in cheaper hotel bathrooms or the smaller places to eat – the latter might just rinse their bowls and chopsticks with lukewarm water, or sometimes tea. Market-bought fruit and vegetables should be washed carefully, as many are grown in mainland China where pesticide and fertilizer use is uncontrolled. Meat and fish are often sold alive and cooked soon afterwards, which guarantees freshness, but shellfish may have been dredged out of the sometimes less-than-clean bays and waters around the islands. **Water** is safe to drink everywhere (except from old wells on some of Hong Kong's outlying islands), though bottled water always tastes nicer. If you come down with **stomach trouble**, the best advice is not to eat anything for 24 hours, drink lots of water or weak tea and take it easy until you feel better. Once on the mend, start on unspiced foods like soup or noodles, though if you don't improve quickly, get medical advice.

Take summer **heat** seriously; temperatures

For all **emergencies** in Hong Kong or Macau (ambulance, police, fire), dial ⓣ999.

rise well into the thirties and the humidity can be almost paralysing. **Prickly heat** skin rashes can be countered by showering often, using talcum powder and wearing light cotton clothing. Make sure you **drink** plenty of water – at least a couple of litres daily in hot weather – especially if you're hiking. Wearing **sunglasses** and a hat is also a good idea during the summer.

While **AIDS** is not as prevalent as in some other Southeast Asian cities, don't contemplate unprotected sex, and if you have acupuncture, ensure that new needles are used.

Pharmacies, Chinese medicine, doctors and hospitals

Pharmacies can advise on minor ailments and will prescribe basic medicines: they're all registered, and (in the centre of Hong Kong, less so in Macau) usually employ English-speakers. They are generally open daily 9am–6pm; Watsons are a big, Hong Kong-wide chain with branches in Macau too. If you're after treatment using **Traditional Chinese Medicine** (see box below), ask at your accommodation or the Hong Kong Tourism Board offices for recommended practitioners. Alternatively, you can try one of the many **Chinese herbal medicine shops**, found throughout Hong Kong and Macau, which are stacked from floor to ceiling with lotions, potions and dried herbs. The people in these shops are not likely to speak English, but if you can describe your ailment they'll prescribe and mix for you a herbal remedy. Note, however, that many Chinese herbal prescriptions are not one-off cures but might need weekly follow-up visits, and that herbalists are not required to have formal training to set up shop – although many do.

For a **doctor**, look in the local phone directories' Yellow Pages (under "Physicians and Surgeons" in Hong Kong; "*Medicos*" in Macau), or contact the reception desk in the larger hotels. Many doctors have been trained overseas, but you should ask for one who speaks English. You'll have to pay for a consultation (around HK$400) and any medicines they prescribe; ask for a receipt for your insurance.

Hospital treatment is infinitely more expensive, at upwards of HK$3000 a day, which makes it essential to have some form of medical insurance. Casualty visits are free, however, and hospitals in both territories have 24-hour casualty departments. Finally, both doctors and **dentists** are known as "doctor" in Hong Kong, so be sure you're not wasting your time at the wrong place. Having dental work done costs a lot, so if you possibly can, wait until you get home for treatment.

Traditional Chinese Medicine

Traditional Chinese Medicine (TCM) works on the principle that, to function properly, there must be a healthy flow of **chi** (energy) around the body. According to Chinese beliefs, *chi* circulates along lines known as **meridians**, each of which originates in an organ and travels to the body's extremities. If the *chi* flow becomes irregular – through injury or illness – energy will pool in parts of the body and be absent in others, causing illness. TCM works on restoring the body's *chi* balance with **acupuncture** – where fine needles are inserted into key points along meridian lines to either increase or decrease *chi* flow – and by prescribing the patient combinations of **medicinal herbs** which help tonify (accepted terminology) and regulate energy in the body. Certain **martial arts**, such as tai chi, are also believed to be good for the health because they exercise the meridian system, thereby regulating the body's *chi* flow and preventing illness. Though there is considerable scepticism outside China as to TCM's effectiveness, there seems to be a case to be made for its use in certain chronic illnesses, to assist recovery after surgery, or simply to maintain good health.

Medical contacts

Ⓦ **www.cdc.gov/travel** US government travel advice, listing precautions, diseases and preventive measures by region.
Ⓦ **www.fitfortravel.scot.nhs.uk** UK NHS website carrying information about travel-related diseases and how to avoid them.
Ⓦ **www.healthinasia.com** An unintentionally amusing set of pages written by expat doctors in Hong Kong; also contains a useful list of phone numbers and addresses of clinics in the SAR.
Ⓦ **www.info.gov.hk/dh** Hong Kong's Department of Health webpage.
Ⓦ **www.istm.org** The website of the International Society for Travel Medicine, with a full list of clinics specializing in international travel health.
Ⓦ **www.tmvc.com.au** Contains a list of all Travellers Medical and Vaccination Centres throughout Australia, New Zealand and Southeast Asia, plus general information on travel health.
Ⓦ **www.tripprep.com** Travel Health Online provides a comprehensive database of necessary vaccinations for most countries, as well as destination and medical service provider information.

In the UK and Ireland

British Airways Travel Clinics 213 Piccadilly, London (Mon–Fri 9.30am–5.30pm, Sat 10am–4pm, no appointment necessary); 101 Cheapside, London EC2 (Mon–Fri 9am–4.30pm, appointment required; Ⓣ0845/600 2236); Ⓦwww.britishairways.com/travel/healthclinintro.
Dun Laoghaire Medical Centre 5 Northumberland Ave, Dun Laoghaire, Co. Dublin Ⓣ01/280 4996, Ⓕ01/280 5603.
Glasgow Travel Clinic 3rd floor, 90 Mitchell St, Glasgow G1 3NQ Ⓣ0141/221 4224.
Hospital for Tropical Diseases Travel Clinic 2nd Floor, Mortimer Market Centre, off Capper St, London (Mon–Fri 9am–5pm by appointment only; Ⓣ020/7388 9600, Ⓦwww.masta.org).
MASTA (Medical Advisory Service for Travellers Abroad) 40 regional clinics (call Ⓣ0870/6062782, Ⓦwww.masta.org for the nearest).
Nomad Pharmacy surgeries Ⓦwww.nomadtravel.co.uk. Surgeries: 52 Grosvenor Gdns, Victoria, London SW1W 0AG Ⓣ020/78323/5823; 43 Bernard St, London, WC1N 1LE Ⓣ020/7833 4114; and 3–4 Wellington Terrace, Turnpike Lane, London N8 0PX Ⓣ020/8889 7014; all have walk-in and appointment clinics from Monday to Saturday.
Travel Medicine Services PO Box 254, 16 College St, Belfast 1 Ⓣ028/9031 5220.
Tropical Medical Bureau Grafton Buildings, 34 Grafton St, Dublin 2 Ⓣ1850/487 674, Ⓦwww.tmb.ie.

In the US and Canada

Canadian Society for International Health 1 Nicholas St, Suite 1105, Ottawa, ON K1N 7B7 Ⓣ613/241-5785, Ⓦwww.csih.org.
International SOS Assistance 3600 Horizon Blvd, Suite 300, Trevose, PA 19053, USA 19053-6956 Ⓣ1-800/523-8930, Ⓦwww.intsos.com.
MEDJET Assistance Ⓣ1-800/963-3528, Ⓦwww.medjetassistance.com.
Travel Medicine Ⓣ1-800/TRAVMED, Ⓦwww.travmed.com.

Australia and New Zealand

Travellers' Medical and Vaccination Centres 27–29 Gilbert Place, Adelaide, SA 5000 Ⓣ08/8212 7522; call Ⓣ1-300/658 844 Ⓦwww.tmvc.com.au. Contact for details of clinics across Australia and New Zealand.

Information, websites and maps

Both Hong Kong and Macau maintain tourist offices in several cities abroad. However, you'll get better, more detailed information once you're there.

Tourist offices abroad

Hong Kong Tourism Board (HKTB)

Australia Level 4, Hong Kong House, 80 Druitt St, Sydney, NSW 2000 Ⓣ02/9283 3083, Ⓔsydwwo@hktb.com.
Canada 3rd Floor, 9 Temperance Street, Toronto, ON M5H 1Y6 Ⓣ416/366 2389, Ⓔyyzwwo@hktb.com.
UK 6 Grafton St, London W1S 4EQ Ⓣ020/7533 7100, Ⓔlonwwo@hktb.com.

US Suite 2050, 10940 Wilshire Boulevard, Los Angeles, CA90024-3915 ⓣ310/208 4582, ⓔJeffS@hktb.com; 115 East 54th Street, New York, NY 10022-4512 ⓣ21/2421 3382, ⓔnycwwo@hktb.com; 130 Montgomery Street, San Francisco CA94104 ⓣ41/5781 4587, ⓔsfowwo@hktb.com.

Macau Government Tourist Office (MGTO)

Australia Level 17, Town Hall House, 456 Kent Street, Sydney NSW 2000 ⓣ02/9264 1488, ⓔmacau@worldtradetravel.com.
New Zealand Level 5, Ballantyne House, 101 Customs Street East, PO Box 3779, Auckland ⓣ09/3085206, ⓔmacau@aviationandtourism.co.nz.
UK 11 Blades Court, 121 Deodar Road, London SW15 2NU ⓣ20/8877 4517, ⓔsharon@representationplus.co.uk.
US 3601 Aviation Blvd. Suite 2100, Manhattan Beach, CA 90266 ⓣ310/643-2630, ⓔmacau@myriadmarketing.com; 501 5th Avenue, Suite 1101, New York NY 10017 ⓣ646/277-0690, ⓔmacau@myriadmarketing.com.

Tourist offices in Hong Kong

The **Hong Kong Tourism Board** (**HKTB**; ⓣ2508 1234 daily 8am–6pm, ⓦwww.hktb.com) are well informed and helpful in advising on restaurants, accommodation, sights, tours and activities, including transport schedules across the SAR; in addition, they organize **free courses** on *tai chi*, Cantonese Opera, tea appreciation, pearl grading, and more, for which you need to sign up for a day in advance. They have three main **offices**, all staffed by English-speakers: at the airport's arrival hall (daily 7am–11pm, accessible to arriving passengers only); Ground Floor, The Centre, 99 Queen's Rd Central, Central (daily 8am–8pm); and at the Star Ferry Concourse, Tsim Sha Tsui (daily 8am–6pm).

Tourist offices in Macau

The **Macau Government Tourist Office** (**MGTO**; ⓣ333000 daily 8am–7pm, ⓦwww.macautourism.gov.mo) is far more laid-back than its Hong Kong counterpart, but they still have plenty of brochures and advice on offer. The main offices are at the Jetfoil Terminal (daily 9am–10pm) and in the middle of Macau at Largo do Senado 9 (daily 9am–6pm); there are also useful counters at the Portas do Cerco (9am–1pm & 2.30–6pm), and the airport (9am–1.30pm, 2.15–7.30pm & 8.15–10pm). Their **Hong Kong office** is at the Macau Ferry Terminal, Shun Tak Tower, Connaught Road, Central (9am–1pm & 2.15–5.30pm; ⓣ2857 2287); you can usually get discounted rates for mid-range hotels here prior to departure.

Useful websites

ⓦ**http://english.hongkong.com** An easy-to-use concise site with handy snippets of information on everything in Hong Kong, from lifestyle through entertainment, travel and banking.
ⓦ**www.cityguide.gov.mo** Well-laid-out site, with lots of illustrations of Macau and useful information such as transport timetables and phone numbers. Also some good ideas for walking tours.
ⓦ**www.hktb.com**. Detailed and up-to-date site from The Hong Kong Tourism Board featuring festivals, weekly events, shopping, food and entertainment listings, plus full visa and visitor information.
ⓦ**www.macautourism.gov.mo**. Full of useful information from the Macau Tourist Office although it's oddly organized and garishly designed. Plenty of ideas for things to do and places to go, with good photos.
ⓦ**www.scmp.com**. The online edition of *The South China Morning Post*, Hong Kong's English-language daily, with a useful careers page, classified listings and news rundown. However, you can't read more than a snippet of the articles unless you subscribe.
ⓦ**www.ypmap.com/eng** Hong Kong's *Yellow Pages* site is excellent for finding anything from cinemas to shops and restaurants. You can search by street, business or building name, and it also lets you zoom in and search for bus and minibus routes.

Maps

As well as the **maps** in this book it's worth getting hold of the user-friendly *Hong Kong Rough Guide Map* printed on rip-proof, waterproof paper. The HKTB also provides a good map covering the tourist districts of Kowloon and the north shore of Hong Kong Island; if you're planning to venture further afield, you'll need something more comprehensive – try the paperback-format *Hong Kong Guidebook*, a couple of hundred pages of bilingual maps, street and building indexes, transport timetables and other listings, available for HK$60 from bookshops (see p.247).

For maps of the islands and New Territories – especially the *Countryside Series*, essential for hiking – try the **Government Bookshop**, Fourth Floor, Murray Building, Garden Road, Central (Mon–Fri 9am–5pm, Sat 9am–noon ⓣ2537 1910). Alternatively, you can get books and maps before you leave home from any of the outlets listed below.

In **Macau**, the only maps you should need are those in this book and the free street maps – showing all the bus routes – handed out by the MGTO at their offices.

Map outlets

In UK and Ireland

Stanfords 12–14 Long Acre, London WC2E 9LP ⓣ020/7836 1321, ⓦwww.stanfords.co.uk. Also at 39 Spring Gardens, Manchester ⓣ0161/831 0250, and 29 Corn St, Bristol ⓣ0117/929 9966.
Blackwell's Map and Travel Shop ⓦmaps.blackwell.co.uk/index.html. Branches all over the UK; check the website for details.
The Map Shop 30a Belvoir St, Leicester LE1 6QH ⓣ0116/247 1400, ⓦwww.mapshopleicester.co.uk.
National Map Centre 22–24 Caxton St, London SW1H 0QU ⓣ020/7222 2466, ⓦwww.mapsnmc.co.uk.
National Map Centre Ireland 34 Aungier St, Dublin ⓣ01/476 0471, ⓦwww.mapcentre.ie.
The Travel Bookshop 13–15 Blenheim Crescent, London W11 2EE ⓣ020/7229 5260, ⓦwww.thetravelbookshop.co.uk.
Traveller 55 Grey St, Newcastle-upon-Tyne NE1 6EF ⓣ0191/261 5622, ⓦwww.newtraveller.com.

In US and Canada

110 North Latitude US ⓣ336/369-4171, ⓦwww.110nlatitude.com.
Book Passage 51 Tamal Vista Blvd, Corte Madera, CA 94925 and in the historic San Francisco Ferry Building ⓣ1-800/999-7909 or ⓣ415/927-0960, ⓦwww.bookpassage.com.
Globe Corner Bookstore 28 Church St, Cambridge, MA 02138 ⓣ1-800/358-6013, ⓦwww.globecorner.com.
Longitude Books 115 W 30th St #1206, New York, NY 10001 ⓣ1-800/342-2164, ⓦwww.longitudebooks.com.
Travel Bug Bookstore 3065 W Broadway, Vancouver, BC, V6K 2G9 ⓣ604/737-1122, ⓦwww.travelbugbooks.ca.
World of Maps 1235 Wellington St, Ottawa, ON, K1Y 3A3 ⓣ1-800/214-8524 or ⓣ613/724-6776, ⓦwww.worldofmaps.com.

In Australia and New Zealand

Mapland 372 Little Bourke St, Melbourne ⓣ03/9670 4383, ⓦwww.mapland.com.au.
Map Shop 6–10 Peel St, Adelaide ⓣ08/8231 2033, ⓦwww.mapshop.net.au.
Map World 371 Pitt St, Sydney ⓣ02/9261 3601, ⓦwww.mapworld.net.au. Also at 900 Hay St, Perth ⓣ08/9322 5733, Jolimont Centre, Canberra ⓣ02/6230 4097 and 1981 Logan Road, Brisbane ⓣ07/3349 6633; 173 Gloucester St, Christchurch ⓣ0800/627 967, ⓦwww.mapworld.co.nz.

Costs and money

It's difficult to pinpoint an average daily cost for staying in Hong Kong and Macau, though it's true to say that both places are more expensive than most other Southeast Asian destinations. If you've just come from China or Thailand, for instance, you're in for a substantial increase in your daily budget. However, once you've accounted for your room and a decent meal every day, most of the extras are fairly cheap: snacking as you go from the street, or lunching on *dim sum*, is excellent value; public transport costs are among the lowest in the world; and the museums and galleries are mostly free.

For **banking information** and opening hours in both territories, see Hong Kong, p.44, Macau, p.45.

Currency

Hong Kong's currency is the **Hong Kong dollar**, written as HK$ or just $, and divided into 100 cents (written as c). **Notes** come in HK$20, 50, 100, 500 and 1000 denominations; there's a nickel-and-bronze HK$10 coin; **silver coins** come as HK$1, 2 and 5; and **bronze coins** as 10c, 20c and 50c.

At the time of writing the **rate of exchange** was HK$14.2 to the pound sterling, HK$7.8 to the US dollar and HK$5.9 to the Australian dollar – check the latest rates at ⓦwww.xe.com. There's no black market and money, in any amount, can be freely taken in and out of the territory.

Macau uses the **pataca**, made up of 100 avos. You'll see prices written as M$, ptcs or MOP$ (as in this book), all of which mean the same thing. **Coins** come as 10, 20 and 50 avos, and MOP$1, 2, 5 and 10; **notes** in denominations of MOP$10, 20, 50, 100, 500 and 1000.

The pataca is pegged to the Hong Kong dollar, though is officially worth roughly three percent less. In practice, **you can use Hong Kong dollars throughout Macau** to pay for anything, on a one-for-one basis – and should be given Hong Kong dollars in change if you do. You can't use patacas in Hong Kong, however, so spend them all before you leave Macau.

Hong Kong costs

At the bottom end of the scale, staying in hostels and dormitories and eating cheap Chinese meals at street stalls, you can survive in Hong Kong for HK$150 a day. Eat out more, or go to better restaurants, take a taxi or two, have a drink in a bar, and you're looking at HK$300 a day. If you upgrade to a room with en-suite facilities, eat three meals a day and don't stint on the extras, your daily expenses will exceed HK$600 – though if you're staying in one of the better hotels, this figure won't even cover your room.

Macau costs

Living costs in Macau are 10–20 percent less than in Hong Kong: you'll pay slightly more for cheaper beds, but will get much better value in the larger hotels. Meals, too, are good value: wine and port is imported from Portugal and untaxed, and an excellent three-course Portuguese meal with wine and coffee can be had for as little as MOP$120. Transport costs are minimal, since you can walk to most places, though buses and taxis are in any case extremely cheap.

Carrying money

It's a good idea to buy at least a few Hong Kong dollars from a bank at home before you go; that way you don't have to use the airport exchange desk (which has poor rates) when you arrive. However, probably the most convenient way to bring money to Hong Kong or Macau is by using a **debit/bank card** issued by your bank to draw funds directly from your home account through the ubiquitous **automatic teller machines** (ATMs) scattered around the two SARs. Your card needs to be marked with the "Cirrus-Maestro" logo, and your PIN number must be compatible with ATMs here – check with your bank in both instances. One of the best features of this method is that you pay official exchange rates, without having to haggle or shop around for the best deals. **Charges** are usually for a set fee per transaction – check with your bank.

You can use all major **credit cards** in Hong Kong but watch out for the **three-percent commission** that many places try to add to the price. American Express, MasterCard and Visa cardholders can also use regional ATMs to withdraw funds, though these are considered cash advances, with interest accruing daily from the date of withdrawal.

Travellers' cheques are another popular option, and are one of the safest, as cheques can be cancelled and reissued to you if lost or stolen – make sure you keep the purchase agreement and a record of cheque serial numbers safe and separate from the cheques themselves. However, it's expensive: you pay a **fee** to buy the cheques, and then pay **commission** every time you cash them at either a bank or currency exchange counter, both of which are ubiquitous in Hong Kong and Macau. It's best to shop around and ignore places advertising "no commission" on the deal – they just make up the difference by offering an even worse rate.

Having **money wired** from home is never convenient or cheap, and should be considered a last resort. The companies listed below typically charge eight to ten percent of the sum transferred. Alternatively, you can go to one of the major international banks and get them to have your bank telex the money to a specific branch in Hong Kong. This will take a couple of working days, and will cost about £25/$40 per transaction.

Money-wiring companies

Travelers Express/MoneyGram Ⓦwww.moneygram.com. US Ⓣ1-800/444-3010; Canada Ⓣ1-800/933-3278; UK, Ireland and New Zealand Ⓣ00800/6663 9472; Australia Ⓣ0011800/6663 9472.
Western Union Ⓦwww.westernunion.com. US and Canada Ⓣ1-800/CALL-CASH; Australia Ⓣ1800/501 500; New Zealand Ⓣ0800/005 253; UK Ⓣ0800/833 833; Republic of Ireland Ⓣ66/947 5603. Customers in the US and Canada can send money online.

Arrival

Most travellers arrive at Hong Kong International Airport, on Chek Lap Kok, just off the north coast of Lantau Island. Arriving by sea is another possibility, either on a cruise ship, or more likely by ferry from nearby parts of the Pearl River Delta. Many people reach Macau by going first to Hong Kong and taking the regular high-speed ferries from there. It's also possible to enter Hong Kong or Macau overland from China.

By air

Hong Kong International Airport, also known as **Chek Lap Kok** (Ⓦwww.hongkongairport.com), is about 34km from the centre of the city. The terminal, designed by British architect Sir Norman Foster, was built on land formed by flattening a small rocky islet and connecting it to the neighbouring island of Lantau. There are foreign-exchange facilities (with poor rates), a left-luggage office and an office of the Hong Kong Hotels Association (see p.181), which can help you find a room with its member hotels. The **Hong Kong Tourism Board** (see p.29) has a desk in the transit area, open from 7am–11pm.

The quickest way between the airport and the city is on the **Airport Express train** or AEL (every ten minutes 5.50am–12.48am). Carriages have air-conditioning and a reasonable amount of luggage space, but no toilets. One-way **tickets** can be bought with cash or credit cards from machines or customer service desks in the arrival halls. There are **three stops** on the line: Tsing Yi (12min; HK$60), Kowloon in Tsim Sha Tsui (20min; HK$90), and Hong Kong Station in Central (23 minutes, HK$100); all child tickets are half-price. From Kowloon and Hong Kong stations, you can catch **free shuttle buses** to local hotels between about 6am and 11pm; you don't have to be staying at any of the hotels to use the service. Hong Kong Station is also linked to the MTR station at Central – it's a five-minute walk between the two.

A cheaper but less convenient alternative is to catch bus #S51 or #S61 from the airport to **Tung Chung** (HK$4), and then use the MTR line (p.36) to reach the city or New Territories – it's about HK$23 from here into Kowloon.

The cheapest way of all from the airport into the city (and to most hotels) is by **Airbus** from outside the terminal. There are ten routes (some of which are detailed in the box p.34) with regular departures between 6am and midnight, and there's plenty of room

In-town check-in

If you have a late flight out, one way to get rid of your luggage after leaving your hotel is to use the **in-town check-in** service, at either the Hong Kong Station in Central or Kowloon Station in Tsim Sha Tsui, which allows you to check in your luggage up to one day in advance of departure (check which airlines offer this service on the airport website). Deposit carry-on luggage that you don't want to lug around town for the rest of the day at **left luggage offices** at the stations (6am–1am). You can also use the free shuttle buses from major hotels in Tsim Sha Tsui and on Hong Kong Island to reach Hong Kong Station and Kowloon Station.

for luggage. The airport customer-service counters sell tickets and give change; on the buses themselves you'll need to have the exact fare. The average journey time is about an hour. English-language announcements on board the buses tell you where to get off for the main hotels.

Taxis from the airport cost roughly HK$300 to Tsim Sha Tsui and about HK$350 to Hong Kong Island, so it's cheaper than taking the AEL for a group of four, though there may be extra charges for luggage and for tunnel tolls – on some tunnel trips the passenger pays the return charge too. **Rush-hour traffic** can slow down journey times considerably, particularly if you're using one of the cross-harbour tunnels to Hong Kong Island.

If your flight arrives after midnight or before 6am, you may want to use one of the nine **night-bus** services. The most useful are the N11 to Causeway Bay (every 30min), the N21 to the Tsim Sha Tsui Star Ferry pier (every 20min), and the N23 to Wan Shan via Yau Ma Tei and Kowloon City (roughly every hour); alternatively, you'll have to take a taxi, which shouldn't charge any extra at night.

Those arriving **by helicopter** from Macau with East Asia Airlines will touch down on the helipad above the Macau Ferry Terminal (see "By sea" below), where they'll clear customs.

By sea

Ocean-going **cruise liners** stopping at Hong Kong dock at the Harbour City Ocean Terminal in downtown Tsim Sha Tsui, just a short walk from MTR stations and the Star Ferry across to Hong Kong Island

Ferries **from China** originating at Zhuhai, Shenzhen, Zhaoqing and various riverside settlements between here and Guangzhou (Canton), mostly terminate at the **China Ferry Terminal** on Canton Road, Tsim Sha Tsui, Kowloon. It's about a fifteen-minute walk from here to the nearest MTR station on Nathan Road, less to much of the area's accommodation, though there are plenty of taxis too. Some ferries **from Macau**, along with some services from local Chinese ports, use the **Macau Ferry Terminal** in the Shun Tak Centre, Connaught Rd, Sheung Wan, Hong Kong Island; Sheung Wan MTR Station and bus terminus are next door.

Airbus routes

#A11 to North Point via Sheung Wan, Central, Admiralty and Wan Chai (daily 6am–midnight, every 15–25min; HK$40).

#A21 to Hung Hom KCR Station via Mongkok, Yau Ma Tei, Jordan and Tsim Sha Tsui (daily 6am--midnight, every 10min; HK$33). Goes past all the hotels and guest houses lining Nathan Road.

#A31 to the New Territories and Tsuen Wan (Discovery Park) via Tsuen Wan MTR Station (daily 6am–midnight, every 15–20min; HK$17). Travels via *Panda Hotel*.

#A35 to Mui Wo, Lantau Island (daily 6.30am–12.25am, at least hourly; HK$14).

#A41 to the New Territories and Sha Tin via Sha Tin KCR Station (daily 6am–midnight, every 15–20min; HK$20).Travels via *Regal Riverside* and *Royal Park*.

By train and bus

Express trains from Guangzhou arrive at Hung Hom Railway Station in Kowloon, also known as the **Kowloon–Canton Railway Station**. The easiest way into Tsim Sha Tsui from here is to catch the KCR line train one stop to East Tsim Sha Tsui Station; alternatively, for other destinations there is a bus stop and taxi rank outside. For Queen's Pier in Central, Hong Kong Island, take the high-speed ferry – walk down the steps out of the station towards the harbour: the pier is just to the right.

Local trains **from Guangzhou** drop you in the Chinese city of Shenzhen, from where you walk across the border to Lo Wu on the Hong Kong side and pick up the regular KCR trains to Kowloon: it's a fifty-minute ride, terminating at East Tsim Sha Tsui Station in Kowloon.

It's also possible to arrive **by bus** from Guangzhou and a couple of nearby Chinese cities. Services are run by the China Travel Service (CTS; see p.272 for their Hong Kong contact details) and stop along the way in Sheung Shui, Sha Tin and at Kowloon Tong MTR Station, before terminating at either Hung Hom Station or CTS branch offices in Mongkok or Wan Chai.

Arrival in Macau

Macau International Airport is located at the eastern end of Taipa Island. From the airport, the **airport bus** #AP1 (MOP$6) runs across the Ponte Governador Bobre de Carvalho bridge and stops outside the Jetfoil Terminal before heading on to the *Hotel Lisboa* and the Portas do Cerco at the border.

Hong Kong **turbojets** and **catamarans** dock at the Jetfoil Terminal in the Porto Exterior, on the eastern side of the Macau peninsula. There's a **money-exchange** office and ATMs here (though you don't need to exchange Hong Kong dollars as they're accepted everywhere in Macau), and a **left-luggage office** on the second floor of the terminal building (daily 6.30am–midnight) and 24-hour luggage lockers on the ground and first floors. The terminal's ground floor **Visitor Information Centre** (8am–7pm) hands out maps.

It takes around twenty minutes to **walk into central Macau**; otherwise, **buses** from the stops directly outside the terminal run into the centre, past several of the main hotels and out to Taipa and Coloane: #3, #3A, #10, #28A, #28B and #32 all go past the *Lisboa*; the #10 or #10A run to Largo do Senado; and the #28A goes on to Taipa Island. Other transport options from the terminal are taxis and pedicabs – for details see p.40.

Ferries from Shekou (Shenzhen) dock at the Porto Interior on the west side of the peninsula, from where it's a short walk to the main avenue, Avenida de Almeida Ribeiro; bus #3A from here stops at Largo do Senado, the *Lisboa*, and Jetfoil Terminal.

Crossing into Macau **from Zhuhai** lands you at either the Portas do Cerco (open 7am–midnight), from where bus #10 or #3 runs down to Avenida de Almeida Ribeiro; or on the Lotus Bridge (open 9am–5pm), between the islands of Taipa and Coloane – any north-bound bus will take you from here into central Macau.

Transport

Hong Kong has one of the world's most efficient integrated public transport systems. Underground and overground trains, trams, buses and ferries connect almost every part of the territory, and services are extremely cheap and simple to use.

Finding sights

Chinese characters for all of Hong Kong and Macau's sights mentioned in the text, along with some important streets, are given in boxes at the end of each chapter – use them if you're having trouble communicating on public transport or in asking directions on the street.

The MTR

Hong Kong's underground **MTR** (Mass Transit Railway, ⓦwww.mtr.com.hk) is the fastest public transport in the territory, and the most expensive – the harbour crossing from Central or Admiralty to Tsim Sha Tsui costs around HK$9, considerably more than the Star Ferry. **Hours of operation** are daily 6am–1am, with trains running every few minutes; the first and last train times are posted on boards at the stations. Avoid travelling during the morning and evening **rush hours** (8–9.30am & 5.30–7pm); in the morning especially, the crowds piling onto the escalators and trains are horrendous – avoid taking heavy luggage onto the train at these times.

There are five colour-coded lines (see the colour map at the back of this book) and useful **interchange stations** include Kowloon Tong (Kwun Tong Line) with the KCR East railway (see opposite), and at Mei Foo (Tsuen Wan Line) with the KCR West railway. The MTR station at Central also provides a link to the airport railway and the Tung Chung line – it's a five-minute walk between the two stations.

There's a **no-smoking** policy on all trains; you're not supposed to eat or drink anything either. There are also **no toilets** on any of the MTR platforms. However, everything is marked and signposted in **English**, as well as in Chinese characters, so you shouldn't get lost.

Tickets

Tickets cost from HK$4 to around HK$26 for a one-way journey. There are no returns and tickets are only valid for ninety minutes, so don't buy one for your return journey at the same time. Feed your money into the machines on the station concourse and you'll get your ticket, which looks like a thin plastic credit card. Some machines don't give change and some take only coins, but there are small change machines in the stations, and you can change notes or buy tickets at the information desks. **Children** under 12 pay half-price with a Child Ticket, also available from the machines.

To **use the system**, you feed your ticket into the turnstile, walk through and pick it up on the other side. At the end of your journey, the turnstile will retain your ticket as you exit.

If you are planning to use public transport a lot, it's worth buying an **Octopus Card**, a rechargeable stored-value ticket which gives reduced-rate travel on the MTR, KCR lines, LR (Light Rail), the Airport Express (AEL), trams, most buses, most ferries (including the Star Ferry) and minibuses. An adult Octopus card costs an initial HK$150, which includes a refundable HK$50 deposit and HK$100 usable value (you don't get the HK$50 back if you return the ticket within three months, however). When it runs out you simply add credit at machines in the MTR or over the counter at any *7-Eleven* store. An added benefit is that you don't have to feed it into the turnstile but can leave it in your wallet or bag and pass the entire thing over the sensor pad on the top of the turnstile. The cards are available from the MTR, AEL, KCR East Rail, LR and Hong Kong New World First Ferry ticket offices, and can also be used like a debit card to buy goods in *7-Eleven* stores.

Octopus also offer a **Tourist Pass** (HK$50) valid for 24hrs from the first time that you use it and allowing unlimited travel on the MTR (but not the AEL); and **Airport Express Tourist Card** (HK$200/300 including a HK$50 refundable deposit) for use on the AEL (either single or return according to price) and 72hrs unlimited travel on the MTR after the first time you use it. It also gives you HK$20 for use on the other forms of transport on which the Octopus card is valid (see above).

As everything is completely automated on the MTR, it seems simple enough to leap the turnstiles and **travel without a ticket**

– which, indeed, is what you'll see some people doing. The stations, however, are patrolled by inspectors and swept by TV cameras – there's a fine of HK$5000 if you're caught.

New Territories trains

There are two main **train networks** in the New Territories – the KCR Network and the Light Rail (LR) – plus the Airport Express (AEL), which as well as serving the airport also has stops at two places en route (see p.33). You're likely to use the AEL if you arrive or depart by air, though you probably won't have occasion to use the KCR and the LR unless you intend to do a bit of out-of-the-way sightseeing. As on the MTR, all stations, signs and trains are marked in English.

The KCR network

The **KCR network** (Ⓦwww.kcrc.com) serves the New Territories with three lines: **KCR East**, the **Ma On Shan Line**, and KCR West (see the colour map at the back of the book). Additional routes are **under construction** to link KCR East with KCR West at East Tsim Sha Tsui, and from Hung Hom to northwestern Hong Kong Island. See "Into mainland China", p.41 for more details on using the KCR to leave Hong Kong.

The ticketing and turnstile system is the same as that on the MTR. One-way **tickets** cost from around HK$3.50 (the Kowloon Tong–Mongkok section) to HK$9 (for the journey from Kowloon to Sheung Shui). **Children** under 3 travel free, those under 12 pay half-fare. There's a **first-class** compartment, staffed by a guard, for double the standard fare. You'll pay a HK$100 fine if caught travelling without a ticket, or travelling first-class with an ordinary ticket.

Kowloon Tong is the interchange station for the KCR and MTR; just follow the signs between the two. More importantly, **Sheung Shui** is the last stop that you can can get off at without a Chinese visa, despite the fact that most trains terminate one stop further on at Lo Wu, the border crossing for China.

The air-conditioned trains **operate** from around 5.30am to 1am, running every three to ten minutes or so. They're generally less crowded than MTR trains (except during rush hour at the Kowloon stations – Kowloon Tong and Mongkok), but be aware that **pickpockets** tend to ply their trade on this route. Again, there's **no smoking** and no eating on board, but there are **toilets** on all the station concourses.

The Light Rail (LR)

The **Light Rail** (Ⓦwww.kcrc.com) is a tram-like network linking the major western New Territory towns of Yuen Long, Tin Shui Wai, Siu Hong and Tuen Mun with both their outlying suburbs and the KCR West line. LR trains are electric, running alongside – and down the middle of – the New Territories' roads, and the system is zoned. Automatic ticket machines on the platforms tell you which zone your destination is in and how much it'll cost. Fares are comparable to the KCR, around HK$4–6 per journey; feed your money in and wait for your ticket. Tourists are unlikely to use the Light Rail system extensively, though it's useful for trips to the Hong Kong International Wetland Park (see p.137) and nearby areas of the New Territories; see the colour map at the back of the book.

Buses and minibuses

Double-decker **buses** are operated by three companies: New World First Bus (Ⓦwww.nwfb.com.hk for schedule), Citybus (Ⓦwww.citybus.com.hk) and KMB (Ⓦwww.kmb.com.hk) which between them cover just about every corner of the SAR. **Bus fares** range from HK$1.20 to around HK$35 a trip – the amount you have to pay is posted at most bus stops and on the buses as you get on. Put the exact fare into the box by the driver (who is unlikely to speak English); there's no change given, so keep a supply of coins with you.

Buses run from around 6am to midnight, there is also a skeleton night bus service (all bus numbers prefixed with "N" run overnight). Not all buses are air-conditioned (those that are cost more), and they can get very crowded during rush hour. However, on longer journeys, to the south of Hong Kong Island and out in the New Territories, they're an excellent way to see the countryside.

Each double-decker bus is marked with

the destination in English and a number. "K" after the number means that the bus links with a stop on the KCR line; "M"-suffixed buses stop at an MTR station; buses with an "R" only run on Sundays and public holidays; and "X" buses are express buses with limited stops.

Two other types of bus are good for short hops, such as scooting up and down Nathan Road: red-striped **minibuses**, and green-striped **maxicabs**. Both seat sixteen people and charge HK$2–18 (exact fare only) depending on distance, the main difference being that minibuses can be flagged down almost anywhere along their route, whereas maxicabs only pull up at stops. Their destination is shown on a card on the front, usually in Chinese characters with a tiny English version. When they want **to get off**, the Chinese shout *yau lok*; in practice, you can say almost anything as long as you make it clear you want to alight. Hours of operation are from around 6am until well after midnight on some routes.

The Hong Kong Tourism Board puts out some very useful **bus route maps**, including some maxicab routes, with the Chinese characters for all the major destinations in Kowloon, Hong Kong Island and the New Territories. Timetables (in English) are also posted at most bus stops. We've also suggested useful bus routes throughout the Guide.

Trams

Double-decker **trams** rattle along the north shore of Hong Kong Island, from Kennedy Town in the west to Shau Kei Wan in the east, via Western, Central, Admiralty, Wan Chai and Causeway Bay; some detour around Happy Valley and the racecourse. Not all trams run the full distance, so check the destination (marked in English) on the front and sides before you get on. From Central, east to Causeway Bay takes around forty minutes, to Shau Kei Wan around fifty minutes, and west to Kennedy Town around half an hour.

Climb aboard at the back. If you're staying on for a long journey, head upstairs for the views. Otherwise, start working your way through to the front and, when you get off, drop the **flat fare** (HK$2 for adults, HK$1 for senior citizens and children) in the box by the driver: there's no change given. Trams operate from 6am to 1am, though services on some parts of the line finish earlier; avoid rush hours if you actually want to see out of the window. For **information**, call Hong Kong Tramways ⓣ2548 7102.

The most famous tram of all is the **Peak Tram**, not really a tram at all but a funicular railway, which climbs swiftly from the Lower Peak Tram Terminal on Garden Road to the Peak Tower on Victoria Peak (with a couple of local commuter request stops on the way) – see p.62 for more details.

Ferries

On a clear day, the **cross-harbour ferries** provide an unforgettable first sight of Hong Kong Island, with countless boats zipping across the harbour. Services are cheap, reliable and run every day of the week: the only days to watch out for are in **typhoon** season, when crossings sometimes become very choppy and can be suspended altogether.

The quickest and most famous service is the **Star Ferry** (ⓣ2366 2576; ⓦwww.starferry.com.hk), a seven-minute crossing between Tsim Sha Tsui and Central on one of ten double-decker, green and white passenger ferries. Ferries run every few minutes 6.30am–11.30pm; it costs just HK$2.20 to travel on the upper deck, HK$1.70 on the lower deck. Check you're in the right channel at the ferry pier, feed your coins into the relevant turnstile and join the waiting hordes at the gate, which swings open when the ferry docks.

There are several other cross-harbour ferry services, too, operated either by Star Ferry, New World First Ferry or Discovery Bay Transportation with regular crossings throughout the day (every five to twenty minutes). These include the **Tsim Sha Tsui** to **Wan Chai** (7.30am–11pm; HK$2.20); the **Wan Chai** to **Hung Hom**, Whampoa (7am–7pm; HK$5.30); the **Central** to **Hung Hom**, Whampoa (7.20am–7pm; HK$5.30); and the high-speed ferry from **Queen's Pier** in Central to **Tsim Sha Tsui East** near Hung Hom KCR terminus (every 20min, 7.40am– 8.20pm; HK$4.50); there are also links from **North Point** to Hung Hom and

Kowloon City. While you may have no real cause to use any of these services, they're worth thinking about simply as trips in their own right: splendid, cheap sightseeing.

Quicker harbour crossings are provided by a fleet of **high-speed ferries**, most usefully the one that links Central (Queen's Pier, in front of City Hall) with Tsim Sha Tsui East, stopping at the pier close to the Hung Hom KCR Station (7.40am–8.20pm, every 20min; HK$4.50). In addition, a 24-hour service speeds from Central Star Ferry Pier to Discovery Bay on Lantau (see p.169), while another series of ferries and hoverferries serve the **outlying islands** from Central and elsewhere; for full details see p.155.

The location of the **ferry piers** is currently in a state of flux while land reclamation work continues in Central and Kowloon: for up-to-date information, contact the HKTB.

Taxis

Hong Kong's **taxis** are relatively cheap – many people treat them as a branch of public transport. You can flag them down in the street or pick one up at the **ranks** you'll find at major MTR and KCR stations and at both Star Ferry terminals. Taxis can't drop or pick up on yellow lines. Look for a red "For Hire" flag in the windscreen; at night the "Taxi" sign on the roof is lit. Make sure the driver turns the meter on when you get in (though rip-offs are rare). On **Hong Kong Island** and **Kowloon**, taxis are red: minimum charge is HK$15 (for the first 2km) and then it's HK$1.40 for every 200m. In the **New Territories**, taxis are green and slightly cheaper. The island of **Lantau** has its own pale blue taxis, though there's no taxi service on any other island.

Taxis can be extremely hard to come by when it rains, during typhoons, on race days, after midnight and at driver change over time (around 9.30am and again at 4pm). Many drivers don't speak English, although they'll know the names of major hotels – and they should have a card somewhere in the cab with major destinations listed in Chinese and English. Otherwise you'll need to have someone write down where you're going on a piece of paper to show to the driver. If you get really stuck, gesture to the driver to call his control centre on the two-way radio, and state your destination into the microphone. Someone there will translate.

Although the red taxis are supposed to work on Hong Kong Island and in Kowloon, drivers will often only pick up fares on one side or the other. In practice, this means that if you want to use the **cross-harbour tunnel**, the driver is allowed to charge you double the toll on top of the fare, since they assume they won't get a fare back. More annoying is the practice of drivers heading back to base and putting a sign in their window saying either "Hong Kong" or "Kowloon"; they'll only take you if you're headed their way, but more often than not will still charge you double the actual toll. If you're not happy with this – and that might depend on how difficult it is to get a taxi at the time – check before you set off, and be prepared to kick up a fuss and get out. You'll also have to pay tolls (HK$5–15) on top of your fare at the other tunnels in the territory, such as the Aberdeen tunnel and the Lion Rock tunnel to Sha Tin – there should be a yellow sign inside each taxi telling you how much the tolls are. You'll also have to pay an extra HK$5 for each piece of **luggage**.

If you want to pursue a complaint, call the 24-hour Hong Kong Police hotline (Ⓣ2527 7177), but make sure you've taken a note of the taxi licence number beforehand.

Renting cars and bikes

Renting your own car in Hong Kong isn't a sensible idea. The public transport system is so good that it's rarely quicker to drive, and in any case one dose of rush-hour traffic would put you off driving forever. If you really need a car, out in the New Territories, say, or on Lantau, it's always cheaper just to take a taxi. There's also the problem of parking: finding a space in the centre is nigh impossible, and the multistorey car parks are generally expensive and located where you least want them. If you're determined, see p.269 for the addresses of **car rental** agencies and central **car parks**.

Bike rental is more feasible, though again, not in crowded central Hong Kong or Kowloon. There are several places in the New Territories where it's fun: in particular, the cycle lanes around Sha Tin which stretch all the way along Tolo Harbour to Tai Po and then on to Tai Mei Tuk (Plover Cove). You can rent bikes from Tai Wai (see p.125), Tai Po (see p.131) or from Plover Cove Country Park itself (see p.132). The less congested outlying islands are also excellent places to cycle: there are bikes for rent at Mui Wo on Lantau, Cheung Chau and the rather hilly Lamma Island just outside Yung Shue Wan. Expect to pay around HK$40–50 a day per bike.

Organized tours

There are a huge range of **organized tours** of Hong Kong, and if you're only staying a couple of days some may be worth considering – the more exotic tram- and boat-related extravaganzas especially. Some of the better ideas are detailed below. Also, if you really can't bear to make your own arrangements, a whole range of companies will organize your trip to Macau or China, though this is extremely easy to do yourself. For more help, try one of the **travel agencies** below.

China Travel Service Floor 4, CTS House, 78–83 Connaught Rd, Central (ⓣ2789 5401, and 27–33 Nathan Road (entrance in Peking Road) ⓣ2315 7188; ⓦwww.chinatravelOne.com. Local tours and China trips with the official Chinese government organization.

Gray Line Tours 5th Floor, Cheong Hing Building, 72 Nathan Rd, Tsim Sha Tsui ⓣ2368 7111, ⓦwww.grayline.com.hk. An international organization whose Hong Kong arm runs predictable coach tours around the SAR (HK$300 upwards) plus longer trips to Macau and China.

Hong Kong Archaeological Society Block 58, Kowloon Park, Tsim Sha Tsui ⓣ2723 5765 (ask for the honorary secretary). Field trips, lectures and excavations.

Hong Kong Dolphinwatch Ltd 1528A Star House, Tsim Sha Tsui, ⓣ2984 1414, ⓦwww.hkdolphinwatch.com. Popular boat trips out to north Lantau waters to spot rare pink dolphins; half-day trip for HK$420.

Hong Kong Tourism Board Any of the HKTB offices (see p.30 for addresses) can book you onto one of their tours, which include everything from escorted visits to various attractions to harbour cruises and full-day New Territories tours (recommended for the more remote heritage trails and ancient sites).

Splendid Tours & Travel Sheraton Hotel Lobby, Level 2, Tsim Sha Tsui, Kowloon ⓣ2316 2151, ⓦwww.splendidtours.com. Offers moderately priced standard harbour cruises, Lantau Island day-trips, Macau excursions and New Territories visits.

Transport in Macau

You'll be able to **walk** almost everywhere in Macau, though to reach Taipa and Coloane and a couple of the more far-flung sights, you'll need transport. **Buses and minibuses** operate on circular routes daily from 7am until 11pm; a few stop running after 6–8pm, though the short distances mean you shouldn't get stuck. **Fares** are low: around MOP$2.5 for any single trip on city routes; slightly more for trips to Taipa or Coloane. The airport bus costs MOP$6 – pay the driver as you get on with the exact fare.

The main **terminals** and bus stops are outside the Jetfoil Terminal; in front of the *Hotel Lisboa;* at Barra district in the southwest of the peninsula (near the Maritime Museum and A-Ma Temple); along Avenida de Almeida Ribeiro; and at Praça Ponte e Horta. Details of individual buses are given in the Macau chapter where useful.

Taxis, pedicabs, car and bike rental

It's cheap enough to get around Macau by **taxi**, and you'll find ranks outside all the main hotels and at various points throughout the enclave. All rides are metered: minimum charge is MOP$10 (for the first 1500m), after which it's MOP$1 for every 250m, plus MOP$3 for each piece of luggage. Going by taxi to the islands of Taipa and Coloane, there's a MOP$5 surcharge (from Taipa to Coloane it's MOP$2), though there's no surcharge if you're coming back the other way. There's also a MOP$5 surcharge if you are picked up at the airport.

Outside the Jetfoil Terminal and the *Hotel Lisboa* you'll be accosted by the drivers of **pedicabs** – three-wheeled bicycle rickshaws. They're more suited for short tourist rides – say around the Praia Grande – than for serious getting around, since Macau's hills prevent any lengthy pedalling. You're supposed to bargain for rides, which cost around MOP$40–50 for a short turn along the harbour and MOP$150 for an hour's sightseeing, but bear in mind that some of the wiry drivers are more than 70 years old.

Renting a car doesn't make an awful lot of sense: it's easy to get around cheaply by public transport and on foot and also extremely difficult to find parking spaces in central Macau. You might, however, want to pay for the novelty of driving a **moke** – a low-slung Jeep – particularly if you intend to see a bit of Taipa and Coloane, where transport is less common. See "Directory" (p.319) for details.

Renting a **bicycle** is the best bet if you want a little more mobility, though be warned that the traffic in the centre is as manic as in Hong Kong, and that you're not allowed to ride over the Ponte Governador Bobre de Carvalho. Bike-riding is most enjoyable on the islands.

Organized tours

There's are endless **tour combinations** available – half-day whisks around the peninsula and islands, from around MOP$110 a head, to pricey three- or four-day trips that take in Zhuhai and parts of Guangdong province. Most can be booked in Hong Kong, though it's generally cheaper to book in Macau. For details contact one of the tour operators below – all offer the same tours at broadly similar prices, though CTS is often slightly

Into mainland China

To enter China, you'll need a **visa**, which in Hong Kong are issued at the Consulate Department of the Chinese Ministry of Foreign Affairs building on Kennedy Road, in Central (Mon–Fri 9am–4pm); and in Macau through the CTS, Rua de Nagasaki 7 ⓣ706655, ⓕ703689. However, it's actually cheaper and faster to arrange a visa through a **travel agency** (see Directory, p.272) or through your accommodation, many of which offer the service. **Fees** vary between around HK$200 and HK$600, according to whether you want a single-entry or double-entry, one-month, three-month, or six-month visa, and whether you want fast (same-day) processing or two to three days. Bring a passport photo with you. Agents can also arrange hotel accommodation and onward journeys to all major cities in China.

From Hong Kong

The simplest route into China **from Hong Kong** is by **direct train to Guangzhou** from Kowloon's Hung Hom KCR Station to Guangzhou East Station; there are a dozen trains daily, and the trip takes under three hours (around HK$200 one way). Tickets are obtainable in advance from CTS offices (see Directory, p.272), or on the day from Hung Hom KCR Station. As a cheaper alternative, ride the KCR up to Lo Wu, cross into Shenzhen on foot and pick up one of the hourly trains to Guangzhou from there – in all, this costs around HK$100.

The other land route is by **bus**. CTS (see Directory, p.272 or ⓦhttp://ctsbus.hkcts.com), runs frequent services to Shenzhen and Guangzhou; the Guangzhou run takes about 3hr 30min and costs HK$150 one-way.

By **boat**, there are around six fast ferries daily to **Shenzhen** (Shekou) each from the Macau Ferry Terminal on Hong Kong Island, and from the China Ferry Terminal on Canton Road, Kowloon. Tickets cost HK$105–170 depending on class and time of day, and the crossing takes under an hour. Further departures from the China Ferry Terminal take in towns around the Pearl River Delta – not of much use for tourists – and to **Zhaoqing** in eastern Guangdong province.

Finally, you can **fly** from Hong Kong into all major Chinese cities on regional Chinese carriers. Note, however, that all air fares from Hong Kong are far more expensive than those out of either Shenzhen or Guangzhou, even if you pay for a night's accommodation in these cities along the way. Good-value air tickets from Hong Kong, Shenzhen or Guangzhou can be booked through travel agents in Hong Kong such as the CTS or Shoestring Travel.

From Macau

From Macau, the quickest way to China is to cross the land border into Zhuhai, from where you can catch a bus to Guangzhou (MOP$55; 3hr). You can also book direct buses to Guangzhou with Macau's CTS for MOP$75, or **fly** to a dozen or so cities across China – though, as with air fares into China from Hong Kong, it's cheaper to fly to Chinese destinations from Guangzhou.

cheaper. The same tours can usually be booked through hotels too, but booking direct will save you MOP$10–50.

China Travel Service Rua de Nagasaki 7 ⓣ706655, ⓕ703689; or desks at the Grandeur hotel (ⓣ781233), Lisboa (ⓣ377666) and Grandview (ⓣ837788). Tours and China visas.

China International Travel Service Av. da Prai Grande Trav. de I. S. de Carvalho 8-10 (ⓣ715454, ⓕ715648.

Gray Line Tours 2nd Floor Jetfoil Terminal ⓣ725813.

New Sintra Tours 2nd Floor, Jetfoil Terminal ⓣ728050.

Communications

Both Hong Kong and Macau's communications are fast and efficient. The phones all work and the postal system is good, sending mail home is quick and relatively cheap, and the poste restante system is well organized.

Mail

Post offices throughout Hong Kong are open Monday–Friday 9.30am–5pm and Saturday 9.30am–1pm. The main GPO building, at 2 Connaught Place, Central, by the Star Ferry on Hong Kong Island, and the main post office at 10 Middle Road in Tsim Sha Tsui stay open longer – Monday–Saturday 8am–6pm and Sunday 9am–2pm. Letters sent **poste restante** will go to the GPO building on Connaught Place (collection Mon–Sat 8am–6pm) – take your passport along when you go to collect them. Letters and cards sent airmail take three days to a week to reach Britain or North America. **Surface mail** is slower, taking weeks rather than days; rates are listed in a leaflet available from post offices.

If you're sending **parcels** home, they'll have to conform with the post office's packaging regulations. Either take your unwrapped parcel along to a main post office – together with your own brown paper and tape – and follow their instructions, or buy one of their cardboard boxes. The post office will have the relevant forms to **insure** your parcels, as well as the **customs declaration** that must be filled in for all goods sent abroad by post. Your parcel will go by surface mail unless you specify otherwise – the price obviously increases the bigger the parcel and the further it has to go.

The main post office in **Macau** is on Largo do Leal Senado, just off Avenida de Almeida Ribeiro (Mon–Fri 9am–6pm, Sat 9am–1pm), and is where the **poste restante** mail is sent.

Telephone numbers

The Hong Kong Chinese consider certain **phone numbers** to be unlucky, principally because the words for some of the numbers sound like more ominous words – 4 (*sei*), for example, which sounds like the Cantonese word for "death". Lots of people won't accept the private numbers they're allocated by the telephone company for this reason, and there's a continuous struggle to change numbers. Conversely, other numbers are considered lucky because they sound fortuitous – particularly 3 (longevity), 8 (prosperity) and 9 (eternity) – and people will pay or bribe to have these included in their telephone number. The same applies, incidentally, to car number plates: each year there's a government auction of the best ones, some of which fetch thousands of dollars.

Useful telephone numbers

Hong Kong

Collect calls ☎10010
Directory enquiries (English) ☎1081
Emergencies (ambulance, police or fire) ☎999
IDD and cardphone enquiries ☎10013
International operator ☎10013
International operator assistance for foreign credit card calls ☎10011
Time and temperature ☎18501
Tourist information (multilingual) ☎2508 1234
Weather (English) ☎187 8066
Calling Macau from Hong Kong ☎001 + 853 + number.

Macau

Directory enquiries (Chinese and English) ☎181
Emergencies ☎999
Time (English) ☎140
Calling Hong Kong from Macau
☎00 + 852 + number.

Calling Hong Kong and Macau from home

Hong Kong Dial the international access code + ☎852 + number.
Macau Dial the international access code + ☎853 + number.
International access codes UK, Ireland and New Zealand ☎00; US and Canada ☎011; Australia ☎0011.

Calling home from Hong Kong and Macau

To call US and Canada: international access code +1+ area code + number.
To call Australia: international access code + 61+ area code + number.
To call New Zealand: international access code + 64 + area code + number.
To call UK and Northern Ireland: international access code + 44 + area code minus initial 0 + number.
To call Republic of Ireland: international access code + 353 + area code + number.
To call China: international access code + 86 + area code + number.
International access codes Hong Kong ☎001; Macau ☎00.

There's also a post office at the Jetfoil Terminal (Mon–Sat 10am–7pm). Otherwise, little booths all over Macau sell **stamps** (*selos* in Portuguese), as do the larger hotels, and there are post offices on Taipa and Coloane. Letters and cards sent from Macau to Europe and North America take around the same time as from Hong Kong – between five days and a week.

Phones

Making a local call from a private phone in **Hong Kong** is free. All telephone numbers contain eight digits and there are no area codes. Public **coinphones** cost HK$1 for five minutes, while there are also credit card phones and **cardphones**. You'll find phones at MTR stations, ferry terminals, in shopping centres and hotel lobbies, while most shops and restaurants will let you use their phone for free. You can buy **phone cards** from PCCW–HKT outlets (see under Mobile Phones overfeaf for addresses) and from tourist offices and 7-Eleven stores; they come in units of HK$50, HK$100, HK$200 and HK$300. However, for overseas calls it's much cheaper to buy **discount phone cards** where you dial an access number, enter a PIN supplied with the card, and then dial the overseas phone number; costs to the UK, US or Australia are just a dollar or two per minute. Different cards give discounts for specific regions only, so you might have to shop around until you find the right one – Worldwide House in Central has dozens of places selling them on the second and third floors.

In **Macau**, local phone calls are free from private phones, or MOP$1 from a payphone (there are groups of payphones around the Largo do Senado and at the Jetfoil Terminal). Hotels, however, may charge up to MOP$3 for each local call – check before you dial. For **international calls**, you'll want to buy a **phonecard** from the telephone office at the back of the main post office, the Jetfoil Terminal, the airport, the *Fortuna*, *Lisboa* and *Grandeur* hotels or CTM shops around town. They come in denominations of MOP$50, MOP$100 and MOP$150, and can be used in most public phones.

For **international calls**, use the International Direct Dialling (IDD) phones found in both SARs.

Mobile phones

If your mobile phone is GSM-compatible then the cheapest way to use it is to buy a **pre-paid SIM** card, to replace the one you use in your home country (giving you a new number). Simply slot the HK$300 stored-value cards into your phone to make local and overseas calls to more than 200 countries (apart from the US and Canada). You pay for both outgoing and incoming calls; recharge vouchers are available to top up the value. The alternative is to set up **auto-roaming** with your mobile company before leaving home, though this is usually much more expensive.

Two companies in Hong Kong, **CSL** (Ⓦprepaid.hkcsl.com) and **SmarTone-Vodaphone** (Ⓦwww.smartone-vodafone.com.hk), sell pre-paid SIM cards. You can buy them from 7-Eleven stores, some supermarkets and direct. SmarTone outlets include Ground Floor, CNT Tower, 338 Hennessy Rd, Wan Chai; 56 Percival St, Causeway Bay; and Ground Floor, National Court, 240–252 Nathan Rd, Jordan; CSL cards are sold at PCCW-HKT shops (main branches at 161–163 Des Voeux Rd, Central; 42–44 Yee Wo St, Causeway Bay; and 168–176 Sai Yueng Choi St, Mongkok.

Email and Internet access

Internet and **email** access is available in Hong Kong at branches of the *Pacific Coffee Company* and other cybercafés and net bars (see p.198), or in the business centres of major hotels. All libraries have public-use terminals where you can surf for free, but you almost always have to book in advance. City Hall library (9th Floor, City Hall High Block, Central; Mon–Thurs 10am–7pm, Fri 10am–9pm, Sat & Sun 10am–5pm) and the Central library (66 Causeway Rd, Causeway Bay; Mon, Tues, Thurs & Fri 10am–9pm, Wed 1pm-9pm, Sat & Sun 10am–6pm) also have a computer room where you can use word-processing software, printers and scanners. In Macau your options are more limited, but there are a few Internet bars – see p.320.

Opening hours and public holidays

Hong Kong has a fairly complicated set of opening hours for different shops and services. Generally, offices are open Monday–Friday 9am–5pm, and some open Saturday 9am–1pm; banks, Monday–Friday 9am–4.30pm, Saturday 9am–12.30pm; shops, daily 10am–7/8pm, though later in tourist areas; and post offices, Monday–Friday 9.30am–5pm, Saturday 9.30am–1pm. Museums tend to close one day a week; check the text for exact details. Temples often have no set hours, though they are usually open from early morning to early evening; produce markets tend to kick off at dawn (when they're busiest) and peter out during the afternoon, though other markets (such as Kowloon's Temple Street Night Market and Jade Market) have varying opening times, which are given in the text.

Public holidays in Hong Kong and Macau

January 1 New Year.
January/February Three days' holiday for Chinese New Year.
March/April Easter (holidays on Good Friday, Easter Saturday and Easter Monday).
April Ching Ming Festival (Cleaning Ancestors' Graves).
May Labour Day, Buddha's Birthday.
June Dragon Boat Festival (boat races to commemorate the patriotic poet-official Qu Yuan).
July 1 HKSAR Establishment Day (Hong Kong only).
September Mid-Autumn Festival (special mooncake pastries are eaten).
October 1 Chinese National Day.
October Cheung Yeung Festival (hill-climbing events).
November 2 All Souls' Day (Macau only).
December 8 Feast of Immaculate Conception (Macau only).
December 20 Macau SAR Establishment Day (Macau only).
December 22 Winter Solstice (Macau only).
December 25 and 26 Christmas.

On **public holidays** and some religious festivals most shops and all government offices in both Hong Kong and Macau are closed. See p.237 for details of festivals in Hong Kong.

Macau

In Macau, **opening hours** are more limited, with government and official offices open Monday–Friday 8.30/9am–1pm and 3–5/5.30pm, Saturday 8.30/9am–1pm. Shops and businesses are usually open throughout the day and have slightly longer hours. Macau's mostly Cantonese population celebrates the same Chinese religious and civil holidays and **festivals** as in Hong Kong (apart from Hong Kong's Tai Chiu festival). Hong Kong's Tin Hau festival is called the **A-Ma** festival in Macau, and takes place around the end of April.

Many of the public holidays associated with Portugal were scrapped after the handover in December 1999, and have been replaced by a couple of dates from the mainland – namely October 1 for **China's National Liberation Day**, and December 20 to mark the **Macau SAR Establishment Day**. In addition the Portuguese keep alive the following celebrations though neither are public holidays:

Lent (first day): procession of Our Lord of Passos. An image of Christ is carried in procession from the church of Santo Agostinho to the Sé for an overnight vigil and then returned via the Stations of the Cross.

May 13: procession of Our Lady of Fatima, from São Domingos church to the Penha chapel to commemorate a miracle in Fatima, Portugal, in 1913. The biggest annual Portuguese religious celebration.

Crime and safety

Hong Kong and Macau are both very safe places for tourists, certainly compared to other Asian cities. The only real concern is the prevalence of pickpockets: the crowded streets, trains and buses are the ideal cover for them. To guard against being robbed in this way, keep money and wallets in inside pockets, sling bags around your neck (not just over your shoulder) and pay attention when getting on and off packed public transport.

In both Hong Kong and Macau, dial ☎999 for any emergency service (police, ambulance or fire).

Apart from this, **avoiding trouble** is a matter of common sense. Most of the streets are perfectly safe, as is Hong Kong's MTR underground system, which is clean, well lit and well used at night. Taxis, too, are reliable, though it's still wise to use registered taxis from proper taxi ranks only.

In both SARs, it's rare that you'll be wandering around areas of the city at night that are a bit dodgy and, if you are, there's nothing you can do to avoid standing out. The best advice if you're lost, or somewhere vaguely threatening, is to look purposeful, don't dawdle and stick to the main roads. If you are **held up and robbed** – an extremely unlikely event – hand over your money and *never* fight back.

More common problems are those associated with **drunkenness** in Hong Kong. If it's your scene, be careful in bars where the emphasis is on buying hugely expensive drinks for the "girls": if you get drunk and can't/won't pay, the bar gorilla will help you find your wallet. And unless you like shouting and fighting, try to avoid the bars when the sailors of various fleets hit the city.

Police and offences

Probably the only contact you'll have with the olive- or blue-uniformed **Hong Kong Police** (who are armed) is if you have something stolen, when you'll need to get a report for your insurance company. In this case, contact one of the police stations, whose addresses are given on p.271. In **Macau**, police wear a dark blue uniform in winter, and sky-blue shirts and navy blue trousers in summer. The main police station, where you should go in the event of any trouble, is listed on p.319.

There are a few **offences** you might commit unwittingly. In Hong Kong, you're required to carry some form of **identification** at all times: if you don't want to carry your passport around, anything with your photograph will do, or your driving licence. Residents (and those thinking of staying and working in Hong Kong) need a special ID card. As a Westerner it's unlikely you'll be stopped in the street and asked for ID, though you might be involved in the occasional police raid on discos and clubs, when they're usually looking for known Triad members, illegal immigrants and drugs. They'll prevent anyone from leaving until they've taken down everyone's details from their ID.

Buying, selling or otherwise being involved with **drugs** is extremely unwise. If you're caught in possession, no one is going to be sympathetic, least of all your consulate.

Other than these things, you'll be left pretty much alone, though don't think of **bathing topless** on any of Hong Kong or Macau's beaches: you'll draw a lot of attention to yourself, offend some people and in any case it's illegal.

Sexual harassment

Harassment is not common, and women travelling in Hong Kong and Macau are more likely to be hassled by foreign expats than by Chinese men. To minimize risks try to avoid travelling alone late at night on Hong Kong's MTR, or during rush hour when men might take advantage of the crush for a quick grope. For local women's organizations in Hong Kong, see p.272.

Organized crime: the Triads

Hong Kong's **Triads** (see p.232) are directly and indirectly responsible for most of the drug dealing, prostitution, corruption and major crime in the territory. Needless to say, the average visitor won't come into contact with any of this, though drug addicts support their habit by pickpocketing and mugging, and the shops and restaurants you visit may be supplied by a Triad-related company.

Travellers with disabilities

Physically disabled travellers, especially those reliant upon wheelchairs, will find Hong Kong easier to manage than they might have imagined, despite the steep streets and busy intersections. There are special access and toilet facilities at the airport, as well as on the main Kowloon–Canton East Railway (KCR) and Light Rail (LR) system, and at MTR stations. The AEL and MTR have carriages with wheelchair spaces and waist-level poles, though other forms of public transport are not so accessible – some buses have wheelchair access but trams are virtually out of bounds.

Wheelchairs are able to gain access to the lower deck of cross-harbour and outlying island ferries, and taxis are usually obliging. There are fewer facilities for visually disabled visitors, though assistance is offered by braille signage in KCR lifts and clicking poles at the top and bottom of escalators.

The HKTB issues a useful and comprehensive free booklet *Hong Kong Access Guide for Disabled Visitors* (available online at Ⓦwww.hkcss.org.hk), listing facilities for the disabled in public buildings, hotels, restaurants and recreational buildings. The HKTB's own website also includes a Barrier-free Travel page (Ⓦwww.discoverhongkong.com/eng/travelneeds/disabled/index.jhtml) with links to Hong Kong websites for disabled travellers.

Macau is far less easy to negotiate for physically disabled travellers. The streets are older, narrower, rougher and steeper, and it lacks the overhead ramps, wide, modern elevators, etc that make Hong Kong relatively approachable; contact the MGTO (Ⓦwww.macautourism.gov.mo) before you travel for details of accommodation and transport facilities.

Contacts for travellers with disabilities

In the UK and Ireland

Irish Wheelchair Association Blackheath Drive, Clontarf, Dublin 3 Ⓣ01/818 6400, Ⓦwww.iwa.ie.
Tripscope The Vasapll Centre, Gill Ave, Bristol BS16 2QQ, Ⓣ0845/7 58 56 41 Ⓦwww.tripscope.org.uk.

In the US and Canada

Access-Able Ⓦwww.access-able.com.
Directions Unlimited 123 Green Lane, Bedford Hills, NY 10507 Ⓣ1-800/533-5343 or 914/241-1700. Travel agency specializing in bookings for people with disabilities.
Mobility International USA 451 Broadway, Eugene, OR 97401 Ⓣ541/343-1284, Ⓦwww.miusa.org.
Society for the Advancement of Travelers with Handicaps 347 5th Ave, New York, NY 10016 Ⓣ212/447-7284, Ⓦwww.sath.org.
Wheels Up! Ⓣ1-888/38-WHEELS, Ⓦwww.wheelsup.com.

In Australia and New Zealand

ACROD (Australian Council for Rehabilitation of the Disabled) PO Box 60, Curtin ACT 2605; Ⓣ02/6282 4333 (also TTY), Ⓦwww.acrod.org.au.
Disabled Persons Assembly 4/173–175 Victoria St, Wellington, New Zealand Ⓣ04/801 9100 (also TTY), Ⓦwww.dpa.org.nz.

Working or studying

Hong Kong has always been full of expats working in the territory although, nowadays, all foreigners seeking a job must already have obtained a work visa before arriving in the SAR, and these are only issued with copious supporting documentation from locally based firms. It is possible to study here, but the cost of living doesn't make it an attractive proposition unless you're being sponsored: it's far cheaper to study Cantonese or other Chinese languages, for example, over the border in Guangdong province.

Finding work

Before you start looking for work, remember that you're up against a well-educated, multilingual local population who are themselves facing increasing unemployment in the face of cheaper labour conditions on the Chinese mainland. The government also imposes stringent conditions on recruiting from abroad – employers have to show that the job cannot be done by a local person. For details on what you'll need to apply for a **work visa**, contact the **Immigration Department**, Immigration Tower, 7 Gloucester Rd, Wan Chai, Hong Kong ⓣ2824 6111, ⓦwww.immd.gov.hk.

The only likely openings are for **skilled and highly specialized work**, usually requiring fluency in English and/or other languages. **Teaching English** is your best bet: to get a job with an official language school, such as the British Council, you'll need a degree and a TEFL qualification, while for government and international schools you'll need an officially recognized teaching qualification from your home country.

Useful publications and websites

An idea of the sorts of jobs available (including TEFL) can be gleaned from the "classifieds" section of the *South China Morning Post* (ⓦwww.scmp.com). Career Global (ⓦwww.caterergloball.com) has a good list of jobs in the Hong Kong hospitality industry; Going Global (ⓦwww.goinglobal.com) publishes a Hong Kong-specific guide for finding work in the SAR; and *Vacation Work* (ⓦwww.vacationwork.co.uk) publishes books on summer jobs abroad and how to work your way around the world. In addition, ⓦwww.studyabroad.com is a useful website with listings and links to study and work programmes in Hong Kong.

Hong Kong

Hong Kong

1

Hong Kong Island

To many people – visitors and residents alike – **Hong Kong Island** *is* Hong Kong. Seized by the British in 1841, the colony coalesced around the island's enormous north-shore harbour (the name "Hong Kong" approximates the Cantonese *Heung Gang*, or "Fragrant Harbour") and created its initial wealth here, despite contemporary disappointment that all Britain had grabbed was a barren rock just 15km broad and 11km long. Here, the rich, industrious and influential carried on their business, building warehouses, offices and housing, in support of which communications, roads and transport developed as best they could. The island still doesn't look planned, though it has taken a kind of mad, organizational genius to fit buildings into the space allowed by the terrain. First impressions are of an organic mass of concrete and glass, stretching back from the water to the encroaching green hills behind. This is **Central**, the economic hub of the island and territory, whose streets hold as tightly constructed a grouping of buildings as can be imagined: there's little available space to drive or even walk at ground level, and the only way left to build is up.

The wealth generated in this urban concentration is part of the reason that Hong Kong exists at all, and brash, commercial Central and adjacent **Wan Chai** are interesting for just that – though the island's north shore also encompasses the more traditional district of **Western** (Sheung Wan and Kennedy Town), and the tourist and shopping zone of **Causeway Bay**. There are rural pockets and walks, too, that make Hong Kong Island an attractive target for a few days' gentle sightseeing. Half an hour's bus ride from the city, the island's **south side** or **east coast** hold a diverse series of attractions: beaches, small villages and seafood restaurants, an amusement park, markets and walks. Closer to Central, you can escape the city by getting on top of it, either by a walk through the

Hong Kong Island Trail

The best way to see much of the island is to walk, whether by pounding the city streets or, if you want some greenery, by following the well-signposted **Hong Kong Island Trail**, which runs for 50km from Victoria Peak (p.71) to Big Wave Bay, just north of Shek O (p.95) in the southeast. Rather than attempting the whole route at once, it's best to take in different sections as you visit nearby places on your way around the island. There are eight sections in all, varying in length from four to just under nine kilometres. The HKTB can give details, but for a map – one of the Countryside Series – you should visit the Government Bookshop (see p.247); there are also basic maps and information available from the Department of Agriculture, Fisheries and Conservation ⓦwww.afcd.gov.hk.

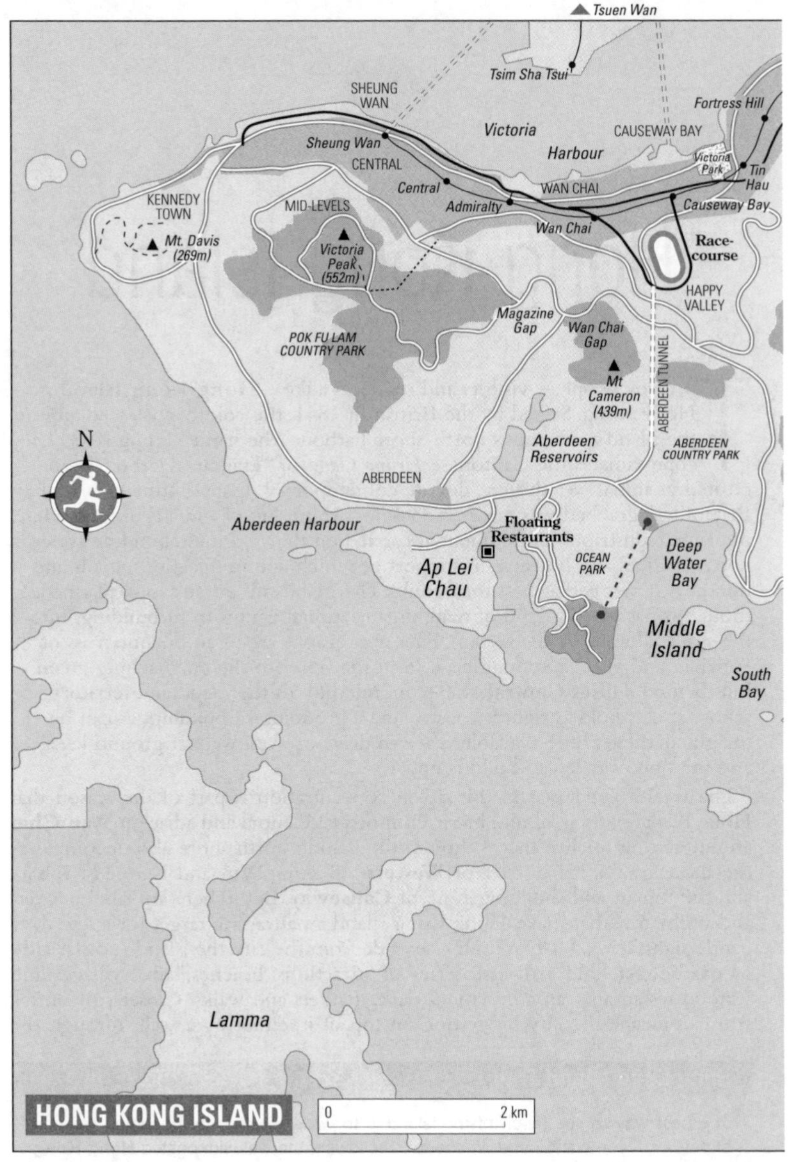

residential areas of **Mid-Levels** or **Wan Chai Gap**, or by going one better and scaling **Victoria Peak** itself, the highest point on the island, reached by the famous Peak Tram, a perilously steep funicular railway.

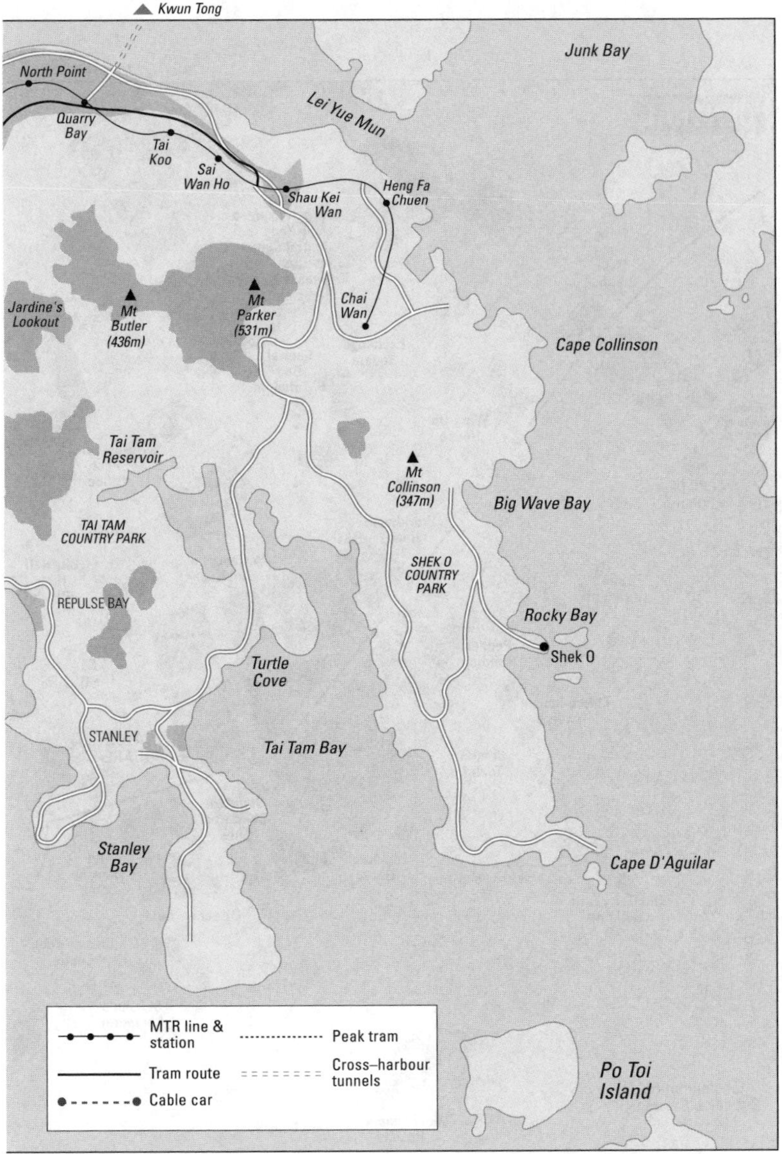

Central

The financial, business and administrative heart of the territory, **CENTRAL** is packed into a narrow strip of land, much of it reclaimed, on the northwest side of Hong Kong Island. It forms the southern edge ofVictoria Harbour and is just a few minutes from the mainland by ferry. Still technically the "capital" of Hong

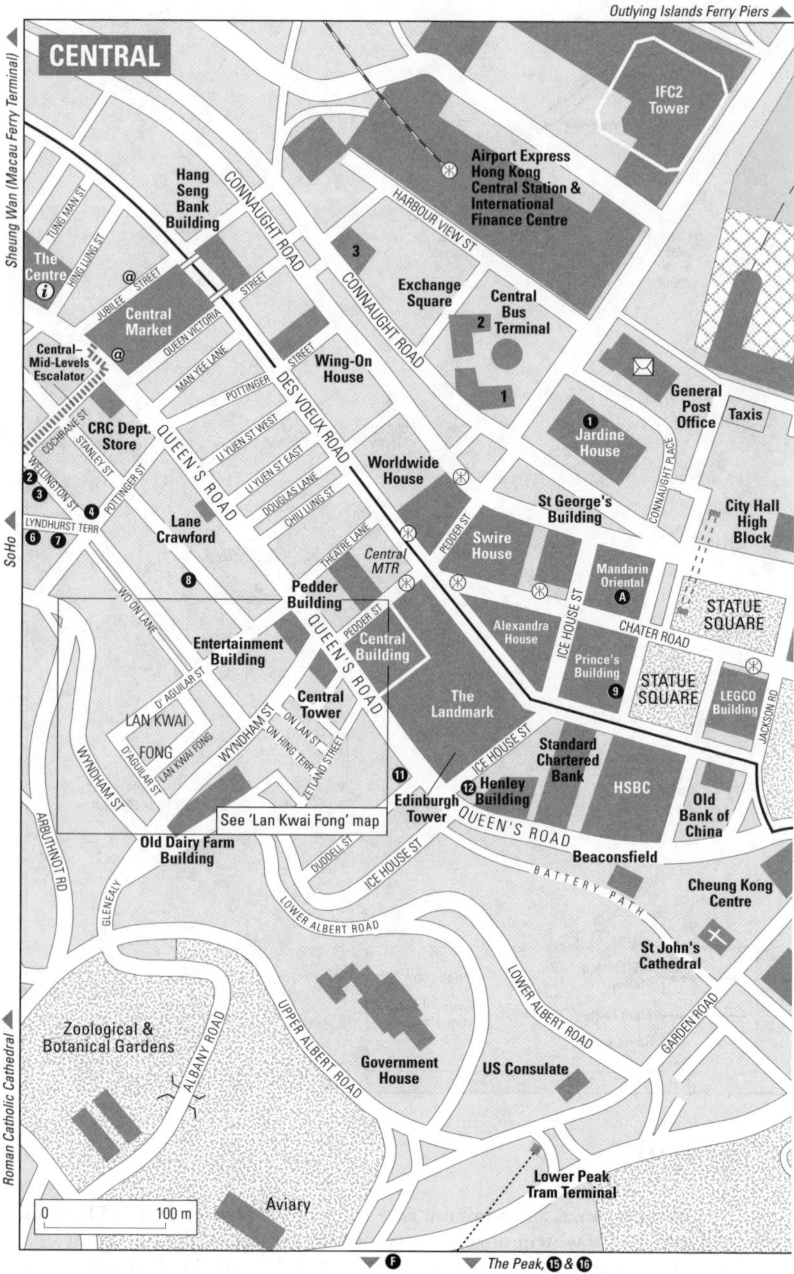
CENTRAL
Outlying Islands Ferry Piers
Sheung Wan (Macau Ferry Terminal)
SoHo
Roman Catholic Cathedral
The Peak, 15 & 16
F
IFC2 Tower
Airport Express Hong Kong Central Station & International Finance Centre
Hang Seng Bank Building
CONNAUGHT ROAD
HARBOUR VIEW ST
Exchange Square
Central Bus Terminal
The Centre
Central Market
Central–Mid-Levels Escalator
JUBILEE STREET
QUEEN VICTORIA STREET
MAN YEE LANE
POTTINGER ST
TUNG MAN ST
HING LUNG ST
Wing-On House
DES VOEUX ROAD
General Post Office
Taxis
Jardine House
CRC Dept. Store
COCHRANE ST
STANLEY ST
WELLINGTON ST
LYNDHURST TERR
QUEEN'S ROAD
LI YUEN ST WEST
LI YUEN ST EAST
DOUGLAS LANE
CHIU LUNG ST
Worldwide House
St George's Building
CONNAUGHT PLACE
City Hall High Block
Lane Crawford
THEATRE LANE
Central MTR
PEDDER ST
Swire House
Mandarin Oriental
Pedder Building
Alexandra House
ICE HOUSE ST
CHATER ROAD
STATUE SQUARE
WO ON LANE
Entertainment Building
Central Building
Prince's Building
LEGCO Building
JACKSON RD
D'AGUILAR ST
LAN KWAI FONG
WYNDHAM ST
Central Tower
ON LAN ST
ON HING TERR
ZETLAND STREET
The Landmark
Standard Chartered Bank
HSBC
Henley Building
Edinburgh Tower
Old Bank of China
See 'Lan Kwai Fong' map
Old Dairy Farm Building
ARBUTHNOT RD
DUDDELL ST
Beaconsfield
BATTERY PATH
Cheung Kong Centre
GLENEALY
LOWER ALBERT ROAD
St John's Cathedral
GARDEN ROAD
UPPER ALBERT ROAD
ALBANY ROAD
Zoological & Botanical Gardens
Government House
US Consulate
Lower Peak Tram Terminal
Aviary
0
100 m

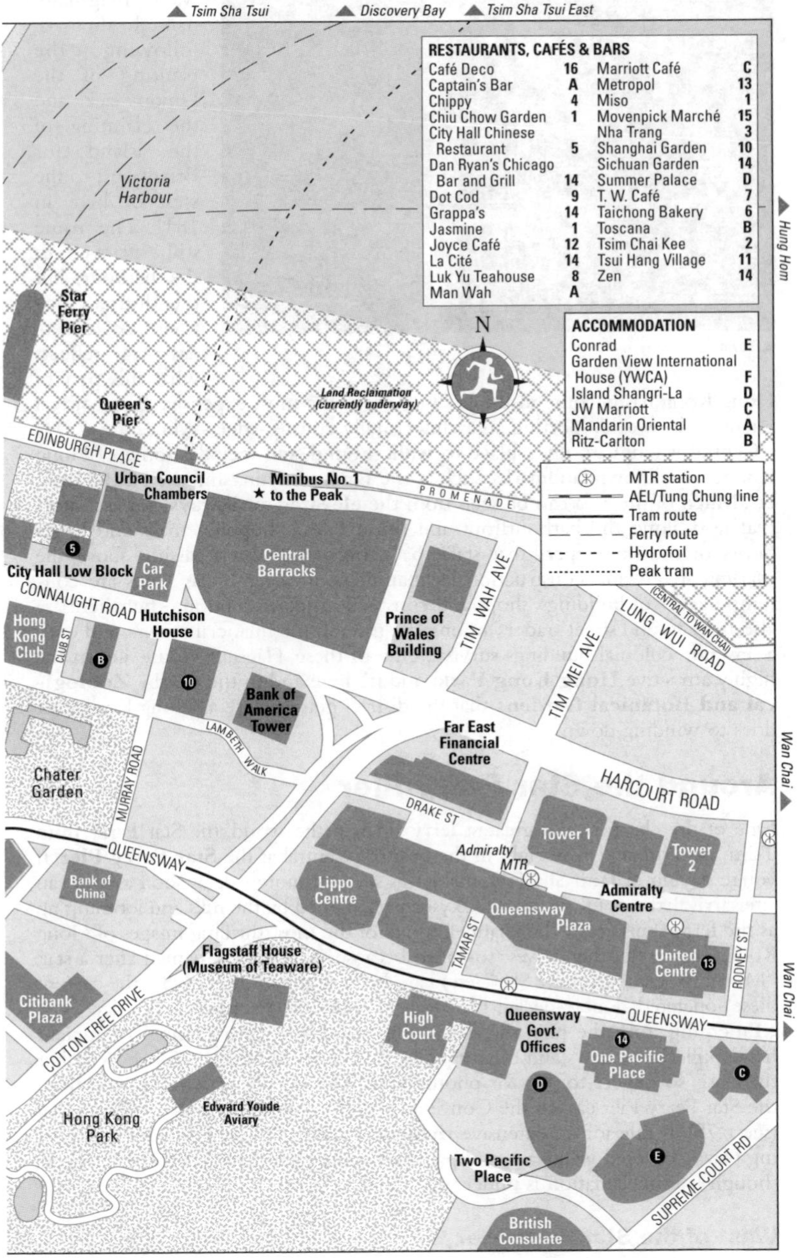

Tsim Sha Tsui
Discovery Bay
Tsim Sha Tsui East

RESTAURANTS, CAFÉS & BARS

Café Deco	16	Marriott Café	C
Captain's Bar	A	Metropol	13
Chippy	4	Miso	1
Chiu Chow Garden	1	Movenpick Marché	15
City Hall Chinese Restaurant	5	Nha Trang	3
Dan Ryan's Chicago Bar and Grill	14	Shanghai Garden	10
Dot Cod	9	Sichuan Garden	14
Grappa's	14	Summer Palace	D
Jasmine	1	T. W. Café	7
Joyce Café	12	Taichong Bakery	6
La Cité	14	Toscana	B
Luk Yu Teahouse	8	Tsim Chai Kee	2
Man Wah	A	Tsui Hang Village	11
		Zen	14

ACCOMMODATION

Conrad	E
Garden View International House (YWCA)	F
Island Shangri-La	D
JW Marriott	C
Mandarin Oriental	A
Ritz-Carlton	B

MTR station
AEL/Tung Chung line
Tram route
Ferry route
Hydrofoil
Peak tram

N

Victoria Harbour
Star Ferry Pier
Queen's Pier
Land Reclamation (currently underway)
Hung Hom
EDINBURGH PLACE
Urban Council Chambers
Minibus No. 1 to the Peak
PROMENADE
City Hall Low Block
Car Park
Central Barracks
CONNAUGHT ROAD
Hutchison House
Hong Kong Club
CLUB ST
Prince of Wales Building
TIM WAH AVE
CENTRAL TO WAN CHAI
LUNG WUI ROAD
TIM MEI AVE
Bank of America Tower
LAMBETH WALK
Chater Garden
MURRAY ROAD
Far East Financial Centre
HARCOURT ROAD
Wan Chai
DRAKE ST
Tower 1
Tower 2
Admiralty MTR
QUEENSWAY
Bank of China
Lippo Centre
Queensway Plaza
Admiralty Centre
TAMAR ST
United Centre
RODNEY ST
Flagstaff House (Museum of Teaware)
Citibank Plaza
COTTON TREE DRIVE
High Court
Queensway Govt. Offices
QUEENSWAY
Wan Chai
One Pacific Place
Edward Youde Aviary
Hong Kong Park
Two Pacific Place
SUPREME COURT RD
British Consulate

▲ Elevated walkway in Central

Kong, the district was originally named Victoria, following the planting of the Union Jack and the claiming of the island for Britain just to the west of here in 1841. The name still survives in the harbour, but the district's no-nonsense latter-day tag reflects what this part of Hong Kong has become in the last fifty years: the most expensive piece of real estate in the world, sporting an architecturally cutting-edge skyline.

Central is emphatically a place to **walk** around, and includes some of Hong Kong's best-known landmarks, such as the Bank of China and the HSBC towers. Much of the area can be seen from the **elevated walkways** and escalators that lead along the harbourfront and through the shopping malls and lower floors of the skyscrapers that stack back from the water, passing above the snarling streets and construction jackhammers. Nearly all the sights are contemporary – of buildings, shops and conspicuous consumption – but there are also markets and street traders among the monolithic financial towers, and even a few rare colonial buildings survive. One of these, Flagstaff House, lies in the highly attractive **Hong Kong Park**, and it's here and in the nearby **Zoological and Botanical Gardens** that the district gets as close as Hong Kong ever does to winding down.

Around the Star Ferry Pier

One of the cheapest and greatest ferry rides in the world, the Star Ferry from Tsim Sha Tsui lands you right in the heart of Central at the **Star Ferry Pier**. If you're staying in Tsim Sha Tsui, make this seven-minute ride as soon as you can after arrival: the sight of Central's skyscrapers, framed by the hills and looming up as the ferry skips across the channel, is one of the most thrilling images of Hong Kong. The ferries themselves (so-called because each ferry is named after a star: "Morning Star", "Evening Star", etc) have been running since 1898 – the current diesel-operated, double-decker boats carry about 100,000 passengers a day.

Emerging from the pier, the first things you'll see are a number of ancient hand-pulled rickshaws and their equally aged runners; both are for show rather than use, so expect to pay for photographs. This whole waterfront area, from the Star Ferry Pier east to the Convention and Exhibition Centre in Wan Chai (see p.78), is due for an extensive **makeover** into a "Civic Corridor", involving plazas, covered walkways, and parkland – the plans have yet to be finalized, though land reclamation is under way.

West of the Star Ferry Pier

Immediately west of the Star Ferry Pier is the waterfront **General Post Office**, which faces **Jardine House**, headquarters of the Jardine group and easily recognized by its porthole windows – a design that has inspired a ruder name among locals. Built in 1972 as the then tallest building in Asia, within ten years it needed to be completely refaced in aluminium, since its original tiles kept falling off.

Past the post office, steps ascend to the **elevated walkway and footbridge** system that runs alongside the harbour and deeper into Central – a good place to gain a first impression of the city. The walkway leads west, passing the Airport Express terminal, then turns to run above Connaught Road for about half a kilometre before reaching the Macau Ferry Terminal. Offshoots head off over Connaught Road into various shopping centres, one of which leads to Central Market and the starting point of the Mid-Levels escalator (see p.74).

Head shorewards and the walkway descends to the **Outlying Islands Ferry Piers**, which serve many of the territory's islands, as well as a bus terminal. (See p.155 for details of ferry departures from here.) On the way you pass the **International Finance Centre**, a business and shopping complex built over the Airport Express terminus, whose **IFC2 Tower** is currently Hong Kong's tallest structure at 420m high – more than twice the height of Jardine House, and even higher than the Peak Tram's upper terminus. This eighty-eight-storey monolith houses the Hong Kong Monetary Authority, and entrance is restricted – you can't even ride the lifts.

Inland from the International Finance Centre, and accessible by a raised walkway, are the three pastel-pink, marble and glass towers of Hong Kong's **Stock Exchange**, housed in Swiss architect Remo Riva's **Exchange Square**. The adjacent open piazza (with sculptures by Henry Moore and Elizabeth Frink) and fountains are sometimes the venue of free lunchtime concerts, making it a good place for an alfresco sandwich. Everything inside the exchange itself is computer-operated: the buildings' environment is electronically controlled, and the brokers whisk between floors in state-of-the-art talking lifts. There's exhibition space, too, inside **The Forum**, the restaurant and meeting area in the middle of the complex.

Underneath Exchange Square (reached by escalators) is Hong Kong's **Central Bus Terminal**, also referred to as Exchange Square Bus Terminal. Buses leave from here for Aberdeen, Stanley, Repulse Bay and The Peak among other places.

East of the Star Ferry Pier

East of the Star Ferry Pier, the two blocks of the **City Hall** are a mean exercise in 1960s civic architecture, all the worse given that the previous City Hall – a grand mid-nineteenth-century French classical structure – was, with Hong Kong's usual disregard for its older buildings, knocked down to make way for them. The Low Block, to the east, has a theatre and a concert hall (plus a café, a gift shop, a *dim sum* restaurant with harbour views, and clean, free public toilets), as well as an enclosed garden through which parade regular wedding parties. The High Block, to the west, holds a succession of libraries, a recital hall and various committee rooms.

Just to the east, **Central Barracks** – until 1997 the headquarters of the British military forces in Hong Kong – is now the base for the People's Liberation Army of China. The barracks was formerly known as HMS Tamar, after the supply ship that served as the Royal Navy's administrative HQ from 1897, and includes the adjacent **Prince of Wales Building**, which looks as if its base has been partly cut away by a giant axeman (Minibus #1 leaves from just behind here for The Peak). It was at the waterfront here in 1997 that the British staged their sunset lowering of the Union Jack, with HMS *Britannia* floodlit at the

Victoria Harbour

Central is the best place from which to ponder the magnificent **Victoria Harbour**, one of the major reasons that the British took possession of Hong Kong Island in the first place. This was once the busiest deep-water harbour in the world, though the waterfront warehouses – or "godowns" – are long gone, and the money-making has shifted into the office buildings of Central, many of which are built upon land reclaimed from the sea. In 1840, the harbour was 2km wide; now it is half that width. As well as affecting the view, this narrowing of the harbour has drastically reduced its ability to flush itself clean. This could prove catastrophic since the water is already dangerously polluted, as a peer over the side of any Star Ferry will prove: 1.5 million cubic litres of untreated sewage are discharged here daily, and new sewage treatment facilities at Stonecutters Island are still some years from completion.

Despite this, it's still difficult to beat the thrill of crossing the harbour by boat. Apart from the Star Ferry, there are many other **ferry** routes and **harbour cruises** worth taking, all of them with fine views of the port and its vessels. Alternatively, you can **walk** along a landscaped waterfront all the way from Queen's Pier to Wan Chai's Convention and Exhibition Centre, or simply park yourself near the Outlying Islands Ferry Piers for a view of the maritime activity that originally made Hong Kong great – junks, ferries, motorboats, container ships, cruise liners, hoverferries and sailing boats. Twenty thousand ocean-going ships pass through the harbour every year, with scores of thousands of smaller boats heading from here on their way to the Pearl River estuary and China.

quay behind. After the handover, the space was supposed to be redeveloped for government offices, but cost-cutting put that plan on hold, and its future is now uncertain.

From the Star Ferry Pier to Statue Square

The pedestrian underpass from the Star Ferry concourse emerges into **Statue Square**, heart of the late nineteenth-century colony, though now uncomfortably bisected by Chater Road, and with the original colonial buildings – along with a cricket pitch – replaced by a visionless late twentieth-century mish-mash of concrete, ponds and sculpture. The northern piece is bounded to the east by the **Hong Kong Club**, a bastion of colonial privilege since Victorian times, and now housed inside a modern, bow-fronted tower. At the opposite side of the square, the **Mandarin Oriental Hotel** – regularly rated "best hotel in the world" – hides an opulent interior inside a typically dull, box-like casing. Taking tea or a drink inside is one way for the riff-raff to get a glimpse, or you can march in and use the toilet facilities, which, as well as being almost the last word in urinary comfort, offer telephones, grooming facilities and chaise longues.

Across Chater Road in the southern half of Statue Square, is the **statue** itself: that of Sir Thomas Jackson, a nineteenth-century manager of the Hongkong and Shanghai Bank. Otherwise, this area is a major focus for dense crowds of the territory's 200,000 Filipina *amahs*, or maids, who gather here on Sundays, their day off. People from the Philippines have been coming to Hong Kong for a century and now form the territory's largest immigrant grouping. Most are women who come to work here as maids, sending money back home to support their families. At weekends and public holidays they descend upon all available spaces in Central, where they picnic, shop, read, sing and have their hair cut.

The LEGCO Building

One of the most important of Central's surviving colonial buildings sits on the eastern side of Statue Square. Built in 1898, the former Supreme Court (now the **LEGCO Building** – home of Hong Kong's Legislative Council), a granite structure with dome and colonnade, is the only colonial structure left in the square. It's as safe from future development as anything can be in Hong Kong, though unfortunately you can't go into what is the territory's nearest equivalent to a parliamentary building.

The HSBC building and around

Crossing the southern half of Statue Square and busy Des Voeux Road puts you right underneath one of Hong Kong's most extraordinary buildings, Sir Norman Foster's headquarters for the **Hongkong and Shanghai Banking Corporation** (HSBC), opened in 1986. It cost around a billion US dollars to complete, although the structure itself is far more impressive than any statistics. The whole battleship-grey building is supported on eight groups of giant pillars, and it's possible to walk right under the bank and come out on the other side – a necessity stipulated by the *feng shui* belief that the old centre of power on the island, Government House, which lies to the south of the bank, should be accessible in a straight line by foot from the main point of arrival on the island, the Star Ferry. You look up through the glass underbelly into a sixty-metre-high atrium, the floors suspended from coathanger-like structures and linked by long escalators that ride through each storey, and open offices ranged around the central atrium. The public banking facilities are on the first two floors of this, so you can ride the first couple of escalators from street level to have a look. The bronze lions at the front were saved from the previous building (torn down to make way for this one) – one still shows damage from World War II shrapnel.

The Standard Chartered Bank and the Bank of China

Next door to the HSBC is the headquarters of the **Standard Chartered Bank**, a curiously stepped tower squeezed between opposing blocks that – by design – just overtop the HSBC's building.

The only serious conceptual rival to Foster's creation, however, is the Chinese-American architect I.M. Pei's **Bank of China**, slightly along to the east, across Garden Road. Built between 1985 and 1990, Pei's angular, dark glass building is architecturally striking, though the knife-like profile pointing skywards offends *feng shui* sensitivities. Local lore has it that the Bank of China and the HSBC continually tried to outdo each other in the height of their buildings, so that the *taipan* of one could sit in his top-floor office and spit on the head of his rival (presumably, the HSBC roof is fairly moist, as the Bank of China is presently some 145m higher at 315m).

The **Old Bank of China**, which the new Bank of China Tower superseded, still stands next to the HSBC. A solid stone structure dating from 1950, it's not open to the public since it's now occupied by another bank and, at the top, the ritzy members-only **China Club**.

Along Queen's Road and Des Voeux Road

Queen's Road is Central's main street, as it has been since the 1840s when it was on the waterfront and described by contemporaries as a "grand boulevard". Just west of the Standard Chartered Bank, Queen's Road is dissected by **Ice House Street**, named after a building that once stored blocks of ice for use in the colony's early hospitals, imported from the United States since there were no commercial ice-making facilities in Hong Kong. A wander up Ice House Street to the junction with Lower Albert Road gives you a view of a later storage building, the early twentieth-century **Old Dairy Farm Building**, in brown and cream brick, which today houses the *Fringe Club* (see "The Arts and Media", p.231) and the *Foreign Correspondents' Club*, a members-only retreat for journalists, diplomats and lawyers.

To the west, beyond Ice House Street, Queen's Road and parallel **Des Voeux Road** take in some of the territory's most exclusive shops and malls, including **The Landmark** shopping complex, on the corner of Pedder Street and Des Voeux Road, boasting an impressive fountain in the huge atrium. You'll doubtless pass through at some point since the Landmark is a key hub in the **pedestrian walkway** system that links all the major buildings of Central to the Airport Express terminal, Star Ferry and harbour.

It's worth leaving the indoor walkways at some stage to reach **Pedder Street** itself, where the early twentieth-century **Pedder Building**, now filled with discount clothes outlets and businesses, is a solid old structure that's somehow escaped demolition over the years. Back across the street, between The Landmark and the Central Building, you should be able to make out a red oval plaque that marks the approximate position of the 1841 waterfront – a remarkable testament to the quantity of land reclaimed since then.

West to Central Market

It doesn't matter which of the two main streets – Queen's Road or Des Voeux Road – you follow west from Pedder Street, though it's useful to know that **trams** run straight down the latter, either to Western or east into Wan Chai. Stay on foot, though, until you've walked the few hundred metres west to Central Market (see below), and you'll pass the parallel cross-alleys of **Li Yuen Street East** and **Li Yuen Street West**, which run between the two main roads. Both are packed tight with stalls touting clothes and accessories: the contents of the two alleys are much the same – women's clothes, silkwear, children's clothes, fabrics, imitation handbags and accessories. Emerge from Li Yuen Street East onto Queen's Road and you're opposite the more upmarket shopping experience of **Lane Crawford**, one of the city's top – and most staid – department stores, with a smart café at the top and aisles full of heavily made-up charge-card queens.

Just beyond Lane Crawford, on the same side of the street, the steps of Pottinger Street are lined with small stalls selling ribbons, flowers, locks and other minor items, looking much as they have done since the 1940s. Pottinger Street leads up to Hollywood Road and SoHo, in Mid-Levels, which have so far managed to resist redevelopment.

Slightly further on, the district's western end is marked by **Central Market** (daily 6am–8pm), which – like all markets in Hong Kong – is about the most fun you can have outside a hospital operating room. Fish and poultry get butchered on the ground floor, meat on the first, with the relative calm of the fruit- and veg-selling taking place one floor higher. It's virtually all over by midday (although the smell remains), so aim to get here early and, if you've the stomach for it, take a break at one of the food stalls inside. There's a shopping arcade on the upper floor, from where the **Central–Mid-Levels escalator link** takes off, snaking up the hill above street level (see p.74 for details).

Just west of Central Market at 99 Queen's Road Central is **The Centre**, by night one of the most eye-catching features of the island's skyline. Designed by architect Denis Lau, who was responsible for Central Plaza in Wan Chai (see p.80), the building's horizontal bars of light change colour constantly and perform a dancing light show nightly at 9pm: the best place to view the spectacle is from The Peak or from the Kowloon waterfront. The Centre's basement also houses the head office of the **Hong Kong Tourism Board** (HKTB; daily 8am–6pm).

South of Queen's Road: Lan Kwai Fong

The network of streets south of Queen's Road – Stanley, Wellington, D'Aguilar and Wyndham streets – contains a fancy array of shops, galleries, restaurants and bars in which the emphasis is firmly Western. You may well find yourself eating and drinking in this area, particularly off D'Aguilar Street, on a sloping L-shaped lane known as **Lan Kwai Fong**. This once housed a major flower market, but Lan Kwai Fong is now known exclusively for its burgeoning array of trendy pubs, bars, restaurants and clubs. They've spread out of the Fong itself, into D'Aguilar Street and others, so the name is now used to refer to the entire area (for full details, see chapters 7 and 8). They're all late-opening – you can eat and drink here until 5am – and mostly frequented by expats and Chinese yuppies. Every August, the area takes part in the **Hong Kong Food Festival**, with outdoor events and food promotions.

From the Zoological Gardens to St John's Cathedral

Perching on the slopes overlooking Central are the low-key **Zoological and Botanical Gardens**, opened in 1864 (entrances on Glenealy and on Albany Road; daily 6am–7pm; free). There's a nice mix of shrubs, trees and paved paths

here, with spectacular close-ups of the upper storeys of the Bank of China Tower and the HSBC, though the main draw is a small aviary, home to cages of rare cranes, songbirds, and all kinds of ducks. West across Albany Road (via the underpass) is a collection of apes, including gibbons and orang-utangs, along with one jaguar. To get here direct from the Star Ferry Pier area, catch buses #3B or #12 heading east along Connaught Road.

Follow the path near the orang-utang cage that slopes downwards from the northwest corner of the Gardens towards Arbuthnot Road, followed by a left up a driveway, and you'll reach the city's **Roman Catholic Cathedral**, finished in 1888 and financed largely by Portuguese Catholics from Macau. If it's open, take a look at the stained-glass west windows, made in Toulouse.

Government House and St John's Cathedral

Below the gardens, on Upper Albert Road, **Government House** was the official residence of Hong Kong's colonial governors from 1855 to 1997. It's a strange conglomeration of styles, with several additions having been made over the years, the most unusual being those of a young Japanese architect who added the turret during the Japanese occupation of Hong Kong in World War II. Hong Kong's first chief executive, Tung Chee-hwa, was rumoured to have been put off from living here by Government House's notoriously bad *feng shui*, although he could equally have been trying to emphasize the territory's break with its colonial past. His successors may think differently, though the house is currently used only for receptions and official functions – the gardens, however, famous for their rhododendrons and azaleas, are opened to the public for a few days every year in early spring.

Down Garden Road, past the **Lower Peak Tram Terminal** (see p.72), is the other dominant symbol of British colonial rule, the Anglican **St John's Cathedral**, founded in 1847 but damaged during World War II when the Japanese army used it as a club. Supposedly the oldest Anglican church in the Far East, it's the only building in Hong Kong that is freehold, as opposed to standing on land leased from the government – presumably, the colonial administrators felt God would accept nothing less than perpetuity. Despite being dwarfed by almost everything around, its pleasant aspect gives you an idea of the more graceful proportions of colonial Hong Kong. The main doors, incidentally, were made from the wood of the supply ship HMS *Tamar*, which was docked down at the harbour for nearly fifty years until 1941, and which lent its name to the British Naval HQ. There's also an interesting bookstore in the grounds selling souvenirs and cards.

You can regain Central's lower reaches by continuing down Garden Road, past the contorted towers of **Citibank Plaza** towards the **Cheung Kong Centre** and the Bank of China. But it's rather more appealing to cross the leafy cathedral grounds to the early nineteenth-century redbrick building at the edge of the hill known as **Beaconsfield**, after Disraeli, the Earl of Beaconsfield. It has had several uses: once the French Mission Building; subsequently the Victoria District Court; it's now where the Court of Final Appeal sits – the body set up to take the role of the UK's House of Lords following the handover. From Beaconsfield, a path drops down to Queen's Road near the HSBC building.

Hong Kong Park

An alternative route from the Zoological Gardens is to head down **Cotton Tree Drive**, which sounds charmingly rural but is in fact choked with traffic. However, beyond the Lower Peak Tram Terminal, on the eastern side of the drive, is the attractive **Hong Kong Park** (daily 6am–11pm; free), which contains the elegantly colonial Flagstaff House and its Museum of Teaware.

▲ Edward Youde Aviary, Hong Kong Park

Beautifully landscaped in tiers up the hillside, the park contains an interesting **conservatory** with dry and humid habitats for its orchids, cacti, and trees, as well as the superb **Edward Youde Aviary** (daily 9am–5pm; free), named after a former governor. This is designed as an enormous mesh tent, inside which is a piece of semitropical forest and its resident bird species. Wooden walkways at branch height bring you face to face with some 800 hooting birds, mostly Southeast Asian and Australasian species; they can be surprisingly hard to spot amongst the canopy, despite their bright colours. As you exit the aviary at the lower end, there are some pools of water for aquatic birds – you can see the pelicans being fed at 10am and 3pm. Elsewhere in the park (and throughout Mid-Levels) you may see flocks of cockatoos. Native to Indonesia, these are escaped pets that have bred successfully. Whilst very pretty – white with yellow crests – they have a habit of damaging trees by ripping off branches and bark.

The rest of Hong Kong Park features ornamental lakes, a visual arts display centre, a children's playground, a bar-restaurant and a sadly under-used open-air theatre. It's also a popular **wedding** spot (there's a registry office inside the park), so bridal parties framed by Central's surrounding skyscrapers are a common sight. To get to the park, take bus #12 from Connaught Road and get off at the first stop on Cotton Tree Drive; from Admiralty MTR, take bus #12A.

Flagstaff House: the Museum of Teaware

At the northern corner of the park, in the lee of the massive Bank of China building, is **Flagstaff House**. Built in 1844 as the office and residence of the Commander of the British Forces in Hong Kong, this cool, white, shuttered building, with its simple pillars and surrounding garden, stands in elegant contrast to the skyscrapers all around. Its survival is down to the donation by one Dr K.S. Lo of his fine teaware collection to the Urban Council (now the Leisure and Cultural Services Department), which promptly restored the house and opened the **Museum of Teaware** inside (Mon & Wed–Sun 10am–5pm; free). The house alone – with its high-ceilinged rooms and polished wooden floors – is worth seeing, but the displays of teaware and related items from China throughout the ages are engaging, too, and there are some explanatory English notes.

Admiralty

Latterly, Central has expanded east, with a batch of striking new buildings down **Queensway**, beyond Hong Kong Park, into the area known as **ADMIRALTY**.

All the buildings are connected by overhead walkways, which you can join from the bottom of Cotton Tree Drive and use to go further into Central or east to Pacific Place. Most of the land here was originally part of the old colonial Victoria Barracks, which were decommissioned at the turn of the 1980s; Hong Kong Park, too, sits on former military turf.

The **Lippo Centre**, at the junction of Cotton Tree Drive and Queensway, is an eye-catching, segmented hexagonal structure, designed by American architect Paul Rudolph and formerly owned by the Australian entrepreneur Alan Bond (after whom it used to be named). Supported on huge grey pillars, interlocking steel and glass spurs trace their way up the centre's twin towers, while in the central lobby a ten-metre-high stone relief of a dragon and junk dominates.

Walkways connect the Lippo Centre to other office and retail buildings, including the Queensway Plaza and Hutchison House, from where you can get back to the walkways that lead around Central's office blocks and across Queensway to the Government Offices and the modern **High Court** building – a disappointingly squat, grey block – and, along from it, to the vast development of **Pacific Place**, with yet more shops, offices, cinemas, restaurants and three luxury **hotels** – the *Island Shangri-La Hotel*, the *Conrad* and the *JW Marriott*. Admiralty MTR has several entrances in the neighbourhood, one at the Lippo Centre itself, another at Queensway Plaza, which brings you out near buses and taxis.

Western District: Sheung Wan to Kennedy Town

The oldest settled parts of Hong Kong Island are all in **WESTERN DISTRICT**, which starts only a few hundred metres from the skyscrapers and office blocks of Central. Not long after the seizure of the island, the British moved out of Western, leaving what was a malarial area to the Chinese, who have been living and trading here ever since. Full of traditional businesses, small temples and crowded residential streets, it's by no means a homogeneous mass, and encompasses several quite distinct areas.

Sheung Wan, at the western end of the MTR Island Line, is the part of the district closest to Central. This area is what's generally thought of as "Western", a web of street markets and traditional shops that unfolds back from the **Macau Ferry Terminal**, which you can reach by the walkway from the Star Ferry Pier in Central. South of Sheung Wan, climbing up the island's hillside, **Hollywood Road** is one of the more important of the district's thoroughfares, where you'll find the famous **Man Mo Temple**; nearby, the **Tai Ping Shan** district conceals a set of lesser-known temples. Further west, you can skip the less appealing bits of Western by taking the bus to the **University of Hong Kong**, where there's a fine collection of Chinese art in the **University Museum and Art Gallery**. Or take the tram direct to its terminus at **Kennedy Town** – the island's westernmost point of interest – a slightly down-at-heel district focused around its waterfront warehouses and wharfs.

Sheung Wan

SHEUNG WAN begins immediately west of Central Market, its streets a mixture of traditional Chinese shops and merchants, tucked into the narrow

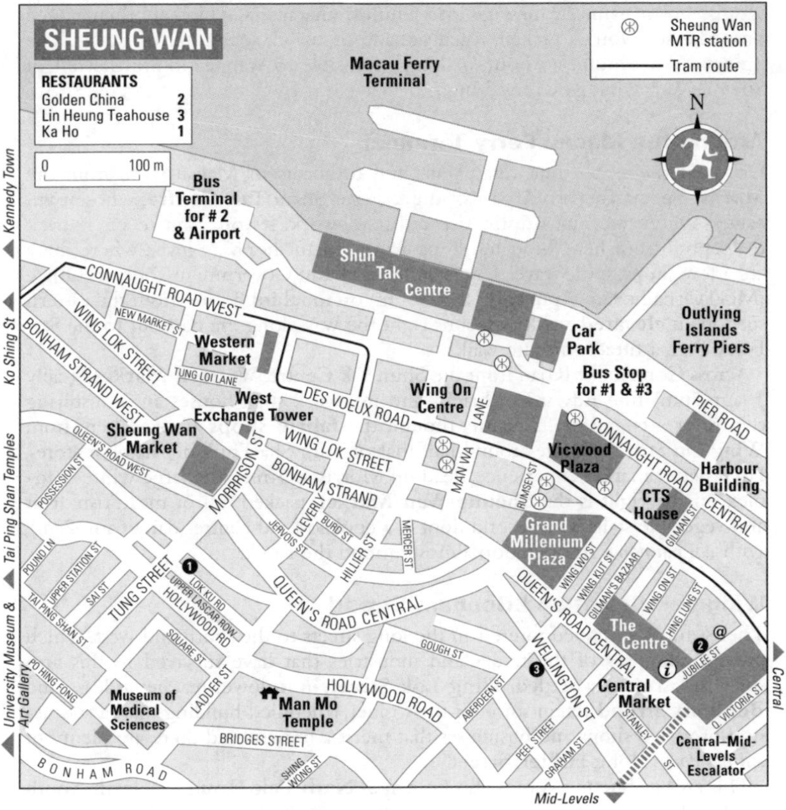

lanes that run between the main roads. Some of the trades have been lost as redevelopment rips out old alleys, especially true of the nooks and crannies immediately west of Central Market, between Bonham Strand and Queen's Road Central to the south, and Des Voeux Road to the north, where skyscraper developments such as The Centre are pushing out the older buildings. However, you should still find enough to occupy a morning's stroll. You can follow the routes outlined below, or simply wander as you fancy: it's difficult to get lost since the main roads are always close by, and once you start climbing you know you're heading away from the harbour.

From Central Market to Man Wa Lane

Heading west down Des Voeux Road, a couple of blocks up on the left is **Wing On Street**, formerly known as "Cloth Alley" because of the fabric stalls that used to cluster here. They've now been relocated to Western Market (see overleaf), although neighbouring alleys such as **Wing Kut Street** feature stalls selling calligraphy brushes as well as clothes, accessories, socks and scarves. Further west, **Man Wa Lane** is full of stalls specializing in carving seals, or "chops", as the carved name stamps they make here are called. The traders here are used to tourists, and many stalls display signs and prices in English. The craftsmen will translate your name or message into Chinese characters, which are then carved onto the seal you've picked, usually made of wood, soapstone or plastic. The process takes around an hour, making it possible to wander round the rest of Sheung Wan while you're waiting.

Around the Macau Ferry Terminal

Down at the waterfront, catamarans and turbocats to Macau leave from the **Macau Ferry Terminal**, part of the massive **Shun Tak Centre**, whose twin towers are encased in a distinctive red framework. If you want to circle back to Central from here, head inside up to the main shopping level, where there are a few shops, some travel agents and the Macau Government Tourism Office (MGTO; daily 9am–1pm & 2.15–5.50pm) on the third floor – from the eastern section an **elevated walkway** runs right the way along the harbour to the Star Ferry Pier, a fifteen-minute walk.

Across Connaught Road from the Shun Tak Centre, **Western Market**'s (daily 10am–7pm) fine Edwardian brick- and ironwork shell houses an uninspiring two-floor arts and crafts centre, though the **fabric shops** (moved here from Wing On Street) charge around half that of Tsim Sha Tsui's department stores. For a better market experience, head up Morrison Street: the large white complex on the right is the **Sheung Wan Market**, packed full of meat, fish, fruit and vegetable stalls. The second floor is a cooked food centre (daily 6am–2am), with *dai pai dong*s in operation almost around the clock.

Wing Lok Street and Bonham Strand

There's more sustained interest in the long streets to the south and west, which provide glimpses of the trades and industries that have survived in this area since the island was settled. **Wing Lok Street**, in its lower reaches at least, and **Bonham Strand** retain some of their older, balconied buildings and a succession of varied shops and businesses that merit a browse, and there are plenty of *dai pai dong*s along **Hillier Street**.

This area of Sheung Wan is also known as **Nam Pak Hong** – "North–South Trading Houses" – and many of the businesses are herbal and medicinal wholesalers, stocking a vast range of marine produce along with dried plants and animals. In particular, Bonham Strand's shops display expensive **bird's nests** (actually the salivary "cement" that holds together the nests of cave-roosting swiftlets) and **ginseng roots**. The nests are used to make **bird's nest soup**, a speciality of Hong Kong restaurants and said to promote longevity; as the nest is tasteless, however, the dish's quality rests in the soup itself. Ginseng – which comes in several varieties – is prescribed for a whole host of problems, from saving those faced with imminent death by illness (which wild ginseng is purported to delay for three days) to curing impotence or hangovers. Some of the larger ginseng trading companies have their offices along **Bonham Strand West**, the most venerable ones boasting impressive interiors of teak and glass. Here you'll see people sorting through newly arrived boxes of ginseng root, chopping it up and preparing it for sale.

Ko Shing Street, at the western end of Bonham Strand West, is devoted to the wholesale medicinal trade. Great sacks and wicker baskets are taken off a line of trucks by men carrying a wicked hook in one hand: they spear the sacks and hoist them onto their shoulders, dumping them onto the pavements where others unload and sort their contents. The shops here, open to the street, display ginseng alongside antlers, crushed pearls, dried seahorses and all the assorted paraphernalia of Chinese **herbalists**. In keeping with the traditional nature of the trade, some of the names are straight from the nineteenth century – one business here has a sign proclaiming it to be the "Prosperity Steamship Company".

Ko Shing Street bends back round towards Connaught Road West (along which the tram runs). The stretch from here to as far west as Centre Street is devoted to stores selling dried mushrooms, salted and preserved fish, dried squid, oysters, sea slugs, seahorses, sharks' fins, scallops and seaweed. They make for colourful displays and, even if the priciest goods are out of your range, you could always pick up a string of Chinese sausages or a bottle of oyster sauce.

Hollywood Road and around

Hollywood Road, running west from the end of Wyndham Street in Central, and the steep streets off it, forms one of Western's most interesting areas, a run of antique shops and curio and furniture stores. There's some wonderful Asian applied art here – furniture, old and new ceramics, burial pottery, painted screens, prints, jewellery and embroidery – and a group of more upmarket antique shops at the eastern end of Hollywood Road. As you move further west towards Upper Lascar Row the selection becomes more mixed (and prices get lower), with any number of smaller places selling bric-a-brac and junk, as well as "genuine" antiques. The western end of Hollywood Road is also known for its coffin sellers, and there are a few surviving shops, as well as some that sell funeral clothes for the dead, made from silk.

Man Mo Temple and the Sun Yat-sen Trail

Follow Hollywood Road west and just before the junction with Ladder Street is the **Man Mo Temple** (daily 8am–6pm), one of Hong Kong's oldest, built in the 1840s and equipped with impressive interior decorations from mainland China. It's not as dark and smoky as some other Chinese temples, but there's still plenty of atmosphere with scented fumes rising off the hanging, pyramidal incense coils. The name of this busy temple derives from the words for "civil" (Man) and "martial" (Mo), the former attribute belonging to the god of literature, Man Cheong, who protects civil servants (he's the red-robed statue wielding a writing brush); the other to the "martial" deity, Kuan Ti (represented by another statue, in green, holding a sword). Kuan Ti is based on the real-life warrior Guan Yu of the Three Kingdoms Period (around 220 AD), who is protector of – among other things – pawnshops, policemen, secret societies and the military. On the left by the main door as you enter, the carved nineteenth-century chairs (which look like shrines) in the glass cases were once used to carry the statues through the streets at festivals. The other altars in the temple are to Pao Kung, the god of justice, and to Shing Wong, a god of the city, who protects the local neighbourhood.

Just beyond the temple, on Bridges Street near the junction with Shing Wong Street, a sign indicates the start of the short **Sun Yat-sen Historical Trail**, an easy-to-follow walk around eleven sites related to the revolutionary who became first president of the Chinese Republic following the overthrow of the Manchu (Qing) dynasty in 1911. The core sights are here around Hollywood Road, though the full trail starts further west at the junction of Eastern Street and High Street. The trail itself is only really of interest to history buffs since all the sites have long since gone, their locations marked by red plaques – you can pick up an illustrated brochure with a map of the trail from the HKTB.

Ladder Street to Possession Street

▲ Antique shop on Upper Lascar Row

Back outside the temple, Hollywood Road is crossed by **Ladder Street**, a steep flight of steps linking Caine Road, in the Mid-Levels, with Queen's Road. Built to ease the passage of sedan-chair bearers as they carried their human loads up to the residential areas along Caine Road in the nineteenth century, it's the only surviving street of its kind, one of several that used to link Central and Western with Mid-Levels. The lower part retains some of its older, shuttered houses, their balconies jutting out over the steps.

Turn right, down the steps, and immediately on the left, **Upper Lascar Row** is what's left of the area known to the late-nineteenth-century citizens of Hong Kong as "Cat Street". The names have various interpretations: *lascar* is an Urdu word, meaning an East Indian seaman, and the area is probably where these seamen lived – the "Cat Street" tag is thought to derive from its consequent role as a red-light area. The other theory is that Cat Street was a "thieves' market", all the goods at which were provided by cat burglars. These days, Upper Lascar Row is a mixture: an increasing number of upmarket antique outlets occupy the shops, while the flea-market vendors have moved to the pavement outside, with old banknotes, coins, jade, watches and jewellery spread out on the ground alongside broken TVs and other junk. The flea market really only comes alive at weekends, while the antique shops are open every day, although some close on Sunday. There is also one gallery of shops, the **Cat Street Galleries** (Mon–Fri 11am–6pm, Sat 10am–6pm), selling a mixture of modern china, contemporary paintings and antiques in showrooms ranged over several floors, with a relaxing coffee shop, too.

Hollywood Road continues west past **Possession Street**, where on 26 January, 1841 the British landed, claiming the island by planting the Union Jack. Though there's nothing of interest in the street itself, its location hundreds of metres south of the harbour is a reminder of how completely land reclamation has altered Hong Kong's shoreline over the years.

Tai Ping Shan

Up Ladder Street from the Man Mo Temple and off to the right lies the district of **TAI PING SHAN**, or "Peaceful Mountain". One of the earliest areas of Chinese settlement after the colony was founded, it belied its name by becoming a haunt of the early Hong Kong Triad societies, and a place whose overcrowded slums were notorious for outbreaks of **plague**. The slums were levelled after a particularly virulent epidemic in 1894 that killed 2500 people, after which a Bacteriology Institute was built on the site; it was here that French researcher **Alexandre Yersin** discovered that plague was spread to humans by fleas that had previously fed on infected rats (and so had the plague bacteria, *yersinia pestis*, named after him). The institute is now the **Museum of Medical Sciences** (Tues–Sat 10am–5pm, Sun 1–5pm; $10), to the right off the top of Ladder Street and housed in an attractive Edwardian building – though the exhibits, comprising dated medical equipment, are less interesting than the area's history.

Down **Tai Ping Shan Street** itself, beyond Bridges Street, there's a cluster of old neighbourhood temples at the junction with Pound Lane. Raised above the street, the temples are easily missed, seeming more a part of someone's house than a place of worship, an impression that persists until you see the incense sticks and are hassled for money by the old women sitting outside. First, reached by climbing the steps on the left of the Pound Lane junction, is the **Kuan Yam Temple**, dating to 1840 and dedicated to the Buddhist goddess of mercy. The altar in the main hall of the green-tiled **Shui Yuat Temple**, opposite and down the steps, holds a statue of the god Shui Yuat Paak, known as the "Pacifying General" and revered for his ability to cure illnesses – the statue was brought here during the 1894 plague outbreak. One of the rooms off the main hall is used by fortune-tellers, and you should also look for the rows of Tai Sui in the temple – a series of statues of sixty different gods, each one related to a specific year in the sixty-year cycle of the Chinese calendar. In times of strife, or to avert trouble, people come to pray and make offerings to the god associated with their year of birth. Further along the street, towards the junction with Upper Station Street, you'll find more shrines, as well as stalls selling incense, oranges and other offerings.

The most interesting temple is further down the street, past the little red Earth God shrine at the junction with Pound Lane that protects the local community. The **Kwung Fuk** ancestral hall was last rebuilt in 1895 after the local plague-inspired demolitions, to store the bodies of those awaiting burial back in China, and to hold the ancestral tablets of those who had died in Hong Kong, far from their own villages. Usually, such halls are for the sole use of one family or clan, but this one is used by anyone who wishes to have an ancestral tablet made for their relatives – there are around 3000 people commemorated here. Several small rooms hold the ancestral tablets – little wooden boards with the name and date of birth of the dead person written on them, and sometimes a photograph, too. Behind the altar there's a courtyard, whose incinerator is for burning the usual paper offerings to the dead, on the far side of which is a room lined with more tablets, some of them completely blackened by years of incense and smoke.

West to Kennedy Town

If you've followed the route through Western district this far, it's unlikely you'll want to **walk** on to Kennedy Town, as it's a long haul from Central. Either head straight there on the **tram** down Des Voeux Road, or follow the route outlined below, which takes you most of the way by **bus**, and allows you to stop off at a couple of points of interest along the way.

The University Museum and Art Gallery

Up past the Museum of Medical Sciences, you can catch bus #3B from Bonham Road to the **University Museum and Art Gallery** (UMAG) at 94 Bonham Rd (Mon–Sat 9.30am–6pm, Sun 1.30–5.30pm; ⓦwww.hku.hk/hkumag; free), opposite an old, yellow-plastered house of the type that once lined this residential road.

An outstanding museum of Chinese art, the collection is in two adjacent buildings, the **T.T. Tsui Building** and the **Fung Ping Shan Building**, through which you enter (the two are linked on the second floor). Inside, the quality of the quiet and uncrowded exhibition of ceramics, bronzes, furniture, scroll paintings and (especially) of contemporary art makes it worth a detour on the way to Kennedy Town.

The collection is rotated, so not all the items are on display at any one time, and there are often visiting exhibitions. However, among the permanent sections are a unique group of **Nestorian bronze crosses**, relics of the Yuan Dynasty (1271–1368 AD) from the Ordos region of northern China. The bronzes were decorations for a heretic Christian group that had survived in central and east Asia since the fifth century AD; most are cruciform in shape, though a few are bird-shaped (also a Christian symbol), star-shaped or circular, or use a swastika pattern. The **ceramics** collection ranges from Neolithic pottery through to the later ruling dynasties. Items from the Tang Dynasty (618–907 AD) include some remarkably realistic glazed camels and horses from tombs, and a selection of three-coloured pottery – dishes, jars and even an arm- and head-rest. There's also white ceramic ware from the Sui to the Song Dynasties, including two Song Dynasty ceramic pillows, one round and one rectangular, both decorated with black-and-white line drawings. More colourful are the Ming (1368–1644) and Qing (1645–1911) Dynasty bowls and dishes, displaying rich blues, greens and reds. In other rooms you can find a selection of woodcarvings and some Ming and Qing dynasty furniture, laid out as a room. In addition to the swords, vessels, bird figures and decorative items, the contemporary Chinese paintings are also worth a look.

From the University to Lu Pan Temple

From the museum, you can walk up into the car park and through the grounds of the **University of Hong Kong**, whose buildings have stood here since its foundation in 1912, when it had less than a hundred students (today it has eight thousand). Architecturally, it's less than gripping, though you might as well walk around to Loke Yew Hall on your left, inside which quiet cloisters planted with high palm trees make for a bit of a break from the traffic outside.

Follow the road through the grounds, cross Pokfulam Road by the footbridge and then walk up its right-hand side (you'll have to dodge under a subway initially). A few hundred metres up, after no. 93 and just before the garages, a white-tiled flight of steps leads down on the right to a terrace overlooking the elaborate, multicoloured roof carvings of figures and dragons on top of the **Lu Pan Temple**. It's the only temple in Hong Kong dedicated to Lu Pan, the "Master Builder", blessed with miraculous powers with which (according to legend) he repaired the Pillars of Heaven and made carved birds that could float in the air. He's commemorated every year on the thirteenth day of the sixth moon (see "Festivals", p.237), when building and construction workers hold a feast and make offerings to him here. At most other times of the year it's dark and empty inside, but take a look at the interesting carvings on either side of the door and above the two internal doors.

From the temple's terrace, steps continue down and turn into a wide, stepped path, Li Po Lung Path. Follow this down to Belcher's Street, at which point you're in Kennedy Town.

Kennedy Town

Most people come out to **KENNEDY TOWN** for the ride on the tram, and then catch the first one back again to Central. This offers good views of the moored junks and warehouses, but doesn't begin to give you the real flavour of the place – a sort of downmarket Sheung Wan, supporting a mixture of maritime and trade businesses. Much of the district (named after Sir Arthur Kennedy, governor from 1872 to 1877) is built on reclaimed land, piled high with decrepit tenements, the streets busy with traders and jammed traffic. Since the mid-nineteenth century, it has seen its goods arrive and leave by sea, at a harbour that still retains its working flavour, though like so many areas of the island's north coast it's being changed by land reclamation.

If you've walked down from the university (see opposite), make for the **tram terminus**, to your left at the end of Catchick Street, passing the large covered market of Smithfield on the way. The **Kennedy Town Abattoir Market** is where the trams turn round before heading back to Central. The waterfront strip a couple of blocks down is known as the **Praya**, a Portuguese word meaning "waterfront" (used more commonly in Macau) that's evidence of the once-strong Portuguese influence in the whole of the South China Sea. The Praya is lined with cranes unloading into the waterfront **godowns** (warehouses). The tram runs back along part of the Praya, but before you go take a walk through the maze of small streets back from the shore, where there's no shortage of cheap restaurants.

Victoria Peak

As one of Hong Kong's main attractions, you have to visit **VICTORIA PEAK** (or simply "The Peak") sooner or later, and since you're going up primarily for the views, try to do so on a clear day. It's a fine ride up, by bus or tram, and the little network of paths and gardens at the top provides one of the world's most spectacular cityscapes – little wonder that this is *the* place to live in the territory, as it has been since the 1870s.

Yet even on the murkiest days The Peak is worth the journey. It's cooler up here, the humidity is more bearable, there's foliage and birdlife, and there's a choice of quiet, shady **walks**. Bring a picnic and enjoy the respite from the crowds below.

The Peak

The 552-metre heights ofVictoria Peak give you the only perspective that matters in Hong Kong: down, and over the towers of Mid-Levels and Central, and the magnificent harbour. It did not take long for the new British arrivals to flee the malarial lower regions of Hong Kong Island and set up cool summer homes here. The first path up to The Peak, as everyone soon learned to call it, was made in 1859, and within twenty years it was a popular retreat from the summer diseases and heat below. Access was difficult at first, by sedan chair only, ensuring it remained the preserve of the colony's wealthy elite. Things changed in the late 1880s with the opening of the Peak Tram, and the first road connection was made in 1924, since which time the territory's power-brokers and administrators have settled it properly with permanent houses – and, latterly, apartment buildings – that rival each other in terms of position, views and phenomenal rental value. Initially, the Chinese weren't allowed on The Peak except to carry up Europeans and supplies on their backs, let alone to settle: now, of course, money is the only qualification necessary for residence. Among the super-rich currently maintaining houses up here are Martin Lee, barrister and leader of the Democratic Party; the chairman and deputy chairman of HSBC; members of the Hotung family, the first Chinese to live on The Peak; and various consul-generals, business people and assorted celebrities.

Getting there: the Peak Tram and other routes

Since 1888, the **Peak Tram** – actually a funicular railway – has been transporting passengers from a terminal close to St John's Cathedral to the end of the line at Victoria Gap, a 1.4-kilometre ride that climbs up to around 400m above sea level. It's an extraordinary sensation, the 27-degree gradient providing an odd perspective of the tall buildings of Central and Mid-Levels, which appear to lean in on the tram as it makes its speedy journey. Despite renovations and upgradings of the terminals and trams, the experience today is fundamentally the same as when the tram first opened, and it's reputed to be the safest form of transport in the world: there's never been an accident yet, and the track brakes fitted to the wheels can stop the tram on the steepest part of the system within six metres.

Most tourists take the tram right to the top, which disguises the fact that for the whole of its life it's been primarily a commuter system. There are four intermediate stops at which you can flag the tram down – at Kennedy, Macdonnell, May and Barker roads – but unless you've been up before and have time to explore on the way, stick with the journey right to the top.

The tram departs from the **Lower Peak Tram Terminal** (on Garden Road, just up from Citibank Plaza in Central) daily from 7am to midnight, every 10–15 minutes; the journey takes eight minutes and **tickets** cost $30 return, $20 one-way. From outside the Star Ferry Pier, you can catch bus #15C (Mon–Sat 10am–11.45pm) to the tram. Be warned that on Sundays and public holidays the queues for the tram can be interminable: get here early.

You can also reach Victoria Gap by **bus** #15, which runs from the Central Bus Terminal, underneath Exchange Square, a splendid ride up the switchback road to The Peak, offering just as spectacular views as those from the tram; it costs less, too – $9.20 one-way – though takes at least half an hour. You can also catch it just outside the Star Ferry Pier. The other service is the #1 minibus from Lung Wui Road just behind the Prince of Wales Building, a slightly quicker bus ride, though it costs a few dollars more. You can do the trip by **taxi** as well, though this will cost around $80 from the Star Ferry Pier. Fitness fanatics can **walk** up, too, though for most people walking down is a more realistic option. See below for routes.

Walks around The Peak

The trams pull up at the terminal in the **Peak Tower**, an incomparably ugly concrete structure generally referred to as the Flying Wok. Its sole virtue is the superb views from the top terrace, which encompass the harbour and Tsim Sha Tsui's land re-clamation projects and progressively receding buildings, right into the New Territories. Inside are **Ripley's Believe It or Not Odditorium** (daily 9am–10pm; $90) and **Madame Tussaud's** (daily noon–8pm; $95), where wax re-creations of kungfu hero Jackie Chan and former Chinese president Jiang Zemin rub shoulders. Further splendid views can be had across the road from the upper terrace of the **Peak Galleria**, a touristy shopping complex with a computerized fountain outside and high-class stores and restaurants with views inside – the *Café Deco Bar and Grill* is the best place here for coffee or lunch, though there's always a wait for window tables. **Buses and taxis** stop at ranks underneath the Galleria.

You're not yet at the top of The Peak itself. Four roads pan out from the tower, one of which, **Mount Austin Road**, leads up to the landscaped **Victoria Peak Garden** – all that remains of the old governor's residence here, which was destroyed by the Japanese during their occupation of the territory in World War II. It's a stiff climb, but you're rewarded by more of those views that leave your stomach somewhere in Central.

Nearly everyone makes **the circuit of The Peak**, a circular walk that takes around an hour depending on how many times you stop for photo calls. A noticeboard beside the Peak Tower details the various walks – follow the green arrows for Victoria Peak Garden, the blue arrows to descend Old Peak Road to May Road tram station, and the yellow arrows for the Harlech and Lugard roads walk.

Start at **Harlech Road** and you'll save the very best views for last. It's a shaded path for most of the route, barely a road at all, and you'll be accompanied by birdsong and cricket noises as you go: other wildlife is less conspicuous, but you might catch sight of the odd monkey or alarmed snake. First views are of Aberdeen and Lamma; as you turn later into **Lugard Road**, Stonecutters Island, Kowloon and Central eventually come into sight – with magnificent views of the latter especially, just before you regain the Peak Tower. It's a panorama that is difficult to tire of – if you can manage it, come up again at night when the lights of Hong Kong transform the city into a glittering box of tricks, the lit roads snaking through the buildings, with Kowloon glinting like gold in the distance.

Walks from The Peak

More adventurous types can make one of several **walks from The Peak** that scramble steeply downhill to either side of the island. None takes more than a couple of hours, but you'll need to carry some water if you're going to tackle them during the heat of the day, as there are no facilities en route.

Head down Harlech Road from the Peak Tower and after about five minutes a signposted path runs down to **Pok Fu Lam Reservoir**, a couple of kilometres away to the south and a good target for picnics and barbecues. You can reach the same place by way of Pok Fu Lam Reservoir Road, which starts close to the car park. Either way, once you're there, the path runs past the reservoir to join the main Pok Fu Lam Road, from where you can catch any of several buses back to Central.

You could also do this walk and then catch a bus in the other direction, on **to Aberdeen**, but if you're feeling energetic it's more fun to walk there direct from The Peak. To do this, follow Peel Rise (down, and then off, Peak Road) for around an hour, a lovely shaded and signposted walk down the valley, passing an immense cemetery on the way into Aberdeen. Huge swathes of graves are strung across the terraces, which are cut into the hillside above the town, from where there are great views of the town's harbour.

Finally, if you follow Harlech Road to just past the junction with Lugard Road, **Hatton Road** makes a steep descent down to the streets above the **University of Hong Kong**, one possible approach to Kennedy Town or Mid-Levels.

Mid-Levels and SoHo

The area halfway up The Peak, back from Central is known – reasonably enough – as **MID-LEVELS**, incorporating the newly gentrified region of **SOHO**. A notch or two down the social scale from The Peak, it retains a reputation as a swanky, if rather dull, residential area – although the forest of apartment buildings may strike you as having a rather depressing concrete-jungle quality.

Easiest access to the area is by the **Central–Mid-Levels Escalator** link, an eight-hundred-metre-long series of elevated walkways, escalators and travelators that cuts up the hillside from Central Market (at the footbridge across Queen's Road by the corner of Jubilee Street) along Cochrane Street and across Hollywood Road, Caine Road and Robinson Road, ending at Conduit Road. It is capable of carrying 30,000 people a day on a one-way system, which changes direction during the day depending on the flow of passengers: uphill from 10.20am to midnight, downhill from 6am to 10am. All told, it's a twenty-minute ride from bottom to top.

Caine Road to Robinson Road

Mid-Levels proper begins just above **Caine Road**, which leads past the Roman Catholic Cathedral (see p.62) to Shelley Street, a left turn up which – at no. 30 – is the **Jamia Mosque**, or Shelley Street Mosque, an important place of worship for the territory's fifty thousand Muslims. A mosque has stood on this site since the 1850s, though the present building dates from 1915, a pale-green structure set in its own quiet, raised courtyard above the surrounding terraces. The cool interior isn't always open, but the courtyard behind should be accessible, flanked by three-storeyed houses with wooden, railed balconies hung about with drying washing.

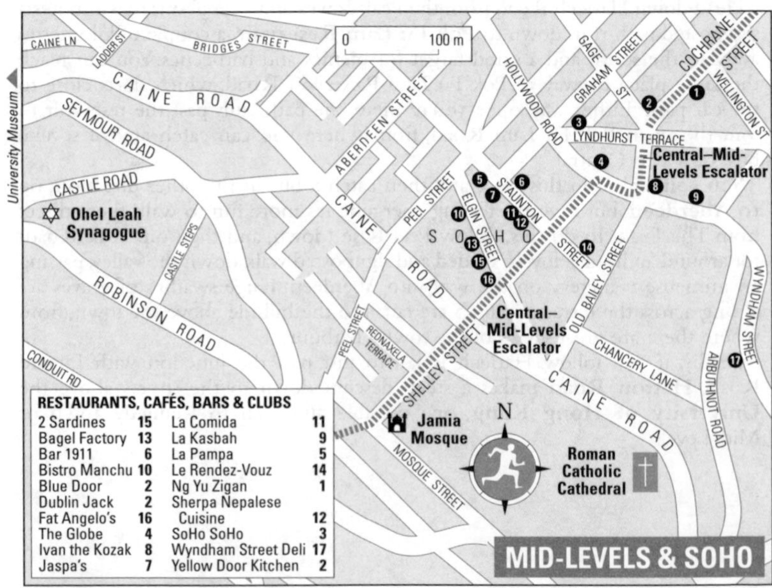

This part of Mid-Levels is very peaceful, with plenty of incidental interest in the peeling residential terraces around. One of the terraces off the other side of Shelley Street is **Rednaxela Terrace**, an unlikely name even for Hong Kong until you reverse the letters – it's actually a misspelling of Alexandra and named after the wife of King Edward VII, Queen Victoria's son.

Continue up Shelley Street and you'll come out on busy **Robinson Road**. Head west along here, and at no. 70 stairs lead down to the whitewashed **Ohel Leah Synagogue** (the name means "Tent of Leah"), lurking in its own quiet leafy hollow below the main road. The territory's best-known synagogue, it was built by the wealthy Sassoon family in memory of their mother and finished in 1902. Great care has recently been taken to restore the oak-carved and painted interior, although unfortunately security concerns make it difficult simply to drop in for a look round – if you want to go in, bring ID and ask at the entrance.

SoHo

One welcome side-effect of the escalator's construction has been the opening up of a whole new area of old streets and houses that have largely been preserved from redevelopment because the steepness of the hill made them hard to get to. This area has been rechristened **SoHo**, as in South of Hollywood Road, although it now also extends north into Peel Street, Wellington Street and Gage Street, these northerly extensions being sometimes referred to as "BoHo" or Below Hollywood Road. There are literally dozens of restaurants and bars here, with more opening (and closing and changing their name and cuisine) every month. The area is interesting in the daytime, too: many of the old-style shophouses remain, and while the tide of gentrification (florists, interior decorators, antique shops) is strong, you'll still find the sort of practical outlets – butchers, hardware shops and rice sellers – that tell you this is still a real Chinese neighbourhood.

Wan Chai Gap

The other hillside section of town, east of The Peak, is a better bet than Mid-Levels for an extended walk: the tree-planted paths leading to **WAN CHAI GAP** offer some fine views and a couple of rather peculiar points of interest. As the approach to the walk is by the #15 bus, it's a tour you can make on your way back from The Peak if you wish.

Along Bowen Road

Get off the #15 bus on Stubbs Road at the stop closest to the Highcliff Apartments and Monte Rosa, two apartment buildings whose signs you can't miss if you're watching out for them. Steps opposite the apartments lead down to **Bowen Road**, which runs west above the city, right the way back to the Peak Tram line.

A short way along Bowen Road, a red-railed path runs up to the right to an **Earth God Shrine**, a painted red image on the rock fronted by a neat altar, at which there are usually incense sticks burning and small food offerings lying about. Protectors of the local community, earth gods have been worshipped for centuries on the mainland; in Hong Kong, you still find them tucked into street corners and against buildings, but this is easily the most spectacularly sited, with views over the Happy Valley racecourse below and the gleaming, teeming tower blocks beyond.

Continue along shaded Bowen Road – a marvellous walk at rooftop level – passing further shrines. After about fifteen minutes you'll reach the **Lover's Stone Garden**, or Lover's Rock. This steep, landscaped area is dotted with more shrines and incense burners, through which steps lead up past a motley succession of red-painted images, tinfoil windmills (representing a change in luck), burning incense sticks, and porcelain religious figures. At the top is the **Yan Yuen Sek**, "Lover's Rock", a nine-metre-high rock pointing into the sky from the top of the bluff. It's one of several focuses of the Maidens' Festival (see p.240), held in mid-August, and since the nineteenth century, unmarried women, wives and widows have been climbing up here to pray for husbands and sons. There are also superb views from here.

Beyond the garden, passing various other small shrines along the way, it's about another ten minutes to the junction with **Wan Chai Gap Road**, where a sharp right leads down into Wan Chai itself, past the Pak Tai Temple (p.81). The left turn heads back up to Stubbs Road to Wan Chai Gap proper and the Police Museum.

The Police Museum

Returning back up to Stubbs Road, a signpost at the junction with Wan Chai Gap Road points to the **Police Museum** (Tues 2–5pm, Wed–Sun 9am–5pm; free), housed in the old Wan Chai Gap Police Station, 100m up Coombe Rd at no. 27, on the hill to the right behind the children's playground: bus #15 from Central Bus Terminal stops nearby, at the junction of Stubbs Road and Peak Road. Inside, exhibits chart the history of the Royal Hong Kong Police Force (officially formed in 1844, though there was a volunteer force as early as the initial 1841 landing, and there are displays of old photos, uniforms and guns, as well as police statements, seized counterfeit cash and a tiger's head (a huge beast shot in Sheung Shui in 1915). Another room displays every kind of drug you've ever heard of and, perversely, shows you exactly how to smuggle them – hollowed-out Bibles and bras stuffed with heroin are just some of the more obvious methods. There's also a mock-up of a heroin factory and a Triad room, complete with ceremonial uniforms and some very offensive weapons retrieved by the police.

Back on Peak Road, you can wait for the #15 bus up to The Peak or follow Wan Chai Gap Road down into Wan Chai. Coombe Road itself climbs on to **Magazine Gap**, another of the hillside passes, from where – if you've got a decent map and lots of stamina – you can eventually hit The Peak from yet another direction.

Wan Chai

East of Central, long, parallel roads run all the way to Causeway Bay, cutting straight through **WAN CHAI**, a district noted for its bars, restaurants and nightlife. Wan Chai first came to prominence as a red-light district in the 1940s, though its real heyday was twenty years later when American soldiers and sailors ran amok in its bars and clubs while on R&R from the wars in Korea and Vietnam. Richard Mason immortalized the area in his novel, *The World of Suzie Wong*, whose eponymous heroine was a Wan Chai prostitute. (Oddly, for the 1960 film of the novel, Wan Chai itself wasn't deemed photogenically sleazy enough, filming taking place around Hollywood Road instead.)

▲ A tram serving Wan Chai

Set against those times, present-day Wan Chai is fairly tame, though its eastern stretch is still a decent venue for a night out. However, the westernmost part of Wan Chai, beyond Queensway, belies its seedy image: as the rents have increased in Central, businesses have moved into the area, a development that acquired extra momentum with the opening of the enormous **Convention and Exhibition Centre** (CEC) and its extension. **Walking** through Wan Chai, you can follow one of three parallel main roads – Lockhart Road, Jaffe Road or Hennessy Road – all of which reach down to Causeway Bay. If you're going by **tram**, note that it detours down Johnston Road instead, which is fine for the Pak Tai Temple and Queen's Road East, but not so handy if you're aiming for the Arts Centre, Convention and Exhibition Centre or the waterfront – for these, take the #18 **bus** from Connaught Road Central, the MTR to Wan Chai or the **Star Ferry** from Tsim Sha Tsui to Wan Chai Ferry Pier. The tram from Central to Causeway Bay via Wan Chai runs along Des Voeux Road, Queensway, Johnston Road, Hennessy Road, then Yee Wo Street or Percival Street.

The Arts Centre and Academy for Performing Arts

Since 1976, much of Hong Kong's arts and drama has been centred on the fifteen-storey **Hong Kong Arts Centre** at 2 Harbour Rd. Despite the competition posed by the Cultural Centre in Tsim Sha Tsui (see p.103), it's still a leading venue for drama, film screenings and various cultural events. It also houses the Goethe Institute and, on the fifth floor, the Pao Sui Loong Galleries (daily 10am–8pm; free), which maintain temporary exhibition space for contemporary art: local and international painting, photography and sculpture. For events and box office details, see p.231.

Close by, on Gloucester Road, the building with the triangular windows houses the **Academy for Performing Arts** (APA). Here, many of the productions are performed by the students themselves – from local works to Shakespeare – though in addition you'll regularly come across visiting shows, as well as modern and classical music and Chinese and Western dance. Other than during performances, the facilities are only open to the students.

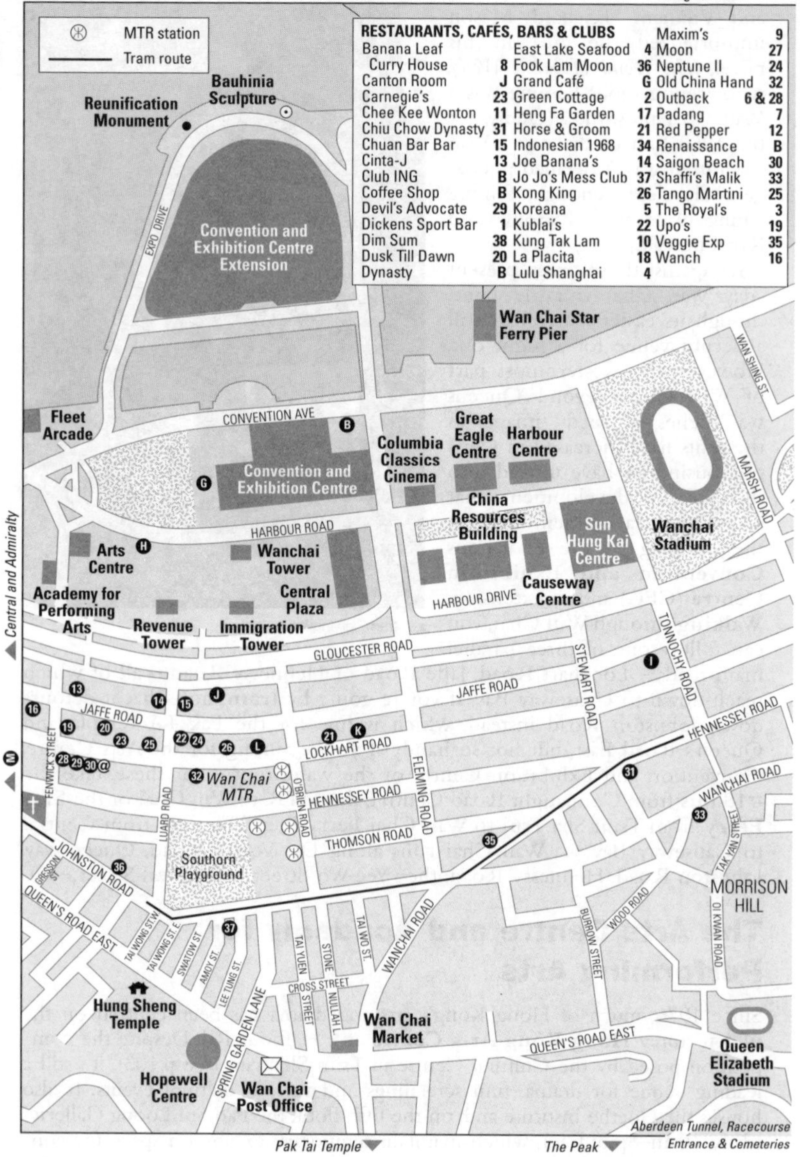

The Convention and Exhibition Centre and around

Ongoing land reclamation and redevelopment means that the Wan Chai harbourfront is continuously mutating. Huge buildings loom over the water, the grandest of which is the **Convention and Exhibition Centre**, resembling,

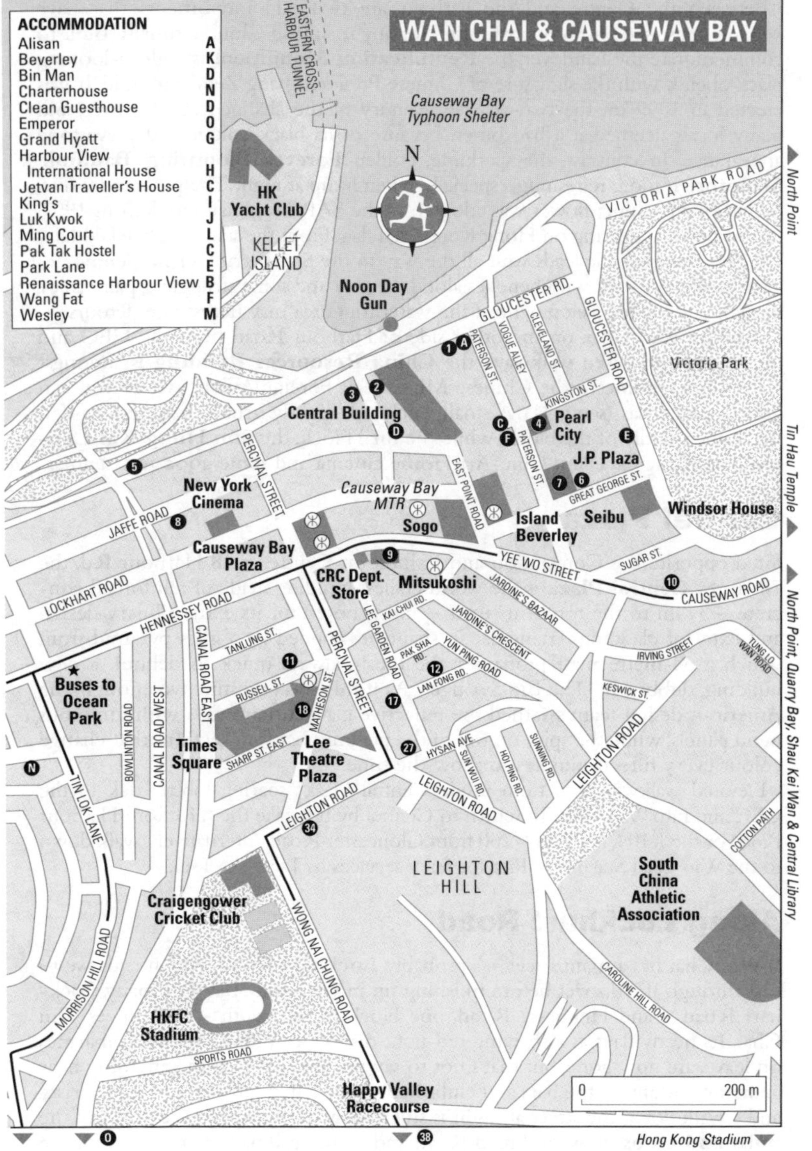

more or less, a giant manta ray. The curved-roofed **CEC Extension**, joined by a bridge to the original centre, was where the British formally handed Hong Kong back to the Chinese in June 1997, and when there are no events going on, you can visit the hall where the ceremonies took place. On the eastern side of the Convention Centre, services for Tsim Sha Tsui leave from the **Wan Chai Ferry Pier** (daily 7.30am–11pm).

Between the Centre and the harbour are two odd monuments that have become must-see photo opportunities for any mainland Chinese tourist. Built to commemorate the handover, the **Reunification Monument** is a glum-looking black obelisk with the signature of Chinese President Jiang Zemin in gold. It was erected in 1999 on the two-year anniversary of the changeover of power, and many locals deemed it a bad omen because of its black colour and gravestone appearance. In contrast, the sparkling, golden **Forever Blooming Bauhinia Sculpture** is more refreshing, especially when lit up at night. The pink and white, orchid-like bauhinia flower was adopted as the SAR's regional emblem in 1997, its five petals appearing on Hong Kong's red flag. From the statues, a bricked harbourfront promenade leads west all the way to the Star Ferry Pier in Central. It's a fairly pleasant walk with benches along the way and some struggling palm trees, though current redevelopment of the waterfront area may necessitate detours.

Back in Wan Chai, on the other side of Harbour Road from the CEC and joined to it by raised walkways, the **China Resources Building** is, amongst other things, home to the Chinese Ministry of Foreign Affairs, where you can get Chinese visas (see p.41). A small, enclosed, slightly grubby Chinese garden sits in the middle of the block, while the final block, the **Sun Hung Kai Centre**, houses the excellent Cine-Art House cinema and some good restaurants.

Central Plaza

Sited opposite the Convention and Exhibition Centre, at 18 Harbour Rd, the 78-storey **Central Plaza** is the world's tallest building made of reinforced concrete – 374m to the top of its mast – and is noted for its extraordinary design and exterior cladding. Triangular in shape, it's topped by a glass pyramid from which a 64-metre mast protrudes: the locals, always quick to debunk a new building, dubbed it "The Big Syringe". As if this wasn't distinctive enough, the American design team swathed the reflective glass curtain walls with luminous neon panels, while the spire on top of the pyramid has four sections that change colour every fifteen minutes to show the time.

Elevated walkways run from inside Central Plaza's soaring lobby back to the CEC and into Wan Chai. To return to Central by bus, take the #18 from Harbour Road or the #104, #115 or #260 from Gloucester Road. Alternatively, walk down to the Wan Chai Star Ferry Pier for ferry services to Tsim Sha Tsui.

Along Lockhart Road

If Wan Chai has a main street, it's probably **Lockhart Road**, which runs west–east through the district before finishing up in Causeway Bay. For many, Lockhart Road – and Hennessy Road, one block to the south – epitomizes Wan Chai. Its heady days as a thriving red-light district, throbbing with US marines on leave, are now gone, but that's not to say the area has become anything near gentrified. Many of the bars and clubs here make a living from fleecing tourists, and a walk down the street at night is still a fairly lively experience. Most of the **pubs and clubs** between Luard Road and Fleming Road are rowdy until the small hours, and it's easy to get a late meal in the hundreds of restaurants along and around Lockhart Road. If there's a merchant or naval fleet in town, Wan Chai occasionally echoes with the sounds of yesteryear, though the most pleasant experience is to stroll down here on Sunday. This is a day off for the Filipina housemaids all over the territory and, after meeting at Statue Square in Central (see p.58), many head for Wan Chai, where the bars and clubs around Lockhart Road open their doors early for some wild singing and dancing.

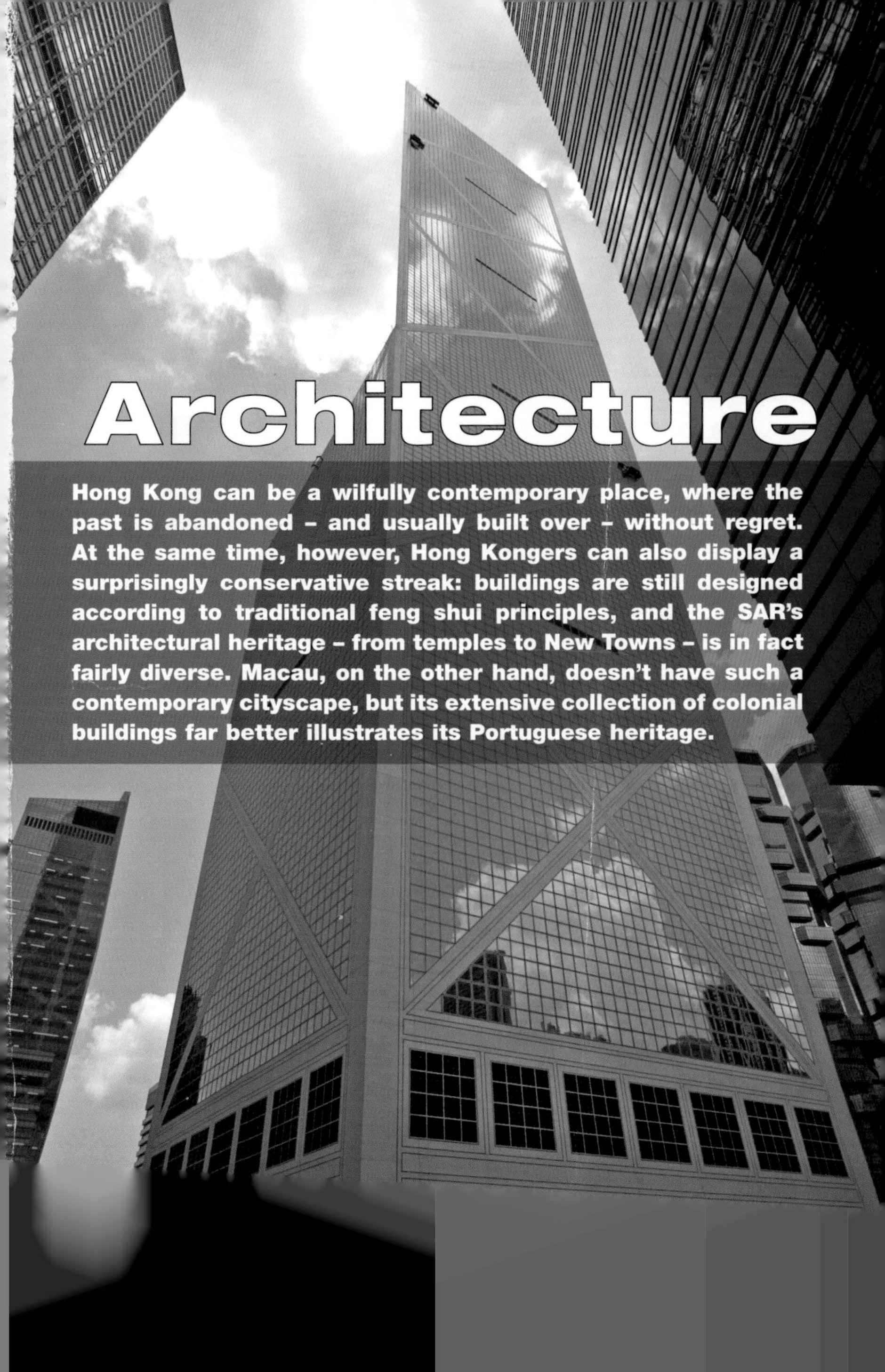

Architecture

Hong Kong can be a wilfully contemporary place, where the past is abandoned – and usually built over – without regret. At the same time, however, Hong Kongers can also display a surprisingly conservative streak: buildings are still designed according to traditional feng shui principles, and the SAR's architectural heritage – from temples to New Towns – is in fact fairly diverse. Macau, on the other hand, doesn't have such a contemporary cityscape, but its extensive collection of colonial buildings far better illustrates its Portuguese heritage.

Geomancy compass

Feng shui

Whatever the scale of a building project, the Chinese consider divination using **feng shui** (literally "wind and water") an essential part of the initial preparations. *Feng shui* is a form of **geomancy**, which assesses how buildings must be positioned so as not to disturb the spiritual attributes of the surrounding landscape, which in a city such as Hong Kong naturally includes other buildings. This reflects Taoist cosmology, which believes that all components of the universe exist in a balance with one another, and therefore the disruption of a single element can cause potentially dangerous alterations to the whole. It is vital, therefore, that structures are favourably oriented according to points on the compass and protected from local "**unlucky directions**" (features that drain or block the flow of good fortune) by the immediate arrangement of other buildings, walls, hills, mountain ranges or water. Geomancy further proposes ideal forms for particular types of structure, and carefully arranges spaces and components within a building according to time-honoured formulae – even the angle of the escalators in the HSBC building was fixed according to *feng shui*. It's not difficult to spot smaller manifestations of *feng shui* around buildings in Hong Kong, such as mirrors hung above doors or woks placed outside windows to deflect bad influences. Water features create positive *feng shui* (it is believed that wealth is borne along by the water), hence the price of harbour-view real estate. By contrast, the old Government House has very bad *feng shui*: it's cut off from the sea, is overlooked by high buildings, and some of the surrounding skyscrapers are placed so that their corners point towards it – the *feng shui* equivalent of being stabbed.

The earliest buildings

Before the British arrived, Hong Kong's settlements comprised fishing villages and self-contained, clan-based farming villages. Fishing communities were semi-nomadic, and have left little trace of their buildings, though the **Tanka village** of **Tai O** on Lantau Island (see p.171) gives an idea of how any available materials might have been used, its stilt houses perched above the water and made from a jumble of corrugated-iron sheeting and driftwood. More substantial examples of traditional farming settlements survive in **Hakka walled villages**, such as **Sam Tung Uk** at Tsuen Wan in the New Territories (see p.138), whose architectural features can be explained by both *feng shui* and the functional need of villagers to defend themselves from potentially hostile neighbours. The rectangular houses are arranged in a grid pattern inside a protective wall, with both house doors and village entrance facing south, a

Queen's Road East and around

If the brashness of Lockhart and Hennessy roads isn't to your taste, head south towards the more traditional streets between Johnston Road – where the tram runs – and **Queen's Road East**, where all the traditional Chinese trades, from pawnbrokers to printers, can be found. Buses #15 and #61 run from Central to **Wan Chai Market**, another of the island's municipal meat, fish, fruit and veg indoor markets.

The Pak Tai Temple

From the market, Stone Nullah Lane (*nullah* is a ravine or gutter) leads uphill; off to the left, down Lung On Street, is the **Pak Tai Temple**, decorated with colourful, handmade roof pottery and woodcarvings. The temple is dedicated to Pak Tai, Military Protector and Emperor of the North, whose task it is to maintain harmony on earth (and prevent flooding). He's represented inside the main hall by a tall, seventeenth-century copper statue, seated on a throne facing the door. Up the steps behind, four figures of warriors and scholars guard a second image of the ebony-faced and bearded god, resplendent in an embroidered jacket with a writhing dragon motif. In a room off to the left craftsmen practise the age-old Chinese art of making **burial offerings** from paper and bamboo – delicate works of art that are burned in order to equip the deceased for the afterlife. Around the walls hang half-finished and finished items: a car, an apartment building, houses, money, furniture and aeroplanes, all painted and coloured.

From the temple, you can climb the steps at the back up to Kennedy Road, turn right onto Wan Chai Gap Road and follow this road left up to Bowen Road to join the walk described under "Wan Chai Gap", on p.75.

From Wan Chai Post Office to Johnston Road

Queen's Road East leads back towards Central, a route that traces out the nineteenth-century shoreline. It's a good street for browsing, with many shops selling products made from **rattan**, a tropical cane or palm used extensively here for making furniture. It's all fairly cheap, and often very elaborate. You'll soon pass an old, whitewashed building, the former **Wan Chai Post Office**, opened in 1912 and positively ancient by Hong Kong standards, before reaching the circular **Hopewell Centre**, whose main asset is a revolving *dim sum* restaurant on the sixtieth floor.

A hundred metres or so further along, the **Hung Sheng Temple** at no. 131 is built right into the rocks that bear down upon Queen's Road East at this point. A long, narrow temple, it started life in the mid-nineteenth century as a shrine by the sea to the scholar Hung Sheng, a patron saint of fishermen because of his reputed skill in forecasting the weather.

Opposite the temple, over the main road, **Tai Wong Street West** runs through to Johnston Road, the bottom half of the alley filled with birdcages, the air thick with the calls of songbirds, budgies and their dinner – crickets tied up in little bags. A couple of streets further up is **Gresson Street**, which has a produce market where you can buy freshly peeled bamboo shoots and **preserved eggs** (see box overleaf) among the more usual items. Johnston Road itself is a handy place to finish up, as you can catch the **tram** from here, either back to Central or on to Causeway Bay.

Hundred-year-old eggs

Every Hong Kong market sells a variety of fresh eggs – ducks, quails, pigeons and geese, as well as chickens – which are inspected under a light by traders for their freshness. Most also contain a massive range of preserved eggs, including the so-called **"hundred-year-old eggs"**. These are made using duck eggs, which are covered with a thick mixture of lime, ash and tea leaves, soaked for a month and then wrapped in ash and rice husks for around six months, when they are peeled and eaten with pickled ginger. They're an acquired taste: green and black inside, with a strong odour, they have a jelly-like consistency and a rich yolk. Salted eggs, too, are produced, covered with a black paste made from salt and burnt rice – in street markets you'll see men plunging the eggs into murky vats of the paste and stirring slowly. These eggs are Cantonese delicacies, which you can try in plenty of restaurants as an appetizer. Failing that, buy a moon cake during the Mid-Autumn Festival (see "Festivals", p.241), which uses the preserved yolk as a filling.

Causeway Bay

CAUSEWAY BAY, a dense shopping and residential district between Wan Chai and Victoria Park, was one of the original areas of settlement in the mid-nineteenth century. There are a few low-key attractions here, and the rattling tram ride from Central is fun, but there's nothing at Causeway Bay you can't find elsewhere in the territory – it's neither as upmarket as Central, nor inexpensive as Tsim Sha Tsui.

The Bay and the Noon Day Gun

Before land reclamation, Causeway Bay was just that – a large, natural bay, known as Tong Lo Wan in Cantonese, that stretched back into what's now Victoria Park and the surrounding streets. The British settled here in the 1840s, erecting warehouses along the waterfront and trading from an area they called East Point. Filled in since the 1950s, all that's left of the bay is the **typhoon shelter**, with its massed ranks of junks and yachts, and **Kellet Island**, now a thumb of land connected to the mainland and harbouring the Hong Kong Yacht Club. Development around here really got under way with the opening of the two-kilometre-long **Eastern Cross-Harbour Tunnel** in the early 1970s, which runs under Kellet Island to Kowloon. With the improved access that this brought (though massive congestion at peak hours threatens its benefit these days), hotels, shops and department stores moved in, effectively turning Causeway Bay into a self-perpetuating tourist ghetto. White high-rises now girdle the typhoon shelter, and although it's not the prettiest of the territory's harbour scenes, there is something stirring about the hundreds of masts and bobbing boats that carpet the water.

Right on the waterfront stands one of Hong Kong's best-known monuments, the **Noon Day Gun**, made famous by one of Noel Coward's better lyrics:

In Hong Kong
They strike a gong
And fire off a noonday gun
To reprimand each inmate
Who's in late

from *Mad Dogs and Englishmen*

Apart from a few local street names, this is the only relic of the influence that the nineteenth-century trading establishments wielded in Causeway Bay, in particular Jardine, Matheson & Co., which had its headquarters here. The story, recorded on a plaque by the gun, is suitably vague, but it's said that the small ship's gun was fired by a Jardine employee to salute one of the company's ships, an action that so outraged the governor – whose traditional prerogative it was to fire off salutes – that he ordered it to be fired every day at noon for evermore. Some of the short harbour cruises (see "Organized Tours", p.41) take in the daily noon firing of the gun, and there's a more elaborate ceremony every New Year's Eve, when it is fired at midnight. The easiest way to reach the gun is to go through the underground *Wilson* car park on Gloucester Road, next to the *Excelsior*; a tunnel runs under the road and emerges right next to the gun. After all the fuss in print, though, it's simply a gun in a railed-off garden.

From the gun, walk further up the tatty promenade towards Victoria Park, and you can negotiate the hire of a **sampan** with the women from the typhoon shelter. Settle on a price and you'll be paddled into the shelter, whereupon other sampans will appear to sell you fresh seafood and produce, which is cooked in front of you and washed down with beer bought from other boats – you'll need to bargain every step of the way.

Victoria Park

The eastern edge of Causeway Bay is marked by the large, green expanse of **Victoria Park**, one of the few decent open-air spaces in this congested city. It's busy all day, from the crack-of-dawn martial arts practitioners to the old men spending an hour or so strolling with their songbirds in little cages along the paths. Amid the paved areas and groves of trees and flowers, there's also a swimming pool, childrens' playground, jogging track and a pebbled path that people walk on in socks to massage their feet; you might catch a soccer match on the lawn, too. The park hosts some lively festivals, including a flower market at Chinese New Year, a lantern display for the Mid-Autumn Festival and the annual candle-lit vigil for the victims of Tiananmen Square on June 4.

At the park's southeastern corner, up Tin Hau Temple Road (by the Tin Hau MTR station), lies Causeway Bay's **Tin Hau Temple**, a couple of centuries old, surrounded by high-rises and sited on top of a little hill that once fronted the water. Tin Hau is the name given locally to the goddess of the sea, and her temples can be found throughout Hong Kong, often – as here - marooned far inland by land reclamation.

Central Library

The sandy yellow Neoclassical building facing Victoria Park on Causeway Road is Hong Kong's **Central Library** (Mon, Tues, Thurs & Fri 10am–9pm, Wed 1–9pm, Sat & Sun 10am–6pm), a massive twelve-storey affair that was the

SAR's biggest and most costly construction project since the airport. Opened in May 2001, it's been unfairly compared to an ugly shopping mall, but inside it is expansive and airy, with an impressive central atrium and floor-to-ceiling windows. It boasts 1.2 million books, more than five hundred public-access computer terminals with Internet, a children's toy library on the second floor, an art and photo exhibition gallery and lecture theatre on the ground level, and state-of-the-art technology throughout – books are whisked around the building on a mechanized conveyance system using overhead rails. During the week, the library isn't too packed and you shouldn't have to queue to use the Internet or read a newspaper from home – there are more than four thousand newspapers, magazines and journals in the reading area on the fifth floor – on one of the comfy chairs. There's a small gift shop and a branch of *Delifrance* on the first floor.

Shopping in Causeway Bay

Doing your shopping in Causeway Bay means splitting your time between two main sections. The grid of streets to the north, closest to Victoria Park, contains the modern shops and businesses, many of them owned by the Japanese who moved here in the 1960s. There are large **Japanese department stores** here – Mitsukoshi and Sogo on Hennessy Road and Seibu on Gloucester Road – stuffed with hi-tech, high-fashion articles, open late and normally packed with people. The other main store here is the CRC Department Store on Hennessy Road, one of the biggest of the stores specializing in products from mainland China, such as silk and porcelain. Above the Sogo supermarket – a good place for cheap takeaway sushi, sit-down Japanese snacks and coffee – the **Island Beverley** shopping mall (entrance on Great George Street) showcases the work of young designers, while more quirky shops, including a pet emporium, trendy hairdressers and countless boutiques, can be found hidden away in cosy rooms on the second floor of buildings in Lockhart Road. **Vogue Alley**, a covered Art Nouveau-ish mall running between Kingston Street and Gloucester Road, has clothes as well as restaurants and bars. Benches and a fountain make it a pleasant place to rest your feet.

The area **south** of Yee Wo Street is immediately different. It's the original Causeway Bay settlement and home to an interesting series of interconnected markets and shopping streets. **Jardine's Bazaar** and **Jardine's Crescent**, two narrow, parallel lanes off Yee Wo Street, have contained a street market since the earliest days of the colony (their names echoing the trading connection) and they remain great places to poke around. Cheap clothes abound, while deeper in you'll find a noisy little market and all manner of traditional shops and stalls selling herbs and provisions. There are similar sights the further back into these streets you go: **Pennington Street**, **Irving Street**, **Fuk Hing Lane** and others all reward making a slow circle through them, perhaps stopping for some tea or to buy some herbal medicine.

Times Square and Lee Theatre Plaza

The most startling fixture in the Causeway Bay shopping scene is the beige blockbuster of a building that is **Times Square**, at Matheson and Russell streets. Spearing skywards from a comparitively small space at ground level, it exemplifies Hong Kong's modern architecture, where space can only be gained by building upwards and distinction attained by unexpected design: a vertical shopping mall supported by great marble trunks and featuring a cathedral window and giant video advertising screen. From the massive open-plan lobby,

Tram routes from Causeway Bay

From Causeway Bay to Central: Yee Wo Street, Hennessy Road, Johnston Road, Queensway, Des Voeux Road.
From Causeway Bay to Happy Valley: Percival Street, Leighton Road, Wong Nai Chung Road, Morrison Hill Road, Ting Lok Lane, Hennessy Road.
From Causeway Bay to Shau Kei Wan: Causeway Road, King's Road, Shau Kei Wan Road.

silver bullet-lifts whiz up to the various themed shopping floors – levels nine to thirteen, Food Forum, are devoted to restaurants and bars, the best of them reviewed in chapters 7 and 8; at ground level there's a cinema and access to Causeway Bay MTR station.

Another fine example of the city's architectural trends lies nearby, at the end of Percival Street, where the architect of the **Lee Theatre Plaza** – faced with an awkward corner on which to build – obviously took New York's Flatiron Building as a starting point. Up soars the steel, glass and marble tower of shops, offices and restaurants, presenting its sharp rib to the front – which is then chopped out above atrium level, leaving the building resembling a face without a nose.

Happy Valley

Travel south on the branch tram line from Causeway Bay and you're soon in **HAPPY VALLEY**. After Western district, which was soon discovered to be rife with malaria, Happy Valley was one of the earliest parts of the island to be settled, in the hope that it would be healthier and more sheltered. But it belied its name, turning into a particularly muddy malarial swamp during the wet season. Everyone moved out, the land was drained and the flattest part turned into a racecourse in 1846, which survives and thrives famously today, and gives the area its Cantonese name of *Pau Ma Tei* ("Racecourse").

Ponies aside, there's not a great deal to see in Happy Valley, though a walk up the main **Sing Woo Road** reveals a small market and plenty of good restaurants. The area is a popular haunt among expats, many of whom live locally – witness the **Craigengower Cricket Club** at the junction with Leighton Road. Ride on the top deck of the tram past here, however, and you'll discover that there is in fact no cricket pitch inside the walls, crown-green bowling being the preferred sport. Trams for the racecourse from Causeway Bay and Wan Chai/Central arrive at the Happy Valley tram terminus at the back (southern end) of the racecourse, on Wong Nai Chung Road, where the spectator entrance is.

Happy Valley Racecourse

The only legal gambling allowed in Hong Kong is on horseracing, and the **Happy Valley Racecourse** is the traditional centre of this multimillion-dollar business (there's also a second racecourse at Sha Tin in the New Territories). It's controlled by the Hong Kong Jockey Club, one of the colony's power bastions since its foundation in 1884, with a board of stewards made up of the leading lights of Hong Kong big business. A percentage of the profits go to social and charitable causes – you'll see Jockey Club schools and clinics all over the territory – and such is the passion for betting on horses in Hong Kong (or, illegally, betting on anything) that the racing season pulls in over $80 billion.

The season runs from September to mid-June and there are usually meetings every Wednesday night. Weekend racing is at Sha Tin, but although that course is more modern it doesn't have the intense atmosphere of Happy Valley, which, with its tight track and high stands, is rather like a Roman amphitheatre. Entrance to the public enclosure is $10, where you can mix with a beery expat crowd, watch the horses being paraded before each race, and pump the bilingual staff to make sense of the intricate accumulator bets that Hong Kong specializes in. Other options include joining the hard-bitten Hong Kong punters up in the stands, mostly watching the action on TV ($20, plus all the cigarette smoke you can handle), or signing up for the HKTB's **Come Horseracing Tour** ($540-790 depending on the event), which will take you to the course, feed you before the races, get you into the members' enclosure and hand out some racing tips: you need to be over 18 and to have been in Hong Kong for less than three weeks – take your passport to any HKTB office at least a day before the race.

On the second floor of the main building at the racecourse, the **Hong Kong Racing Museum** (Tues–Sun 10am–5pm; free) presents various aspects of Hong Kong's racing history, from the early days in Happy Valley through the construction of the site at Sha Tin to the charitable projects funded by the Jockey Club. Racing buffs can also study champion racehorse characteristics and famous jockeys in the museum's eight galleries and cinema.

The cemeteries

It's tempting to think that the series of **cemeteries** staggered up the valley on the west side of the racecourse is full of failed punters. In fact, they provide an interesting snapshot of the territory's ethnic and religious mix: starting from Queen's Road East and climbing up, the five mid-nineteenth-century cemeteries are officially Muslim, Catholic, Protestant Colonial (the largest, with a berth for Lord Napier, the first Chief Superintendent of Trade with China), Parsee and Jewish. For a quick look, the #15 bus (to The Peak from the Central Bus Terminal) runs past them, up Stubbs Road, though the best views are the virtually airborne ones from Bowen Road, the path that runs to Wan Chai Gap (see "Wan Chai Gap", p.75). The #6 (to Stanley) also goes by. If you want to explore them at closer quarters (most are open daily 8am–6pm), take the Happy Valley tram around Wong Nai Chung Road; there's a stop close to the Catholic and Colonial cemeteries, from where you can walk around to further entrances on Stubbs Road.

The South Side

Apart from The Peak, the other great escape from the built-up north end of Hong Kong Island is to the **south side**, a long, fragmented coastline from Aberdeen to Stanley punctured by bays and inlets. Unfortunately, a large proportion of the Hong Kong population escapes there too, particularly at the weekend. It's worth braving the crowded buses and roads, however, for some of the territory's best **beaches** and a series of little villages that pre-date the arrival of the British in the mid-nineteenth century – though none of them is exactly traditional or isolated these days. Most have somewhere to eat, and you needn't worry about getting stuck, as the **buses** are all very regular and run until late in the evening.

The quickest and most obvious trips are to **Aberdeen** and **Repulse Bay** in the west, and most find time to move on to **Stanley**, too, which is probably the most interesting place to aim for if you've only got time for one excursion. If you have children in tow, then **Ocean Park** – Hong Kong's oldest theme and adventure park – is a great outing.

Aberdeen

ABERDEEN was one of the few places on the island already settled when the British arrived in the 1840s – the bay here was used as a shelter for the indigenous Hoklos and Tankas, who fished in the surrounding archipelago. It's still really the only other large town on the island, with more than sixty thousand people, several hundred of them living as they've done for centuries, on sampans and junks tied up in the harbour (though they're gradually being moved into new housing estates). The British named the town that grew up here after their colonial secretary, the Earl of Aberdeen, but the Cantonese name – *Heung Gong Tsai*, or "Little Hong Kong" – better reflects the attractions of its fine harbour. To reach Aberdeen, catch **bus** #7 from the Outlying Islands Ferry Piers (via Pokfulam Road, getting off on Aberdeen Main Road); the #70 from Exchange Square in Central via Admiralty MTR; or #72 from Moreton

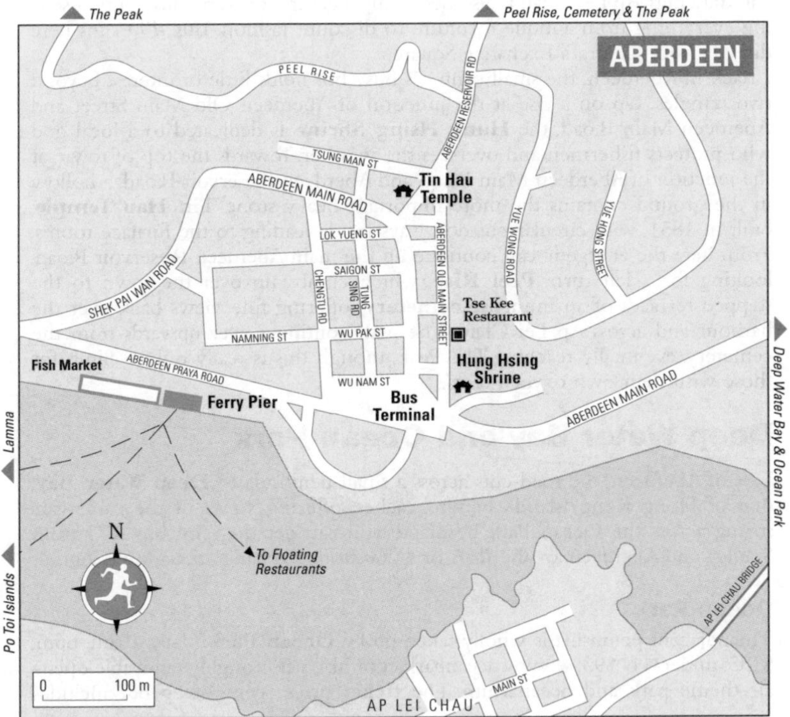

Terrace in Causeway Bay – any of which take around fifteen minutes. There's also a **boat** connection between Aberdeen and nearby Lamma Island (see p.157), and across to Po Toi island (see p.93).

The harbour and town

Arriving by bus, you'll either be dropped at the Bus Terminal or on Aberdeen Main Road, but it makes no difference since the central grid of streets is fairly small. Making your way down to the **harbour** first will help you understand the importance of water to the town. Cross the main road by the pedestrian footbridge to the long waterfront; before going any further, check out the excellent **fish market** here (best early in the morning), where fishermen sell their catches direct to restaurants. Around the ferry pier you'll be hailed by women touting the **sampan rides** that are the main reason to visit Aberdeen: a bit of bargaining should get you a thirty-minute ride for around $50 a head. The trip offers photogenic views of houseboats jammed together, complete with dogs, drying laundry and outdoor kitchens, as well as boatyards and three **floating restaurants**, which are especially spectacular when lit up at night – though their food isn't up to much (see p.202).

Sampans also run across to the large island just offshore, **Ap Lei Chau** ("Duck's Tongue Island"); there's also a connecting bridge, with bus services. This is one of the territory's main boat- and junk-building centres. Wandering around the yards is fascinating, particularly if you can find someone to tell you what's going on. The workshops here are mostly family-owned, the skills handed down through generations, with only minimal reliance on proper plans and drawings. Ap Lei Chau is also becoming a centre for warehouse outlets selling everything from antique furniture to discount fashion. Bus #90 runs here directly from Central's Exchange Square.

Back in Aberdeen, the small centre is busy but holds little of interest beyond two temples. Up on a rise at the junction of Aberdeen Old Main Street and Aberdeen Main Road, the **Hung Hsing Shrine** is dedicated to a local god who protects fishermen and oversees the weather. Towards the top of town, at the junction of Aberdeen Main Road and Aberdeen Reservoir Road, a hollow in the ground contains the more important heavy stone **Tin Hau Temple**, built in 1851, with circular-cut doorways inside leading to the furnace rooms. From here the energetic can continue up the main Aberdeen Reservoir Road, looking for a left turn, **Peel Rise**, which climbs up over the town to the stepped terraces of an immense **cemetery**, offering fine views back over the harbour and across Ap Lei Chau. The path continues ever upwards from the cemetery, eventually reaching The Peak, though this is really only a climb for those with their own oxygen tents.

Deep Water Bay and Ocean Park

East of Aberdeen, the road cuts across a small peninsula to **Deep Water Bay**, one of Hong Kong Island's better beaches, offering views of the cable-cars strung across the Ocean Park headland; you can get there on bus #73 from Stanley and Aberdeen, or the #6A or #260 from Exchange Square in Central.

Ocean Park

The adjacent peninsula is wholly taken up by **Ocean Park** (daily 10am–6pm; $185, under-11s $93; ⓦwww.oceanpark.com.hk), a thoroughly enjoyable open-air theme park and oceanarium. The **ticket** price seems steep but includes everything on offer, enough to take up most of a day. A couple of **warnings**, though: the food on sale inside is either junk snacks or pricey meals, so you might want to take your own picnic (although officially you're not allowed to take your own food in). Also, try to go early if you want to get your money's worth. It'll take a good four hours to see all parts of the park, wait in line for a couple of rides and see the marine shows – with kids, and in the busy summer season, expect it to take longer, and expect to have to wait for all the popular rides. If you can, avoid going on Sundays and public holidays.

In the face of fierce **competition** from Disney over on Lantau Island, the park is busy repositioning itself, and is scaling back fairground rides in favour of a focus on wildlife and the natural world. One of the star attractions is a pair of giant pandas, An-An and Jia-Jia, for whom a special $80-million, two-thousand-square-metre complex has been created, complete with kitchen, clinic, fake mountain slopes and misting machines to mimic a mountain atmosphere.

The first section, the **Lowland** area, is a landscaped garden with greenhouses, a butterfly house, various parks, a theatre and a kiddies' adventure playground. There's also a 3D film simulator and a popular dinosaur discovery trail, with full-size moving models. This is also the departure point for the **cable car**, which hoists you 1.5km up the mountainside, high above Deep Water Bay, to the **Headland** section. Here, you'll find a mix of rides including the frightening "Dragon Roller-Coaster" built on the headland so that it feels like you'll be thrown into the sea at 80km per hour, and the self-explanatory "Abyss Turbo Drop". There's also one of the world's largest reef aquariums, with a massive atoll reef that's home to more than two thousand fish, including giant rays and sharks.

Bus routes to Ocean Park

The easiest way to get to Ocean Park is to take the Citybus Tour, which includes return transport – from Admiralty MTR or the Star Ferry Pier in Central – and entrance to the park. A number of ordinary bus services also pass the park. Unless otherwise shown, buses run every ten to fifteen minutes until around midnight.

From Aberdeen

#48 (direct), #70 and #72 from Aberdeen Main Road. Get off at the stop before Aberdeen Tunnel.

From Admiralty MTR

Citybus #629. The all-in-one bus and entrance ticket costs $209 (children $105), with one child free for each paying adult.

From Causeway Bay

#72A, #72, #92, #96 and #592 from outside the Hennessy Centre to Aberdeen. Get off just after emerging from Aberdeen Tunnel and follow the signs along Ocean Park Road; at weekends, the #72A stops right outside Ocean Park.

From the Star Ferry Pier in Central

Citybus #629 to Ocean Park. The all-inclusive bus and entrance ticket costs $209 (children $105), with one child free for each paying adult.

The #6 minibus (daily except Sun and public holidays) leaves from just in front of the Star Ferry Pier between City Hall and Edinburgh Place car park.

From Central Bus Terminal, Exchange Square

#41A, #70, #75, #90 and #97. Get off just after emerging from Aberdeen Tunnel and follow the signs along Ocean Park Road (about a 10min walk).

From Repulse Bay/Stanley

Bus #73 runs past the park en route to Aberdeen.

Looming over the lot is the **Ocean Park Tower**, 200m above sea level, giving superb vistas from its viewing platform and panoramic elevator. After this, you can head down the other side to the **Tai Shue Wan** area, by way of one of the world's longest outdoor escalators. There are fine views on the way down, more rides at the bottom, and access to **Middle Kingdom**, a Chinese theme park with pagodas, traditional crafts and entertainment such as Chinese opera.

Repulse Bay

The next bay along, **REPULSE BAY**, has lost whatever colonial attraction it once had, when the grand *Repulse Bay Hotel* stood at its centre, hosting tea dances and cocktail parties. The hotel was torn down without ceremony in the 1980s (the only surviving portion is the ludicrously expensive *Verandah* restaurant, at 109 Repulse Bay Rd) and the hill behind the bay is now lined with flash apartments contained within a high-rise wall washed in pink, yellow and blue. The **beach** itself is clean and wide, though the water quality isn't great, and it's backed by a concrete promenade containing some unmemorable cafés. On summer afternoons tens of thousands of people can descend on the sands – the record is 70,000 – but the atmosphere is always fairly downmarket. Connoisseurs of kitsch may want to amble down to the little Chinese garden at the end of the prom, where a brightly painted group of goddesses, Buddha statues, stone lions and dragons offer some tempting photo opportunities.

The people packing the beach are mostly oblivious to Repulse Bay's fairly grim history during World War II. The old hotel was used as a base by British troops, but in 1941, after three days of fierce fighting, the Japanese took the hotel, capturing and executing many of the defenders. Others were taken off to prison camps. The bay here had always been an attractive target for new arrivals: the name itself comes from the ship HMS *Repulse*, from which the nineteenth-century British mopped up the local pirates operating out of the area. If the beach is too crowded for comfort, try the nearby beaches at **Middle Bay** and **South Bay**, fifteen minutes' and thirty minutes' walk south around the bay respectively.

To get to Repulse Bay, take **buses** #6, #6A, #61, #64, #66 (not Sun) or #260 from Exchange Square in Central, or #73 from Aberdeen. Buses #6, #6A, #260 and #73 continue through Repulse Bay to Stanley, a fine ride.

Stanley

The major attraction on the south coast is **STANLEY**, sited on its own little peninsula and with much more appeal than all the other villages along the coast of the island. You could easily spend a day here, certainly if you're planning to do any shopping in the market, or use it as a jumping-off point for the nearby Po Toi island.

Stanley has been one of the main areas of settlement throughout the island's history. Prior to Britain's seizure of the island there were already two thousand people living here, earning a decent living from fishing; today, it's a small residential place, popular with Westerners as it's only 15km from Central, and fairly lively at most times of the year. The name, incidentally, is down to another nineteenth-century colonial secretary, Lord Stanley, but as with Aberdeen the original Cantonese name is much more evocative – *Chek Chue* (literally "Red Pillar"), which is either a reference to the red-flowering kapok trees here, or a euphemism for "robber's lair", after the pirates who once used the village as a base.

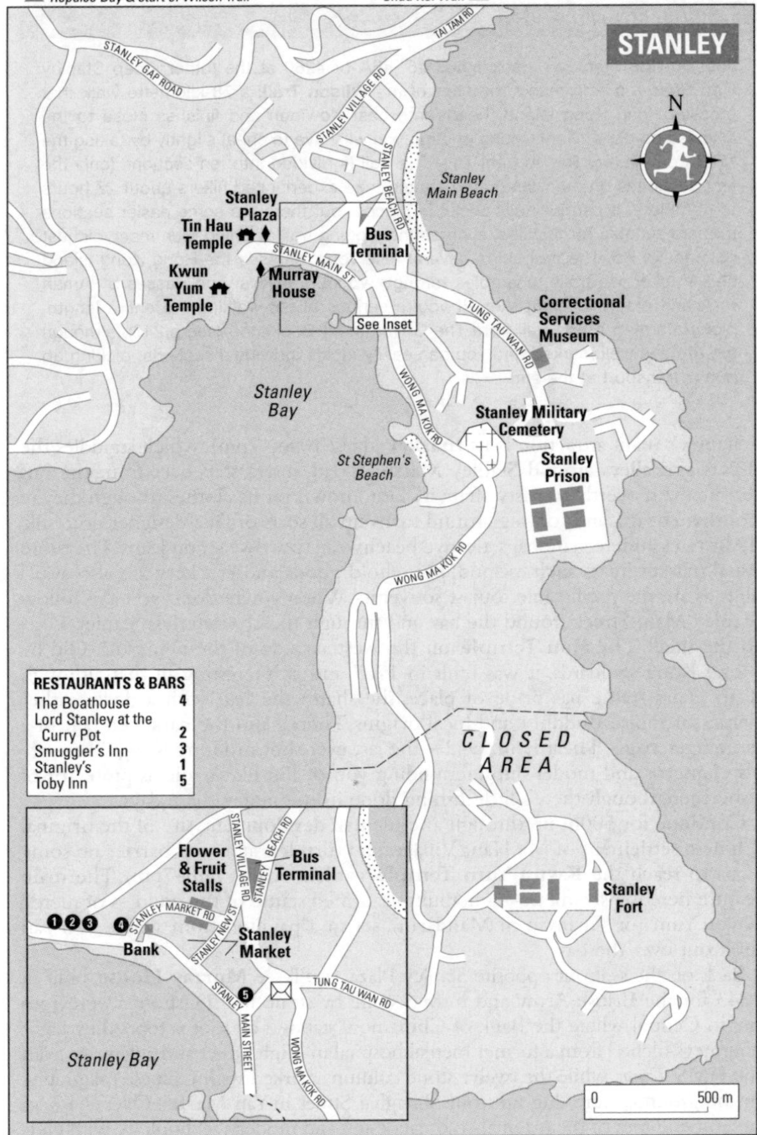

Around the village

The bus will drop you at the **bus terminal** on Stanley Village Road, and the **main beach** is just a couple of minutes' walk away, down on the eastern side of the peninsula. This is narrow and stony, ringed by new development, and for swimming there's actually a much better one, St Stephen's Beach, about ten minutes out of the centre in the opposite direction (see p.93).

The Wilson Trail

Just outside Stanley – get off bus #6, #6A or #260 at the rather steep Stanley Gap Road – a sign marks the start of the **Wilson Trail**, a 78-kilometre walk that crosses Hong Kong Island, heads into east Kowloon and finishes close to the Chinese border at Nam Chung (though you will have to cheat slightly by taking the MTR from Quarry Bay to Lam Tin). The trail is divided into ten sections (only the first section is on the island), and should take experienced hikers about 27 hours to complete. It can be quite tricky in places, but there are some easier sections that are suitable for families, such as the jogging trail at Shing Mun reservoir, just outside Tai Po. The trail skirts several reservoirs, crosses the Hong Kong Island and MacLehose trails, shambles through wooded valleys, and passes by Amah rock and plenty of campsites. If you're serious about walking the entire length, pick up a map of the trail from The Government Bookshop (see p.247), although the route is well marked and you can easily tackle individual sections, picking up public transport at the end.

Stanley's main attraction is its **market** (daily 10am–7pm), which straddles the streets and alleys around Stanley Market Road, just a step over from the bus terminal. An overtly touristy affair, it's best known for its clothes (though they're not that cheap), and rooting around turns up all sorts of fake designer gear, silk, T-shirts, cashmere, handbags, tie-dye beachwear, sportswear and jeans. The more usual market items such as food, household goods and crockery are also available, as are the predictable tourist souvenirs. When you're done, you can follow Stanley Main Street around the bay and through the characterless Stanley Plaza to the small **Tin Hau Temple** on the western side of the peninsula. Old by Hong Kong standards, it was built in 1767 and is interesting in that although Tian Hau's statue has pride of place, she shares the hall with a dozen other deities of Taoist, Buddhist and local origins. There's also the darkened pelt of a large tiger, bagged nearby in 1942 – the last ever shot in Hong Kong. There are also lanterns and model ships, reminding you of Tin Hau's role as protector of fishermen, though there's little fishing done from Stanley these days.

Continue for 500m up through a residential development, site of the original Chinese settlement of Ma Hang Village, and turn left at a road barrier up some steps to reach the **Kwun Yum Temple** gardens (daily 7am–7pm). The main feature here is a six-metre-high, multiple-armed statue of the goddess of mercy, Kwun Yum (or Guanyin in Mandarin), set in a pavilion from where you can look out over the bay.

Back on the seafront opposite Stanley Plaza, you'll see **Murray House**, built in 1843 for the British Army and moved stone by stone in 1982 from its previous site in Central where the Bank of China now stands. The roof is topped by eight chimneys filched from a former mental hospital in High Street and a flagpole from the HMS *Tamar*, while the twelve stone columns marked with Chinese calligraphy in the grounds were dug up from Shanghai Street in Yau Ma Tei. Overall, it's an unsatisfying mix of the original colonial design and modern technology, with gliding escalators and a fibre-optic lighting system that glows different colours at night. Inside, displays describe the architectural feats achieved during its reconstruction, while the top two floors have been given over to restaurants, whose mediocre fare is balanced by fine views across the bay from their balconies.

To St Stephen's Beach and Stanley Fort

From Murray House, follow Stanley Main Street south into Wong Ma Kok Road, and after about fifteen minutes (just after the playing field), you'll see signposted steps leading down to **St Stephen's Beach**, a nice stretch of clean sand with a short pier, a watersports centre, barbecue pits, showers and decent swimming. If you miss the steps to the beach, you can take the side road on the right a little further on, by St Stephen's School.

A few minutes on down the main road, the **Stanley Military Cemetery** has some graves dating back to the mid-1840s, but is mostly full of those killed defending Hong Kong from the Japanese in 1941 and later in the war. It's a poignant spot to stop and remember the brave stand that many of the soldiers took, especially since the other significant landmark, **Stanley Prison** – where hundreds of civilians were interned in dire conditions by the Japanese during the war – is just over the way. Nowadays, it's a maximum-security prison, housing (among others) convicted murderers who were on Hong Kong's death row until 1993, when capital punishment was abolished. The death sentence hadn't been carried out since 1966, but the fear was that China might have carried out the penalty after 1997 if it had remained in law. Before you reach the prison, the small **Correctional Services Museum** (Tues–Sun 10am–5pm; free) has a couple of simulated cells, a mock gallows, scores of apparatus for chastisement (including a wooden flogging frame and a cat-of-nine-tails), and a room full of products made by the prisoners.

Above the prison – though reached on a separate road – is **Stanley Fort**, formerly a British military base. The area is closed to the public (signs here say "Caution – Troops Marching"), though there's nothing to stop you going as far as you're allowed for the views over Stanley Bay.

Practicalities

Stanley isn't far beyond Repulse Bay, reached on **buses** #6, #6A or #260 (an express) from Exchange Square in Central, the #73 from Aberdeen/Repulse Bay, or – coming around the other side of the island – #63 from North Point and Causeway Bay and bus #14 from Sai Wan Ho and Shau Kei Wan (which is on the MTR and tram route; see below). The journey takes about forty minutes from Central and is a terrific ride, the road sometimes swooping high above the bays. There's nowhere **to stay** in Stanley, and the last bus leaves around midnight, though minibus #40 to Causeway Bay runs until 4am.

You can get something cheap **to eat** at the *dai pai dong*s on both sides of Stanley Market Road – noodles and the like, and there's fresh fruit on sale, too. More formally (and expensively), there are several good **restaurants** – in particular, *Lord Stanley at the Curry Pot* (see p.214 for review), or, if you haven't come to Hong Kong to eat Western food, Cantonese seafood places such as the *Toby Inn*, which, despite the name, gets plenty of Chinese custom. Stanley being the *gweilo* hangout it is, there are also a couple of **pubs** on Stanley Main Street, the most thoroughly colonial of which is *Smuggler's Inn*. You'll also find a **post office**, a couple of **banks** and a **supermarket** at Stanley Plaza.

Po Toi island

St Stephen's beach is the jumping-off point for a visit to the southerly **Po Toi island**, an hour's ferry ride away. Like all the minor outlying islands, its population is dwindling, but its glassed-in, prehistoric rock carvings of spirals and fish, and steep granite cliffs and boulders make for a good half-day's stroll and some secluded swimming. There's a small Tin Hau **temple** near the ferry pier at Tai Wan, and a spread of seafood restaurants that only really see any business on a Sunday. Fans of John Le Carré will know this island as the setting where the denouement to his *The Honourable Schoolboy*, a thriller largely set in Hong Kong, takes place.

On Sundays only, **ferries** leave St Stephen's Beach for Po Toi island at 10am and 11.30am, returning at 3pm, 4pm and 6pm. At other times, you can get to the island from Aberdeen (see p.87), but these **ferries** are less useful as they leave Aberdeen on Tuesday, Thursday and Saturday at 9am and Sundays at 8am, then come straight back again, and there's nowhere to stay on the island. Phone the HKTB (☎2508 1234) or, if you speak Chinese, the ferry company, (☎2554 4059) for more details.

The East Coast

Aside from a couple of low-key attractions – a string of trendy **restaurants and bars** in Quarry Bay, and a **museum** perched on a cliff in Shau Kei Wan – there's little incentive to travel much further **east** than Causeway Bay, although the tram ride is fairly entertaining – along King's Road, through **North Point**, the northernmost point of Hong Kong Island, and the residential areas of **Quarry Bay** and **Tai Koo Shing** before reaching **Shau Kei Wan** at the end of the line. Once, this whole stretch was lined with beaches, but the views these days are of high-rise apartments. Improvements in transport infrastructure are making the area more popular: the **Eastern Island Corridor**, a highway built above and along the shoreline, provides some impressive views if you're speeding along it in a car, while the tunnelled **MTR** link across the harbour from Quarry Bay gives much quicker access to Kowloon. It's probably best to go out on the tram – around half an hour from Causeway Bay to the end of the line – and return by MTR; each stop along the tram route also has its own MTR station.

Beyond Shau Kei Wan, heading south, you soon escape into more rural surroundings. Some of the island's best beaches are on its east coast, the ones around **Shek O** particularly, while you've a better chance of avoiding the crowds if you take one of the high hill walks from **Tai Tam Reservoir** that run over the centre of the island.

North Point

If you're going to jump off the tram anywhere before Shau Kei Wan, the otherwise ordinary **NORTH POINT** has a good **market** on Marble Street, a couple of blocks up from North Point Ferry Pier, selling cheap summer clothes and farm produce. Just opposite MTR exit B2, at no. 423 King's Rd, the **Sunbeam Theatre** is an excellent place to watch Chinese opera without any tourist hype, while its cinema is the cheapest in Hong Kong, and shows mainland Chinese art-house films (usually with English subtitles). Check with the HKTB before coming out here though, as there are rumours of the theatre's imminent closure. Down at the ferry pier, there's a fresh fish market, while the **ferries** run across to Hung Hom in Kowloon (daily 7.15am–7.35pm). **Buses** #10 to Central and Kennedy Town, and #63 (not Sun) and #65 (Sun only) to Stanley also leave from the ferry pier. You can also take the purple **MTR** Tseung Kwan O Line across the harbour to Kowloon, though you'll need to change again on the other side to reach Tsim Sha Tsui.

Quarry Bay and Tai Koo Shing

Further east, the tram runs through **QUARRY BAY**, where the second cross-harbour tunnel terminates. Opposite the MTR exit on King's Road – from where you can take the green Kwun Tong Line across to Kowloon – a string of westernized bars and a scattering of upmarket restaurants line Tong Chong Street and a few of its side streets. The region, dubbed "Little Lan Kwai Fong", is particularly popular with the expat journalists who work in the area; both *CNN* and the *South China Morning Post* have their offices nearby. None of the restaurants or bars merits a special trip, but if you're in the area, you could grab a midday sandwich from *Sprouts* at no. 23 Hoi Kwong St, or a speciality Belgian beer at the *East End Brewery* on Tong Chong Street.

If you're on the tram, the only other likely stop is **TAI KOO SHING**, a massive new development just beyond Quarry Bay. If you don't have time to see one of the New Territories' instant cities that have sprung up over recent years, then Tai Koo Shing will do just as well – a large-scale residential city with its own monster shopping and entertainment complex, **Cityplaza**, featuring shops, skating rinks (ice and roller), restaurants, free children's shows, a state-of-the-art cinema and lots more indoor entertainment – not a bad place for a wet day. Tai Koo Shing has its own MTR station, from which you can walk straight into Cityplaza.

Shau Kei Wan

The tram and bus #2 from Central finish their run near the MTR station in **SHAU KEI WAN**. Continue east along the coast (via Shau Kei Wan Main Street East from the tram or bus, or Exit B2 and follow the signs from the MTR), past a small boatyard and **Tam Kung temple**, dedicated to the protective deity of fishermen and focus for a festival on the eighth day of the fourth lunar month (around mid-May). Another 200m and you're at the **Hong Kong Museum of Coastal Defence** (Mon–Wed & Fri–Sun 10am–5pm; $10, free on Wed; ⓦwww.lcsd.gov.hk/museum/history), which sprawls across the site of the Lei Yue Mun Fort, built by the British in 1887 to defend the eastern approach to Victoria Harbour. The bulk of its indoor section is set in the renovated redoubt, the exhibition rooms reached by a maze of brick tunnels. The museum covers all stages of Hong Kong's marine history, starting with the efforts of the Guangdong armed forces, moving on to the British Navy's escapades, and the Japanese occupation (known as the "Abyss of Misery") and ending with the "mighty and civilized force" of the People's Liberation Army. Exhibits worth looking out for include an opium-pipe display, moving letters from prisoners-of-war under the Japanese, and the richly embroidered satin army uniforms of Ming and Qing Dynasty soldiers, studded with iron rivets. Outside, accompanied by stunning views of the rugged eastern end of Victoria Harbour, you can follow a marked trail past an army of British tanks, restored gun emplacements, underground magazines, a torpedo station, HMS *Tamar*'s anchor and a gunpowder factory.

Shek O and around

The easternmost limb of land on the island holds the enjoyable beach and village of **SHEK O**, reached by bus #9 from the Shau Kei Wan bus terminal (right next to the MTR), a glorious half-hour ride down a winding road, with splendid views of Tai Tam Reservoir as well as Stanley and the south coast. On Sunday afternoons only, you can also get here direct from Exchange Square in Central on bus #309, which runs hourly 2.10–6.10pm (returning from Shek O hourly 3–7pm).

The bus drops you at the small bus station in Shek O village. Walk down the road to the roundabout and the **beach** is ahead of you, behind the car park. It's one of Hong Kong's best: wide, with white sand and fringed by shady trees, though it can get very full at the weekend. There's a mini-golf course next to the beach to help while away the afternoon; bikes for rent from the back of the car park; and a few **restaurants** in the village, including the *Happy Garden Vietnamese Thai* (see p.217) on the roundabout, the similar *Cheong Shing*, or upmarket *Shek O Chinese Thai Seafood Restaurant*. There are a couple of expat bars here, too, such as the *Bamboo Club*, which does pizzas and fried seafood and, on Sunday, extra snack stalls open, serving the crowds who come down to swim.

The bucket-and-spade shops and basic restaurants in the village don't give the game away, but Shek O is actually one of the swankiest addresses in Hong Kong, and there are some opulent houses in the area. You can get a flavour of things by walking through the village and following the path up to **Shek O Headland**, where you'll be faced with yet more sweeping panoramas. To the right is **Cape D'Aguilar**; to the left, **Rocky Bay**, a nice beach, though with heavily polluted water – which means the sand is generally empty.

Heading back to Shau Kei Wan from Shek O, you don't have to return to the bus station but can instead take a **minibus** from the car park: they're more frequent and a little quicker.

Big Wave Bay

For more space and fewer people, head further north to **Big Wave Bay**, terminus of the Hong Kong Island Trail (see p.51), where there's another good beach (clean enough to swim from, unlike Rocky Bay), barbecue pits and a refreshment kiosk. You'll have to walk from Shek O, which takes about half an hour: if you're heading straight here, get off the bus on the way into Shek O at the fork in the road just before the village.

Turtle Cove and Tai Tam Reservoir

The second of the bus routes down the east side of the island, the #14 (also from Shau Kei Wan), runs down the other side of Tai Tam Bay to Stanley, calling at **Turtle Cove**, a popular beach with all the usual facilities.

On the way back you could call at **Tai Tam Reservoir**, the first in Hong Kong and starting point for several excellent **hill walks** (maps available from the Government Bookshop; see p.247). The easiest is northwest to Wong Nai Chung Gap, a two-hour walk along Tai Tam Reservoir Road to the Gap, just beyond which is Happy Valley (walk on to Stubbs Road and you can pick up the #15 bus into Central). A longer walk (around 4hr) goes due north along Mount Parker Road, between Mount Butler and Mount Parker, to Quarry Bay, from where you can pick up the MTR or tram back into Central.

Places	
Aberdeen	香港仔
Admiralty	金鐘
Ap Lei Chau	鴨脷洲
Causeway Bay	銅鑼灣
Central	中環
Happy Valley	跑馬地
Hong Kong	香港
Hong Kong Island	香港島
Kennedy Town	堅尼地城
North Point	北角
Quarry Bay	鰂魚涌
Repulse Bay	淺水灣
Shau Kei Wan	筲箕灣
Shek O	石澳
Sheung Wan	上環
Stanley	赤柱
Tai Koo Shing	太古城
Tin Hau	天后
Wan Chai	灣仔
Sights	
Academy for Performing Arts	香港演藝學院
The Bank of China	中國銀行大廈
Central Library	中央圖書館
Central Plaza	中環廣場
The Centre	長江實業中心
China Ministry of Foreign Affairs	中國外交部
City Hall	大會堂
Correctional Services Museum	懲教博物館
Exchange Square	交易廣場
Happy Valley Racecourse	跑馬地馬場
Hong Kong and Shanghai Bank	香港上海匯豐銀行大廈
Hong Kong Arts Centre	香港藝術中心
Hong Kong Island Trail	香港島徑
Hong Kong Museum of Coastal Defence	香港海防博物館
Hong Kong Park	香港公園
IFC2	國際金融中心二期
Kwong Fuk Ancestral Hall	廣福義祠
Mandarin Oriental Hotel	香港文華東方酒店
Man Mo Temple	文武廟
Museum of Medical Sciences	香港醫學博物館
Ocean Park	香港海洋公園
Pacific Place	太古廣場
The Peak	山頂
The Police Museum	警隊博物館
Shui Yuat Temple	水月宮
Statue Square	皇后像廣場
Tam Kung Temple	譚公廟
Times Square	時代廣場
University of Hong Kong	香港大學
Victoria Park	維多利亞公園
Wan Chai Convention and Exhibition Centre	香港會議展覽中心
Western Market	西港城
Zoological and Botanical Gardens	香港動植物公園

Streets	
Bowen Road	寶雲道
Des Voeux Road	德輔道
Gloucester Road	告士打道
Hennessy Road	軒尼詩道
Hollywood Road	荷李活道
Lan Kwai Fong	蘭桂坊
Lockhart Road	駱克道
Queen's Road	皇后大道
Transport	
bus stop	巴士站
ferry pier	渡輪碼頭
MTR station	地下鐵車站
Lower Peak Tram Terminal	纜車總站
Macau Ferry Terminal	港澳碼頭
Outlying Islands Ferry Piers	港外線碼頭
Star Ferry Pier	天星碼頭

2

Kowloon

The peninsula on the Chinese mainland, which became part of Hong Kong in 1860 – almost twenty years after the British nabbed the island over the water – is called **Kowloon**, an English transliteration of the Cantonese words *gau lung*, "nine dragons". The dutiful historical explanation of the name is that the fleeing boy-emperor of the Song Dynasty, who ran to the Hong Kong area to escape the Mongols in the thirteenth century, counted eight hills here, purported to hide eight dragons – a figure that was rounded up to nine by sycophantic servants who pointed out that an emperor is himself a dragon. Since that flurry of imperial attention, Kowloon's twelve square kilometres have changed from a rolling green peninsula to one of the most built-up areas in the world.

There was an unruly Chinese village here, at the tip of the peninsula, since the very earliest days of the fledgling island colony across the harbour, alongside fortified walls and battlements protecting a Chinese garrison. But after the peninsula was ceded to the British, development gathered pace, and colonial buildings and roads were laid out as the growing population spread across from Hong Kong Island. Today, that gradual development – from village to colonial town – has been subsumed into the packed, frenetic region of Kowloon that is **Tsim Sha Tsui**, which takes up the tip of the peninsula. This is where many visitors stay, eat and – almost Tsim Sha Tsui's *raison d'être* – shop, finding endless diversion in a cluster of commercial streets that have few equals anywhere in the world. There's also a more traditional side to Kowloon, however, seen in the areas to the north – **Yau Ma Tei** and **Mongkok** – where there are older, explorable streets and buildings that have retained their Chinese character.

Kowloon proper ends at **Boundary Street**, about 4km north of the harbour. In 1860, before the New Territories were added to the colony (in 1898), this formed the frontier between Hong Kong and China. Nowadays, although technically part of the New Territories, the areas immediately above Boundary Street are sometimes known as **New Kowloon**, and have a few attractions for the visitor. Mostly, they're densely populated shopping and residential areas, but people ride out here for a couple of minor diversions, as well as for one of Hong Kong's best temples and the trip to the seafood-eating village of **Lei Yue Mun**, to the east.

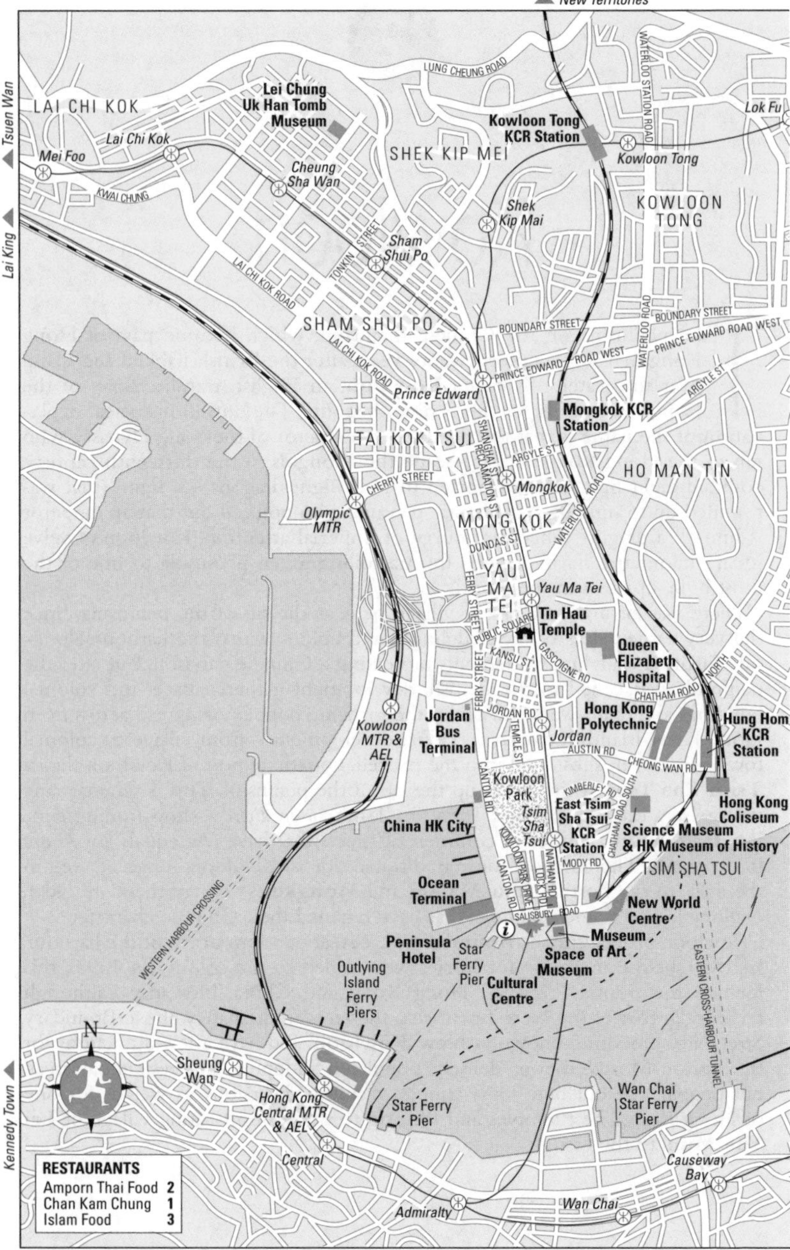
New Territories
Tsuen Wan
Lai King
Kennedy Town
LAI CHI KOK
Lei Chung Uk Han Tomb Museum
Kowloon Tong KCR Station
Lok Fu
Lai Chi Kok
Mei Foo
Cheung Sha Wan
SHEK KIP MEI
Kowloon Tong
KOWLOON TONG
Shek Kip Mai
Sham Shui Po
SHAM SHUI PO
Prince Edward
Mongkok KCR Station
TAI KOK TSUI
HO MAN TIN
Mongkok
Olympic MTR
MONG KOK
YAU MA TEI
Yau Ma Tei
Tin Hau Temple
Queen Elizabeth Hospital
Hong Kong Polytechnic
Hung Hom KCR Station
Kowloon MTR & AEL
Jordan Bus Terminal
Jordan
Kowloon Park
Hong Kong Coliseum
China HK City
Tsim Sha Tsui
East Tsim Sha Tsui KCR Station
Science Museum & HK Museum of History
TSIM SHA TSUI
Ocean Terminal
New World Centre
Peninsula Hotel
Star Ferry Pier
Museum of Art
Space Museum
Cultural Centre
Outlying Island Ferry Piers
WESTERN HARBOUR CROSSING
EASTERN CROSS-HARBOUR TUNNEL
Sheung Wan
Hong Kong Central MTR & AEL
Star Ferry Pier
Wan Chai Star Ferry Pier
Central
Causeway Bay
Admiralty
Wan Chai
LUNG CHEUNG ROAD
WATERLOO STATION ROAD
KWAI CHUNG
TONKIN STREET
LAI CHI KOK ROAD
BOUNDARY STREET
PRINCE EDWARD ROAD WEST
ARGYLE ST
WATERLOO ROAD
SHANGHAI ST
RECLAMATION ST
CHERRY STREET
DUNDAS ST
FERRY STREET
PUBLIC SQUARE
KANSU ST
GASCOIGNE RD
CHATHAM ROAD NORTH
JORDAN RD
TEMPLE ST
AUSTIN RD
CHEONG WAN RD
CANTON RD
KIMBERLEY RD
CHATHAM ROAD SOUTH
KOWLOON PARK DRIVE
NATHAN RD
LOCK RD
MODY RD
SALISBURY ROAD
RESTAURANTS
Amporn Thai Food 2
Chan Kam Chung 1
Islam Food 3

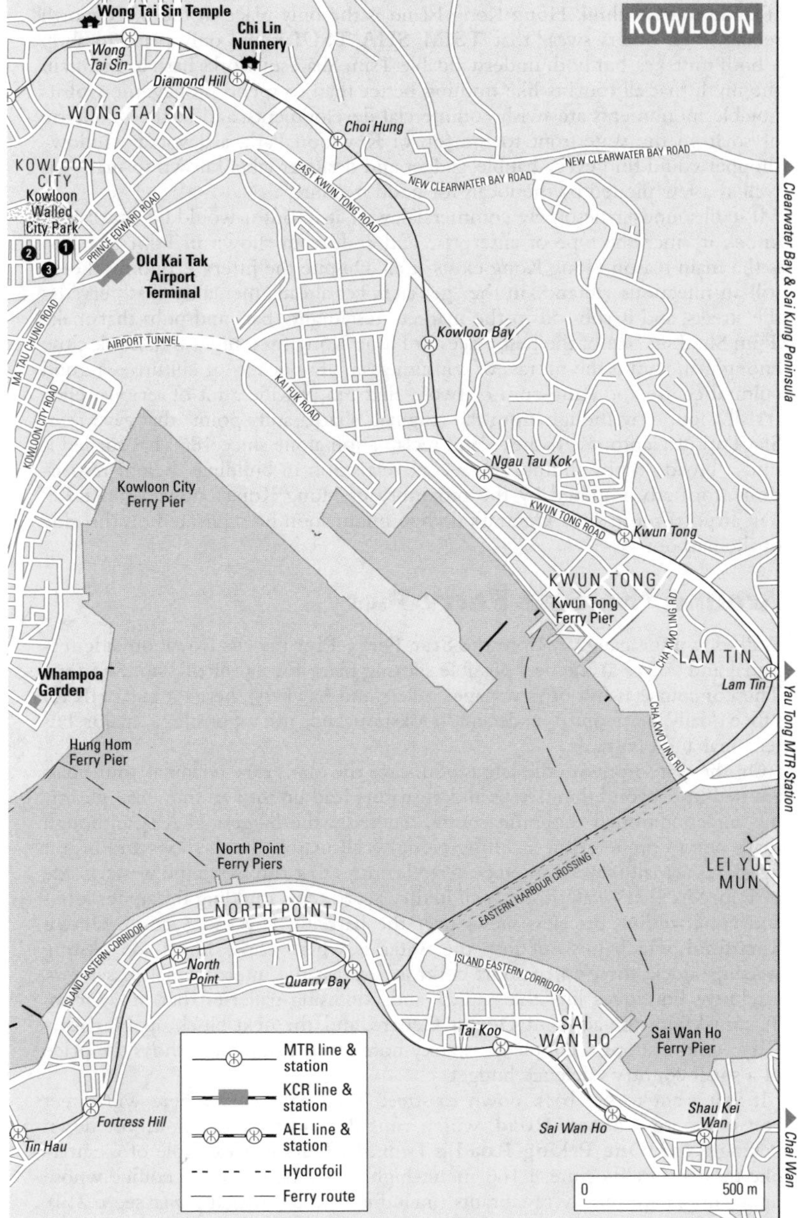

▶ Clearwater Bay & Sai Kung Peninsula
▶ Yau Tong MTR Station
▶ Chai Wan

Tsim Sha Tsui

If some tourists think Hong Kong Island is the only place in the SAR worth seeing, then others swear that **TSIM SHA TSUI** is the only place to shop – both mistakes, but both understandable. Tsim Sha Tsui works hard to maintain the myth that all tourists like nothing better than to spend money: most of its notable monuments are swish commercial developments, and in the kilometre or so from the waterfront to the top of Kowloon Park, a devoted window-shopper could find every bauble, gadget and designer label known to man – as well as a few pirated by the locals for good measure.

If it all sounds gruesomely commercial, well, it is. But it would be churlish to knock it, since the type of enterprise and endeavour shown in Tsim Sha Tsui is the main reason Hong Kong exists at all. Despite the jittery economy, there's still an infectious vibrancy in the "get rich, get ahead" mentality that pervades the streets, and it rubs off in the markets, restaurants, bars and pubs that make Tsim Sha Tsui one of the best places in Hong Kong for a night out. Look close enough, and amid the morass of consumerism are pockets of culture – a good cultural centre and a museum or two – that can provide a bit of serious relief. It's all a long way, though, from the original "sharp, sandy point" that gave Tsim Sha Tsui its Cantonese name – land reclamation alone since 1860 has turned it into a broad, stubby thumb, and recent relaxation in buildings' height restrictions (formerly imposed by the proximity of Hong Kong's now defunct Kai Tak airport) means that Central's skyline might soon be replicated on this side of the harbour.

Around the Star Ferry Pier

Walk down the gangway from the **Star Ferry Pier** into its Kowloon-side terminal and you're at the best possible starting place for a tour of Tsim Sha Tsui. The concourse is full of newspaper sellers and hawkers; there's a busy HKTB office (daily 8am–6pm), a decent bookshop and, just opposite, a major bus terminal and taxi rank.

On the waterfront, on the left as you leave the Star Ferry terminal, tour boats are tied up. Beyond them, steps and escalators lead up into an immense, gleaming, air-conditioned shopping centre, reputedly the biggest in Asia (although that's not a unique claim in Hong Kong) – all marble, swish shops and bright lights. It's actually several interconnected centres that run along the western side of Tsim Sha Tsui's waterfront, with luxury apartments studding the upper levels and commanding priceless views over the harbour. The first section, **Ocean Terminal**, which juts out into the water, is where cruise liners and visiting warships dock; there's a passport control here for the international passengers. Exclusive boutiques line the endless and confusing galleries that link Ocean Terminal with the adjacent **Ocean Centre**, and, the next block up, **Harbour City** – more shops, a couple of swanky hotels, and clothes and shoes the price of a small country's defence budget.

If you want to get back down to street level, signs everywhere will direct you out onto **Canton Road**, which runs due north. East off it, just down Peking Road, **One Peking Road** is Tsim Sha Tsui's first example of Central-like modern architecture, a 160-metre-high, glassy, bow-fronted edifice whose upper floors are mostly restaurants (including the renowned *Aqua*; see p.214), all with excellent harbour views. Back on Canton Road, continue north and you'll pass the **China Ferry Terminal**, a block of shops and restaurants around the ticket offices and departure lounges for ferry and hydrofoil trips to China and Macau. Further up is the adjacent **China Hong Kong City** – more of the same, though without the ferries.

The Hong Kong Cultural Centre

Back at the Star Ferry Pier, over Salisbury Road, the slender, 45-metre-high **clocktower**, dating from 1921, is the only remnant of the grand train station that once stood on the waterfront here – the beginning of a line that linked Hong Kong with Beijing, Mongolia, Russia and Europe. The station was demolished in 1978 to make way for a new waterfront development, whose focal point is the architectural nonentity that is the **Hong Kong Cultural Centre**. Given six hundred million Hong Kong dollars and a prime harbour-side site, the architect managed to come up with a drab pink-tiled building that has few friends and – astonishingly – no windows. The plain exterior is shaped like a vast winged chute; a brick skirt runs around the entire complex, forming a sort of wedge-shaped cloister, while out in the landscaped plaza, lines of palm trees sit either side of a man-made water channel. The nearby two-tiered walkway offers great views of Hong Kong Island, particularly at night, and is usually full of courting couples, amateur photographers and fishermen. From here, the waterfront promenade goes to Hung Hom.

Whatever you think of the Cultural Centre, it represents an optimistic attempt to position Hong Kong as one of Asia's major cultural hubs. Inside, the centre contains three separate venues – a concert hall, grand theatre and studio theatre – as well as a good book- and gift-shop and a café. Its foyer hosts free exhibitions and events most days (see chapter 10 for other events and box-office details). Adjacent blocks harbour an art museum, a space museum, a library, cinema, restaurants and a small formal garden. If you're unable to catch a performance inside the Cultural Centre, consider taking one of the daily **guided tours** of the complex (book in advance; $10), although tours are sometimes cancelled when the theatres are being used for performances or rehearsals – call first to check. Tickets are available in advance from the box office (daily 10am–8pm; ⓣ2734 9009), situated in the foyer.

▲ The clocktower, Tsim Sha Tsui

The Museum of Art

With the opening of the Cultural Centre came the eagerly awaited establishment of Hong Kong's **Museum of Art** (Mon–Wed & Fri–Sun 10am–6pm;

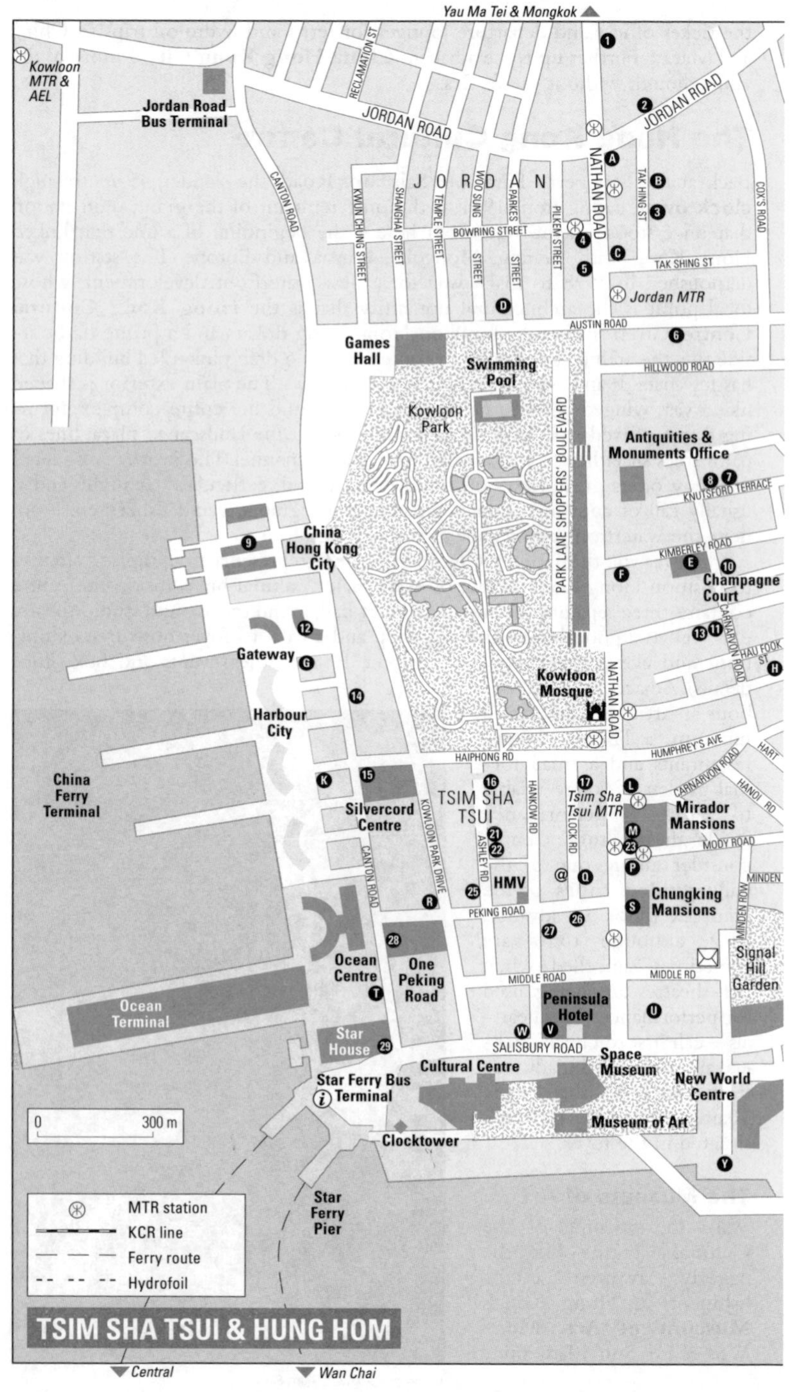
Yau Ma Tei & Mongkok
Kowloon MTR & AEL
Jordan Road Bus Terminal
JORDAN ROAD
RECLAMATION ST
NATHAN ROAD
J O R D A N
CANTON ROAD
KWUN CHUNG STREET
SHANGHAI STREET
TEMPLE STREET
WOO SUNG STREET
PARKES STREET
PILKEM STREET
BOWRING STREET
TAK HING ST
COX'S ROAD
TAK SHING ST
Jordan MTR
AUSTIN ROAD
HILLWOOD ROAD
Games Hall
Swimming Pool
Kowloon Park
PARK LANE SHOPPERS' BOULEVARD
Antiquities & Monuments Office
KNUTSFORD TERRACE
KIMBERLEY ROAD
Champagne Court
China Hong Kong City
CARNARVON ROAD
HAU FOOK ST
Gateway
Kowloon Mosque
Harbour City
HAIPHONG RD
HUMPHREY'S AVE
HART
HANOI RD
China Ferry Terminal
TSIM SHA TSUI
Silvercord Centre
KOWLOON PARK DRIVE
HANKOW RD
LOCK RD
Tsim Sha Tsui MTR
Mirador Mansions
ASHLEY RD
MODY ROAD
CANTON ROAD
HMV
MINDEN
MINDEN ROW
PEKING ROAD
Chungking Mansions
Ocean Centre
One Peking Road
MIDDLE ROAD
MIDDLE RD
Signal Hill Garden
Ocean Terminal
Peninsula Hotel
Star House
SALISBURY ROAD
Cultural Centre
Space Museum
New World Centre
Star Ferry Bus Terminal
Museum of Art
0 300 m
Clocktower
Star Ferry Pier
MTR station
KCR line
Ferry route
Hydrofoil
TSIM SHA TSUI & HUNG HOM
Central
Wan Chai

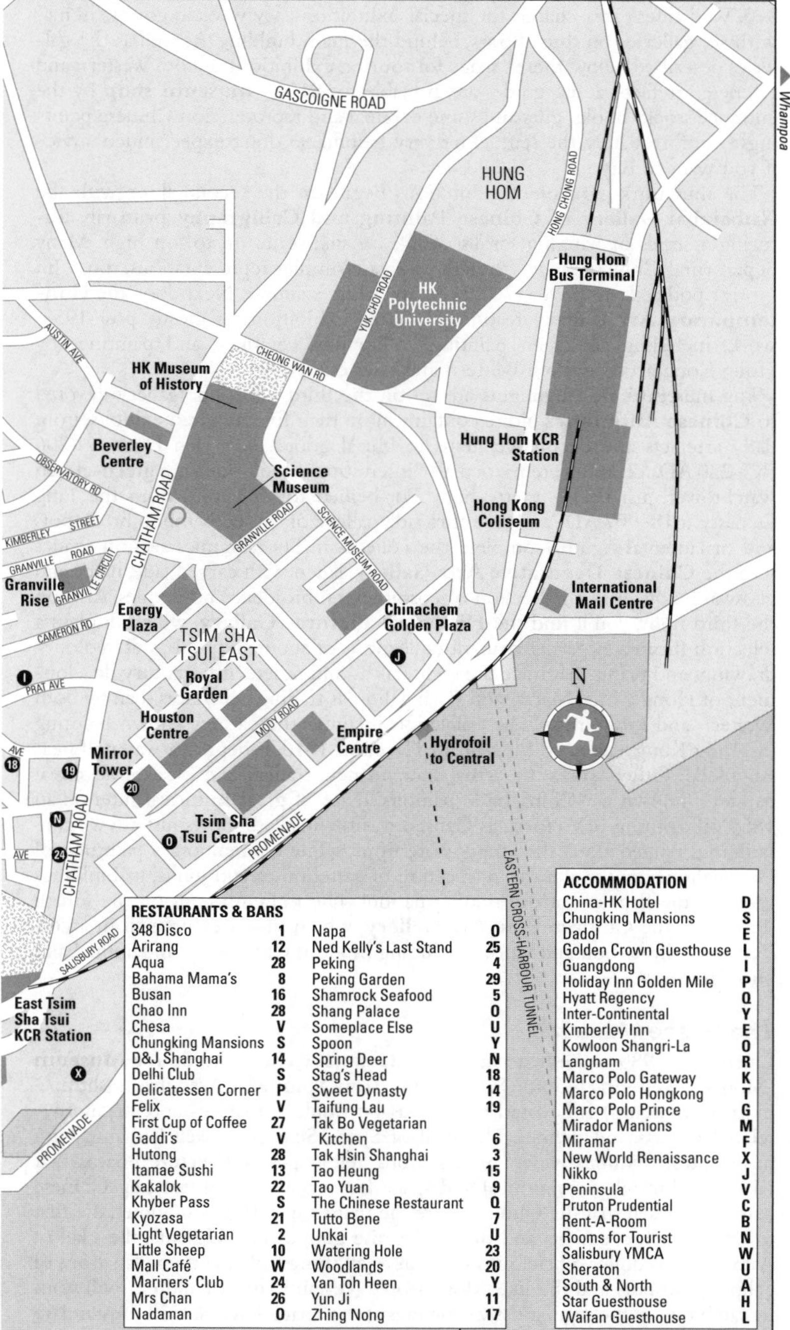
Kowloon City
New Territories & Guangzhou
Whampoa
Central
GASCOIGNE ROAD
HUNG HOM
HONG CHONG ROAD
Hung Hom Bus Terminal
HK Polytechnic University
YUK CHOI ROAD
CHEONG WAN RD
AUSTIN AVE
HK Museum of History
Beverley Centre
OBSERVATORY RD
Science Museum
Hung Hom KCR Station
Hong Kong Coliseum
CHATHAM ROAD
KIMBERLEY STREET
GRANVILLE ROAD
GRANVILLE ROAD
SCIENCE MUSEUM ROAD
GRANVILLE CIRCUIT
Granville Rise
Energy Plaza
CAMERON RD
TSIM SHA TSUI EAST
Chinachem Golden Plaza
International Mail Centre
PRAT AVE
Royal Garden
Houston Centre
MODY ROAD
Empire Centre
Hydrofoil to Central
N
Mirror Tower
Tsim Sha Tsui Centre
PROMENADE
EASTERN CROSS-HARBOUR TUNNEL
SALISBURY ROAD
East Tsim Sha Tsui KCR Station
PROMENADE
RESTAURANTS & BARS
348 Disco 1
Arirang 12
Aqua 28
Bahama Mama's 8
Busan 16
Chao Inn 28
Chesa V
Chungking Mansions S
D&J Shanghai 14
Delhi Club S
Delicatessen Corner P
Felix V
First Cup of Coffee 27
Gaddi's V
Hutong 28
Itamae Sushi 13
Kakalok 22
Khyber Pass S
Kyozasa 21
Light Vegetarian 2
Little Sheep 10
Mall Café W
Mariners' Club 24
Mrs Chan 26
Nadaman O
Napa O
Ned Kelly's Last Stand 25
Peking 4
Peking Garden 29
Shamrock Seafood 5
Shang Palace O
Someplace Else U
Spoon Y
Spring Deer N
Stag's Head 18
Sweet Dynasty 14
Taifung Lau 19
Tak Bo Vegetarian Kitchen 6
Tak Hsin Shanghai 3
Tao Heung 15
Tao Yuan 9
The Chinese Restaurant Q
Tutto Bene 7
Unkai U
Watering Hole 23
Woodlands 20
Yan Toh Heen Y
Yun Ji 11
Zhing Nong 17
ACCOMMODATION
China-HK Hotel D
Chungking Mansions S
Dadol E
Golden Crown Guesthouse L
Guangdong I
Holiday Inn Golden Mile P
Hyatt Regency Q
Inter-Continental Y
Kimberley Inn E
Kowloon Shangri-La O
Langham R
Marco Polo Gateway K
Marco Polo Hongkong T
Marco Polo Prince G
Mirador Manions M
Miramar F
New World Renaissance X
Nikko J
Peninsula V
Pruton Prudential C
Rent-A-Room B
Rooms for Tourist N
Salisbury YMCA W
Sheraton U
South & North A
Star Guesthouse H
Waifan Guesthouse L

$10, Wed free; extra charge for special exhibitions; ⓦwww.lcsd.gov.hk/hkma) with six galleries on three floors, behind the main building. As well as the galleries described below, there's space for touring exhibitions of both Western and Chinese artefacts; audio guides are available for $10. A **museum shop** by the entrance stocks books, gifts and some original and reproduction Chinese paintings – unfortunately, the staff aren't very helpful, so don't expect much advice if you want to buy.

The museum's permanent exhibitions begin on the second floor with the **Xubaizhai Gallery of Chinese Painting and Calligraphy**, primarily featuring a series of hanging scrolls of ink on silk, some up to 4m high. Many depict rural Chinese scenes, though there are simpler representations, too – Jin Nong's podgy *Lone Horse* (1761) is an appealing example. Next door, the **Contemporary Art Gallery** features changing exhibitions of mostly post-1950s work, including silkscreen painting, calligraphy, ceramics, and paintings by Hong Kong artists in both Western and Chinese styles.

The museum's real highlights are up on the third floor. The gallery devoted to **Chinese Antiquities** alone contains more than five hundred exhibits, from daily artefacts and decorative items to burial goods. The Han Dynasty (206 BC–220 AD) ceramics are particularly interesting – look out for a green-glazed watchtower, just over a metre high. Pot-bellied tomb figures from the Tang Dynasty (618–907 AD) and an entire side gallery of carved bamboo brush pots and ornamental figures complete the collection. The ceramics section shades into the **Chinese Decorative Arts Gallery**, laden with carved jade, ivory and glassware, as well as a collection of costumes, embroidery and textiles. Also on the third floor, you'll find the **Historical Pictures Gallery**, which displays a selection (from a larger permanent collection) of about sixty oils, watercolours, drawings and prints that trace the eighteenth- and nineteenth-century development of Hong Kong, Macau and Guangzhou as trading centres, as seen by both Western and local artists. The collection includes the earliest known painting of Hong Kong; executed by William Havell in 1816, it depicts a waterfall near Aberdeen. Other works, by army draughtsmen, traders and local professional painters (known as "China trade painters"), are of great historical interest: an 1854 oil painting of Victoria, as Central was then called, shows just a few score buildings ranged along the empty waterfront, while contemporary paintings of Guangzhou show it as a thriving centre of warehouses and junks, its buildings sporting the flags of various trading nations. The museum ends on the fourth floor with the **Chinese Fine Art Gallery**, which shows exhibits from a collection of three thousand works, including modern Chinese art and animal and bird paintings.

The Space Museum

Opened in 1980 as the first stage of the Cultural Centre, the **Space Museum** (Mon & Wed–Fri 1–9pm, Sat & Sun 10am–9pm; $10, Wed free; ⓦhttp://hk.space.museum) is devoted to a hands-on display of space- and astronomy-related objects and themes. The Hall of Space Science is well laid out, with push-button exhibits, video presentations, telescopes and picture boards that take you through astronomical and space history, with an interesting Chinese bias – you learn that the Chinese were the first to spot Halley's Comet, the first to chart star movements and the first to use gunpowder. Upstairs, the Hall of Astronomy is duller, a brief introduction to all things solar, with explanations of eclipses, sunspots and the like. Most people (certainly most children) will want to catch one of the regular daily showings at the Space Theatre ($32 for standard or $24 for the cheap front stalls; 6- to 15-year-olds, students and senior citizens

$16 for standard and $12 for cheap; under-6s free), which has a choice of films shown on the massive Omnimax screen, providing a thrilling Sensurround experience. Call ☎2721 0226 for show times.

Along Salisbury Road

Over the road from the Space Museum stands an equally recognizable monument, and one of Tsim Sha Tsui's few throwbacks to colonial times: the **Peninsula Hotel**. Built in the 1920s, its elegant wings reaching around a fountain, the hotel used to lord it over the water before land reclamation robbed it of its harbourside position – a newer, central tower, boasting top-floor picture windows and the *Felix* restaurant, has restored its erstwhile views. It was the *Peninsula* that put up the travellers who had disembarked from the Kowloon–Canton railway; for decades the glitterati frequented it along with other grand Asian colonial hotels like the *Taj Mahal* in Bombay and *Raffles* in Singapore. It's still one of the most expensive places to stay in Hong Kong and one of those with the most social clout; even if your budget won't stretch to a room here, you can drop into the opulent lobby for afternoon tea – serenaded by a string quartet – and window shopping in the glitzy arcades. Note that if you're dressed "inappropriately" (no shorts or sandals) you'll be gently steered to the door, whatever the size of your bank balance.

Further along Salisbury Road, past the *Sheraton Hotel* at the bottom of Nathan Road, the *New World Renaissance Hotel* and the *Inter-Continental* form part of the waterfront **New World Centre** – a hotel and shopping complex built on reclaimed land. The lobby of the *Inter-Continental* has twelve-metre-high windows looking out over the harbour, which make a humble drink a spectacular affair; if you work your way outside to the **waterfront promenade**, you can walk all the way up to Hung Hom or back to the Star Ferry Pier.

Nathan Road

Between the *Peninsula* and the *Sheraton* hotels, **Nathan Road** is Tsim Sha Tsui's – and Kowloon's – main thoroughfare, running north from the waterfront all the way to Boundary Street. This is the commercial artery for the whole area, buildings crowding to a point in the distance, festooned with bright neon signs. It's always packed and noisy, split by fast-moving traffic that stops occasionally at the periodic lights to allow an ocean of people to cross from side to side.

Turn-of-the-twentieth-century photographs show Nathan Road as a tree-lined avenue, with grass verges and no traffic. Built originally in 1865 (and called Robinson Road), there was little prospect of its development until Sir

▲ Nathan Road

Matthew Nathan, a professional engineer, took up the governorship of Hong Kong in 1904. Under his orders the road was widened and extended as far north as Yau Ma Tei, but even with the gradual enlargement of Tsim Sha Tsui, the road remained so underused it gained the sobriquet "Nathan's Folly". In 1950, there was only one building more than ten storeys high and not until the 1960s was there real development, when large hotels began to appear in Tsim Sha Tsui and the shopping arcades sprouted.

Shopping on Nathan Road

Today, other than eating and drinking in the surrounding streets, most pedestrians on Nathan Road are intent on trawling the **shops** that have provided the road with its modern tag, the "Golden Mile". It's not just the neon along here that glitters, but the windows, too – full of gold and silver, precious stones, hi-fis and cameras, watches and calculators, clothes, shoes and fine art. Window-shopping can be more of a struggle than elsewhere in Hong Kong since, apart from the crowds, you also have to contend with hustlers and the pavement hawkers selling goods at knock-down (and knock-off) prices – you'll soon tire of the insistent offers of a "copy watch".

As well as the mainstream jewellery and hi-fi shops, Nathan Road has its own **shopping centres**, some of which are as impressive as those elsewhere in Hong Kong, alongside a couple of fairly grim mansion blocks, whose crowded ground floors contain numerous downmarket shops and stalls. The best known is **Chungking Mansions**, at nos. 36–44, on the east side before the *Holiday Inn*, which is notorious for its plethora of guesthouses and Indian restaurants, although there are some great places to buy cheap silk, T-shirts and other clothes at the shops on the ground and first floors. **Mirador Mansions**, further up on the same side of the road (nos. 56–58), has more of the same.

The side streets off both sides of Nathan Road are alive with similar possibilities. On the east side, **Granville Road** in particular is famous for its bargain clothes shops, some of them showcasing the work of new, young designers, though you'll also find clothes, accessories and jewellery stores all the way along **Carnarvon**, **Cameron** and **Kimberley** roads. On the west side of Nathan Road, department stores and shopping centres reign: there's a large Yue Hwa Chinese Products store at the corner of Peking Road and Kowloon Park Drive, with HMV's megastore nearby. For full details of shopping in Tsim Sha Tsui and elsewhere, see chapter 12.

> **Buses** that head up and down **Nathan Road** include the #1, #1A, #2, #6, #6A, and #9. The **MTR** is less useful for short hops; the five stops on Nathan Road are Tsim Sha Tsui (for Chungking Mansions and Kowloon Park), Jordan (for Jordan Road), Yau Ma Tei (Waterloo Road), Mongkok (Argyle Street) and Prince Edward (Prince Edward Road) – with around 3km between the first and last.

Kowloon Park

There's breathing space close by in **Kowloon Park** (daily 6am–midnight), which stretches along Nathan Road between Haiphong Road and Austin Road. Typically, for such a built-up territory, it's not actually at ground level, but suspended above a "Shoppers' Boulevard"; steps lead up into the park from Nathan Road. Parts of it have been landscaped and styled as a Chinese garden with fountains, rest areas, children's playground, and two bird collections – the wildfowl (including flamingos and mandarin ducks) outside in landscaped ponds, the parrots and others contained in a small aviary. There's also an outdoor and indoor swimming complex (daily 8am–noon, 1.30–6pm & 7.30–10pm; $21), an indoor games hall and a sculpture walk (illuminated at night) featuring work by local artists.

The southeastern corner of the park is taken up with an open area known as the **Kung Fu Corner**. Full of practitioners from about 6am every morning, it also hosts free displays of various martial arts between 2.30pm and 4.30pm every Sunday. Below it, at 105 Nathan Rd, is the large **Kowloon Mosque**, built in the mid-1980s for nearly $30 million to serve the territory's fifty thousand Muslims (of whom about half are Chinese). It replaced a mosque originally built in 1894 for the British Army's Muslim troops from India, and retains its classic design, with a central white marble dome and minarets – surprisingly, it doesn't look out of place, standing above the street. Sadly, however, you're not allowed in for a further investigation of the mosque and Islamic Centre it contains.

Leave the park at the southern end and you can drop down to Haiphong Road and its covered **market** at the Canton Road end (daily 6am–8pm).

Tsim Sha Tsui East

After the rambling streets and businesses of Tsim Sha Tsui, **TSIM SHA TSUI EAST** couldn't be more different. Starting at the New World Centre, all the land east of Chatham Road is reclaimed, and the whole of the district has sprung up from nothing over twenty years. It is almost exclusively a wedge of large hotels, connected shopping centres and expensive restaurants and clubs, which you can bypass by sticking to the **waterfront promenade** that follows the harbour around from the Cultural Centre. From here there are superb views across the harbour to Hong Kong Island. Halfway up the promenade, a five-minute walk beyond the *Shangri-La*, there's a small pier from where you can catch a **hydrofoil** over to Queen's Pier in Central on Hong Kong Island. Maxicab #1 runs from the Star Ferry Pier to Granville Square, in Tsim Sha Tsui East.

Hong Kong Science Museum

The **Hong Kong Science Museum**, at 2 Science Museum Rd (Mon–Wed & Fri 1–9pm, Sat, Sun & public holidays 10am–9pm; $25, Wed free; ⓦhk.science.museum), is an enterprising venture worth spending a few hours in, especially if you have children. Its three floors of hands-on exhibits are designed to take the mystery out of all things scientific – since this includes everything from the workings of kitchen and bathroom appliances to the finer points of robotics, computers, cellular phones and hi-fi equipment, even the most Luddite of visitors should be tempted to push buttons and operate robot arms with abandon. Don't miss the fascinating hands-on look at brain perception in the human body section in the basement, or the World Population Meter, which counts up – at a frighteningly fast rate – the earth's population. Avoid Sundays if you can, and try to go early or late in the day, since the attraction palls if you have to wait in line for a turn at the best of the machines and exhibits. To get there, take bus #5, #5C or #8 from the Star Ferry Pier.

Hong Kong Museum of History

Opposite the Science Museum, at 100 Chatham Rd South, stands the $390-million **Hong Kong Museum of History** (Mon, Wed–Sat 10am–6pm, Sun 10am–7pm; $10, free on Wed; @hk.history.museum). Housing an ambitious exhibition, the "Story of Hong Kong", it trawls through some four million years of the region's history, using videos, light shows, interactive software and life-size reproductions of everything from patches of prehistoric jungle to a 1913 tram, which you can scramble around. The museum even smells right: its most interesting section is a reproduction of a 1930s street with tea shops that smell of tea, and a herbalist's niche filled with a bitter pungent aroma. Perhaps what's most surprising is that these shops don't look much different from those in business now, almost a hundred years later, in nearby Mongkok and Sheung Wan. Although the early Chinese settlers and the British invaders are well documented, there is little material on Hong Kong's more recent immigrants, the large ethnic populations of Indians, Nepalese and Filipinos, and scant coverage of events after the 1997 handover.

Hung Hom

Keep to the Tsim Sha Tsui East promenade, past the line of hotels, and eventually (beyond the International Mail Centre) steps take you up into the labyrinthine corridors and overhead walkways that feed into one of several destinations in **HUNG HOM**, the next neighbourhood to the north. All told, it's a twenty- to thirty-minute walk from the beginning of the promenade. Alternatively, green minibus #6 from Hankow Road goes this way via Austin Road.

The most noticeable building is the **Hong Kong Coliseum**, completed in 1983, an inverted pyramid that contains a 12,500-seater stadium, used for sports events and concerts. Remarkably, it's built over the concourse and platforms of the **Hung Hom Kowloon–Canton Railway (KCR) Station**, relocated here in 1975 once it had been decided to demolish the old station down by the Star Ferry Pier. This is where you'll have to come if you want to take the train to China, a route that has been in existence since 1912 and that provides a link with London via the Trans-Siberian Express. There are also KCR trains to the New Territories from here. To get to the Kowloon KCR Station, take bus #5C or #8A from the Star Ferry Pier, or minibus #6 as above.

Ten minutes' walk east of the KCR station, near the ferry pier, is **Whampoa Garden**, an upper-middle-class housing and commercial development built around the old Kowloon dockyard: bus #8A runs here directly from the Star Ferry Pier via Hung Hom KCR Station. The Kowloon dockyard operated on this site from 1870 to 1984, but with the land filled in around it, the dock now supports a hundred-metre-long concrete "ship", open to the public and stacked with shops, restaurants and recreational facilities. Climb up to the top deck for a surreal view of the surrounding buildings – across to tenth-floor apartments from a ship that looks like it could sail at any minute. North of here is the main Hung Hom shopping area, which has a few **factory outlets** selling clothes and jewellery in the block of streets between Man Yue Street and Hok Yuen Street and in the Kaiser Estates building. You can reach these directly on bus #5C from the Star Ferry Pier/Hung Hom KCR Station.

Just beyond Whampoa Garden is the **Hung Hom Ferry Pier**, from where services go to Central, Wan Chai and North Point, though these services terminate around 7pm.

Yau Ma Tei

About twenty minutes' walk north from the Star Ferry Pier up Nathan Road – take bus #1, #1A, #2, #6, #6A, #7 or #9, or the MTR to Jordan or Yau Ma Tei – you enter an older part of Kowloon, **YAU MA TEI**, one of the first areas to be built upon after the British acquired Kowloon in 1860 and now, with a pleasing symmetry, at the heart of Hong Kong's most wide-ranging development programme. The **West Kowloon Reclamation Project** has reclaimed an entire district from the water on the west side of the peninsula here, with the new land earmarked for residential, office and retail buildings centred on the **West Kowloon rail terminal**, from which the Airport Express and Tung Chung MTR lines head out west to the airport.

The name of the district – completely out of place amongst today's modernity – recalls the sesame seed farming that the first inhabitants made their living from (*ma* is sesame). The most interesting streets are the long straight ones north of Jordan Road, on the west side of Nathan Road, which – like Western district on Hong Kong Island – conceal a wealth of traditional shops, businesses, markets, and even a temple of some repute: in particular, Yau Ma Tei is the site of the **Jade Market** and the **Temple Street Night Market**, neither of which should be missed.

The streets

Starting from Jordan Road, it barely matters which street you follow north. Most are a pot-luck mix of endless fascination, such as **Shanghai Street**, containing an eclectic and attractive mix of shops and stalls selling items as diverse as bright red Chinese wedding gowns, embroidered pillow cases, lacquered shrines, statuettes, chopping blocks, incense and kitchenware. It is also famous for its red and yellow Chinese signs, offering a range of exotic and specialist sexual services.

Running parallel and to the west is **Reclamation Street**. Here, between **Nanking** and **Kansu** streets, you'll find one of the most intense street markets in the area, concrete proof that the Chinese prefer to buy their food while it's still hopping about. You'll see fish, frogs and turtles cut up on slabs while still alive, calf's heads on the pavements, trays of chicken hearts and livers, and butchers wielding bloodied cleavers. Just to the east, down **Saigon Street**, there's a small enclave of pawnshops and mahjong schools. At the end of the open-air market, at Kansu Street, the **Yau Ma Tei Covered Market** is a more sober affair. Just west of here on the opposite side of the road is the Jade Market (see p.113), while a block to the north, at 627 Public Square St, is the old colonial **police station**, still in service. Heading east from here will bring you to the Tin Hau Temple (see p.113).

Reclamation Street recommences a block east of the police station and continues to run north. There's a large wholesale **fruit market** at the junction with Waterloo Road, with wicker baskets and tiered boxes of oranges stacked under shelters, the interior alleys echoing to the clack of mahjong tiles. Immediately north of here, the street is clogged with traders and workers handling steel rods, metal drums and heavy-duty kitchen equipment, and there's also the odd shop specializing in Buddhist utensils and decorations – shrines, joss sticks, urns and pictures by the windowful.

The next street to the west, **Canton Road**, is another old thoroughfare that is now split into two. At the southern end, near the junction with Public Square

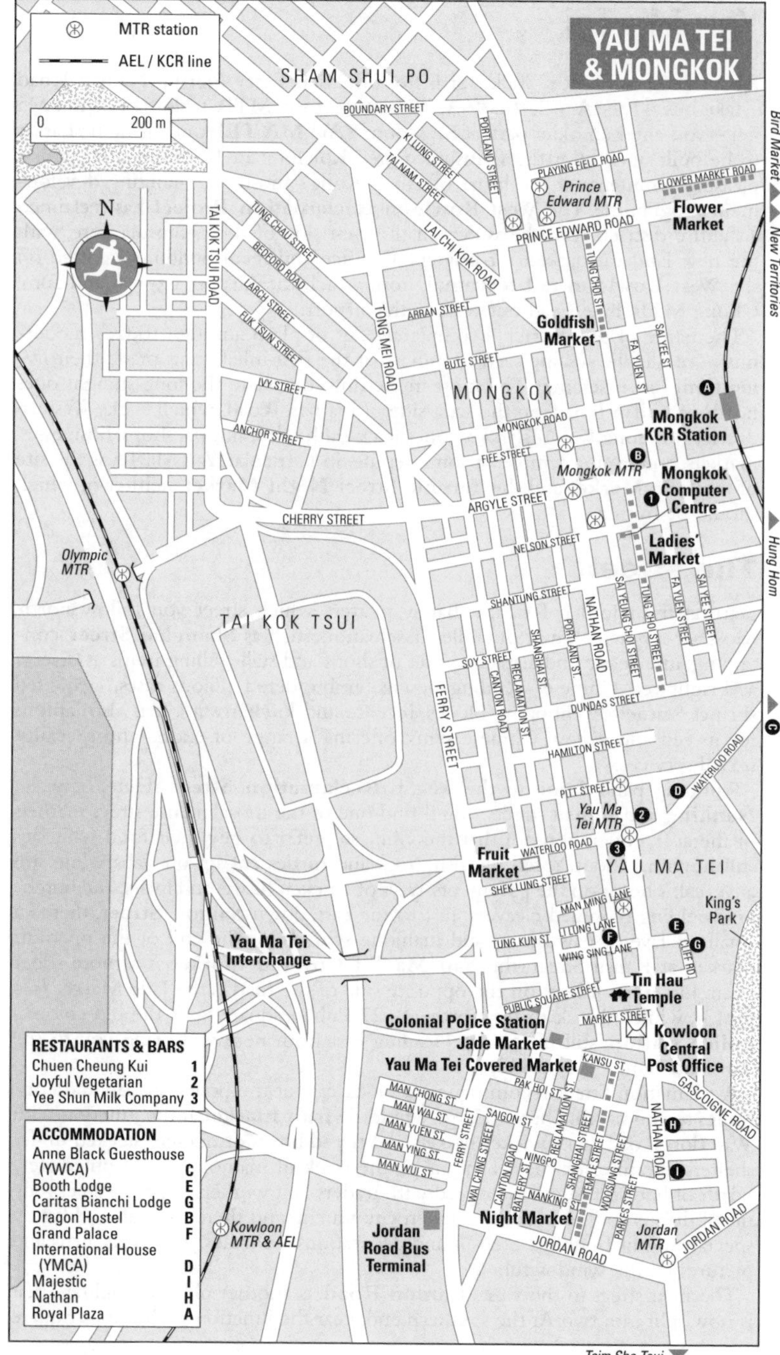
YAU MA TEI & MONGKOK
MTR station
AEL / KCR line
0 200 m
N
SHAM SHUI PO
BOUNDARY STREET
KI LUNG STREET
TAI NAM STREET
PORTLAND STREET
PLAYING FIELD ROAD
FLOWER MARKET ROAD
Prince Edward MTR
Flower Market
Bird Market
New Territories
PRINCE EDWARD ROAD
LAI CHI KOK ROAD
TAI KOK TSUI ROAD
TUNG CHAU STREET
BEDFORD ROAD
LARCH STREET
FUK TSUN STREET
TONG MEI ROAD
ARRAN STREET
TUNG CHOI ST
Goldfish Market
FA YUEN ST
SAI YEE ST
BUTE STREET
IVY STREET
MONGKOK
ANCHOR STREET
MONGKOK ROAD
Mongkok KCR Station
FIFE STREET
Mongkok MTR
Mongkok Computer Centre
ARGYLE STREET
CHERRY STREET
NELSON STREET
Ladies' Market
Hung Hom
Olympic MTR
SHANTUNG STREET
TAI KOK TSUI
SAI YEUNG CHOI STREET
TUNG CHOI STREET
FA YUEN STREET
SAI YEE STREET
NATHAN ROAD
PORTLAND ST
SHANGHAI ST
RECLAMATION ST
SOY STREET
CANTON ROAD
FERRY STREET
DUNDAS STREET
HAMILTON STREET
WATERLOO ROAD
PITT STREET
Yau Ma Tei MTR
Fruit Market
WATERLOO ROAD
YAU MA TEI
SHEK LUNG STREET
MAN MING LANE
King's Park
TUNG KUN ST
LI LUNG LANE
WING SING LANE
CLIFF RD
Yau Ma Tei Interchange
Tin Hau Temple
PUBLIC SQUARE STREET
MARKET STREET
Colonial Police Station
Jade Market
Kowloon Central Post Office
Yau Ma Tei Covered Market
KANSU ST
PAK HOI ST
GASCOIGNE ROAD
MAN CHONG ST
MAN WAI ST
MAN YUEN ST
MAN YING ST
MAN WUI ST
FERRY STREET
SAIGON ST
WALCHING STREET
CANTON ROAD
BATTERY ST
NINGPO
RECLAMATION ST
SHANGHAI STREET
TEMPLE STREET
WOOSUNG STREET
NATHAN ROAD
NANKING ST
PARKES STREET
Night Market
Kowloon MTR & AEL
Jordan Road Bus Terminal
JORDAN ROAD
Jordan MTR
JORDAN ROAD
Tsim Sha Tsui
RESTAURANTS & BARS
Chuen Cheung Kui 1
Joyful Vegetarian 2
Yee Shun Milk Company 3
ACCOMMODATION
Anne Black Guesthouse (YWCA) C
Booth Lodge E
Caritas Bianchi Lodge G
Dragon Hostel B
Grand Palace F
International House (YMCA) D
Majestic I
Nathan H
Royal Plaza A

Street, are jade and ivory shops (mahjong sets a speciality), while the middle section from Waterloo Road as far as Dundas Street is a varied produce market, less stomach-turning than the one in Reclamation Street. The wholesale market trade is encamped around the Pitt Street junction, whilst the section around Dundas Street has twitching fish and shrimps in shallow plastic buckets. The northern section, from Dundas Street to Soy Street, is devoted to mechanical and electrical shops – hardware, engines and engineering works piled high at the side of the road. Look out for the medicinal tea shops with their copper and brass urns decorated with dragons – you can stand on the street and drink a bowlful for around $5.

Tin Hau Temple

That Yau Ma Tei was once a working harbour is clear from the presence of the **Tin Hau Temple** (daily 8am–6pm), just off Nathan Road on Public Square Street, even if following successive bouts of land reclamation it's now way inland. The small area fronting the complex is usually teeming with men sitting around or gambling at backgammon and mahjong, and people may ask for alms as you go in. The main temple, around a century old, is dedicated to Tin Hau, the goddess of the sea, but there are three other temples here, too: the one to the left is dedicated to Shea Tan, protector of the local community; to the right are ones to Shing Wong, the city god, and Fook Tak, an earth god.

Jade Market

You'll find the **Jade Market** (daily 9am–6pm, though all the best stuff goes before lunch) underneath the Gascoigne Road flyover on Kansu Street (Jordan or Yau Ma Tei MTR). Several hundred stalls display an enormous selection of coloured jade, from earrings and jewellery to statues, and though there's some serious buying and bargaining going on here between dealers, it's a lot of fun just to poke around the stalls to see what you can turn up for a few dollars. In part, jade owes its value to the fact that, as an extremely hard stone, it's very difficult to carve; it's also said by the Chinese to bestow "magical", or at least medicinal, qualities on the wearer. Certain shapes represent wealth (deer), good luck (tiger) or power (dragon). Basically, there are two kinds: nephrite (which can be varying shades of green) and the rarer jadeite, much of which comes from Burma and which can be all sorts of colours. A rough guide to quality is that the jade should be cold to the touch and with a pure colour that remains constant all the way through; coloured tinges or blemishes can reduce the value. However, since the scope for being misled is considerable, if you don't know what you're doing you're best advised to stick to small trinkets – rings, pendants, paperweights, earrings – if all you want is a souvenir.

Temple Street Night Market

Although **Temple Street Night Market** (north from the junction with Jordan Road) opens in the afternoon, it still really only comes to life after dark. The most famous market in the area, from around 6pm until 11pm it's crammed with stalls selling tourist-oriented gear, including clothes (for men particularly), Bruce Lee dolls, household goods, watches, CDs, cassettes and jewellery, while fortune tellers and herbalists set up stalls in the surrounding streets. If you're lucky, there'll also be impromptu performances of Cantonese opera. About halfway up you'll see stalls laden with an amazing array of shellfish: a couple of plates of sea snails, prawns, mussels or clams, with a beer or two, won't be expensive, and it's a great place to stop awhile and take in the atmosphere. More formal meals, hardly more costly, can be found a little further up, where there's a covered *dai pai dong*. Again, fish and seafood are the speciality, and some of the stalls here even have English menus if you want to know exactly what you're getting.

Mongkok

North of Yau Ma Tei is **MONGKOK**, one of the oldest sections of Kowloon, and one of the most densely populated areas in the world. Mongkok is also known as the home of Hong Kong's Triad gangs, and the living conditions here give a few indications as to why secret societies flourish in this area. Almost within touching distance across the roads, decrepit apartment buildings are stuffed to the gills with people living in some fairly grim conditions, though, as elsewhere in Hong Kong, attempts to move them out have taken time. Despite a certain down-at-heel atmosphere, Mongkok, like the rest of the SAR, is extremely safe, and worth a visit to see how a lot of the population lives: besides several unusual **street markets**, Mongkok is also a good place to shop for **electronic goods** and accessories, with lower prices than Tsim Sha Tsui and less chance of being ripped off – though note that the district is at the heart of Hong Kong's massive pirated software industry.

To the north, you're within striking distance of **Boundary Street**, which until 1898 and the acquisition of the New Territories marked the boundary with China.

▲ Shopping in Mongkok

The Ladies' Market

At Tung Choi Street, a huge women's clothes market, sometimes known as the **Ladies' Market** (daily noon–10.30pm; nearest MTR is Mongkok, eastern Nelson Street exit) stretches for four blocks north from Dundas Street to Argyle Street. It's a good place to pick up bargain skirts, dresses, T-shirts, children's clothes, small electrical items and watches; prices are very fluid, however, and bargaining is the order of the day. Since the same gear turns up on stall after stall, have a good look around before making a move for anything.

The Goldfish Market to the Flower Market

Still on Tung Choi Street, directly north of the Ladies' Market, is the **Goldfish Market**, its shops festooned with plastic bags containing all kinds of ornamental and tropical fish. Goldfish are a variety of carp, a popular symbol of good fortune. You'll often see drawings of carp – particularly in pairs – or carp-shaped lanterns in temples or on display during Chinese festivals. Consequently, great care is taken with their breeding, and some can cost thousands of dollars.

One block east of Tung Choi Street is **Fa Yuen Street**, where there's another mixed street market during the day. The next street east, **Sai Yee Street**, has a number of wedding shops and photo studios, with pictures of idealized Chinese brides in their windows. At the junction with **Bute Street**, a pedestrian walkway links these streets directly to the **Mongkok KCR** station.

A block north of the top end of Tung Choi Street, just to the east of Prince Edward MTR, is **Flower Market Road**. There are dozens of inexpensive flower and plant shops here (daily 10am–6pm), and at the weekend many more vendors bring in trucks full of orchids, orange trees and other exotica. It's particularly good around Chinese New Year, when many people come to buy narcissi, orange trees and plum blossom to decorate their apartments.

The Bird Market

Mongkok's **Bird Market** is housed in a purpose-built Chinese-style garden (daily 7am–8pm) in **Yuen Po Street**, at the point where Flower Market Street meets the KCR flyover. There are two or three dozen stalls crammed with caged songbirds, parakeets, mynah birds, live crickets tied up in little plastic bags (they're fed to the birds with chopsticks), birdseed barrels and men varnishing newly made bamboo cages – minus bird they start at $60 or so, though the more elaborate ones run into the hundreds. Little porcelain bird bowls and other paraphernalia cost from around $10. It's also interesting just to watch the local men who bring their own caged birds here for an airing and to listen to them sing. Taking your songbird out for a walk is a popular pastime among older Chinese men, one you'll see often in the more traditional areas of town.

New Kowloon

The area north of Boundary Street, so-called **NEW KOWLOON**, has much less going for it than the streets of Tsim Sha Tsui and Yau Ma Tei, but if you've got the time there are one or two districts that show a different side of Hong Kong, and a couple of places close enough to tack onto the beginning or end of a day's sightseeing. All are still firmly in built-up parts of the city, with access being easiest by MTR, except for Kowloon City.

Kowloon City

Boundary Street, Prince Edward Road and Argyle Street all run east from Mongkok, converging on **KOWLOON CITY**, the area immediately surrounding the old **Kai Tak airport** site. An airport first opened here in the 1930s, though it wasn't until 1956 that the impressive runway – almost 4km long – was built right into the middle of Kowloon Bay. Now that the airport has closed and is all but demolished – though for what is still unclear – the region makes you feel like you've stepped back in time forty years, exuding a laid-back air of relative peace and quiet. It's a fascinating mix of old Hong Kong and Thailand: you'll find unsalubrious narrow alleyways packed with mahjong parlours, herbalists and tailors, alongside scores of Thai restaurants (see p.217 for details), Thai hair and beauty salons, supermarkets and even baht moneychangers. Thai script on shop signs is almost as common as Chinese characters, fuelled by an ever-increasing expat Thai population. The network of streets between the Walled City Park (see below), and the abandoned airport in particular, is renowned for its cheap and excellent restaurants, including Vietnamese, Korean, Japanese and Indian as well as Thai and a variety of Chinese cuisines.

The government has ambitious plans to redevelop the area and reclaim large parts of the harbour on both sides of the old runway: the **Southeast Kowloon Development Plan** is intended to create parks, shopping centres, industrial areas and housing for a quarter of a million people on the Kai Tak site; there's also been talk of a cruise ship terminal. Unusually for Hong Kong, however, the plan has met stiff opposition. Environmentalists say damage to the harbour would be excessive and local residents feel the plans – tower blocks and a park surrounded by motorways – are a badly thought-out and unimaginative use of a wonderful site.

Kowloon City is easily reached by any number of **buses**: take #1, #1A or #5C from outside the Star Ferry Pier in Tsim Sha Tsui; or cross-harbour buses #101, #103 or #111 from the south side of Statue Square in Central or in front of Admiralty MTR station on Hong Kong Island. All these buses stop on Prince Edward Road East – look out for the disused airport building on the right: Kowloon City spreads in a network of streets away from the airport, on the same side as the bus stop.

Kowloon Walled City

For years, one of the more notorious districts of Hong Kong lay close to the airport, between Carpenter and Tung Tau Tsuen roads. **Kowloon Walled City** was a slum of gigantic proportions, which had occupied an anomalous position in Hong Kong since the acquisition of the New Territories by the British in 1898, when the Chinese managed to retain judicial control over it by a legal sleight of hand. Originally the site of a Chinese garrison, and walled in (hence the name), it developed into a planned village, rife with disease but thriving from the trade that a nearby wharf brought. There was constant friction between the British authorities and the residents, who felt able to call on the Chinese government whenever they were threatened with resettlement, and the Walled City became a bizarre enclave, virtually free from colonial rule. During the Japanese occupation of Hong Kong, the walls were dismantled and used to extend the airport, and many of the buildings were destroyed. But any hopes the British had of taking over the district were dashed after the end of the war, when thousands of refugees from the Chinese mainland moved into the Walled City and made it their own. Compromise plans came to nothing, and for years the Walled City remained a no-go area for the police, becoming a haunt of Triad gangs and fugitive criminals, leading some to call it the "cancer of Kowloon".

Sweat-shops and unlicensed factories employed the refugees, who never left the Walled City in case they were arrested; wells were sunk to provide water, and electricity was tapped from the mains; every inch of its tattered surface was covered with wire cages tacked on by the inhabitants to create extra space; there was even a temple and basic restaurants. But life in the city took place amid the most primitive surroundings imaginable: in gloomy, wet corridors, lined with festering rubbish, and with little semblance of order, let alone law. Things improved slightly in the 1970s and 80s, when residents' associations got together and began to clean up the brothels, abortion clinics, unlicensed medical and dental shops, drinking, drugs and gambling dens that infested the six-hectare site. Finally, in 1987 a planned evacuation programme was agreed with the thirty thousand residents, and by 1991 all of them had been rehoused elsewhere and compensated. The site was levelled and turned into the landscaped **Kowloon Walled City Park** (daily 6.30am–11pm), where you can see the restored walls and magistrate's buildings of the original nineteenth-century Qing dynasty military outpost. Bus #1 from the Star Ferry Pier stops on Tung Tau Tsuen Road.

Kowloon Tong

West of the airport, **KOWLOON TONG** is a wealthy, residential area, packed with English and American kindergartens and expensive schools, while nearby Broadcast Drive is home to most of the radio and TV stations in the SAR. You are hardly likely to find yourself strolling around here, though Kowloon Tong is the site of the interchange between the MTR and KCR train systems, itself topped by **Festival Walk**, one of Hong Kong's newest shopping plazas. Kowloon Tong is also noted for its nest of euphemistically tagged "short-time hotels". These aren't as seedy as they might sound: many cater to ordinary couples wanting to get away from tiny apartments and the rest of the family. Head along Waterloo Road and down the adjacent side streets and you can't miss them: all sumptuously decorated and equipped, sitting behind security cameras and grilles.

Wong Tai Sin Temple

There are more strange goings-on a couple of MTR stops east of Kowloon Tong at the massive and colourful **Wong Tai Sin Temple** (daily 7am–5.30pm; small donation expected), next to Wong Tai Sin MTR station. Built in 1973, it's one of Hong Kong's major Taoist temples, dedicated to Wong Tai Sin, whose portrait was brought to Hong Kong in 1915 from the mainland and moved here from a temple in Wan Chai six years later. Over three million people come to pay their respects here every year. The god, a mythical shepherd boy with the power of healing, has an almost fanatical following, primarily because he's famous for bringing good luck to gamblers, and there are always crowds at the temple, which shows no restraint in its decoration and lavish grounds. As you enter, you'll find hawkers and stalls selling paper money, incense, oranges (very auspicious because of their colour) and Chinese decorations.

You're not always allowed into the main temple building, but from the courtyard you'll still be able to see the altar, which supports the imported image of Wong Tai Sin. On the left is a small hut where you can borrow a pot of bamboo prediction sticks (free). Crowds kneel in front of the shrine shaking the pot until one of the (numbered) bamboo sticks drops out – this stick is then exchanged for a piece of paper bearing the same number, which has a prediction written on it.

Behind the main building is the pleasant **Good Wish Garden** (Tues–Sun 9am–4pm; $2), with Chinese pavilions, carp ponds and waterfalls. Inside this is the smaller Nine Dragon Wall Garden, which houses a copy of the famous mural in the Imperial Palace in Beijing. The whole complex is good for an hour or so; just watching people making offerings and praying for good luck is diverting enough. There's also a clinic here, the upper floor of which offers **Chinese herbal medicine**.

Just inside the main entrance of the temple, on the left, is a covered street of booths. Some sell paraphernalia for worshippers or Chinese medicine, but most are **fortune-tellers**, who read palms, bumps, feet and faces. It's a thriving industry in Hong Kong, and many of these fortune-tellers have testimonials of authenticity and success pinned to the booths, with prices and explanations displayed for the sceptical. There are about 160 practitioners to choose from. Some speak English (there's a map at the end of the building that indicates the English-speakers with a red dot) so if you want to find out whether or not you're going to win at the races, this is the place to ask. Busiest days at the temple are around Chinese New Year, when luck is particularly sought, and at Wong Tai Sin's festival, on the twenty-third day of the eighth lunar month (usually in September).

Diamond Hill

Formerly a run-down scramble of squatter huts, dark alleys and warehouses, **DIAMOND HILL**, one MTR stop east of Wong Tai Sin, now sports modern apartment buildings and a glittering multistorey shopping centre, **Hollywood Plaza**, above the station, complete with an excellent food hall and cinema. But the area's real attraction is the Tang-style **Chi Lin Nunnery**, 5 Chi Lin Drive (daily except Wed 9am–3pm; free), whose beautifully proportioned courtyards and dark timber buildings look Japanese-influenced – though it was in fact the Japanese who borrowed their temple architecture from Tang China and never moved on. Originally built in the 1930s but recently restored at a cost of $90 million, the nunnery is home to a few nuns who run religious, education and social service projects, though you can wander round inside its wooden halls and admire the statues of Buddha and deities in gold and precious wood – look for a very languid one of Avalokitesvara, the original Indian source for Kuan Yam. Access to the nunnery is through the Western Lotus Pond Garden (daily 6.30am–7pm), beautifully tended landscaped grounds with rocks, tea plants, bonsai and fig trees and, of course, lotus ponds.

Diamond Hill is also the stop to catch **buses** to the beaches of Sai Kung and Clearwater Bay (see pp.145 and 147 for bus details); the bus station is directly beneath Hollywood Plaza.

The Lei Cheng Uk Han Tomb Museum

In 1955, between what are now the MTR stations of Sham Shui Po and Cheung Sha Wan, a couple of kilometres northwest of Mongkok, workmen flattening a hillside in order to build a new housing estate unearthed Hong Kong's most ancient historic monument – a Han Dynasty tomb almost two thousand years old. It's been preserved *in situ* and now forms the major part of the **Lei Cheng Uk Han Tomb Museum**, 41 Tonkin St (Mon–Wed, Fri & Sat 10am–1pm & 2–6pm, Sun 1–6pm; free), an offshoot of the Museum of History in Tsim Sha Tsui.

In truth, the small museum is not really worth a special journey, but is interesting if you're in the area. There's a brief explanation of how the tomb was found, with photographs and a few funerary exhibits; the glass-fronted tomb itself is out in the garden, encased in concrete to preserve it. It's easy enough to make out the central chamber, which is crossed by four barrel-vaulted brick niches, but the best idea of what it looked like can be gleaned from the diagrams back inside. A slightly larger musem is planned for the near future, which aims to put Lei Cheng Uk into context with similar finds in mainland China.

To reach the museum, either take **bus** #2, #6 or #6A from the Star Ferry

Pier to Tonkin Street, or the **MTR** to Cheung Sha Wan; take exit A3 and walk north for five minutes up Tonkin Street, past abandoned factories, and it's on your left.

Lei Yue Mun

LEI YUE MUN, as befits its name ("Carp Fish Gate"), sits at the narrowest entrance to the harbour. It's probably the biggest and most commercialized of the places to come and eat seafood in Hong Kong, with around 25 restaurants and as many fresh fish shops, the slabs and tanks twitching with creatures shortly to be cooked. The recognized procedure is to choose your fish and shellfish from a shop, where it will be weighed and priced, and then take it (or you'll be taken) to a restaurant, where it's cooked to your instructions: you generally pay the bill at the end – one to the fishmonger and one to the restaurant for cooking the fish and for any rice and other dishes you may have had. The strongest possible warnings about **rip-offs** are applicable here. You must ask the price of the fish you choose before it's bashed on the head and carted off to a restaurant or you're just inviting someone to choose what will allegedly be the most expensive creature in the tank for you. A good way to proceed is to name a price to the fishmonger that you want to spend. Alternatively, if there's a group of you, get the tourist office or a Chinese friend to ring one of the restaurants before you go and sort out a fixed-price set menu, which can work out fairly inexpensive. Evenings are the best time to come, when you can sit at the restaurant windows and look out over the typhoon shelter.

Getting there

The easiest way is to take the MTR to **Yau Tong**, and take exit A2. Turn left down Cha Kwo Ling Road, passing the Yau Tong Centre and a recreation ground, into Shung Shun Street, which leads down to the waterfront – all in all, a ten- to fifteen-minute walk. At the waterfront you'll find the **Sam Ka Tsuen** typhoon shelter, which is where the ferry from Sai Wan Ho arrives. From here you can walk round to the restaurants or, from behind the ferry terminal, you can take a sampan across to the village of Lei Yue Mun, passing through moored and inhabited fishing boats.

Places	
Choi Hung	彩虹
Diamond Hill	鑽石山
Hung Hom	紅磡
Jordan	佐敦
Kowloon	九龍
Kowloon City	九龍城
Kowloon Tong	九龍塘
Lam Tin	藍田
Lei Yue Mun	鯉魚門
Lok Fu	樂富
Mongkok	旺角
Prince Edward	太子
Sham Shui Po	深水埗
Tsim Sha Tsui	尖沙咀
Tsim Sha Tsui East	尖沙咀東

Whampoa	黃埔
Wong Tai Sin	黃大仙
Yau Ma Tei	油麻地
Sights	
Bird Market	園圃街雀鳥花園
Chi Lin Nunnery	志蓮淨苑
Festival Walk	又一城
Flower Market	花墟
Goldfish Market	金魚街
Harbour City	海港城
Hong Kong Coliseum	香港體育館
Hong Kong Cultural Centre	香港文化中心
Hong Kong Museum of History	香港歷史博物館
Jade Market	玉器市場
Kowloon Park	九龍公園
Kowloon Walled City Park	九龍寨城公園
Ladies' Market	女人街
The Museum of Art	香港藝術館
Ocean Centre	海洋中心
The Peninsula Hotel	半島酒店
The Science Museum	香港科學館
The Space Museum	香港太空館
Temple Street Night Market	廟街夜市
Whampoa Garden	黃埔公園
Wong Tai Sin Temple	黃大仙廟
Streets	
Boundary Street	界限街
Canton Road	廣東道
Granville Road	加連威老街
Nathan Road	彌敦道
Transport	
KCR station	九廣鐵路車站
MTR station	地下鐵車站
China Ferry Terminal	中港碼頭

3

The New Territories

Too many visitors miss out on the best that Hong Kong has to offer – namely the 740 square kilometres of mainland, beyond Kowloon, leased to Britain for 99 years in 1898 and known as the **New Territories**. Around half of the colony's population lives here, both in large new cities and small, traditional villages, and the area is the source of much of Hong Kong's food and water. It's in the New Territories, too, that you'll find the most resonant echoes of the People's Republic. Massive housing estates built around gleaming New Towns don't completely obscure the rural nature of much of the land, and although it's not as easy as it once was to spot water buffalo in the New Territories, some country roads still feature teeming duck farms and isolated houses, while a few decrepit walled villages survive, surrounded by their ancestral lands and with their traditional temples and meeting halls intact. What's more, large parts of the New Territories have been designated country parks, some of them offering excellent hiking. The **Sai Kung Peninsula**, to the east, is the best example, though the adventurous could see the whole of the New Territories from a hiker's viewpoint by following the cross-territory **MacLehose Trail** (see p.151) from Sai Kung to the far west, or the **Wilson Trail** (see p.92) from Sai Kung north to Nam Chung Reservoir by the Chinese border.

Don't expect it to be all peace and quiet. Parts are as busy and boisterous as anywhere in Kowloon, though there is always the impression of more space. Some of the **New Towns** are sights in their own right, containing all the energy and industry of the city centre. In between the new structures and roads are nineteenth-century temples, some fascinating museums, and traditional markets – as well as the walled villages and coastal fishing communities that have managed to retain an identity amid the rapid development. You can get a glimpse of the modern New Territories by riding the MTR to the end of the line at **Tsuen Wan**, from where buses connect with the other major western towns, **Tuen Mun** and **Yuen Long**. Equally rewarding is the **KCR East train route** north, through interesting towns like **Sha Tin** and **Tai Po** to the Chinese border. The last stop on the Hong Kong side, the town of **Sheung Shui**, is currently teetering between a traditional Chinese life and full-blown Hong Kong-style development.

Public transport, both trains and buses, will get you to most places in the New Territories, and minibuses can prove useful, too. In addition to the main KCR East line, there's also the newer **KCR West**, running from the Nam Cheong MTR Station to Tuen Mun, which has made reaching some of the western New Territories' key sights much easier. There isn't any one place that you

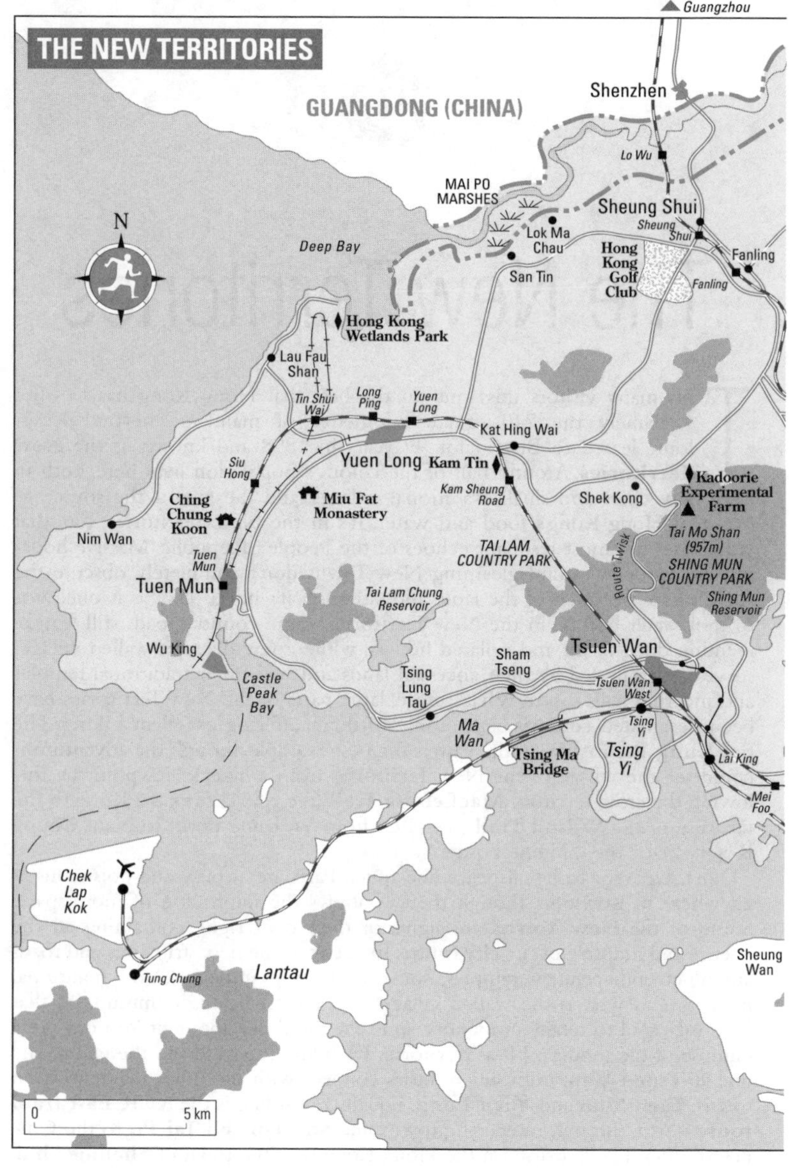

can't get to and back from in a day if you're based in Kowloon or Hong Kong Island; pick up the HKTB's bus route leaflet for the New Territories, which prints many of the destinations in Chinese characters. Note that you can rent bikes at several places, too, particularly at Tai Wai, Sha Tin and Tai Po, all easily reached by KCR.

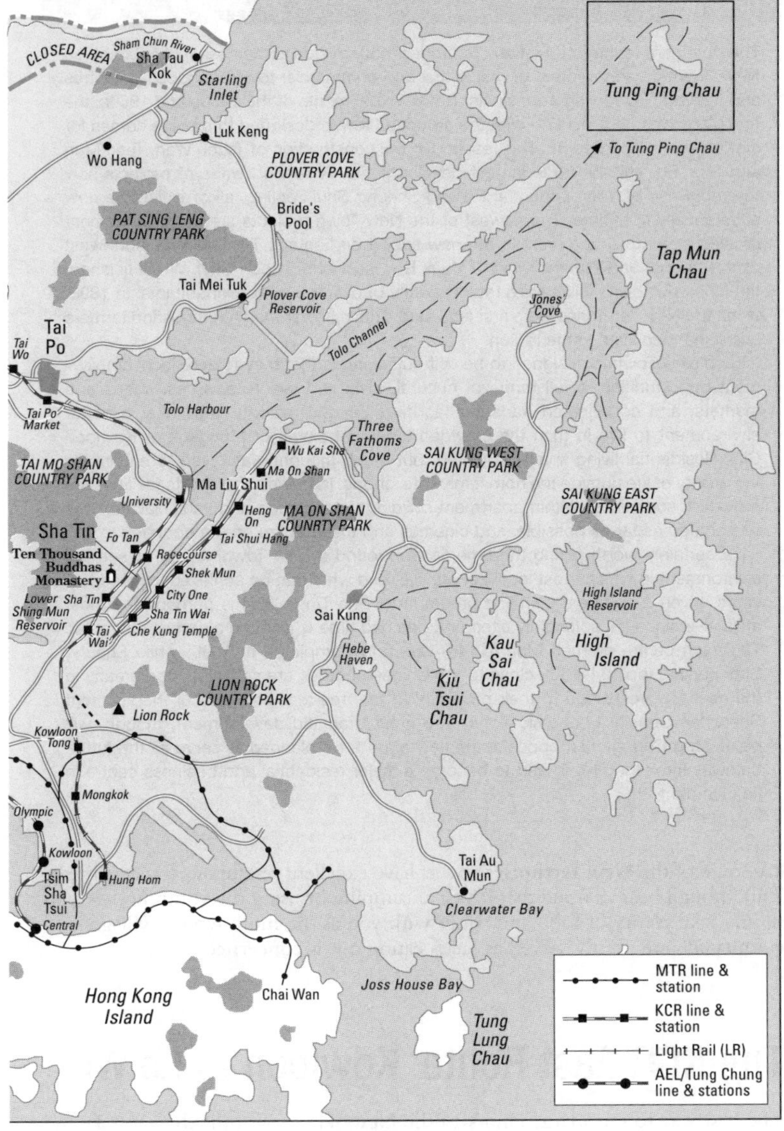

You could tour the greater part of the central and western New Territories on a circular route in a day, using the KCR and buses; it would take at least one more day to see some of the smaller eastern section, where the going is slower. Accommodation is limited to a few youth hostels and campsites (see chapter 6 for a full listing). You shouldn't have too much trouble finding somewhere to

New Towns

The dominant feature of the New Territories' countryside is the seemingly ubiquitous **New Towns**, each a forest of residential and commercial towers, shopping centres and flyovers. Borrowing from similar British experiments of the 1950s and 1960s, the first plans were laid in 1972, with the proposed towns designed to provide homes for almost two million people. This resulted in the construction of Tsuen Wan, Tuen Mun and Sha Tin, still the three largest developments. A second wave of projects saw the rapid rise of Yuen Long, Tai Po and Sheung Shui/Fanling, all of which are now substantially complete. The newest of the New Town projects are the development of sites at Tung Chung (next to the new airport on Lantau), Tin Shui Wai (northwest of Yuen Long) and Tsueng Kwan O (Junk Bay, east of Kowloon City). When finished, the nine new towns will have a total capacity of over 3.5 million inhabitants; in 1898, when the New Territories were first leased to Britain, fewer than ten thousand farmers and fishermen lived in the region.

Each New Town is designed to be self-sufficient, in that they feature local employment opportunities, a full range of cultural, civic and leisure services, shops and markets, and coordinated transport facilities. For the majority, they offer a better environment to live in than the crowded tenement slums of Mongkok or Kowloon City. Residential living space is limited, but much thought was given to enhancing the quality of life outside the home: markets, shops, laundries and sports facilities are provided, sometimes within apartment buildings; pedestrian and vehicular traffic is segregated as far as possible; and cinemas and theatres are on the doorstep.

It's certainly worth taking the time to look round a New Town, if only to see the environment in which most local people live, and what can be achieved in just a few years, given a coherent planning programme. Sha Tin (p.127) is perhaps the most attractive since it's splendidly sited and has had time to acquire a certain character. The town centre of Tuen Mun (p.144) was only completed in 1990; while Sheung Shui/Fanling (pp.134–136), close to the Chinese border, are set to change greatly in the next few years due to their proximity to the free-market antics of the adjacent Shenzhen Special Economic Zone. The most dramatic development, though, will be at Tung Chung. Just opposite the new airport, it's planned to serve as the future gateway into Hong Kong and to become a major residential and business centre in its own right.

eat; some of the New Territories' towns have excellent restaurants (especially Sha Tin), though bear in mind that if you're camping or using the youth hostels, you should take plenty of food and water with you as the more remote villages and countryside are poorly served as far as eating out is concerned.

The KCR East Route: Kowloon to Lo Wu

The best way to see a large chunk of the New Territories quickly is to take the **KCR East line** from its terminus in Hung Hom north to the Chinese border. The whole trip to Sheung Shui, the last stop you can make on the Hong Kong side as a day-tripper, takes around fifty minutes. The route passes through some typical New Towns, such as **Sha Tin** and **Tai Po**, which have mushroomed from villages (or sometimes from nothing) in just a few decades. There are several temples and markets in between, while the stop at the **Chinese University** gives the choice of a scenic ferry ride or a visit to one of the region's better art galleries. **Sheung Shui** itself is probably the most interesting place to break the journey, while from Tai Po and **Fanling** it's only a short bus ride into some quite beautiful countryside to the east, at **Plover Cove** and **Starling Inlet**.

If you're going on into **China**, you'll pass through the border crossing at **Lo Wu**, at the end of the Hong Kong part of the KCR East line, though this is an otherwise restricted area.

Tai Wai

The first stop after the MTR/KCR East interchange at Kowloon Tong is **TAI WAI**, nowadays less a town in its own right (though there's been a village here since the fourteenth century) than an extension of Sha Tin. Its most obvious attraction is **Lion Rock Country Park**, where the two outcrops of Amah Rock and Lion Rock make for a fine half-day hike or, if you're serious, a **rock climb** (see "Listings" p.260). You should be able to see Amah Rock from the train; from the station, take Exit C and turn left (south) towards a large roundabout, where you'll find a pedestrian overpass. Take this diagonally across to Hung Mui Kuk road, and follow it south for about a kilometre to the park entrance – alternatively, take bus #80 from the station and tell the driver where you want to go.

Once at the park, the trail heads up first to **Amah Rock** (in Cantonese, *Mong Fu Shek*, or "Yearning for Husband Rock"). In legend, a woman carrying her child on her back climbed the hill to wait for her husband to return from fishing; when he failed to appear, the gods turned her to stone. Young women make the pilgrimage up here during the annual Maiden's Festival (see p.240). For the more challenging **Lion Rock**, continue beyond Amah Rock, past a shelter at Kowloon Pass, then head left onto the MacLehose Trail (p.151), where you bear right at another, smaller shelter up over rough, rocky terrain to two peaks formed by the Lion's "head" and "rump" – on a clear day the views, over Kowloon and the harbour, are superb.

Cycle paths start from just outside Tai Wai's KCR station and run up through Sha Tin, along the river, before skirting Tolo Harbour all the way to Tai Po and Plover Cove – a popular route and a good way to get to grips with the New Territories. Bikes can be rented from just outside the KCR station and cost around $10 an hour (or $50 a day), though the price rises at the weekend when thousands of locals go cycling. You'll need to leave your passport or a cash deposit. Some bike owners have a sister-shop in Tai Po and allow you to return the bicycle there, if you don't want to cycle all the way back.

Che Kung Temple

Just outside Tai Wai, the austere **Che Kung Temple** is dedicated to the Song dynasty general Che Kung, who protects against the floods and plagues that once stalked this valley. There are two station options: either get out at Tai Wai KCR and follow the signs for five minutes; or change trains at Tai Wai onto the new KCR East extension and ride one stop to Che Kung Temple station.

Built in 1993, the temple is a modern, grim-looking, black-roofed building by the road (the prettier green-roofed building behind is private property), its entrance marked by a crowd of fortune-tellers, palm readers and incense sellers. Inside, beyond the courtyard, is a ten-metre-high, aggressive-looking statue of the general with a drawn sword and a collection of brass fans, which people turn for luck. You can still see the remains of the original three-hundred-year old temple out back, but it is usually closed to the public. Che Kung's festival is held on the third day of Chinese New Year, when the temple is packed with people coming here to pray for good luck.

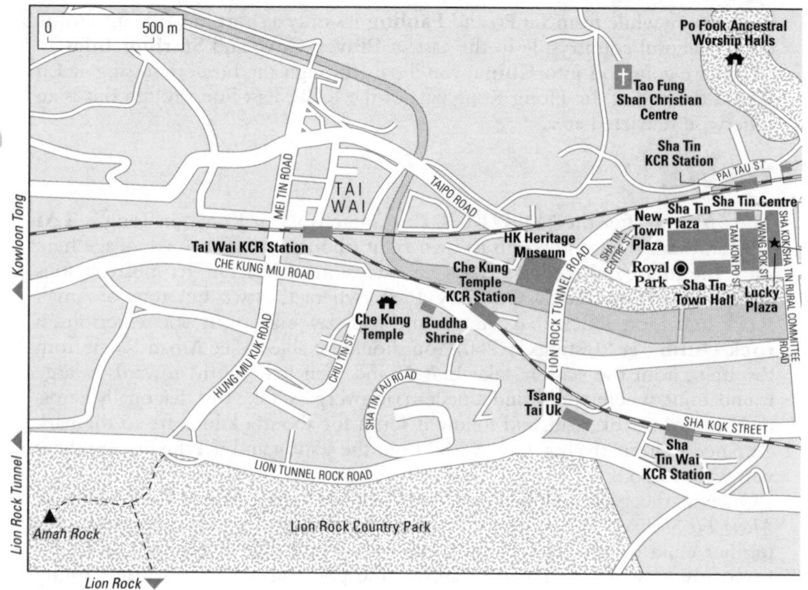

Come out of the temple and keep on up the main road – Che Kung Miu Road – towards Sha Tin and, after another hundred metres or so on the right, you'll find a little covered garden containing a **Four-Faced Buddha Shrine**. This is a symbol more commonly found in Thailand: you're supposed to pray to each face in turn, moving around the shrine in an anticlockwise direction.

Tsang Tai Uk

From the shrine, it's only a ten-minute walk to one of the New Territories' lesser-known walled villages, **TSANG TAI UK**. Signs guide you up the main road (which becomes Tai Chung Kiu Road as it approaches Sha Tin) to Sha Kok Street on the right: walk down here, and the village is behind the recreation ground to the right, looking very out of place amongst nearby highrises and expressways.

The area is believed to have been settled around 1500, though the first **Hakka** people migrated here only during the eighteenth century. Tsang Tai Uk means "The Tsangs' Mansion", though it's actually a rectangular, walled village of grey stone, built in the 1870s by a wealthy stonemason to house families of his clan. Fortress-like clan villages are a Hakka speciality, as these people – concentrated today in Hong Kong and the southern mainland provinces – were dislodged by warfare millennia ago from their original lands in central China, and have never been sure of their welcome in places they subsequently settled. Indeed, *hakka* translates as "guest family", indicating their status as outsiders.

Although there are also some modern structures inside the thick, protective outer wall, older features include traditional courtyard homes, an ancestral hall, and two wells; each corner of the outer wall sports a square watchtower, adorned with faded stone decoration. A triple gateway leads into the village, which is based around a central courtyard, with wide alleys running its length split by a network of high-ceilinged rooms and storerooms. Most of the Tsang

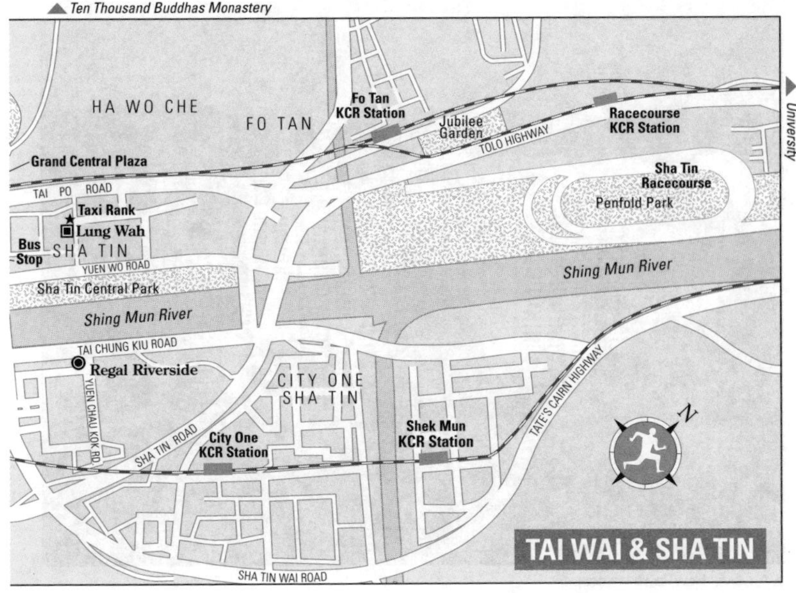

family have moved out, but the community is still very much lived in, its alleyways choked with bicycles, gas canisters, discarded furniture and drying washing. Overall, it's a lot more appealing than more frequently visited villages in the Kam Tin area near Yuen Long (see p.142).

Sha Tin

Built on both sides of the Shing Mun River in the southern New Territories, **SHA TIN** is one of the most interesting stops on the KCR East line. The name means "sandy fields", a relic of the days when the area consisted of arable land made fertile by sediment washed down by the river. This productive land supported farming villages, like Tai Wai, for centuries, though it's only since the 1970s that Sha Tin has taken on its ultramodern appearance. Much of the New Town building here has occurred on land reclaimed from the mud and sand, which you can still see and smell in the murky channelled river.

The town – home to more than half a million people, and still growing – splits into several areas served by separate KCR stations: Tai Wai, covered above; to the north, Fo Tan, a residential area overlooking the racecourse; while Sha Tin town itself is reached from the central KCR station, also called Sha Tin. The station exit leads into **New Town Plaza**, a huge shopping and recreation centre, which offers an accurate view of contemporary local life and manners: solidly Chinese, with crowded shops and good-value restaurants full of local families. If you're here at the right time, you can join the crowds of kids who gather to watch the central musical fountain with its coloured lights and ten-metre sprays (displays at 12.45pm, 9.30pm, plus 10.00am and 5.30pm at weekends).

Head through the plaza and there are walkway connections to other nearby shopping centres, as well as the pleasant eight-hectare **riverside park** (daily

▲ A typical New Town cityscape

7am–11pm) and Sha Tin Town Hall, a popular place for weddings and also the venue for some excellent theatre and international dance troupes including ballet and the Shaolin Monks. Opposite the town hall is **Snoopy's World** (daily 9am–10pm; free), an outdoor playground ideal for small children, with body painting, games and a little boat ride.

A ten-minute walk south through the riverside park (follow the signs to the museum) brings you to the **Hong Kong Heritage Museum** (Mon & Wed–Sat 10am–6pm, Sun & public holidays 10am–7pm; $10, Wed free; ⓦwww.heritagemuseum.gov.hk), an enormous orange-roofed structure based on the traditional design of Si He Yuan, a compound with houses laid out around a central courtyard. The SAR's largest museum, with twelve exhibition halls on three floors, it showcases Hong Kong's culture through displays of art, music, dance, history, literature and theatre. The highlight is the **Cantonese Opera Heritage Hall**, where you can admire the flamboyant costumes, embroidered shoes, stage props, mock-ups of traditional stage sets and artists' dressing rooms, accompanied by the crashing cymbals of Chinese opera. You can even daub your face in virtual make-up to see how you would look as an opera star. The museum's other permanent exhibitions include the **T.T. Tsui Gallery of Chinese Art** featuring fine Chinese ceramics, bronze, jade, laquerware and stone sculptures, as well as Tibetan Buddhist statues and thangka paintings; while **The New Territories Heritage Hall** has archeological remains dating back to 4000 BC, accounts of Hong Kong's various Chinese ethnic groups, plus mock-ups of early hardware and medicine shops and explanations of ancestral worship, feasts and festivals. The museum also houses six temporary exhibition galleries, while children should head to the **Children's Discovery Gallery** on the ground floor, where they can dress up in traditional costume, dance with cartoon characters, play at being archeologists and make a bird out of felt.

However, the town's best-known sight is the **Sha Tin Racecourse**, which, together with Happy Valley, is the only legal betting outlet in Hong Kong. It's packed on race days, and the season is from September to June, with meet–

ings usually held on Wednesday evenings or Saturday and Sunday afternoons; the biggest annual event is the Hong Kong Derby in March, a two-kilometre race for four-year-olds, which attracts an international crowd and is reputedly one of the richest horseraces in the world. At other times, you can get into **Penfold Park** (closed Mon and race days) and its bird sanctuary, which are in the middle of the track. On race days, KCR trains stop at Racecourse station; at other times, get off the train at Fo Tan – the track and park are behind the Jubilee Garden estate.

The Ten Thousand Buddhas Monastery

A little way northwest of Sha Tin is the **Ten Thousand Buddhas Monastery** (daily 10am–5pm; free), an appealing shabby temple dating from the 1960s, set at the peak of Po Fook Hill. Its red and gold pagoda is visible from just outside the KCR station, right behind and above a larger white-and-green complex of Chinese buildings that house the Po Fook Ancestral Worship Halls. About four hundred steps lead up to the monastery, and the five hundred life-sized, gold-painted statues of arhats (Buddhist saints) flanking the track might take your mind off the climb. You emerge onto a terrace beside the main temple, which has an undistinguished exterior but houses around thirteen thousand small black-and-gold Buddha statues, each about a foot high and sculpted in a different posture, lining the walls to a height of thirty feet or more. The building also contains the embalmed and gilded body of a monk, the founder of the monastery. Outside on the terrace there's a small pagoda, along with brightly painted shoddy concrete statues of Chinese deities, including a lion and elephant (representing the Buddhist gods of Wisdom and Benevolence). You can buy **vegetarian lunches** here, either off the menu or from a more basic canteen selection (which is actually better value).

The **Po Fook Ancestral Worship Halls** (9am–5pm; free) are also worth a look. They include landscaped gardens, a temple complex and dozens of small shrines, each containing the memorial plaques and ashes of different families. You may see a funeral here, complete with the paper offerings, which are burnt so as to join the deceased in the afterlife. The vans in the lower car park decorated with plastic flowers are the hearses.

To reach the hill and the temple, exit Sha Tin KCR following the sign for "Buses/Grand Central Plaza". Go down the ramp to the left of the bus terminal and walk past the old houses on the left towards the modern, glass Grand Central Plaza building. Turn left there, and after about 20m you reach the entrance to the Po Fook Ancestral Worship Halls. A path to the monastery leads off to the right, between the entrance way and a public car park. Keep going left, passing some shacks after a couple of hundred metres, and you'll find the steps.

Tao Fung Shan

On the next ridge, the **Tao Fung Shan Christian Centre** (daily 9am–5pm) is a complex of buildings built in the 1930s in a Chinese style, though this time the pagoda at the top holds a small Christian chapel. To get there, take the ramp by the bus terminal, but instead of walking straight on for the Ten Thousand Buddhas Monastery, turn back sharp left, parallel to the rail tracks, through Pai Tau village. You'll see a wooden post in front of a large tree, with a green arrow and logo. The path on the right leads up above the village, and, after about ten minutes' climb, brings you out on the main Tao Fung Shan Road, where it joins Pak Lok Path. Keep on up the road for another fifteen minutes or so and you can't miss the centre.

At the top, a marked path leads through pretty grounds to a large, white stone cross, which faces directly out over the river. Away to the left are the blocks of Sha Tin and Fo Tan, while just visible through the apartment buildings at the foot of the hills opposite is Tsang Tai Uk village, a low, grey splash among the towers.

The views aren't the only reason to make the climb. In the grounds is a **porcelain workshop** (Mon–Fri 9am–12.30pm & 2–5pm, Sat 8.30am–12.30pm), where you can see good-quality porcelain being hand-painted. The decorated plates run to hundreds of dollars, but you can pick up a souvenir here – a cup and saucer, jug or decorated tile – for around $50.

Steps from the centre lead down to the **cemetery**, below the stone factory, just outside the main entrance, where there's the grave of Tao Fung Shan's founder, the Norwegian evangelist Karl Ludwig Reichelt (1877–1952), whose idea it was to convert Buddhist monks to Christianity. In part, this explains the centre's orthodox Buddhist look: Reichelt hoped that the buildings would dupe wandering Buddhist monks seeking sanctuary, and it certainly worked – until World War II, Tao Fung Shan was a prosperous Christian centre, although it has struggled to attract devotees in more recent times.

University, Ma Liu Shui and Tung Ping Chau

Beyond Sha Tin, the main KCR East line runs upriver before turning to hug the edge of Tolo Harbour. Just before the turn, there's a stop called **UNIVERSITY**, which serves Hong Kong's **Chinese University**, the campus spread back from the harbour up the hillside.

A shuttle bus from outside the station runs every 15–30 minutes up the steep hill to the central campus. If you get off at the second stop, at the top by the Sir Run Run Shaw Hall, the university's **Art Museum** (Mon–Sat 10am–4.45pm, Sun 12.30–5.30pm; free) is over to the left, in the middle of a block of buildings surrounding a square. The well-lit, spacious split-level galleries usually display items from the museum's own wide collection of Chinese paintings, calligraphy and ceramics dating from the Ming Dynasty onwards. Local and mainland Chinese museums often send touring exhibitions of art and archeological pieces here, too (check details online at ⓦwww.cuhk.edu.hk/ics/amm).

Ma Liu Shui

The other reason to come here is for services from the ferry pier at **MA LIU SHUI**. From University KCR, follow the sign to the Ferry Pier out of the station, turn left, cross the highway by the flyover and descend to the waterfront – a ten-minute walk. Ferries go from here through **Tolo Harbour** and the Tolo Channel – either stay on board for the scenic round trip or jump off at Tap Mun Chau or another of the minor stops along the way; see p.152 for details, or contact the Tsui Wah Ferry company (ⓣ2527 2513).

Tung Ping Chau

Ferries also run from Ma Liu Shui to the island of **Tung Ping Chau**, about as far away from central Hong Kong as you can get – which explains why hardly anyone goes there. Way to the northeast, beyond Tap Mun Chau and off the Chinese coast (close enough for illegal immigrants from the mainland to have swum here), it's long been abandoned by its inhabitants, and is now a marine park. It's a flat place, its apex just 37m high, but there are some good beaches and the odd overgrown trail along its banana-shaped, four-kilometre length.

The **ferry** runs only at weekends, leaving Ma Liu Shui at 9am (Sat & Sun) and 3.30pm (Sat only), returning at about 5.15pm; the journey takes ninety minutes and costs $80 return. This should give you quite long enough on the island, though some people come equipped with camping gear and everything else necessary for a pleasant night's stay – like an enormous bottle of something alcoholic. The campsite is at Kang Lau Shek, at the eastern end of the island; there's no fresh water.

Tai Po

Beyond University, the rail line runs alongside the sea. At **TAI PO**, on the western point of Tolo Harbour, you're roughly halfway up the KCR East line. A market town since the seventeenth century, the manageable town centre is gradually being overwhelmed by new industrial and housing developments. Nonetheless, there's enough to warrant a short stroll, and regular buses from the station – called Tai Po Market – enable you to escape into the unspoiled hiking and picnic areas around Plover Cove.

The Town

Amongst its New Town modernity, Tai Po houses a few small temples and the **Hong Kong Railway Museum** (Mon & Wed–Sun 9am–5pm; free), which

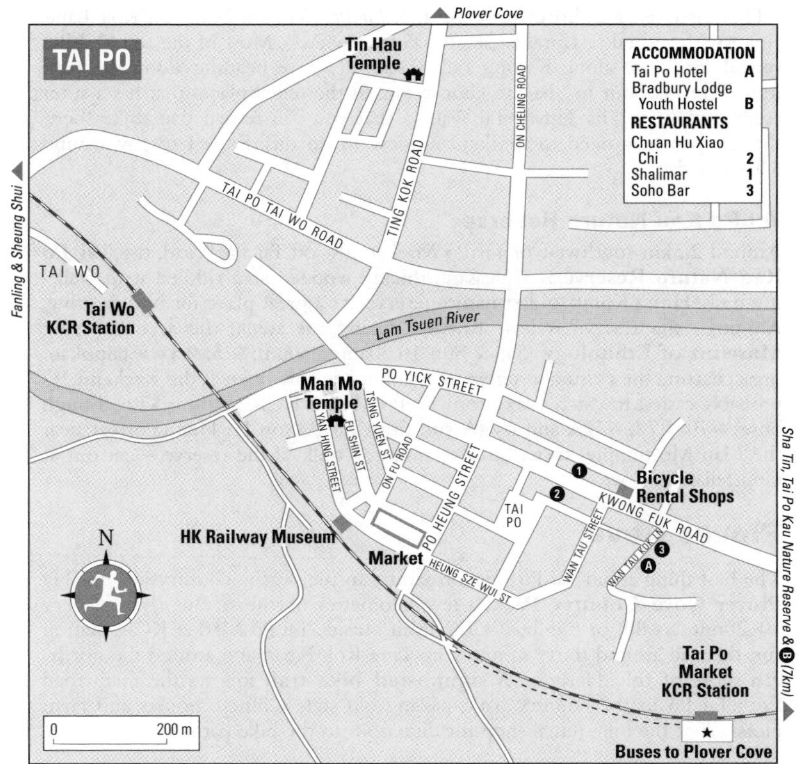

occupies the site and buildings of the old Tai Po Market Railway Station at 13 Shun Tak St. The small exhibition includes photographs of the KCR's opening ceremony in 1910 and recordings of engine and whistle sounds of various 1950s trains, while outside on the preserved tracks you can see coaches dating back to 1911. The other nearby diversion is the beautiful **Man Mo Temple** (dawn to dusk), on Fu Shin Street, surrounded by outdoor market stalls and built about a hundred years ago as a shrine to the Taoist gods of war and literature. Towards the main altar, look up and you'll see prayers written on red plastic plaques dangling inside the enormous hanging incense coils, which can burn for weeks. For around $70, one of the temple workers will write you a personal prayer (you can dedicate it to yourself or someone else) and hang it up with the others. Little English is spoken, however. Outside, there are plenty of interesting old shops around here, too, selling dried seafood, religious paraphernalia and other Chinese wares.

Tai Po's other attractions are across the river, which separates the old town from the new industrial developments. Over the bridge, Ting Kok Road leads up to the town's **Tin Hau Temple**, a few hundred metres up on the left. It's a particularly old relic, built around three hundred years ago and reflecting Tai Po's traditional importance as a fishing centre. It's also one of the main centres for celebration and devotion during the annual Tin Hau festival (late April/May), when the whole place is decorated with streamers, banners and little windmills: come then and you're likely to catch a Cantonese opera performance on a temporary stage over the road.

There is one basic **hotel** in town, the *Tai Po Hotel* on Wan Tau Kok Lane, along with several restaurants (see p.205 for reviews). Most of the town's **bike rental** shops are along Kwong Fuk Road: if you're heading along the path from Tolo Harbour to Sha Tin choose one of the rental places that has a sister establishment in Sha Tin or Tai Wai, so that you can return your bike there, though you may need to speak Cantonese to do this. Expect to pay around $40–50 a day.

Tai Po Kau Nature Reserve

Around 2.5km southwest of Tai Po Market, just off Tai Po Road, the **Tai Po Kau Nature Reserve** is a pleasant, thickly wooded area riddled with walking trails. Hong Kong's oldest nature reserve, it's a great place for bird spotting. Although the reserve is less crowded during the week, the accompanying **Museum of Ethnology** (Sat & Sun 10.30am–6.30pm; $25; Ⓦwww.taipokau.org), charting the cultural progress of mankind, is only open at the weekend. It's probably easiest to catch a taxi from Tai Po Market KCR Station ($20), though buses #70, #72, #72A and #74A run from Tai Po (on Po Heung Street near the Man Mo temple) to within five minutes' walk of the reserve – get out at Constellation Cove.

Plover Cove

The best thing about Tai Po is its proximity to the nearby countryside, notably **Plover Cove Country Park**, a few kilometres northeast. Bus #75K (every 10–20min; $4.80) or minibus #20C from outside Tai Po Market KCR Station run there in around thirty minutes, up Ting Kok Road and around the northern shore of Tolo Harbour. A **signposted bike trail** follows the main road from Tai Po to the country park, passing old-style Chinese houses and farm plots: ask at the bike rental shop for directions to the bike path.

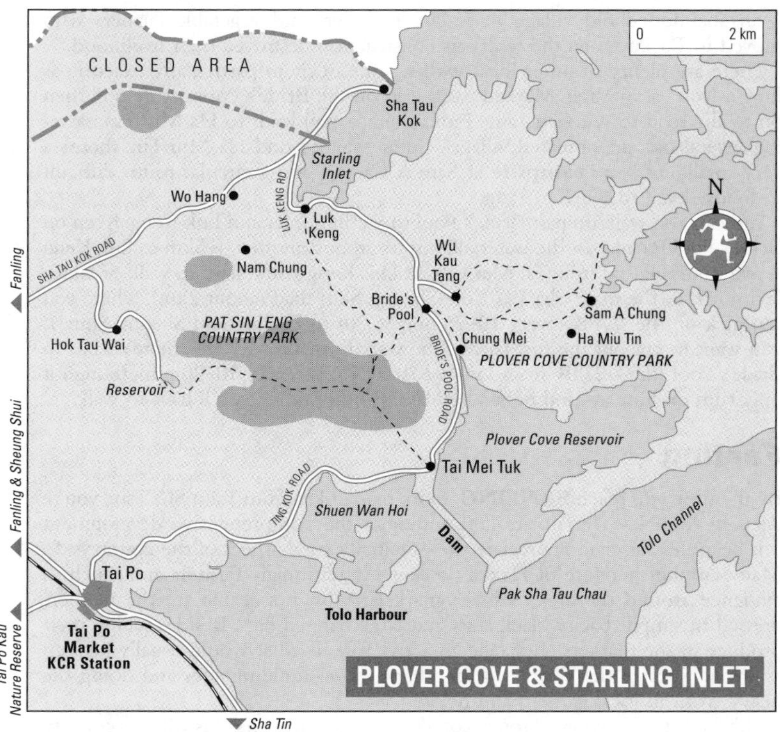

Tai Mei Tuk

The bus terminates at the few houses of **TAI MEI TUK** at the edge of the Plover Cove Reservoir. The bay here was once part of the harbour and has since been dammed to provide a huge freshwater supply for Hong Kong. Under the water is a sunken village – the population was moved to Sai Kung. Close to the terminus there's a clutch of restaurants, food and drink stalls, and a line of **bicycle and tricycle rental** places ($30–65 a day, $120 for the tricycles). There's also the *Bradbury Lodge Youth Hostel* (see p.183 for details), which you'll need to book in advance. Over the road, the little peninsula by the main dam shelters a barbecue site, and there's a watersports centre where you can rent rowing boats and windsurfers. There's also a **visitors' centre** (daily except Tues 9.30–11.30am & 1.30–4.30pm) with useful information boards on local flora, fauna and geology, as well as hiking advice; the five-kilometre-long **Pat Sin Leng Nature Trail** running between here and Bride's Pool (see below) scrambles up to a five-hundred-metre-high ridge for views of the reservoir.

Local walks

The only road, Bride's Pool Road, heads north, alongside the reservoir and past endless barbecue sites to **Bride's Pool** – around an hour's stroll along a road that gets a fair bit of traffic at the weekend. A series of waterfalls, it's home to more barbecue sites and lots of picnickers, though you can escape the worst of the crowds by taking the trail thirty minutes back downriver to Chung Mei

– an abandoned old village of scallop gatherers and vegetable farmers who moved to Tai Po when the reservoir construction destroyed their livelihood.

There are plenty of other local **walks**, none of them particularly exacting as long as you carry water. Marked paths lead off the Bride's Pool nature trail then on to the road to Wu Kau Tang. From there, a trail leads to Ha Miu Tin, skirting several old, depopulated villages. Some way beyond Ha Miu Tin, there's a very small and basic **campsite** at Sam A Chung, and a circular route, difficult to follow, back to Wu Kau Tang.

You can also walk on past Bride's Pool to Starling Inlet and Luk Keng. Keep on Bride's Pool Road, past the waterfall, and it's around another 4–5km to Luk Keng – two hours all told from Tai Mei Tuk. At Luk Keng you'll have to walk or take a taxi north to the main Sha Tau Kok–Sheung Shui road (about 2km), where you can pick up the #78K (every 10–25min; $6.20) to Fanling and Sheung Shui. If you want to cut out the first part of the walk from Tai Mei Tuk, there's a bus to Bride's Pool (the #275R from Tai Po Market KCR, every 10–20min), though it only runs on Sundays and public holidays; at other times, you'll have to walk.

Fanling

By the time you reach **FANLING**, more than 20km from Tsim Sha Tsui, you're deep in the New Territories and – despite the comprehensive development – it becomes easier to appreciate the essentially rural aspect of the countryside. Many families here are of Hakka descent – traditionally farmers and much in evidence around the area's vibrant markets. Most noticeable are the women, dressed in simple, baggy black suits and large fringed hats. Besides selling their produce in the markets, they take an active role in what would usually be seen as "male" jobs in the West – hauling barrows on building sites and doing the heavy work in local gardens and fields.

Although this is where Hong Kong's chief executive has his official country house, the town of Fanling itself is eminently missable. Much of it is being rebuilt and merged with neighbouring Sheung Shui to form another massive new housing development. One reason to stop here is for the large **Fung Ying Seen Koon** Taoist temple (daily 9am–6pm) opposite the KCR station, serving vegetarian lunches (11am–4.30pm), with sculpted gardens, fortune-tellers and contemporary ancestral halls – small rooms stacked floor to ceiling with tiny

ancestral tablets. Look out for the incense sales centre where you can watch women folding coloured paper into replica objects thought to be useful in the afterlife – money, boats, mobile telephones, watches, rings, jade jewellery and even cigarettes – ready for burning. The swanky **Hong Kong Golf Club**, founded in 1889 (and open to visitors; see p.258) is also in town, as is the **Jockey Club**'s luxurious stable complex at Bea's River.

The main tourist attraction, however, is the nearby **Luen Wo market** (Luen Wo Hui) on Wo Mun Street, well worth a visit if you haven't seen a full-blooded Chinese affair before – it's a ten-minute bus (#77K) or minibus (#52A) ride from outside Fanling KCR Station (bus #70 from the Jordan Bus Terminal – near the Kowloon Airport Express Station on Wui Cheung Road – also goes direct, an hour's ride). Get there by 10am to see it at its best; if you do, you'll be able to breakfast very cheaply. The Chinese eat *congee* and a doughnut stick from one of the little noodle stalls around the covered market; for a few dollars more, other places will sell you a plate of duck or pork and rice.

Sha Tau Kok, Starling Inlet and Luk Keng

East of Fanling, the new development peters out into the rural border area with China. Bus #78K from outside Fanling's KCR Station runs up to **SHA TAU KOK**, a twenty-minute ride past quiet farming and fishing villages dotted along the valley. Just before you get to Sha Tau Kok the road passes two villages (Wo Hang and Man Uk Pin) that are known for their Mid-Autumn Festival (see p.241) celebrations, when unmanned hot-air balloons built out of bamboo and rice paper, 3–5m high, are launched at night. In still conditions the balloons have been known to fly thousands of metres up and well into the Chinese mainland. The Sha Tau Kok area is not one you can easily explore, since the village itself lies in a restricted area abutting the Chinese border, but it's a pleasant ride. At Starling Inlet, there's a checkpoint on the road, where you'll be politely turfed off the bus. You'll have to wait for the return bus; the Sha Tau Kok locals have passes that enable them to cross in and out freely.

You can see more of this pretty area by instead taking the #56K maxicab from Fanling KCR Station, which turns off the Sha Tau Kok road at Starling Inlet and runs around the cove and its mangrove swamps to **LUK KENG**. This is a very peaceful village, with a couple of noodle stalls on the road by the bus stop and two more old Hakka villages in the valley plain behind. The area is a popular wintering place for birds, egrets in particular. If you walk down the main Luk Keng Road, it soon becomes Bride's Pool Road (see "Plover Cove" on p.132); about five minutes from Luk Keng bus stop there's a noticeboard showing the path to Bride's Pool. It also indicates a circular half-hour "Family Walk", which takes you out along the inlet and then cuts back high above the villages and water to regain the main road. There are magnificent views as you go, across to the high-rises of the border town of Sha Tau Kok and China beyond, and down to the fish farms and junks of Starling Inlet itself.

A much longer hike is accessible by taking the #52K maxicab from Fanling KCR. This drops you at **Hok Tau Wai** (where there's a campsite), around 4km from Fanling, from where a trail runs past a small reservoir over the top of the Pat Sin Leng Country Park and down to Tai Mei Tuk at Plover Cove – a lengthy walk but easily done in a day.

Sheung Shui

A few minutes beyond Fanling, **SHEUNG SHUI** is as far as you can go on the KCR without continuing into China. Only 3km from the border, it's worth a visit as an unpretentious place to see ordinary people going through their daily activities.

The town divides into two areas. The main part, just five minutes on foot from the KCR station using the overhead walkways, is known as **Shek Wu Hui**, an interconnected block of streets that can't be bettered as an example of a down-to-earth New Territories' market town. There are cheap clothes stalls, *dai pai dongs*, herbalists' shops and Hakka women on their way to market laden down with goods and bags. The **food market**, in the alleys behind San Hong Street (off the main San Fung Avenue), is one of the best in the territory, certainly the one that comes closest in appearance to those over the border. The covered stalls are stuffed with fruit and veg, preserved eggs and beancurd, while in a separate section live fish are picked from the slabs and clubbed on demand. It's no place for the squeamish, particularly when you notice the more peripheral trades going on in between the stalls: vendors selling from buckets of tied crabs and jumping prawns; the frog seller who dispatches the beasts with a hatchet across the back, keeping the legs and throwing the twitching bodies away; the woman who spends all day wringing the necks of tiny birds, taken from a squeaking cage, and placing the pathetic plucked carcasses on a slab.

The other part of Sheung Shui is **Po Sheung Tsuen**, aka Sheung Shui Wai, the original village over to the west of the town. Head down the main San Fung Avenue from the KCR station, turn left into Po Wan Road and walk between the two sections of the park (the Jockey Club playground) up to the main Po Shek Wu Road, where you'll see the China Light and Power building over the way. Cross at the lights and go down the steps straight ahead of you, just to your right. Walk along by the side of the small drainage channel and through the car park, and behind the new apartment buildings is the old village. It's an almost medieval raggle-taggle of buildings with dank alleys between the houses, just wide enough for one person to walk down. The houses are a strange mixture, some brand new with bright tiling, others just corrugated iron and cheap plaster. The only thing to see is the large local ancestral hall, **Liu Man Shek Tong** (Wed & Thurs, Sat & Sun, 9am–1pm & 2–5pm), built in the eighteenth century. Giving directions to this is pointless, since the name and numbering system for the alleys is hopelessly confusing, but you'll stumble across it sooner or later and be glad that you did: unlike many such places in more touristy parts of Hong Kong, this one is firmly in use by the locals and still stands in its original crumbly surroundings, carved and decorated in traditional fashion.

Practicalities

Buses use the bays outside the KCR station, while most **minibuses** leave from San Fat Street, a two-minute walk west. There's no shortage of **restaurants** here: for a plate of meat and rice, or bowl of noodles, the *Ming Yuen* on the corner of San Fat and Fu Hing streets, is worth a try, while the *Malaysia Restaurant*, also on San Fat Street (no. 26), serves decent Malaysian food, as well as European lunches and dinners. For something a little different, the *Better Olé*, a little further along Fu Hing Street, is a very popular steak-cum-curry house. For bargain meals, head to the **dai pai dongs** in the town's market – they're all at the eastern end of San Shing Avenue.

The Border: San Tin & the Mai Po Marshes

The **border with China** follows the course of the Sham Chun River across the narrow neck of the New Territories' peninsula, and remains a formal barrier to travel under the "one country, two systems" policy that governs Hong

Kong's relationship with the mainland. The main crossing point at **LO WU**, the final stop on the KCR line, is **off limits** unless you've valid documents for continuing into China, but there are a couple of accessible areas at San Tin and the adjacent Mai Po Marshes, a remote wetlands reserve for birdlife.

San Tin

If rural peace and quiet appeals, head for the traditional Chinese dwellings at the nearby village of **SAN TIN**, a few kilometres west of Sheung Shui. Take bus #76K (marked Yuen Long West) from Choi Yuen road, outside Sheung Shui KCR Station, and get off in San Tin by the Esso service station.

Walk up the street beside the post office, just off the main road, and within five minutes you'll be at **Tai Fu Tai** (daily except Tues 9am–1pm, 2–5pm; free), a fine example of a nineteenth-century home built for a wealthy Chinese family of the Man clan, who originally settled this area in the fifteenth century. There are some excellent murals inside, carved wood panels, and glazed friezes in high relief. Built in 1865, this is considered one of the most beautiful buildings of its kind remaining in Hong Kong – and you'll have the place to yourself. From here, continue through the maze of quiet streets and you'll find three ancestral halls. The best of these, the **Man Lun Fung Ancestral Hall**, was built in the mid-seventeenth century and restored in 1987. It's still in regular use as a place for worship and meeting by local people; the forest of wooden tablets commemorates men of the clan.

Mai Po Marshes

Just north of San Tin, the **Mai Po Marshes** have been designated a site of international importance for migratory waterfowl such as Dalmatian pelicans and black-faced spoonbills, and are also home to other wildlife, including otters. The Mai Po Nature Reserve, at the centre of the marshes, has floating hides for bird-watching, which is best between October and May, though getting here is a bit problematic at present – contact Hong Kong Outdoors (Ⓦwww.hkoutdoors.com) for the latest.

Also in the Mai Po marshes, at **Tin Shui Wai**, some disused fishponds are being converted into the SAR's first major eco-tourism site, the **Hong Kong International Wetland Park** (Ⓣ3152 2666), which was closed at the time of writing for construction of its final stage. The park's purpose is to replace some of the valuable marshland lost to development in the area and to act as a buffer zone between the development and Mai Po marshes, hopefully attracting a similar selection of wildfowl as the marshes whilst being slightly more accessible. There's no direct way here from San Tin, however, though it is easy to **get here** from Kowloon: first, take the KCR West rail to Tin Shui Wai, then catch the Light Rail "Circular" line to Wetland Park Station.

The West: Tsuen Wan, Yuen Long and Tuen Mun

Access to the **western New Territories** is primarily along the **KCR West line**, which runs from Nam Cheong on the MTR line northwest, via the New Towns of **Tsuen Wan** and **Yuen Long**, to the line's terminus at **Tuen Mun**. The towns themselves are interesting exercises in urban planning, but not of immense appeal from a touristic viewpoint, though there are a few temples, museums, and old-style walled villages to check out. The area features some good walks, too, including a fantastic climb up Hong Kong's highest peak, **Tai Mo Shan**. Using the towns as transit points, it's easy to reach everything on buses and the tram-like **Light Rail** (LR) system.

Tsuen Wan

A stack of grey high-rises nestling between the hills, **TSUEN WAN** ("Shallow Bay") overlooks Tsing Yi island and the greater harbour beyond. In 1898 the town had only three thousand inhabitants, mostly farmers; now, around a million people live or work in the area, and the place has the futuristic, concrete-bound look favoured by planners all over Hong Kong, with flyovers and walkways spinning off in all directions, and signposts pointing into interlinking malls and gardens. There is also the usual complement of shops, stores, and a market, but the main reasons to linger here are the first-rate Sam Tung Uk Museum and several attractive **walks** on the town's outskirts.

The Sam Tung Uk Museum

The Tsuen Wan area was completely depopulated following the orders of the seventeenth-century Manchu government to abandon the coastal villages in response to constant pirate attacks. It wasn't populated again until the end of

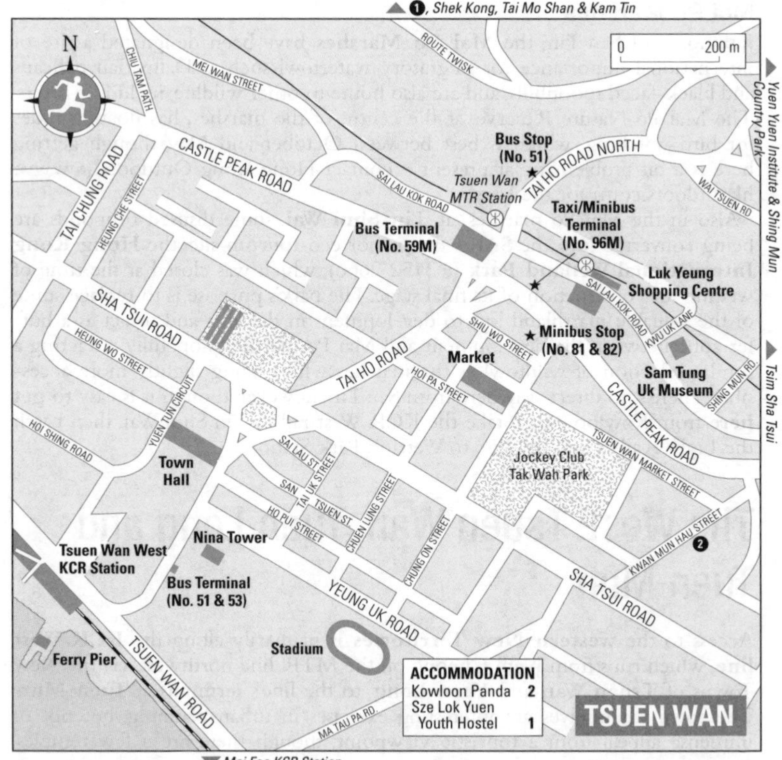

the century, and permanent settlements only developed later, typified by the eighteenth-century Hakka walled village that survives today as the **Sam Tung Uk Museum** (daily except Tues 9am–5pm; free). The museum is on Kwu Uk Lane; exit left from the MTR and it's about 200m.

Founded by a clan originally from China's Fujian province, Sam Tung Uk was a farming village – the name means "three-beamed dwelling", a reference to the three-roofed halls that form the central axis of the village, with new housing added on both sides as the village grew. At the entrance there's an **orientation room**, which tells the story of the village's restoration; one photograph shows Sam Tung Uk in 1977, surrounded by similar villages when Tsuen Wan was just a twinkle in a planner's eye, revealing the speed of Hong Kong's development. As the New Town went up around it, the villagers moved out, and in 1981 Sam Tung Uk was declared a monument – cleaned, stripped and renovated to its original condition, with the furniture and most of the exhibits actually collected from two contemporary Hakka villages over the border in Guangdong.

The basic layout is of three connected halls: a common room for villagers, with carts and sedan chairs; a central hall for banquets and gatherings; and the ancestral hall, which faced the main entrance. Everywhere, the walls are whitewashed and cool, the buildings sporting low lintels and well-crafted beamed roofs. The rooms, connected by narrow streets – corridors really – display traditional farming implements, some beautiful blackwood furniture, as well as more ordinary chairs, tables, cooking utensils and cleaning tools. The ancestral hall has been painted in its original bright red and green colours, giving an idea of what you're missing in other parts of Hong Kong, where the halls are often ingrained with decades' worth of dust and dirt. Outside, the **gardens** have been landscaped to show how there would have been a threshing ground and a fishpond, and there's a gatehouse beyond, which would have guarded the entrance to the village.

Shing Mun and Kam Shan country parks

Fifteen minutes east of Tsuen Wan by bus, **Shing Mun Country Park** is a fine target if you've got a couple of spare hours and want to get out into more rural surroundings. Maxicab #82 from Shiu Wo Street, two blocks south of the MTR, runs straight to the **Country Park Visitors' Centre** (daily except Tues 9.30am–4.30pm; ☎2489 1362), and on Sunday there is also minibus #94S from Tsuen Wan Ferry Pier. The visitors' centre has a summertime refreshment kiosk and toilets, and the exhibition hall highlights local history – particularly the World War II defensive system (see below) – flora, fauna and local mining activities. From the centre, a signposted walk runs around the Shing Mun (Jubilee) Reservoir, a relatively easy two-hour hike, much of it shaded by trees, with great views of the surrounding hills.

A minor detour from the hike around the reservoir takes you to the **Shing Mun Redoubt**, a twelve-acre underground hilltop fortification built by the British in 1939 as part of the New Territories' defence (known as the "Gin Drinker's Line") against possible Japanese invasion. Based on a series of tunnels – each named after a London street or area – the system was taken by the Japanese after a short but bloody battle in 1941. Large parts of the system still remain intact, covered by undergrowth: if you're intent upon exploring, take a torch and be careful, since the tunnels aren't maintained. To get there from the visitors' centre, walk around the reservoir in an anticlockwise direction; when you see a big overhead sign marked "MacLehose Trail (Stage Six)", leave the road and join the trail – the tunnels start about ten minutes after the sign, mostly on the left-hand side of the track.

This section of the **MacLehose Trail** itself heads south towards Smuggler's Ridge, a ninety-minute climb that takes you into the neighbouring **Kam Shan Country Park**, known for its wild macaque monkeys. This part of the trail ends at the Kowloon Reservoirs and the park entrance, from where you can pick up buses back to Jordan MTR (#81).

Yuen Yuen Institute

To complete the tour of Tsuen Wan's outskirts, take maxicab #81 from Shiu Wo Street (two blocks south of Tsuen Wan MTR) to the **Yuen Yuen Institute** (daily 8.30am–5pm), a ten-minute ride into the green hills overlooking the city; the bus may be marked "Lo Wai Village". It's a working temple dedicated to Taoism, Buddhism and Confucianism – which makes for an interesting mix of styles. The main building is a replica of Beijing's Temple of Heaven, and there are also bonsai trees, a collection of rocks (contemplated by scholars as an aid to meditation), and a dining room with very good vegetarian food. Lunch is around $60.

Practicalities

Tsuen Wan's **MTR station** is just north of the centre, conveniently close to the Sam Tung Uk museum. The **KCR station** is 750m south across the centre on the waterfront – bus #301M connects the two.

Buses stop all over the place in Tsuen Wan. From a small depot just east of the KCR station near the **Nina Tower**, you can catch bus #53 (every 20–30min; $6.70) along Castle Peak road to nearby beaches (and on around the coast to Tuen Mun, p.144); and bus #51 (every 20–30min; $7.60) along Route Twisk, via Tai Mo Shan Country Park, to Kam Tin (see p.142). You can also catch bus #51 at the Tai Ho Road overpass, just west of the MTR station. **Shiu Wo Street**, a couple of blocks south of the MTR, near the market, has the minibus and maxicab stops for the country parks and the Yuen Yuen Institute.

Tsuen Wan has one of the New Territories' few **hotels**, the *Kowloon Panda* (see p.191 for details); inside is the *Yuet Loy Heen* **restaurant**, on the second floor, which serves highly rated *dim sum* from 7am to 2.30pm; the seafood choices are especially good.

West of Tuen Mun: Castle Peak Road

Two parallel roads run along the **coast** of the western New Territories beyond Tsuen Wan: the new, fast highway, Tuen Mun Road, and the quieter and original **Castle Peak Road**. Finished in 1919, this road is the one to follow if you want to see any of the shoreline, as it winds around the **beaches** and small headlands between Tsuen Wan and Tuen Mun, before cutting up through the inland region to Yuen Long and continuing to Lok Ma Chau. The coastal part of the route is best done on bus #53 from Tsuen Wan: see "Practicalities" above for details.

Tsing Yi Island, which dominates the entire first half of the coastline, across Rambler Channel from Tsuen Wan, is home to container terminals, oil depots and other industrial concerns. The various noxious emissions haven't helped the water quality, which is already hit by the junk flowing out of Tsuen Wan's harbour. Consequently, the water hereabouts is off-limits for swimming.

The beaches and Sham Tseng

The **beaches** nearest to Tsuen Wan are all pretty much affected by the polluted water, but the sands are generally fine. You'll pass **Approach Beach** and **Ting**

Kau, while further on are **Ho Mei Wan** and **Gemini** beaches; beyond Sham Tseng come **Angler's** and **Dragon**.

If none of these appeal, consider stopping at **SHAM TSENG** itself, a little roadside village about fifteen minutes out of Tsuen Wan. Get off at the stop after the massive San Miguel brewery, directly opposite which there's a line of nine or ten **restaurants**, all specializing in roast goose and duck. The *Chan Kee*, right opposite the factory, has an English menu and tables under a marquee where you can spend a very pleasant lunchtime eating goose and swigging the local San Miguel beer. Stay on the #53 bus, and Castle Peak road continues around to Tuen Mun and beyond – see p.144.

Route Twisk: Tai Mo Shan and Shek Kong

From Tsuen Wan, it's possible to abandon the KCR West line and continue northwest to Yuen Long by road along the circuitous **Route Twisk**, via a high pass that is sometimes blocked partly by landslides during the typhoon season. (Twisk, incidentally, stands for "Tsuen Wan Into Shek Kong".) Bus #51 leaves every 20–30min from Tsuen Wan's Nina Tower bus terminal near the Tsuen Wan Ferry Pier, or from the bus stop on the flyover just north of the MTR station (see opposite for further details).

Tai Mo Shan and the MacLehose Trail

It's a splendid climb in the bus up the hillside above Tsuen Wan, with great views back to the sea. The road twists past bamboo groves and banana trees, while the occasional clearings off to the side harbour picnic sites perched on the edge of a hill. After 4–5km, just above the village of Tsuen Kam Au, the bus stops at an entrance to the **Tai Mo Shan Country Park**, which contains Hong Kong's highest peak, **Tai Mo Shan**, 957m above sea level. The climb is straightforward enough – a concrete track runs from Route Twisk to the peak – and can be combined with a night in the nearby **Sze Lok Yuen Youth Hostel** (see p.183 for details), which you reach by getting off the #51 at the junction with the smaller Tai Mo Shan Road – the hostel is signposted, around 45 minutes' walk up the road; turn right onto a small concrete track after passing the car park. You'll need to bring your own food. There's a visitors' centre near the bus stop with details of all the other local trails, including the walk to the magnificent series of waterfalls at **Ng Tung Chai**, in the north of the park.

At either the hostel or the peak, you're just off the **MacLehose Trail** (Stage 8), 22km from its western end at Tuen Mun (see p.151 for further details on the MacLehose Trail). If you fancy a short day's hike, join the trail here and walk west to Tin Fu Tsai (6km), from where you can drop down the 3–4km to the coast at Tsing Lung Tau for buses east or west along the coast. There's also a **campsite** in the Tai Mo Shan Country Park, by the management centre, over on the western side of Route Twisk.

Shek Kong and Kadoorie Farm & Botanical Gardens

The #51 bus climbs up over the pass and rattles down the winding road into the **Shek Kong** (pronounced "Sek" Kong) area, through richly forested slopes, offering sweeping views of the plain below and of the runway formerly used by the Shek Kong military garrison.

To the east of Shek Kong is the **Kadoorie Farm and Botanical Gardens** (Mon–Sat 9.30am–5pm, free). Founded by the Kadoorie family in the 1950s, the farm's original purpose was as an experimental breeding station. It now also serves as a sanctuary for abandoned and injured animals – endangered species such as owls, birds of prey and snakes saved by the police on their way to the cooking pot often end up here – so it's popular with children. To get there, take bus #64K from Tai Po KCR and get off on Lam Kam Road. They like you to call one or two days in advance on ⓣ2488 1317, or check their website at ⓦwww.kfbg.org.hk.

Kam Tin

The #51 bus ends its ride in **KAM TIN** – it's also on the KCR West line as **Kam Sheung Road KCR** – an area famous for its surviving **walled villages**. One of them at least is firmly on the tourist map, but there are a couple of others in the area displaying the same characteristic buildings and solid defensive walls.

Kat Hing Wai is the most obvious walled village, 200m down the main road from the bus stop – from the KCR station, take Exit B, cross the small footbridge, turn left and follow Kam Sheung Road to the intersection, turn right, and it's 100m. The square walls enclose a self-contained village, encircled by a moat, which has been inhabited for nearly four hundred years by members of the Tang clan, who once farmed the surrounding area. Their ancestors moved here from central and southern China almost eight hundred years ago, fortifying villages like these against pirate attacks and organizing their lives with little reference to the measures and edicts of far-off imperial China. As late as 1898, this village was one of those prepared to see action against the new British landlords, when local militias were raised to resist the handing over of the New Territories to Britain. As punishment the British confiscated the iron gates of the village – they were returned in 1925 after having been found in Ireland.

Today, the buildings are as defensively impressive as ever, with guardhouses on each corner, but otherwise Kat Hing Wai is rather sad, with lots of bad modern buildings and TV aerials. Most of it is now geared to tourists: the main street is lined with tacky souvenir stalls and Hakka women posing for photos in their "costume" (still normal dress in many parts of the New Territories). They'll want money if you try and take a photo, and it'll cost you a dollar to set foot through the gate in the first place.

More rewarding is **Shui Tau Tsuen**, a few hundred metres back down the main road (towards Tsuen Wan) on the right; at the Mung Yeung Public School, follow the lane down and over the bridge. The village is much bigger, though not as immediately promising. New building on the outskirts has destroyed the sense of a walled settlement, and many of the old buildings are locked or falling down; but the elegant carved roofs are still apparent, and a walk around the tight alleys reveals the local temple and an ancestral hall, and gives at least some impression of normal village life. The other village in the area is **Wing Lung Wai**, up the main road in the opposite direction, beyond Kat Hing Wai, though this is mostly fenced off and inaccessible to visitors. You can, however, get into the market here for the usual mix of noise and activity.

Practicalities

Kam Tin's main drag is traffic-choked Kam Tin Road, lined with hardware stores, grocers, restaurants, bars and even discos – slightly surprising in the middle of nowhere until you realize that this used to be the site of a big British military base. There are **cafés** all the way along serving noodles and the like. Scarcely any more formal, but providing a change, the *Shahjahn Restaurant*, opposite the bus stop and next to the post office, serves reasonably priced Nepalese and Indian food.

Moving on to Yuen Long and Tuen Mun, your best bet is the KCR West train; you can also catch **bus** #77K or minibus #18 to Yuen Long or Sheung Shui; bus #51 runs back to Tsuen Wan, while #64K passes the walled villages on its run between Tai Po KCR and Yuen Long.

Yuen Long

YUEN LONG is a built-up New Town with more than 120,000 residents, much the same as all the other New Towns and unrecognizable as the coastal fishing village it once was. The most interesting time to be here is for the big annual **Tin Hau Festival** celebrations, a throwback to the town's fishing days. The town is also renowned for the quality of its **moon cakes**, the small lotus-seed cakes with a preserved egg yolk that are eaten during the Mid-Autumn Festival – some of the best around are the Wing Wah moon cakes made by the *Tai Wing Wah Restaurant*, 11 Tai Lee St.

There are still visible relics of an older life in the surrounding countryside, however – small temples and ancestral homes scattered across the fragmented coastline. Unfortunately, they're difficult to reach and mostly run-down, though the government has preserved a series of buildings in nearby **Ping Shan**, including the thirteenth-century Tang's Ancestral Hall, the largest in Hong Kong, along with the territory's sole remaining historical pagoda, the green-bricked Tsui Shing Lau. If you're keen to see them, you can get a map and brochure of the two-kilometre **Ping Shan trail** from the Antiquities and Monuments Office (ⓦ www.lcsd.gov.hk/CE/Museum/Monument); the #53 bus from outside Yuen Long KCR Station runs past the start of the trail.

Practicalities

Around 2km across, Yuen Long is neatly split into east and west sections by the Shanpak canal. Yuen Long **KCR Station** is just east of the city; out the front (Exit F) is a major **bus and minibus** terminus – the #53 from Tsuen Wan ends up here, as does the #K65 to Lau Fau Shan – plus the **Light Rail** terminal (Exit B or E), part of the system that runs all over the area between here and Tuen Mun to the southwest, as well as up to Hong Kong International Wetland Park (see p.137) – take the green line #761.

Just north of the centre and actually bridging the canal, **Long Ping KCR Station** is an alternative access point, better placed to reach a second large bus station about 200m south in **On Tat Square** (take Exit C from the station), just off the main Castle Peak Road: from here you can catch bus #77K to Fanling, bus #76K to Mai Po Marshes, or the #64K to Tai Po Market KCR Station.

Lau Fau Shan

The main reason to visit Yuen Long is to take the bus out to nearby **LAU FAU SHAN**, an oyster-gathering and fishing village a few kilometres northwest. It's the most unusual of the places in Hong Kong in which to eat seafood: a ramshackle settlement built – literally – on old oyster shells. It's also the least visited of the seafood villages, so prices are realistic and a basic meal can be had without much fear of being ripped off. To **get there**, take the #K65 bus from the KCR station (see above).

The ride takes around twenty minutes, through some fairly drastic constructions necessary to protect the local villages from floodwater. The bus stop in Lau Fau Shan is right by the only street, Ching Tai Street, which leads down to the water past a succession of small restaurants, fishmongers' stalls and dried seafood provisions stores, many staffed by ladies in traditional Hakka dress. The oysters are turned into excellent oyster sauce, which is on sale everywhere. The main fish market is at the very end of the street. The dried foods – oysters, scallops, mussels and fish used to make soups – are interesting, but are something of a delicacy; a packet of dried scallops costs up to $500. Walk through the fish market to the main jetty, on either side of which, stretching away into the distance, are enormous dunes made out of piles of millions of old, opened oyster shells, among which are scattered fishing pots, wooden skiffs and wading birds looking for food. The village here looks out over Deep Bay and across to the skyscrapers of the Chinese mainland – a fine prospect.

There are plenty of **restaurants** in the village, all pretty reliable. Choose a fish and they'll bring it wriggling to your table for inspection before whisking it away to be cooked; the deep-fried oysters are also thoroughly recommended, a massive crispy plateful, easily enough for three, will cost about $100.

Southwest to Tuen Mun

Though the KCR West continues southwest to Tuen Mun, a couple of sights along the way make it worth opting for the Light Rail line from Yuen Long instead. Start off by catching the brown, dark blue, or red lines (#615, #610, or #614 respectively) to **Lam Tei** station; cross the road and the **Mui Fat Monastery** is just on your left. The only part of the monastery you can get into is the tall, square temple set back from the main road, a garish edifice whose entrance is guarded by two golden dragons, their bodies writhing up the building (pigeons nest in their manes), the usual pair of lions, and two six-tusked elephants. There are three floors inside, the top one overwhelming in its opulence, with three large golden Buddhas, massive crystal chandeliers, marble tablets, 10,000 little Buddha images lining the walls and a bell and a skin drum hanging at either side. On the middle floor is a decorated dining room that serves **vegetarian lunches** (noon–3.30pm; from $40 a dish). Outside in the grounds, you'll see a glass-roofed complex of buildings being built; this will house a worship hall, Buddhist library, office and various cultural facilities.

Ching Chung Koon Temple

Back on the #615 Light Rail line, it's another short ride to Ching Chung Station and adjacent **Ching Chung Koon Temple** (daily 7am–7pm), a large Taoist complex. You'll enter alongside an ornamental **garden**, built in traditional style, with imported Chinese rocks, a pool and pagodas. Beyond are various halls, gardens and shrines, built in 1949 and dedicated to Lu Sun Young, an eighth-century "immortal" blessed with magical and curative powers. The main temple is flanked by small pavilions housing bells and drums, used to signal prayer times. **Vegetarian lunches** (a set meal served for a minimum of two people) can be booked in the room to the left, while next door is the **ancestral hall**, unusually large and crammed full of photos and records of the dead. People pray here for their ancestors' souls, and occasionally you might catch a commemoration service, with chanting monks accompanied by drums, cymbals and flutes. The best time to see this is at either of the annual festivals that commemorate the dead: Ching Ming or Yue Lan (see pp.238 and 240 respectively).

Tuen Mun

Once you finally reach it, **TUEN MUN**, a large and straggling town of nearly half a million people, doesn't have immense appeal. The name of the town means "channel gate", a reminder that this was once an important defensive post, guarding the eastern approaches to the Pearl River estuary. These days it's a standard New Town, sporting the obligatory parkland, plus a shopping and commercial development – **Tuen Mun Town Plaza** – which at least makes an attempt at variation: there's a fake Georgian square around a fountain, planted inside the plaza.

The reality is that you're probably here to catch a connection out. The KCR West terminus and LR share the same **train station** in the centre of town, where you can catch the KCR back to Kowloon via Yuen Long and Tsuen Wan. Alternatively, **bus** #53 runs direct to Tsuen Wan along the coast; you can catch it by taking Exit B from the train station and following Pui To road to the bus stop on Castle Peak Road.

A final option is to ride a **ferry to Tung Chung** on Lantau Island (p.175); the pier is at the main **LR terminus** (lines #507, #610, #614, #615, #614P and #615P teminate here), about 2.5km south of the KCR station.

The East: Clearwater Bay and the Sai Kung Peninsula

To visit the eastern limb of the New Territories you'll need to set aside another couple of days: one for the popular beaches and magnificent Tin Hau Temple at **Clearwater Bay**; another to visit the beautiful **Sai Kung Peninsula**, with its fishing town, nearby islands, and tremendous outdoor appeal – definitely one of Hong Kong's highlights. Sai Kung is about the closest Hong Kong gets to real isolation, though on weekends and holidays even the large country parks here aren't big enough to absorb all the visitors. Happily, most people stick to two or three spots – those prepared to do some walking will be able to find a bit of space.

Access to both areas is by bus from **Diamond Hill MTR Station**, on the Kwun Tong line (all the buses leave from the main bus station underneath Hollywood Plaza).

To Clearwater Bay

Bus #91 (and #91R on Sun) from Diamond Hill MTR (also stopping outside Choi Hung MTR) runs east and then south along **Clearwater Bay Road**, a pleasant half-hour's ride through striking countryside, dotted with expensive villas with precarious views over the bays below. About ten minutes out of Choi Hung (ask the driver to stop at Tseng Lan Shue village), you can pick up the Wilson Trail, and follow it east and south past Junk Bay and round to Lam Tin, or west towards Lion Rock and Sha Tin. The trail is marked by yellow signs near the underpass just outside the village (see p.92 for more details).

Back on the road, about halfway between Diamond Hill and Clearwater Bay, you'll pass the **Shaw Brothers'** and **Clearwater Bay film studios**, where countless Cantonese movies are churned out every year, before dropping down to **Tai Au Mun**, which overlooks **Clearwater Bay** itself. There's a bus stop here, where you can get off for the first, smaller **beach** (known as #1 beach), though the bus does continue down the hill to stop at the terminus next to the much bigger #2 beach. You can count on this being packed on a sunny week-

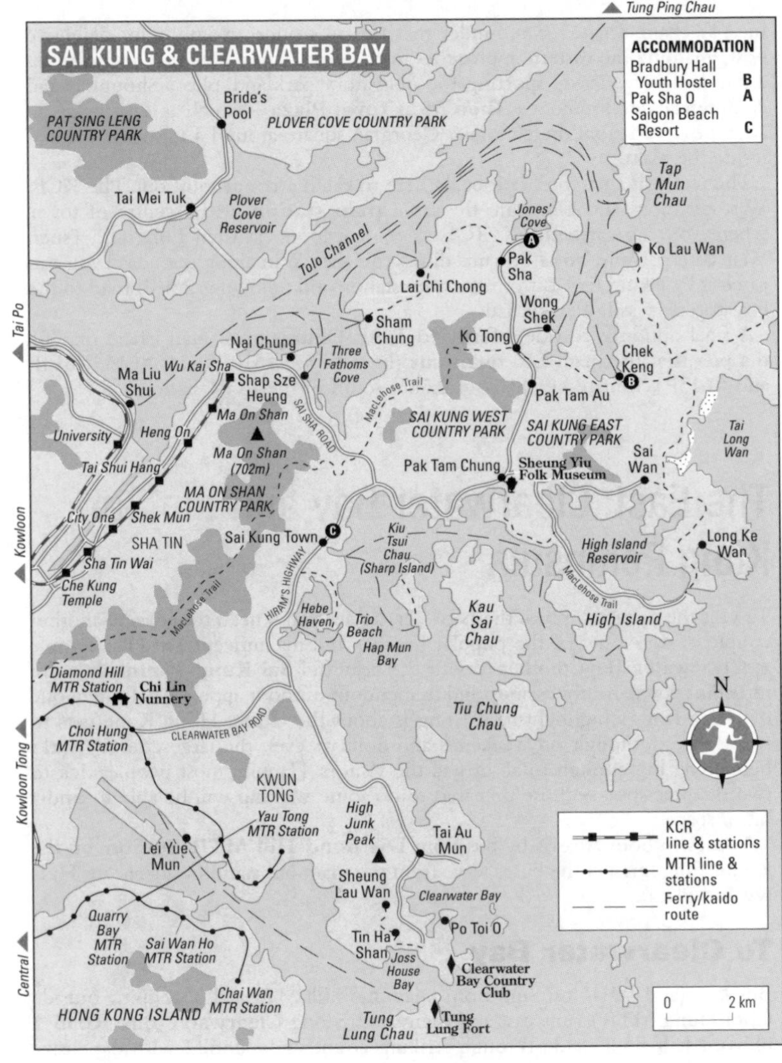

end, despite its size, and you should take your own food if you've come for the day, as there's only a snack kiosk here. A path connects the two beaches if you want to check on space at either one. Incidentally, minibus #103 departs from here back to Tseung Kwan O and/or Kwun Tong – both with MTR stations – every 9–15 minutes; make it clear to the driver where you're heading, as the drop-off points for these stations are not obvious.

Joss House Bay and back

From the bus terminus, you can follow the road for another 4.5km, though it's more fun to take the ridgetop **walking track** for part of the way – follow the road for about 700m, and you'll see a sign pointing the way. This follows the ridge to its 273-metre summit, taking in marvellous views of the sea, peninsula, Tung Lung Chau, and small craft, before descending back to the road at the peninsula's narrow neck. On one side of this neck is the tiny fishing and seafood village of **Po Toi O**, which is guarded by two temples, one on each side of the narrow bay in which the village is set. On the opposite side is a beautifully sited **Tin Hau Temple**, which faces out from its terrace over **Joss House Bay**. Founded in 1266, this is the major site of the annual Tin Hau celebrations in Hong Kong, and there's a long pier below the terrace where thousands of passengers disgorge from the special chartered junks and ferries to come to pay homage to the goddess of the sea. The temple entrance is guarded by two small stone lions with round stones in their mouths: turn the stones three times for luck. Inside are incense spirals, a drum, and stalls selling religious items. A small track leads to a nearby rock bearing a Song Dynasty inscription from 1274, recording a visit made by an officer in charge of salt administration – the oldest-known dated inscription in Hong Kong.

Across the peninsula's neck, the road circuits around the curved headland to the **Clearwater Bay Golf and Country Club**, though to use the tennis, swimming and golf facilities of this luxury resort, visitors must join HKTB's "Sports and Recreation Tour".

Tung Lung Chau

Lying just to the south of the peninsula, the small island of **TUNG LUNG CHAU** maintains a restored eighteenth-century Chinese fort on its northern shore. Overlooking the Fat Tong Mun passage, the **Tung Lung Fort** kept a strategic eye on ships sailing to Hong Kong, but was finally abandoned to the elements at the beginning of the nineteenth century. It remained overgrown until 1979, when its rectangular walls and interior were restored and opened to the public. There's also an **information centre** here (daily except Tues 9am–4pm). Tung Lung's other historic attraction is Hong Kong's largest **rock carving**, a representation of a dragon some two metres tall; take the path from the fort and head back past the ferry pier – around 1.5km in all.

Despite the island's proximity to the Clearwater Bay peninsula, it is reached by a thirty-minute **ferry journey from Sai Wan Ho**, on the Island MTR line on Hong Kong Island (Sat & Sun only; $28). Only two or three ferries make the journey a day, with the first one leaving at 9am and the last returning at 5.30pm; they dock roughly halfway between the fort and the rock carving. Alternatively, several ferries a day leave from the **Sam Ka Tsuen ferry pier,** near the seafood restaurants of Lei Yue Mun in Kowloon, reached by bus #14C or taxi from Kwun Tong MTR (Sat & Sun only; $25); the first one leaves at 9pm, and the last one returns at 4.30pm.

Sai Kung Town and its beaches

North of Clearwater Bay, beaches and coves spread over a large area, incorporating a series of island retreats, good walking trails and even a folk museum. The whole area is known as **Sai Kung**, and is divided into two main **country parks**, with several approaches and various little centres. The main centre is the rapidly developing resort of **SAI KUNG TOWN**. Bus #92 from Diamond Hill MTR or Choi Hung MTR (6am–11pm, every 10min; $5.90) and maxicab #1A from Choi Hung MTR both take around half an hour or more, following Clearwater Bay Road before heading north along Hiram's Highway, passing the boating resort of Hebe Haven on the way. Alternatively, take bus #299 (6am–

▲ Sai Kung Town harbour

midnight, every 15min; $9) from New Town Plaza in Sha Tin.

The Town

Sai Kung Town is a pleasant blend of local fishing port and low-key tourist retreat. The bus and maxicab terminal is just back from the sea (minibuses stop further back, next to the sports centre), with a large part of the adjacent seafront promenade devoted to fish and seafood **restaurants**, most of which have outside seating overlooking the bay. A walk down the seafront takes you to the daily **fish market** (6–11am) in the older part of town, overlooking the junks tied up in the harbour. Alternatively, you can wait to bargain when the fishing boats pull in around 2pm and start offering their catches to customers on the waterfront from nets at the end of four-metre-long poles. *Tung Kee Seafood*, at the end of the quayside closest to the bus terminal, will cook your purchase for you, or try their speciality "bamboo fish": carp, stuffed with preserved turnip and grilled over charcoal outside on a hand-rotated bamboo pole – either way, count on around $150 a head.

There's a fairly strong expat presence in town, so if you wander through the few streets back from the quay you'll also come across a few **pubs**, such as *Steamers Bar*, at A2–3 Chan Man St, and the *Duke of York*, at 42–56 Fuk Man Rd, as well as a bakery, Ali Oli, at 11 Sha Tsui Path, selling scrumptious cheesecakes, bread rolls and steak and onion pie – a good place to get a picnic if you're thinking of heading out to one of the beaches or the country park. **Canoes**, **sailing boats**, **windsurf boards** and **dinghies** can all be rented at the sports centre next to Sai Kung's only **hotel**, the *Saigon Beach Resort* (see p.192), a ten-minute walk north of the town towards Ma On Shan.

Nearby islands and beaches

Along the Sai Kung Town quayside you'll be accosted by people selling tickets for *kaidos*, which run across to **islands and beaches** in the vicinity. It's sometimes a bit tricky to work out exactly where the boats are going, as there are no signs and few people speak English, but if you don't really mind and just want to hit a beach, take off with the first that offers itself – they leave and return at regular intervals all day, so you shouldn't get stuck anywhere you don't want to.

The most popular trip is the short run across to **Kiu Tsui Chau** (or Sharp Island), whose main beach at Hap Mun Bay, where the *kaidos* dock, is fine, though it's small and can get mobbed at the weekends. There are barbecue pits and a snack bar, and a rough trail leads up through thick vegetation to the island's highest point. Most of the rocky coast is inaccessible, though *kaidos* also run from Sai Kung Town to Kiu Tsui, a small bay to the north of the island. Be warned that getting back to Sai Kung Town from Hap Mun Bay can be a bit of a scrum: you have to leave on a boat with the same coloured flag as the one that you came on, and, as there's no such thing as a queue in Hong Kong, it can be a fight to get on the boat.

Other *kaidos* and ferries run from Sai Kung Town on the longer route to **High Island**, now actually part of the mainland peninsula since dams linked it to form the High Island Reservoir. *Kaidos* also run from the yachting centre of **HEBE HAVEN** (Pak Sha Wan) across to a peninsular beach, called **Trio Beach**, south of Sai Kung Town: the bus to Sai Kung passes Hebe Haven first, or you can always walk the 2–3km from Sai Kung to the beach. Ferries to Hong Kong's only public **golf course** on Kau Sai Chau depart from the pier just past the bus station every twenty minutes ($45 return).

The Sai Kung Peninsula

It takes a little more effort to get the best out of the rest of the **Sai Kung Peninsula**, which stretches all the way north to the Tolo Channel and encompasses some supremely isolated headlands and coves. The whole region is one giant, 7500-hectare **country park**, split into two sections, **Sai Kung East** and **Sai Kung West**, along with neighbouring **Ma On Shan Country Park**, which reaches down to Sha Tin. There have been settlements here since the fourteenth century, mostly fishing villages, though the area was never widely populated: even thirty years ago most places in Sai Kung could be reached only on foot. Despite increasing popularity, Sai Kung has still not been spoiled, neither by crass tourist developments nor the post-SARS surge in weekend-trippers after a breath of unpolluted country air. Following the marked paths through the grasslands and planted forests is very relaxing after a spell in the city: there's plenty of birdlife, some spectacular coastal geological formations due to the peninsula's volcanic history, and lots of quiet places just to plonk yourself down and tear into a picnic. If you're doing any serious walks, you'll find the *Countryside Series Sheet 4 (Sai Kung and Clearwater Bay)* and the *Pak Tam Chung Nature Trail* **maps**, both available from the Government Bookshop (p.247), useful. Recommended **tour operators** include NEI (ⓣ2486 2112, ⓦwww.kayak-and-hike.com) for hiking and **kayaking** around the coastline; Asiatic Marine (ⓦwww.asiaticmarine.com) for **scuba diving**, "seafaris", and kite-boarding; and **hiking** specialists Explore Sai Kung (ⓣ2243 1083, ⓔjudy@accomasia.com).

The best place to start is Sai Kung Town, from where regular buses run to many of the places covered in this section. The **MacLehose Trail** runs right across the peninsula, while you can see most of the more isolated northern coast from the **ferry** that departs twice daily from Ma Liu Shui for Tap Mun Chau (see p.153).

Pak Tam Chung

Pak Tam Chung in Sai Kung Country Park can be reached from Sai Kung Town on bus #94, marked Wong Shek Pier (6am–9pm, hourly; $4.20); or from Diamond Hill on bus #96R (Sun and public holidays only, 7.30am–6.20pm, every 20min; $12.10). Pak Tam Chung marks the start of the MacLehose Trail, although there's nothing much here apart from a bus terminal, a **visitors' centre** where you can pick up local hiking and transport information (daily except Tues 9.30am–4.30pm; ⓣ2792 7365) and the nearby **Sheung Yiu Folk Museum** (daily except Tues 9am–4pm; free). The museum is a thirty-minute walk from the bus terminal along the seashore down the **Pak Tam Chung Nature Trail**, a pleasantly shady and signposted route that includes woodland laid out according to the principles of *feng shui*. It's based around an abandoned village, Sheung Yiu, founded 150 years ago by a Hakka family who made their living from the produce of a local lime kiln. The kiln itself is on the outskirts of the village, on the path as you approach; the lime from it was used for local agriculture and building purposes. Further on, the village is a line of whitewashed houses built on a high terrace overlooking the water and defended by a thick wall and gate tower, which kept off the pirates who roamed the area in the nineteenth century. The tile-roofed houses, including an equipped kitchen house, have been restored and filled with farming implements, typical Hakka clothes and diagrams showing how the kiln worked.

The MacLehose Trailhead: High Island Reservoir and Tai Long Wan

Keep on the Pak Tam Road from Pak Tam Chung, past the turn-off for the museum, and the **trailhead** for the eastern end of the cross-New Territories **MacLehose Trail** is just a few minutes' walk ahead. The first two stages of this hundred-kilometre route run off to the south from here, through the Sai Kung East Country Park, a twenty-kilometre hike around **High Island Reservoir** and then north to Ko Tong, on Pak Tam Road, from where you can continue the trail or cut back to Pak Tam Chung. This part of the trail takes the best part of a day to complete, but there are no fewer than seven **campsites** along the way, one of which, at Long Ke Wan on the southeastern edge of the reservoir, has a fine beach. Less committed hikers could shorten the route by just walking around the reservoir and back to the trailhead down Sai Wan Road, which branches off the trail about three-quarters of the way round (at Sai Wan), heading directly back to Pak Tam Chung.

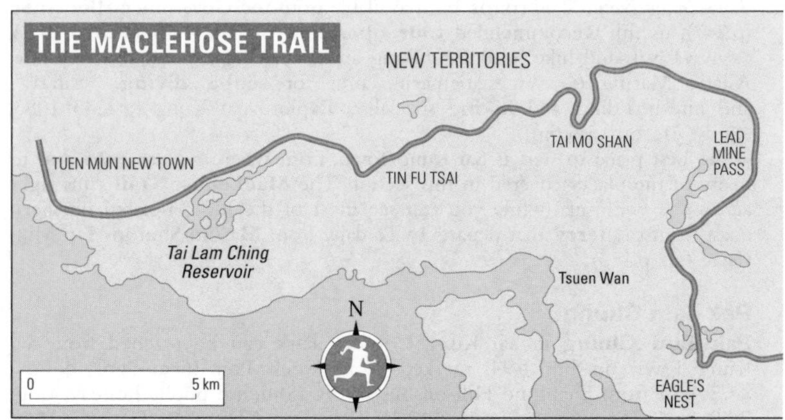

The MacLehose Trail

The **MacLehose Trail** (named after a former governor) is a hundred-kilometre-long hiking route that stretches from Pak Tam Chung on the Sai Kung Peninsula to the new town of Tuen Mun (see map below). It links seven different country parks and is divided into ten different signposted stages, each of which connects with public transport and some of which are provided with campsites, so that you can make a day's hike or complete the whole trail, as you wish. There's one official IYHF youth hostel right on the trail at Tai Mo Shan, as well as a couple close to the trail at Wong Shek. You could do the whole trail in four or five days, but most people take it slower, particularly if they're attempting it in the summer, when the going is hot; the easternmost sections are the most attractive. An annual charity race sets teams a 48-hour target for the course; the winners usually manage it in well under 24, while the record (set by Gurkha troops) is just 13.

Information on the trail, including 1:20,000 route **maps**, is available from the Government Bookshop (see p.247). Alternatively, pick up the *Hiker's Guide to Hong Kong* from bookshops, which gives a stage-by-stage breakdown of the trail, including a grading system of the difficulty of each section.

If you're looking for a beach at the end of a walk, then a path just beyond Sai Wan leads north to the bay of **Tai Long Wan** (Big Wave Bay) – a much better target from Pak Tam Chung if you're not interested in completing any part of the MacLehose Trail for its own sake. It'll still take three to four hours for the round trip (around 12km by concrete path), but the beach of unspoiled white sand, one of the finest in the territory, is very definitely worth it. The small village of Ham Tin, next to Tai Long Wan beach, has a couple of outdoor restaurants serving basic food and drinks, though they're usually only open at the weekend.

Wong Shek, Chek Keng and Jones' Cove

Bus #94 (also #96R on Sun and public holidays from Diamond Hill MTR) continues on across the neck of Sai Kung East Country Park to **WONG**

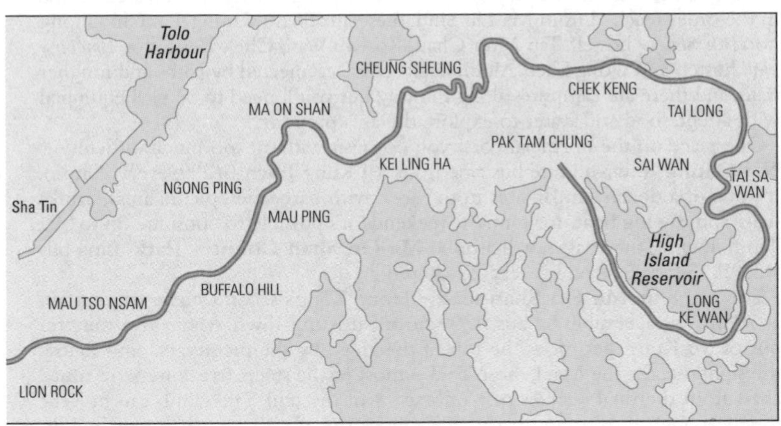

SHEK – little more than a pier and a few barbecue pits really, and only worth coming out to if you're going to be staying at one of the nearby youth hostels or catching the *kaido* north to the island of **Tap Mun Chau** (see opposite).

Two of Hong Kong's more remote **youth hostels**, both with over a hundred beds, are in the Wong Shek area (for booking details, see "Accommodation", p.184). The most popular, *Bradbury Hall* (not to be confused with *Bradbury Lodge*) is near **CHEK KENG**, the next village and bay to the east. You can either reach it directly on the ferry from Ma Liu Shui (see below); or by getting off the bus at the top of the pass, at Pak Tam Au, before you reach Wong Shek, and following the signposted path down to Chek Keng – a 45-minute walk. The hostel is right next to the sea (which, for once, is clean enough to swim in), and there's space for **camping**, too; you can get cold drinks and basic **meals** in the village.

The other hostel, *Pak Sha O*, is at **JONES' COVE**, to the north – **Hoi Ha Wan** on some maps. Again, you could come by ferry from Ma Liu Shui, getting off at either Lai Chi Chong or Wong Shek and following the signs; around an hour's walk. But it's easier to take the #94 bus, getting off just before Wong Shek at Ko Tong. Take Hoi Ha Road, on the left, and it's around a thirty-minute walk to the hostel – though taxis are available if you hang around, and on Sundays and public holidays there's a maxicab service. Hoi Ha **beach** is around another fifteen minutes' walk from the hostel, and again, you can get simple food and cold drinks in the village.

The Northern Coast and the Tolo Channel

The most remote section of the Sai Kung peninsula is its **northern coast**, though you can easily see it by taking the **ferry from Ma Liu Shui** to Tap Mun Chau island (see opposite). The pier is a signposted ten-minute walk from the University KCR Station; current departures are at 8.30am and 3pm, with an extra departure at 10.35am on Saturday and Sunday (Mon–Fri $16; Sat & Sun $25). The return service leaves Tap Mun Chau daily at around 4.30pm, with additional departures at 10.15am (Mon–Fri) and 1.45pm (Sat & Sun).

Ma Liu Shui lies at one end of the **Tolo Channel**, which divides the New Territories' two most rural areas: Plover Cove and Sai Kung. The 75-minute **ferry** ride makes for a fine half-day trip if all you're going to do is stay on board and soak up the views: the early morning departure runs up the channel for Tap Mun Chau calling on the way at isolated bays along Sai Kung's northern coast. In the order reached from Ma Liu Shui, these are: Sham Chung, Lai Chi Chong (for *Pak Sha O* hostel), Tap Mun Chau, Ko Lau Wan, Chek Keng (for *Bradbury Hall* hostel) and Wong Shek. All these places are connected by paths and rougher trails, and there are campsites along the way, but you'll need to be well equipped with a tent, food and water to explore the area properly.

One place on the northern coast you can visit without too much difficulty is **Nai Chung**, a ten-minute bus ride from Sai Kung Town (#299; every 20min). It's one of a dozen similar sites in the area, with barbecues, picnic areas, drinks stalls, and rowing boats for rent. At weekends, it's possible to continue on to Sha Tin following the coast north around **Ma On Shan Country Park** using bus #289R (Sat & Sun only; every 20–30min).

The climb up **Ma On Shan** itself – Hong Kong's second highest mountain at 702m – is accessible by bus #299 from Sai Kung Town. About five minutes out of Sai Kung, get off at the top of the ridge by the picnic area and follow the signposts for the MacLehose Trail – most of the steep, five-kilometre route, apart from the final peak, is part of Stage 4 of the trail. The climb can be very tough, though the extraordinary views make the effort more than worthwhile. You'll need decent footwear and plenty of water.

Tap Mun Chau

Right up in the northeast of the territory at the mouth of the Tolo Channel, **TAP MUN CHAU** island, although awkward to reach, is becoming an increasingly popular destination. There's not much to see: the relative isolation is the main draw.

The quickest way to **get here** is by *kaido* from Wong Shek – a twenty-minute crossing. There are currently seven services daily on weekdays and twelve at the weekend (Mon–Fri first boat leaves at 7.45am, last at 6pm; Sat & Sun, first at 8am, last at 6.05pm), but check with the HKTB first. The alternative approach is by ferry from Ma Liu Shui Ferry Pier (see opposite for details). Perhaps the best option is to cross from Wong Shek by *kaido* and pick up the return ferry to Ma Liu Shui.

Both ferry and *kaido* dock in a sheltered inlet on the island's west side that contains the only **village** – a single line of crumbling houses and small shops overlooking the fish farms that constitute the only industry. It's a run-down, ramshackle kind of place, nice and quiet, with the houses on the only street open to the pavement. There's a Tin Hau temple along here, too (to the left of the pier), the venue for a large annual festival, while to the right of the pier a fishermen's quarter straddles the low hill – nets and tackle stacked and stored in the huts and houses, many built on stilts over the water.

A couple of paths spread across the island, which is surprisingly green, leading to its English name of "Grass Island". After you've ambled around, the only thing to do is to head back to the main street and its one good **restaurant**, the *New Hon Kee*; left from the ferry pier, and it's on the first corner. There's no English sign, but there is an English menu, which offers reasonable seafood, fried rice and beer in a room overlooking the water.

Don't miss the last ferry whatever you do – be at the pier in plenty of time. There's no accommodation on Tap Mun Chau, and even the restaurant owners don't live on the island but back in the New Territories.

Places	
Bride's Pool	新娘潭
Clearwater Bay	清水灣
Fanling	粉嶺
Fo Tan	火炭
Joss House Bay	大廟灣
Kam Tin	錦田
Kiu Tsui Chau	橋咀洲
Lam Tei	籃地
Lau Fau Shan	流浮山
MacLehose Trail	麥理浩徑
Mai Po Marshes	米埔濕地
New Territories	新界
Pak Tam Chung	北潭涌
Ping Shan Heritage Trail	屏山文博徑
Plover Cove Country Park	船灣郊野公園
Sai Kung	西貢
Sham Tseng	深井
Shatin	沙田
Sheung Shui	上水
Starling Inlet	沙頭角海
Tai Long Wan	大浪灣

Tai Mei Tuk	大尾督
Tai Mo Shan Country Park	大帽山郊野公園
Tai Po	大埔
Tai Po Market	大埔墟
Tai Wai	大圍
Tap Mun Chau	塔門洲
Tsuen Wan	荃灣
Tuen Mun	屯門
Tung Lung Chau	東龍洲
Tung Ping Chau	東坪洲
Wilson Trail	衛奕信徑
Wong Shek	黃石
Yuen Long	元朗
Sights	
Che Kung Temple	車公廟
Chinese University	香港中文大學
Ching Chung Koon Temple	青松觀
Clearwater Bay Country Club	清水灣鄉村俱樂部
Fung Ying Seen Koon	蓬瀛仙館
Hong Kong Heritage Museum	香港文花博物館
Hong Kong Railway Museum	香港鐵路博物館
Kadoorie Farm and Botanical Gardens	嘉道理農場
Kat Hing Wai Walled Village	吉慶圍圍村
Liu Man Shek Tong Ancestral Hall	廖萬石堂
Luen Wo Market	聯和墟圍村
Mui Fat Monastery	妙法寺
New Town Plaza	新城市廣場商場
Po Fook Ancestral Worship Halls	寶福社堂
Sam Tung Uk Museum	荃灣三棟屋博物館
Shatin Racecourse	沙田跑馬場
Shui Tau Tsuen walled village	水頭村圍村
Ten Thousand Buddhas Monastery	萬佛寺
Tsang Tai Uk walled village	曾大屋圍村
Yuen Yuen Institute	圓玄學院
Transport	
Ma Liu Shui Ferry Pier	馬料水渡輪碼頭
KCR station	九廣鐵路車站
LR station	輕便鐵路車站

The outlying islands

Hong Kong Island is only one of 260-odd other islands scattered in the South China Sea that, together with the Kowloon peninsula and New Territories, make up the Hong Kong Special Administrative Region. The vast majority of these **outlying islands** are tiny, barren and uninhabited; others are restricted areas, used as detention centres or for rehabilitating drug addicts. The few you are able to visit form some of the SAR's less cluttered reaches, and the southwestern trio of **Lamma**, **Cheung Chau** and **Lantau** are popular with locals and tourists alike: Lantau is actually much bigger than Hong Kong Island, and staying there overnight is an attractive possibility.

None of the islands is exactly uncharted territory. Several were already inhabited by the Chinese long before Hong Kong became British territory, and the easily accessible ones have become increasingly developed over the years; even so, many places can still feel relatively deserted.

One major draw is the **beaches** – not a bad idea given the crowded state of the sands on Hong Kong Island, although they may well be packed if you go at the weekend or on a public holiday. Pollution, however, means that swimming is often not an option – the local papers print water-quality ratings for the main venues every week – but there are other reasons to visit. Lantau is a popular spot for **hiking**, and its cross-island trail, old villages and monasteries make it easily the most interesting island to head for. Lamma and Cheung Chau are noted for their **seafood restaurants** and food stalls; while the quieter and less visited islands – including Peng Chau – still offer a slice of the traditional Chinese life that was once lived all over the region. And if nothing else, the islands make excellent escapes when the pace of the city palls: there are **hotels** on Lantau, Lamma and Cheung Chau, and a couple of **hostels** on Lantau – see "Accommodation" (p.192–193 and p.183) for details.

There's a good **map** of the southwestern islands – Lantau, Cheung Chau, Peng Chau and Lamma – in the Countryside Series (available from the Government Bookshop; see p.247). The HKTB dishes out printed **ferry and hydrofoil timetables** for all the major routes, which are well worth picking up, since the times given below are all subject to change.

Getting there

Regular **ferries** run from Hong Kong Island to Lamma, Cheung Chau, Peng Chau and Lantau, while faster (and more expensive) **hydrofoils** run to Mui Wo (Silvermine Bay) and Discovery Bay, both on Lantau, Cheung Chau and Peng Chau. Most services depart from the **Outlying Islands Ferry Piers** on Hong Kong Island, just west of the Star Ferry Pier. There are exceptions, though, so

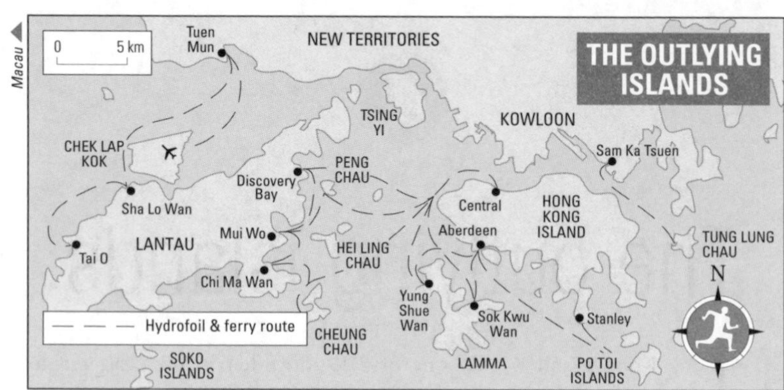

check "Travel details" at the end of each island account for specific information. Access to a couple of places is by **kaido**, a small ferry or licensed, motorized sampan. Some **inter-island connections** are also made by *kaido*; these are less frequent than the ferries and though there are timetables on some of the routes, you'll often just have to ask around. If you don't mind splashing out, arranging a **charter boat** is easy enough: enquire at ferry piers on the islands, look in the classified sections of the newspapers or *HK Magazine*, or ring the HKTB (☎2508 1234). For organized **tours** of the islands by boat, see p.41.

The islands covered in this chapter are the main ones in the southwest of the territory, to which there are regular ferries from Central and Kowloon. However, other *minor islands*, accessible from various points on Hong Kong Island and in the New Territories, are covered elsewhere: Ap Lei Chau p.88; Tung Ping Chau p.130; Po Toi islands p.147; Tap Mun Chau p.153; and Tung Lung Chau p.147.

Using the ferries

You can't reserve seats on the ferries: it's first come, first served, so get there early at busy times. **Tickets** to all main destinations start at $11 one-way for a normal ferry, and $22 for a fast ferry. Children under 12 pay half-price at all times. All return tickets are double the price of a single. If you can, especially at the weekend, buy a return ticket on all services so you won't have to queue on the way back; most services also accept the Octopus card (see p.36). The *Island-Hopping Pass* ($30) offered by First Ferries, who run the services to Lantau, Peng Chau, and Cheung Chau islands, is a waste of money as you'd never get around all these places in the single day allowed by the pass, and see nothing if you tried to do so.

None of the journeys is very long – around an hour maximum on all the main routes – and if you can't get a seat, you can always lounge on deck; coming back into Hong Kong, especially, the views are fabulous. Some of the ferries also have a small **bar** selling coffee, sandwiches, hot noodles, cold drinks and beer. On a public *kaido* (not chartered), you generally pay the fare to the person operating the boat. It will usually only be around $5–10, though foreigners can expect to pay more than the locals on some routes, and you may have to bargain. Sometimes, when there's no regular service, you'll need to charter the whole boat – the text tells you when it's necessary and roughly how much it will cost; again, expect to haggle.

When to go

Services to all the main islands are busier (and, in some cases, more frequent) on **Sunday**, with enormous queues at the piers. If you're planning to stay **overnight** on any of the islands, be prepared to pay double or more at the weekend, and book well in advance. **Midweek** is much quieter, and some places can seem positively secluded. Note that major disruption to the timetables can occur during the **typhoon season** (June–Oct), when ferry services can be abandoned at very short notice – contact the ferry companies direct using the details at the end of each island account.

Lamma

The closest inhabited island to Hong Kong – Aberdeen is only around 3km from its northern point – **LAMMA** is an elongated fourteen square kilometres of land inhabited by some 5000 people, including a now-dwindling expat population seeking a more mellow existence than that offered by city life. Motorized traffic is limited to four-wheel bikes carting trailers, and the only downsides are an unsightly power station and limited quarrying operations. Well-marked paths link the main settlement, *Yung Shue Wan*, with small beaches,

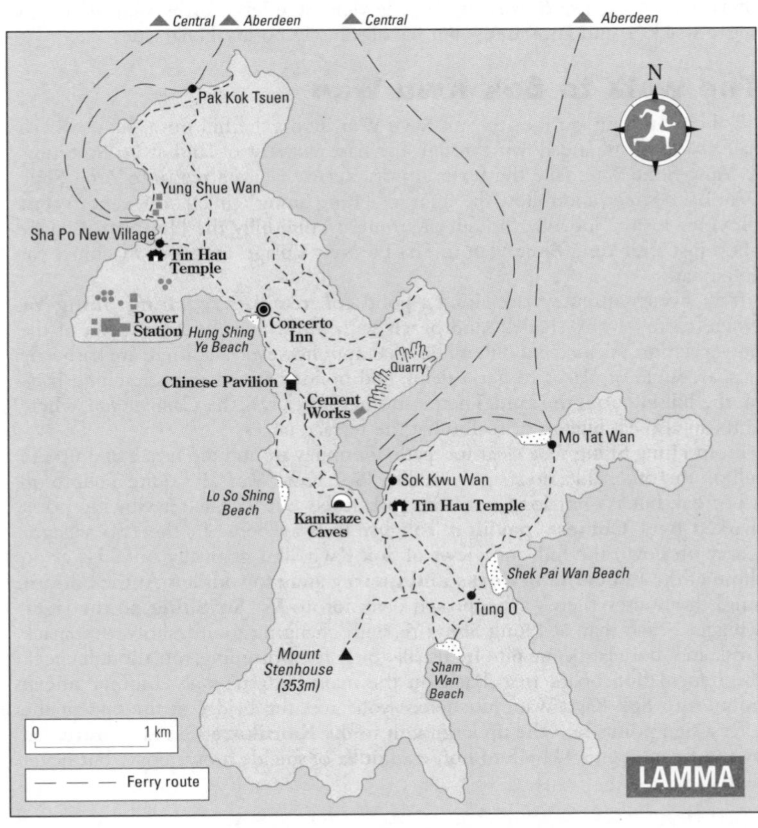

green hilltops, and pleasant seascapes, and you can round off an easy couple of hours' walking with a meal at the tiny village of *Sok Kwu Wan*, famed for its seafood restaurants. Both Yung Shue Wan and Sok Kwu Wan are connected to Hong Kong Island by regular ferries, so whichever one you arrive at there's no need to retrace your steps.

Yung Shue Wan

YUNG SHUE WAN ("Banyan Bay") is a pretty, tree-shaded village at the northwestern end of the island where the bulk of Lamma's residents live, with a few hotels, small grocery stores, a **bank** with an ATM (though there's often no cash available after Saturday afternoon), a **post office**, and eating places catering for both Chinese and Western palates. The seafront esplanade is **Yung Shue Wan Main Street**, at the end of which a typically gloomy, century-old **Tin Hau temple** overlooks the water.

If you've come to Lamma for a walk, there's nothing much to stop you heading off straight away, though there are several **places to stay** (see p.192). Current pick of several **seafood restaurants** are waterfront tables at *Lamma Seaview Man Fung Restaurant* (☎2982 0719) and *Sampan Seafood*, both near the pier and offering fresh crab, abalone, and fish from live tanks, plus a long list of budget rice or noodle combination dishes, which will set you up nicely for an afternoon's walk. *The Bookworm Café*, 79 Main St, offers worthy vegetarian and vegan snacks – and **Internet** – but has absolutely no local character.

The walk to Sok Kwu Wan

It's about an hour on foot to Sok Kwu Wan, across the hill from the northern half of the island and down through the narrow waist of land at Lo So Shing. In Yung Shue Wan, take the turning just after 64 Main Street into Yung Shue Wan Back Street, and follow the signs to "Hung Shing Yeh". If you want to **rent bicycles** for the journey, though the route is quite hilly, the Hoi Nam Bicycle Shop just after Yung Shue Wan in Sha Po New Village, rents out machines for $50 a day.

It's a twenty-minute walk along a good concrete path to **Hung Shing Ye**, where there's a tiny, shaded sand beach with unfortunately close views of the power station. It's nice enough when it's empty, however, and there are barbecue pits, a couple of places to get a drink and holiday apartments stretching back up the hillside from the sand. There's another hotel, too, the *Concerto Inn*, where you can also eat pigeon or seafood at the terrace tables.

From Hung Shing Ye, a clear footpath continues around the beach and up the hill on the other side, now signposted to "Sok Kwu Wan". It's quite a climb on a hot day, but it's not long until the path levels out to reach a viewing point marked by a **Chinese pavilion**, roughly halfway between the two villages. Carry on down the hill, and views of Sok Kwu Wan gradually unfold – as do those of the vast **cement works and quarry** away to your left. At the bottom, amid the houses, there's a signposted diversion to **Lo So Shing**, to the right, a bigger beach than at Hung Shing Ye, with changing rooms, showers, a snack kiosk and more barbecue pits. It's usually okay for swimming, too, though check the information board first. Back on the main path, it's only another fifteen minutes to Sok Kwu Wan. Just before you cross the bridge at the end of the inlet a sign points into the undergrowth to the **Kamikaze Caves**, constructed by the Japanese in 1944–45 to house a flotilla of suicide motor boats, but never used.

Sok Kwu Wan

The bay at **SOK KWU WAN** is devoted to fish farming. Floating wooden frames cover the water, interspersed with rowing boats, junks and the canvas shelters of the fishermen and women. A concrete path runs the 100m through the village, from the obligatory Tin Hau temple to the main pier, along which Sok Kwu Wan's **seafood restaurants** form a line. They're the only real reason to come here, though what was once a low-key array of simple eating houses has turned into a range of more polished restaurants, with outdoor tables overlooking the bay, and large fish tanks set back on the street. Some restaurants have special set-menus in English posted on the walls, but always ask the price first, certainly if you're choosing your fish straight from the tank. As there's not much between them in terms of appearance and service, the easiest way to pick a restaurant is to look for the busiest. A couple of the more entrepreneurial establishments, *Rainbow Seafood* (Ⓣ2982 8100) and *Winstar Seafood* (Ⓣ2982 8338) have set up a free ferry service between Sok Kwu Wan and Central/ Aberdeen for customers; phone to check first.

There are a few fairly basic **holiday apartments** in the village: ask at the *Peach Garden Seafood Restaurant* (Ⓣ2982 8581) halfway along the main street, for details.

Mo Tat Wan and Mount Stenhouse

If you arrive early enough, there are a couple of other targets around Sok Kwu Wan to occupy the time before dinner. It's a 25-minute walk (left as you step off the ferry pier) to **MO TAT WAN**, another small beach village, usually quieter than the others on the island. It's one of the oldest settlements in Hong Kong, here in some shape or form for over three hundred years. The *kaido* service to Aberdeen from Sok Kwu Wan calls in regularly every day; there's a timetable posted at Sok Kwu Wan Pier.

Lamma travel details

Ferries and fast ferries

From **Central**, you can reach Yung Shue Wan in 35min by ordinary ferry and 20min by fast, while it takes 25min (fast ferry only) to Sok Kwu Wan. From **Aberdeen**, it's 25min to Yung Shue Wan via Pak Kok Tsuen (fast ferry only).

Outlying Islands Ferry Piers to: Yung Shue Wan (Mon–Sat 31 daily, every 20–30min, first at 6.30am, last at 12.30am; Sun 28 daily, first at 7.30am, last at 12.30am); Sok Kwu Wan (Mon–Sat 11 daily, Sun 16 daily; first at 7.20am, last at 11.30pm).

Aberdeen to: Yung Shue Wan and Pak Kok Tsuen (Mon–Sat 9 daily, first at 6.30am, last at 7pm; Sun every 30min, first at 7.30am, last at 7.30pm); Mo Tat Wan then on to Sok Kwu Wan (Mon–Sat 12 daily, first at 6.50am, last at 10.40pm; Sun every 45min, first at 7.30am, last at 7.50pm).

Yung Shue Wan to: Outlying Islands Ferry Piers (Mon–Sat 29 daily, first at 6.20am, last at 11.30am; Sun 27 daily, first at 6.40am, last at 11.30pm); Aberdeen (Mon–Sat 11 daily, first at 6.30am, last at 8.15pm; Sun 15 daily, first at 6am, last at 8.45pm).

Sok Kwu Wan to: Outlying Islands Ferry Piers (Mon–Sat 11 daily, Sun 16 daily; first at 6.45am, last at 10.40pm); Mo Tat Wan and then on to Aberdeen (Mon–Sat 12 daily, first at 6.05am, last at 10.05pm; Sun every 45min, first at 6.15am, last at 10.05pm).

For up-to-date ferry information, contact Hong Kong and Kowloon Ferry Ltd (Ⓣ2815 6063, Ⓦwww.hkkf.com.hk) and for Sok Kwu Wan–Aberdeen services, Chuen Kee Ferry Ltd (Ⓣ2525 1108).

A path from Mo Tat Wan leads the kilometre or so to the bigger beach of **Shek Pai Wan** on the southeastern coast, from where you can continue – past Tung O – to the smaller **Sham Wan** beach, perhaps the remotest on the island, and worth heading to if only for that reason.

Cast around a bit, either in Sok Kwu Wan or at Shek Pai Wan and Sham Wan, and it's not difficult to find one of the paths that lead eventually to the summit of **Mount Stenhouse** (also known as Shan Tei Tong), 353m up in the middle of the island's southwestern bulge. It's quite a climb, particularly since the paths aren't wonderful, but you'll be rewarded with some fine views. It should take around two hours from Sok Kwu Wan to climb up and down again; take plenty of water.

Cheung Chau

A fifty-minute ferry-ride southwest of the city, **CHEUNG CHAU** is the most densely populated of the outlying islands: 23,000 people live here, the central waist of its dumb-bell shape is crammed with buildings, and its harbour and typhoon shelter are busy day and night. The island is one of the oldest settled parts of Hong Kong (relics dug up here have been dated back to the Bronze Age), with a prosperity based on fishing, supplemented in the past with smuggling and piracy. There's a life here that's independent of the fortunes of Hong Kong, manifest in a surviving junk shipyard, many working temples and one of Hong Kong's best annual festivals.

Concrete **paths** cover the entire island and, despite the name (meaning "long island" in Cantonese), you can whip around the place fairly quickly. Like Lamma, no cars are allowed, though you'll have to listen out for the buzz of the motorized scooter-like work vehicles as you walk along – the paths aren't really wide enough for you both. Much of the relatively undeveloped parts of the island are taken up by youth camps, and the two or three fine beaches are regularly crowded. But for all that, traditional life thrives in the main village, with its fishing boats and stalls; there are some excellent views as you go; and – as ever – sampling Cheung Chau's seafood is a good reason to visit.

▲ Cheung Chau Village's waterfront

Cheung Chau Village

The ferry from Central picks its way through the breakwaters and junks to dock at **CHEUNG CHAU VILLAGE**, where the island's population and activity is concentrated. The waterfront road, or **Praya** (the full name is Pak She Praya Road) is the setting for a decent-sized daily **market**, where fishermen, fruit-and-veg sellers and cultivated pearl traders rub elbows (you can even get pearls taken straight from the oysters and set in a piece of jewellery of your choice). From opposite the ferry pier, Tung Wan Road leads across the island's waist to Tung Wan Beach (see overleaf), a short walk through a couple of twists and turns lined with stalls and shops – the place to snap up bamboo hats and other essential beach gear. Just beyond the pier, down Tung Wan Road, you'll see an ancient banyan tree, whose base is often cluttered with makeshift altars. During World War II the Japanese were said to have hung their victims from its branches.

One block in from the water, the main thoroughfare, **San Hing Street**, leads up about 500m to the **Pak Tai Temple**, built in 1788 and today facing basketball courts. Not surprisingly, on an island once totally dependent on fishing, the inhabitants deemed it prudent to dedicate a temple to Pak Tai, God of

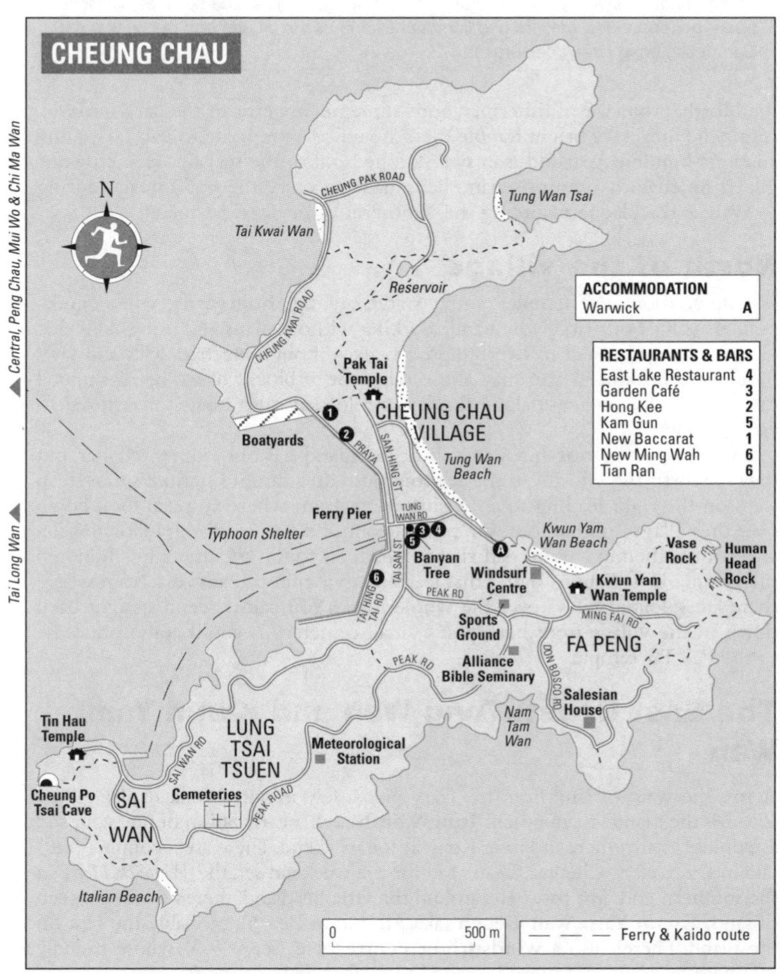

Cheung Chau Bun Festival

Every year, in late April/early May, Pak Tai Temple hosts the four-day **Cheung Chau Bun Festival,** or "Tai Chiu", held since the ravages of a series of eighteenth- and nineteenth-century plagues that supposedly appeased the vengeful spirits of those wrongly killed by Cheung Chau's pirates. Outside the temple, several sets of bamboo scaffolding are erected, each around 20m high and topped with pink and white buns. Up until 1978, at midnight on a designated day, people were encouraged to clamber up the frames to grab the buns, which would bring good luck – the higher the bun, the better the luck. This particular activity was stopped after a couple of the towers collapsed and 24 people were injured; these days the buns are just handed out from the bottom of the frames. The festival's other great draw is the teams of costumed children riding on floats through the streets, some of their peers strapped onto stilts on which they glide over the crowds. The village is packed for the four days of the festival – extra ferries are laid on from Hong Kong – and it's a fascinating time to come: as well as the displays, there is a host of religious services, Chinese opera performances, unicorn and lion dances and all the bluster and bustle that the Cantonese bring to any celebration.

the North, protector of fishermen and "supreme emperor of the dark heaven". Inside the unusually bright temple there are relics appropriate to Pak Tai's status: an eight-hundred-year-old iron sword, fished out of the sea; a golden crown; a gilded nineteenth-century sedan chair, made to carry the god's image during festivals; and a plaque recording the 1966 visit of Princess Margaret.

North of the village

Just down from the temple, at the water, are the **boatyards**, where junk-builders still labour largely by hand, working without plans and using skills that haven't changed much in five hundred years – though electric drills and saws have been introduced. You may also catch sight of blocks of ice being shipped out of the adjacent ice-making factory and loaded onto boats for removal to Hong Kong.

Beyond here, the **northern** stretch of the island has only views to offer, but they're worth the effort. On the seafront, just after the fire station, some steep steps on the right lead up to a housing estate, from where you can look down over the village and harbour. Or continue around the headland, following the waterfront Cheung Kwai Road: there's a path off to the left after a few hundred metres (marked "Family Trail") that leads up to a hilltop **reservoir**, from where there are splendid views over the whole island. You can descend straight back down to the village from here, past a small cemetery – you'll come out close to the Pak Tai Temple.

The East Coast: Tung Wan and Kwun Yam Wan

Across the waist of land from the ferry pier, a few minutes' walk up Tung Wan Road, is the island's main beach, **Tung Wan Beach**: nearly 800m of fine sand and as popular as anywhere in Hong Kong at the weekend. There are a couple of restaurants, as well as Cheung Chau's bid for the weekend set, the *Warwick Hotel*, at the southern end. Just past here, around the little headland, there's another sweep of sand, **Kwun Yam Wan Beach** (aka Afternoon Beach), probably the best on the island. There's also a **windsurfing centre** here (see p.263) whose friendly café with beach-view terrace is a good place for a beer or snack.

A walk around the island

If you've got a couple of hours, the **southern** part of the island offers a good circular walk along tree-shaded paths. From the waterfront in the village, close to the ferry pier, jump on a *kaido* to **Sai Wan**, across the harbour at the south-western tip of the island ($3). It's a five-minute crossing, and on the way the *kaido* sometimes calls at one or two of the junks in the harbour, depositing people laden with shopping at their floating homes. Alternatively, you can reach Sai Wan by walking along the harbourfront promenade (20min).

From Sai Wan's pier, a path leads up to one of the island's several **Tin Hau** temples, where there's a pavilion overlooking the harbour. A path runs over the brow of the hill to a rocky bluff, part of which has been landscaped. Follow everyone else scrambling over the rocks and you'll come to the so-called **Cheung Po Tsai Cave**, touted as the HQ of a notorious Cheung Chau pirate. Whether it was or wasn't, the adventurous and agile can climb through the underground passage here: you'll need a flashlight, and the scramble is fairly hard going, though faint hearts will be shamed by the queue of elderly women risking the drop into the abyss with their grandchildren.

Back on the main path, there's a **barbeque area** with covered seating and toilets, from where you can take a side-path down between the rocks onto a small rocky beach – though you might have to wade at this point if the tide is in – and back up to another headland covered in large, rounded granite boulders with some superb views over the sea on a calm day. The path continues down to Pak Tso Wan, known as **Italian Beach** – small and sandy, though a little grubby. Return to the road, which ascends through a series of **cemeteries**, and the **Aeronautical Meteorological Station**, into Lung Tsai Tsuen, once a separate village but now a southern outpost of the main village. Just after the Alliance Bible Seminary building, take Fa Peng Road to the right and then follow Don Bosco Road, which leads down to a small beach with another **Tin Hau temple** and Salesian House, a religious retreat, before doubling back to **Fa Peng Knoll**, the island's eastern bulge. Turn left here, and the path runs down past **Kwun Yam Temple** to Kwun Yam Wan beach, only a short walk from the centre of the village. Alternatively, a path from Fa Peng leads around the eastern headland, climbing down the cliffside to view a series of weirdly shaped **rocks** that have supposedly self-explanatory names – Vase Rock, Human Head Rock and Loaf Rock; they could equally be called Big Splodge Rock, Amorphous Rock and Vague Shape Rock.

Practicalities

Cheung Chau has no shortage of **holiday apartments** to let – most come with bathroom and kitchen and many overlook the beach. Prices start at around $150 per night during the week, or $220 at weekends. To rent them, head to the stalls opposite the ferry pier, though not all the stallholders speak English. The only time to avoid, or book months in advance, is during the Bun Festival in late April or early May. The most expensive place to stay is the *Warwick Hotel*, overlooking Tung Wan Beach; for details, see p.193.

For **eating**, most of the village's waterfront Praya is lined with small restaurants, and at night, the whole street is decked out with tables and chairs. Further north towards the Pak Tai Temple, there's a strip of very popular seafood restaurants, including the *New Baccarat* and the *Hong Kee*, which serve delicious garlic-fried prawns, scallops and Yang Chow fried rice. In the opposite direction, *New Ming Wah* is popular with Chinese for its seafood and waterfront tables overlooking all sorts of small craft; next door, the Tian Ran specializes in all

Cheung Chau travel details

Ferries and fast ferries

Ordinary ferries (55min) run alternately with fast ferries (40min) between Central and Cheung Chau, while all sailings from Tsim Sha Tsui use fast ferries.
Outlying Islands Ferry Piers to: Cheung Chau (daily, every 30min around the clock).
Star Ferry Pier, Tsim Sha Tsui, via Mui Wo (Lantau) to: Cheung Chau (Sat 2pm, 4pm & 6pm; Sun 10am, noon, 2pm, 4pm & 6pm).
Cheung Chau to: Outlying Islands Ferry Piers (daily, every 30min around the clock, except no service between 11.45pm and 2.20am); Star Ferry Pier, Tsim Sha Tsui (Sat 3.05pm, 5.05pm, & 7.05pm; Sun 11.05am, 1.05pm, 3.05pm, 5.05pm & 7.05pm).

Inter-island ferries

Cheung Chau to: Chi Ma Wan and Mui Wo (both on Lantau) and on to Peng Chau (daily, roughly every 2hr, first at 6am, last at 10.50pm; not every departure calls at every stop, so check the timetable at the pier).
For ticket prices and other ferry details, see p.156. For up-to-date ferry information, contact the New World First Ferry Company (ⓣ2131 8181, ⓦwww.nwff.com.hk).

sorts of sweet desserts – glutinous rice balls, grass jelly, mango and sago drinks – and also staple light meals such as prawn wonton soup. Behind the banyan tree next to a Park'N'Shop store, Kam Gun does excellent dim sum 7am–noon on the first floor – there's no English sign or menus, but it's easy to find. Tung Wan Road also offers a good selection of eating and **drinking** possibilities: the expat *Garden Café*, just past the banyan tree, offers club sandwiches and beer while a few doors up, the friendly staff at the *East Lake Restaurant* serve similar seafood fare to the Praya restaurants. To stock up on **picnic** food, there's a Wellcome supermarket on the seafront and a Park'N'Shop near the banyan tree. Note that if you're on Cheung Chau during the Bun Festival, the island goes **vegetarian** for a few days – no great hardship, since the food on offer remains excellent.

There are **bike rental** shops on the road between the Pak Tai Temple and the Praya, as well as at the northern end of the Praya itself. To rent a **kaido** for an hour's tour around Cheung Chau's waters (roughly $150), head to the small pier just south of where the main ferries dock. The HSBC **bank**, at the northern end of the Praya, opens on Saturday mornings, and there are several ATMs around town.

Peng Chau

There are both fast and slow direct ferries to **PENG CHAU**, a tiny horseshoe-shaped blob of land forty minutes from Hong Kong and just twenty minutes from its larger neighbour, Lantau. Although there are no obvious attractions, the quiet streets are a pleasant alternative to the busy antics of Lantau's Mui Wo. You could see the whole of Peng Chau in a couple of hours, then settle down to a steak at the friendly expat *Jungle Bar*, 38C Wing Hing St (closed Mon).

Wing On Street, just back from the pier, is a typical island street: part market, part residential, with an eighteenth-century Tin Hau temple, noodle shops, Chinese herbalists and no traffic. Some shops sell hand-painted porcelain, a local cottage industry. Signs point you in the direction of **Tung Wan**, the island's only real beach. It's five minutes' walk away and is pretty enough, with a barbecue site and a few fishing boats. Really, though, you won't want to hang around, unless you've been tempted into one of the **seafood restaurants**, where the food is as good and as cheap as on any of the islands.

Peng Chau travel details

Ferries and fast ferries

Ordinary ferries (40min) and fast ferries (25min) run roughly alternately.

Outlying Islands Ferry Piers to: Peng Chau (daily, roughly every 45min, 7am–midnight, plus one service at 3am).

Peng Chau to: Outlying Islands Ferry Piers (daily, roughly every 45min, first at 6.15am, last at 11.30pm, with one service at 3.25am).

Inter-island ferries

Peng Chau to: Mui Wo and Chi Ma Wan (both Lantau) and on to Cheung Chau (daily, roughly every 2hr, first at 5.40am, last at 11.40pm; check the timetable at the pier).

Kaido

Peng Chau to: Tai Shui Hang (Trappist Monastery, Lantau; six daily, 7.45am, 9.05am, 11.15am, 12.15pm, 2.20pm & 4.20pm).

For ticket prices and other ferry details, see p.156. For up-to-date ferry information, contact the New World First Ferry Company (ⓣ2131 8181, ⓦwww.nwff.com.hk).

Hei Ling Chau

A fairly frequent service runs from the quayside to **Hei Ling Chau**, an island south of Peng Chau and around twice its size, though don't get on the ferry by mistake, since part of the island is used as a drug rehabilitation centre – the chattering day-trippers are actually visiting relatives.

Lantau

By far the biggest island in the territory, **LANTAU** and its charms could occupy several days. Twice the size of Hong Kong Island, it's wild and rugged enough in parts to make hiking an attractive option; the beaches include Hong Kong's best; and there's a full set of cultural diversions, including several monasteries, the newly opened Disneyland, and the world's largest seated outdoor bronze Buddha statue.

Most people's first sight of Hong Kong is of Lantau, as the **airport** is sited at Chek Lap Kok island, just off Lantau's north coast. and the airport expressway and rail line run along the island's north shore, previously one of the more isolated stretches of Hong Kong coastline but now considerably developed, especially around the New Town of **Tung Chung**. There is still room to get away from it all, even so: more than half the island is designated country park, and the circular **Lantau Trail** loops for 70km around its southern half, passing campsites and the island's two youth hostels along the way. For detailed information on the trail's twelve stages, pick up the free *Lantau Trail* leaflet, published by the Country Parks Authority (CPA), which lists the route stages and picks out the relevant camping and transport details. There's a CPA booth at the ferry pier in *Mui Wo*, although don't count on too much help in English. You don't have to tackle the whole thing: there are a couple of easy stages and other half-day walks accessible from Mui Wo. Don't underestimate the trails, though: parts are steep and unshaded, which can take its toll in the tropical heat and humidity. Take a hat, sunscreen and water.

The main ways to reach Lantau are by **ferry** from Hong Kong Island and Kowloon to the eastern settlements of Mui Wo and **Discovery Bay** respectively, or by **MTR** to Tung Chung and Disneyland; there are also several **buses** from Kowloon to Tung Chung. Once here, **local buses** are run by the New Lantao Bus Company, which connects nearly all the places covered below, as do the island's distinctive pale blue **taxis**.

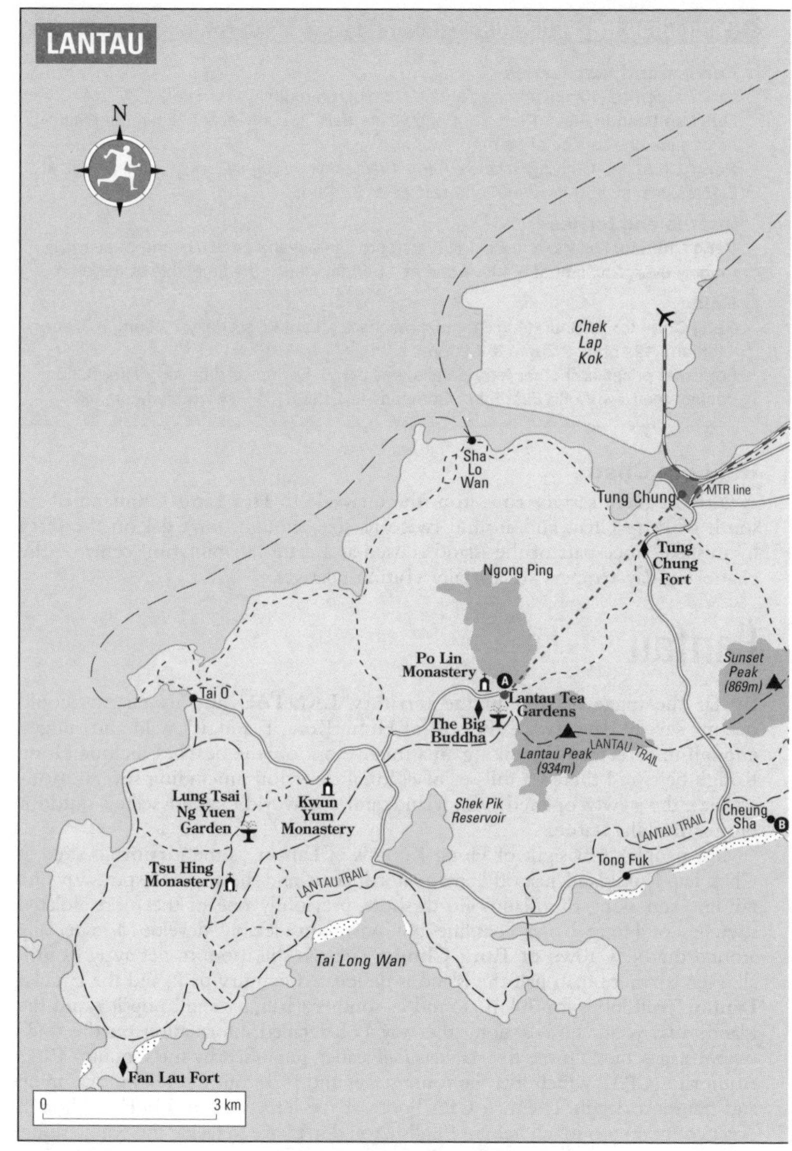

Mui Wo (Silvermine Bay)

All ferries from Hong Kong dock at **MUI WO** ("Plum Cove"), also known in English as Silvermine Bay, after the silver mine that once brought prosperity to the village. The mine has long since been boarded up, but the walk there is pleasant enough – about a kilometre inland from the village and close to a

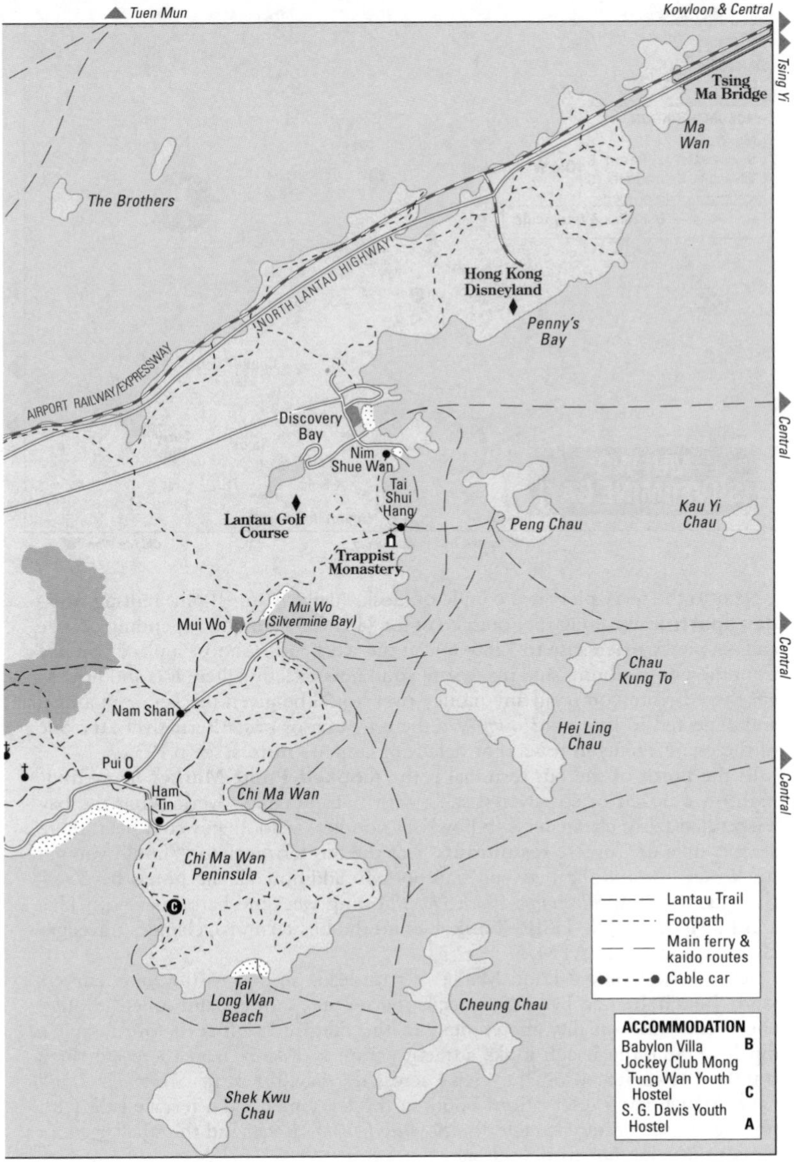

Lantau Trail
Footpath
Main ferry & kaido routes
Cable car

ACCOMMODATION
Babylon Villa B
Jockey Club Mong Tung Wan Youth Hostel C
S. G. Davis Youth Hostel A

waterfall. The village itself is actually about the least interesting place on the island, and most people head from the ferry straight to the **bus terminal** outside, where queues build up quickly for buses to the most popular destinations on the island – take the #2 for Ngong Ping (the Big Buddha), #3M for Tung Chung, or #A35 for the airport. **Taxis** leave from the same square.

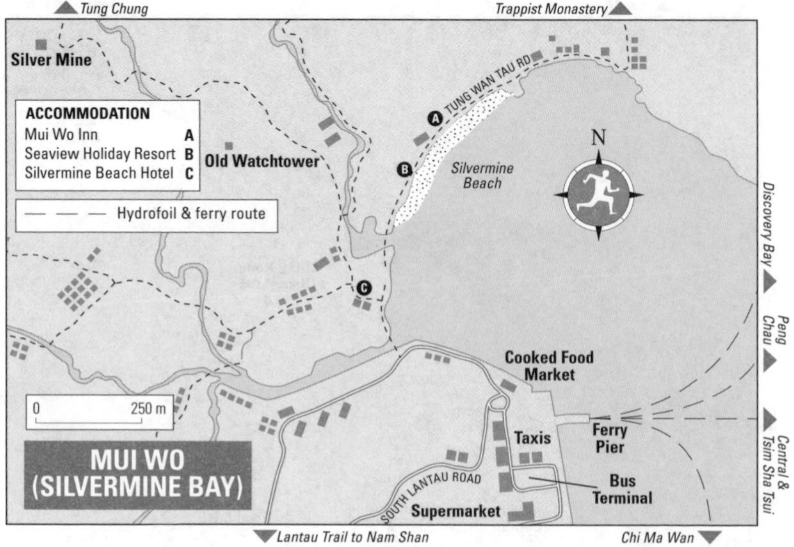

Next to the ferry pier are a couple of kiosks (daily 10am–10pm) renting **holiday apartments** along the south coast for $180–350 a night, depending on size and sea views; prices rise to $280–600 at the weekends. Choose a place you like from the photo albums, and make sure you know exactly where it is and how to get there before you hand any money over. You'll be given the keys and a map and expected to find your own way there by taxi or bus. Alternatively, try one of the estate agents in town. For details of Lantau's **hotels**, see p.193.

To the north of the bus terminal is the **Cooked Food Market** (6am–midnight) – a dozen or so covered stalls with outside tables overlooking the bay. They're all fairly cheap, serving bowls of noodles, seafood and cold beer; there are a couple of Chinese **restaurants** near the bus terminal, too, should you get stuck here for a while between transport. In addition, all the hotels have restaurants, with the *Silvermine Beach Hotel* hosting weekend barbecues with Thai and Indian food. The HSBC **bank**, behind the bus terminal, changes travellers' cheques, and has an ATM.

Beyond the Cooked Food Market, a path leads around to the long, curved, sandy **beach**, backed by restaurants, barbecue pits, showers and toilets, though check the water-quality meter next to the lifeguard's office before taking a dip here. Still, the beach looks attractive from a distance, and there are three **hotels** that capitalize on the views across the bay: the large *Silvermine Beach Hotel* (which has a reservations booth at the ferry pier and a terrace café with bay views), the rather characterless *Seaview Holiday Resort* and the smaller, more pleasant *Mui Wo Inn*, further along.

It's possible to **rent bicycles** near the ferry pier and along the beach at Mui Wo (around $10 an hour, or $40 for a day), though given the island's steep hills and excellent bus service, there's no compelling reason to do so (although mountain biking is becoming an increasingly popular activity on Lantau's trails). Mui Wo is also the starting and finishing point of the **Lantau Trail**.

North: to the Trappist Monastery and Discovery Bay

One of the best short hikes from Mui Wo is over the hills to the Our Lady of Joy Monastery, better known simply as the **Trappist Monastery**, in the next bay north. It takes around an hour and a half. Head along the seafront Tung Wan Tau Road (past the hotels) to the end, cross the bridge over the river and follow the path as it loops round to the right. A signpost to the left directs you up some steps and onto the bare hills; there are some excellent views as you go – over Peng Chau and to Hong Kong Island in the distance – and a detour to the peak on your left offers a view over the golf course above Discovery Bay. Otherwise, stick to the path to the right of the peak, which brings you out at the Trappist Monastery. Founded by refugees from mainland China, the institution (which is closed to the public) used to run a dairy that sold milk throughout Hong Kong, though they sold up years ago – the Trappist insignia on milk cartons is now just a brand name. If you follow the road downhill past the monastery to the sea (marked by large crucifixes signifying the Stations of the Cross), you'll find a **kaido** service across to Peng Chau (from where you can return directly to Central), though there are only a few daily crossings, the last one at 4.30pm.

Discovery Bay and Disneyland

Before you reach the *kaido* stop below the monastery, a signposted path to the left points towards Discovery Bay, an easy walk from here that takes about half an hour and passes through a sprawling – and illegal – squatter camp. Not far beyond is the edge of **DISCOVERY BAY** ("Disco Bay" to the *gweilo* locals), a fast-growing New Town popular with young families, with its own artificial beach, restaurants, shops, markets, banks and watersports facilities. The atmosphere is nightmarish, a too-perfect copy of idealized middle-American suburbia, with happy blonde families zipping about in golf carts, and very few Chinese faces. The main attraction is the 24-hour **hydrofoil** back to Hong Kong (every 20min during peak hours), which delivers you next to the Star Ferry Pier in Central in half an hour. There's also a high-speed ferry service that shuttles between Discovery Bay and Mui Wo, and **bus links** to Tung Chung (#DB01R) and the airport (#DB02R), via the 650-metre-long **Discovery Bay tunnel**.

Northeast of Discovery Bay, Penny's Bay has now been filled in by the construction of **Hong Kong Disneyland** (ⓦwww.hongkongdisneyland.com), which is also connected to Kowloon by an expressway and a stop on the MTR Tung Chung line. Still under construction at the time of writing, this entertainment superpower will offer such delights as "Main Street USA", a shopping mall dolled up to resemble a typical Midwest Town around 1900; "Tomorrowland", featuring a spaceship flight-simulator and giant rollercoaster; and "Fantasyland", in which the Tarzan and Lion King franchises will rub shoulders – all filled by a bevy of familiar cartoon characters. Doubtless this will all prove incredibly popular with Hong Kong's Chinese, even if Disney's one Chinese character, Mulan, is strangely absent.

Chi Ma Wan Peninsula

The other short walk from Mui Wo is to the **CHI MA WAN PENINSULA**, a foot of land around 4km south of the ferry pier. The most direct route is to follow the first section of the Lantau Trail as far as Nam Shan (where there's a campsite) and then switch to the last section of the trail, following it south to the peninsula: you'll come out on Chi Ma Wan Road, which runs east–west across the neck of the peninsula.

East along the road it's only a short walk to **Chi Ma Wan** itself. From the pier, there's a handy **ferry** service, either back to Mui Wo or on to Cheung Chau to the south. With a good map, you could make your way around the peninsula clockwise from Chi Ma Wan (there's another campsite at the peninsula's easternmost point), but it's easier to take in the **western side** around **Pui O**, reached on buses #1, #2, #3, #4 or #7P from the Mui Wo Ferry Pier, or bus #3 or #3M from Tung Chung.

From the bus stop on the main road at Pui O, follow the signpost to **Ham Tin**. A concrete footpath leads you across the fields and alongside the river to a small temple, from where another signpost points up towards **Mong Tung Wan** – just under an hour's walk, with lovely views over Pui O beach. The quiet bay has a **youth hostel**, the *Jockey Club Mong Tung Wan Hostel* (see p.183) made up of white bungalows set back from the harbour – a nice, clean place, though packed to the gills on Saturday nights from June to August. Camping is allowed here, and there are barbecue pits outside. The path from the hostel leads down to a tiny harbour, where you could swim, though it's rocky and a little murky. You can travel direct to Cheung Chau from here by *kaido* at around $100 for the boat.

Yi Long and Tai Long Wan

A footpath runs on from Mong Tung Wan around the peninsula, climbing steeply above the coast, and you can clamber down to good beaches at a couple of places, the best being **Tai Long Wan**, which has some long and usually empty sands. It's hard going on foot, though; it's easier to take a *kaido* from Cheung Chau's waterfront ($80–100, depending on numbers).

The south coast: Pui O to Fan Lau

Lantau's best beaches are all on the **south coast**, and most are easily accessible by **bus** from Mui Wo; bus #1 (to Tai O), #2 (to Po Lin Monastery) and #4 (to Tong Fuk) run along the coast, so you can get off wherever you like.

Pui O beach is the closest to Mui Wo, around a fifteen-minute bus ride away (see above). It's an excellent spot (if you can overlook the piles of rubbish on the way to the beach) and popular with the expat population, with barbecue pits, a free campsite at its eastern end and, back on the main road, the *Namaste Indian Restaurant* (closed Tues). The *JK Club*, also on the main road, has Sunday barbecues and is a friendly place for a quiet drink in the evening.

The next beach along, at **Cheung Sha**, is considered by many to be the best in the SAR. There are a couple of cafés here, serving simple Chinese food, as well as *The Stoep*, on the beach (for South African and Mediterranean cuisine), a campsite, and the option to rent a holiday apartment through agencies in Mui Wo or a room at beachside *Babylon Villa* (see p.193).

Cheung Sha beach stretches all the way down to the unfortunately named **Tong Fuk** (more cheap Chinese cafés as well as *The Gallery*, an English-style pub only open on Sundays), where the road strikes inland to reach the **Shek Pik Reservoir**, an impressive construction whose surroundings have been landscaped to provide picnic areas and walking trails. There's a beach below the reservoir at Tai Long Wan, a short walk away. The road up to Tai O/Po Lin (see p.173) skirts the reservoir; crane your head up to the opposing hilltop for a first view of the seated Buddha – his back to you at this point.

The pink dolphins

The waters around the western end of Lantau are where Hong Kong's few remaining **pink dolphins** (the Indo-Pacific humpback dolphin) are most likely to be found. These rose-coloured creatures are beautiful but rare: WWF (formerly the World Wildlife Fund) estimates that around 120 are now left, the remainder having been killed by a combination of polluted waters, disturbance by fishermen and, arguably, various developments around Lantau. You can visit the dolphins on trips organized by Hong Kong Dolphinwatch (Ⓣ2984 1414; Ⓦwww.hkdolphinwatch.com; trips last five hours and cost $320 for adults, $160 for children aged 3–11), who also raise money to help protect these threatened creatures. The WWF does not support the tour, arguing that frequent motorboat trips out to view the dolphins are harmful to the animals; Dolphinwatch does not dispute this, though the tours form only a tiny amount of the marine traffic using these extremely busy waters, and hopefully increase awareness about these incredibly endangered animals.

A longer walk from Shek Pik follows a section of the Lantau Trail, past a couple of fairly isolated campsites to **FAN LAU**, 5km away on the southwestern tip of the island. It takes around two hours to walk from Shek Pik, via Kau Ling Chung. There are two excellent beaches here, a large east-facing stretch and a smaller one a few minutes' walk across the headland, as well as the remains of a 1300-year-old rectangular **fort**, from which there are fine views across the water. Built to garrison troops, the fort overlooked a strategic sea route into the Pearl River estuary, but was abandoned at the beginning of the last century. The Lantau Trail swings north from Fan Lau, with Tai O village around two to three hours' walk further on.

Tai O and around

The largest village on Lantau, **TAI O**, on the western coast, was once the centre of a thriving salt export trade to China, as well as being one of Hong Kong's oldest fishing settlements. The saltpans are still visible, though locals

▲ Fishing boats to Tai O

have converted them into fish-breeding ponds – an enterprise that hasn't stopped the village population declining as people move to the city to look for jobs. There are still around two thousand people left though, with plenty of interest in the village's old streets, tin-roofed **stilt-houses**, shrines and temples, all of which, despite increasing tourism, remain fairly low-key.

The village is in two halves: a land side, where the **buses** stop (#1 from Mui Wo, #11 from Tung Chung, and #21 from Po Lin Monastery) and an island settlement, across a narrow creek lined with fishermen's houses built on stilts. To get there from the bus stop, walk down to the main street, follow it round to the right, and then turn left by the vendors selling live seafood. Plenty of restaurants and shops line the way, dried fish being a particular speciality; there's also a tiny **museum** (free), displaying everyday artefacts such as washboards, vases, a threshing machine, and a cutlass. At the bridge, operators offer short **boat trips** around the island ($10–25 depending on where you want to go).

On the island side are more small shops, a market, shacks alive with the clack of mahjong tiles, and a few local **temples**. One – originally founded in the Ming dynasty – is dedicated to Kuan Ti, the god of war and righteousness, to whom people pray for protection. Another, the renovated Hau Wong Temple (spelt with Mandarin pronunciation on local signs as "Hou Wang"), is a five-minute walk away along Kat Hing Back Street, at the end of the village on a small headland facing the sea. Built a little later, in 1699, it contains the local dragon-racing boat, some sharks' bones, a whale's head found by Tai O's fishermen and a lovely carved roof-frieze displaying two roaring dragons. If you're taking the ferry out of Tai O, you'll pass a third temple, the Hung Shing Temple, on the way down Shek Tsai Po Street towards the pier, about fifteen minutes on foot from the village centre.

Inevitably, Tai O offers plenty of places **to eat**. Try the *Relax* or *Good View Seafood* restaurants on the land side, or cross to the island where, at the end of the street, the *Fook Moon Lam* (11am–9.30pm) next to the market has a short English-language menu featuring good fresh scallops and prawns. There's a small HSBC **minibank** (Mon & Thurs 9.15am–4pm) with an ATM, just after the bridge on the island side. The **ferry pier** is opposite the bus station, with boats run by the Lee Tat Ferry Company (☎2985 5868, Chinese-speaking only) to Tuen Mun, stopping off in Sha Lo Wan, a small village with a beach and fishing opportunities on the northwest tip of Lantau.

Kwun Yum Monastery, Lung Tsai Ng Yuen and Tsu Hing Monastery

On the way to or from Tai O, not far from the village, the #1 and #21 buses stop at the **Kwun Yum Monastery**, where you can get a simple vegetarian meal. A half-hour's walk up from here is the **Lung Tsai Ng Yuen** ornamental garden, at its best in February and March, and a further kilometre beyond this is the **Tsu Hing Monastery** – situated in one of the most isolated spots on the island and guarded by a six-metre-long stone dragon. The monks and nuns here aren't really geared up to receiving visitors, though no one will object if you turn up and have a vague interest in Buddhism: Sunday is the recommended visiting day. There is accommodation available, too, but only for those seriously interested in a meditational retreat. The return walk via Lung Tsai Ng Yuen, then directly to Tai O, takes about an hour.

The Po Lin Monastery and Lantau Peak

The one place that everyone makes for in Lantau is the **Po Lin Monastery**, home of the **Big Buddha**, in the central **Ngong Ping** region, north of the Shek Pik Reservoir. There's often a massive queue for the #2 bus from Mui Wo after the ferry comes in, especially at the weekend, but it's worth the wait – partly for the fifty-minute ride past the reservoir and slowly up the valley, with swirling views below to the coast. By the time you read this you should also be able to get to the Big Buddha by **cable car**, from Tung Chung MTR Station – the project was nearing completion at the time of writing.

Po Lin Monastery and the Big Buddha

The **Po Lin Monastery** was established in 1927 on the Ngong Ping plateau, surrounded by mountains, including Lantau Peak itself. The temple complex is on a much grander scale than is usual in Hong Kong, reminiscent more of a Beijing opera set than a place of worship – an impression of grandeur enhanced by other features of the site such as the huge bronze urn, a gift from the mainland Chinese government to mark the 1997 handover. The hundred monks and nuns here led a relatively peaceful existence until the 1970s, when the main temple and its pavilions were opened to the public, since which time they've been besieged by swarms of people posing for photos on the temple steps and in the gardens. The main temple houses a noted group of three statues of the Buddha – fairly restrained under the circumstances, at only around three metres high each. There's nothing at all restrained about the temple itself, though, which is painted and sculpted in an almost gaudy fashion, its surfaces awash with vibrant gold, red, pink, orange and yellow.

All this pales into insignificance besides the gigantic but serene **Tian Tan Buddha** statue, more popularly known as the **Big Buddha** (daily 10am–5.30pm), at the top of a flight of 268 steps up the hillside in front of the monastery. The bronze figure seated in a ring of outsized lotus petals is 34m high and weighs 250 tonnes – roughly the same as a jumbo jet. It was built at a reputed cost of $68 million and, following its consecration in 1993, is now Lantau's top tourist attraction. Climb the steps for supreme views over the surrounding hills and down to the temple complex – there's no charge. Inside the base are four paintings depicting the Buddha's spiritual journeys, while if you've bought a meal ticket (see below), you'll also be allowed into the (rather dull) exhibition galleries underneath the statue.

Everything else in the complex is firmly aimed at the weekend tourist invasion, too. Inside the temple courtyard there's a huge **dining hall** (11.30am–5pm), usually awash with chatter, where you can get a filling meal of fairly straightforward vegetarian food, orthodox enough to avoid the use of garlic, ginger or onions. Buy **meal tickets** ($60, or the "deluxe" meal, served in air-conditioned surroundings, for $100) just beside the restaurant's entrance; in the covered area here, there's a long counter selling takeaway **vegetarian dim sum** – mostly sweet dishes – which you can eat at the adjacent tables.

Just to the left of the steps for the statue, a path leads the few hundred metres up to the **Lantau Tea Gardens**, once Hong Kong's only tea-producing estate. It contains the little *Tea Gardens Restaurant*, where you can sit outside, eat fried rice and drink a beer – the tea is good, too. Despite its proximity to the monastery, it's usually fairly peaceful. Signs just beyond the restaurant indicate the paths to Lantau Peak, the Po Lam Zen Monastery and the *S. G. Davis Youth Hostel*. You'll need to book ahead if you want to stay at the hostel (see p.183); take bus #S1 ($3.50) from the airport to Tung Chung bus terminal, then bus #23 (Mon–Sat $16; Sun $25) to the end of the line.

Chek Lap Kok and the new airport

During the 1980s, with the old airport at Kai Tak at saturation point and the danger of the flight approach amongst the buildings of Kowloon a major concern, Hong Kong's need for a new airport was generally acknowledged. Despite this, plans for a new airport, announced in 1989, were highly controversial and led to a long-running spat between the British authorities in Hong Kong and the Chinese government, who saw it as a plot to spend Hong Kong's reserves – and give work to British construction companies – before the handover. What was surprising was the choice of site – isolated **Chek Lap Kok island,** off the north coast of Lantau – and the sheer scale of the proposals, which were to make the airport and its associated developments the world's largest civil engineering project. Before the redevelopment Chek Lap Kok had supported a dwindling population of around two hundred. Now the island has been completely levelled, forty thousand tonnes of explosive were used to blast out 75 million cubic metres of rock, and reclamation more than doubled its size. The airport platform is 6km long, while the dimensions of the airport buildings on the reclaimed island are no less staggering: the terminal building alone is twice the size of those of London Heathrow and New York's JFK airports put together. It is currently designed to handle 35 million passengers a year, a figure that will rise to more than eighty million by 2040.

The construction of the airport has been only the start of an entire new phase of development in Hong Kong: the Airport Core Programme (ACP), comprising ten major projects including the building of the world's longest road and rail suspension bridge – the 2.2-kilometre Tsing Ma bridge – linking northeastern Lantau with Tsing Yi district in the New Territories. Some of these were needed to provide transport links – the siting of Chek Lap Kok in one of the more inaccessible corners of Hong Kong meant the territory's communications and transport infrastructure had to be redrawn almost from scratch – whilst entire New Towns and industrial areas have grown up along the new transport routes in areas such as Tsing Yi, Tai Kok Tsui and West Kowloon. Tung Chung, Hong Kong's gateway town if you're arriving by air, is designed to house 60,000 people and is linked to the SAR's downtown by the six-lane North Lantau Highway, the 32-kilometre Airport Express Railway and the Tung Chung MTR line.

Naturally, there were objections to a scheme of such magnitude. The residents of Tung Chung have seen their village and way of life transformed, some say ruined; fishermen on nearby Cheung Chau claim that the dumping of mud from the project has killed the fish; while environmental groups have pointed to the detrimental effect on species such as the pink dolphin, which once inhabited the waters around Chek Lap Kok. More vociferous objections came from the Chinese government, worried – perhaps with some justification – that the airport was a last, grand gesture from a departing British government that wouldn't have to foot the bill after 1997 if things went wrong. The cost was astronomical: estimates put the entire ACP budget at around $155 billion, of which the airport site accounted for around $70 billion. For a while there was real concern that arguments over the cost would derail the entire project, though the airport finally opened in July 1998.

Lantau Peak

A very steep path leads up from the Tea Gardens to the 934-metre-high peak of Fung Wong Shan, as **Lantau Peak** is properly known, the second highest in Hong Kong, and renowned as an excellent venue for sunrise watching. The two-kilometere-long trail takes about an hour; the views – as far as Macau on a clear day – are justly famous.

The peak is on the Lantau Trail, and depending on how energetic you feel, the path then heads east, reaching the slightly lower **Tai Tung Shan**, or "Sunset Peak", after about 5km. A fairly sharpish two-hour descent from there puts you on the road at Nam Shan, within shouting distance of Mui Wo (see p.176 for bus details).

Tung Chung

Lantau's main north coast settlement, **TUNG CHUNG**, faces Chek Lap Kok island. The airport project (see box) jump-started this almost forgotten fishing village out of twentieth-century obscurity into what has become one of the fastest-growing New Towns in Hong Kong: two of the fourteen local settlements were torn down to make way for access roads and an MTR station; the bridge from the airport was completed; and high-rises have sprouted like bamboo after rain.

It's still worth heading out here to see the relics of the old Tung Chung, and the bus ride (#3 or #13 from Mui Wo) alone is sufficient reason to come, climbing slowly over the hills before rattling down the valley to the town, which focuses a huge **transit centre** containing department stores, cafés and restaurants, the MTR and bus stations, and the nearly completed cable car to the Big Buddha. The road north out of Tung Chung leads past the nineteenth-century **Battery**, while a kilometre or so back inland, the road winds to **Tung Chung Fort** (a signposted, fifteen-minute walk from the transit centre), whose six cannons and stone crenalated walls currently protect a school. There was a fortress here as long ago as the seventeenth century, though this building dates back only to 1817, built on the orders of the viceroy of Guangdong (Canton province) to defend Lantau's northern coast. If the guns were fired today they'd take out some large tower blocks between here and the sea.

There are some good **walks** in the vicinity, most obviously the one up to **Po Lin Monastery**, a pleasant three-hour hike passing several smaller temples scattered along the Tung Chung valley. Longer hikes are those to Mui Wo and along the coastal path to Tai O, both of which take around five hours; don't forget to take water, suncream, strong shoes and a hat. Walking track and **cable car** aside, there's also a **bus** (#23) to and from the Po Lin Monastery, with frequent services, especially on Sundays; it's a fifty-minute ride. You can also ride the **MTR** from here back, via Yan O (for Disneyland), to Kowloon and Hong Kong Island.

Lantau travel details

Ferries and fast ferries

Between Central and Mui Wo, roughly every third sailing is by ordinary ferry (about 55min), while fast ferries (40min) operate at other times; between Tsim Sha Tsui and Mui Wo, the two services alternate.

Outlying Islands Ferry Piers to: Mui Wo (every 30min, first at 6.10am, last at 12.30pm).

Star Ferry Pier, Tsim Sha Tsui to: Mui Wo (Sat 2pm, 4pm & 6pm; Sun 10am, noon, 2pm, 4pm & 6pm).

Mui Wo to: Outlying Islands Ferry Piers (roughly every 30min, first at 5.55am, last at 11.30pm); Star Ferry Pier, Tsim Sha Tsui (Sat 2.40pm, 4.40pm & 6.40pm; Sun 10.40am, 12.40pm, 2.40pm, 4.40pm & 6.40pm).

Tai O to: Sha Lo Wan then on to Tuen Mun, New Territories (Mon–Fri 8am & 4.30pm; Sat 8am, 3pm & 5.30pm; Sun 8am, 10.15am, 2pm, 4pm & 6pm).

Tai Shui Hang (Trappist Monastery) to: Peng Chau (Mon–Sat 8.10am, 9.30am, 11.30am, 12.30pm, 2.45pm & 4.30pm; Sun 8.10am, 10.15am, 12.30pm, 3pm & 4.45pm).

Tuen Mun to: Chek Lap Kok (daily every 15–30min between 6am and 11pm); Sha Lo Wan then on to Tai O (Mon–Fri 9.15am & 5.30pm; Sat 9.15am, 4pm & 6.30pm; Sun 9.15am, 11.15am, 3pm, 5pm & 7pm).

Chek Lap Kok to: Tuen Mun, New Territories (daily every 15–30min between 6am and 11pm).

Discovery Bay to: Star Ferry Pier, Central (24hr service; every 20–30min at peak times).

Star Ferry Pier, Central to: Discovery Bay (24hr service; every 20–30min at peak times).

Inter-island ferries

Mui Wo to: Peng Chau (11 daily, first at 6.35am, last at 11.59pm); Chi Ma Wan then on to Cheung Chau (10 daily, first at 6am, last at 10.50pm).

Discovery Bay to: Mui Wo (Mon–Fri 7.25am, 11am, 3pm, 4.10pm & 6.10pm; Sat & Sun 7.25am, 8.40am, 10.35am, 1.10pm, 3pm, 4.10pm, 6.10pm & 7.50pm).

Mui Wo to: Discovery Bay (Mon–Fri 7.45am, 11.20am, 3.20pm, 4.30pm & 6.30pm; Sat & Sun 7.45am, 9am, 10.55am, 1.30pm, 3.20pm, 4.30pm, 6.30pm & 8.10pm).

Kaido

Kaido services operate on the following routes with varying degrees of regularity; specific details are given in the text where appropriate.

Tai Shui Hang–Nim Shue Wan.

Tai Long Wan–Cheung Chau.

Mong Tung Wan–Cheung Chau.

Buses

On regular services, fares are between $4 and $12 one-way; air-con services cost about a third more. You pay on board; fares are just under double on Sundays and public holidays. The #2 air-con bus from Mui Wo direct to Po Lin Monastery costs $16 ($25 on Sun).

#1 Mui Wo–Tai O (via Pui O and Kwun Yam Temple): roughly every 30min until 1.10am.

#2 Mui Wo–Ngong Ping (Po Lin Monastery): Mon–Sat every 20–60min, first at 7.50am, last at 6.40pm; Sun first at 8am, last at 6.20pm.

#3 Mui Wo–Tung Chung: roughly every hour, first at 6.25am, last at 10.15pm.

#4 Mui Wo–Tong Fuk (via Nam Shan and Cheung Sha beach): Mon–Sat hourly until 7.25pm, Sun every 30min until 8.20pm.

#7 P Mui Wo–Pui O (via Nam Shan): Sat pm & Sun only; Sat 7 departures, first at 2.30pm, last at 7.25pm; Sun every 30min until 6.20pm.

#11 Tung Chung–Tai O: Mon–Sat every 45min, Sun every 30min, first at 6.20am, last at 1.20am.

#21 Tai O–Ngong Ping: 7 daily, first at 7.45am, last at 3pm.

#23 Tung Chung–Ngong Ping: Mon–Sat every 15–30min, Sun roughly every 15min, first at 8.10am, last at 6.10pm.

Airport–Mui Wo: daily every 40min, first at 6am, last at midnight.

#DB01R Tung Chung–Discovery Bay: daily roughly every hour, first at 5.30am, last at 1.30am.

For up-to-date ferry information, contact the New World First Ferry Company (Ⓣ2131 8181, Ⓦwww.nwff.com.hk), which runs services between the airport, Tung Chung and Tuen Mun.

For Discovery Bay ferry service, call Discovery Bay Transportation Services Ltd (Ⓣ2987 7351).

For ferries between Tai O, Sha Lo Wan and Tuen Mun, call Lee Tat Ferry Company (Ⓣ2985 5868); no English spoken.

For bus information, call New Lantao Bus Company (Ⓣ2984 9848).

Moving experiences begin with Cathay Pacific.

Flying with Cathay Pacific is a moving experience because we believe your journey is just as important as your destination. We have been proudly flying visitors to our home and hub in Hong Kong, one of the world's most inspirational cities, for 60 years. We now fly to over 90 destinations worldwide, so with us there are plenty of opportunities to be moved.

To fly Cathay Pacific call 020 8834 8888 or visit **www.cathaypacific.com**

Now you're really flying.

www.cathaypacific.com

BOARDING PASS CATHAY PACIFIC
FROM: LONDON HEATHROW
TO: AUSTRALIA & NEW ZEALAND
BOARDING PASS CATHAY PACIFIC
FROM: LONDON HEATHROW
TO: ASIA

Move even farther with Cathay Pacific.

We fly to 27 destinations across Asia and Australasia.

Cathay Pacific helps move you to even more fascinating and inspiring places. From London Heathrow via Hong Kong we offer connections to 20 destinations across Asia and 7 across Australasia, and a total of over 90 destinations worldwide.

To fly Cathay Pacific call 020 8834 8888 or visit **www.cathaypacific.com**

Now you're really flying.

www.cathaypacific.com

Places	
Cheung Chau	長洲
Cheung Sha	長沙
Chi Ma Wan	芝麻灣
Discovery Bay	愉景灣
Lamma Island	南丫島
Lantau Island	大嶼山
Mo Tat Wan	模達灣
Mui Wo	梅窩
Peng Chau	坪洲
Sok Kwu Wan	索罟灣
Tai O	大澳
Tong Fuk	塘福
Tung Chung	東涌
Yung Shue Wan	榕樹灣
Sights	
Big Buddha	天壇大佛
Cheung Po Tsai Cave	張保仔洞
Disneyland	香港迪士尼樂園
Pak Tai Temple	北帝廟
Po Lin Monastery	寶蓮寺
Shek Pik Reservoir	石壁水塘
Trappist Monastery	修道院
Tung Chung Fort	東涌炮台
Transport	
Chek Lap Kok airport	赤鱲角飛場

Hong Kong listings

Hong Kong listings

Accommodation

Accommodation in Hong Kong doesn't have to be a major expense. There are plenty of rock-bottom choices, starting at around $60 a night for a **bed** in a dormitory (even cheaper if you stay in an IYHF hostel), which are bearable if all you're doing is passing through. However, for extended stays – even just three or four nights – they cease to be an attractive proposition: they're often crowded, dirty and hot. If you can afford a little more, then a room in a **guesthouse** with fan or air-conditioning starts at around $200 for a double, slightly more with an attached bathroom. Above that, some of the three- and four-star **hotels** offer deep discounts when their occupancy rate is looking low; and almost everywhere offers deals on **long-term stays** of one month or more. If money is no object, Hong Kong also has some of the world's finest hotels, offering an unparalleled degree of comfort and service.

There isn't really a high or a low season so far as hotel bookings are concerned and, given the sheer number of options, **booking in advance** isn't strictly necessary if you don't mind a bit of legwork. However, advance booking is a good idea during Chinese New Year, which falls in January or February, or during popular sports events such as the Rugby Sevens, when there will be fewer options than usual. For peace of mind, therefore – and certainly if you want to guarantee space in one of the plusher hotels – it's as well to have at least your first night's accommodation sorted out before you arrive.

Another reason to book ahead is to secure a **better deal** – rooms at cheaper places can always be` bargained down in price over the phone, while plusher hotels have their own websites, often advertising package rates. Other options include dedicated websites such as Ⓦwww.hotels-in-hong-kong.com, which features discounts, packages and various offers for mostly mid- to upmarket hotels; or the **Hong Kong Hotels Association** (Ⓦwww.hkha.org), though they only deal with hotels that are members of their association. They also have offices at the A and B Halls in the airport (daily 6am–midnight; Hall A Ⓣ2383 8380; Hall B Ⓣ2769 8822).

The bulk of the cheaper dormitories, guesthouses and lower-range hotels are Kowloon-side, with a scattering in Causeway Bay on Hong Kong Island – though there are also a number in the New Territories and Outlying Islands. Mid-range and upmarket hotels are concentrated in Kowloon and Central.

Dormitory accommodation

The cheapest beds in Hong Kong are those found in **dormitory-style accommodation**, mostly in privately run guesthouses and hostels,

Australia Youth Hostels Association Australia ⓣ02/9261 111, ⓦwww.yha.com.au.

Canada Hostelling International/Canadian Hostelling Association ⓣ800/663 5777 or 613/237 7884, ⓦwww.hostellingintl.ca.

England and Wales Youth Hostel Association (YHA) ⓣ0870/770 8868, ⓦwww.yha.org.uk and ⓦwww.iyhf.org.

Ireland An Oige ⓣ01/830 4555, ⓦwww.irelandyha.org.

New Zealand Youth Hostels Association of New Zealand ⓣ03/379 9970, ⓦwww.yha.co.nz.

Northern Ireland Hostelling International Northern Ireland ⓣ028/9032 4733, ⓦwww.hini.org.uk.

Scotland Scottish Youth Hostel Association ⓣ0870/155 3255, ⓦwww.syha.org.uk.

USA Hostelling International–American Youth Hostels (HI–AYH) ⓣ301/495 1240, ⓦwww.hiayh.org.

though there are also a number of IYHF **youth hostels**, mostly located far from the centre in the New Terrirories.

IYHF youth hostels

There are seven official International Youth Hostel Federation (IYHF) **youth hostels** in Hong Kong, of which three are regularly used by foreign travellers: *Ma Wui Hall* on Hong Kong Island, and *Jockey Club Mong Tung Wang* and *S.G. Davis*, both of which are relatively close to Chek Lap Kok Airport. The others are in fairly remote parts of the New Territories, but well placed for hiking trips, or just to escape central Hong Kong. They are all very cheap – $30–80 per person, $150–540 for a double to six-bed room, if available – and have cooking and washing facilities. You'll need an IYHF membership card to use them, available from the national organizations in your home country (see the box below), or you can buy a "Welcome Stamp" ($30 per night) at your first Hong Kong hostel – buying six is the equivalent of having annual international membership. You can reserve rooms via the **head office** of the Hong Kong Youth Hostels Association, Room 225, Block 19, Shek Kip Mei Estate, Kowloon (Mon–Fri 10am–7pm; Sat 10am–5pm; ⓣ2788 1638, ⓦwww.yha.org.hk).

Given their remote locations, it's essential to book beds at the hostels **in advance**, either through the head office, or by contacting hostels direct. The HKTB office in the airport arrivals hall has a leaflet on how to reach the *Ma Wui Hall*, *S.G. Davis* and *Bradbury Lodge* hostels; use the free phones to check on space with the warden or the head office. The hostels are **closed** between 10am and 4pm on weekdays, and between 1 and 2pm at weekends (some also close one day midweek), and there are separate dormitories for men and women – couples must take two-person rooms. On Friday and Saturday nights throughout the year, the New Territories hostels are nearly always packed with groups of young Chinese: go in midweek and you'll often be on your own. You'll also need a sheet **sleeping bag**, which you can rent at the hostel for a few dollars, and **food** – many are far from shops.

Mount Davis

Ma Wui Hall Mount Davis, Hong Kong Island ⓣ**2817 5715.** Hong Kong's most popular and accessible hostel, above Kennedy Town on top of Mount Davis, with superb views. It's open 7am–midnight, there are cooking facilities, lockers, air-conditioning and 163 beds, including two- to six-person rooms. Getting here, however, is complicated, unless you catch the infrequent shuttle bus ($10) from the ground floor of the Shun Tak Centre (Macau Ferry Terminal) – phone the hostel for times. Otherwise, catch bus #5 from Admiralty or minibus #54 from the Outlying Islands Ferry Piers in Central and get off near the junction of Victoria Road and Mount Davis Path; walk back 100m from the bus stop and you'll see Mt Davis Path branching off up the hill – the hostel is a 35-minute walk. If you have a lot of luggage, get off the bus in Kennedy Town and catch a taxi from there (around $50 plus $5 per item of luggage).

New Territories

Bradbury Hall Chek Keng, Sai Kung Peninsula ☎2328 2458. 92 beds, plus camping facilities.
Bradbury Lodge 66 Tai Mei Tuk Rd, Tai Mei Tuk, Tai Po ☎2662 5123. 94 beds and two- to four-bed rooms.
Pak Sha O Hoi Ha Rd (Jones' Cove), Sai Kung Peninsula ☎2328 2327. 112 beds, plus camping facilities.
Sze Lok Yuen Tai Mo Shan, Tsuen Wan ☎2488 8188. 92 beds, plus camping facilities.

Lantau

For Lantau hostels, see map on pp.166–167.
Jockey Club Mong Tung Wan Chi Ma Wan peninsula ☎2984 1389. 88 beds; closed 1–2 days a week, camping facilities available; see p.170.
S.G. Davis Ngong Ping ☎2985 5610. 46 beds, plus camping facilities available; see p.173.

Other hostels

Mostly located in Tsim Sha Tsui, dormitories in non-IYHF hostels are generally clean enough, even if they barely conform with the SAR's stringent health and safety restrictions. Typically, you'll pay around $80 for a bed in a dorm, sharing with other backpackers. There will normally be separate shower and laundry facilities, and sometimes a TV room and cooking facilities. The dorms are generally friendly places, good for meeting people, but can be cramped and are in no way secure. *Cosmic Guesthouse* (p.189), *Golden Crown Guesthouse* (p.187), and *Travellers' Hostel* (p.189) are among the places with dorm space – see the listings below for more information.

Guesthouses, YMCAs and hotels

Most budget travellers end up in one of Tsim Sha Tsui's **guesthouses**. Given the high rents in Hong Kong, expect shoe-box-sized rooms, with basic decor, paper-thin walls and a turnover that's fast and furious (qualities shared by many of the owners). These places are not necessarily dives, however, and there are at least a lot of them – if one doesn't appeal, an alternative option will be just a short walk away.

Many guesthouses are contained inside large mansion blocks on and around **Nathan Road** in Tsim Sha Tsui, most notoriously **Chungking Mansions** (36–44 Nathan Rd) and nearby **Mirador Mansions** (56–58 Nathan Rd). Both are ugly, giant buildings whose lower levels are given over to small shops selling a huge array of daily necessities, the rest filled by countless small guesthouses and budget hostels packed away amongst a warren of dingy corridors. Prior to 1997, a good slice of customers were British backpackers, stopping off in Hong Kong to top-up their finances by taking short-term work; nowadays, the majority are small-businessmen from Africa and the Indian subcontinent. Other mansion blocks in the area tend to be less overwhelming, if slightly more expensive, so don't panic if neither Chungking nor Mirador suit.

When **renting your room**, *always* ask to see it first, and don't be afraid to try and bargain the price down. If you're staying a few days, you'll often be able to get a reduction, but be wary about paying the whole lot at once: if the guesthouse turns out to be roach-infested or noisy, or both, you'll have a hard job getting your money back if you want to leave early. The best advice is to take the room for one night and see what it's like before parting with more cash.

Check that the **air-conditioning** unit actually works and isn't too noisy – some places make an extra charge ($10–20 per night) for its use; other rooms simply come equipped with a ceiling fan. **Bathrooms** are rarely that: rather, a wardrobe-sized alcove with toilet and hand-held shower – usually better than sharing what can be fairly grim communal facilities. Most rooms also come with TV, though the reception in places like Chungking Mansions can leave a lot to be desired. Guesthouses nearly all charge per room, which usually sleeps two (sometimes three) people, so **single travellers** will find themselves paying over the odds – some guesthouses offer single rooms, but these are often fairly claustrophobic.

There are several **YMCAs** and **religious organizations** offering accommodation somewhere in between the most expensive of the guesthouses and the cheapest of the regular hotels. The rooms are all well appointed (with air-con and TV) and comparatively spacious. Most importantly, at these prices, you can start to pick and choose the area you want to stay in; some of the places below are in excellent locations. Rooms at all of them can be booked with the Hong Kong Hotels Association (see p.181).

At the top end of the scale, Hong Kong has some of the world's finest and most expensive **hotels**, competing for the massive business custom that passes through: the *Peninsula*, the *Mandarin Oriental* and the *Conrad* are often mentioned in surveys of the world's best hotels. There are many cheaper, mid-range hotels around, too, though beware those at the lower end of this range, which are little more than guesthouses – the YMCAs might prove better value. With most hotels, the only choice to be made is location, since most are fitted with everything that you could possibly want – business centres, gyms and restaurants, hair stylists and gift-shops.

Lots of hotels don't distinguish between singles and doubles; you're just charged for the room. Breakfast is not usually included, but is worth negotiating over. It pays to shop around, since most places offer discounts and deals at odd times of the year, while booking through a **travel agent** or **inclusive package or tour** will often reap a cheaper rate. Count on adding a ten-percent **service charge** and a three-percent government **tax** to the quoted room price. Add an extra twenty percent to the prices quoted below for **harbour views** (if available).

Finally, if you're after a long-term stay, budget-end accommodation might give one free night if you stay a week, whereas some hotels – mostly mid-range ones - offer monthly rates at approximately the cost of ten nights.

Central

On the whole, this is the most expensive area in Hong Kong to look for a room. There are no guesthouses and the hotels are of international quality and price – the locations, though, are superb. The #A11 Airbus from the airport passes most of the Central hotels; otherwise, take the MTR to either Central or Admiralty (for Pacific Place).

For the accommodation listed below, see map on pp.54–55.

Conrad Pacific Place, 88 Queensway ⓣ2521 3838, ⓦwww.conrad.com.hk. Spiffy modern hotel with large well-equipped rooms that suffer from a lack of character despite all their comforts. But the hotel takes full advantage of its position on the upper floors of one of the Pacific Place towers with great views from all rooms, and superb restaurants. $2950

Garden View International House (YWCA) 1 Macdonnell Rd ⓣ2877 3737, ⓦww.wywca.org.hk. Slightly expensive at full rate, though an excellent location near the botanical gardens and Lower Peak Tram Terminal, just fifteen minutes' walk from Central. However, often has discounted rates, and a weekly package for seven consecutive nights. Book in advance. Take the Airbus to Central Bus Terminal and then green maxicab #1A from just outside the Star Ferry Pier or a taxi (about $30). $1250

▲ A room at the *Mandarin Oriental*

Island Shangri-La Pacific Place, Supreme Court Rd ⓣ2877 3838, ⓦwww.shangri-la.com. Classy hotel at Pacific Place, with the best Peak or harbour views of the lot, particularly from the top-floor Cyrano's bar. Rooms are set around a central atrium holding a magnificent Chinese landscape painting spanning more than forty floors. $2500

JW Marriott Pacific Place, 88 Queensway ⓣ2810 8366, ⓦwww.marriott.com. Flash Pacific Place complex, exuding Hong Kong luxury. The 602 rooms are on the small side but bright and comfortable, and all with views of the city, harbour or hills. $3000

Mandarin Oriental 5 Connaught Rd ⓣ2522 0111, ⓦwww.mandarinoriental.com. The Mandarin is considered by many to be the best hotel in the world: there's no faulting the service (the staff run into hundreds), facilities (the rooms have antiques and balconies, the corridors eighteenth-century Chinese textiles) or location. You don't need to stay here to appreciate its atmosphere – people-watching in the lobby is a great way to see Hong Kong's finest at work and play. The café is a favourite lunch spot, the *Chinnery Bar* is where bankers come to unwind, and the *Mandarin Grill* is where government officials have their power lunches. If you really want to put the staff through their paces, they claim that the restaurants will prepare any dish that has ever appeared on the menu over the last thirty years. $2000.

Ritz-Carlton 3 Connaught Rd ⓣ2877 6666, ⓦwww.ritzcarlton.com. In a prime city centre location, it's probably the best alternative in Central to staying at the Mandarin Oriental. Rooms (just over 200 of them) are eminently comfortable, and there's a high staff–guest ratio. $2000

Wan Chai & Causeway Bay

Wan Chai, Hong Kong's business entertainment district, offers few accommodation bargains, geared as it is towards the business community and upmarket package tours – though last-minute discounts can often slash advertised prices. Access is by buses #1, #18, or Airbus #A11; Wan Chai MTR puts you close to most hotels, as does the Wan Chai Ferry Pier.

Causeway Bay, however, compares well with Tsim Sha Tsui for budget travellers: there are well over a hundred cheap hostel rooms within five minutes' walk of the MTR station, mainly at the Great George Building, Fairview Mansions and Hyde Park Mansions in Paterson Street, and the Central Building in Jaffe Road. Access is by Airbus #A11, tram or Causeway Bay MTR.

For the accommodation listed below, see map on pp.78–79.

Wan Chai

Beverley Floor 4, 175-191 Lockhart Road ⓣ2507 2026, ⓕ2877 9277. Rooms are reasonably spacious and clean, though the lurid pink wallpaper and tacky, illuminated bed trim might put you off. Management amenable to a little bargaining; altogether a good deal. $500

Grand Hyatt **1 Harbour Rd ⓣ2588 1234, ⓦwww.hongkong.grand.hyatt.com.** Part of the Convention and Exhibition Centre complex (along with the neighbouring Renaissance Harbour View), and bulging with harbour views; it's aimed mainly at business trade – luxurious rather than tasteful, and bristling with bars, restaurants, pools, gardens, tennis courts and a health club. $2243

Harbour View International House **4 Harbour Rd ⓣ2802 0111, ⓔhvihymca@netvigator.com.** Good location and views, next door to the Arts Centre and handy for Wan Chai Ferry Pier. The spacious doubles come with all basic facilities, though the bathrooms are a bit of a squeeze. No sports centre or swimming pool, but guests can use the facilities of the Tsim Sha Tsui YMCA. Monthly rates are a good deal. $1200

Luk Kwok **72 Gloucester Rd ⓣ2866 2166, ⓦwww.lukkwokhotel.com.** Famous as the setting for The World of Suzie Wong (see p.147), though the rebuilt brown-marble and glass exterior and staid, mid-range rooms pack none of the romance of the novel. $1650

Ming Court **2nd Floor, 137–147 Lockhart Rd, Hong Kong Mansions (opposite Exit C on Wan Chai MTR), ⓣ2135 8692.** This "love" hotel sports seventeen clean, lilac-painted rooms with all the basic amenities – bathroom, air-con and TV. No view to speak of from the tiny windows, but fair value for money. No English spoken. $600

Renaissance Harbour View **1 Harbour Rd ⓣ2802 8888, ⓦwww.renaissancehotels.com/hkghv.** Splendid views and the same expense-account business clientele as the Grand Hyatt – you get to use the Grand Hyatt's facilities, too, including the largest hotel swimming pool in Hong Kong. A favourite with aircrews, and the breakfast comes well recommended. $2500

Wesley **22 Hennessy Rd ⓣ2866 6688, ⓕ2866 6633.** Knock-down room rates in a quiet and comfortable modern hotel, close to the Arts Centre. Don't expect much luxury at this price; the gloomy rooms are done out in grey and views are restricted to the sides of high-rises with glimmers of the harbour if you crane your neck. But all are equipped with standard hotel amenities including mini-bar and satellite TV. Good-value monthly rates. $800

Causeway Bay

Alisan **Flat A, 5th Floor, Hoito Court, 275 Gloucester Rd ⓣ2838 0762, ⓦhttp://home.hkstar.com/~alisangh.** Long-term, tidy guesthouse favourite with helpful management; rooms are the usual compromise between space and cost, but all have air-con, TV, shower and phone. $320

Bin Man **1st Floor, Room F, Central Building, 531 Jaffe Rd ⓣ2833 2063, ⓕ2838 5651.** Fantastic name for this small and friendly guesthouse with tiny clean rooms and attached bathroom. $280

Charterhouse **209–219 Wanchai Rd ⓣ2833 5566, ⓦwww.charterhouse.com.** Elegant, good-sized rooms done out in warm beige, and some with views of the Happy Valley Racecourse, though smug staff prefer dealing with Mainland tour groups, rather than Westerners. Coming by MTR, take the Times Square exit. $1200

Clean Guesthouse **1st Floor, Room N, Central Building, 531 Jaffe Rd ⓣ2833 2063.** Lives up to its name, a very clean and friendly hostel, perhaps the best in this building, with towels, slippers and soap all provided. $280

Emperor **1 Wang Tak St, Happy Valley ⓣ2893 3693, ⓦwww.holidaycity.com/emperor-hongkong.** A lovely hotel in a peaceful location, ideal for children, and away from the crushing crowds of Causeway Bay. The medium-sized rooms are nothing special but cheery and comfortable, with all the standard hotel facilities. It's a ten-minute walk from Causeway Bay MTR, or you can take the Happy Valley tram up Tin Lok Lane. Special offers, and discounted rates for long stays. $1780

Jetvan Traveller's House **4th Floor, 4a Fairview Mansions, 51 Paterson St ⓣ2890 8133, ⓔjetvanhus@yahoo.com.** This guesthouse has eight rooms, all with telephone, air-con, TV and bathroom, though rather cramped – some are also windowless. Book ahead. $350.

King's **300 Jaffe Road ⓣ3188 2277, ⓕ3188 2626.** Quirky boutique hotel with a "cyber" theme resulting in a sort of minimalist sci-fi decor. Rooms come with IDD computers and plasma-screen TVs, and deals can slash rates. $1000

Pak Tak Hostel **7th Floor, Block A, Hyde Park Mansions, 53 Paterson St ⓣ2890 7067, ⓕ2576 8475.** This fourteen-roomed guesthouse has a range of doubles and twins all with attached bath, air-con, telephone and TV. The rooms are bright and clean, with larger windows than most other budget choices. $350

Park Lane **310 Gloucester Road ⓣ2293 8888, ⓦwww.parklane.com.hk.** Smart business or upmarket traveller option overlooking Victoria Park; well placed for MTR. $2300.

Wang Fat **3rd floor, Paterson Building, 47 Paterson St ⓣ2895 1015, ⓦwww.wangfathostel.com.hk.** A recently renovated, bright and clean hostel with slightly more elbow room than most, a free laundry service and multilingual manager. Dorms $120, rooms $350.

Tsim Sha Tsui & Hung Hom

Tsim Sha Tsui and the surrounding areas are supremely well sited for shops, bars, restaurants and nightlife. The main drag, Nathan Road, runs the gamut from high-class hotels such as the *Sheraton* and *Miramar* to the myriad cheap guesthouses in Chungking Mansions and other buildings. In the streets east and west of Nathan Road, there's a similar mix: it's just to the west of the road that you'll find possibly the two best-sited hotels in the territory, the colonial *Peninsula* and the affordable *Salisbury YMCA*. The area east of Chatham Road is all built on land reclaimed since the 1970s, with a string of upmarket hotels along the waterfront in Tsim Sha Tsui East. The #A21 Airbus comes within striking distance of most accommodation in the Tsim Sha Tsui and Hung Hom area; Tsim Sha Tsui MTR and East Tsim Sha Tsui KCR stations also put you within walking distance of all the places listed below.

Staying up around Jordan Road, just north of Kowloon Park, is no great hardship. You're within walking distance of Tsim Sha Tsui (and the streetlife of lower Yau Ma Tei), and although there's no let-up in noise you usually get a little more for your money. Jordan MTR is the most convenient station.

For the accommodation listed below, see map on pp.104–105.

Along Nathan Road

Golden Crown Guesthouse **5th Floor, Golden Crown Court, 66–70 Nathan Rd ⓣ2369 1782, ⓕ2368 1740.** Golden Crown Court is by far the least awful of the blocks along Nathan Road, and this is a very friendly place, though there's not much space in the five-bed dorms. The other rooms are a good size and fairly clean, however. Dorms $80 per person, rooms $250

Holiday Inn Golden Mile **50 Nathan Rd ⓣ2369 3111, ⓦwww.goldenmile.com.** Right next door to Chungking Mansions, this standard Holiday Inn has relatively spacious rooms, with plenty of singles. There's also a pool, a popular bar and several restaurants. $2500

Hyatt Regency **67 Nathan Rd ⓣ2311 1234, ⓦwww.hongkong.regency.hyatt.com.** Spectacular lobby and ground-floor shopping arcade, perfectly positioned for shopaholics: seventeen floors and over seven hundred rooms, all very decently equipped with marble bathrooms and hairdryers. $1130

Miramar **118–130 Nathan Rd ⓣ2368 1111, ⓦwww.miramarhk.com.** Right opposite Kowloon Park, this is a fairly garish hotel, great value for money if you're after a mid-range place, and bursting with shops and restaurants. It's enormous (the rooms are much larger than average), and it's often full. Check the website for package deals. $1200

Sheraton **20 Nathan Rd ⓣ2369 1111, ⓦwww.sheraton.com/hongkong.** Lording it over the bottom of Nathan Road, the Sheraton is swanky and expensive, though for the price of a cocktail you can ride the exterior lift to the Sky Lounge for superb harbour views; yuppies congregate in the basement *Someplace Else* bar. The rooms are tastefully decorated and large, and it is worth looking out for regular special discount packages. $3600

Waifan Guesthouse **5th Floor, Golden Crown Court, 66-70 Nathan Road ⓣ2302 4812, ⓦwww.ictravelhk.com.** Clean, relatively roomy option, with helpful and remarkably calm owner. $280

Chungking Mansions, 36–44 Nathan Rd.

Chungking Mansions is not the place for anyone overly concerned with hygiene or worried about fire, though most of the **guesthouses** themselves are alright, and some are really good. The building's ground and first floors are shopping arcades, with the guesthouses on the floors above. There are five sets of **lifts**, labelled A to E, two for each block – one for the even floors, one for the odd floors. Noticeboards tell you which guesthouses are on each floor: the numbers, A3, B4, etc, are the address on that floor for each guesthouse. Confusingly, once you're up in the mansions, some of the blocks connect with each other by corridors: one wrong turn through a swing door and you could be coming down Block C having gone up Block B. Searching for a room, it's best to leave one person downstairs with the luggage as the lifts are very small. If you're really going to shop around, go straight to the top floor of a block and work your way down, as big queues often form for the lifts (especially Blocks A and B). A few owners run more than one place, so don't worry if you're packed off to another block or another floor when you try to check in: just make sure to see the room first and establish the price.

▲ Chungking Mansions

Dragon Inn Block B, 3rd Floor ⓣ2368 2007, ⓔdragoinn@asiaonline.net. Well-organized, friendly hostel-cum-travel agent, with 21 clean and basic rooms including singles with shared bathroom and en-suite triples. Security cameras and ever-present staff make this place feel safe: a good choice on the 3rd floor. $170

Fortunate Guesthouse Block A, 11th Floor ⓣ9581 6606, or 2367 9490. Clean, modern guesthouse that would do well for a group of friends or family: two of the rooms have four beds. Otherwise, the clean doubles come with air-con, TV and own bathroom. $180

Hawaii Guesthouse Block A, 14th Floor ⓣ2366 6127. One of the bargains in the mansion, with en-suite air-con rooms the same price however many people occupy them – though three would be pushing it. Singles with shared bathroom $80, air-con use $10 extra. $160

Park Guesthouse Block A, 15th Floor, A1 ⓣ2368 1689, ⓕ2367 7889. This long-established guesthouse has very tidy box-like singles and doubles, some with fridges and shower. Don't believe them if they tell you some rooms have sea views, though. $160

Peking (and New Peking) Guesthouse Block A, 12th Floor, A2 ⓣ2723 8320. The new block boasts spanking, spacious new rooms with tiled floor, fridge and big windows. Some of the big doubles could fit four people. The old block has cheaper, smaller and older, but still presentable, rooms. Welcoming manager. $180

Tai Wan Hotel Block A, 3rd Floor ⓣ9406 2379, ⓔtaiwan.hotel@hotmail.com. New and very clean, with bigger rooms than most and a reception area staffed full-time make this place a cut above average. $170

Tom's Guesthouse Block A, 8th Floor, A5 ⓣ2722 4956; Block B & C, 16th Floor, C1 ⓣ2367 9258 or 9194 5923. Pleasant sets of rooms with a friendly owner flitting between them; the cheapest rooms are in Block A. The rooms are tidy and the guesthouse feels safe; you get the use of a fridge, there's chilled water on demand, and the bathrooms are clean and decent. $170

Travellers' Hostel Block A, 16th Floor ⓣ2368 7710, ⓔmrspau@yahoo.com.hk. This well-known hostel occupies the whole of the 16th floor: it has a noticeboard, Internet access, a shared kitchen, and a lounge with satellite TV. Dorm rooms have seven beds with lockers, and there's a range of fairly shabby singles and doubles on offer, with a $10 charge per night for air-con use. Eccentric long-term expat residents can be irritating. Dorms $80 per person, rooms $160

Welcome Guesthouse Block A, 7th Floor, A5 ⓣ2721 7793, ⓔGuestHouseHK@hotmail.com or ⓔgloriak@netvigator.com. A recommended first choice; air-con doubles with and without shower, and some singles. Nice clean rooms, luggage storage, laundry service, and China visas available. Very friendly owners who sometimes run tai chi lessons in Kowloon Park in the morning. $160

Yan Yan Guesthouse Block E, 8th & 12th Floors ⓣ2366 8930. Reception on 8th floor. Singles, doubles, triples, and four-person rooms with all facilities. Being in Block E, it's a bit more relaxed and quieter; all in all, good value for money. Air-con charged at discretion of management – if used sparingly free, if used constantly $20 per day. $160

Mirador Mansions, 56–58 Nathan Rd.

Despite the cockroach debris on the stairs, the lines of dripping washing in the corridor and the interminable wait at the lifts, **Mirador** is cleaner, less sleazy and more manageable than its larger neighbour, Chungking. Rooms are clean and well equipped, albeit tiny.

Cosmic Guesthouse 12th Floor, A1, A2, F1 and 6th Floor, F3; reception on 12th Floor, ⓣ2739 4952. English-speaking staff and rooms ranging from dorm to deluxe doubles with bathroom and good-sized windows. Luggage storage $10 a night. The eight-bed dorms are on the grubby side, but the individual rooms are clean. Dorms $70 per person, rooms $180

Garden Hostel 3rd Floor, F4 ⓣ2311 1183. Mirador's finest guesthouse; friendly and laid back with a large sofa-filled and pot-planted garden to chill out in with some secondhand books. They have more than fifty beds, and their eight-bed dorms are split into male- and female-only. The individual rooms are white-tiled to the ceiling and fairly spartan, which makes them clinical but exceptionally clean. Dorms $60 per person, rooms $160

East of Nathan Road

Dadol 1st Floor, Champagne Court, 16–20 Kimberley Rd ⓣ2369 8882, ⓕ2311 0250. There are more than forty well-kept rooms with carpet, bathroom, TV, telephone and air-con in this clean hotel. Although a "love" hotel, popular with young couples at lunchtime for one-hour rental, the atmosphere is not sleazy and the staff, who speak some English, welcome regular travellers and also offer single rooms. $270

Guangdong 18 Prat Ave ⓣ3410 8888, ⓦwww.gdhhotels.com. Mainland Chinese-operated hotel within staggering distance of some of the better bars and restaurants. Rooms, although good-sized, are rather plain and characterless, and decorated in 1980s synthetic fibres. $1080

Kimberley Inn 1st Floor, Champagne Court, 18–20 Kimberley Road ⓣ2723 9280, ⓕ2723 6870. Larger, more comfortable rooms than average in this guesthouse-cum-hotel, but more expensive, too. Management are friendly but don't speak much English, so haggling is out for most tourists. $400

Rooms for Tourist 6th Floor, Lyton House Building, 36 Mody Rd ⓣ2366 0579 or 2721 8309. A friendly and stylish hostel with a deadpan manager, and fresh orchids in the bathroom. The en-suite rooms are well sized, clean and simple. $250

Star Guesthouse Flat B, 6th Floor, 21 Cameron Road ⓣ2723 8951, ⓦwww.starguesthouse.com.hk. Friendly owner Charlie Chan offers a comfortable range of singles, doubles and triples in two locations along the road; some rooms are tiny, however, so ask to see a few. More expensive than Mirador or Chungking, but worth it for the cleaner, calmer atmosphere. $300

West of Nathan Road

Langham 8 Peking Rd ⓣ2375 1133, ⓦwww.langhamhotels.com. It's all dim lighting and heavy fabrics in this hotel whose lobby is hung with dripping chandeliers. Serious

prices for rooms with all the usual comforts, including a pool. It's at the Canton Road end of the street and is camouflaged as a shopping centre. $2200

Marco Polo Hongkong, Marco Polo Gateway, Marco Polo Prince Harbour City, Canton Rd ⓣ**2113 1888,** ⓦ**www.marcopolohotels.com.** The massive Harbour City complex houses three different hotels under the same Marco Polo umbrella. They're all fairly fancy, if not overwhelming, and you can use each hotel's facilities at will. Only the *Hongkong* (the largest) has harbour views; those at the *Prince* overlook the park. $2050

Peninsula Salisbury Rd ⓣ**2920 2888,** ⓦ**www.peninsula.com.** Possibly the grandest hotel in Hong Kong, the *Peninsula* has been putting visitors up in unrivalled style since the late 1920s. Its elegant colonial wings have been overshadowed by the new central tower, which provides harbour views to match the style and quality of the hotel – the top-floor bar-restaurant, *Felix*, is the work of designer Philippe Starck. Service is impeccable, as you might expect. At least put on some "smart-casual" clothes and drop in for afternoon tea in the splendid lobby, or have a drink at *Felix* (though the food is overrated). See p.107 for more on the hotel's history. $2600

Salisbury YMCA 41 Salisbury Rd ⓣ**2268 7000,** ⓦ**www.ymcahk.org.hk.** This is the best semi-cheap hotel location in this part of town. The facilities are excellent, including two indoor pools, fitness centre, squash court and a good café. The air-con doubles with TV and shower are booked up weeks in advance; there are also 56 budget beds available in four-bedded dorms, though you can't stay more than seven days in these. Dorm beds $210 per person, rooms $700

Tsim Sha Tsui East & Hung Hom

Inter-Continental 18 Salisbury Rd ⓣ**2721 1211,** ⓦ**www.hongkong-ic.intercontinental.com.** Rival to the *Peninsula* and actually the preferred hotel of many international business tycoons. An extraordinary glassed-in lobby (in which mere mortals can take a drink) and a twisting marble staircase that pops up in fashion shoots. As well as its waterfront site, it has its own pool, a top-rated Cantonese restaurant and is connected to the New World Centre, a huge shopping mall. With a fistful of credit cards, you need never leave. $3300

Kowloon Shangri-La 64 Mody Rd ⓣ**2721 2111,** ⓦ**www.shangri-la.com.** This huge, opulent hotel has 725 luxurious rooms, a pool, health club, eight restaurants and bars, an entire executive level and a 24-hour business centre. Inside, the design makes the usual extravagant use of marble, crystal and splashing fountains. $2500

New World Renaissance 22 Salisbury Rd ⓣ**2369 4111,** ⓦ**www.renaissance.com.** One of Tsim Sha Tsui East's oldest hotels, the sprawling red-brick New World Renaissance has comfortable rooms, with huge bathrooms, and the service meets all the usual high-class hotel standards. $1900

Nikko 72 Mody Rd ⓣ**2739 1111,** ⓦ**www.hotel-nikko.com.hk.** Plush Japanese-owned business hotel, popular with Japanese package tours. It has all the contemporary luxury you'd expect, and is only a step away from Hung Hom KCR Station. $2400

Jordan

China-HK Hotel 1st Floor, Parkes Mansion, 1–11 Parkes Street (Austin Road) ⓣ**2730 8023,** ⓕ**2723 5398.** Real hotel rather than a guesthouse, with a permanently staffed reception area, and large beds, though rooms themselves are not much bigger. Surrounded by inexpensive restaurants. $400

Pruton Prudential 222 Nathan Rd ⓣ**2311 8222,** ⓕ**2311 4760.** Great city-views and a swimming pool on the roof do a lot to attract custom, and the MTR exit couldn't be closer. The rooms are modern, large, bright and cheery, and the helpful staff are complemented by plenty of beefy security men. It is, however, a tad expensive. $1100

Rent-A-Room 2nd Floor, Flat A, Knight Garden, 7–8 Tak Hing St ⓣ**2366 3011,** ⓦ**www.rentaroomhk.com.** No sign; look for "Knight Garden" about halfway down street. Rented apartments rather than a typical guesthouse; rooms are large, with fridge, wardrobes, kettle, telephones, optional Internet link, and access to washing machines. Not cheap overnight, but excellent value for long-term rental. $450

South & North 5th Floor, 5G, National Court, 242–252 Nathan Rd ⓣ**2730 9768 or 2369 0869.** A very clean, albeit tiny hotel, but the seven tiled rooms are comfortable enough and have everything you need, including a fridge, shower and toilet, air-con and clean sheets. Single rooms available. $280

Yau Ma Tei & Mongkok

Comparative hotel prices start to drop once you get into Yau Ma Tei, and you can pick up some bargains, especially at the hotels operated by religious organizations. Not many tourists choose to stay as far out as Mongkok, however, though there are a couple of decent options, and you're close to the Bird Market and Ladies' Market. Regular buses run up and down Nathan Road, or you can get to all the places listed below (see map on p.112) via nearby MTR stations.

Yau Ma Tei

Booth Lodge 7th Floor, 11 Wing Sing Lane ⓣ2771 9266, ⓦwww.boothlodge.salvation.org.hk. A smart, Salvation Army hotel just off Nathan Road, close to the Jade and Night markets. Rooms are comfortably functional (though cheaper rooms are fairly small), and there's a pleasant restaurant and outdoor café terrace. Breakfast buffet included. $700

Caritas Bianchi Lodge 4 Cliff Rd ⓣ2388 1111, ⓕ2770 6669. Almost next door to Booth Lodge, and around twice as big, the air-con rooms in this Roman Catholic-run hotel have bath and TV. Continental breakfast is included, and there's a restaurant serving cheap lunches and dinners. Long-term packages available. $820

Grand Palace 1B Wing Sing Lane ⓣ2771 8088, ⓦwww.grandpalacehotel.hk. Mainland Chinese-run hotel that hardly lives up to its name, with rooms not much bigger than those of Tsim Sha Tsui's guesthouses. It is, however, clean, helpful, and well placed for the night market. $400

International House (YMCA) 23 Waterloo Rd ⓣ2771 9111, ⓦwww.ymcaintlhouse-hk.org. Smart and well-equipped YMCA guesthouse with some budget single rooms for men; you can't book these in advance, so just turn up early. Rooms come with air-con, bath and TV; laundry service, too. The restaurant serves a good buffet breakfast. $680

Majestic 348 Nathan Rd ⓣ2781 1333, ⓦwww.majestichotel.com.hk. One of the better hotels in this area, above a shopping complex and two-screen cinema. The rooms are comfortable, if a little heavy on the pine furniture. $950

Nathan 378 Nathan Rd ⓣ2780 9798, ⓦwww.nathanhotel.com. Good-value, newly renovated business venue, with fairly spacious rooms featuring broadband Internet connections. $880.

Mongkok

Anne Black Guesthouse (YWCA) 5 Man Fuk Rd, off Waterloo Rd ⓣ2713 9211, ⓦwww.ywca.org.hk. Basic singles and doubles with shower at pretty good rates; men can stay here, too. It's a little bit of a way from Mongkok KCR Station: head east along Argyle Street, over the rail line, until you reach Soares Avenue; turn south down here, cross over Waterloo Road into Pui Ching Road, and Man Fuk Road is first on the left – about a fifteen-minute walk in all. $700

Dragon Hostel Room 707, 7th Floor, Sincere House, 83 Argyle St ⓣ2395 0577, ⓦwww.dragonhostel.com. Guesthouse with helpful management and comparatively large single, double, and family rooms that present a good deal when compared with what you'd get for the same price in Tsim Sha Tsui. Long-stay rates available. $250

Royal Plaza 193 Prince Edward Rd West, ⓣ2928 8822, ⓦwww.royalplaza.com.hk. This smart hotel sits on top of Mongkok KCR Station with an entrance in the Grand Century Place shopping plaza. The 469 rooms are pleasant enough and come with all the usual hotel amenities but are fairly characterless. Good prices for a hotel that offers fountain-and-piano-in-the-lobby opulence, a forty-metre swimming pool, gym, an enormous ballroom, and a library. $1580

The New Territories

Most people tend to see the New Territories on a day-trip, but if you want a night away from the manic centre, stay either at one of the youth hostels (see p.183) – which are all fairly remote – or one of the major hotels below.

Kowloon Panda 3 Tsuen Wah St, Tsuen Wan, ⓣ2409 1111, ⓦwww.pandahotel.com.hk. See map on p.138. Easily accessed on the MTR (though admittedly at the end of the line) or the #A31 Airbus, the enormous, one-thousand-roomed Panda has plenty of space, some rooms with water views, and masses of facilities (including a pool and two good restaurants), plus offers the chance to see a bit of New Town life at first hand. $600

Saigon Beach Resort Tai Mong Tsi Rd, Sai Kung ⓣ2791 1068, ⓕ2792 3035. See map on p.146. Perfect location, right by the beach around 1km from Sai Kung Town, with thirty rooms, all boasting a sea view. There's an excellent bar and restaurant overlooking the sea and a watersports centre nearby. The building itself is an ugly concrete box, though the rooms have been recently renovated. Rates shoot up at the weekend. $1000

Regal Riverside Tai Chung Kiu Rd, Sha Tin ⓣ2649 7878, ⓦwww.regal-hotels.com. See map on pp.126–127. The New Territories' best hotel – though there's not a lot of competition – but stuck out on the other side of the Shing Mun River, making it a ten-minute trek to Sha Tin KCR Station and its New Town amenities. Comfortable, with large rooms and bathrooms; often appears on holiday packages, and is good for families. $600

Royal Park 8 Pak Hok Ting St, Sha Tin ⓣ2601 2111, ⓦwww.royalpark.com.hk. See map on pp.126–127. A red-brick tower that blends in well with the surrounding court buildings and residential high-rises, and convenient for Sha Tin KCR Station. Well-appointed rooms with big windows, and plenty of facilities including a gym, swimming pool and sauna. The hotel also runs a shuttle bus to Tsim Sha Tsui. $1400

Tai Po Hotel 2nd Floor, 6 Wun Tau Kok Lane ⓣ2658 6121, ⓦwww.yp.com.hk/taipohotel. See map on p.131. Ideal if you want to explore Plover Cove, this basic hotel has fifty small-tiled rooms with air-con and attached bathroom. Everything is clean, although well worn, and the staff are friendly. Triples also available. $400

The Outlying Islands

Outlying Islands' accommodation is best booked in advance, especially at the weekend, when half of Hong Kong heads out of the urban areas, and guesthouse prices can also double. On the other hand, there are often discounted rates for staying a few days mid-week. As well as the places listed below, you'll find plenty of travel agents and touts near the piers renting out holiday apartments (see relevant section in text) and there are two youth hostels on Lantau (see p.183).

Lamma

For the accommodation listed below, see map on p.157.

Bali Holiday Resort Yung Shue Wan ⓣ2982 4580. Newish, spacious rooms in apartment block, with or without views and kitchenettes – more modern than Man Lai Wah but further back from the water. Weekly and monthly rates. $350

Concerto Inn 28 Hung Sing Yeh Beach, Yung Shue Wan ⓣ2982 1668, ⓦwww.concertoinn.com.hk. Lamma's best hotel, offering rooms with balconies overlooking the beach, satellite TV and a video and fridge in every room – some have kitchens, too. The restaurant is sited on a nice garden terrace. $480

Katmandhu Guesthouse 39 Main St, Yung Shue Wan ⓣ & ⓕ2982 0028. Attached to Bubbles Laundry. Rooms are no-frills, dark little cells with hard mattresses but are all self-contained with shower unit, microwave, TV and DVD. Little natural light inside, but a cheap, cleanish bed for the night. $250

Man Lai Wah Hotel Yung Shue Wan ⓣ2982 0220, or 2982 0600. Right by the ferry pier, overlooking the harbour, this hotel has nine compact rooms stocked with ageing furniture, and beds with well-used squeaky mattresses. However, this is made up for by the small balconies with sea views; they also have attached bathroom and TV and DVD. $350

Cheung Chau

For the accommodation listed below, see map on p.161.

Warwick East Bay ⓣ2981 0081, ⓦwww.warwickhotel.com.hk. Overlooking Tung Wan Beach, this is the obvious – if most expensive – place to stay: a concrete box whose rooms have balconies, private baths and cable TV. There's also a terrace café and a swimming pool. They also offer a babysitting service and long-stay rates. $700

Lantau

For the accommodation listed below, see map on pp.166–167.

Babylon Villa Cheung Sha Lower Village ⓣ2980 3145, ⓕ2980 3024. A standard British "bed and breakfast" by the sea. There are three cosy rooms in one of three colour themes: pink, blue or yellow, with minibar, bathroom and TV. Everything's a bit cramped, but the setting is romantic, there's a small terraced dining room and a pile of secondhand books and magazines. This is a no-smoking hotel. Room rate includes breakfast for two people. $800

Mui Wo Inn Mui Wo ⓣ2984 7725, ⓕ2984 1916. A short walk beyond the Silvermine Beach, this kitsch little hotel with a small kidney-shaped swimming pool has fairly plain rooms; the front ones have balconies and lovely sea views, while the rooms out back are cheaper but not so nice. $280

Silvermine Beach Hotel Mui Wo ⓣ2984 8295, ⓦwww.resort.com.hk. Overlooking the beach at Silvermine Bay, this is comfortable, almost luxurious, and great value for money compared to the hotels back in the centre of Hong Kong Island (though it's owned by Kowloon's Miramar). There's a swimming pool, gym, sauna, tennis courts and all the usual business paraphernalia. $880

Camping

There are around forty official **campsites** throughout the SAR, most in the various country parks. There are large concentrations on Lantau and on the Sai Kung Peninsula in the New Territories; several of the most usefully sited are detailed in the text. All of them cost just a few dollars (or are free) but you can't reserve a space, so getting there early at the weekend or on a public holiday is a good idea. All the sites have basic facilities: toilets, barbecue pits and a water supply. But generally you'll need to take your own food and equipment, and be prepared to walk to most of them as they're often well away from shops and villages. There's a free combined information sheet/map of the sites, called *Campsites of Hong Kong Country Parks*, available from the HKTB.

You can sometimes **camp at the youth hostels** on Lantau and out in the New Territories; see the list on p.182 and call first to check before setting out. Camping this way, you'll be able to use the hostel facilities, too.

6

Eating

Don't underestimate the importance of food in Chinese culture. Meals are a shared, family affair, informal but always full of opportunities to show respect for others by the way the food and drink is served, accepted and eaten. As a visitor, especially as a foreigner, the nuances might pass you by, but it will soon become apparent that the Hong Kong Chinese live to eat – every café and restaurant is noisy and packed, the shrill interiors a world apart from the more restrained ambience favoured in the West. Almost everyone eats out regularly – even if it's only at one of the many busy street stalls - and the vast Chinese restaurants organize their opening hours around the long working days of most of the population.

As well as the joys of eating some of the best **Cantonese** food available anywhere, including that great breakfast institution, **dim sum**, the city offers a variety of **regional Chinese** restaurants, from Beijing and Shanghai to Sichuan. There's also a colossal range of **world cuisine** represented, leaving you to choose between curry houses, sushi bars, British pub-style food, sophisticated Southeast

A food index

Asian cuisine, American and European restaurants, hotel lunchtime buffets, pizzerias, vegetarian, South American, Chinese and Western fast-food chains, and **dai pai dongs** (street stalls) shovelling calorific fuel into office workers.

Food needn't be expensive, certainly if you stick to Chinese and Asian restaurants. The important thing is to retain your spirit of adventure at all times: some of the best dining experiences in Hong Kong are in the most unlikely looking places, and some of the best food is eaten almost in passing, on the street or taken quickly in a *dim sum* restaurant or café.

The **listings and reviews** below should help you decide where and what to eat in Hong Kong. We've started with cafés, coffee shops, delis and street food, followed by *dim sum* restaurants and Chinese food in its various guises, succeeded by all the other cuisines available in the SAR, listed in alphabetical order. At the end of the chapter are details about buying your own food in markets and supermarkets. **Vegetarian** restaurants, and those that serve vegetarian meals, are included throughout; most of the purely vegetarian places are either Cantonese or Indian/Pakistani – there's a round-up on p.219. To go straight to the listings for the kind of food you want to eat, check the **food index** opposite.

The **opening hours** given throughout are daily, unless otherwise stated. Chinese restaurants tend to close early, and the kitchen is usually winding down by 9pm or so. Don't count on being able to use **credit cards** everywhere. Many restaurants – especially the smaller ones – will only take cash, so always check first if you're unsure.

While the listings below are a good starting point, Hong Kong's restaurant scene is extremely volatile, with fashion and events taking a continuing toll: the 2002 SARS scare, when tourism ceased and Hong Kongers avoided social contacts for fear of contracting the disease, was reputedly responsible for the closure of one in three of Kowloon's restaurants. The free weekly **magazines**, *BC* and *HK Magazine*, review places of the moment, or you can fork out $120 for **restaurant guides** by *Hong Kong Tatler* (conservative and upmarket) or *BC* (caustic and more adventurous).

Two factors you might want to consider when choosing your restaurant are **hygiene** and MSG. While the ingredients used in most restaurants – particularly Chinese – are extremely fresh, the conditions in which they are handled can leave a lot to be desired. Things to look out for are the general cleanliness of the staff, the condition of the kitchen and utensils, the water in which live fish and seafood are kept and whether cooked and fresh food are handled separately. **MSG**, or monosodium glutamate, is also a common additive in many Chinese restaurants (and is also sold in supermarkets for domestic use). It acts not on the food but by stimulating your sense of taste – in other words, part of your nervous system. Large amounts can produce an allergic reaction in some people, and if you feel slightly "buzzy" after a meal, that's why. Some restaurants have a policy of no MSG, and you can get (or at least try to get) others to leave it out.

Cafés, coffee shops, delis and fast food

Whether you're looking for breakfast, coffee and cake, sandwiches, burgers or ice-cream, you'll be spoilt for choice in Hong Kong. Cafés and hotel/department store coffee shops are ubiquitous, while all the familiar Western burger and pizza joints are represented. Burger bars are also, incidentally, the cheapest places to get a cup of coffee, a cold drink or a welcome blast of air-conditioning. Other Western delights include a growing number of sandwich bars and delis, a few specialist ice-cream shops and some fine independent coffee bars.

Tea, coffee and soft drinks

Tea is to China what wines are to France, and specialist tea shops stock a truly bewildering variety of leaves from famous tea-growing districts around the mainland, costing from a few dollars per 100g to several hundred. Cheap restaurants always dish out a plastic cupful when you sit down; at *dim sum* joints the staff should ask what sort of tea you'd like (though often foreigners are automatically brought a pot of jasmine); and at more formal meals tea might be served before or after the meal, but very rarely with it.

You can get **non-Chinese tea** in cafés and snack bars (but rarely in Chinese restaurants): it's generally Lipton's and comes hot or cold on request, often with a slice of lemon. Tea with milk – usually the condensed variety – is rarer, though a local concoction, yin-yang coffee, mixes tea, coffee, and milk to produce a brew that frankly does nothing for any of them. For the real thing, venture into one of the big hotels for **afternoon tea** (see box on p.200), something that is well worth doing at least once for the atmosphere alone.

Coffee is widely available, though not overly popular with the Chinese. In cheap cafés it's invariably instant and weak and, again, served with condensed milk and sugar unless you specify otherwise. However, there's a well-established band of European and American cafés, where you can get a familiar and unnecessarily complex list of americano, espresso, cappuccino, mocha and latte. Some of these places double as cybercafés offering Internet access (see box on p.198). You'll also get a decent cup of coffee in most of the larger hotels and many European restaurants.

All the usual international fizzy **soft drinks** are available from stalls and shops everywhere, as are a variety of fruit juices – though the small boxed ones are packed with sugar and additives. Cups of freshly squeezed fruit juice off the street are cheap, between $5 and $10 for orange or more exotic coconut or mixed fruit concoctions. You could also try the local soft drinks: Vitamilk is a plain or flavoured soya milk drink – a few dollars a carton – while lemon tea, chocolate milk, iced teas and lots of other infusions all come cold and in cartons. Regular milk isn't drunk very much by the Cantonese, but there are, surprisingly, several milk bars around town, or you can buy it in supermarkets.

A couple of Chinese chains sell Asian-influenced snacks (radish cake, chicken wings and the like), and there are lots of Chinese **cake shops**, too, dealing in freshly baked custard tarts, roast pork buns, sweet beanpaste buns and a host of others – many exceedingly sweet. **Chinese cafés**, often just hole-in-the-wall affairs, dish out polystyrene and foil boxes of more substantial food – rice and meat, noodles and so on – which you can generally take away or eat perched on a stool for around $20–40 a go.

Hong Kong-wide

Café de Coral Over a hundred branches around Hong Kong with bright, plastic interiors and a daily turnover of 300,000 customers seeking Chinese fast food. Noodles, chicken wings, fried rice, radish cakes, salads and sandwiches at low prices. Generally daily 8am–8pm.

Délifrance Pseudo-French deli-cafés selling croissants, baguettes, cakes and coffee from seventeen outlets strung between The Peak; Central and north Hong Kong Island; Kowloon; Sha Tin, Tsuen Wan and Kwai Fung in the New Territories; and Tung Chung on Lantau. Those in business areas might only operate Mon–Fri 8am–6pm, others generally daily 8am–8pm.

Häagen-Dazs The best ice-cream in Hong Kong – the chain also does cakes and drinks. Branches (among others) at Central; The Peak; Times Square, Causeway Bay; and the Hyatt Regency Hotel, Tsim Sha Tsui. Daily 10am–8pm.

Maxim's Barbecued chicken legs, hamburgers, salads, roast-meat dishes, drinks and sandwiches. Garish and synthetic-tasting cakes, too. At MTR and KCR stations, and at the Star Ferry piers. Generally daily 9am–8pm.

Oliver's Super Sandwiches Reliable but crowded deli and sandwich shop chain, also serving breakfast, afternoon tea and baked potatoes. Avoid the insipid pasta dishes. Branches around Central; Wan Chai; Causeway Bay; and Kowloon. Mon–Sat 8am–6pm.
Pacific Coffee Company (see "Cybercafés" p.198) Stylish coffee-shop chain with great coffee, good fruit juices, cookies and sandwiches, plus international newspapers and friendly staff. The biggest attraction is the comfy sofas into which you can sink with your coffee and relax. Opening hours vary depending on the locality (Mon–Sat 8am–6pm in Central) but roughly daily 8am 9pm.
rbt Twelve outlets, mostly in Kowloon. Originally specializing in Taiwanese "frothy" tea (rbt stands for "real brewed tea", though the Chinese name translates as "immortal's footprint forest"), this place has branched out into Pearl Sago drinks, Taro milk tea, fruit teas and coffees served in a glass boot, as well as weird Asian-Western meals, such as fried jacket potato with tofu. Cute furnishings make them popular with teenagers. Mon–Sat 7am–10pm, Sun 8am–6pm.
Starbucks Coffee The international coffee imperialists are here to compete against the local *Pacific Coffee Company*. Opening hours vary depending on the branch, but generally daily 8am–8pm.

Central, SoHo & The Peak

Unless otherwise stated, the places listed below are marked on the map on pp.54–55.

Bagel Factory 41 Elgin St, SoHo. See map on p.74. Bagels smeared in a wide range of flavoured cream cheeses, as well as chunky pies, quiches and pasta salads. The Soho Bakery next door and under the same ownership sells home-baked calorie-laden cakes, marble cheesecakes and pastries. Only a handful of places to sit down, but you could always take your bagel to the nearby botanical gardens. Daily 8am–9pm.
La Cité Basement, The Mall, One Pacific Place, 88 Queensway, Central. Smart bistro-cum-café that pushes all the right buttons – soup, snacks and set lunches, or just teas and coffees while you take the weight off your shopping feet. Daily 11am–11pm.
Dan Ryan's Chicago Bar and Grill 114 The Mall, One Pacific Place, 88 Queensway, Central. American restaurant (see p.212) serving classic breakfasts at weekends – eggs, pancakes and all the trimmings. Very good for children. Served Sat & Sun 7.30–11am.
Jaspa's 28–30 Staunton St, SoHo. See map on p.74. Chunky breakfasts including doorstopper toast, big bowls of muesli, and grilled Turkish bread with strawberries. Breakfast served daily 7–11am.
Joyce Café The Galleria, 9 Queen's Rd, Central. In a league of its own for stylish café surroundings, and expensive, although there are set breakfast menus (7.30am–noon). The menu is mostly soups, sandwiches, pastas and salads, with East-West fusion and health-food overtones. Mon–Sat 10am–9pm.
Mandarin Oriental Hotel 5 Connaught Rd, Central. Power-breakfast (served 7–11am in the *Grill Room*) where around $250 gets you unlimited stabs at an enormous buffet, from fresh fruit juice and cereals, eggs and all the works, through to strudels and cheese. Sunday brunch (11am–3pm) is similarly stylish, though costs around $350. For coffee, all-day snacks and light meals, *The Cafe* (7am–1am) is the favoured see-and-be-seen haunt, although its breakfast gets mixed reviews.
Marriott Café Marriott Hotel, One Pacific Place, 88 Queensway, Central. Western/Asian snacks and meals in an elegant hotel coffee shop whose long hours are a boon in this district. Daily 7am–1am.
Movenpick Marché Levels 6 & 7, The Peak Tower, The Peak. Good, inexpensive fresh food from this Swiss chain. Salads, sandwiches, soups and daily hot dishes, plus Swiss ice-cream. The sixth-floor café has an outside terrace. Daily 11am–11pm.
Taichong Bakery 32 Lyndhurst Terrace, Central. Takeaway Cantonese roast pork buns and custard tarts, so popular that long queues form as each batch is removed from the oven.
T.W. Café 2–10 Lyndhurst Terrace, Central. Not only fine coffee, but also large set breakfasts of egg and toast, fried fillet of sole, or chicken steaks for around $25. Window bar for people watching.
Wyndham Street Deli 36 Wyndham St, SoHo. See map on p.74. European-style deli offering moderately priced sandwiches, pastas, grills and salads, plus wonderful cakes and desserts. Good, reasonably priced (for Hong Kong) wine list. Mon–Sat 7am–11pm, Sun 9am–6pm.

Breakfast

The usual Chinese **breakfast** is *congee*, available from some early-opening restaurants or street stalls. The traditional Cantonese way to start the day is *dim sum*, served either in restaurants – some of which specialize in it – or makeshift stalls catering to passers-by. Western cooked and Continental breakfasts are available in most of the bigger hotels, and in an increasing number of cafés, coffee shops and some pubs. Check the reviews under "Cafés, coffee shops, delis and fast food" and "Dim sum" for full details of where serves what.

Wan Chai

The places listed below are marked on the map on pp.78–79.

Grand Café **Grand Hyatt, 1 Harbour Rd.** Hotel coffee shop with some of the finest window seats in the SAR and stylish, elegant surroundings. The food matches these step for step – always pricey, but top quality. Daily 6.30am–1am.

Renaissance Harbour View Hotel **1 Harbour Rd.** Near the Grand Hyatt, the *Coffee Shop* offers equally spectacular views, with slightly cheaper prices. Daily 7am–10.30pm.

Tsim Sha Tsui, Hung Hom & Yau Ma Tei

Unless otherwise stated, the places listed below are marked on the map on pp.104–105.

Chungking Mansions **36–44 Nathan Rd, Tsim Sha Tsui.** Take your pick from Nepalese, Indian or Pakistani cuisine – cheap curried breakfasts for those with cast-iron constitutions. Daily 8am–10pm.

Delicatessen Corner **Basement, Holiday Inn Golden Mile, 46–52 Nathan Rd, Tsim Sha Tsui.** German-style lunch boxes, soups, salads and sandwiches. Daily 7.30am–11.30pm.

First Cup of Coffee **12 Hankow Road, Tsim Sha Tsui.** Open 7am–1am for extremely good coffee from around $15 a cup, plus home-made croissants, torte, biscuits and toasted sandwiches.

Mall Café **Ground Floor, YMCA, 41 Salisbury Rd, Tsim Sha Tsui.** Favourite Tsim Sha Tsui spot for a leisurely breakfast – Continental,

Cybercafés

Not surprisingly in a city obsessed with technology, there are many cafés where you can log on for free whilst enjoying a decent cup of coffee or a snack. Juices, sandwiches, newspapers and magazines are also often available. Pacific Coffee Company (see p.197 for more) outlets are scattered around Kowloon and Hong Kong Island (for the most spectacular views while surfing the net head up to The Peak), but the rest of the cybercafés are more or less concentrated in Tsim Sha Tsui and Wan Chai.

Avanti Network Shop 54–62 Lockhart Rd, Wan Chai. Loud techno-music filled cyberbar; a $30 drink or snack gives you one hour on the net. Mon–Sat 7am–midnight.

It Fans Jubilee St, Central. Broadband-connected netbar, mostly full of young network-gaming students, Filipinos and Indonesians. Mon–Thurs $16 per hour, Fri–Sun $18 per hour.

Joint Professional Centre Ground Floor, The Center, 99 Queen's Rd, Central. Just opposite the HKTB's office, this small Internet café is usually deserted – so ideal for uninterrupted surfing – and has a fast connection. Surfing is free provided you buy a drink or a snack. Mon–Fri 9am–9pm, Sat 9am–5pm.

Pacific Coffee Company Customers are allowed to surf for a maximum of twenty minutes; even so, in the busier branches you'll probably have to wait your turn, and then put up with others, cup in hand, ready to pounce on the machine when you leave. Generally Mon–Sat 8am–6pm in Central, daily 8am–9pm elsewhere.

Shadowman 7 Lock Rd, Tsim Sha Tsui. Convenient for all the backpacker's hostels, this café offers twenty free minutes on their high-speed Macs if you buy a drink or one of the light meals or snacks (halal food) – otherwise, it's about $1 per minute. Daily 8.30am–midnight.

English or Chinese for $30–40 – set lunch or sandwich. The Hong Kong daily papers are available. Daily 7am–midnight.

Yee Shun Milk Company 519 Nathan Rd, Yau Ma Tei. **See map on p.112.** Lovely old *cha chan teng* whose speciality is bowls of sweetened steamed milk served either hot or cold. You can also fill up on fruit or milk shakes, sandwiches, toast and steamed eggs. Daily 8am–9pm.

New Territories

Coffee Shop, University of Science and Technology Clearwater Bay Rd, Tseung Kwan O, Kowloon. Snacks, sandwiches, salads, hot dishes and specialist coffees – a hot dish or large sandwich costs around $20–30. There's a large outdoor terrace with great views of the coastline. Get there by bus #91M or #91 from Diamond Hill MTR or #298 from Lam Tin MTR.

Street food: dai pai dongs

A short walk through some of the densely populated parts of the SAR offers you a vast choice of street food – dozens of different snacks, all at incredibly cheap prices. Hygiene shouldn't be too much of a concern; most of the snacks are fairly innocuous anyway, made out of fresh or preserved ingredients, while more elaborate food – noodles and the like – is freshly cooked in front of you.

The freelance street stalls you'll see all over the SAR are called **dai pai dongs**, literally "big licence stalls" after the permits that used to be issued for them. The mobile mini-kitchen variety are technically illegal nowadays but you still see them around in backstreets; there are also semi-permanent sit-down affairs in various markets, and especially out on the islands, where they tend to group together into informal restaurants. Don't worry about language or menus – most only have a repertoire of two or three dishes, and all the ingredients will be on view, so just point to what you want and expect to pay, on average, $10 for a basic dish. Common snacks are fish, beef and pork balls (threaded onto bamboo sticks and dipped in chilli sauce), fresh and dried squid, spring rolls, steamed buns, *won ton* (stuffed dumplings), simple noodle soups, pancakes, *congee*, cooked intestines, tofu pudding and various sweets. More elaborate offerings might include seafood, mixed rice and noodle dishes, stews, soups and bottled beer.

Unfortunately, the alfresco *dai pai dong*'s days may be numbered, with local government trying to get them banned for health reasons, and moved indoors. But for now, the following central Hong Kong and Kowloon locations are the most accessible places to sample *dai pai dong* food. Every New Territories town has its own particular area for *dai pai dongs*, as do the outlying islands; see the text for more details. All the *dai pai dongs* listed overleaf open daily from 6am until around midnight and sometimes even later, unless otherwise stated.

▲ *Dai pai dong* on Temple Street

Afternoon tea

Sipping a cup of British-style tea, with proper milk and all the trimmings, in one of the SAR's most splendid hotels has become something of a Hong Kong institution. The lobby lounges are generally the places to head for, among which the **Peninsula** (Salisbury Rd, Tsim Sha Tsui) is the most magnificent – all gilt and soaring pillars, and a string quartet playing as you drink tea and munch scones. Other marvellous venues for afternoon tea are the **Inter-Continental** (Salisbury Rd, Tsim Sha Tsui); the *Lobby Lounge* at the **Island Shangri-La** (Two Pacific Place, 88 Queensway, Central); the *Tiffin Lounge* at the **Grand Hyatt** (1 Harbour Rd, Wan Chai) and the *Mandarin Oriental* (5 Connaught Rd, Central). At all these places, expect to pay around $150 upwards per person for a set tea. Dress code is "smart casual"; you may find that blue jeans, whatever their condition, are not acceptable.

Cooked Food Market Urban Council Complex, 345 Queen's Rd, Central. The Cooked Food Market on the second floor is one of the more authentic culinary experiences in town: no frills, no foreigners. Daily 6am–2am.

Graham Street Market At the bottom of Stanley Street, Central. Daily 6am–9pm.

Haiphong Road Bottom of Kowloon Park, Tsim Sha Tsui. Late morning–late.

Hau Fook Street Off Carnarvon Road, between Cameron Road and Granville Road, Tsim Sha Tsui. The street tables here serve basic Cantonese and Shanghai food, especially seafood.

Fa Yuen Street and **Nelson Street** In Mongkok have night-time tables.

Kowloon City Market 3rd Floor, Cooked Food Hall, 100 Nga Tsin Wai Rd, Kowloon City. The first Chinese eatery, called Lok Yuen, on the left as you walk in (it has no English name), is famous for its iced tea with condensed milk (*dong lai cha*) and pork chops (*chu pa*). Daily 7am–5.30pm.

Kung Wo Beancurd Factory 118 Pei Ho St, Sham Shui Po. There's no English sign, but you'll see it just behind the market stalls diametrically opposite Sham Shui Po MTR exit B2. This simple traditional canteen is famous for its very cheap home-made beancurd, dished up hot and fried and stuffed with meat or fish. Daily 7.15am–8pm.

Temple Street Yau Ma Tei. Reliable seafood-based street food at the Temple Street Night Market, full of noisy Chinese youths and groups of nervous-looking tourists – establish prices when you order, and check your change carefully to avoid rip-offs. Daily 7–11pm; see p.113.

Dim sum

Restaurants specializing in *dim sum* **open early** in the morning, from around 7am, and serve right through lunch up until around 5pm; nearly all regular Cantonese restaurants also serve *dim sum*, usually from 10am or11am until 3pm. In addition, most shopping plazas in residential areas have at least one *dim sum* restaurant, and they are often the best places to head for an authentic, bustling and good-value meal, though don't expect anyone to speak English. If you can't make breakfast, the best time is before the lunch rush – say around noon – as after lunch there won't be much left. The opening hours given in the reviews below are the *dim sum* hours for that particular restaurant: most of the places convert into regular restaurants for the evening session.

Central

Unless otherwise stated, the places listed below are marked on the map on pp.54–55.

City Hall Chinese Restaurant 2nd Floor, City Hall Low Block ☎2521 1303. Harbour views and a good range of *dim sum* served throughout the day. You'll have to wait for a lunchtime table; take a ticket at the door. Mon–Sat 10am–3pm, Sun 8am–3pm.

Jasmine Shop 5, Lower Ground Floor, Jardine House, 1 Connaught Place ☎2524 5098. One of a chain offering dependable *dim sum* in upmarket surroundings and served by staff who are used to novice visitors. Daily 11am–3pm & 6–11pm.

Luk Yu Teahouse 24–26 Stanley St ☎2523 5464. Famous as much for its 1930s vibe – heavy ceiling fans, dark wooden furniture, shell lamps, and *dim sum* carried around tables in tin trays by elderly staff – as for its food, whose quality is frankly not up to the hefty price tag (at least $100 a head). Even so, it's worth a trip to impress a business client or just for the

Dim sum restaurants

Most *dim sum* restaurants are enormous and noisy, often with tables on several floors; in the smarter places, staff with two-way radios check on space before letting you through. In many, the decoration is completely over-the-top: they're used for wedding receptions and parties and are covered in dragons, swirls, painted screens and ornate backgrounds that can easily cost millions of Hong Kong dollars.

Going in, you'll either be confronted by a maître d', who'll put your name on a list and tell you when there's space, or often you can just walk through and fight for a table yourself. It's busiest at lunchtime and on Sunday when families come out to eat, when you'll have to queue. This is not an orderly concept: just attach yourself to a likely looking table where people appear to be finishing up, and hover over the seats until they leave. Any hesitation and you'll lose your table, so keep an eye out.

It's best to go in a group if you can, in order to share dishes. As all the tables seat about ten or more, you'll be surrounded by others anyway, which is fun if the experience is new to you.

How to order, how to pay

Once you've secured a table, you'll be asked what sort of tea you'd like or, more likely, brought a pot of jasmine by default (see box on p.000). There's usually no extra charge for tea, and when you want a refill, just leave the lid off the teapot and it'll be topped up. You'll also be left with an all-important order card, on which your selection will be marked up.

At this stage, if you're Chinese, you'll have already started to wash your chopsticks and rinse your bowls in the hot tea or water: everything should be clean anyway, but it's almost a ritual with some people.

Ordering is what makes many *dim sum* restaurants such fun: traditionally, the selection is wheeled around in trolleys stacked with bamboo steamers in which the dumplings are cooked; each steamer contains a small plate with three or four little dumplings, or a single serving of more substantial dishes. Somewhere, too, there'll be people frying stuffed vegetables at mobile stands, others with trays of spring rolls and cakes, and different trolleys dispensing noodle soups, *congee* and other food. Just flag down the trolleys as they pass and see what you fancy by lifting the lids. Each time you pick something, the basket or plate will be dumped on the table, and a mark made on the order card according to the size of the dish (small, medium, large, and special). In some *dim sum* restaurants you'll have to order your dishes from the kitchen, in which case there'll invariably be a menu on the table – if it's in Chinese only and nobody speaks English, have a look at what others are eating and point.

When you've finished, leave your chopsticks over the pile of rubble left on your table and flag down a waiter, who will take your card. They'll count the number of empty baskets/plates on the table, check it off against the ticks on your order card, and go away to prepare the bill. Most things cost between $10 and $40 a serving, so even if you absolutely stuff yourself, it's hard to spend more than $90–120 a head in a group, perhaps rising to $150 if you eat in one of the fancier or more famous *dim sum* places. On top of this, you'll nearly always pay a ten-percent service charge.

ambience; you'll need to book at weekends. Daily 7am–6pm.

Metropol **4th Floor, United Centre, 95 Queensway ☎2865 1988.** Seating for over a thousand in this downtown business venue – even so, you'll need to reserve a table most days. Daily 8am–midnight.

Summer Palace **5th Floor, Island Shangri-La Hotel, Two Pacific Place, 88 Queensway ☎2820 8552.** Superb – but expensive – *dim sum* in relaxed, stylish and reasonably quiet surroundings. Daily 11.30am–3pm.

Tsui Hang Village **2nd Floor, New World Tower, 16–18 Queen's Rd ☎2524 2012.** Get there early for the good *dim sum* in splendid, traditional surroundings. Sat 11am–5.30pm, Sun 10am–5.30pm.

Yung Kee **32–40 Wellington St ☎2522 1624.** **See map on p.61.** Classic Cantonese restaurant that gets mobbed for its fine *dim sum*, in particular the roasted goose. Mon–Sat 2–5pm, Sun 10am–5.30pm.

Zen **The Mall, One Pacific Place, 88 Queensway ☎2845 4555.** Sharp designer-style and expertly cooked *dim sum*, which means considerably higher prices than usual (around $100 a head). A rather casual attitude to reservations when they're busy. Daily 11.30am–3pm & 5.30–11pm.

Sheung Wan

The places listed below are marked on the map on p.65.

Ka Ho **328 Lok Ku Rd, just around from antiques shops on Upper Lascar Row ☎2815 8133.** A staunchly Chinese venue without a hint of English spoken, perhaps a little intimidating for first-time *dim sum* but good quality and low prices – everything is under $10. Daily from 6.30am.

Lin Heung Teahouse **160–164 Wellington St ☎2544 4556.** This great place relocated here from Guangzhou (Canton) around 1950, and they've been so busy since that they haven't had time to change the furnishings or allow their ancient staff to retire. Little English spoken, but a fantastic atmosphere if you like crowded, lively venues with inexpensive food. Daily from 7.30am.

Wan Chai & Causeway Bay

The places listed below are marked on the map on pp.78–79.

Canton Room **1st Floor, Luk Kwok Hotel, 72 Gloucester Rd ☎2866 2166.** Fine *dim sum* served in this rather splendid hotel dining room with wood panelling and Art Deco touches. Daily 11.30am–3pm.

Dim Sum **63 Sing Woo Rd, Happy Valley ☎2834 8893.** Old-style wooden booths make this a nice, cosy place to experiment with *dim sum* – there are over eighty varieties on the menu, and staff are patient with foreigners. **Daily** 11am–4.30pm & 6–11pm.

Dynasty **Renaissance Harbour View, 1 Harbour Rd ☎2802 8888.** Harbour views from one of Hong Kong's best hotels. Excellent, creative but pricey *dim sum*. Mon–Sat noon–3pm, Sun 11.30am–3pm.

East Lake Seafood **4th Floor, Pearl City, 22–36 Paterson Street ☎2504 3311.** Cheerful, noisy placed packed with local Chinese daily from 7am to noon.

Maxim's **2nd & 3rd Floors, Hennessy Centre, Hennessy Rd ☎2895 2200.** A down-to-earth *dim sum* place, where the relatively cheery trolley-pushers muster up the odd word of English. The deep-fried crispy chicken is particularly delicious. Daily 7.30am–5pm.

Aberdeen

Jumbo Floating Restaurant **Shum Wan Pier Drive, Wong Chuk Hang ☎2553 9111.** **See map on p.87.** A Hong Kong institution, this floating restaurant serves *dim sum* from 10.30am onwards, but the food is nothing special and it's overpriced. Daily 10.30am–4.30pm.

Tsim Sha Tsui

The places listed below are marked on the map on pp.104–105.

The Chinese Restaurant **2nd Floor, Hyatt Regency, 67 Nathan Rd ☎2311 1234.** Elegant traditional teahouse surroundings, complete with booth seating and deferential waiters, make for one of the finer *dim sum* experiences. Pricey, but worth every cent. Daily 11.30am–3pm.

Tao Heung **Floor 3, Silvercord Court, 30 Canton Rd** (entrance beside cinema on Haiphong Rd) **☎2375 9128.** Come early for a window-seat facing Kowloon Park. No trolleys, but they have an English menu, and their selection is first-rate and inexpensive – try the white radish cake, roast pork *sheung fan* (stuffed rice noodles), and their beef rissoles with celery. Daily from 7.30am.

△ Dim sum at *Luk Yu Teahouse*

Dim sum menu reader

Savouries

Steamed prawn dumplings	蝦餃
Steamed beef-ball	牛肉丸
Steamed spare ribs in spicy sauce	排骨
Steamed pork and prawn dumpling	燒賣
Steamed bun stuffed with barbecued pork	叉燒包
Gelatinous rice-flour roll stuffed with shrimp/meat	長粉
Steamed glutinous rice filled with assorted meat, wrapped in a lotus leaf	糯米雞
Deep-fried stuffed dumpling served with sweet and sour sauce	餛飩
Half-moon-shaped steamed dumpling with meat/shrimp	粉角
Congee (thick rice gruel, flavoured with shredded meat and spring onion)	春卷
Spring roll	羅蔔糕
Turnip cake	鳳爪
Chicken feet	釀豆腐
Stuffed beancurd	鳳爪
Taro/yam croquette	蕃薯糊角
Crabmeat dumplings	蟹肉角
Shark's fin dumplings	魚鰭餃
Curried squid	咖喱魷魚
Steamed, sliced chicken wrapped in beancurd	雞絲粉卷
Fried, stuffed green pepper	釀青椒
Deep-fried beancurd roll with pork/shrimp	鮮春卷
Steamed dumpling with pork and chicken	豬肉雞水餃
Steamed chicken bun	雞包仔
Barbecued pork puff	叉燒酥
Mixed meat croquette	咸水角

Sweets

Water-chestnut cake	馬蹄糕
Sweet beancurd with almond soup	豆腐花
Sweet coconut balls	糯米池
Steamed sponge cake	馬來糕
Mango pudding	芒果布丁
Sweet lotus-seed paste bun	蓮蓉糕
Egg-custard tart	蛋撻

Tao Yuan **1st Floor, China Hong Kong City, 33 Canton Rd ☎2736 1688.** *Dim sum* for a clientele that couldn't be more critical: Chinese travellers from the adjacent departure level for China ferries. It's usually packed. Mon–Sat 11am–midnight, Sun 10am–midnight.

Tai Po

Chuan Hu Xiao Chi **4–10 Tai Ming Lane, Tai Po ☎2657 6838.** **See map on p.131.** Just off the main square towards the *Tai Po Hotel*, this kitsch little restaurant with green booths, sunflower-yellow walls and wooden tables serves tasty Sichuan and Shanghai-inspired *dim sum*. Daily 11.00am–11.30pm.

Vegetarian dim sum

The majority of *dim sum* restaurants have enough options on their menus to keep most vegetarians happy; however, there are also a few specialist vegetarian-only places, such as those listed below.

Kung Tak Lam **Lok Sing Centre, 31 Yee Wo St, Causeway Bay ☎2890 3127.** **See map on pp.78–79.** Inexpensive Shanghai vegetarian *dim sum* with more than 150 choices. No meat, no MSG, organic vegetables. Try one of the delicious pan-fried fake meats. Daily 11am–11pm.

Light Vegetarian **Ground Floor, New Lucky House, 13 Jordan Road, Kowloon ☎2384 2833.** **See map on pp.104–105.** Large sit-down *dim sum* selection, plus take-away at the front. Mid-range, very comfortable. Daily from 10.30am.

Tak Bo Vegetarian Kitchen **106 Austin Rd, Tsim Sha Tsui ☎2723 2770.** **See map on pp.104–105.** Point to what you want from the window and eat inside; it's all cheap and very tasty. Try the electric pink-and-yellow steamed buns. Daily from 10.30am.

Restaurants

If you've mastered the *dim sum* experience, no Chinese or Asian restaurant in Hong Kong need hold any fears. Most places have menus in English, and the only real problem is that often the English-language menu is much less extensive and exciting than the Chinese one: you may have to point at what other Chinese diners are eating if you want seasonal, traditional food.

Most Cantonese restaurants open early in the morning and, in certain parts of the city, such as Tsim Sha Tsui and Wan Chai, can stay open until midnight or beyond. The ones that do *dim sum* start serving their regular menu from mid- to late afternoon onwards. In the evenings, most local people like to eat early, which means that kitchens start closing at around 9pm. Other regional Chinese and Asian restaurants keep pretty much the same hours, though they perhaps won't open until 11am or so. Western restaurants generally have shorter hours, but you'll never have a problem finding somewhere to eat up until around midnight.

You'll find that many restaurants located in residential blocks – such as *Chung-King Mansions*' Indian establishments – call themselves **clubs**. This is to get around restaurant licensing laws, and technically you need to be a member to eat at them; though in all these places, entering the restaurant confers temporary membership. Real clubs, which do require you to be a member, or guest of a member, to eat there (such as the *Foreign Correspondents' Club*), are not covered in this guide.

For the intricacies of **eating and ordering** in a Chinese restaurant, see the box on p.201. To ask for **the bill**, you say *mai dan*, though – with the wrong intonation – this can also mean to "buy eggs". Sign language works just as well. Nearly all restaurants will add a ten-percent **service charge** to your bill, and if small plates of nuts and pickles are brought with tea, you'll pay for them, too – wave them away if you don't want them. In places where there's no service charge, leaving ten percent or a few dollars from your change is fine. Even if you've paid service, the waiter may wave your change airily above your head in the leather wallet that the bill came in; if you want the change, make a move for it or that will be deemed a tip, too.

Chinese

Lots of Chinese restaurants offer a set tourist menu, which can be good value but is unlikely to be very adventurous. If you're going on into China, you might want to try some regional food here first, though – naturally enough – Hong Kong's restaurants are best for southern Chinese fare.

Central

Unless otherwise stated, the places listed below are marked on the map on pp.54–55.

Jasmine Shop 5, Lower Ground Floor, Jardine House, 1 Connaught Place ☎2524 5098. Popular member of the *Maxim* restaurant chain with a decent – if unsurprising – moderately priced menu. There'll be plenty that's recognizable, all well cooked and served by English-speaking staff. Daily 11am–3pm & 6–11pm.

Man Wah Mandarin Oriental Hotel, 5 Connaught Rd ☎2522 0111. If you've got the cash for one extravagantly priced Cantonese meal, blow it here on some beautiful food – the steamed crab with ginger shouldn't be missed – and spectacular views. If they don't take your breath away, the bill will. Reservations are essential. Daily noon–3pm & 6.30–11pm.

Tsim Chai Kee Near the corner of Wellington and Cochrane streets. Tiny place offering either prawn *won ton* or fishball noodle soup for $11 a serving – but they're some of the best in Central, and you'll have to queue to get a seat at lunchtime.

Tsui Hang Village 2nd Floor, New World Tower, 16–18 Queen's Rd ☎2524 2012. Named after the home town of Sun Yat-sen, the restaurant is well thought of – the food and decor are traditional and prices moderate for this part of the city. Mon–Fri 11am–3pm & 5.30–11.30pm, Sat 11am–11pm, Sun 10am–11.30pm.

Tsui Wah 17–19 Wellington St. See map on p.61. Multistorey institution serving a huge array of inexpensive Cantonese fast food, but fishball noodle soup is the thing to go for – the stock is very good quality – along with Hai Nam Chicken or sweet desserts. Packed to bursting at lunchtimes. Open mid-morning to early evening.

Yung Kee 32–40 Wellington St ☎2522 1624. See map on p.61. Four-storey eating-house and a great Cantonese institution, known for its exceptional roast goose, *chao siu* pork and pigeon – the best you will find anywhere. Very reasonable prices considering. Daily 11am–11.30pm.

Zhong Guo Song 6 Wo On Lane ☎2810 4141. See map on p.61. Tiny place with no decor, but the food is fresh, well presented, and inexpensive. Large (but uninteresting) vegetarian selection; no MSG, and minimum oil. Mains $50 or so.

Zen The Mall, One Pacific Place, 88 Queensway ☎2845 4555. Hi-tech surroundings, imaginative Cantonese food and competent, English-speaking staff. Osmanthus clams with broccoli and prawns, and squid with glass noodles and garlic are typical examples. Daily 11.30am–3.00pm & 5.30–11pm. Count on $100 per main dish.

Sheung Wan

Golden China 9 Jubilee St ☎2545 1472. See map on p.65. There's a small English sign, but don't expect any to be spoken inside – no problem, however, as this small, comfortable Cantonese diner has a limited menu along the lines of roast duck or roast pork and rice; portions $22–30. Has been catering to Central's office workers since 1963. Daily 8am–late afternoon.

Wan Chai & Causeway Bay

The places listed below are marked on the map on pp.78–79.

Chee Kee Wonton Ground Floor, 52 Russell St. Small, low-key haunt (whose sign is in Chinese only – look for the packed interior hung with Chinese prints and antique-style wooden stools) serving some of the tastiest *won ton* noodles in town. Soups are $24. Daily 11am–8pm.

Fook Lam Moon 35–45 Johnston Rd ☎2866 0663. Amongst Hong Kong's finest and most famous Cantonese restaurants, this is not the place to come if you're skimping on costs. House specialities include bird's nest soup, abalone, crispy piglet and crisp-skinned chicken. Daily 11.30am–3pm & 6–11pm.

Heng Fa Garden 1st Floor, 57 Lee Garden Rd ☎2915 7797. This popular, inexpensive restaurant has no English sign; it's located just before the turn-off into Lan Fong Rd on the opposite side of the road. The main reason for coming here is the desserts, such as sticky bean pudding, although there's also a full menu of noodle and *congee* dishes, and the dumplings and steamed egg are recommended. Daily 11.30am–midnight.

Veggie Exp 1st Floor, Ming Fung Building, 140 Wanchai Rd ☎2115 8880. Interesting vegetarian place with an unusual range of Cantonese and regional dishes (tofu and persimmon, for example), plus medicinal dishes – such as burdock and herb soup – that are rarely served in other vegetarian restaurants. Dishes containing egg are marked on the menu. Daily 11am–11pm. Mains around $50, set menus from $108.

Aberdeen

The places listed below are marked on the map on p.87.

Floating restaurants Shum Wan, Wong Chuk Hang. Docked in Aberdeen Harbour, Hong Kong's famous floating restaurants are, in truth, overpriced, mediocre and jammed with package-tour groups. However, if you still hanker after a meal in surroundings that look like a set from *The Last Emperor*, both the *Jumbo* (☎2553 9111; daily 10.30am–11.30pm), or the *Tai Pak* (t2554 1026; daily 10.30am–10.00pm) have their own private boat that will run you there across the harbour.

Tse Kee 80 & 82 Old Main St. Well-known basic noodle and fishball restaurant. There are two separate entrances, which can be confusing. Daily 10.30am–6pm.

Tsim Sha Tsui

The places listed below are marked on the map on pp.104–105.

Kakalok Cnr of Ashley Rd and Ichang St. A fast-food joint to end them all: noodles, rice, chicken, fish, whatever, all fried. Has the distinction of serving the cheapest fish and chips in Hong Kong ($15), and has fed many hard-up backpackers over the years. No seats, but Kowloon Park is 100m away. Daily mid-morning–late.

Light Vegetarian Ground Floor, New Lucky House, 13 Jordan Rd ☎2384 2833. Airy, busy place with a big selection of classic Cantonese and Shanghai vegetarian dishes: taro fish; a "bird's nest" basket with fried vegetables; pumpkin soup served in a pumpkin; "yin-yang" mushroom, corn and spinach soup; vegetarian duck. Around $55 a dish.

Shamrock Seafood 223 Nathan Rd ☎2735 6722. Cantonese and Chiu Chow seafood, along with a couple of the inescapable roast meat dishes, plus a fair vegetarian selection. Nothing startling, just a good, reliable and not too pricey place to eat with crowds of locals. Most mains $70 and above.

Shang Palace Basement 1, Kowloon Shangri-La Hotel, 64 Mody Rd, Tsim Sha Tsui East ☎2733 8754. Pricey but capable restaurant that seems to cook everything well, including pigeon, complete with over-the-top Imperial decor. It's busy at lunchtime – go early. Mon–Sat noon–3pm & 6.30–11pm, Sun 10.30am–3pm & 6.30–11pm.

Sweet Dynasty 88 Canton Rd ☎2199 7799. A bustling restaurant specializing in cheap desserts packed with taro, coconut milk and fruit. They also do a range of noodle, *congee* and weird dishes including stewed snow frog's fat with lotus seeds and red dates. Daily 10am–midnight.

Yan Toh Heen Inter-Continental Hotel, 18 Salisbury Rd ☎2721 1211. Reckoned one of Hong Kong's best for cutting-edge Cantonese cooking – and for the excellent service and amazing harbour views. Count on $800 a head for the works, though a $600 set-menu relieves the pain a little. Reservations essential. Daily noon–2.30pm & 6–11pm.

Yun Ji 16 Granville Rd. Not somewhere to cross the city for, but does excellent Cantonese one-plate rice, noodle, and soup dishes for around $25 a dish. Daily 7am–9pm.

Yau Ma Tei & Mongkok

Joyful Vegetarian 530 Nathan Rd, Yau Ma Tei ☎2780 2230. See map on p.112. Offers a range of inexpensive Chinese vegetarian greats, all

juicy with crispy skin. In one version, goose is flavoured with sour plum, a technique from **Chiu Chow** (Chaozhou) in southern China, where **sweet and sour** dishes with fruit also originated; the town's biggest contribution to local menus, however, is translucent *fun gwor* dumplings (popular in Hong Kong's *dim sum* restaurants). **Hakka** dishes – derived from the people of the same name – have also been absorbed by the Hong Kong palate, including the occasional use of preserved vegetables, chicken baked whole under a pile of crushed salt, and stewed tofu cubes stuffed with minced pork.

The cornerstone of Cantonese cooking is creating a balance of flavour, texture and colour

Dim sum

A traditional way of starting the day is with **dim sum**, which literally translates as "little heart". The name refers to the core element of a *dim sum* meal: dozens of types of small dumplings stuffed with vegetables, meat or seafood, and boiled, fried, baked or steamed – crunchy *har gau*, minced prawns wrapped in transparent rice-flour skins, are the hallmark of a good restaurant. These are backed up by spring rolls, prawn toast, sweet and savoury cakes, and other snacks, along with small servings of main-meal dishes such as squid with black beans, rice and cooked meats in lotus leaves, meat or seafood rissoles, curried squid, chicken feet, turnip cake, and stuffed peppers. Unusually, *dim sum* meals also feature sweet **desserts**, such as coconut jelly and custard tartlets, a very foreign concept in Chinese food. *Dim sum* is also known as **yum cha**, "drink tea", as a pot always accompanies a meal.

Taste and texture

Cantonese seasoning involves minimal use of sugar, soy sauce, rice wine and vinegar to tease out underlying fresh, sweet tastes; stronger spices such as chilli, salted black beans and five-spice powder (made from cumin, coriander seed, star anise, cinnamon and cardamom) are sparingly employed only to offer a contrast. The object is always to season without being obvious – any heavy-handedness and diners would immediately suspect that what they are eating is not fresh. Nothing illustrates this better than seafood, awful when old but delicate and fresh when straight out of the sea: mullet and bream, prawns, crabs, abalone, octopus and lobster are all eaten, with many restaurants allowing diners to pick their own straight from the tank. As a general rule, seafood is best eaten steamed, lightly seasoned with soy, ginger, spring onion and some fermented black soyabeans. Any Cantonese restaurant will have a signature seafood dish – even if it's just a fishball soup – but for freshness and atmosphere, it's hard to beat the outdoor places on Lamma and Cheung Chau islands.

As in all Chinese cooking, texture is also vital to the success of a dish. The Cantonese most enjoy well-defined textures, such as the crunchiness of a really fresh, lightly cooked prawn, or the smooth resilience of steamed beef balls with fresh coriander (which actually get their texture and juiciness from added fish paste). Vegetables are also mainly used to provide contrasting textures, from mushrooms to green beans, bean sprouts, taro, carrot, aubergine, and especially *pak choi* (Chinese broccoli), served steamed with garlic or oyster sauce. Though most people eat a far greater quantity of vegetables than meat, the Chinese believe that only meat can provide essential energy, and avoiding it is unhealthy in the long term. However, for both physical and spiritual reasons, people do eat vegetarian dishes fairly regularly, and there is a sophisticated **vegetarian cuisine**, which uses gluten and tofu in all its forms to mimic meat. White steamed **rice** is the Cantonese staple, along with broad **rice noodles** (*hefen*); fried rice is considered a special dish.

Another source of texture are **preserved ingredients** such as birds' nests and sea cucumber, which are actually completely flavourless in themselves and are thus served in a slow-cooked meat **stock**, sieved and skimmed until all fat and residues are removed and only the requisite "fresh" flavour remains. Stock recipes are often fiercely guarded by their creators, and especially tasty ones (sometimes containing medicinal herbs) can make a restaurant's reputation.

Tea

Chinese **tea** falls into three broad categories: **green**, where the leaves are picked and then dried straight away, producing a green- or yellow-tinted brew; **black**, where the leaves are fermented before drying, for a dark red infusion; and **oolong**, where the leaves are part-fermented before drying, creating a yellow or light red brew. Famous varieties that are popular in Hong Kong include *heung pin cha* (jasmine, a green tea scented by mixing in flowers during the drying process), green *longjing* ("Dragon Well"), *tiet kwunyam* ("Iron Buddha", a popular type of *oolong*-style tea), and black *bolei* (pu'er tea), the favoured accompaniment to a *dim sum* meal for its supposed fat-reducing properties. Drinking tea is usually an informal affair, though there are regional tea ceremonies, the best known of which is *gongfu cha* from the Chiu Chow region involving tiny cups of fragrant *oolong*.

Another brew integral to Chinese life is **medicinal tea**, sold from open-fronted shops with cups or bowls ranged on a counter alongside ornate brass urns, each hung with a label naming the concoction in Chinese. Medicinal teas are made from various astringent medicinal herbs (the Cantonese term, *fu cha*, translates as "bitter tea"); two popular in winter for driving off colds are *ng fa cha* (five-flower tea) and *ya sei mei* (twenty-four flavour tea).

The cuisines

Cantonese cuisine is the most common cooking style found in Hong Kong, along with Chiu Chow and Hakka, which are essentially variations on the Cantonese theme. However, many types of regional Chinese food are also found here, either at specialist restaurants or as individual dishes in places that are otherwise firmly Cantonese – the waiter should always be able to point you towards the house speciality.

Beijing (Peking)

Beijing food is a northern, colder-climate style of cooking that relies more on pickles and meat, and favours wheat noodles and heavy dough dumplings instead of rice. One speciality is the Mongolian hot-pot of sliced meat, vegetables and dumplings cooked and mixed together in a stock that's boiled at your table in a special stove; you dip the raw ingredients in, eat them once cooked and then drink the resulting soup at the end of the meal. The most famous Beijing food of all is Peking duck, a recipe that's existed in China for centuries – slices of skin and meat from a barbecued duck, wrapped in a pancake with spring onion and radish and smeared with plum sauce. The local ducks are usually rather fattier than what you may be used to at home. If you order this, be sure to ask for the duck carcass to be taken away after carving and turned into soup with vegetables and mushrooms, which is then served later.

Shanghainese

Shanghainese is also a heavier cuisine than Cantonese, using more oil and spices, as well as preserved vegetables, pickles and steamed dumplings. Where the southern cuisines are interested in fresh flavours, Shanghai's is more concerned in emphasizing each ingredient's characteristic taste, with a bias towards sweetness. Meals often start with cold dishes such as smoked fish; and might include "drunken chicken", cooked in rice wine; or "red-cooked" pork, stewed in an aromatic stock containing soy sauce, sugar and aniseed. Seafood is also widely used, particularly fried or braised eels, while the great speciality is the expensive hairy crab – sent from Shanghai in the autumn, it is steamed and accompanied by ginger tea; the roe is considered a delicacy.

Sichuan (Szechuan)

Totally at odds with the above regions, Sichuan food takes little interest in original tastes or freshness, instead constructing pungent flavours with a heavy use of garlic, chillies and aromatic Sichuan pepper. Salted bean paste is a common cooking agent. Marinades are widely used, and specialities include spicy tofu, smoked duck (marinaded in wine, highly seasoned and cooked over camphor wood and tea leaves), and "strange-flavoured" chicken (served with a soya-sesame-vinegar sauce). Other dishes you'll see are braised aubergine, pork with raw garlic purée, and braised beans. You'll get through a lot of beer with a Sichuan meal.

– weekends are always packed. Not much English spoken, but there's an English menu; try the salt-baked chicken or tofu cubes stuffed with mince. Daily 11am–midnight.

Chiu Chow

Chan Kam Chung 56–58 South Wall Rd, Kowloon City ☎2383 3114. See map on pp.100–101. There's no English sign – look for the first restaurant on the left with seafood tanks outside as you come from the walled city park. This simple, inexpensive Chinese kitchen has been going for thirty years; you'll have to point to what you want (no English menu), but it's worth it for the atmosphere. The goose comes recommended; wash it down with tiny cups of *gongfu* tea. Daily 11am–12pm.

Chao Inn 7th Floor, One Peking Rd, Tsim Sha Tsui ☎2369 8819. See map on pp.104–105. You'll need to book window tables for harbour views, and the moderately priced food – cuisine from Chaozhou in Guangdong province – is also a cut

Shark's fin

If there's one dish that epitomizes both the Chinese propensity for eating unlikely animal body parts and their willingness to pay through the nose for the privilege, it's shark's fin. Many Cantonese restaurants offer it up as thick, fibrous shark's fin soup, not so much an acquired taste but an outrageously expensive one: suffice to say that if there's a cheap bowl of shark's fin on the menu, it isn't the real thing.

Quite how and why it came to be eaten in the first place is unclear, though the Chinese claim medicinal properties for the fin – being high in cartilage, it's believed to reinforce bone and help arthritis sufferers. Whatever the truth of this, the wider concern is that eating shark's fin soup is putting many shark species at risk. Economic growth in Southeast Asia and the Pacific Rim has fuelled demand for shark's fin, and, consequently, shark fishing is now very big business. Numbers are declining rapidly and since the shark is an important part of the food chain, the destruction of large numbers of them has disturbing implications for the marine environment.

For this reason alone, there's a growing move to boycott the eating of shark's fin products. If you need any more convincing, it's worth noting that shark flesh is not usually eaten in the Far East, so the fish are killed just for their fins. These are cut off while the shark is still alive and then the fish is thrown back into the sea, where – without its fins to give it mobility – it drowns.

above average, especially the roast goose. 10am-10pm.

Chiu Chow Dynasty 2nd Floor, Emperor Group Centre, 288 Hennesy Rd, Wan Chai ⓣ2832 6628. See map on pp.78–79. Gloomy decor – the interior isn't spacious enough for the heavy wooden furniture – but top Chiu Chow fare, including imitation cold-meat platter, sour-plum goose, deep-fried duck with taro, and the biggest range of Chiu Chow dumplings in town. $80 and up per main. Daily 11am–11pm.

Chiu Chow Garden Basement, Jardine House, 1 Connaught Place, Central ⓣ2525 8246. See map on pp.54–55. Chiu Chow food from the *Maxim* people. Always reliable and not expensive; goose a speciality. Daily 10am–3pm & 5.30pm–midnight.

Beijing (Peking)

Hutong 28th Floor, One Peking Rd, Tsim Sha Tsui ⓣ3428 8342. See map on pp.104–105. Part of the Aqua chain, similarly smart, expensive, and gifted with stunning views. Minimalist chic takes on northern Chinese food (with a few Sichuan-inspired items); the house speciality is slow-cooked lamb ribs served on a wooden plate

Peking 227 Nathan Rd, Jordan ⓣ2730 1315. See map on pp.104–105. Don't be put off by the fairly glum decor; this moderately priced place serves some of the best Beijing food in Hong Kong, with the duck especially recommended. Daily 11am–10.30pm.

Peking Garden 3rd Floor, Star House, Tsim Sha Tsui ⓣ2735 8211. See map on pp.104–105. One branch of a moderately priced, high-quality chain serving mostly northern cuisine, though with a nod to a couple of eastern dishes. Try the smoked vegetable rolls, "drunken chicken", fish with black vinegar, or, of course, Peking duck. Daily 11.30am–3pm, 5.30–11.30pm.

Spring Deer 1st Floor, 42 Mody Rd, Tsim Sha Tsui ⓣ2366 4012. See map on pp.104–105. Long-established, good-value place noted for its barbecued Peking duck (which is carved at the table) among a barrage of authentic dishes, such as baked fish on a hot plate, smoked chicken, and beancurd with minced pork. Daily noon–10.30pm.

Taifung Lau 29-31 Chatham Rd, Tsim Sha Tsui ⓣ2366 2494. See map on pp.104–105. The elderly, gloomy furnishings will never win any awards, but the northeastern Chinese food is good. Copious lamb and beef dishes – including Mongolian hot-pot (which you need to order a day in advance) – along with Peking duck, and Shandong preserved chicken. Most mains $100–150, though you can ask for half portions. Daily noon–11pm.

Shanghainese

D&J Shanghai 2nd Floor, Hanley House, 68-80 Canton Rd, Tsim Sha Tsui ⓣ3113 6993. See map on pp.104–105. Good place for Shanghai cold dishes, hot meals, or just a quick snack of *xioalong bao* (steamed pork buns).

Slightly tourist-inflated prices – mains $50 and up. Daily 11am–midnight.

Lulu Shanghai 3rd Floor, Pearl City, Paterson St, Causeway Bay ☎2882 2972. See map on pp.78–79. Fairly smart affair; try the cold, marinated sliced duck; sautéed fresh prawns; steamed dumplings; and fish slices served in a taro "cup" with pine nuts and sweetcorn kernels. Count on $120 a head. Daily 11.30am–2pm & evenings.

Ng Yu Zigan 26 Cochrane St, Mid-Levels. See map on p.74. Small English sign over the doorway reads "Between Wu Yue". Great snacks and light meals, including spicy noodles, stewed Dongpo pork, little dumplings and marinated cucumber slices; use of raw garlic and chillies may prove too pungent for some. Order a selection to share at around $25 a dish. Daily 8am–9pm.

Shanghai Garden Hutchison House, 10 Harcourt Rd, Central ☎2524 8181. See map on pp.54–55. Scrumptious authentic Shanghai fare (though a few regional dishes creep in); prices are fairly high. Daily 11.30am–3pm & 5.30–11.30pm.

Tak Hsin Shanghai 4–6 Tak Hing St, Jordan ☎2317 0663. See map on pp.104–105. Simple, everyday dishes served in equally unpretentious but comfortable surrounds – the steamed sliced pork with bamboo shoots, chicken *qiguo* (steam-pot), and beans with salted cabbage are all good. Photo-menu makes ordering easy. Around $50 a dish.

Zhing Nong 23a Lock Rd, Tsim Sha Tsui ☎2366 3187. See map on pp.104–105. Shanghai with definite Sichuanese leanings, and a cramped interior serving cold noodle dishes, Shanghai steamed pork buns, crispy pork and noodle soup, cold shredded chicken and seasonal hairy crabs. Most dishes under $50; closes 9pm sharp.

Sichuan (Szechuan)

Chuan Bar Bar 20 Luard Rd, Wan Chai ☎2527 8388. See map on pp.78–79. A smart Sichuanese restaurant-bar hung with wooden screens and serving chilli fish fillets, "strange-flavoured' chicken, beancurd and bamboo shoots, aubergine with hot garlic sauce, and more. Mains around the $50 mark; good-value set lunches and dinners.

Kong King 117 Lockhart Rd, Wan Chai ☎2520 0988. See map on pp.78–79. Difficult to categorize exactly, but includes classic Sichuanese "sizzling rice" (deep-fried rice cake with a light seafood soup poured over it at the table), and handmade noodles with shredded pork and preserved vegetables; also a big range of northern-style dumplings. You can eat well here for $100 a head. 11am–3pm & 6–11pm.

Red Pepper 7 Lan Fong Rd, Causeway Bay ☎2577 3811. See map on pp.78–79. The name says it all – hot food and a favourite with expats, which means higher-than-warranted prices and pushy staff. The smoked duck and beancurd are standard favourites. Best booked in advance, since it can get very busy. Daily noon–11.45pm. Set meal for two $158; otherwise, count on $70 per main.

Sichuan Garden The Mall, One Pacific Place, 88 Queensway, Central ☎2845 8433. See map on pp.54–55. Another moderately priced *Maxim's* restaurant – try the camphor-smoked duck, fish in hot and spicy soup, sautéed beef in a pungent sauce, or sizzling rice. Mon–Sat 11.30am–3pm & 5.30–11.30pm, Sun 11am–3pm & 5.30–11pm.

Yellow Door Kitchen 6th Floor, 37 Cochrane St, Mid-Levels ☎2858 6555. See map on p.74. Entrance on Lyndhurst Terrace next to Dublin Jack. This refreshing and friendly place offers an authentic Sichuanese menu including such rarely served (to foreigners) items as bitter melon, and they'll make it as hot as you'd get in China if you ask. Mon–Fri noon–2.30pm; and Mon–Sat from 6.30pm. Set dinner at $220 a head will leave you full for a day.

Other Chinese regions

Bistro Manchu 33 Elgin St, SoHo ☎2536 9218. See map on p.74. Moderately priced Manchurian food of the hearty stew and dumpling variety – northern Chinese with a bit of Mongolian and Korean thrown in, served in stylish East-meets-West surroundings. Daily noon–2.30pm & 6–11pm.

Islam Food 1 Lung Kong Rd, Kowloon City ☎2382 2822. See map on pp.100–101. This excellent, friendly no-frills restaurant focuses on the traditional food of China's Muslim minority peoples, but also serves some Beijing, Shanghainese and Sichuan dishes. The beef-cakes are renowned locally. Daily 11am–11pm.

Little Sheep 1st Floor, 26 Kimberley Rd, Tsim Sha Tsui ☎2722 7633. See map on pp.104–105. Inexpensive mainland Chinese chain loosely based on Mongolian hot-pot, offering a range of thinly sliced meats, vegetables and noodles to cook yourself at the table in bubbling vats of stock – ask for "white" (plain stock) or "red" (very spicy). Not much English spoken. Daily 11am–2pm & 6pm–late.

Manchu Manchu Ground Floor, 17–22 Lan Kwai Fong, Central ☎2536 0968. See map on p.61. Fairly smart affair with paper lanterns, wood panelling, and not one concession to southern Chinese tastes on its menu. Interesting items include wood-ear fungus and cabbage, chicken leg stuffed with one-hundred-year-old eggs, mutton soups, and sesame-pine nut pastries. Mains around $100. Noon–3pm & 6–11pm.

African

La Kasbah 17 Hollywood Rd, Mid-Levels ☎2525 9493. See map on p.74. Heavy wooden doors open into a red-lit intimate restaurant thumping to the sounds of exotic Arabic beats. Waiters wear fezzes while you dine on expensive North African delicacies and sip mint tea. Mon–Sat 6.30–11.30pm.

The Stoep 32 Lower Cheung Sha Village, Lantau Island ☎2980 2699. A relaxed, moderately priced restaurant serving jugs of Pimms by the sea. Mediterranean and meaty South African cuisine, including the scary-sounding Boerewors – a home-made sausage. Daily 11am–11pm.

American

Al's Diner 37 D'Aguilar St, Central ☎2869 1869. See map on p.61. Straightforward and inexpensive diner food – burgers, dogs, chilli and sandwiches – and late opening at weekends for ravenous clubbers. Mon–Thurs 11am–12.30am, Fri & Sat 11am–3.30am, Sun 6pm–12.30am.

Dan Ryan's Chicago Bar and Grill 114 The Mall, One Pacific Place, 88 Queensway, Central ☎2845 4600. See map on pp.54–55. Bumper American-size portions of ribs, burgers, steaks, salads and home-made desserts. You'll get enough food to sink a battleship, but it doesn't come cheap at $200 for a steak. Daily 11am–midnight.

Napa 21st Floor, Kowloon Shangri-La Hotel, Tsim Sha Tsui ☎2733 8752. See map on pp.104–105. Excellent Californian food in stunning Art Deco surroundings, with possibly the best view of the harbour available anywhere. Expect to pay highly for the privilege. Daily noon–3pm & 6.30–11pm.

Australian

Moon 1 Hysan Ave, Wan Chai ☎3110 2002. See map on pp.78–79. Faddish fusion menu aimed at local yuppies, with dishes including pasta, noodles, char-grilled steak, and Thai red curry. Good-value set dinners for two at $200, and a Sunday buffet until 3pm for $108. Daily 11.30am–11.30pm.

Ned Kelly's Last Stand 11a Ashley Rd, Tsim Sha Tsui ☎2376 0562. See map on pp.104–105. Laid-back, Aussie bar with live jazz (see "Live music", p.225) and a filling range of mid-range tucker – meat pies much in evidence. Daily 11.45am–1.45am.

Outback Branches at Fenwick Street, Wan Chai, and Great George Street, Causeway Bay. US chain of Australian-style grill restaurants, which basically means plenty of steak, burgers, chips and carbonated drinks served amongst didgeridoo decor. Awful in a way, but if you're after a steak for $128, this is the place.

British

British food, like the rest of their influence, is on the decline in Hong Kong, with the following restaurants the last of a once-widespread crowd. For no-nonsense portions of fish and chips, steak-and-kidney pie or an all-day English breakfast, most pubs can do the honours; see the next chapter for full pub and bar listings.

Chippy 51 Wellington St, Central. See map on pp.54–55. Tiny diner serving up mushy peas, bangers and mash, and pie and chips, along with slightly classier items such as pasta and a glass of wine. Entrance facing the steps leading down to Stanley St. Mon–Fri 11am–3pm & 6–10.30pm, Sat 11am–7pm. Plate of battered cod and fries costs $85.

Dot Cod B4 Basement, Prince's Building, 10 Chater Rd, Central ☎2810 6877. A busy Brit-style seafood restaurant and oyster bar that is literally seething at lunchtime with city-types tucking into cod and chips, olive-oil roast cod, lobster and whitebait among others. They also do grilled kipper breakfasts. Mon–Sat 7.30am–midnight. Expensive at $168 for cod and chips.

Jimmy's Kitchen 1–3 Wyndham St, Central ☎2526 5293. See map on p.61. British-pub-like interior, complete with horse brasses and dark woodwork; and an upmarket pub menu – pan-fried cod, oyster chowder and lamb fillets. Also does great martinis. Pricey at $100 a head without drinks. Daily 11.30am–3pm & 6–11pm.

SoHo SoHo **The Workstation, 43–45 Lyndhurst Terrace, SoHo ☎2147 2618. See map on p.74.** Modern British cooking offering traditional ingredients with a twist, served in chic surrounds with dark walls and glass partitions. The menu changes regularly. Weekday lunchtime specials from $145, and set dinners from $190, are good value. Mon–Sat noon–2.30pm, 7–10.30pm.

Buffets and set meals

Most of the larger hotels put on self-service buffets – for breakfast, lunch or afternoon tea, and sometimes for dinner, too. Many also offer two- or three-course set meals. Check advertisements for special deals. Buffet lunch (around $110) is usually noon–2.30pm, dinner ($160–250) 6.30–10pm, but ring for exact times; ten-percent service is added in all cases, and drinks are usually extra.

Filipino

Cinta-J **69 Jaffe Rd, Wan Chai ☎2529 6622. See map on pp.78–79.** Great dark restaurant-bar serving good-value meals of soups, casseroles and seafood (and a long Happy Hour Mon–Fri 5–10pm). Daily 11am–5am.

French

2 Sardines **43 Elgin St, SoHo ☎2973 6618. See map on p.74.** Small restaurant that has built itself a big reputation for reliable, reasonably priced French food. Daily noon–2pm & 6pm–11pm.

Arc Brasserie **8–13 Wo On Lane, Central ☎2234 9918. See map on p.61.** Extensive menu of French bistro classics such as onion soup, mussels, snails, baked wild mushrooms and roast duck breast, served in a laid-back lounge-like setting. The signature dish is goose liver, and the desserts are wonderful. Daily 11am–11pm. Around $500 per person for a full meal.

Gaddi's **1st Floor, Peninsula Hotel, Salisbury Rd, Tsim Sha Tsui ☎2366 6251. See map on pp.104–105.** One of the most respected Western restaurants in Hong Kong, in a conservative kind of way. Extraordinary food, extraordinary prices (at $1000 per person for a full meal); advance booking and smart dress essential. Noon–2.30pm & 7–11pm.

Le Rendez-Vous **5 Staunton St, SoHo ☎2905 1808. See map on p.74.** This tiny, cosy café serves huge crepes, both sweet and savoury. A romantic and fairly inexpensive venue for a candlelit evening dine. Daily 10am–11.30pm.

Spoon **Inter-Continental Hotel, 18 Salisbury Rd, Tsim Sha Tsui ☎2313 2256. See map on pp.104–105.** Like most of Hong Kong's foodies, you'll either love or hate this cutting-edge restaurant serving extremely odd, intriguing dishes. You might find it safer to stick to the set menu (changes daily), though even this is expensive. Daily 6pm–midnight.

Stanley's **1st & 2nd Floors, 90b Stanley Main St, Stanley ☎2831 8873. See map on p.91.** Chic French restaurant in Stanley village, which – despite high prices - is winning a lot of friends with its imaginative, regularly changing menu, and bay views. Try to book in advance. Noon–midnight.

Indian, Pakistani and Nepalese

Central & SoHo

Ashoka **57–59 Wyndham St, Central ☎2524 9623. See map on p.61.** Very popular northern Indian restaurant serving good-value set lunches and dinners, and several vegetarian choices, including large thalis. Daily 10am–10.30pm.

Gunga Din's Club **Lower Ground Floor, 59 Wyndham St, Central ☎2523 1439. See map on p.61.** Among the very best of Hong Kong's small, club-like Indian restaurants. Prices are extremely reasonable; booking recommended. Daily 11.30am–2.30pm & 6–10.30pm.

Sherpa Nepalese Cuisine **11 Staunton St, SoHo ☎2973 6886. See map on p.74.** Friendly restaurant with an interesting range of vegetarian dishes, and excellent roti (Nepali bread). Serves a good-value set lunch. Daily 11am–3pm & 6–11pm.

Wan Chai

The places listed below are marked on the map on pp.178–179.

Jo Jo's **1st Floor, 86–90 Johnston Rd, Wan**

Chai (entrance on Lee Tung St) ⓣ2527 3776. Hardly luxury surroundings, but a deservedly popular, inexpensive spot with tandoori specialities and views out onto the busy street. Daily 11am–3pm & 6–11pm.

Shaffi's Malik 185 Wanchai Road ⓣ2572 7474. Claims to be the oldest Indian restaurant in town – nothing spectacular, but good, tasty staples such as sheek kebabs, chicken tikka, *saag paneer* and naan. Good-value set lunches ($38), and set meal for two ($180). Daily 11am–3pm and 6–11pm.

Stanley

Lord Stanley at the Curry Pot 6th Floor, 90b Stanley Main St ⓣ2899 0811. See map on p.91. Very friendly little restaurant with ocean views from its sixth-floor windows, and delicately judged Indian food from all regions. The set lunch is fair value, but you can't go wrong choosing à la carte either. Daily noon–3pm & 6–10.30pm.

Tsim Sha Tsui

The places listed below are marked on the map on pp.104–105.

Delhi Club Block C, 3rd Floor, Chungking Mansions, 36–44 Nathan Rd ⓣ2368 1682. An Indian-Nepali curry-house *par excellence*, despite the spartan surroundings and slapdown service. The ludicrously cheap set meal would feed an army, and there's a good range of vegetarian dishes, mutton specialities and clay oven-cooked naan. Daily noon–2.30pm & 6–11.30pm.

Khyber Pass Block E, 7th Floor, Chungking Mansions, 36–44 Nathan Rd ⓣ2782 2768. Mess-hall seating at long tables, good – if unoriginal – food such as chicken tikka and *saag paneer*, and low prices. Daily noon–3.30pm & 6–11.30pm. $30–50 a dish.

Woodlands Mirror Tower, 61 Mody Rd ⓣ2369 3718. Part of an international chain, this is an inexpensive vegetarian Indian restaurant, whose menu describes each dish in detail. Snacks as well as full meals, including biryani and excellent thalis, the portions large enough to share. Always popular, with friendly service. Daily noon–3.30pm & 6.30–11pm.

Indonesian

The places listed below are marked on the map on pp.78–79.

Indonesian 1968 28 Leighton Rd, Causeway Bay ⓣ2577 9981. Recommended place with canteen-style surroundings, and staff who'll help you get the best out of the inexpensive menu – the chargrilled fish, curries and spicy aubergine get top marks. Daily 11.30am–11pm.

Padang J.P. Plaza, 22–36 Paterson St, Causeway Bay ⓣ2881 5075. This unpretentious place does a good run of *rendang*, satays, grilled seafood, mutton curry and – especially – durian-flavoured desserts. A little pricey for what you get, but good. Mains from $50.

International

Aqua 29th Floor and Penthouse, One Peking Road, Tsim Sha Tsui ⓣ3427 2288. See map on pp.104–105. Sunken slate tables and superlative harbour views are the setting for consuming an unexpectedly successful blend of Italian and Japanese dishes. The atmosphere is informal, and the prices high. Reservations essential. Mon–Thurs noon–2am, Fri–Sun 10.30am–2am.

Café Deco Levels 1 & 2, Peak Galleria, 118 Peak Rd, The Peak ⓣ2849 5111.See map on pp.54–55. Unrivalled views and a stylish Art Deco interior define this expensive, upmarket café serving gourmet pizzas, curries and grilled meats. Or just call in for a drink, or cake and coffee; at night, there's often live jazz. Mon–Thurs 11.30am–midnight, Fri & Sat 11.30am–1am, Sun 9.30am–midnight.

Felix 28th Floor, Peninsula Hotel, Salisbury Road, Tsim Sha Tsui ⓣ2315 3188. See map on pp.104–105. This restaurant was designed by

▲ Dining at *Aqua*

Philippe Starck, and the incredible views of Hong Kong Island in themselves warrant a visit. The Eurasian menu, however, is not as good as it should be at over $500 a head, but many people just come for a martini at the bar. Restaurant 6–11pm; bar 6pm–2am.

Jaspa's 28–30 Staunton St, SoHo ⓣ2869 0733. See map on p.74. A mix of hearty European and Mexican meals, with a wide vegetarian selection. Ideal for children, as each table comes with wax crayons and a paper tablecloth. Mon–Sat 10.30am–10.30pm, Sun 9am–10.30pm.

Mariners' Club 11 Middle Rd, Tsim Sha Tsui ⓣ2368 8261. See map on pp.104–105. Genuine club, though nonmembers are allowed to use the restaurant, which does filling breakfasts ($40), and Chinese-, Indian- and Western-style lunch and dinner buffets ($55–105).

M at the Fringe 2 Lower Albert Rd, Central ⓣ2877 4000. See map on p.61. Stylish restaurant much favoured by the glitterati for its boldly flavoured, health-conscious dishes – meat, fish and veggie – whose influences span the world. Reservations advised. Mon–Sat noon–3pm & 6pm–12.30am, Sun 7–12pm. Count on $300 a head for a three-course meal without drinks.

Post '97 1st Floor, 9–11 Lan Kwai Fong, Central ⓣ2810 9333. See map on p.61. Relaxed brasserie surroundings and an eclectic, expensive menu of Mediterranean and American food, plus a daily vegetarian choice. There's also coffee and herbal teas, while brunch specials are served all day on Sunday. Mon–Fri 9am–2am, Sat & Sun 24hr.

Roc Garden at the Fringe, 2 Lower Albert Rd, Central. See map on p.61. Vegetarian lunchtime buffet for $65 a head, with afternoon/evening tapas $20–45 a serving; there's a bar, balcony tables, and a rooftop garden with barbecue area. All a very good deal; no bookings.

Italian

Fat Angelo's 49a–c Elgin St, SoHo ⓣ2973 6808. See map on p.74. Extremely popular, noisy Italian joint serving up enormous pizzas and a range of pasta dishes. Two people can happily share one dish, making a fairly inexpensive night out. Daily noon–midnight.

Grappa's 132 The Mall, One Pacific Place, 88 Queensway, Central ⓣ2868 0086. See map on pp.54–55. A good place to meet or eat, whether you want a glass of wine, a snack or a full meal. Despite being fairly pricey the restaurant is usually full, but turnover is quick. Daily 9am–midnight.

Toscana Ritz-Carlton, 3 Connaught Rd, Central ⓣ2532 2062. See map on pp.54–55. Fashionable Tuscan restaurant in one of the fanciest of the city's hotels. Stylish Italian food, some of it good value, in posh surroundings. But style comes at a price. There are set lunches and dinners, too, from around $320. Daily 11am–3pm & 6–11pm.

Tutto Bene 7 Knutsford Terrace, Tsim Sha Tsui ⓣ2316 2116. See map on pp.104–105. Located on a small lane just north of Kimberly Rd, this popular expatriate hangout is one of several "Mediterranean" restaurants in the vicinity. Good Italian food in a pleasant atmosphere, with tables spread out on the pavement. Mon–Thurs & Sun 6.30pm–midnight, Fri–Sat 6pm–1am.

Upo's East Town Building, 16 Fenwick St, Wan Chai ⓣ2861 0077. See map on pp.78–79. Staid place with chequered cloths, exposed beam decor and a menu of well-presented Italian favourites. Children under 12 not allowed after 6pm. Fairly pricey for what you get – most mains above $100.

Japanese

Department stores For informal Japanese food, try the inexpensive supermarkets in Sogo, 555 Hennessy Rd, Wan Chai; the Great Food Hall, One Pacific Place, 88 Queensway, Central and department stores, which feature takeaway sushi and Japanese snack bars.

Itamae Sushi 14 Granville Rd, Tsim Sha Tsui. See map on pp.104–105. Conveyor-belt sushi at front, tables and menus at back, fish tanks in between. Looks upmarket, but pretty reasonable at $10–40 per colour-coded plate of an almost entirely raw seafood selection. Expect to queue; no reservations. Daily 11.30am-midnight.

Kyoto Joe 21 D'Aguilar St, Central ⓣ2804 6800. See map on p.61. Modern Japanese restaurant with at least two dining areas and bars; very popular with the expat crowd and serving reliable (and a bit expensive) lightweight Japanese meals. About $150 per head.

Kyozasa 20 Ashley Rd, Tsim Sha Tsui ⓣ2739 1336. See map on pp.104–105. Homely Japanese country food such as soba noodles and tofu. Low prices and plain decor – the menu items are written on brown paper and hung on the walls – makes this a relaxing and unpretentious place to eat, and recommended by the crowds of Japanese who consistently pack out this tiny restaurant. Daily noon–2.30pm, 6.30–11pm.

Miso Lower Ground Floor, Jardine House, Connaught Rd, Central ☎2845 8773. See map on pp.54–55. This ultramodern, ultra-cool restaurant will cook any Japanese delicacy you want (though not cheaply). The menu includes standards such as rolls, cones, sushi and saki, which are lapped up by a business crowd. Mon–Sat 11.30am–3pm & 6–10.30pm.

Nadaman Basement 2, Kowloon Shangri-La, 64 Mody Rd, Tsim Sha Tsui ☎2877 3838. See map on pp.104–105. Traditional, minimalist Japanese dining room where most of the business clientele tucks in at the sushi bar or spends big on the other house specials, such as the *kaiseki*, a set dinner of various small, beautifully presented dishes. Daily noon–3pm & 6.30–11pm.

Unkai 3rd Floor, Sheraton Hotel, 20 Nathan Rd, Tsim Sha Tsui ☎2369 1111. See map on pp.104–105. If you're going to blow your money on one expensive Japanese meal, this is the place to do it. The food here is authentic and beautifully presented. Daily noon–2.30pm & 6.30–10.30pm.

Korean

Nearly all Korean restaurants in Hong Kong feature a "barbecue" (*bulgogi*) as part of the menu – the table contains a grill, over which you cook marinaded slices of meat, fish or seafood; assorted pickles (including *kimchi* – spicy, pickled cabbage), rice and soup come with the meal. One odd feature of many restaurants is the ginseng-flavoured chewing gum handed out when you leave.

Arirang 2nd Floor, The Gateway, 25 Canton Rd, Tsim Sha Tsui ☎2956 3288. See map on pp.104–105. Dependable, moderately priced restaurant offering the usual Korean specialities – barbecued meat platters, spicy cold noodles – plus one free Korean beer for each guest. Daily 10am–midnight.

Busan 29 Ashley Rd, Tsim Sha Tsui ☎2376 3385. See map on pp.104–105. Highly popular barbeque place, which also does good ginseng chicken, cold noodles and seaweed soup. It's a little expensive, though; count on at least $120 a head. Daily 10am–11.30pm.

Koreana Ground Floor, Elizabeth House, 250 Gloucester Rd, Causeway Bay ☎2577 5145. See map on pp.78–79. Decently priced barbecue restaurant with all the standard dishes as well as some interesting vegetable choices and good noodles. Daily 11.30am–3pm, 6pm–midnight.

Malaysian and Singaporean

Banana Leaf Curry House Lockhart House, 440 Jaffe Rd, Wan Chai ☎2573 8187. See map on pp.78–79. One of a chain of bright, loud and inexpensive restaurants, low in atmosphere but good for Malaysian curries, satays, grills, samosas and roti served on a banana leaf. Daily noon–3pm & 6pm–midnight.

Mrs Chan Basement, 63 Peking Rd, Tsim Sha Tsui ☎2368 8706. See map on pp.104–105. Moderately priced Singapore-Malay home cooking, very good if you order the right things – including any of the seafood or satay dishes. Daily 11.30am-10pm.

Mexican

Agave 33 D'Aguilar St, Central ☎2521 2010. See map on p.61. A fine selection of burritos, enchiladas and fajitas, plus more than a hundred types of tequila. This place is not cheap – you'll have to cough up $275 for some of the rarer shots of tequila – but the Mexican chef uses his imported ingredients well and generally pleases the punters. Mon–Thurs 5.30pm–2am, Fri–Sat 5.30pm–4am.

La Placita 13th Floor, Times Square, 1 Matheson St, Causeway Bay ☎2506 3308. See map on pp.78–79. With an arcaded interior modelled on a Mexican village square, staff in ponchos, and pastel paint thrown about like it was on special offer, you know you're in El Mariachi themeland. A good bar to help the enchiladas go down. Daily noon–midnight.

Middle Eastern

Beirut 39 D'Aguilar St, Central ☎2804 6611. See map on p.61. A chic but cramped setting for Lebanese food, kebabs and mixed grills – though the bar gets just as much custom as the moderately priced restaurant. Mon–Fri noon–11.30pm, Sat noon–midnight, Sun 6pm–11.30pm.

Mongolian

Kublai's 3rd Floor, One Capitol Place, 18 Luard Rd, Wan Chai ☎2529 9117. **See map on pp.78–79.** Mongolian "barbecue" restaurant: pick your own ingredients – noodles, spices, vegetables, sliced meat and fish, and sauces – and then take them to be cooked. Highly entertaining if there's a crowd, and you can keep going back for more – though the whole affair can be a little rushed at busy times. Daily 11am–3am.

Russian/Ukrainian

Ivan the Kozak Ground Floor, 46–48 Cochrane St, Mid-Levels ☎2851 1193. **See map on p.74.** Hard to tell if the deadpan atmosphere is deliberate stereotyping, but the food – chicken Kiev, lamb stew, lots of cabbage and potatoes – certainly is. Portions are decent, good value and tasty, but the highlight here is donning a fur coat and walking into the huge freezer for a shot of vodka and a photo. Mon–Fri noon–10.30pm, Sat & Sun 5–10.30pm.

South American

La Pampa 32 Staunton St, SoHo ☎2868 6959. **See map on p.74.** Moderately expensive Argentinian restaurant that does what it does – barbecued steak, mainly – exceedingly well. You order by weight, it's grilled just how you want it and served with nominal quantities of vegetables. Make sure you have red wine, too. Daily noon–3pm & 6–11pm.

Spanish

La Comida 22 Staunton St, SoHo ☎2530 3118. **See map on p.74.** Relaxed restaurant, pleasant service and with tasty, good-value tapas, but not much else. The evening crowds are proof of its consistently good food. Daily 11am–11pm.

Swiss

Chesa 1st Floor, Peninsula Hotel, Salisbury Rd, Tsim Sha Tsui ☎2315 3169. **See map on pp.104–105.** The Peninsula's top-price Swiss restaurant serves great fondue and superb meat and fish dishes. Reservations essential. Daily noon–2.30pm & 6.30–10.30pm.

Thai

There are some classy Thai restaurants spread all over Hong Kong, but the best places are in Kowloon City, near the old Kai Tak airport site – take buses #11 (from Kowloon Airport Express Station), #5, #5C and #9 (from Tsim Sha Tsui Star Ferry Pier) or #14 (from the China Ferry Terminal) and get off on Prince Edward Road East, in front of the Regal Kai Tak Hotel.

Amporn Thai Food 3rd Floor, Cooked Food Hall, Kowloon City Market, 100 Nga Tsin Wai Rd, Kowloon City ☎2716 3689. **See map on pp.100–101.** Head to the third floor of the market, and Amporn Thai Food takes up most of the Cooked Food Hall. Don't be put off by the plastic stools and tables and the clattering din – this place is the real thing. There's no English menu, but the staff are friendly and can speak a little English; the Thai steamboat and fresh prawns are recommended. Daily noon–midnight.

Happy Garden Vietnamese Thai Near the bus stop, main corner, Shek O. One of several laid-back places with outdoor tables, luridly coloured drinks, and excellent food – try the morning glory with *blechan* beef, or huge Thai fish cakes. Mains around $60. Daily noon–10pm.

Thai Lemongrass 3rd Floor, California Tower, 30–32 D'Aguilar St, Central ☎2905 1688. **See map on p.61.** Chic surroundings and high-quality, expensive food covering many of Thailand's local cuisines. Mon–Thurs noon–2.30pm & 6.30–11pm, Fri & Sat noon–2.30pm, 7–11.30pm, Sun 6.30–10.30pm.

Vegetarian food

Most restaurants have vegetable, mushroom and beancurd (tofu) dishes on the menu, or you can order a regular noodle dish without the meat. Bear in mind, though, if you're a purist, that many Chinese dishes start off life with a meat stock; waiters will sometimes also insist that light meats such as chicken or fish are not really meat. If you really eat nothing of animal origin, it's better to say "I eat vegetarian food" (*ngor sik tzai*), or Buddhist monk's food as it's thought of, which is an accepted concept. To avoid any problems, it's easiest to eat in one of the excellent **Chinese vegetarian restaurants**, where the food is based on tofu, yam, taro and gluten, which can be shaped into – and made to taste of – its meaty counterpart (you even call it by the same names). Some of these places also serve excellent vegetarian *dim sum*, which is fortunate, as you'll have a hard time getting meat-free items in a real *dim sum* restaurant.

Other than these places, you're best off in the SAR's **Indian and Pakistani restaurants** (p.213), which have lots of non-meat choices, or a hotel buffet (p.213), which will always have a good salad bar and other vegetarian options. A meal at one of the **Buddhist monasteries** in Hong Kong will also consist of strictly vegetarian food; see especially Lantau (chapter 4) and the various temples in the New Territories (chapter 3).

Vegetarian restaurants

The places listed below are completely vegetarian, and are reviewed elsewhere in this chapter.

Joyful Vegetarian 530 Nathan Rd, Yau Ma Tei; see p.207.
Light Vegetarian 13 Jordan Rd, Jordan; see p.205.
Veggie Exp 1st Floor, Ming Fung Building, 140 Wanchai Rd, Wan Chai; see p.207
Woodlands Mirror Tower, 61 Mody Rd, Tsim Sha Tsui; see p.214.

Vietnamese

Green Cottage 32 Cannon St, Causeway Bay ☎2832 2863. See map on pp.78–79. This popular, family-run Vietnamese restaurant serves up, amongst other things, thirty different types of noodle soup (*pho*) in pleasant but cramped surroundings. Everything is good value for money, in particular the curry duck with French bread. Daily 10.30am–10.30pm.

Indochine 1929 2nd Floor, California Tower, 30–32 Lan Kwai Fong, Central ☎2869 7399. See map on p.61. The very elegant Indochine serves up some of the tastiest Vietnamese food in the SAR. There's a whiff of French colonial style about the place – stuffed snails feature on the menu – and every dish is a winner. Reservations advised. Mon–Sat noon–late, Sun 6pm–late.

Nha Trang 88–90 Wellington St, Central ☎2581 9992. See map on pp.54–55. First-rate Vietnamese food, whose crisp, clean, and sharp flavours make a nice break from more muggy Chinese fare.

Special diets

Some of the Pakistani restaurants in Chungking Mansions advertise themselves as serving **halal** food, as does the occasional Chinese Muslim restaurant.

For **kosher** food, enquire about the kosher kitchen and restaurant at the Ohel Leah synagogue, 76 Robinson Rd, Mid-Levels ☎2801 5442, or contact the Jewish Community Centre, 70 Robinson Rd, Mid-Levels ☎2801 5440. There's also the *Shalom Grill*, 2nd Floor, Fortune House, 61 Connaught Rd, Central ☎2851 6300, serving kosher Middle Eastern food and couscous.

Any other dietary requirements can probably be catered for by the biggest hotel restaurants; it's always worth a phone call. Or check the list of **supermarkets** given under "Markets, supermarkets, bakeries and barbecues" (opposite) if you want to play safe and buy your own provisions.

The grilled prawn and pomelo salad, rice-skin rolls, and lemongrass beef are excellent, and two can eat very well for $200.

Saigon Beach 66 Lockhart Rd, Wan Chai ⓣ2529 7823. See map on pp.78–79. Good little restaurant that's a draw with young travellers and locals because they stick to the basics and cook them well. They do a large selection of inexpensive spicy, meat-filled French baguettes. Daily noon–3pm & 6–10pm.

Markets, supermarkets, bakeries and barbecues

With hot food and snacks so cheap in Hong Kong, there isn't much incentive to buy picnic food. There are, however, supermarkets right across Hong Kong that may be useful if you're going to use any of the hundreds of barbecue sites throughout the SAR, if you're on a special diet, or if you simply want to know exactly what it is you're eating. Be warned, though, that for anything recognizably Western, you'll pay a lot more than you would at home.

Markets

A walk around a Cantonese market is a sight in itself, and several are detailed in the text, including Hong Kong Island's Central Market (p.60), Sheung Wan market (p.64) and Luen Wo and Sheung Shui markets (p.135) in the New Territories. A market is where the bulk of the population buys its fresh food, shopping at least once a day for meat, fish, fruit and vegetables. All the towns and residential buildings, especially in the developments in the New Territories, have a market hall.

They can look a bit intimidating at first, but no one minds you wandering around and checking out the produce. Prodding and handling **fruit and veg** is almost expected: just pick out the items you want and hand them over. They'll invariably be weighed on an ingenious set of hand-held scales and, although the metric system is in official use, will be priced according to traditional Chinese weights and measures – most food is sold by the **catty**, which equals 1.3lb or 600g. Some stallholders will let you sample some of the more obscure fruit: one to watch for is the durian, a yellow, spiky fruit shaped like a rugby ball, that is fairly pricey and decidedly smelly – very much an acquired taste.

Buying **meat and fish** is also straightforward, though if you're going by sight alone make sure that the pretty fish you're pointing at isn't extremely rare and very expensive. It's perfectly alright to have several things weighed until you find the piece you want. For the best fish, either get to the market early in the morning, or come back in the mid-afternoon when the second catch is delivered. Every market will also have a **cooked meat** stall selling roast pork, duck and chicken, which can perk up a picnic lunch no end.

Supermarkets

There are plenty of supermarkets around, but apart from a couple of notable exceptions, they're pricey and concentrate on tinned and packet foods. SAR-wide supermarket chains include Wellcome and Park 'N' Shop (see below). They're generally open daily from around 8am to 8pm, though stores throughout the SAR vary their hours.

Hong Kong-wide supermarkets

Park 'N' Shop including branches at Ground Floor, Hang Seng Bank Building, Central; 1st Floor, Admiralty Centre MTR level; and Shop 5, Festival Walk, Kowloon Tong (this branch has a wider than average range of Western goods).

Wellcome including branches at 2nd Floor, The Forum, Exchange Square, Central; 84 Queen's Rd Central, Central; Shop 2b,

Lower Basement, The Landmark, Central; and 78 Nathan Rd, Tsim Sha Tsui.

Specialist stores

City'super **Times Square, 1 Matheson St, Causeway Bay.** Large Western supermarket and delicatessen.

Great Basement **One Pacific Place, 88 Queensway, Central**. Upmarket Japanese food hall, selling top-quality fresh produce, alongside an enormous range of international foodstuffs including Harrods' teas.

Indian Provision Store **Ground Floor, 65–68 Chungking Mansions, 36–44 Nathan Rd, Tsim Sha Tsui.** Indian spices, sweets and pickles, as well as tins and dairy products.

Oliver's Delicatessen **2nd Floor, Prince's Building, Central.** A Mecca for Hong Kong's expat community, stocking bread, wine, cheese, biscuits, meat and a huge range of other Western products.

Sogo **East Point Centre, 555 Hennessy Rd, Causeway Bay.** There's a Japanese supermarket inside the department store – takeaway Japanese snacks and food as well.

Bakeries

The bread sold in supermarkets tends to be white and rather sweet, so you're better off buying it from the bakeries you'll find in every market and on most street corners. It'll be substantially the same but will at least be fresher, and costs only a few dollars for a small sliced loaf. Brown and wholemeal are usually available only from shops patronized heavily by expats. Cakes from bakeries are cheap, too, only a dollar or two for very sweet, rather synthetic creations. More elaborate cream cakes and buns are sold from the *Maxim's* chain of shops, which you'll find in most MTR and KCR stations, as well as at the Star Ferry piers. If you're looking for fresh bread or cakes that are closer to Western tastes, such as apple strudel, try the Western-style supermarkets and delis, such as Park 'N' Shop and Wellcome, or The Soho Bakery (excellent brioche and baguettes) at 41 Elgin St, Central, or Ali Oli (11 Sha Tsui Path, Sai Kung).

Barbecues

Almost everywhere of scenic interest you go in Hong Kong (and at some youth hostels and campsites) there are special barbecue pits provided in picnic areas. They're inordinately popular, and getting the ingredients together for a barbecue isn't difficult. Supermarkets sell fuel, barbecue forks, rubbish bags and all the food, as do kiosks at some of the more enterprising sites; either buy ready-made satay sticks, or pick up cuts of meat and fish from the market.

7

Nightlife: bars, pubs and clubs

If you're not making eating your sole evening's entertainment, then Hong Kong has plenty of **bars**, **pubs and clubs** in which you can while away the night. Although several of the pubs are British in style – complete with homesick expats, horse brasses and dartboards – lots of other bars are American or Australian, with food and drink to match. And because Hong Kong doesn't have so much of that desperately trendy edge that bedevils London and New York, most of them are good, down-to-earth fun – though you still need to dress in "smart casuals". Most of the newer, trendier bars and clubs are in Central, especially **Lan Kwai Fong** and **SoHo**, the chic eating and drinking area around the Mid-Levels escalator between Lyndhurst Terrace and Robinson Road, where new bars and restaurants open almost every week. There are other possibilities at **Tsim Sha Tsui**, whose well-established pubs and discos are much favoured by travellers staying in the nearby guesthouses. Traditionally, **Wan Chai** has played host to the less refined, late-opening, hard-drinking dens, although rising rents in Central have encouraged more sophisticated establishments to move into the area.

Most bars are **open** from around lunchtime until well after midnight; some, especially in Lan Kwai Fong and Wan Chai, stay open until breakfast, and a few keep serving drinks around the clock, particularly at the weekend. Many don't have a specific closing time at all – if it's busy, they stay open till 4 or 5am, if it's quiet, they shut at 1 or 2am: where this is the case, we have simply said "late" for the closing time. If there's a DJ or it's a **club night**, you might have to pay to get in: from around $60 at the smaller places up to $400 at the flash designer clubs. Some include a drink or two in the entry price, and lots only charge an entrance fee on the busy Friday and Saturday nights. Many bars also put on **live music**, usually pseudo-folk (singer-guitarists mangling *Yesterday*) or jazz: these are picked out in the lists below, but for fuller details of live music, turn to the following chapter.

The **music** played is generally mainstream European and American pop and dance music, although there's a minuscule Indie scene, while plenty of places also play Canto-pop (see "Live Music", p.227), and others have Japanese-style karaoke lounges. Many of the newly opened stylish joints in SoHo have behind-the-bar DJs spinning club and funk music; some have a resident DJ every night, others have one or two special club nights, usually on Friday and Saturday. **Rave** parties (tickets $400 upwards) are held periodically with guest DJs, usually at

Alcoholic drinks

The most readily available alcoholic beverage is beer – lager-style and served ice cold. San Miguel and mainland-brand Tsingtao are the top contenders, though bars and restaurants (and lots of supermarkets) also sell British bitter, Guinness and untold other foreign beers, designer or otherwise, draught or bottled, Belgian to Venezuelan. In a supermarket, beer costs around $8–12 for a small can. In most restaurants, it's around $25–30 for the same can; while in bars and pubs, this can rise dramatically – anything from $38 upwards for a small bottle, $50–65 for a draught pint.

Drinking **wine** in a bar or restaurant is similarly expensive, starting at around $40 a glass, $200 a bottle for even the most average of wines – considerably more for anything halfway decent – though in a supermarket a bottle of European plonk will set you back as little as $30, with a decent tipple costing from $60 upwards. You can also get wine from the Chinese mainland (Dynasty is a common label) but it's not terribly drinkable. Most internationally known **spirits** are available in bars and restaurants, again at a price. Cheaper, though rougher, are the various brands of Chinese spirits (*bok jau*, literally translating as "white spirit" and made from sorghum), the cheaper examples of which are best left for cooking, or stripping paint.

HITEC, 1 Trademark Drive, Kowloon Bay, or the Hong Kong Convention and Exhibition Centre in Wan Chai. Keep an eye out for flyers, check local **listings magazines** *BC* and *HK Magazine* or the *South China Morning Post*'s *24/7* supplement, or pick up *Absolute*, a free local clubbing and style magazine from bars, designer fashion chains (DKNY, Bauhaus, and Ad:Hoc) or HMV stores. Finally, look out for big **club nights on the mainland**; well-known DJs frequently host riotous nights in nearby Guangzhou and Shenzhen (*24/7* carries regional information).

The main drawback is that pubbing and clubbing – or at least drinking – is comparatively **expensive**, and you'll need a fairly substantial amount of money to party every night (see the box above).The main thing to watch out for in this respect is the prevalence of **happy hour**, where you'll get two-for-one drinks. They generally last a lot more than an hour: sometime between 5pm and 8pm is usual (though some places sell cheap drinks all afternoon); many places also try to lure you back in with the same deal at around 11pm–1am. Blackboards and notices in pubs and bars have details, or check the reviews below. In addition, many bars now feature a **ladies' night** in the week where women get in free and are either offered cheap or free drinks, while men are charged a (hefty) entrance fee. It may be a sad way to lure in extra male punters, but it dramatically cuts the cost of a night out for the girls: check adverts in the listings magazines. Finally, it's worth noting that in the newer, trendier bars you're expected to **tip the bar staff** – ten percent will cover it.

Lan Kwai Fong

The places listed below are marked on the map on p.61.

Bit Point 31 D'Aguilar St ⓣ2523 7436. German theme-bar, concentrating on meals until around 10pm, after which the bar starts selling industrial quantities of lager and schnapps as the jukebox blares. Mon–Sat noon–2am, Sun 4pm–late; happy hour 4–9pm.

Bulldog Ground Floor, 17 Lan Kwai Fong ⓣ2523 3528. Fourteen-metre-long bar, plasma screen TVs tuned to world sports, dartboard, plus heaps of private nooks and crannies – this bar and grill is for kicking back in and getting rowdy over a game of soccer. Sun–Thurs noon–2am, Fri & Sat noon–4am; happy hour 5–8pm.

California Ground Floor, California Tower, 30–32 Lan Kwai Fong ⓣ2521 1345. Expensive American bar and restaurant with a tiny dance floor on which the local yuppies strut their stuff. It's been around for too long to be at the cutting edge of anything, but can still be fun on occasion. Mon, Tues & Thurs noon–1am, Wed, Fri & Sat noon–4am, Sun 6pm–midnight.

C Bar Ground Floor, California Tower, 30–32 D'Aguilar St ☎2530 3695. Tiny corner-bar, with just a few stools, whose big draw is frozen cocktails dispensed with a giant syringe. The associated C Club downstairs pulls in hip and very young crowds with Ibiza DJs playing house music. A fun and rowdy place. Mon–Thurs 7.30pm–1am, Fri–Sat 7.30pm–2am, Sun 2–10pm.

Club 64 Ground Floor, 12–14 Wing Wah Lane ☎2523 2801. Down-at-heel, back-alley drinking den playing blues and rock to an enthusiastic, vaguely Indie crowd most nights, many of whom spill out onto the pavement later. Drinks are affordable and happy hour is a long 2.30–9pm. Mon–Sat noon–2am, Sun noon–6pm.

D26 26 D'Aguilar Street, ☎2877 1610. Small, low-key bar; a good place for a warm-up drink or if you actually want a conversation with your companions.

Insomnia 38–44 D'Aguilar Street ☎2525 0957. Street-side bar open from 8am–6am where, for part of the time at least, conversation is possible. Further in, the house band plays covers at maximum volume to an enthusiastic dance crowd.

Keg 52 D'Aguilar St ☎2810 0369. Decked out in wood and metal trim to resemble the inside of a barrel, this place has a big range of imported beers, including Ruddles and Hoegaarden. Fri & Sat 5pm–2am, Sun–Thurs 5pm–1am.

Post '97 9 Lan Kwai Fong ☎2186 1816. A disco downstairs and a vaguely arty, bohemian atmosphere in the bar upstairs, with a strong gay presence on Friday nights. Serves fry-ups, sandwiches and all-day breakfasts.

Schnurrbart Ground Floor, Winner Building, 27 D'Aguilar St ☎2523 4700. Long-standing German bar with herring and sausage snacks, and some of the best beer around. Serious headaches are available courtesy of the 25 different kinds of schnapps – try the butterscotch. Mon–Thurs noon–12.30am, Fri & Sat noon–1.30am, Sun 6pm–12.30am.

Wooloomooloo Cnr D'Aguilar and Wyndham streets. Smart Aussie bar, more or less, with good, loud rock 'n' roll, sports TV, and plenty of beers.

SoHo

The places listed below are marked on the map on p.74.

Bar 1911 27 Staunton St ☎2810 6681. Ignore the "members only" sign. This is one of SoHo's best-established and most popular joints, offering comfortable seats and reasonable noise levels if you want to talk. Not a bargain, but nowhere in this area is. Mon–Sat 5pm–midnight, Sun 5–11pm.

Blue Door 5th Floor, 37 Cochrane St. Sadly, Hong Kong's only jazz club, with top-quality live music and jazz Saturday night 10.30pm–12.30am.

Gay nightlife

In recent years, the gay scene has quietly expanded in Hong Kong, and there are a few clubs and bars geared specifically to a gay crowd. Most popular are **Propaganda**, 1 Hollywood Rd, Central (☎2868 1316; Mon–Thurs 9pm–3.30am, Fri & Sat 9pm–6am), which has a decent-sized dance floor, adjacent chill-out bar quiet enough to have a conversation, and a pricey cover charge of $200 most nights; and **Works**, 1st Floor, 30–32 Wyndham St, Central (☎2868 6102; Tues–Thurs 7pm–1.30am, Fri–Sun 9pm–late), an industrial-looking warehouse of a club with plenty of dark corners and a $60 cover charge. A couple of mainstream joints host gay nights, or have an obviously mixed crowd.

While the above venues are male-dominated, lesbian nightlife is a more local affair, restricted to karaoke-lounge-type bars or dimly lit clubs playing loud Canto-pop. A cover charge of around $120, which includes one drink, is standard. Most venues are hidden away in commercial buildings in Causeway Bay: try **Oasis** (14th Floor, Evernew House, 485 Lockhart Rd, Causeway Bay ☎2575 8878), **Hermie** (13th Floor, Circle Plaza, 499 Hennessy Rd, Causeway Bay ☎3107 0000) and the popular **Virus** (6th Floor, Allways Centre, 468 Jaffe Rd, Causeway Bay ☎2904 7207).

Bars with views

The places below all offer excellent views while you drink, mostly of the harbour, and most charge more than usual for the privilege.

Café Deco Levels 1 & 2, Peak Galleria, 118 Peak Rd, The Peak ☎2849 5111. See p.226 for review. The terrace is particularly pleasant in hot weather.

Felix 28th Floor, *Peninsula Hotel*, Salisbury Rd, Tsim Sha Tsui ☎2920 2888. See p.214 for review. Cocktails here cost the same as in any regular bar in Hong Kong, while the men's toilets have the best views in the SAR.

Flying Machine 14th Floor, *Regal Airport Hotel*, 38 Sa Po Rd, Kowloon City ☎2718 0333. Views over the old airport runway and the eastern harbour.

Oasis Lounge 8th Floor, *Renaissance Harbour View Hotel*, 70 Mody Rd, Tsim Sha Tsui East ☎2721 5161.

Sky Lounge 18th Floor, *Sheraton Hotel*, 20 Nathan Rd, Tsim Sha Tsui ☎2369 1111.

Dublin Jack **37 Cochrane St ☎2543 0081.** Irish pub, just under the escalator exit for Lyndhurst Terrace. Draught Guinness, big portions of tasty Irish food, and room to stand outside, as well as well over a hundred different varieties of whiskey, too. Mon–Fri 8am–2am, Sat–Sun 11am–2am; happy hour noon–8pm.

The Globe **39 Hollywood Rd ☎2543 1941.** Cosy, friendly bar serving snacks, with a great jukebox and the best beer in SoHo, including British and European ales and Belgian wheat beer. Popular with locals after work – can get rowdier later on. Mon–Fri 7.30pm–late, Sat & Sun 10.30pm–late.

Central

Captain's Bar **Mandarin Oriental Hotel, 5 Connaught Rd ☎2521 0111. See map on pp.54–55.** Knowledgeable bar staff can provide you with every cocktail known to man, and the atmosphere is lively. Excellent Filipino band play nightly 9pm–2am. Not cheap. Daily 11am–2.30am.

Fringe Club **2 Lower Albert Rd ☎2521 7251. See map on p.61.** The ground-floor bar of this theatre and art-gallery complex has good-value beers and live music, while there's also a popular rooftop bar. Mon–Thurs noon–midnight, Fri & Sat noon–3am; happy hour 4–9pm.

▲ Cocktail in the bar at *Felix*

Wan Chai

The places listed below are marked on the map on pp.78–79.

Carnegie's **53–55 Lockhart Rd ☎2866 6289.** Noise level means conversation here is only possible by flash cards, and once it's packed, hordes of punters keen to revel the night away fight for dancing space on the bar. Home of the much-talked-about topless barman on a Wednesday night; occasional riotous club nights, too, and regular live music. Daily 11am–3am, often later.

Club ING **4th Floor, Renaissance Harbour View Hotel, 1 Harbour Rd ☎2824 0523.** Glitzy, extravagant dance club, which hosts good club nights – a ladies' night on Thursdays, and men's night on Fridays when beer is $10 a bottle for guys. Sun–Wed 9.30pm–3am, Thurs–Sat 9.30pm–4am.

Devil's Advocate **48–50 Lockhart Rd ☎2865 7271.** Hugely popular at the moment, especially with young office workers and expats – rotten jukebox selection, though. Cheap soft drinks at lunchtime. Daily 11am–late.

Dusk Till Dawn **76 Jaffe Rd ☎2528 4689.** The colour scheme is vaguely Mediterranean, but this is not the place for a quiet drink – loud live music, raucous staff, and equally rowdy punters. Daily afternoon–late; happy hour 5–11pm.

Horse and Groom 161 Lockhart Rd ☎2507 2517. Large, dark venue with wreaths of wrought iron and neon. The cheap drinks and Western pub food attract a good mixed crowd of expats and locals. Mon–Sat 11am–4.30am, Sun 7pm–4am; happy hour Sat 6–9pm, Sun 8–10pm.

Joe Banana's 23 Luard Rd ☎2529 1811. Lively, unsophisticated American bar with a late disco, fake palms, occasional live music, and marathon weekend opening hours; happy hour noon–10pm. You need to be (or look) 21 and there's a strict door policy – men need a shirt with a collar. Mon–Thurs 11.30am–5am, Fri & Sat 11.30am–6am, Sun 5pm–5am.

Neptune II 98–108 Jaffe Rd ☎2865 2238. Dingy but good-natured club, the backdrop for mostly Western pop, interspersed with bouts of the Filipino house band playing cover versions. The clientele is mainly Filipina, too – which means significant numbers of Western men on the prowl. Daily 6pm–7am.

Old China Hand 104 Lockhart Rd ☎2527 9174. Pub for hard-core drinkers, hung-over clubbers (who come for breakfast), embittered, seedy expats acting the part, and those with a taste for loud music. Mon–Sat 24hr, Sun 9am–2am.

Tango Martini 3rd Floor, Empire Land Commercial Centre, 81–85 Lockhart Rd ☎2528 0855. This lounge-style bar-and-restaurant features comfy tiger-print couches and chairs and more than 201 martinis, setting it apart from most of Wan Chai's gritty establishments. Chic and expensive, you'll either love it or hate it. Mon–Fri noon–3pm & 6pm–2am, Sat & Sun 6pm–2am.

Wanch 54 Jaffe Rd ☎2861 1621. A Wan Chai institution, this tiny, unpretentious bar is jostling and friendly and has live music – usually folk and rock – every night. Also serves cheap chunky cheeseburgers and sandwiches. Mon–Sat 11am–2am, Sun noon–2am.

Causeway Bay

The places listed below are marked on the map on pp.78–79.

Dickens Sports Bar Lower Ground Floor, Excelsior Hotel, 281 Gloucester Rd ☎2837 6782. This bar prides itself on re-creating an authentic British atmosphere: the kitchen dishes up genuine British pub grub, the TV airs British sitcoms, and there are English papers to read. One of the few decent hotel bars. Mon–Thurs & Sun 11am–2am, Fri & Sat 11am–3am.

The Royal's 21 Cannon St ☎2832 7879. Not a single Westerner to be seen in this dark, rowdy Chinese bar, where you can watch the locals playing dice, accompanied by loud Canto-pop. Daily 11am–2am.

Tsim Sha Tsui

The places listed below are marked on the map on pp.104–105.

Bahama Mama's 4–5 Knutsford Terrace ☎2368 2121. Beach-bar theme and outdoor terrace that prompts party-crowd antics. Has one of Hong Kong's only football tables, and is one of the rare bars that is popular with both gweilos and local Chinese. For the best crack, stump up the cover charge and come along on club nights where a mixed music policy offers everything from garage to world. Mon–Thurs 5pm–3am, Fri & Sat 5pm–4am, Sun 6pm–2am.

Ned Kelly's Last Stand 11a Ashley Rd ☎2376 0562. Dark Australian bar with great live traditional jazz after 9pm; good beer and meaty Aussie food served at the tables. It's a real favourite with travellers, and good fun. Daily 11.45am–1.45am.

Someplace Else Basement, Sheraton Hotel, 20 Nathan Rd ☎2721 6151. The Sheraton's upmarket singles' bar, whose large, rowdy two-floor bar-restaurant has live music, free popcorn nibbles, Tex-Mex and Asian snacks and a good cocktail list. Daily 11am–2am; happy hour 4–8pm.

Stag's Head Hart Avenue, Tsim Sha Tsui ☎2369 3142. Popular pub attracting expats and tourists alike; almost always has beer, spirit and wine promotions during noon–10pm happy hours.

Watering Hole Basement, 1A Mody Rd ☎2312 2288. An enormous subterranean bar with darts and a small selection of beers. The decor is nondescript, but there's a good mix of locals, expats and tourists, the bar staff are friendly, and it's big enough to harbour lots of dark nooks and crannies. Daily 4pm–1pm.

Elsewhere

348 Disco Majestic Centre, 348 Nathan Rd, Jordan ☎2332 8132. See map on pp.104–105. The most famous club for locals, its entranceway is flanked by giant robots, skulls and twisted metal. All very loud and Canto-dance inside – a typical Asian hi-tech disco. Rich kids have their own glass case holding reserved bottles of whiskey or cognac; there's pricey karaoke next door, and a weekend cover charge of $150–200 for the disco. Daily 7pm–9am.

Boathouse 86–88 Stanley Main St, Stanley ⓣ2813 4467. See map on p.91. A marine-themed bar housed in a pretty blue house with a small roof garden, serving such dishes as Guinness-marinated baby back ribs. Daily noon–midnight.

Café Deco Level 1 & 2, Peak Galleria, 118 Peak Rd, The Peak ⓣ2849 5111. See map on pp.54–55. Stupendous views from the picture windows and great Deco surroundings make this one of the island's highlights. Come for a meal, or just a drink; stop and listen to the jazz band. Mon–Thurs & Sun 10am–midnight, Fri & Sat 10am–1am.

Duke of York 42–56 Fuk Man Rd, Sai Kung ⓣ2792 8435. A long-standing local expat haunt with darts, chessboards, lots of seating, big-screen sports, and pork scratchings. Occasional live bands. Daily noon–2am.

East End Brewery 23–27 Tong Chong St, Quarry Bay ⓣ2811 1907. Situated amid a string of bars and fancy restaurants, this pub attracts the early evening business crowds who flock here to sample one of 38 different microbrews from the US or a Belgium speciality beer. Sat–Thurs 11.30am–12.30am, Fri 11.30am–1am.

Smuggler's Inn 90a Stanley Main St, Stanley ⓣ2813 8852. See map on p.51. A grungy little bar with cheap snacks and indifferent staff, but it's very popular with locals who shut themselves in after midnight to bop to loud music. Daily 10am–2am.

8

Live music

Hong Kong is never the first place that touring Western bands think of, but even so the **live music** scene can be fun, despite the lack of venues. Apart from the Hong Kong Coliseum and the Queen Elizabeth Stadium, where the megastars play, there's no real middle-ranking concert hall for rock and pop music. If you're in Hong Kong during a quiet period for Western bands, check to see if any of the big names in the home-grown pop music scene are playing.

Cantopop, a bland, Chinese-language blending of Western pop ballads and disco, is easily the most popular music in Hong Kong. Its origins lie in the Cantonese movie musicals of the 1950s and 1960s, whose soundtracks became enormously popular in postwar Hong Kong. Until the 1970s, however, most true pop music in Hong Kong was either imported from the West or from Taiwan, whose Mandarin pop (or Mandopop) singers were among the first to receive star treatment. Then Hong Kong-based artist Sam Hui mixed Cantonese lyrics with Western pop music in the mid-1970s, and Cantopop was born. Output is phenomenal – many of the big names routinely record five or more albums per year – and its stars are accorded tremendous status: Tony Leung, the late Leslie Cheung, Andy Lau, Sammi Cheng, Beijing-born Faye Wong, and Kelly Chen are household names in the SAR, and can't appear in public without getting mobbed by fans. Live performances, where fans sit waving coloured light sticks and holding message boards for their heroes, sell out months in advance – try and book before you travel if you're hoping to catch one.

There's also a small **jazz** scene, based around regular gigs in pubs and clubs, while many bars offer evening punters what is euphemistically referred to as **folk** music. You'll never see anyone very exciting, but if all you want to do is drink to the strains of Eagles cover versions, there are ample opportunities. Finally, most of the large **hotels** feature resident bands and visiting "international artists" in their bars – usually from the Philippines. It's invariably mood music and crooning as an accompaniment to expensive cocktail-sipping.

The choice of **Western classical** music is rather more limited – certainly when it comes to local musicians and orchestras. Hong Kong is, however, well established on the international touring circuit, and because of the limited interest in Western classical music you can often get last-minute tickets to see world-class artists when they're in town.

Hong Kong also offers occasional chances to listen to **Chinese classical** music, not only Chinese opera but also concerts featuring traditional Chinese instruments, which most Westerners find rather easier on the ears than the opera.

To find out **what's on**, look in the free listings magazines, *BC Magazine* and *HK Magazine*, available at many of the venues listed below and at bars and restaurants, or check out the *South China Morning Post*'s *24/7* supplement.

Rock and pop

Outside the big venues, less well-known bands tend to appear in bars and pubs, or are served up as PAs ("personal appearances" singing or miming to backing tapes) in one or two of the clubs. If you're here in June, keep an eye out for World Battle of the Bands (Ⓦwww.worldbattleofthebands.com), which makes use of venues such as Central's Fringe Club, and features local rock talent.

You'll find details of forthcoming events in the local press, or contact the places listed below direct. Ticket prices vary, but you'll usually pay $50–100 for local bands and second-rank visiting groups and artists, and more like $300–800 for someone famous. **Tickets** for concerts at major venues can be booked through URBTIX (Ⓣ2111 5999 or Ⓦwww.urbtix.hk) or HK Ticketing (Ⓣ3128 8288 daily 10am–8pm or Ⓦwww.hkticketing.com/eng).

Carnegies Ground Floor **53–55 Lockhart Rd, Wan Chai Ⓣ2866 6289.** Hosts regular gigs by local acts; usually no cover charge.

Chasers **2 Carlton Building, Knutsford Terrace, Tsim Sha Tsui Ⓣ2367 9487.** This rowdy bar, along with its two sister establishments (*Insomnia*, 38–44 D'Aguilar St, Lan Kwai Fong, Central; *Dusk Till Dawn*, 76–84 Jaffe Rd, Wan Chai), rotates six different Filipino-cover bands churning out a wide range of music every night from 9.30pm.

Fringe Club **2 Lower Albert Rd, Central Ⓣ3128 8288.** Rock and pop gigs by local bands and visiting artistes; occasionally free.

Hong Kong Coliseum **9 Cheong Wan Rd, Hung Hom, Kowloon Ⓣ2355 7234.** Everything from major international rock bands, to Cantonese operatic solos and lengthy concerts by Canto-pop superstars.

Queen Elizabeth Stadium **18 Oi Kwan Rd, Wan Chai Ⓣ2591 1346.** Major rock and pop bands.

Folk

Entrance to these bars and pubs is free.

Cinta J **69 Jaffe Rd, Wan Chai Ⓣ2529 6622.** Filipino singers after 9pm.

Delaney's **2nd Floor, One Capital Place, 18 Luard Rd, Wan Chai Ⓣ2804 2880; Basement, Mary Building, 71–77 Peking Rd, Tsim Sha Tsui Ⓣ2301 3980.** Genuine traditional Irish folk at both venues on selected nights.

The Wanch **54 Jaffe Rd, Wan Chai Ⓣ2861 1621.** Solid folk and pub-rock venue, with live music seven nights a week from 9pm to 2am.

Jazz & Blues

Entrance to pub and bar jazz gigs is free, except where stated below.

Blue Door **Floor 5, 37 Cochrane St, Central.** Hong Kong's only jazz club, with live music Saturday night 10.30pm–12.30am.

Café Deco **Levels 1 & 2, Peak Galleria, 118 Peak Rd, The Peak Ⓣ2849 5111.** Regular jazz and cool sounds in The Peak's Art Deco extravaganza (with occasional cover charge for special events).

Chicago Blues **2a Hart Ave, Tsim Sha Tsui Ⓣ2723 7633.** A small, laid-back bar with a core of regular locals who come to listen to live jazz and blues on Thursdays and the weekend. Drinks not expensive, but cover charge on Thursdays and Fridays. Daily 5pm–late.

Fringe Club **2 Lower Albert Rd, Central Ⓣ2521 7251.** Occasional jazz gigs; cover charge for nonmembers.

Ned Kelly's Last Stand **11a Ashley Rd, Tsim Sha Tsui Ⓣ2376 0562.** Trad and Dixieland jazz every night after 9pm from a stomping resident band.

Western and Chinese classical

The main local exponent of Western classical music is the Hong Kong Philharmonic Orchestra (Ⓦwww.hkpo.com), formed in 1975, whose season runs from September through to June, and which regularly employs excellent guest conductors and soloists. Performances are at a variety of venues, primarily the Cultural Centre; information on Ⓣ2734 9009. The Hong Kong Sinfonietta is another professional orchestra, although their performances can be rather ragged.

For **Chinese orchestral music**, watch for performances by the Hong Kong Chinese Orchestra (Ⓦwww.hkco.org), founded in 1977 and the territory's only professional Chinese music group. The orchestra plays one weekend every month at City Hall and the Cultural Centre, performing reworkings of Western classical music on traditional Chinese instruments – a combination not to everyone's taste, but certainly worth hearing. For other Chinese classical music, check with the HKTB, and look out for student concerts at the university and Academy of Performing Arts (APA), which regularly hosts free concerts (see p.230). For details of Chinese opera performances, see p.232.

9

The arts and media

Despite a certain amount of snobbery amongst the local population that the SAR is a repository of Chinese culture, having been largely unaffected by the various turmoils that beset the mainland during the twentieth century, "cultural events" in Hong Kong can be few and far between. This is not for want of trying: the **Cultural Centre** in Tsim Sha Tsui and the **Hong Kong Arts Centre** and the adjacent **Academy for Performing Arts**, in Wan Chai, all host domestic and international dance, opera and music performances. Somehow, though, it all seems a bit artificial; the only art form that commands a mass audience here is **film**, with the cinemas packed for every new Hollywood or Chinese release. That's not to say that you can't experience **Chinese culture**, just that it tends to be at its best when it's informally presented: at the night markets, perhaps, or during religious holidays at temples and on the street.

Cantonese might be the language of the majority in Hong Kong, but there's also good **English-language media** coverage, including television, radio and newspapers.

Information, tickets and venues

Information about cultural events and performances can be picked up at any of the venues listed below. The best sources of detailed **listings** are the free weeklies HK Magazine and BC Magazine (Ⓦwww.bcmagazine.net), available at Western-style bars, restaurants, all *Pacific Coffee* outlets and some other coffee shops and bookshops. There's also the *South China Morning Post*'s *24/7* magazine, which comes free with the Friday edition of the paper. Other sources include the Hong Kong Arts Centre's monthly *Artslink* magazine, the Fringe Club Monthly leaflet and the monthly pamphlet put out by the Hong Kong City Hall and Hong Kong Cultural Centre.

Tickets for most events can be bought at the venues, and from two ticketing companies: **HK Ticketing** (Ⓣ3128 8288 daily 10am–8pm; or Ⓦwww.hkticketing.com/eng); and **URBTIX** (bookings must be made at least 7 days in advance; Ⓣ2111 5999 or Ⓦwww.urbtix.gov.hk). Both also have outlets around town; you can get the addresses off their websites. Tickets for many cultural events are subsidized: seats for local productions cost around $50–120, rising to $250–800 for anything international.

Main venues

Academy for Performing Arts 1 Gloucester Rd, Wan Chai Ⓣ2584 8500. Six separate stages for local and international drama, and modern and classical dance. Box office daily 10am–6pm.

Alliance Française 2nd Floor, 123 Hennessy Rd,

Wan Chai ⓣ2527 7825; Ho Kwan Building, 52 Jordan Rd, Kowloon ⓣ2730 3257. Films and culture at the French Cultural Institute. Box office daily 8.30am–9.30pm.

City Hall **1 Edinburgh Place, Central ⓣ2921 2840.** Drama, concerts, recitals, exhibitions and lectures. Box office daily 10am–9.30pm.

Fringe Club **2 Lower Albert Rd, Central ⓣ2521 7251, ⓦwww.hkfringeclub.com.** Offbeat venue for cabaret, alternative theatre, jazz, concerts and poetry, as well as exhibitions, classes and workshops. Pick up the schedule from the venue; temporary membership available. Box office Mon–Sat 10am–10pm.

Goethe Institute **14th Floor, Hong Kong Arts Centre, 2 Harbour Rd, Wan Chai ⓣ2802 0088, ⓦwww.goethe.de/hongkong.** Films and events at the German Cultural Institute.

Hong Kong Arts Centre **2 Harbour Rd, Wan Chai ⓣ2582 0200, ⓦwww.hkac.org.hk.** Local art, drama, concerts, film screenings, galleries and exhibitions. Box office daily 10am–6pm.

Hong Kong Coliseum **9 Cheong Wan Rd, Hung Hom ⓣ2355 7234.** Hong Kong's largest venue (12,000 seats) for concerts, dance and sports events. Box office daily 10am–6.30pm.

Hong Kong Convention and Exhibition Centre **Expo Drive, Wan Chai ⓣ2582 8888.** Major conventions, exhibitions, concerts and performances. Box office varies according to the promoter; check press for details.

Hong Kong Cultural Centre **10 Salisbury Rd, Tsim Sha Tsui ⓣ2734 2010.** Dance, drama and concerts, drawing on local and international performers. See p.103 for more details. Box office daily 10am–9.30pm.

Ko Shan Theatre **77 Ko Shan Rd (off Chatham Rd North), Hung Hom ⓣ2740 9212.** Hong Kong's first open-air theatre, located in a disused quarry. Film, theatre, Chinese opera and concerts. Box office daily 10am–6.30pm.

Kwai Tsing Theatre **12 Hing Ning Rd, Kwai Chung ⓣ2408 0128.** Hosts international and local dance and drama. Box office daily 10am–9.30pm.

Ngau Chi Wan Civic Centre **2nd Floor, Ngau Chi Wan Complex, 11 Clearwater Bay Rd, Kowloon (Choi Hung MTR) ⓣ2325 1970.** Drama, dance and film. Box office daily 10am–6.30pm.

Queen Elizabeth Stadium **18 Oi Kwan Rd, Wan Chai ⓣ2591 1346.** Stadium with a 3500 capacity for large concerts and sports events. Box office daily 10am–6.30pm.

Sha Tin Town Hall **1 Yuen Wo Rd, New Town Plaza, Sha Tin, New Territories ⓣ2694 2511.** Drama, dance and concerts, with many internationally renowned troupes. Box office daily 10am–9.30pm.

Sheung Wan Civic Centre **345 Queen's Rd, Sheung Wan ⓣ2853 2678.** Drama, concerts, lectures and exhibitions. Box office daily 10am–6.30pm.

Sunbeam Theatre **423 King's Rd, North Point ⓣ2563 2959.** Gloriously old theatre and cinema that shows Cantonese, Beijing and Chaozhou (another southern form) opera almost every night. Untouristy and cheap with tickets from $50 to $300. Sadly, may be closing – phone ahead to check. Box office daily 11.30am–9.30pm.

Tsuen Wan Town Hall **72 Tai Ho Rd, Tsuen Wan, New Territories ⓣ2414 0144.** Large venue for concerts, dance and drama. Box office daily 10am–9.30pm.

Tuen Mun Town Hall **3 Tuen Hi Rd, Tuen Mun, New Territories ⓣ2450 4202.** Local venue for concerts, dance and drama. Box office daily 10am–9.30pm.

Free concerts

There's no shortage of **free music events and concerts** around Hong Kong. At the Cultural Centre's Thursday Happy Hour (6–7pm) you can listen to a range of musicians, while on Saturday afternoons it hosts a mix of music, theatre and dance shows tailored for a family audience: both events take place in the foyer. The Academy for Performing Arts also has regular free concerts performed by its own students in its recital hall – phone first to reserve a ticket (see opposite) – while occasional lunchtime and afternoon recitals take place at St John's Cathedral, Garden Road, Central (ⓣ2523 4157), usually on a Wednesday. In addition, the Leisure and Cultural Services Department (ⓣ2591 1340, ⓦwww.lcsd.gov.hk) arranges evening jazz concerts in the summertime (6–7.30pm) at various outdoor venues and in some shopping centres around the city; phone or check their website to see what's on.

Chinese cultural performances

Chinese cultural performances are widespread in Hong Kong – every town and village has a hall, theatre or outdoor space where traditional opera and dance are put on. All performances are highly theatrical; coming across one by accident can be a real highlight of your stay.

The best known is **Chinese opera**, which you'll see performed locally at festivals, on religious holidays and in some of the larger venues by visiting and local troupes. In Hong Kong, the style is mostly Cantonese (though visiting mainland Chinese groups perform Beijing opera on occasion, too), a musical drama with mime, set songs and responses based on well-known legends and stories. The costumes and garish make-up are magnificent, and although the strident singing and percussion may test Western ears, it becomes compelling after a while – particularly as the story is interspersed with bouts of elaborate swordfighting and acrobatics. Performances often go on for three hours or more, but the ones held in or near temples at festivals are usually informal, with people walking about, chatting and eating right the way through. Opera buffs may also want to visit the excellent Cantonese opera exhibition on the first floor of the Heritage Museum in Sha Tin (see p.128), and the Temple Street Night Market (p.113), where enthusiastic amateurs often perform Cantonese opera.

Other cultural shows you might catch include traditional Chinese **music**, **puppet theatre**, **folk dancing**, **acrobatics, magic** and **martial arts** – all things that soon become evident if you're in Hong Kong for any length of time. Street markets and festivals are good places to look; or check in the local press for specific performances at some of the main venues listed on p.234

Obviously, it's most rewarding to stumble on performances as you travel around the territory: religious festival events (see p.237) and cultural shows out in the New Territories (listed in the press) are put on for the locals and have few pretensions. But if you want to ensure you see at least something of the traditional culture during your stay, the HKTB organizes **free shows** at various locations such as the New World Centre (Tsim Sha Tsui) and Cityplaza (Tai Koo Shing), where there'll usually be a bit of everything on display from opera extracts to glove puppetry. For more information, contact any of the HKTB offices (see p.30).

Arts festivals

There are several main arts festivals in Hong Kong each year. More information about all of them can be obtained from the HKTB, but it's worth knowing that tickets for the best performances can be hard to come by; book well in advance, or be prepared to settle for what performances you can get into.

City Festival (Jan/Feb). An alternative arts festival organized by the Fringe Club, with street performances by local and international artists; check Ⓦwww.hkfringe.com.hk for information.

Hong Kong Arts Festival (Feb/Mar). Wide-ranging international arts festival bringing together leading artists from China and the West. Usually includes opera, theatre, ballet and concerts; check Ⓦwww.hk.artsfestival.org for information.

Hong Kong International Film Festival (April). A month of international films at various venues – very popular and imaginative with screenings of current releases as well as old-world cinema classics. City Hall has specific information if you want to book in advance, or check Ⓦwww.hkiff.org.hk.

International Arts Carnival (July/Aug). Six weeks of acrobatics, puppet shows, clown theatre, mime and magic, aimed at children and families; check Ⓦwww.hkiac.gov.hk for information.

Hong Kong cinema and the world

Despite a population of only seven million, Hong Kong ranks as the world's third largest movie producer (after India and the US), and with a following to match: there are over forty cinemas in the SAR, and they're usually all full. Its popular appeal is made easier by the content: generally easy-to-digest romances, comedies, or high-speed action, with little interest in deeper meanings or the outside world – and certainly not in politics.

World interest in Hong Kong's film industry dates back to 1970s martial arts legend Bruce Lee. Although better known overseas for the Hollywood-financed *Enter the Dragon*, the success in Hong Kong of his earlier film *Fist of Fury* launched a domestic kung fu movie boom, off the back of which sprung Jackie Chan and a much-needed element of slapstick comedy – best seen in Chan's early works, such as *Drunken Master*. As the genre faltered in the 1980s, directors mixed in a supernatural aspect, pioneered by Tsui Hark in *Zu: Warriors from the Magic Mountain* and *Chinese Ghost Story*. Long out of fashion, the kung fu genre has been recently revived by director Stephen Chow, whose Shaolin Soccer and Kung Fu Hustle sport uniquely surreal humour and visuals.

Martial arts remain an inevitable component of Hong Kong's modern action movies, with police thrillers the current favourite theme. This can largely be attributed to John Woo's influential 1980s hits *A Better Tomorrow* and *Hard Boiled*, which feature Chow Yun Fat shooting his way through relentless scenes of orchestrated violence. Woo's many imitators have mostly succeeded only in making pointless, bloody movies whose plots inevitably conclude with the massacre of the entire cast, though recent efforts such as *Infernal Affairs*, starring Andy Lau, Tony Leung, Kelly Chen and Sammi Cheng (all of whom are moonlighting from succesful Canto-pop careers) at least add a little depth to the heroes' moody characters.

In the meantime, Hong Kong's film industry has also churned out endless quantities of (usually tragic) romances, or domestic comedies using a Laurel and Hardy format. These often rely on a knowledge of the ins-and-outs of Chinese daily life and, as neither translate very well, are fairly inaccessible to a Western audience.

At present, Hong Kong's only director interested in anything but light entertainment is Wong Karwai, whose early works such as *Chungking Express* depicted Hong Kong as a crowded, disjointed city where people, though forced together, seemed unable to communicate. His more recent films have added a European sense of style, which worked in the sensuous In the *Mood for Love* but overwhelmed the plot in the obscure, self-referential *2046*.

Film

Cinemas in Hong Kong are usually multi-screen complexes showing a mixture of new Hollywood and local releases. Going to the movies is inexpensive (around $55 a ticket; half-price on Tues) and it's worth taking in one of the **Chinese-language films** if you can: most are the domestic product (see "Hong Kong cinema" box, above), though films from the mainland are increasingly on view as well. Look for a showing with English subtitles. Current films are reviewed in both the English-language daily newspapers, as well as *HK Magazine* and *BC Magazine*. All the major **English-language films** make

▲ Poster for a Chinese-language film

it to Hong Kong soon after release, and are usually shown in their original language, with Chinese subtitles – but check the performance you want isn't a dubbed version.

All the major venues offer computerized booking systems, so you can either phone in advance and let the system select the best available seats, or go in person and pick your seat from those available, shown on the video monitor by the box office (the loge, incidentally, is equivalent to the dress circle). However, as all Hollywood films are subtitled, it's not uncommon for Chinese members of the audience to talk right through them – sometimes on their mobile phones – and most cinemas have the air-conditioning turned up so high you'll need a jacket to stop your teeth chattering.

The **major cinemas**, and a few interesting minor ones, are listed below, but for a full rundown of what's on where, consult the local press. If you're just wandering and fancy a movie, the biggest concentration of cinemas is in Wan Chai and Causeway Bay. There are also regular film shows (often free) sponsored by the Alliance Française and Goethe Institute (see "Main venues" on p.230 for addresses), while occasional film shows are held in the Space Museum (see p.106) and Science Museum lecture halls (see p.109).

The best venues for **art-house cinema** are AMC Festival Walk, Broadway Cinematheque, the Cine-Art House and the Hong Kong Arts Centre, which have year-round showings of good alternative films, many from Europe and East Asia, while real film buffs will want to try to coincide with the annual **film festival** (see the "Arts festivals" box p.232), which always has an excellent and entertaining international programme, though it can be hard to get seats.

AMC Festival Walk Upper Ground Floor, Festival Walk, Kowloon Tong ☎2265 8595. A mammoth eleven-screen cinema showing everything from mainstream Hollywood through Hong Kong cinema to art-house.

Broadway Circuit ☎2388 3188. Eleven cinemas scattered through the SAR; call for nearest locations.

Chinachem Circuit ☎2311 3000, www.cel-cinemas.com. Four cinemas in Kowloon and the New Territories.

Cine-Art House Sun Hung Kai Centre, 30 Harbour Rd, Wan Chai ☎2827 4820. Arty foreign films in two mini-cinemas.

Cinematique Prosperous Gardens, 3 Public Square St, Yau Ma Tei ☎2388 3188. Movie buff's paradise with art-house shows, an excellent film library (for members only), film courses and adjacent café and bar.

Golden Harvest ☎2186 1313. Domestic film studio with six cinemas in Kowloon, Mongkok and Causeway Bay.

Hong Kong Arts Centre 2 Harbour Rd, Wan Chai ☎2582 0200. Seasons of alternative and foreign films and Chinese cinema.

New York Cinema 463–483 Lockhart Rd, Plaza II, Causeway Bay ☎2838 7380. Plush cinema for new Western and Chinese releases.

Sunbeam Theatre 423 King's Rd, North Point ☎2563 2959. One of the cheapest and oldest cinemas; particularly good for arty mainland films.

UA ☎2317 6666. Eight cinemas in Kowloon and Hong Kong Island.

Television and radio

Every hotel and most guesthouses lay on TV and radio for their guests, and you'll be hard pushed to escape them in bars and restaurants – although what you'll get is likely to be quantity rather than quality.

There are four main domestic TV channels, two English-language and two Cantonese, operated by two companies. Television Broadcasts (TVB) runs Jade (Cantonese) and **TVB Pearl** (English); Asia Television (ATV) runs Home (Cantonese) and **ATV World** (English). In addition, domestic and hotel TVs can often receive cable and satellite channels, including ESPN, CNN and BBC World. Hong Kong's broadcasting companies, unlike their mainland counter-

English-language radio stations

RTHK Radio 3 (567 kHz, 1584 kHz, 97.9 mHz, 106.8 mHz). News, finance, current affairs and pop music.
RTHK Radio 4 (97.6 to 98.9 mHz). Western and Chinese classical music.
RTHK Radio 6 (675 kHz). The BBC World Service relay station.
Metro Plus (1044 kHz AM). Local and Asian news and finance, interspersed with music. Half-hourly news and weather. Broadcasts in Cantonese and Mandarin part of the time.
Metro Finance (104mHz, 102.4 to 106.3 mHz FM). 24-hour business radio.

parts, are privately run and uncensored, although it's generally felt that self-censorship is practised instead.

Much of the domestic **English-language programming** – documentaries, soaps and sitcoms – is imported, mostly from the US. In fact, there's a declining interest in English as an essential second language; with China's economy looming ever-larger on the world stage, fluency in Mandarin is increasingly important and TVB Pearl now broadcasts nightly Mandarin-language news, weather and financial reports. Meanwhile, the saving grace of the English-language channels is that both regularly feature **films** in the evening, usually recent Hollywood releases. Other than horse racing and a few major international events, **sport** is not well covered – real fans are better off trying one of the sport-oriented bars in Lan Kwai Fong or Wan Chai.

If you speak Cantonese, try the **Chinese channels** for locally produced drama series and feature films – but on the whole it's a diet of soaps and variety shows.

On the **radio**, there's plenty in English to tune in to. Stations include those operated by the main broadcasting outfit, Radio Television Hong Kong (RTHK; see the box above or tune in online at Ⓦwww.rthk.org.hk); there are commercial stations, too, as well as the BBC World Service.

Full **programme details** for TV and radio are contained in the daily newspapers.

Theatre and the performing arts

Hong Kong has increasingly become the home of local **drama and performance art**, alongside the usual international touring companies and artists who enliven the cultural year. Big musical productions are popular, although the lack of suitable venues limits their numbers. A rundown of **venues** is given on p.230, but check whether **productions** are in English or Cantonese.

Other than straight drama, some of the most exciting local performances are of **dance**, which doesn't have the disadvantage of a language barrier and often mixes Western and Chinese forms very successfully. **Fringe events** are common, too: the Fringe Club (see p.236), especially, hosts its fair share of mime, magic, cabaret and comedy.

Some interesting **local companies** to watch out for, who perform at venues all over the territory, include:

City Contemporary Dance Company Ⓦ**www.ccdc.com.hk**. Very good, full-time professional company; they usually perform at the Hong Kong Arts Centre.

Hong Kong Ballet Company Ⓦ**www.hkballet.com**. Classical and contemporary ballet performances at various venues.

Hong Kong Dance Company Ⓦ **http://prod1.e1.com.hk/hkdance**. Modern and classical Chinese dance.

Hong Kong Singers Ⓦ **www.hksingers.com.** Musical comedy of the Gilbert and Sullivan variety.

Visual arts

Some of the main venues listed above have **gallery and exhibition space** that's worth checking for current displays. Otherwise, keep an eye on the SAR's **museums**, which host occasional lectures and exhibitions. Both the Heritage Museum (see p.128) and the Hong Kong Museum of Art (see p.103) host temporary art exhibitions, while the University of Hong Kong (see p.130) and the Chinese University near Sha Tin (see p.130) have free galleries open to the public. The Leisure and Cultural Services Department's district **libraries** also put on year-round lectures (sometimes in English) and exhibitions that might be of interest.

There are many **private art galleries** in Hong Kong. The *South China Morning Post* highlights a good selection of current exhibitions in its daily What's On section, as does the weekly *HK Magazine*. The places listed below are usually worth dropping in on, though most are closed on Sundays:

Alisan Fine Arts 315 Prince's Building, 10 Chater Rd, Central Ⓣ **2526 1091,** Ⓦ **www.alisan.com.hk.** Mainly Chinese contemporary work of a not-too-challenging variety.

Altfield Gallery 248–49 Prince's Building, 10 Chater Rd, Central Ⓣ **2537 6370,** Ⓦ **www.altfield.com.hk.** China Trade paintings, maps, prints, Chinese furniture and Southeast Asian works of art. Open Sun.

The Fringe Club 2 Lower Albert Rd, Central Ⓣ **2521 7251,** Ⓦ **www.hkfringeclub.com.** Currently houses two galleries, the Montblanc and Nokia Galleries, with the emphasis on local artists, though international multimedia works also shown.

Galerie La Vong 13th Floor, One Lan Kwai Fong, Central Ⓣ **2869 6863.** Leading modern Vietnamese painters.

Gallery On Old Bailey 17 Old Bailey St, Central Ⓣ **2869 7122,** Ⓦ **www.galleryonoldbailey.com.** Largely contemporary Chinese oil paintings, and small sculptures from around the world. Open Sun afternoon.

Hanart TZ Gallery 2nd Floor, Henley Building, 5 Queen's Rd, Central Ⓣ **2526 9019,** Ⓦ **www.hanart.com.** Leading dealer of modern Chinese painters.

John Batten Gallery 64 Peel Street, Central Ⓣ **2854 1018,** Ⓦ **www.johnbattengallery.com.** Specializes in kooky, off-beat art.

Schoeni 27 Hollywood Rd, Central Ⓣ **2542 3143,** Ⓦ **www.schoeni.com.hk.** Exhibitions of both international and Chinese contemporary artists.

Zee Stone Gallery Yu Yuet Lai Building, 43–55 Wyndham St, Central Ⓣ **2810 5895,** Ⓦ **www.zeestone.com.** Modern Vietnamese, Chinese and Tibetan paintings and antique furniture. Open Sun 1–5pm.

Festivals

You're in luck if you can time a visit to coincide with one of Hong Kong's many traditional **Chinese festivals** that bring whole streets or areas in both Hong Kong and Macau to a complete standstill. At the most exuberant festival of all – Chinese New Year – the entire population takes time out to celebrate. With roots going back hundreds (even thousands) of years, many of the festivals are highly symbolic and are often a mixture of secular and religious displays and devotions. Each has its own peculiarities and attractions: not all are as vibrant and lively as New Year, but each offers a unique slice of Hong Kong and Macau and, by extension, China.

Confusingly, not all the festivals are also public holidays, when most things will be closed (see p.45 for a list of public holidays). But all mean a substantial increase in the number of people travelling on public transport, higher prices for certain services, and large crowds in the festival centres. Also, as the Chinese use the **lunar calendar** and not the Gregorian calendar, many of the festivals fall on different days, even different months, from year to year. The likely months are listed below, but for exact details contact the HKTB or MGTO, or look in the HKTB's free publications: *Hong Kong: A Traveller's Guide* and *Where Hong Kong*. The festivals below are dealt with **chronologically**, starting with the Chinese New Year.

Chinese New Year

Most famous and most important of the Chinese festivals, Chinese New Year (known in Chinese as "Spring Festival") is celebrated for the first two weeks of the first month of the lunar calendar, some time in January or February. Decorations go up everywhere, there's a huge flower market in Victoria Park on Hong Kong Island (and in Fa Hui Park and Cheung Sha Wan playground in Kowloon), where locals buy lucky flowers – peach and plum blossom – oranges, lanterns and sweets. You might also catch a lion dance, where pairs of brightly coloured "pantomime" lions (roles performed by local martial arts teams) put on acrobatic routines and parade through the streets visiting businesses, whose owners provide them with food. Oddly, this takes the form of a cabbage, though in Cantonese the words for "cabbage" and "wealth" sound similar, and the whole dance is symbolic of chasing away bad luck and bringing prosperity for the forthcoming year. There's more of this in the red and gold posters pasted to walls and houses all over the SAR: the Chinese characters wish long life, wealth and happiness.

Most years there's a **firework display** over the harbour on the third night – a tremendous spectacle if you can catch it – replacing the traditional custom of privately letting off strings of firecrackers to drive away evil spirits (you might still come across this in remoter corners of the SAR). Other than this – and vast crowds at temples, burning incense to **Cai Shen**, the god of wealth – there's not actually a great deal to see at Chinese New Year. Most offices, banks, official buildings and some shops are closed for three days or even longer (traditional New Year celebrations last fifteen days). It's a family festival, when people clean their houses, settle debts, visit friends and relations, buy new clothes and generally ensure a fresh start for the year. Married couples hand out money (new notes only) in red envelopes (*lai see*) to their families, and tip their doormen, cleaners and other staff in the same way; people on salaries get a bonus; and shop assistants and waiters are feasted by their employers. Families also go out to celebrate: particular **things to eat** include noodles (for longevity), fish (the Cantonese word sounds similar to that for "surplus"), and dumplings (for wealth). To wish someone a "Happy New Year", you say "*kung hei fat choi*".

Arriving in Hong Kong and trying to find a **room** during Chinese New Year is something you should avoid. And don't even think about travelling to China during the festival: everything is jam-packed solid as literally millions of Hong Kong Chinese stream across the border to visit relatives.

Yuen Siu (Spring Lantern) Festival

The Yuen Siu, or Spring Lantern, Festival marks the last official day of the Chinese New Year celebrations (the fifteenth day of the first moon), and so falls about two weeks after the public holidays. Traditionally designed, brightly coloured lanterns symbolizing the moon are hung in restaurants, shops, temples and houses. Yuen Siu is also known as "Lovers' Day", a kind of Chinese Valentine's Day. There's a second lantern festival in September; see "Mid-Autumn Festival", p.241.

Ching Ming Festival

Generally falling in April, Ching Ming is when families visit their ancestral graves to perform traditional rites. The day – the beginning of the third moon, a public holiday – signals the beginning of spring and a new farming year, but it's more noted for the sweeping of graves at the cemeteries. Whole families take along joss sticks, incense and food offerings (roast pork and fruit), which are left for the dead at the graves, while prayers are said for the departed souls and blessings sought for the latest generations of the family. Extra public transport is laid on for trips to the cemeteries, on Hong Kong Island and out in the New Territories, as well as extra ferries to carry people to the outlying islands: it's one enormous scrum.

Tin Hau Festival

A traditional fishing festival, this is one of the most spectacular of the year's events. Falling on the 23rd day of the third lunar month (late April or May), it is in honour of Tin Hau, a legendary fisherman's daughter of a thousand years ago, who could forecast the weather, calm the waves and generally help the fishermen to a decent catch; not surprisingly, she is regarded as the goddess of the sea and of fishermen, and as the protector of sailors. Fishing boats are colourfully decorated with flags, streamers and pennants as fishermen and others who follow the goddess gather at the various Tin Hau temples to ask for luck in the coming year and to offer food, fruit and pink dumplings as a mark of respect. The main temple is the one at Joss House Bay in Sai Kung (p.146), where massive crowds congregate every year, and there is always a good celebration in Yuen Long in the New Territories, another large centre of Tin Hau worship. Special ferry services run out to some of the brightly decorated temples, many of which put on Chinese opera displays, dances and parades.

Birthday of the Lord Buddha

A low-key celebration in May when the Buddha's statue is taken out of the various Buddhist monasteries and "bathed" in scented water. The monasteries on Lantau are an obvious place to head for to see the rites being performed, but there are important monasteries in the New Territories too, at Sha Tin and Lam Tei.

Tam Kung Festival

The second patron saint of the fishing people is Tam Kung, whose festival is celebrated on the eighth day of the fourth lunar month (usually in May) at the temple in Shau Kei Wan on Hong Kong Island (see p.95).

Tai Chiu (Cheung Chau Bun) Festival

A week-long extravaganza in late April/early May (starting on the same day as the Tam Kung Festival, above) on Cheung Chau Island, the Tai Chiu Festival is one of the highlights of the festival year. The buns that give the festival its English name are distributed for luck at the end of the celebrations, which consist of dances, operas, parades – and the famous "floating children" and bun towers. See p.162 for more details; and expect the island and all the transport there and back to be in a state of siege during this time.

Tuen Ng (Dragon Boat) Festival

The Tuen Ng Festival is one of the oldest of Cantonese festivals, held to commemorate the Chinese hero Ch'u Yuen, an adviser to the king who committed suicide by jumping in a river in Hunan Province and drowning, in protest against a corrupt third-century BC government. The local people tried to save him in their boats, while others threw rice dumplings into the water to feed the fish that would otherwise have eaten his body.

Today, the festival is celebrated on the fifth day of the fifth lunar month (sometime in June) with noisy races between dragon boats – narrow rowing boats with a dragon's head and tail – while conical rice dumplings wrapped up in bamboo leaves are eaten, too. The boats are crewed by anything up to eighty people (though most are smaller), the oar-strokes set by a drummer, and the races are accompanied by cymbals and watched from scores of junks and launches. You can see **races** in many places, particularly on the Sha Tin waterfront, where it's become a major spectacle. There are also races at Tai Po, Stanley, Aberdeen, Yung

▲ Dragon Boat Festival

Shue Wan (Lamma) and Mui Wo (Lantau) – see the local press for details or ask the tourist office. Since 1976, there's been an annual International Dragon Boat Race, with teams from all over the world competing.

Birthday of Lu Pan

Held in July, this is a holiday for anyone connected with the building trades. Lu Pan was a master builder in around 600 BC, a skilled carpenter and possessor of miraculous powers. Banquets are held in his honour on his festival day (the thirteenth day of the sixth lunar month), and there are ceremonies at the Lu Pan Temple in Kennedy Town (p.70).

Maidens' Festival

Also known as the Seven Sisters' Festival, the Maidens' Festival is held in mid-August, on the seventh day of the seventh lunar month. It is observed mostly by young girls and lovers, who burn incense and paper and leave offerings of fruit and flowers. The festival dates back more than 1500 years and, like many Chinese festivals, there are many different versions of the legend accompanying it. A common one is that it marks the story of the youngest of seven sisters who was separated from her lover and only allowed to see him once a year – on this date. Like most other Chinese festivals you will see offerings placed on rooftops, by the roadside or burnt in the gutters of quiet streets – a more formal setting can be found at the Bowen Road Lover's Stone Garden above Wan Chai (p.76).

Yue Lan Festival

The Yue Lan Festival is held on the fifteenth day of the seventh lunar month (at some point in August). It's known as the "Festival of the Hungry Ghosts", commemorating the lunar month when ghosts are released from the underworld to roam the earth. It's generally seen as an unlucky day, when accidents or sinister events can happen. To forestall them, people give offerings to the ghosts in the form of paper models of food, cars, houses, money, furniture, etc. – which are then ceremonially burnt so that the ghosts can take them back to the underworld with them. It's not a public holiday, but you may see fires on the pavements and at the roadside during this time where the elaborate models are burnt. See the account of the Pak Tai Temple in Wan Chai (p.81) for more details about the dying craft of making paper models.

Mid-Autumn Festival

Another major festival, the Mid-Autumn Festival is also called the Moon Cake Festival after the sweet cakes eaten at this time – mostly made from sesame and lotus paste and stuffed with an egg. The festival takes place in September, on the fifteenth day of the eighth lunar month, roughly equivalent to the Western Harvest Festival. It purportedly commemorates a fourteenth-century revolt against the Mongols, when the call to arms was written on pieces of paper, stuffed inside the cakes and distributed to the population. Nowadays, the various kinds of moon cake (*yuek beng*) are stacked up in bakeries for the occasion – they're all wonderfully sickly and cost around $100 for a box of four, though the better, more elaborate double-yolk cakes are pricier. The festival is also accompanied by lantern displays on hillsides throughout the SAR. You'll see the charming paper, cellophane or silk lanterns for sale in many shops; many are shaped like animals, flowers, ships or cars. The Peak and various spots in the New Territories are favourite places to go and light your lantern while watching the moon rise – at which point you scoff the cakes. There's a lantern display, too, in Victoria Park on Hong Kong Island, but expect transport to anywhere near a hill (such as the Peak Tram) to be packed. Some more traditional villages in the New Territories celebrate by building large sausage-shaped hot-air balloons out of paper and bamboo, and launching them at night; fuelled and illuminated by burning wadding they can travel hundreds of feet up if the air is still. Tradition links this practice to ancient military signalling, but its true origins are obscure. The day after the festival is a public holiday.

Birthday of Confucius

The Birthday of Confucius in September is marked by low-key religious ceremonies at the Confucius Temple in Causeway Bay.

Cheung Yeung Festival

A public holiday on the ninth day of the ninth lunar month (October), the Cheung Yeung Festival relates to a tale from Han Dynasty times, when a soothsayer advised an old man to take his family to the mountains for 24 hours to avoid disaster. On his return, everything else in the village had died. The same trip to high places is made today in remembrance, with the result again that all transport to hilly areas is packed. Lots of people also take this as another opportunity to visit family graves.

11

Shopping

A lot of people still come to Hong Kong mainly to **shop**, although the stories you may have heard about giveaway prices for cameras, electrical goods and other items haven't been true for some time. This is partly because the stability of the Hong Kong dollar has kept prices high in comparison with other parts of Asia, and partly because of the advent of Internet shopping. But what is incredible here is the **huge range of goods** for sale – most of them cutting-edge – crammed into such a small area. As long as you're not expecting cut-price bargains, you can still find good deals on clothing, mobile phones, computer software and accessories, jewellery, silk and other Chinese arts and crafts, and there are also some specialist niches, like porcelain and antiques, worth investigating. In addition, since Hong Kong is a largely **tax-free zone**, the only imported goods to attract duty are alcohol, tobacco, perfumes, cosmetics and cars, and the prices you pay should reflect that (worth remembering when a sales clerk tries to persuade you that a discount of less than your home sales tax rate represents a big concession).

The key is to approach your shopping as you would at home – with **scepticism**. For big-ticket items – particularly electronics – there is no substitute for **research**: horror stories of visitors being charged three or four times the real price are legion here. If you don't have the information you need, a phone call home or a quick surf on the Internet could save you a lot of money and grief. At the very least, compare prices with the local fixed-price retailers or department stores. Remember that almost every purchase you make will be non-refundable (and being overcharged won't negate that), so keep an eye out for the small print and the warranty, check whether an electronic item will work in your home country, and make sure you know exactly what is and is not included. A **fully itemized receipt** will help.

You'll have no difficulty finding designer gear or electronic goods in Hong Kong. All the big names are sold absolutely everywhere and specific addresses, if you need them, are given in the HKTB's *Guide to Quality Merchants* and a dozen other publications and leaflets. We've listed more mainstream markets, bookshops and department stores that should be useful for anyone staying in Hong Kong, as well as a selection of more unusual shops, any of which can occupy a spare half-hour or so, or provide an offbeat souvenir or interesting purchase.

Shop opening hours vary according to which part of Hong Kong you shop in, and most areas have late-night shopping once a week. Shops generally open seven days a week, though some smaller establishments close on Sunday. Otherwise, the only time shops close is for two to three days around Chinese New Year, and even then by no means all do so. Opening hours for street **markets** (apart from fresh-food markets) are even longer, usually daily until 11pm or midnight, though a couple of exceptions are mentioned in the text.

Shopping hours

Central and Western: daily 10am–7pm.
Wan Chai and Causeway Bay: daily 10am–10pm.
Tsim Sha Tsui, Yau Ma Tei and Mongkok: daily 10am–10pm.
Tsim Sha Tsui East: daily 10am–7.30pm.

Shopping: a survival guide

Although it may sometimes seem like it, not everyone's out to rip you off, but there are some things to be aware of before you part with any cash. The key ground-rule is to **shop around** to get an idea of what things cost. Pirate and fake goods (DVDs and clothes especially) are common, so if you find spectacularly cheap prices always check them out elsewhere. **Parallel imports** (imports which come via a third party, rather than directly from the manufacturer, and so are not covered by warranties) of electronic goods are also on the increase. In itself this may not be a problem, as these imports are usually aimed at local consumers whose demand for the latest models often outstrips supply. But buying parallel imports can cause problems if you are not aware of what they are; guarantees are often invalid and the manufacturer may be unwilling to service them. Often the shop itself will offer a one-year guarantee, but this is fairly useless unless you live in Hong Kong and even then it only covers the repair work – you will be charged for any replacement parts. Not surprisingly, such repairs almost always require replacement parts, and even the smallest, simplest plastic knob will be outrageously expensive. Take your time; find out exactly what's included, ask for demonstrations and – on principle – don't buy the first one you see. If you're being unduly pressurized to buy, you're probably in the wrong shop.

Choosing a shop

For expensive items, it's recommended that you use shops that are members of the **Quality Tourism Services** (QTS) Scheme, run by the Hong Kong Tourism Board (HKTB) and the Association of Better Business and Tourism Services. All members must pass a test and pay an annual membership fee before they can display the QTS symbol in their window – a golden Q encircling a Chinese character, on top of a small red junk. Obviously, only a fraction of Hong Kong's shops and stores are in the QTS scheme and the ones that don't belong aren't necessarily all villains – far from it. But it's a starting point if you're worried.

All the registered shops are listed in the HKTB's *Guide to Quality Merchants* (available free from HKTB offices; see p.30), which has plenty of information on shopping for various items and goods, as well as restaurants. There's also shopping information in the monthly *Where Hong Kong* magazine and *Hong Kong: A Traveller's Guide*, both available from HKTB offices. Advertisements in the *South China Morning Post* and the free *HK Magazine* are also good sources of information.

Lastly, Fiona Campbell's *The Guide to Shopping in Hong Kong* (FDC Services) is a reliable and regularly updated guide to local retail outlets, written as much for locals as for visitors – local bookstores should stock it.

If you have any questions about shopping in Hong Kong, or complaints against QTS members, ring ⓣ2508 1234 (daily 8am–6pm). For general complaints about goods made in Hong Kong, try the Consumer Council on ⓣ2929 2222 or ⓦ www.consumer.org.hk.

Guarantees

Always check the **guarantee** you're given for photographic, electronic or electrical goods. Some are **international**, in which case they should carry the name of the sole agent in Hong Kong for that product, but most are purely **local guarantees,** which are only valid in Hong Kong, usually for a period of twelve months. All guarantees should carry a description of the product, including a model number and serial number, as well as the date of purchase, the name and address of the shop you bought it from and the shop's official stamp. In either case, don't put too much reliance on the protection of a piece of paper. Parallel imports may not carry any kind of guarantee.

Deposits and refunds

You don't need to put down a **deposit** on anything unless it's being made for you. For tailored clothes, expect to put down fifty percent of the price, or a little more. On other items, if the shop tries to insist (to "secure" the item, or to order a new one because they're "out of stock") go somewhere else – there are always plenty of alternatives. Generally, goods are **not returnable or refundable**, though if something is faulty or missing the better shops may replace your goods. It will help if you have your receipt itemized and go straight back to the shop if there's something wrong.

Compatibility

It's important to check that **electronic goods** are compatible with your domestic mains voltage, and that television sets and DVD players are compatible with each other, and with your domestic broadcasting system. Beware of the "bait and switch" scam, when having paid for a certain product, you are then told it can't be used in your home country. The shop refuses to refund the transaction, forcing you to pay more for a "better, compatible" model. Be aware, too, that legitimate DVD films bought in Hong Kong are regionally coded, and may not work in your machine at home – there are no such problems with pirated DVD films, audio CDs or computer software, however.

Customs, shipping and insurance

Before making large purchases, check with the relevant consulate (see p.269) or the HKTB about **customs regulations** for the country you want to import the goods to. The shop may be able to arrange to have your purchase packed and sent overseas, but make sure you have it **insured** to cover damage in transit as well as loss (and of course also ensure that you keep the receipt). To send items home yourself, you need to go to a main post office, where you can also arrange insurance (though check first to see if you're covered by your own travel insurance). Parcels usually take about a month by surface mail and a week by airmail to reach Europe or North America.

Avoiding rip-offs

Having checked all the main points, you still need to be armed against the out-and-out bad guys – or simply against the shopkeepers who see their chance to make some extra profit from an unsuspecting visitor.

❑ Always ask the **price**, and what that price includes. Ask more than once to ensure a consistent answer.

❑ **Bargaining**: for most large items in the bigger shops and department stores, the price will be fixed and you won't be able to bargain, though you might be able to wangle extra accessories and the like before completing the sale. However, it's almost mandatory to bargain in markets and smaller shops, especially for electronic goods, though you should avoid Tsim Sha Tsui (the staff there are too wily) and head to Mongkok instead. Decide the price you want to pay for an item and stick with it, and if you can't get them down to that, politely walk away. Often the staff will call you back and grudgingly agree to your price if it's a fair one. They are more likely to agree to a discount if you buy two or more items.

❑ **Switching goods**: if you've paid for goods, don't let them out of your sight as it's not unknown for bits and pieces to have mysteriously vanished by the time you get home, or for cheaper or damaged gear to have been substituted. Either pack your purchases yourself, or check everything before you leave the shop. If things like camera cases or electrical leads are part of the package, make sure they're there and itemized on the receipt: otherwise if you return later to complain you may be told that they're "extras" which you now have to pay for.

❑ **Fake and pirate gear**: sometimes you know that goods are fakes or copies and it doesn't matter. Pirated DVDs, computer software and CDs for instance, are available in many places. Copies of leading international jewellery brands' signature designs, by local jewellers (in gold and precious stones), are also good value. Fake designer-label gear from markets may also have a certain cachet. But if you want the real thing, don't buy anything from anyone on the street, and don't be tempted by stupid "bargains" – pay the going rate and get receipts and guarantees. In any case, the traffic in pirated items like watches and DVDs is being increasingly stamped on by the customs authorities, who are under heavy international pressure to clean up their act.

Boycotting products

There's almost nothing you can't buy in Hong Kong, which means that there is trade in several products you may not feel entirely happy about, including furs, leather and skin goods made from rare and exotic or endangered species, including **ivory**. There are huge stocks of this in Hong Kong, one of the world's largest markets in the product, and it is still home to a big ivory-processing industry – you'll see the results in shop windows. However, both the Chinese government and the Hong Kong authorities are parties to CITES (the Convention on International Trade in Endangered Species), and since 1990 the Hong Kong authorities have abided more stringently by the rules of the worldwide ban.

There is also a growing trade in **shatoosh**, a fibre even finer than cashmere. It comes from Tibetan antelopes that are shot by poachers (the fur isn't gathered after being rubbed off on thorns, as vendors would have you believe). The shawls produced can go for US$10,000 or more.

The trade in endangered species also rears its head in traditional **Chinese medicine**, which often uses the body parts of critically endangered animals like tigers and rhinos. Surprisingly, many of the medicines carry bilingual ingredient lists – if you're going to buy anything, check first.

Antiques and art galleries

Hong Kong offers good opportunities to buy Chinese **antiques and arts**, although local buyers are very clued up and bargains are consequently rare. For antiques, the best place to start is **Hollywood Road**, though the majority of the customers here are foreigners, and include many dealers. Most of the items come from China, usually by "unofficial" routes. There are no problems in exporting antiques once they are in Hong Kong, but if you're worried, pieces that have left China legitimately will have a small red seal on them.

The type of stock available changes from year to year. What never changes, though, is the premium on really good pieces. However, if you are happy with something that is attractive rather than valuable, you'll have much more choice and leeway for bargaining (which, incidentally, is a must). It's quite possible to get some very nice pieces of embroidery or small Han or Tang figures for a couple of hundred dollars, though they may also be composite – made from remnants of a number of different items. Many of the Hollywood Road shops maintain larger **warehouses** elsewhere (including over the border), so if you're really interested, ask about visiting. Art and antiques more than one hundred years old are usually allowed into most countries duty-free, though check first with your consulate (there's a list on p.269). The shop should provide the necessary **certificate of authenticity**.

If you're interested in more **modern art**, Hong Kong is also a good place to view the work of some of the best Chinese contemporary painters. Once again, the best isn't cheap, not least because there is a local market for modern Chinese art.

Antique shops

The two main hotspots for antique hunting are Hollywood Road in Central and the third floor of Pacific Place in Admiralty. The shops below are all well established, and close on Sundays, unless otherwise stated.

Altfield Gallery 2nd Floor, Prince's Building, 10 Chater Rd, Central ⓣ2537 6370, ⓦwww.altfield.com.hk. Specializes in Southeast Asian furniture, textiles, Burmese Buddha figures and a good selection of Oriental prints, paintings and maps – all expensive but good quality. Hosts regular exhibitions, and has very helpful, unpushy staff. Open Sun 11am–5pm.

Art Treasures Gallery 42 Hollywood Rd, Central ⓣ2543 0430, ⓦwww.art-treasures-gallery.com. Helpful small gallery with a warehouse in Zhu Hai in China. Core specializations are furniture – bargain hard on this – and burial items, but they're also branching out into other things.

Dragon Culture 231 & 184 Hollywood Rd, Central ⓣ2545 8098, ⓦwww.dragonculture.com.hk. Vast selection of burial ceramics and other items (including fossilized dinosaur eggs) in all price ranges.

Dynasty Antiques Ground Floor, 48–50 Hollywood Rd, Central ⓣ2851 1389, ⓦwww.dynasty-antiques.com. Finely restored classic Chinese and Tibetan antique furniture in a cavernous store.

Honeychurch Antiques 29 Hollywood Rd, Central ⓣ2543 2433, ⓦwww.honeychurch.com/hong_kong.html. One of the longest-established galleries, offering a wide selection of small items from throughout Asia, including Japan. Silver, porcelain, books, prints and many other things. Expensive but interesting.

Karin Weber Gallery 32A Staunton St, Mid-Levels ⓣ2544 5004, ⓦwww.karinwebergallery.com. Large selection of mid-price items. Also organizes trips to warehouses in mainland China. Open Sun 2–6pm.

L&E 188 Hollywood Rd, Central ⓣ2546 9886, ⓦwww.lneco.com. New decorative porcelain and old Chinese furniture. They have a warehouse in Aberdeen full of old furniture and china. Packing and shipping can be arranged.

Low Price Shop 47 Hollywood Rd, Central. A Hong Kong institution. More of a stall really, selling bric-a-brac, old photos and general junk. Bargain hard.

Sun Chau Book and Antique Co 32 Stanley St, Central ⓣ2522 8268, ⓦwww.sunchau.com.hk. Quirky shop full of old household bits and pieces such as porcelain, photographs, Cultural Revolution posters and even gramophone records from the 1930s – this is one place where bargains do occasionally surface.

Teresa Coleman 79 Wyndham St, Central ⓣ2526 2450, ⓦwww.teresacoleman.com. One of Hong Kong's best-known dealers, with an international reputation for dealing in Chinese textiles and a good selection of pictures and prints.

Books and magazines

All the bookshops below sell **English-language books**, and many sell overseas newspapers and magazines too. The stall in Theatre Lane, near exit D2 of Central MTR, stocks a particularly wide range of Western magazines and newspapers. There are, of course, hundreds of other bookshops selling Chinese-language books only.

Angelo De Carpi **18 Wo On Lane, Central.** A range of gay and lesbian fiction, studies and joke books, and piles of male magazines.

Bookazine **Ground Floor, Pacific House, 20 Queens Rd, Central.** Excellent selection of foreign magazines and books.

Chaip Coin Co. **Shop 233, 2nd Floor, World-Wide House, 19 Des Voeux Rd, Central.** A tiny shop selling all manner of foreign magazines, from *Viz* through motorcycle magazines to obscure food and fashion publications from the UK, US and Australia.

Collectables **1st Floor, Winning House, 26 Hollywood Rd, Central.** Immense collection of all kinds of books, including a wonderful pile of old *National Geographics*. Also stocks secondhand CDs, VCDs, DVDs and records.

The Commercial Press **3rd Floor, Star House, 3 Salisbury Rd, Tsim Sha Tsui; 9 Yee Woo St, Causeway Bay; and Shop 266–270, 2nd Floor, New Town Plaza, Sha Tin.** Largely Chinese-language books but very good for Chinese-learning texts (both Cantonese and Mandarin), and lots of good contemporary nonfiction (in English) on China and Hong Kong. The main branch in Star House also has a pleasant café.

Cosmos Books **1st Floor, 30 Johnston Rd, Wan Chai; and 96 Nathan Rd, Tsim Sha Tsui (entrance on Granville Rd).** A good stock of Chinese- and English-language novels, art, travel and history books.

Dymocks **Star Ferry Concourse, Central; Shop 115–116, 1st Floor, Prince's Building, 10 Chater Rd, Central; Shop 2007–2011, Level 2, International Finance Centre, Central; and Shop F–G, 2nd Floor, Windsor House, 311 Gloucester Rd, Causeway Bay.** Fine selection of English-language novels, travel guides, dictionaries, maps and books on Hong Kong and China, and foreign newspapers.

Government Publications Centre **Queensway Government Offices, Low Block, Ground Floor, 66 Queensway, Admiralty.** Official government publications, Hong Kong maps, exhibition catalogues and books on local flora, fauna, politics, environment, industry and anything else you can think of.

Hong Kong Book Centre **Basement On Lok Yuen Building, 25 Des Voeux Rd, Central.** Cramped, library-like interior, but well stocked with novels and travel books, and good on Chinese history and politics. Also has foreign newspapers.

Lotus Born Buddhist Art and Books **1st Floor, 57 Hankow Rd, Tsim Sha Tsui.** Only a few of the Buddhist texts are in English, but they also sell a large selection of Buddhist chants on CD and tape. The peaceful music and white Buddha shrine make this shop a haven from the packed streets below.

Page One **Basement One Times Square, 1 Matheson St, Causeway Bay; Shop 3002, 3rd Floor, Harbour City, Canton Rd, Tsim Sha Tsui; and Shop 30, LG1, Festival Walk, Kowloon Tong.** Perhaps the best bookshops in Hong Kong, selling a huge selection of English-language books and magazines from fiction through to archeology and computer manuals. They also stock a healthy number of gay and lesbian books and magazines. The vast Kowloon Tong branch has a café selling great cakes to munch while you read.

Swindon Book Co. Ltd **Star Ferry Concourse, Tsim Sha Tsui; and 13–15 Lock Rd, Tsim Sha Tsui.** A good general bookshop with a large section on travel, local interest and Chinese culture.

Tai Yip Chinese Art Book Gallery **72 Wellington St, Central; First Floor, Central Library, 66 Causeway Rd, Tin Hau (near Causeway Bay); and Hong Kong Heritage Museum, 1 Man Lam Rd, Sha Tin.** Some books and magazines on Chinese arts and crafts – new and secondhand. Also books, funky stationery and gifts relating to Hong Kong and China.

Times Bookshop **Shop P315–316, 3rd Floor, World Trade Centre, 280 Gloucester Rd, Causeway Bay; and Basement, Golden Crown Court, 66–70 Nathan Rd, Tsim Sha Tsui.** Fairly standard not-too-expensive bookshop with a reasonable section of books and some nice stationery.

Traveller's Home **2nd Floor, 55 Hankow Rd, Tsim Sha Tsui.** An eclectic range of secondhand books, travel guides in both English and Chinese, plus regular presentations by local travel writers and photographers.

China and porcelain

Porcelain has been a traditional export of Hong Kong for hundreds of years, and is still a good buy. The available quality varies enormously – from the cheapest household blue and white (still very pretty) to museum-quality replicas of old patterns.

Chinese Arts and Crafts China Resources Building, 26 Harbour Rd, Wan Chai; 230 The Mall, Pacific Place, 88 Queensway, Admiralty; Star House, 3 Salisbury Rd, Tsim Sha Tsui; and Nathan Hotel, 378 Nathan Rd, Yau Ma Tei. A good selection of all types and qualities of china in traditional styles, plus a few antique pieces.

▲ Porcelain for sale in Central

Hing Cheung Fu Kee Chinaware Co. 17 Staunton St, SoHo. A down-to-earth warehourse-style shop with piles of cheap Chinese teapots and plateware.

Lee Fung Chinaware 18 Shelley St, Mid-Levels. You'll pass this as you ride the Mid-Levels escalator up. Good-quality selection of china, well displayed.

Wah Tung China Ltd 59 Hollywood Rd, Central. Very high-quality selection, representing all the major decorative trends in Chinese porcelain. They pack and dispatch worldwide.

Chinese and Oriental products stores

These stores specialize in **products made in mainland China**, including silk clothes and underwear, cashmere, fabrics, furniture, porcelain, antiques, herbal medicines, electrical goods, household linen, jewellery and decorative items.

Chinese Arts and Crafts Asia Standard Tower, 59 Queen's Rd, Central; China Resources Building, 26 Harbour Rd, Wan Chai; 230 The Mall, Pacific Place, 88 Queensway, Admiralty; Star House, 3 Salisbury Rd, Tsim Sha Tsui; and Nathan Hotel, 378 Nathan Rd, Yau Ma Tei. The largest and best branches are those in Star House and Wan Chai, and the new Central branch is the plushest. Some items are very good value, and it's always worth a look around, although some of the silks and linens can be found cheaper in Stanley Market.

CRC Department Store Chiao Shang Building, 92 Queen's Rd, Central; and Lok Sing Centre, 488 Hennessy Rd, Causeway Bay. Cheap department-store products plus Chinese specialities such as medicines, foodstuffs, porcelain and handicrafts.

Chun Sang Trading 3–4 Glenealy, Central. Inexpensive Chinese-made cotton and linen products – embroidered sheets, cushion covers and tablecloths.

Yue Hwa Chinese Products Emporium 39 Queen's Rd Central, Central; 22–36 Paterson St, Causeway Bay; 301–309 Nathan Rd, Yau Ma Tei; 1 Kowloon Park Drive, Tsim Sha Tsui; 54–62 Nathan Rd, Tsim Sha Tsui; and 24–32 Paterson St, Causeway Bay. Long-standing department store, particularly good for Chinese medicines.

Clothes

For the addresses of the **big-name designers** – from Armani to Valentino, as well as local Hong Kong whizz-kids – look no further than the HKTB Guide to Quality Merchants, which lists them all in exhaustive detail. Otherwise, simply check out stores as you wend your way around the city. Be aware, though, that Western designer clothes are often significantly more expensive here than they are back home because of the extra cachet attached to foreign labels.

Clothing and shoe sizes

Dresses							
US	8	10	12	14	16	18	20
UK	10	12	14	16	18	20	22
Continental	40	42	44	46	48	50	52
Women's shoes							
US	4.5	5.5	6.5	7.5	8.5	9.5	
UK	3	4	5	6	7	8	
Continental	35.5	36.5	37.5	38.5	39.5	40.5	
Men's suits/coats							
US	36	38	40	42	44	46	
UK	36	38	40	42	44	46	
Continental	46	48	50	52	54	56	
Men's shirts							
US	14	15	16	17			
UK	14	15	16	17			
Continental	36	38	41	43			
Men's shoes							
US	6	7	8	9	10	11	
UK	6	7	8	9	10	11	
Continental	39	41	42	43	44	46	

For cheaper clothes shopping, check out the main local **fashion chain stores** – Giordano, U2, Baleno and Bossini – for decent-quality, value-for-money casual wear, including shirts, chinos, jackets, skirts and socks. There are countless branches in all areas of the city. Alternatively, track down the factory and **warehouse outlets** (see overleaf), whose bargain prices for designer shirts and jackets really start to save you money. For other ideas, visit the various **markets** (p.254) that specialize in clothes. The Chinese products stores are also worth checking for fabrics, silk clothing, cashmere and padded winter jackets.

For local designers and more off-beat designs, head to the Beverley Commercial Building, 87–105 Chatham Rd, two blocks north of Granville Road, a street renowned for its cheap boutiques. More young designers have outlets nearby in the Rise Commercial Building, 5–11 Granville Circuit, and in Granville Rise, while the Island Beverley, 1 Great George St, Causeway Bay (the entrance is via an escalator above SOGO's supermarket) is packed with original designs from locals, many with a strong Japanese influence. Be aware that these clothes are made for the local market and larger Western figures might not find much to fit them here. All three centres open in the afternoon and close around 10pm.

Local designers

Blanc De Chine 2nd Floor, Pedder Building, 12 Pedder St, Central. Designs loosely based on traditional Chinese clothes, in silk and cashmere using muted colours.

Joyce Ground Floor, New World Tower, Central; Shop 334, Pacific Place, 88 Queensway, Admiralty; and 23 Nathan Rd, Tsim Sha Tsui. Hong Kong's most fashionable boutique offers its own range of clothing, as well as many top overseas designer brands.

Shanghai Tang Pedder Building, 12 Pedder St, Central. The store is beautifully done up in 1930s Shanghai style, making it a must to visit, if not to buy. It specializes in new takes on traditional Chinese designs – often in vibrant colours – and can also make things to order (see below). Some household items and gifts are available, too. Watch out for the regular, competitive sales.

Vivienne Tam Shop 209, Pacific Place, 88

Queensway, Admiralty; Shop 219, Times Square, 1 Matheson St, Causeway Bay; Shop G310–311, Harbour City, Tsim Sha Tsui; and Shop 55, LG1, Festival Walk, Kowloon Tong. Funky shirts and dresses in David Hockney-meets-Vivienne Westwood style, often featuring Chairman Mao and other icons of the East.

Walter Ma **9 Queen's Rd Central, Central.** Party clothes for Hong Kong's smart set.

Factory and warehouse outlets

One unusual aspect of shopping in Hong Kong is the chance to buy from a wide variety of factory and warehouse outlets. These are in commercial buildings, not shops, and sell clothes, fabrics and jewellery direct to the public. They can open and close very quickly – consult the HKTB brochure, *Factory Outlets*, for addresses, or pick up a locally published guide like *The Smart Shopper in Hong Kong* or *The Complete Guide to Hong Kong Factory Bargains*. Many outlets can be difficult to find if you don't have the exact address. Be sure to try things on before you buy – marked sizes mean nothing. Prices are competitive, either because there's a low mark-up or because you're buying samples, ends-of-lines or high-quality seconds.

If you just want to browse, **Granville Road** in Tsim Sha Tsui (off Nathan Road) is a good place to look, as are the many stores along **Cheung Sha Wan Road** in Sham Shui Po, Kowloon – catch the MTR to Sham Shui Po. In Central, look for signs in doorways along **Wyndham Street** and **D'Aguilar Street**, and don't forget the **Pedder Building** (12 Pedder St), which is full of discount outlets. In Aberdeen, check out the **Joyce Warehouse**, 21st Floor, Horizon Plaza, Ap Lei Chau, where Hong Kong's most fashionable shop puts all last season's stuff that didn't sell – with discounts up to eighty percent. The same building also houses several other discount outlets.

Tailors

Hong Kong has long been known for the speed and value of its tailors. Whatever you're told, however, don't demand a suit in 24 hours: if you're foolish enough to do so, it either won't fit, will fall apart, or both. Nor should you expect ridiculously low prices, though as a rule-of-thumb a handmade men's suit in Hong Kong costs the same as an off-the-peg version in the West. Bargaining is usually not appropriate, and you'll need to pay about fifty percent of the price as deposit.

When it comes to **style**, the easiest way is to bring the tailor something to copy, perhaps with some alterations. If that's not possible, a picture is useful – most shops have piles of magazines to help you choose. The best way to find a good tailor is personal recommendation – if you don't know anyone try asking in your hotel. Alternatively, look for a tailor who relies on regular clients, not passing tourists; the big hotels, shopping malls or areas around Mid-Levels, Happy Valley and Causeway Bay are promising locations. Ask to look at some of the garments they have under way. Women may want to choose a tailor with an established Western clientele, as they will be used to dealing with the rather different body shape. Some suggestions include:

Italian Tailor **1st Floor, Prince's Building, 10 Chater Rd, Central.** Upmarket men's tailor which makes suits for many local businessmen. Quality fabric selection.

Johnson & Co. **44 Hankow Rd, Tsim Sha Tsui.** Does a lot of work for military and naval customers. Mostly male clientele.

Linva Tailor **38 Cochrane St, Central.** Well-established ladies' tailor, whose core business is making party clothes (*cheongsam*) for local ladies. Also does embroidery.

Margaret Court **Tailoress Floor 8, Winner Building, 27 D'Aguilar St, Central.** Lots of local Western female clients, and a solid reputation for good work, although it doesn't come cheaply. A shirt costs around $300, plus fabric.

Punjab House **Shop J, Ground Floor, Golden Crown Court, 66–70 Nathan Rd, Tsim Sha Tsui.** Former favourite of the British Forces and firefighters; good quality male and female formal wear.

Sam's Tailors **94 Nathan Rd, Tsim Sha Tsui.** A Hong Kong institution, as much for Sam's talent for self-publicity as for the quality of his clothes. A long list of distinguished clients.

Shanghai Tang **12 Pedder St, Central.** This boutique's tailoring service specializes in modern adaptations of traditional Chinese styles for men and women, and has a fabulous selection of fabrics. They are very geared up to helping visitors and can arrange quick fittings and the posting of finished garments.

Fabrics

All tailors keep a selection of fabrics or samples, but if you want to choose your own, or don't have time to wait for theirs to arrive in stock, there are a number of fabric shops around town, particularly in Li Yuen streets East and West; at the junction of Queen's Road and Wellington Street; in D'Aguilar Street; and at Western Market in Sheung Wan.

Electronic goods and software

Hong Kong is an excellent place to stock up on electronic goods and software. In many cases there's no tax on these items, and the locals want nothing but the very latest model – creating big discounts on older versions. This holds most true for mobile phones, computers and MP3 players; for other types of electronics, such as **cameras and DVD players**, expect less competitive prices.

Scams in selling these products abound (see p.242); don't plan to buy anything without a good idea of the lowest price you can get it for at home. In general, avoid hard-core tourist shopping areas such as Nathan Road in favour of outlets along Sai Yeung Choi Street or Fa Yuen Street in **Mongok**. **Department stores** – Chinese and Western – make good reference points, as do the fixed-price retail chains such as Fortress, which has branches all over Hong Kong. The electronics shops in the **Prince's Building** (10 Chater Rd, Central), or in **hotels** such as the *Furama* on Connaught Road in Central are also pretty straight and may not be as expensive as you think. **Stanley Street** in Central has a good range of camera shops. See also "Secondhand" (p.255).

Mongkok is again the place to look for **pirated computer software**, though the shops selling it are discreetly hidden away in the dark innards of other buildings. While not strictly illegal in Hong Kong, you'll find that your own country will have very different views on the matter should you be caught bringing pirated software home with you – and if for some reason the software doesn't work, don't expect a refund.

For the latest offers on computers and accessories, look at the ads in the *South China Morning Post*'s technology supplement every Tuesday. The main places to head for include:

298 Computer Zone **298 Hennessy Rd, Wan Chai.** Warren-like place, full of shops selling new, secondhand, official and pirated computer gear.

Golden Shopping Arcade **156 Fuk Wah St, Sham Shui Po, Kowloon.** Famous for its supply of cheap computer goods, but also notorious as a centre for pirate software.

Mongkok Computer Centre **8 Nelson St, Mongkok.** Lots of pirated games and a good selection of laptops.

Star House **Salisbury Rd, Tsim Sha Tsui, near the Star Ferry Pier.** Reliable computer mall, including a specialist computer bookshop.

Windsor House **311 Gloucester Rd, Causeway Bay.** Useful Hong Kong-side arcade, which also stocks secondhand computers.

Crafts

In addition to what's available in the Chinese products stores (see p.248), the shops below offer various types of modern arts-and-crafts products from throughout Asia.

Ah Chung Gallery 1st Floor, 28 Cochrane St, Central. A showcase for the work of the owner's brother – very distinctive Chinese art using bright colours and cartoon-like images. Also sells lots of associated stationery and knick-knacks using the design.

Banyan Tree 214–18 Prince's Building, 10 Chater Rd, Central. Antiques, reproduction furniture and pricey Asian handicrafts.

G.O.D. 6th Floor, Horizon Plaza, Ap Lei Chau, Aberdeen; Shop 27, Festival Walk, Kowloon Tong; and Shop 2, 3rd Floor, Discovery Park, Tsuen Wan. Simple, modern household products and furniture for Chinese yuppies. Some very good designs and colours, in natural materials and at reasonable prices.

Good Lacquer Gifts Gallery Shop 206B, 2nd Floor, Pedder Building, 12 Pedder St, Central. Sells pretty Chinese and Vietnamese lacquerware.

King and Country 3rd Floor, Pacific Place, 88 Queensway, Admiralty. An amazing shop which sells beautiful hand-painted lead soldiers and models. Many have military themes, but there are also wonderful sets showing Chinese life, the Qing Dynasty court and a traditional wedding.

Mountain Folkcraft 12 Wo On Lane (off D'Aguilar St), Central. Beautiful handmade folk arts and crafts from Southeast Asia and elsewhere.

Museum Shop Hong Kong Arts Centre, Cultural Centre, Salisbury Rd, Tsim Sha Tsui. Art books and supplies, calligraphy materials, prints, postcards, gifts and stationery.

Welfare Handicrafts Shops Shop 7, Lower Ground Floor, Jardine House, One Connaught Place, Central; and Salisbury Rd (opposite the Cultural Centre), Tsim Sha Tsui. Locally made arts and crafts sold on behalf of charities.

Department stores

There is a vast selection of mammoth, air-conditioned department stores, owned by parent companies from different countries; pick your culture and dive in. Most have cafés and coffee shops inside, too.

Local stores

Lane Crawford 70 Queen's Rd, Central; and Levels 1–3, The Mall, Pacific Place, 88 Queensway, Admiralty. Hong Kong's oldest Western-style department store – the first branch listed is the main one.

Sincere 173 Des Voeux Rd, Central; and 83 Argyle St, Mongkok. A more downmarket store; the Argyle Street branch is good for shoes.

Wing On 211 Des Voeux Rd, Central; 345 Nathan Rd, Yau Ma Tei; and Shop G22–32, Ground Floor, Treasure World, Whampoa Garden, Hung Hom. Standard department store, good for everyday items.

Japanese stores

Mitsukoshi Hennessy Centre, 500 Hennessy Rd, Causeway Bay. A good place for upmarket labels, with an excellent Park'N'Shop supermarket in the basement selling a wide range of Western foodstuffs until late (10pm).

Seibu Pacific Place, 88 Queensway, Admiralty; and Windsor House, 311 Gloucester Rd, Causeway Bay. Upmarket store, carrying a big proportion of European household goods and fashion.

Sogo East Point Centre, 555 Hennessy Rd, Causeway Bay. Ten floors' worth of consumerism, including a good Japanese supermarket.

Food and drink

For a list of **bakeries**, **delicatessens**, **takeaways** and **supermarkets**, consult the relevant sections of chapter 7. You'll find accounts of **markets** where you can buy food throughout the book. The main ones are Central and Sheung

Wan markets (chapter 1); Temple Street Night Market (chapter 2); and Luen Wo Market and Sheung Shui Market (both chapter 3).

For **wines**, **spirits** and other drinks, most of the supermarkets have adequate selections. There are also an increasing number of wine shops, mostly in Central and Mid-Levels (where some restaurants don't have licences). If you want a bigger selection, try Oliver's Delicatessen at Shop 201–205, Prince's Building, 10 Chater Rd, Central; Citysuper, Times Square, 1 Matheson St, Causeway Bay; The Big Apple Deli, 105–109 Harbour Centre, 25 Harbour Rd, Wan Chai; Great Food Hall, Pacific Place, 88 Queensway, Admiralty; Watson's Wine, D'Aguilar Street, Central; 2 Staunton St, SoHo; and 311 Gloucester Rd, Causeway Bay. Most of these sell a range of Western foods (cheese, bread, chocolates) too.

When buying food in markets, you need to know that **Chinese weights and measures** are different from Western ones. Most things (vegetables, beansprouts, rice, dried foods) are sold by the **catty**, which is the equivalent of 1.3 lb or 600g; the smaller unit is the **tael**, equivalent to 1.3 oz or 38g. That said, unless you can speak and read Chinese, you'll probably find that simply picking up the amount you want and handing it to the stallholder is the best way to go about things. Fruit is sold by the piece or the pound, meat and fish by the ounce.

Jewellery

Jewellery **prices** are low in Hong Kong (since precious stones can be imported without paying duty) and there are literally thousands of jewellers, reflecting the local population's love for glitter and sparkle. Most of their designs tend towards the flashy – this is a town where you wear your wealth on your sleeve, or your finger – although many also do pieces that are extremely close to the signature designs of some of the most famous international jewellers. Alternatively, given time they can make or copy to your requirements. Again if you're buying, shop around, take what you hear with a pinch of salt, and check the fixed-price shops before venturing to Nathan Road or to Queen's Road Central.

If you're looking for **jade**, there's a special Jade Market in Kansu Street, Yau Ma Tei (p.254). If you need help or information on buying **diamonds**, contact the Diamond Importers' Association Ltd, Room 1707, Parker House, 70 Queen's Rd, Central ☎2523 5497. For **opals**, a fun place to visit is The Opal Mine (Burlington House, Ground Floor, 92 Nathan Rd, Tsim Sha Tsui), which also has an informative exhibition on the mining of opal in Australia, where ninety percent of the world's supply comes from.

Elissa Cohen Jewellery **209 Hankow Centre, 5–15 Hankow Rd, Tsim Sha Tsui.** Individual designs, lots of pearls.

Gallery One **31–33 Hollywood Rd.** A huge selection of semiprecious beads and necklaces – amber, amethyst, tiger's eye, crystal and much more. They will string any arrangement you want.

Johnson & Co. **1st Floor, 44 Hankow Rd, Tsim Sha Tsui.** Straight, middle-of-the-road jeweller, not too pushy.

Just Gold **Ground Floor, Shop 139, Pacific Place, 88 Queensway, Admiralty; 452 Hennessy Rd, Wan Chai; Shop A2, 27 Nathan Rd, Tsim Sha Tsui; and Unit UG14, Festival Walk, Kowloon Tong.** Local chain specializing in fun, fashionable, cheapish designs for young women. They have the licence for Mickey Mouse gold jewellery – very popular locally.

Kai-Yin Lo **3rd Floor, Pacific Place, 88 Queensway, Admiralty; Shop M6, Mandarin Hotel; and Shop BE11a, Peninsula Hotel, Salisbury Rd, Tsim Sha Tsui.** Hong Kong's best-known jewellery designer, who also sells in New York. Makes interesting use of old jade, carvings and semiprecious stones. Expensive, but nice to look.

New Universal Jewelery Company **10 Ice House St, Central.** Reliable, quality jewellers with

wide range of styles. Competitive prices.
Regal Jewelery Empire Centre, 68 Mody Rd, Tsim Sha Tsui East. Good, large selection of gold, including some very well-known designs. Unfortunately the sales force are very shark-like. You need to be an experienced and persistent bargainer.

Markets: clothes, fabrics and bric-a-brac

The cheapest clothes and fabrics can be found in markets, but shop around and haggle. You won't be able to try anything on and you'll never be able to take anything back, but be sensible and you shouldn't go too far wrong.

Jade Market Kansu St, Yau Ma Tei. Jade jewellery, artefacts and statues; p.113.
Jardine's Bazaar Causeway Bay. Clothes and household goods; p.84.
Li Yuen Street East and West Central. Women's and children's clothes; p.60.
Man Wa Lane Sheung Wan. Traditional Chinese seals; p.65.
Marble Street North Point. Shirts and shorts; p.94.
Stanley Market Stanley Village. Silk, cashmere, and some fake designer labels a speciality; p.92.
Temple Street Yau Ma Tei. The SAR's best night market: clothes, tapes, watches, jewellery, and digital bits and pieces; p.113.
Tung Choi Street Mongkok. Women's and children's clothes and accessories; p.114.
Upper Lascar Row (Cat Street) Central. Flea market; p.68.
Western Market Sheung Wan. Fabrics, arts and crafts; p.66.

CDs, VCDs and DVDs

Most mainstream CDs can be found in Hong Kong: prices are generally around twenty to thirty percent lower than in the UK (and slightly higher than in the US). Check out the locally produced Canto-pop releases, as well as recordings of mainland Chinese artists. Note that artists are almost always filed under first names. If you come across market barrows selling CDs, they're almost certainly pirate copies. Also widely available are VCDs and DVDs of movies, from old Hollywood classics through Hong Kong mass-produced titles to newly released blockbusters. If you head for the independent outlets along **Hennessy Road** from Causeway Bay to Wan Chai, or along **Nathan Road** from Mongkok to Jordan, you'll get VCDs for as little as $10 and DVDs for $50–150.

Chungking Mansions 36–44 Nathan Rd, Tsim Sha Tsui. Cheap tapes and CDs at various stalls inside Nathan Road's most labyrinthine shopping centre – particularly good for Bollywood music.

HMV 1st Floor, Central Building, Central Ground Floor; Windsor House, 311 Gloucester Rd, Causeway Bay; and Sands Building, Peking Rd, Tsim Sha Tsui. Megastores with listening stations and a mammoth choice, as good for world and Canto-pop as for Western releases.
Hong Kong Records Shop 252, The Mall, Pacific Place, 88 Queensway, Admiralty. Good mixture of styles and prices; no vinyl in sight, despite the name.
Monitor Records 4–16 Tak Shing St, Jordan. The widest selection of CDs in Hong Kong, with titles going for $30 less than in high-street chains. As well as mainstream pop you'll find dance, funk and all kinds of club music, world music and even very select genres such as darkwave

medieval, darkwave gothic to darkwave neofolk. Amazingly, there's also a good collection of vinyl.

Works Records 38 Hankow Rd, Tsim Sha Tsui. Scruffy shop selling a diverse range of bootleg CDs (mainly from Germany) from artists across the board; all kinds of musical genres from mainstream pop through drum'n'bass to thrash metal. Not cheap.

Secondhand

Bizarrely, Hong Kong is rather a good place to buy secondhand stuff, or – as it's coyly known locally – "pre-owned". The local population is so fashion- and brand-conscious that there is a lot of turnover, and apartments are so small people don't have room to keep last season's stuff.

Cameras try the shops in Stanley Street, Central; or David Chan Co, 15 Champagne Court, 16 Kimberley Rd, Tsim Sha Tsui; Tin Cheung Camera Co., 26 Tung Yung Building, 100 Nathan Rd, Tsim Sha Tsui; or Hing Lee Camera Co., 25 Lyndhurst Terrace, Central.

Clothes The Pedder Building, 12 Pedder St, Central, has some outlets such as La Place which deal in upmarket secondhand clothes. Oxfam has two stores (Shop 8, Lower Ground Floor, Jardine House, One Connaught Rd, Central; and Shop 28, Lower Ground Floor, Silvercord Centre, 30 Canton Rd, Tsim Sha Tsui) which stock everything from cast-off designer gear to shabby togs. Other options include Retrostone (1st Floor, 504 Lockhart Rd, Causeway Bay) for secondhand jeans and beaded accessories, and Beatniks (Shop A–C, Yuet Wah Ct, 19–21 Shelter St, Causeway Bay; Shop 1, Ground Floor, Rise Commercial Building, 5–11 Granville Circuit, Tsim Sha Tsui; and Shop 2, Ground Floor, 54C Granville Rd, Tsim Sha Tsui), selling pricey clothes, including denim, supposedly all imported from New York.

Computers try outlets in 298 Computer Zone, 298 Hennessy Rd, Wan Chai; or Windsor House, 311 Gloucester Rd, Causeway Bay.

Watches Berne Horology (Kam On Building, 176A Queen's Rd, Central) and Henrie Collection (Shop 9B, Champagne Court, 16 Kimberley Rd, Tsim Sha Tsui) sell everything from antique clocks and watches through to old egg-timers, gramophone players and sundials.

Shopping malls

Even if you hate shopping, it's impossible to avoid walking through a **shopping mall** sooner or later, since half the pedestrian overpasses and walkways in Central and Tsim Sha Tsui East pass straight through one or more of them. You may as well accept that you're going to see the inside of more shopping malls than you thought existed; you may even enjoy them when the weather is hot or wet since they're air-conditioned. The main concentrations are in **Central**, **Admiralty** and **Tsim Sha Tsui**, with a few in Causeway Bay and a couple of other major malls in the New Territories. Many are sights in themselves: gleaming, climate-controlled consumer paradises, serviced by state-of-the-art lifts, enlivened by galleries, lights and fountains, and sustained by bars, cafés and restaurants. All the important ones are covered in the main guide, but a quick checklist of the best includes:

Cityplaza 111 King's Rd, Taikoo Shing. Popular mid-range mall, with a flashy cinema and an ice rink: caters mainly for local shoppers.

Dragon Centre 37K Yen Chow St, Sham Shui Po. A downmarket shopping plaza, whose top floor is ringed by a snaking rollercoaster above a popular ice rink. There's the usual run of inexpensive chain food outlets, clothes stores and electronics shops, while the ground floor often hosts free jazz concerts or ballroom dancing.

Festival Walk Kowloon Tong. Linked by underpass to Kowloon Tong MTR. One of the newest and shiniest of the Hong Kong malls, designed by the super-trendy Miami architectural practice, Arquitechtonica. The design incorporates feng shui principles, so there are no pointed edges and lots of references to nature – water with the fountains, a glacier with the ice rink, a cave for the food court. There are also more than two hundred shops and an eleven-screen cinema.

Harbour City **700 Tsim Sha Tsui, near the Kowloon Star Ferry Terminal.** A warren-like building incorporating seven hundred shops, the Ocean Centre, Ocean Terminal and the Marco Polo Hong Kong Hotel Arcade. Includes a couple of posh antique shops, a good bookshop, Toys 'R' Us, and a number of local jewellers, as well as the usual boutiques.

The Landmark **Des Voeux Rd, Central. Central MTR.** Five minute's walk from the Star Ferry Pier, you're almost certain to pass through this mall as it's an intersection for Central's raised walkways. Check out the basement for local brands and a good bookshop. The designer boutiques on the upper floors are interesting in the sales.

Pacific Place **88 Queensway, Admiralty.** Linked by underpass directly to Admiralty MTR. One of the swankiest malls around, but in addition to the designer outlets on the upper floors it also has a good range of ordinary shops and local boutiques on the lower ones.

Prince's Building **10 Chater Rd, Central. Next to Chater Square and two minutes from the Star Ferry.** Not really a mall, but it has become a second home for many of Hong Kong's expats because of the deli on the third floor, which stocks loads of foreign foods and wines. Also home to some interesting fashion accessory shops, jewellers and tailors, two good bookshops and stationers, and an expensive but totally genuine antique shop.

Times Square **1 Matheson St, Causeway Bay. Linked by walkway to Causeway Bay MTR; the tram also runs nearby.** The main mall in Causeway Bay, with the usual selection of local and international retailers, plus lots of restaurants, a cinema complex and a forum area often used for special exhibitions.

World-Wide House **19 Des Voeux Rd, Central.** A lively, friendly and offbeat shopping mall, packed with gold shops, cheap boutiques, snack stalls selling cheap Philippine rice-and-fish staples and the cheapest sandwiches in town, as well as a superb magazine shop on the second floor, and a Delifrance on the first floor.

Tea shops

Chinese tea in decorative tins and boxes makes a nice, portable souvenir, and can be bought from any of Hong Kong's numerous **specialist tea shops**, or in prepacked selections from **Chinese products shops** (see p.248). In traditional tea shops the tea is treated like wine, with different vintages and producers. There are dozens of different varieties, and some shops will let you taste before you make your choice. You buy in small amounts, since tea loses its flavour after a while. Most shops also stock teapots – often fanciful creations, shaped as animals, plants or fruits. Some are collector's items, made by well-known potters and priced accordingly.

Best Tea House **3 Lock Rd, Tsim Sha Tsui; and Unit 201, Causeway Bay Plaza II, 463–483 Lockhart Rd, Causeway Bay.**

Ki Chan Tea Co. **174 Johnston Rd, Wan Chai.** Old men distribute the tea leaves from their red and gold cylinders in this no-nonsense, well-established shop.

Ying Kee **Siu Ying Building, 151 Queen's Rd, Central.** Huge selection of Chinese teas and teapots.

12

Sports and recreation

The only drawback to Hong Kong's varied range of **sporting and recreation opportunities** is the inevitable lack of space for such things. One particularly good sports centre is the **South China Athletic Association** (Caroline Hill, Causeway Bay ⓣ2577 4437, ⓦwww.scaa.org.hk), which offers one-month visitors' passes for $50 and has facilities for all kinds of sports and keep-fit activities including several swimming pools. The centre is next to the Hong Kong Stadium football ground, a fifteen-minute walk from exit F of Causeway Bay MTR Station.

Spectator sports are more limited, though there are events throughout the year; you'll find details below. The SAR's main sporting venue is the **Queen Elizabeth Stadium** (see below). The HKTB's website (ⓦwww.discoverhongkong.com) gives details of forthcoming events here or at any of the other major municipal stadiums and sports grounds; and major events are listed in the weekly freebies *HK Magazine*, *BC Magazine* and *Where Hong Kong*, all distributed via bars, restaurants and cafés.

Badminton

You can rent badminton courts for around $60 an hour at any Leisure and Cultural Services Department indoor games hall (ⓣ2414 5555, ⓦwww.lcsd.gov.hk for more information); or you can play at the Queen Elizabeth Stadium, 18 Oi Kwan Rd, Wan Chai (ⓣ2591 1331). You'll need to book in advance and show your passport. More general information is available from the Hong Kong Badminton Association (ⓣ2504 8318). The following are the most central of the indoor games halls.

Fa Yuen Street Complex Indoor Games Hall 13th Floor, 123a Fa Yuen St, Mongkok ⓣ2395 1501.
Harbour Road Indoor Games Hall 27 Harbour Rd, Wan Chai, just in front of the Star Ferry Pier ⓣ2542 2852.
Hong Kong Park Indoor Games Hall 29 Cotton Tree Drive, Central ⓣ2521 5072.
Kowloon Park Indoor Games Hall 22 Austin Rd, Jordan ⓣ2724 3494.

Diving

There's some reasonable diving in Hong Kong's waters, with the coast around Sai Kung and some isolated pinnacles along the Chinese border being the most popular places – you might see anything from seahorses to sharks. A couple of certified companies run courses and dives: an afternoon of diving including all equipment, boat trip and food should come to around $800. Asiatic Marine (ⓦwww.asiaticmarine.com) are particularly good; or try Marine Divers

(Ⓣ2656 9399, wwww.marinedivers.com) or the Ocean Sky Diving Training Centre (Ⓣ2366 3738, Ⓦwww. oceanskydiver.com).

Golf

Golf is a pricey sport in Hong Kong, and you'll have to be keen to play at any of the SAR's clubs. Most, if they are open to nonmembers at all, take them only during the week. You also have to be careful what you wear: tracksuits, T-shirts, collarless shirts, shorts more than four inches above the knee, jeans, vests and bathing gear are all specifically banned from the greens. Less serious golf is catered for by the mini-golf course at Shek O, right by the beach, and a similar set-up, with a driving range, at Sha Tin's New Town Plaza.

Clearwater Bay Golf and Country Club Sai Kung Peninsula Ⓣ2719 1595, Ⓦwww.cwbgolf.org. Green fees on the Executive Nine course are around $400, golf cart and clubs extra; playing the 18-hole championship course starts at $1700.

Discovery Bay Lantau Ⓣ2987 7273. Among the newest of Hong Kong's golf clubs, with a course spectacularly laid out on top of the island's hills. Fees here are around $900 from Monday to Friday, and $1700 at weekends, plus extras.

Hong Kong Golf Club (HKGC) Fanling, New Territories Ⓣ2670 1211, Ⓦwww.hkgolfclub.org. The SAR's major club, and home of the Hong Kong Open, boasts three 18-hole courses at which visitors can play on weekdays for around $1400 per person, plus caddies and clubs. The HKGC also operates a course at Deep Water Bay on Hong Kong Island (Ⓣ2812 7070); visitors pay around $450 plus extras, again on weekdays only (8.30am–3pm). You should book well in advance for all these courses.

Kau Sai Chau Public Golf Course Kau Sai Chau Island, Sai Kung Peninsula Ⓣ2791 3380. Hong Kong's only public golf course (run by the Jockey Club) is a little bit out of the way. You'll have to take a ferry from Sai Kung pier in the New Territories (every 20min; $45 return). Depending on when you play, you'll pay between $300 and $900.

Hiking

One of the most pleasant and unexpected discoveries to be made in Hong Kong is the countryside. Despite the density of its urban areas, nearly three-quarters of the SAR's land is still undeveloped, and – even more surprising – forty percent of the SAR is officially classified as country park. There are 23 different parks in the New Territories and on Lantau and Hong Kong Island, and it's worth making the effort to get out into at least one for the totally different perspective it will give you.

The countryside varies from subtropical vegetation to pine forests and barren hillsides. There are also wonderful views, interesting flora and fauna, and some rare peace and quiet. All the parks are easily accessible by public transport and are well supplied with trails varying in difficulty from afternoon strolls to challenging hikes.

Don't be deceived, however, into thinking that because of their closeness to the city the country parks are easy or tame countryside. They are not. Every year a couple of walkers simply disappear or are found dead, having fallen down slopes or met with accidents. Much of the terrain is mountainous and unshaded and can be dangerous in the tropical sun and humidity if not treated with respect. Wear good shoes and sun protection, take water and – if possible – a mobile phone.

All the SAR's **long-distance hikes** are covered in the text. The four main routes are the Lantau Trail (p.165), the one-hundred-kilometre MacLehose Trail

Betting on the horses

Minimum bet at the racecourses is $10 and you can only bet in multiples of this sum. Aside from simply betting on a win or place, try betting a quinella (predicting first and second horse, in any order); a tierce (first, second and third horse in correct order); double or triple trio (first three horses, in any order, in two or three designated races); or a treble (winners of three designated races). Betting tax is 11.5 percent, rising to 17.5 percent on a more complicated bet.

(p.150), the cross-harbour Wilson Trail (p.92), and the Hong Kong Island Trail (p.51). You can buy various **trail maps** for all these routes from the Government Bookshop (see p.247), or check the **Country and Marine Parks Authority** website Ⓦhttp://parks.afcd.gov.hk.

Horses: racing and riding

The only sport in Hong Kong to command true mass appeal, horseracing is a spectating must if you're here during the season, which runs from September to mid-June. There are two courses, both run by the Hong Kong Jockey Club (Ⓣ2966 8397, Ⓦwww.hkjc.com): the original one at Happy Valley (meetings every Wednesday evening during the season) and a much newer, state-of-the-art affair at Sha Tin in the New Territories, which stages races most weekends during the season. The HKTB can organize tours and tickets for the enclosures; for more on this, or just turning up and spectating, see p.259.

If you want to do some **horse-riding** yourself, there are a few stables throughout the SAR, mostly owned by the Jockey Club, but they're expensive, and the best of them are for members only. The public can, however, get in the saddle at **Tuen Mun Public Riding School**, Lot 45, Lung Mun Road, Tuen Mun Ⓣ2461 3338 (lessons from $360 per hour).

Martial arts

If China has an indigenous "sport", it's the martial arts – not surprising, perhaps, in a country whose history is littered with long periods of civil conflict. Isolated communities often had to defend themselves against bands of marauders, and so developed their own systems of fighting, which were traditionally taught only to community members – meaning that today there are hundreds of Chinese martial arts styles. Most trace their origins back to the Shaolin Temple in China's Henan province, where it is said that Boddhidharma, the sixth-century originator of Zen Buddhism, taught the monks exercises based on animal movements to balance their long periods of inactivity while meditating. These exercises were then developed into fighting routines for defending the temple, and gradually disseminated into the rest of China.

▲ Bruce Lee in *Fist of Fury*

Today, Chinese martial arts tend to be grouped into two types: "**external**" or hard styles, such as Shaolin kung fu, which concentrate on developing physical power; and "**internal**" or soft styles, such as *tai chi*, which concentrate on developing *qi* (chi), an internal force. Only experts can easily tell internal and external styles apart by just watching, despite the techniques being substantially at odds; both produce effective fighting systems, however, though internal arts tend to improve as you age (hence *tai chi*'s popularity with the elderly), whereas the external styles are more effective for younger practitioners.

Get up early enough – around 7am – and you'll see many styles being practiced in the nearest park, especially Kowloon Park in Tsim Sha Tsui (where experts also put on displays every Sun at 2.30pm), and Victoria Park on Hong Kong Island. The large groups moving slowly through their routines are doing **tai chi**; if you see people walking in endless tight circles they're practising **pa kwa**, another internal martial art. Specific southern Chinese styles include **wing chun**, which concentrates on very accurate handwork and became famous as being the first martial art Bruce Lee studied; **choy li fut**; and **hung gar**, associated with the nineteenth-century master Wong Fei Hung.

The HKTB runs free *tai chi* lessons in English, every Tuesday and Wednesday at 8–9am, just outside the Hong Kong Cultural Centre in Tsim Sha Tsui, but if you're serious about studying a Chinese martial art, try contacting one of the following (all speak English):

Hong Kong Chinese Martial Arts Association **687 Nathan Rd, Jordan ⓣ2394 4803.** General advice and contacts.

C.S. Tang ⓣ9426 9253, ⓔcstang@i-cable.com. Traditional styles of tai chi and pa kwa taught by a long-time student of the late pa kwa master Ho Ho Choi.

Mr Kong ⓣ9450 5882. Specializes in his own free-form "propeller hands" style – easy to learn (you can pick up the principles in a few minutes), fun to do, great for health and agility, and an excellent fighting method.

Donald Mak ⓣ9132 8162. Good wing chun instructor.

William Wan ⓣ9885 8336, ⓦwww.kungfuwan.com. Choy li fut and Shaolin styles.

Mountain biking

There are ten official mountain bike trails in the SAR: four trails on Lantau Island, three on the Sai Kung Peninsula, and others at Tai Lam Country Park, Shek O Country Park and Clear Water Bay Country Park (the latter closed on Sundays and public holidays). To ride on these, you'll need a permit from the Agriculture, Fisheries and Conservation Department, 5th Floor, Cheung Sha Wan Government Offices, 303 Cheung Sha Wan Rd, Kowloon (t2317 0482, ⓦwww.afcd.gov.hk). For online maps and more information about the trails, check the Hong Kong Mountain Biking Association's website at wwww.hkmba.org.

Rock climbing

Away from central Hong Kong's office towers, the SAR's countryside offers some excellent rock climbing. Lion Rock (see p.127) near Sha Tin is probably the most popular site, but there are plenty of other recognized routes on rockfaces and crags everywhere from Clearwater Bay and the Saikung Peninsula to outlying parts of Kowloon and Hong Kong Island, as well as on Lamma and Lantau islands.

The best source of **information** is ⓦwww.hongkongclimbing.com, which grades and provides practical details for a score of climbs around Hong Kong;

they also give links to local clubs and associations, as well as details of various **climbing walls** if you want some practice first.

Rugby

Rugby (Union, not League) is generally of a good standard and each Easter three days are devoted to a series of Rugby Sevens matches with international teams – the boisterous crowd is as entertaining as the matches themselves. The event is organized by the Hong Kong Rugby Football Union (Room 2001, Sports House, 1 Stadium Path, So Kon Po, Causeway Bay ⓣ2504 8311, ⓦwww.hkrugby.com), which can provide more information and tell you how to go about joining a team in Hong Kong. Tickets for the three-day event cost around HK$750.

Running

You'll see people jogging at dozens of places throughout the SAR, some of which have marked routes and exercise stops along the way. A few of the most popular spots are along Bowen Road in Mid-Levels; around the roads at the top of Victoria Peak; along the Tsim Sha Tsui East waterfront; around Victoria Park; and in Kowloon Park, off Nathan Road. If you do run or jog, remember that the summer heat and humidity are crippling; run in the early morning or evening and take some water along.

An increasingly wide variety of **races** now take place for walkers and runners – traditional marathons, endurance events and adventure racing. Notable events include the **Hong Kong Marathon** (ⓦwww.hkmarathon.com), held in February, the **MacLehose Trailwalker** in November and the **Action Asia Challenge** in December. You can get information, and entry forms for the Hong Kong Marathon, from the Hong Kong Amateur Athletic Association (ⓣ2504 8215, ⓦwww.hkaaa.com); the HKTB can help with the others. All such events start early, because of the climate.

More offbeat running is provided by the **Orienteering Association of Hong Kong** (Room 1014, Sports House, 1 Stadium Path, So Kon Po, Causeway Bay ⓣ2504 8111, ⓦwww.oahk.org.hk), which maintains an orienteering course in Pokfulam Country Park on Hong Kong Island. Plans are in the pipeline for six more courses in country parks around the SAR, including two on Lantau Island, and one on Monkey Mountain, in Kam Shan Country Park.

Skating

There are a number of ice rinks in Hong Kong; try Cityplaza Ice Palace, Cityplaza, Tai Koo Shing (Tai Koo MTR; Mon–Fri 10am–10pm, Sat & Sun 8.30am–10pm; $40 per day during the week, $50 at the weekend, including skates; ⓣ2885 4697), or The Glacier, Festival Walk, Kowloon Tong (daily 10.30am–10pm; $50–60 per session; ⓣ2265 8888). For skateboarding and rollerblading, check out the Hong Kong Skate Board Community's website (ⓦwww.hkskateboarding.com) for the nearest skate-friendly park – the one locals rate best is the skateboard arena at 1 Lai Wan Rd, Mei Foo, Kowloon, which hosts international competitions.

Soccer

Soccer is played widely throughout the SAR. Hong Kong's First Division is littered with has-been or never-were players from other countries (mostly Britain) – teams are allowed five overseas players. Good local talent is fairly thin on the ground, but games can be entertaining, not least because the foreign players brought in tend to be strikers and consequently face local defences comprising people much shorter than themselves.

If you're sufficiently interested, teams to watch are Happy Valley, South China and Eastern. The "national team", such as it is, usually has a torrid time in the World Cup qualifying matches, making heavy weather against such footballing giants as Bahrain and Lebanon. The best advice for soccer fans is to find a TV on Saturday evenings during the English soccer season, when you get an hour's worth of the previous week's top English matches; most major cup and international matches are televised live, too.

Squash

Squash is about the most popular indoor racket sport in Hong Kong. Book well in advance, and expect to pay around $60 an hour at the public courts listed below. Courts are generally open daily 7am–11pm.

Fa Yuen Street Complex Indoor Games Hall 13th Floor, 123a Fa Yuen St, Mongkok ⓣ2395 1501.
Harbour Road Indoor Games Hall 27 Harbour Rd, Wan Chai, just in front of the Star Ferry Pier ⓣ2542 2852.
Hong Kong Squash Centre 23 Cotton Tree Drive, Central ⓣ2869 0611, ⓦwww.hksquash.org.hk.
Kowloon Park Indoor Games Hall 22 Austin Rd, Jordan ⓣ2724 3494.
Lockhart Road Indoor Games Hall 10th Floor, Lockhart Road Complex, 225 Hennessy Rd, Wan Chai ⓣ2879 5521.
Queen Elizabeth Stadium 18 Oi Kwan Rd, Wan Chai ⓣ2591 1346.
Victoria Park Hing Fat St, Causeway Bay ⓣ2570 6186.

Swimming

If you don't want to risk the water at any of the SAR's beaches – the best of which are covered in the text – then you'll have to take your dip in one of the eighteen crowded swimming pools operated by the Leisure and Cultural Services Department (ⓦwww.lcsd.gov.hk/beach/en/swim-intro.php for details). These pools charge $19 for adults, $9 for children; they open daily (though some are closed Monday afternoons) approximately 6.30am–noon, 1–5pm & 6–10pm from April to December. Alternatively, some of the bigger hotels will let you use their modest-sized pools for a large fee. Try the *Kowloon Shangri-La* ($250; see p.190), the *Sheraton* ($250; see p.187), the *Conrad* ($200; see p.184), and *JW Marriott* ($340; see p.185). Three useful Leisure and Cultural Services Department pools are:

Kowloon Park Nathan Rd, Tsim Sha Tsui ⓣ2724 3577.
Morrison Hill 7 Oi Kwan Rd, Wan Chai ⓣ2575 3028.
Victoria Park Hing Fat St, Causeway Bay ⓣ2570 4682.

Tennis

Public tennis courts are often solidly booked, but if you can get a court you'll pay around $40 an hour during the day and up to $60 in the evening (after 7pm). The Queen Elizabeth Stadium (see opposite) also has facilities for table tennis, which costs about $20 per hour.

Hong Kong Tennis Centre Wong Nai Chung Gap Rd, Happy Valley ⓣ2574 9122, ⓦwww.tennishk.org. Daily 7am–11pm.

King's Park Tennis Courts 15 King's Park Rise, King's Park, Yau Ma Tei ⓣ2385 8985 or ⓣ2388 8154. Daily 7am–10pm.

Victoria Park Hing Fat St, Causeway Bay ⓣ2570 6186. Daily 7am–10pm.

Watersports

As you might expect, there's plenty of choice for watersports in a region of 230 islands. Sailing enthusiasts who are members of an overseas club can contact the prestigious Hong Kong Yacht Club on Kellet Island, Causeway Bay (ⓣ2832 2817, ⓦwww.rhkyc.org.hk), which has reciprocal arrangements with many foreign clubs. The Hong Kong Yachting Association (ⓣ2504 8159, ⓦwww.sailing.org.hk) operates intensive instruction courses at Clearwater Bay. For plain boating and pleasure cruising, contact any of the tour companies listed under "Organized Tours", p.41, or ask the HKTB for recommendations.

You can rent **windsurfing** equipment at quite a few of Hong Kong's beaches: both the government-funded centre at Tei Mei Tuk near Tai Po (ⓣ2665 2591) and Sai Kung's Chong Hing Windsurf Centre (ⓣ2792 6810) offer classes where you can learn the basics fairly cheaply; or try the Windsurf Centre (ⓣ2981 8316; daily 10am–7pm) on Kwun Yam Wan beach on Cheung Chau (p.162), which also offers courses and rental. The Windsurfing Association of Hong Kong (1 Stadium Path, So Kon Po, Causeway Bay ⓣ2504 8255, ⓦwww.windsurfing.org.hk) can help with other enquiries.

Some beachside operations also offer **water-skiing** and **canoeing** (particularly at the Cheung Chau Windsurf Centre); you can get more information from the Hong Kong Water-Skiing Association (ⓣ2504 8168, ⓦwww.waterski.org.hk).

13

Children's Hong Kong

Although Hong Kong doesn't have an enormous amount in the way of specialized children's activities and events, the territory itself can be a playground – the transport, particularly the trams and ferries, is exciting; most of the views and walks more so; and there are several venues with a real family slant, such as Ocean Park and Disneyland. The sections below should give you some ideas for day-to-day activities, and there's also a round-up of dangers to be aware of if you're travelling with small children.

Outings

You can base a day-trip around the places and activities below, all of which can occupy several hours with kids in tow. Some also offer a way to get out of the crowds – lunchtimes in Central and Causeway Bay can be frightening for small children.

Botanical Gardens Central (p.61). A pleasant green area, housing tropical birds and some small mammals. The best-known inhabitant is a jaguar, but don't miss the lemurs, gibbons and orang-utans.

Disneyland Lantau Island (p.169). No Chinese content here, but a host of cartoon favourites and a safari-park-style boat ride populating a middle-America amusement park.

Festival Walk Kowloon Tong MTR, Exit C (p.117). Massive shopping mall with an ice rink, a Rainforest Café, and endless shops.

Hong Kong Park Central (p.62). Across the road from the Botanical Gardens. Enormous walk-

Babysitting

Most large hotels can organize babysitting for you; the HKTB (see p.000) has a full list of those that will oblige, if you want to check before you leave.

Playgroups and information

Playgroups and parent-toddler groups are run by a variety of organizations, although most are aimed at residents rather than short-term visitors. Information is available from – amongst others – the Preschool Playgroups Association (ⓦwww.hkppa.info); St John's Cathedral, Garden Road, Central (ⓦwww.stjohnscathedral.org.hk/playgroup.htm); or the bilingual *Parent's Journal* magazine, available from children's clothes stores and toddler shops.

Clothes and supplies

Hong Kong has several branches of the specialist store Mothercare, of which the most central are Shop 338–340, Prince's Building, Chater Rd, Central; Shop P, 2nd Floor, The In Square, Windsor House, 311 Gloucester Rd, Causeway Bay; and Shop 137, Ocean Terminal, Harbour City, Canton Rd, Tsim Sha Tsui. There are also children's clothes and toy shops in most of the large shopping malls.

in aviary, greenhouses, gardens, picnic areas, restaurant and the best playground in Hong Kong. Also close to the pedestrian walkways that snake off into the hi-tech buildings of Central.

Kadoorie Farm near Kam Tin, New Territories (p.141). Farm with experimental breeding programme, lots of animals, abandoned and injured wildlife, walks, views and plants.

KCR train to Sheung Shui and back New Territories (p.124). A train ride, with stops at traditional markets, brand-new towns and shopping centres, and a railway museum. Start from Festival Walk at Kowloon Tong.

Ocean Park Deep Water Bay, Hong Kong Island (p.88). Multi-ride amusement and theme park, with moving dinosaurs, marine animals, shows, gardens and Hong Kong's giant pandas An-An and Jia-Jia in their purpose-built home. Next door, Middle Kingdom re-creates life in ancient China, with acrobats, lion dancing and the chance to try skills such as calligraphy.

Outlying islands (chapter 4). Ferry rides to all the main islands, where there are beaches, walks, temples, watersports and – on Cheung Chau particularly – cycling trails.

Sea cruises (see "Organized tours", p.41). Cruises lasting anything from an hour to a whole day through the harbour and around the outlying islands; many include lunch. The Dolphinwatch trip to see the endangered pink dolphins is particularly good.

Stanley Village Hong Kong Island (p.90). Beaches, watersports, a covered market, some child-friendly restaurants and a good bus ride there and back.

Victoria Peak (p.71). A trip up on the Peak Tram; easy flat walks around The Peak with great views; the shops of The Peak Galleria; Ripley's "Believe It Or Not!" Odditorium; a space-ride simulator; Madame Tussaud's; panoramic views and picnic areas.

Whampoa Garden Hung Hom (p.110). Huge concrete ship-shaped shopping mall, with musical fountain, coffee shop, ice-skating rink, cinema and children's play area.

Museums and temples

The following places will interest an inquisitive child. The museums are ones where participation is encouraged – operating robots, clambering on old train carriages, exploring a renovated village – and while nearly all the temples in Hong Kong are unusual enough for most visitors, the ones listed below are particularly large and colourful.

Ching Chung Koon Temple Tuen Mun, New Territories (see p.144).

Heritage Museum 1 Man Lam Rd, Sha Tin (see p.128).

Po Lin Monastery Lantau Island (see pp.166–167).

Railway Museum Tai Po Market, New Territories (see p.131).

Sam Tung Uk Folk Museum Tsuen Wa, New Territories (see p.138).

Science Museum Science Museum Rd, Tsim Sha Tsui East (see p.109).

Space Museum Salisbury Rd, Tsim Sha Tsui (see p.106).

Wong Tai Sin Temple Kowloon (see p.117).

Entertainment

Obvious ideas include cinemas, which show the latest films in English; the HKTB-organized cultural shows, with song, dance and mime in various venues; and a (brief) visit to a Chinese opera for the singing and costumes. Some places, like the Arts Centre and local libraries, organize special events for children throughout the school summer holiday: the HKTB will have current information, or call into City Hall and look at the noticeboards.

Coinciding with one of Hong Kong's **festivals** is another way to expose kids to a bit of cultural entertainment. If they're happy with crowds and loud noise they'll particularly enjoy the Cheung Chau Bun Festival (see p.239). Dragon boat

Hazards

• Hong Kong can be extremely hot and humid. Small children should wear a hat and suncream when outside, and drink plenty of liquids.
• Pollution is a growing problem. Air contamination in urban areas – especially Causeway Bay – makes them worth avoiding at peak times, particularly if your child is asthmatic. The seawater in many popular swimming spots may not be healthy for small children with no immunity to local bugs. Don't even think of touching the water in Victoria Harbour.
• Restaurant hygiene may also be an issue, particularly for children who are not used to Chinese food. Use your common sense when choosing where to eat.
• Keep a close eye on children when riding public transport. Tram rides on Hong Kong Island, the Peak Tram and the MTR are all exciting, but they're nearly always packed. Keep kids away from tram windows, and from the edges of the cross-harbour ferries. It's easy to get separated in crowds, although it's very unlikely that anyone will try to abduct them.
• Don't encourage or allow children to play with animals found on the street. Rabies and bird flu are recurrent problems here, and if your child gets bitten or scratched by a stray kitten or bird, you're in for lengthy hospital visits.

racing (see p.239) and any of the colourful Tin Hau celebrations (see p.143) are also popular. Suitable **arts events** include the **Arts Festival** in February and March, and the **International Arts Carnival** in July and August, aimed at families and children with puppets, clowns and acrobats.

Shopping

Shopping can keep children amused, too, especially when it's raining, since if you pick one of the huge shopping malls you don't have to set foot outside for hours on end, even to eat. There's a list of the main malls on p.255; while specific shops that you might want to take in include the enormous Toys 'R' Us (Shop 003, Ground Floor, Ocean Terminal, Canton Rd, Tsim Sha Tsui; 3rd Floor, Windsor House, 311 Gloucester Rd, Causeway Bay; and Shop A197–199, Level I, New Town Plaza, Sha Tin, New Territories); and Wise Kids (Shop 134, Pacific Place, 88 Queensway, Admiralty; Shop 105, The Galleria, 9 Queen's Rd Central; and Shop 905-6, Times Square, Causeway Bay). Mitsukoshi and Sogo, the Japanese department stores in Causeway Bay (see p.84), are good, with games, toys, comics and cafés, as is the entire Festival Walk complex in Kowloon Tong (see p.117). Head to Tai Yuen Street, just off Johnston Road, opposite Southorn Playground in Wan Chai, for Hong Kong's budget toy street, selling all manner of plastic goodies and old-fashioned Hong Kong toys.

Eating

It's good to know that restaurants in Hong Kong (certainly Chinese restaurants) generally welcome children with open arms, and many have high chairs available. Eating is a family affair, as a trip to any *dim sum* restaurant shows, but if your children are unadventurous about their food, there are no problems getting fish and chips, pizzas, hamburgers and the usual more familiar meals. Chapter 7 details all the eating possibilities, but we've listed here a few of the more child-friendly restaurants, some of which provide crayons for scribbling and special children's menus: Rainforest Café (Festival Walk, Kowloon Tong), Häagen-Dazs (see p.196) and Spaghetti House (10 Stanley St, Central; 68 Hennessy Rd, Wan Chai; 1st Floor, World Trade Centre, Causeway Bay; and 1st Floor, Imperial Hotel, Nathan Road, Tsim Sha Tsui, among others). For more of an occasion, visit one of the specialist fish restaurants in Lau Fau Shan or Lei Yue Mun or on one of the outlying islands, where youngsters can pick dinner out of the fish tanks.

14

Directory

Airlines All the airlines in Hong Kong are listed in the Yellow Pages under "Air Line Companies". The main ones include:
Aeroflot ⓣ2537 2611
Air Canada ⓣ2867 8111
Air India ⓣ2522 1176
Air New Zealand ⓣ2862 8988
British Airways ⓣ2822 9000
Cathay Pacific ⓣ2747 1888
China Eastern & China Southern ⓣ2861 0322
Dragonair ⓣ3193 3888
JAL ⓣ2523 0081
KLM ⓣ2808 2111
Malaysia Airlines ⓣ2521 8181
Qantas ⓣ2822 9000
Singapore Airlines ⓣ2520 2233
Thai International ⓣ2876 6888
United Airlines ⓣ2810 4888.

Airport enquiries Hong Kong International (Chek Lap Kok) Airport ⓣ2181 0000, ⓦwww.hongkongairport.com.

Ambulance Call ⓣ999, or the St John's Ambulance Brigade, which runs a free ambulance service, on ⓣ2576 6555 (Hong Kong Island), ⓣ2713 5555 (Kowloon) or ⓣ2639 2555 (New Territories).

Banks and exchange There are banks of every nationality and description throughout Hong Kong, seemingly on every street corner. Opening hours are Mon–Fri 9am–4.30pm, Sat 9am–12.30pm, with small fluctuations – half an hour each side – from branch to branch. Almost all charge commission for exchanging travellers' cheques, which is usually around $50 per transaction, though this can vary widely from bank to bank: always check the rate before committing yourself. Currently, the banks offering the best deals are Wing Lung Bank (branches throughout the SAR), which charges $30 for exchanging either cash or travellers' cheques, and the Citic Ka Wah Bank (branches throughout the SAR), which will exchange American Express travellers' cheques commission-free (up to US$100 per day). There's no commission either if you change American Express or Thomas Cook cheques at their respective offices. You can also change money and cheques at a licensed moneychanger – there are many in Tsim Sha Tsui and Causeway Bay – which stay open late and on Sunday. They generally don't charge commission, but their exchange rates are up to 5-percent lower than the banks', which means that in effect you're paying about HK$50 commission on US$100. If you're changing large amounts, you're better off using a bank. Big hotels also offer exchange services, but again the rates are lower.

Bike rental Not an option in central Hong Kong, though possible on the islands and in the New Territories. There are numerous bike rental shops near the Mui Wo ferry pier on Lantau Island; around the KCR station in Tai Wai; on Sha Tin Rural Committee Road; on the ground floor of Lucky Plaza in Sha Tin; around Tei Mei Tuk reservoir; and on Kwong Fuk Road in Tai Po itself. One day's hire costs between $40 and $60.

British Council 3 Supreme Court Rd, Admiralty ⓣ2913 5100, whttp://britishcouncil.org.hk. There's a small Internet café on the first floor, and a lending library on the third floor (Mon–Fri noon–8.00pm, Sat 10.30am–5.30pm), which costs $700 a year (or $400 for 6 months) to join. Members can borrow books and videos. There's also a reference section, open to anyone, with British newspapers and magazines. For French and

German equivalents, see "Cultural groups" below.

Car parks The biggest firm is Wilson, which has car parks at Kowloon (Hung Hom) Station, City Hall (Central), 310 Gloucester Rd and 475 Lockhart Rd, among other places; other central car parks are at Exchange Square and Central Plaza. Charges are roughly $20 an hour.

Car rental You'll pay from around $580 a day, $2500 a week, for the smallest available car. You need to be over 18 (21 or 25 with some firms), have been driving for at least a year and have a valid overseas driving licence (with which you can drive in Hong Kong for a year) or an international driving licence. Remember that you drive on the left. Agencies include: Avis, Ground Floor, 67 Mody Rd, Tsim Sha Tsui East ⓣ2890 6988, ⓦwww.avis.com.hk; or Hertz, 12th Floor, 9 Queens Rd, Central-toll-free ⓣ8009 62321, ⓦwww.hertz.com. Hiring a car and driver by the day or hour may be cheaper. Try Fung Hing Hire ⓣ2572 0333, ⓦwww.funghingcar.com.hk.

Clothing repairs and alterations The many small shops in World-Wide House, Des Voeux Rd in Central are cheap and reasonably quick.

Consulates and embassies Australia, 23rd Floor, Harbour Centre, 25 Harbour Rd, Wan Chai ⓣ2827 8881
Canada, 14th Floor, 1 Exchange Square, Central ⓣ2810 4321
China, 42 Kennedy Rd, Central ⓣ2106 6303
India, 16th Floor, United Centre, 95 Queensway, Admiralty ⓣ2528 4028
Ireland, 6th Floor, Chung Nam Building, 1 Lockhart Rd, Wan Chai ⓣ2527 4897
Japan, 46th Floor, One Exchange Square, Central ⓣ2522 1184
Korea, 5th Floor, Far East Finance Centre, 16 Harcourt Rd, Central ⓣ2529 4141
Malaysia, 23rd Floor, Malaysia Building, 50 Gloucester Rd, Wan Chai ⓣ2821 0800
New Zealand, 6501 Central Plaza, 18 Harbour Rd, Wan Chai ⓣ2877 4488
Philippines, 14th Floor, United Centre, 95 Queensway, Admiralty ⓣ2823 8500
Singapore, 901–2 Tower 1, Admiralty Centre, Admiralty ⓣ2527 2212
South Africa, 2706 Great Eagle Centre, 23 Harbour Rd, Wan Chai ⓣ2577 3279
Taiwan, 4th Floor, East Tower, Lippo Centre, 89 Queensway, Admiralty ⓣ2528 8316
Thailand, 8th Floor, Fairmont House, 8 Cotton Tree Drive, Central ⓣ2521 6481
UK, 1 Supreme Court Rd, Admiralty ⓣ2901 3000
US, 26 Garden Rd, Central ⓣ2523 9011
Vietnam, 15th Floor, Great Smart Tower, 230 Wan Chai Rd, Wan Chai ⓣ2591 4517

Contraception Condoms are available in supermarkets, and you can buy the Pill without prescription from chemists. For anything else, contact a family planning clinic: the HQ is at Southorn Centre, 130 Hennessy Rd, Wan Chai ⓣ2575 4477.

Counselling and advice Community Advice Bureau, 16C Right Emperor Building, 122–126 Wellington Rd, Central ⓣ2815 5444, ⓦwww.cab.org.hk (Mon–Fri 9.30am–4.30pm), deals with day-to-day problems and advice for newcomers and tourists. The AIDS Concern counselling service is on ⓣ2898 4422 (Thurs & Sat 7–10pm); Alcoholics Anonymous on ⓣ2522 5665 (daily 6–7pm). The Samaritans have an English-speaking 24hr service on ⓣ2896 0000, ⓦwww.samaritans.org.hk.

Country parks The Country and Marine Parks Authority, Agriculture and Fisheries Dept, 12th Floor, 393 Canton Rd, Kowloon ⓣ2733 2235 (Mon–Fri 9am–5pm, Sat 9am–noon) has information and trail maps for all Hong Kong's country parks. Maps are also on sale from the Government Bookshop (see p.247).

Cultural groups Alliance Française, 2nd Floor, 123 Hennessy Rd, Wan Chai ⓣ2527 7825 (Mon–Fri 10am–1pm & 2–6pm; bus #11 passes by) has a French-language library and films; there's a second branch at 52 Jordan Rd, Kowloon ⓣ2730 3257. The Goethe Institute, 14th Floor, Hong Kong Arts Centre, 2 Harbour Rd, Wan Chai ⓣ2802 0088 (Mon–Fri 9.30am–7.45pm) has a general-purpose German-language library (as well as some English-language books), and also newspapers and a video library.

Dentists Dentists are listed in the Yellow Pages under "Dental Practitioners"; or ring the Hong Kong Dental Association (ⓣ2528 5327) for a list of qualified dentists. Treatment is expensive.

Departure tax Airport departure tax is $50 for anyone over 12; this is usually included in the ticket price.

Doctors Look in the Yellow Pages under "Physicians and Surgeons", or contact the reception desk in the larger hotels. Make sure you ask for a doctor who speaks good English. You'll have to pay for a consultation and any medicines they prescribe. Consultations can cost anything between $100 and $800, but average $400 (a visitor is charged $455 for a consultation at a government hospital Out Patients' department); if the medicine is not prescription-only, it's often cheaper to write down the name and pick it up from an ordinary chemist, rather than buy it from the surgery. Ask for receipts for your insurance. It's cheaper to visit the nearest local government clinic (often with the words "Jockey Club" in the title, since that's who partly funds them): they stay open late, and you'll only pay a few dollars if you need a basic prescription or treatment at the casualty desk – though you may have to queue. All the clinics are listed in the Hong Kong phone books (at the beginning, in the Government directory).

Dress Dress as you would in any city where it's normally hot and humid, though bear in mind that a lot of the smarter hotels and restaurants insist on some kind of dress code, usually "smart casual". So no shorts, sandals or flip-flops if you're going for tea at the *Peninsula* and a jacket and tie if you're eating in an expense-account restaurant. For formal dinners, you'll need the penguin suit and tie rental services of Tuxe Top Co. Ltd, 1st Floor, 18 Hennessy Rd, Wan Chai ⓣ2529 2179 and 3rd Floor, Wing Lok House, 16 Peking Rd (entrance in Lock Road), Tsim Sha Tsui ⓣ2366 6311 (both branches open daily 10am–7pm).

Dry cleaning Most laundries (see opposite) offer this service, though it can take a day or two.

Electricity Current is 200 volts AC. Plugs are a mixture of round two- or three-pins, but the most common is the large three square-pinned socket used in the UK. Either way, a travel plug is useful, or you can buy adaptors at the night market, shops on the ground floor of Chungking Mansions, or many other similar places for about $5.

Embassies see "Consulates" (p.269).

Emergencies Call ⓣ999 for fire, police or ambulance; also see "Ambulance", (p.268) "Counselling and advice" and "Doctors" (p.269) and "Hospitals" (above).

Gay life For up-to-date information on gay venues, pick up the Gaystation brochure, which you can find in the gay venues themselves, Page One bookshop (see p.247) and some of the clubs, or log onto ⓦwww.gaystation.com.hk. See the box on p.223 for a list of popular night-time venues; you'll also find a great listings page at ⓦwww.dragoncastle.net/hongkong.shtml. There's a helpline service, Horizons, on ⓣ2815 9268.

Government Bookshop 4th Floor, Murray Building, Garden Rd, Central (Mon–Fri 9am–5pm, Sat 9am–noon ⓣ2537 1910). For maps of the islands, New Territories and other useful publications.

Hospitals Government hospitals are the cheapest; they're listed in the Hong Kong phone book. Hong Kong ID cardholders pay $68 per day if admitted to a public ward; some private beds are also available in public hospitals at a higher charge. Those who aren't local residents pay around $3100 a day (with $19,000 deposit), though casualty visits are free – the government hospitals below have 24hr casualty departments. Private hospitals are more expensive, but the standard of care is higher.

Government Hospitals: Princess Margaret Hospital, 2–10 Lai King Hill Rd, Lai Chi Kok, Kowloon ⓣ2990 1111; Queen Elizabeth Hospital, 30 Gascoigne Rd, Kowloon ⓣ2958 8428; Queen Mary Hospital, Pokfulam Rd, Hong Kong Island ⓣ2855 3838.

Private Hospitals: Hong Kong Baptist Hospital, 222 Waterloo Rd, Kowloon Tong ⓣ2339 8888; Canossa Hospital, 1 Old Peak Rd, Hong Kong Island ⓣ2522 2181; Matilda Hospital, 41 Mount Kellett Rd, The Peak ⓣ2848 0700.

ID cards Available to long-term residents from the Immigration Department, ImmigrationTower, Gloucester Rd, Wan Chai ⓣ2824 6111.

Internet access Internet access is available at larger hotels and branches of the Pacific Coffee Company and other cybercafés, public libraries and some shopping plazas.

Laundry Most hotels offer (expensive) laundry services; guesthouses are usually cheaper. Otherwise, there are laundries in almost every back street, charging by the weight of your washing and taking a couple of hours.

Left luggage There's an office in the departure lounge at the airport (daily 6.30am–1am), and at Hong Kong Station in Central for the Airport Express. Alternatively, you can usually leave luggage at your guesthouse or hotel – but don't leave anything valuable unless you're confident it's secure.

Libraries The main English-language library is the high-tech twelve-floor Central Library at 66 Causeway Rd, facing Victoria Park in Causeway Bay (ⓣ3150 1234, ⓦwww.hkpl.gov.hk; Mon & Tues, Wed 1–9pm, Thurs–Sun 10am–9pm). The library boasts computers, Internet access on every floor, an exhibition gallery, a toy library, stacks of comfortable sofas, 450,000 million publications for lending, a reference library and over 4000 periodicals and newspapers. Without a Hong Kong ID card and proof of address, you can borrow books by showing your passport and paying a $130 deposit for each book, with a maximum of six books. There are 66 other public libraries around the SAR, which you can use in the same way; the most useful is 3rd Floor, City Hall High Block, Edinburgh Place, Central. There's also the British Council library (see p.268).

Lost property Police ⓣ2860 2000; MTR, Admiralty Station (daily 11am–6pm); KCR, 8th Floor, KCR House, Sha Tin, New Territories ⓣ2606 9392 (Mon–Sat 9am–noon). To recover items left in taxis, call ⓣ2385 8288, although you'll pay a steep fee up front – even then, they don't have a very good record for finding anything. To report a lost Visa card, call ⓣ800 900 782, or for a MasterCard call ⓣ800 966 677.

Massage As well as the inevitable sleazy joints, Hong Kong has some fine legitimate massage parlours, largely centred around Wan Chai and Mongkok. Try the Golden Rock Acupressure and Massage Centre of the Blind, 8th Floor, Gold Swan Commercial Building, 438 Hennessy Rd, Wan Chai (ⓣ2572 1322; daily 10am–11.30pm); or the Health Home Acupressure and Massage Centre for the Blind, Suite 1703, 397 Hennessey Rd, Wan Chai (ⓣ2838 6438; daily 9am–11pm). A one-hour session at either costs around $250.

Newspapers There are four English-language newspapers published in Hong Kong. The *South China Morning Post* gives the party line on the various problems besetting Hong Kong, and carries a daily "what's on" listings section. Its only rival is the *Standard*, which is aimed more at the business community but is occasionally very scathing about government shortcomings. The other two papers are the *Asian Wall Street Journal* and the *International Herald Tribune* – the first business-led, the second culled mostly from American newspapers. Published in China, but widely available in Hong Kong, the *China Daily* makes interesting reading in an Alice-in-Wonderland kind of way – straight-down-the-line Beijing government propaganda. There are also over forty Chinese newspapers published daily in Hong Kong of various political hues. Beijing objects to the hard reporting of several of them, though there are a few pro-China papers as balance. British, European and American newspapers are widely available, too, normally a couple of days late. They're on sale at both Star Ferry concourses; or try inside the *South China Morning Post* Family Bookshop in Central's Star Ferry concourse. Many bookshops, including this one, also stock a wide range of local and foreign magazines. For local listings magazines and free sheets, see p.230.

Pharmacies The largest Western-style pharmacy is Watson's (open daily 9am–7pm or later), which stocks toiletries, contact-lens fluid and first-aid items. A number of products are available over the counter that are prescription-only in many Western countries, notably contraceptive pills and melatonin. Watson's has branches all over Hong Kong (for your nearest, phone ⓣ2606 8833), including Entertainment Building, 30 Queen's Rd, Central; Shop 301–307, 3rd Floor, Prince's Building, 10 Chater Rd, Central; and 241 Nathan Rd, Tsim Sha Tsui. Alternatively, try any of the branches of Manning's around town, which sells more or less the same as Watson's, usually a fraction cheaper.

Photocopying There's a photocopy service in all public libraries (see "Libraries" above), the General Post Office next to the Star Ferry Pier in Central (see p.56), and in many photo developers.

Police For emergencies, dial ⓣ999. The Police Headquarters is at Arsenal Street, Wan Chai ⓣ2860 2000. For lost property and general enquiries, call ⓣ2860 2000 and you'll be given the address and telephone number of the local police station that will deal with your loss. For Crime Hotline and taxi complaints, call ⓣ2527 7177; for complaints against the police, call ⓣ2866 7700.

Time Hong Kong is eight hours ahead of the UK (seven in summer), thirteen hours ahead of New York, sixteen hours ahead of Los Angeles and two hours behind Sydney.

Tipping Large hotels and most restaurants will add a ten-percent service charge to your bill. In restaurants where there's no service charge, they'll expect to pick up the dollar coins change. In taxis, make the fare up to the nearest dollar. Porters at upmarket hotels and at the airport aren't carrying your bags for the love of the job – tip at your discretion.

Toilets You'll find public toilets at all major beaches, sights and country parks – there's usually no paper, though there might be an attendant on hand to sell you a couple of sheets. Public toilets are scarcer in the centre, but that's no problem given the number of restaurants and hotels in Tsim Sha Tsui and Central. The swankier the place, the less likely you'll be challenged; indeed, some of the very top hotels have restrooms incorporated into their high-class ground-floor shopping arcades. The finest (and most intimidating) toilet experiences are those in the arcade of the *Peninsula Hotel* (men should go up to the *Felix* restaurant) or the *Mandarin* on Hong Kong Island. Amid brass and marble elegance, attendants turn on the taps, hand over the soap and retrieve the towels; there's talc, eau de toilette, hairbrushes, and when you've finished you can sit on the chaise longue and make phone calls all afternoon. Needless to say, you're expected to tip.

Transport enquiries See "Transport", p.35, for public transport information.

Travel agencies As well as flights to the rest of Southeast Asia and beyond, most of the places below can help with travel to China, including organizing visas. If you're looking for budget flights or tours, you should also check the classified sections of the *South China Morning Post* and *HK Magazine*. One word of warning, however: when making a booking don't hand any money over, even a deposit, until the ticket is confirmed. Many agents offer great deals, and ask for a holding deposit while they put you on a waiting list. You'll find out later that your agent couldn't get you a seat on the great deal but on a more expensive one instead. If you don't buy, then you lose your deposit.

China Travel Service (CTS): Ground Floor, CTS House, 78–83 Connaught Rd, Central ⓣ2853 3533 or 2315 7188, ⓦwww.chinatravel1.com; China Travel Building, Southorn Centre, Wan Chai ⓣ2832 3888; and 1st Floor, Alpha House, 27–33 Nathan Rd (entrance in Peking Rd), Tsim Sha Tsui ⓣ2315 7124 or 2853 3531. Open Mon–Fri 9am–7pm, Sat 9am–5pm, Sun 9am–12.30pm & 2–5pm. China visas, tours, accommodation and train and plane tickets.

Connaught Travel, 4th Floor, Chung Hing Commercial Building, 62 Connaught Rd, Central ⓣ2544 1531, ⓦwww.connaught-travel.com. Efficient, friendly and good air fare rates.

Hong Kong Student Travel Ltd, Hang Lung Centre, Yee Wo St, Causeway Bay ⓣ2833 9909. Very popular place for flights, package tours, boats and trains to China, visas, ISIC and YIEE cards.

Shoestring Travel, 4th Floor, Alpha House, 27–33 Nathan Rd, Tsim Sha Tsui ⓣ2723 2306 (entrance on Peking Rd). Flights, visas and bus tickets to Guangzhou.

Western Union Dozens of agents in Hong Kong – see ⓦwww.westernunion.com for the nearest. Most operate approximately Mon–Fri 9am–7.30pm, Sat 9am–2pm & Sun 9am–5pm).

Women's Hong Kong Women's issues have yet to make much of an impact in Hong Kong. There are, however, a number of associations for women, including the Hong Kong Federation of Women (ⓣ2833 6133, ⓦwww.hkfw.org). There is also a refuge – Harmony House (24hr hotline on ⓣ2522 0434) – for battered women and their children. It's also worth knowing that there's a long-term residential hotel/club for women in Hong Kong, the Helena May (35 Garden Road, Mid-Levels ⓣ2522 6766), but check well in advance if you want to stay – you'll need to ensure they have room and will take a nonmember.

Macau

Macau

15

Macau, Taipa and Coloane

Lying 60km west from Hong Kong across the Pearl River delta, the former Portuguese enclave of **MACAU** occupies a peninsula and a couple of islands that together cover just twenty-six square kilometres. As in Hong Kong, Macau's atmosphere has been shaped by the blending of European and Chinese culture, especially noticeable here in the antique colonial architecture and Portuguese-influenced **Macanese cooking** existing alongside a predominantly Cantonese-speaking population. Whilst very laid-back compared with Hong Kong, Macau attracts millions of big-spending tourists each year – an increasing number from mainland China – to gamble frenetically at its many **casinos**, the only place in China where they have been legalized. The colossal income generated is currently funding a mini-economic boom, featuring the construction of high-rise hotels, flyovers, bridges, and large-scale **land reclamation**.

The **peninsula** that the city of Macau itself occupies is about 4km by 2km at its widest points and easy to negotiate on foot – though the few hills can make for tiring climbing in the heat of the day. It's here that you'll find most of the casinos, restaurants and sights, including the ruined church of **São Paulo** and the adjacent **Fortaleza do Monte** with its informative museum. Other attractions include a couple of **temples** that equal any of the better-known ones in Hong Kong; an excellent **maritime museum**, which illuminates Macau's long association with fishing and trade; and a series of quiet and beautiful **gardens** and squares reflecting the enclave's laid-back approach to life. Many central streets retain a dated, decaying, slightly seedy charm, in particular **Rua da Felicidade**, with its whitewashed buildings, and the area north of the main **Avenida de Almeida Ribeiro**.

Three undulating, ribbon-like bridges link the peninsula with **Taipa** Island, from where a causeway (currently being massively broadened) runs across to the southernmost **Coloane** Island. Both islands are small, easily reached by **bus**, and feature more good restaurants and the odd church and temple; Coloane also has the enclave's only beaches and a few walking trails.

The only trouble you're likely to have in Macau is one of **language**. English signs dry up quickly once you're out of the downtown area, and on Taipa and Coloane you'll probably only see written Portuguese and Chinese – though you'd be unlucky to be unable to locate an English-speaker if you needed one.

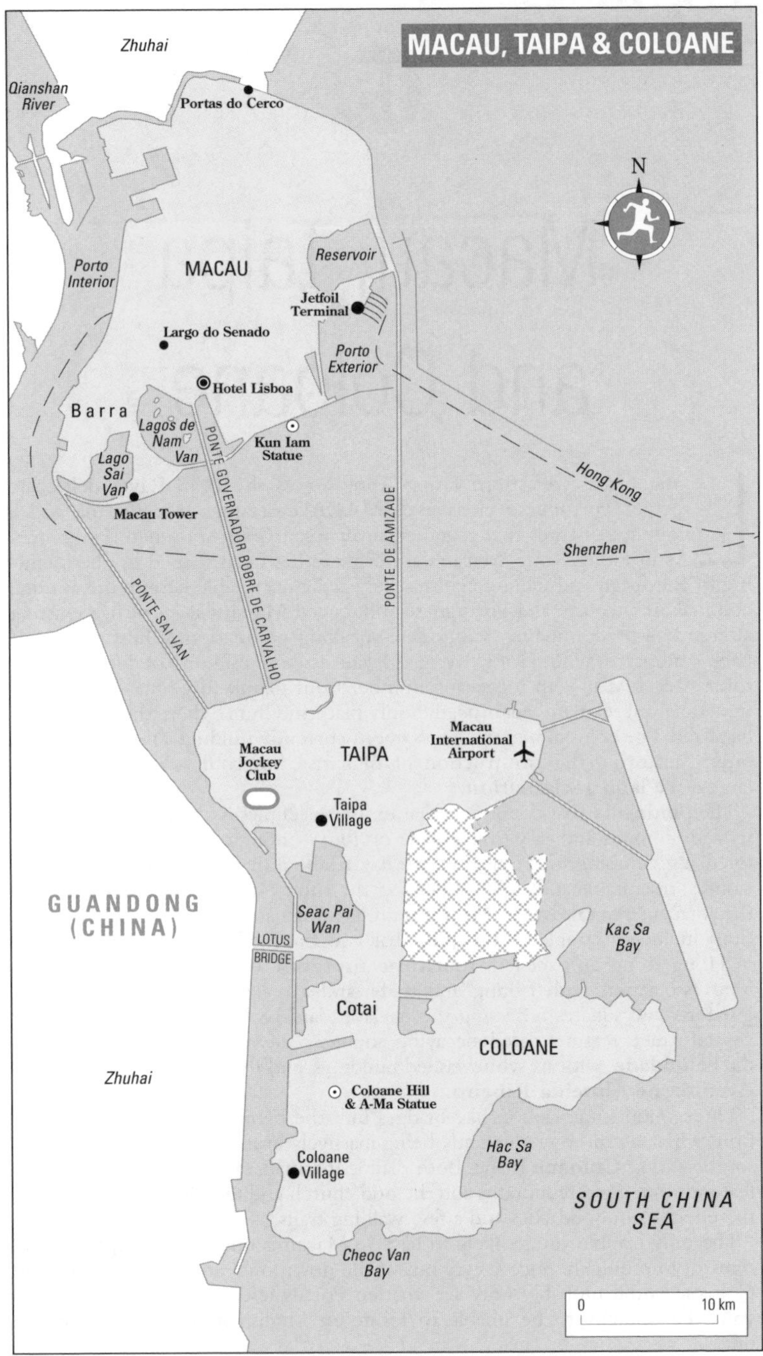
MACAU, TAIPA & COLOANE
Zhuhai
Qianshan River
Portas do Cerco
N
Reservoir
Porto Interior
MACAU
Jetfoil Terminal
Largo do Senado
Porto Exterior
Hotel Lisboa
Barra
Lagos de Nam Van
Kun Iam Statue
Lago Sai Van
Macau Tower
PONTE GOVERNADOR BOBRE DE CARVALHO
PONTE DE AMIZADE
Hong Kong
Shenzhen
PONTE SAI VAN
Macau International Airport
Macau Jockey Club
TAIPA
Taipa Village
GUANDONG (CHINA)
Seac Pai Wan
LOTUS BRIDGE
Kac Sa Bay
Cotai
COLOANE
Zhuhai
Coloane Hill & A-Ma Statue
Hac Sa Bay
Coloane Village
SOUTH CHINA SEA
Cheoc Van Bay
0
10 km

Travelling between Hong Kong and Macau

By sea

There are two departure points for ferries from Hong Kong to Macau. Turbojet (Ⓦwww.turbojet.com.hk) runs between one and four times an hour, round the clock, from the **Macau Ferry Terminal** in the Shun Tak Centre, Central, Hong Kong Island; while First Ferry (Ⓦwww.nwff.com.hk) departs from the **China Ferry Terminal** on Canton Road, Tsim Sha Tsui, Kowloon, around twice an hour between 7am and midnight. Either service takes 55 minutes and costs about HK$140 one-way, though discounts are often available. Ferries are all fast, modern vessels, and arrive at Macau's Porto Exterior Jetfoil Terminal.

Outside peak times **buying a ticket** is rarely a problem and you can often simply turn up and go. In practice, however, it's advisable to **book in advance**, especially at the weekend and on public holidays; you can book anything from same-day departure up to 28 days before you travel. Buying a **return ticket** is also recommended since it saves time at the other end. Aside from the terminals themselves, you can book tickets at the following MTR stations: Tsim Sha Tsui, Mongkok, Tsuen Wan, Kwun Tong, Causeway Bay, Central and Admiralty.

All tickets are for a specific departure time; aim to be at the ferry terminal at least thirty minutes before departure as you'll have to fill in immigration forms before boarding; also allow extra time if you have to pick up pre-booked tickets. You'll be allowed on with a suitcase or rucksack, but anything more and you'll have to check it in at the counter, again at least thirty minutes before departure, and you'll pay an extra $20–40, depending on weight. All services have drinks and snacks for sale on board.

For the **return journery**, all ferry tickets are sold at marked booths on the second floor of Macau's Jetfoil Terminal and at an outlet in the *Hotel Lisboa*'s shopping arcade. Departure frequencies are the same as from Hong Kong, as are the prices – though they're expressed in *patacas*.

By air

There's also a **helicopter service** between Hong Kong and Macau, with 28 flights daily, roughly every thirty minutes (first at 9am, last at 10.30pm) operated by East Asia Airlines (3rd Floor, Shun Tak Centre in Hong Kong Ⓣ2108 4838; Macau Ⓣ727288, Ⓦwww.helihongkong.com), and costing around $1210 one-way ($1310 at weekends) – the journey takes twenty minutes. Departures are from the helipad at Hong Kong's Macau Ferry Terminal, where you can buy tickets from a window adjacent to the turbocat and catamaran ticket offices, and arrive at the helipad on top of Macau's Jetfoil Terminal. For the return journey, you can get tickets from marked booths on the second floor of the Jetfoil Terminal and at an outlet in the *Hotel Lisboa*'s shopping arcade.

Around the peninsula

Macau's **PENINSULA** contains not just the remnants of its colonial past, but also a large and bustling modern quarter. The main artery, which cuts diagonally northwest across the peninsula, begins as Avenida do Infante D. Henrique, changing its name halfway along to **Avenida de Almeida Ribeiro**; it's north of here that you'll find the core of the **old city** and many of its major sights between **Largo do Senado** (Senate Square) and the **Guia** hilltop. South of here are the bright lights and modern development of **Avenida da Amizade** and associated casinos; while south of Avenida de Almeida Ribeiro there's more historic architecture through the narrow lanes of the **southern peninsula**.

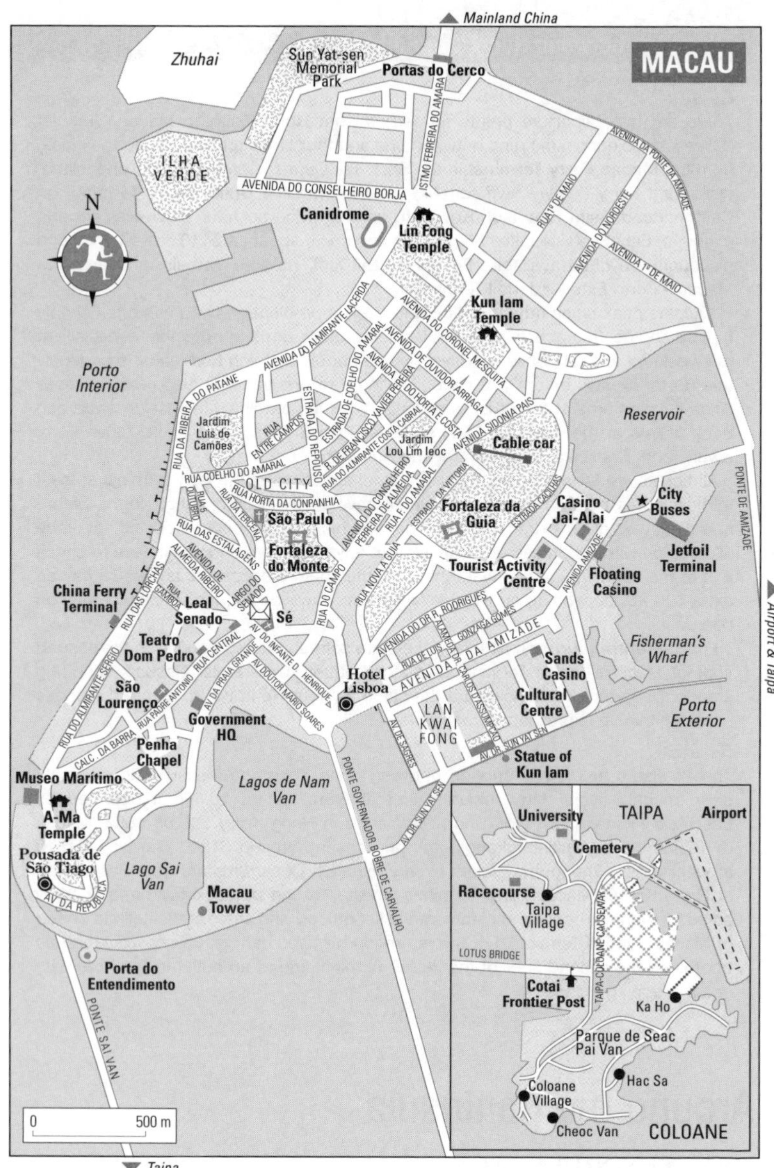

There are also a few sights in the otherwise nondescript north of town on the way to the **Portas do Cerco** (Barrier Gate) and the mainland Chinese border. Just about everything is within walking distance of most accommodation options, though you'll probably need a bus for the northernmost bits of town.

The old centre: Largo do Senado to the Fortaleza da Guia

The best place to start a tour of Macau is in **Largo do Senado**, the old city's main focus, usually full of sociable crowds out shopping during the day, or heading to restaurants in the evening. Just north is the iconic ruined facade of **São Paulo** and the nearby fortified hilltop, **Fortaleza do Monte**, beyond which the older-style streets fade out amongst a couple of city gardens and another defensive post, **Fortaleza da Guia**. You could make an easy circuit of these central sights in about four hours – long enough on a hot day – before heading back to Largo do Senado for a coffee.

Largo do Senado and Leal Senado

Largo do Senado (Senate Square) is the city's public focus, cobbled and surrounded by elegant colonial buildings painted pale pink, yellow or white, whose shuttered upper storey and street-level colonnades exude a wonderful tropical charm. There's a small fountain in the middle, while west down Rua de São Domingos and adjacent streets is a **market**: a quadrangle of clothes stalls and *dai pai dongs* around a covered building which deals mostly in fish and meat. On the east side of the square, **Santa Casa de Misericórdia** (Holy House of Mercy; Mon–Sat 10am–5.30pm; MOP$5) is Macau's oldest social institution, founded in 1569 by Dom Belchior Carneiro, the city's first Catholic bishop. His skull is displayed in a wood-panelled **museum** upstairs, along with porcelain marked with the Jesuit logo "JHS", and other religious artefacts.

The Senate House itself, the **Leal Senado** (Mon–Sun 9am–9pm; free), faces Largo do Senado on Avenida de Almeida Ribeiro. The name means "Loyal Senate", bestowed by a grateful Portuguese monarchy after Macau refused to fly the Castilian flag following the Spanish occupation of Portugal in 1580. Its traditional Portuguese design sports interior courtyard walls decorated with classic blue and white *azulejo* tiling, with an ornamental courtyard out the back. Still in use by the municipal government of Macau, it's something of a civic centre today, housing a small **art gallery** on the ground floor with ever-changing exhibitions, and an upstairs **library** (Mon–Fri 1–7pm), whose wooden shelves are stacked with a large collection of books (many in English) about China dating from the sixteenth century onwards – ask the librarians if you want to have a read. On the next level up, the **Senate Chamber** – a grand room with panelled walls and ceiling and excellent views over the square – is sometimes open to the public when not in use.

Sé and São Domingos

East off Largo do Senado, two small lanes slope a short way uphill to another, smaller cobbled square and the squat **Sé**, Macau's cathedral. It's not a particularly distinguished church – rebuilt in stone in the mid-nineteenth century on top of its original sixteenth-century foundations and completely restored again in 1937 – though it's spacious enough inside, with some fine stained glass, and is flanked by some rather pretty colonial buildings.

At the north end of Largo do Senado, the arcaded buildings peter out in the adjacent Largo São Domingos, which holds Macau's most beautiful church, the fine seventeenth-century Baroque **São Domingos** (usually open afternoons; ring the buzzer at the metal side gate). Built for Macau's Dominicans, its restrained cream-and-stucco facade is echoed inside by the pastel colours on display on the pillars and walls, and on the statue of the Virgin and Child that sits on top of the altar. On May 13 every year, the church is the starting point for a major procession in honour of Our Lady of Fatima.

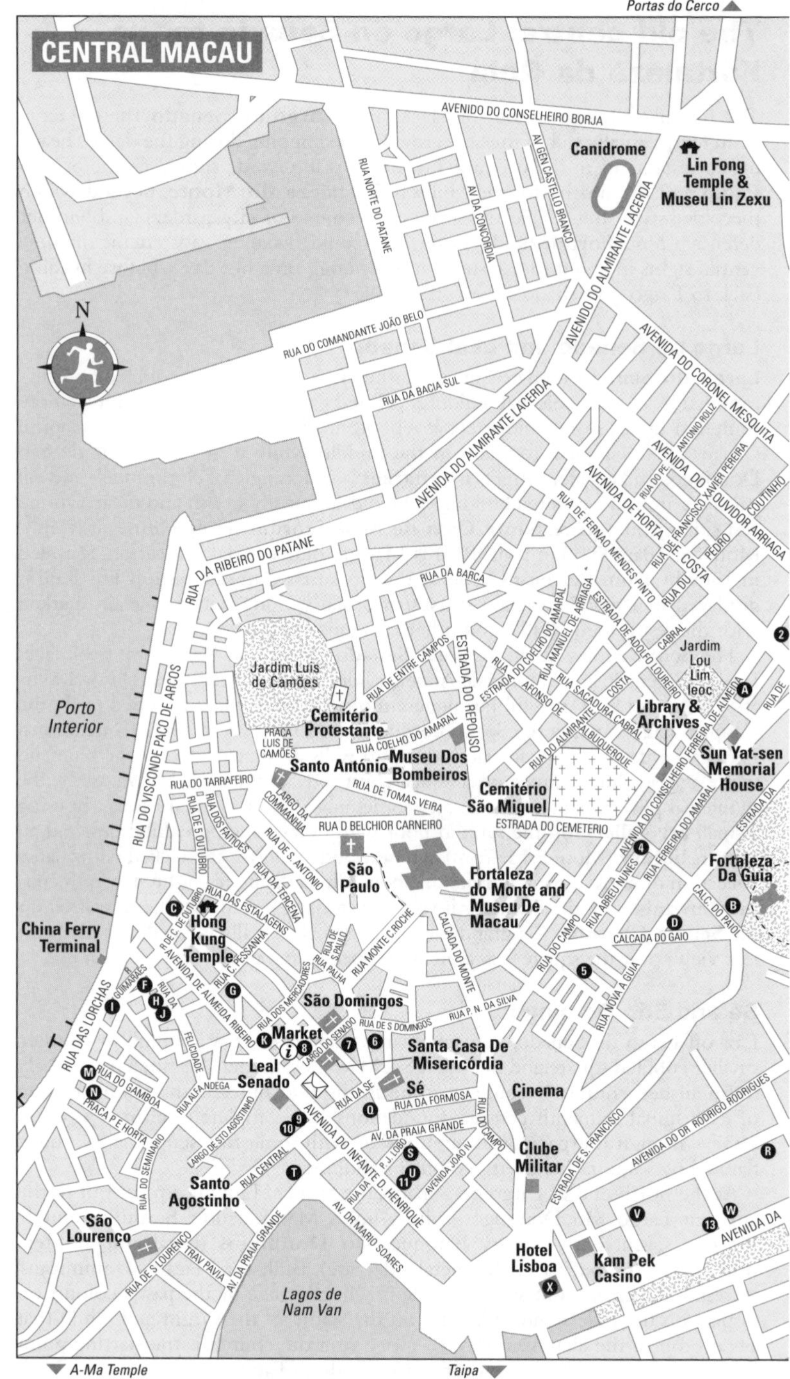
Portas do Cerco
CENTRAL MACAU
N
AVENIDO DO CONSELHEIRO BORJA
Canidrome
Lin Fong Temple & Museu Lin Zexu
RUA NORTE DO PATANE
AV DA CONCORDIA
AV GEN CASTELLO BRANCO
AVENIDO DO ALMIRANTE LACERDA
RUA DO COMANDANTE JOÃO BELO
RUA DA BACIA SUL
AVENIDA DO CORONEL MESQUITA
AVENIDA DO ALMIRANTE LACERDA
AVENIDA DO OUVIDOR ARRIAGA
AVENIDA DE HORTA E COSTA
RUA DE FERNAO MENDES PINTO
RUA DE FRANCISCO XAVIER PEREIRA
RUA DA RIBEIRO DO PATANE
RUA DA BARCA
ESTRADA DO REPOUSO
ESTRADA DE ADOLFO LOUREIRO
RUA MANUEL DE ARRIAGA
ESTRADA DO COELHO DO AMARAL
RUA SACADURA CABRAL
Jardim Lou Lim Ieoc
Library & Archives
Sun Yat-sen Memorial House
Porto Interior
Jardim Luis de Camões
Cemitério Protestante
RUA DE ENTRE CAMPOS
RUA COELHO DO AMARAL
PRAÇA LUIS DE CAMÕES
Santo António
Museu Dos Bombeiros
RUA DE TOMAS VEIRA
Cemitério São Miguel
RUA DO VISCONDE PACO DE ARCOS
RUA DO TARRAFEIRO
RUA D BELCHIOR CARNEIRO
ESTRADA DO CEMETERIO
AVENIDA DO CONSELHEIRO FERREIRA DE ALMEIDA
RUA FERREIRA DO AMARAL
São Paulo
Fortaleza do Monte and Museu De Macau
Fortaleza Da Guia
RUA DE S. ANTONIO
RUA DA TERCENA
RUA DAS ESTALAGENS
RUA MONTE C.ROCHE
CALCADA DO MONTE
RUA ABREU NUNES
RUA DO CAMPO
CALCADA DO GAIO
CALC. DO PAIOL
China Ferry Terminal
Hong Kung Temple
AVENIDA DE ALMEIDA RIBEIRO
RUA DAS LORCHAS
RUA NOVA A GUIA
São Domingos
RUA DE S DOMINGOS
RUA P. N. DA SILVA
Market
Leal Senado
Santa Casa De Misericórdia
Sé
Cinema
RUA DO GAMBOA
PRACA P E HORTA
RUA DA SE
RUA DA FORMOSA
AV. DA PRAIA GRANDE
AVENIDA DO INFANTE D. HENRIQUE
AVENIDA DO DR RODRIGO RODRIGUES
ESTRADA DE S. FRANCISCO
Clube Militar
Santo Agostinho
RUA CENTRAL
LARGO DE STO AGOSTINHO
RUA DO SEMINARIO
AV. DR MARIO SOARES
AVENIDA DA
São Lourenço
RUA DE S LOURENÇO
TRAV PAVIA
AV. DA PRAIA GRANDE
Hotel Lisboa
Kam Pek Casino
Lagos de Nam Van
A-Ma Temple
Taipa

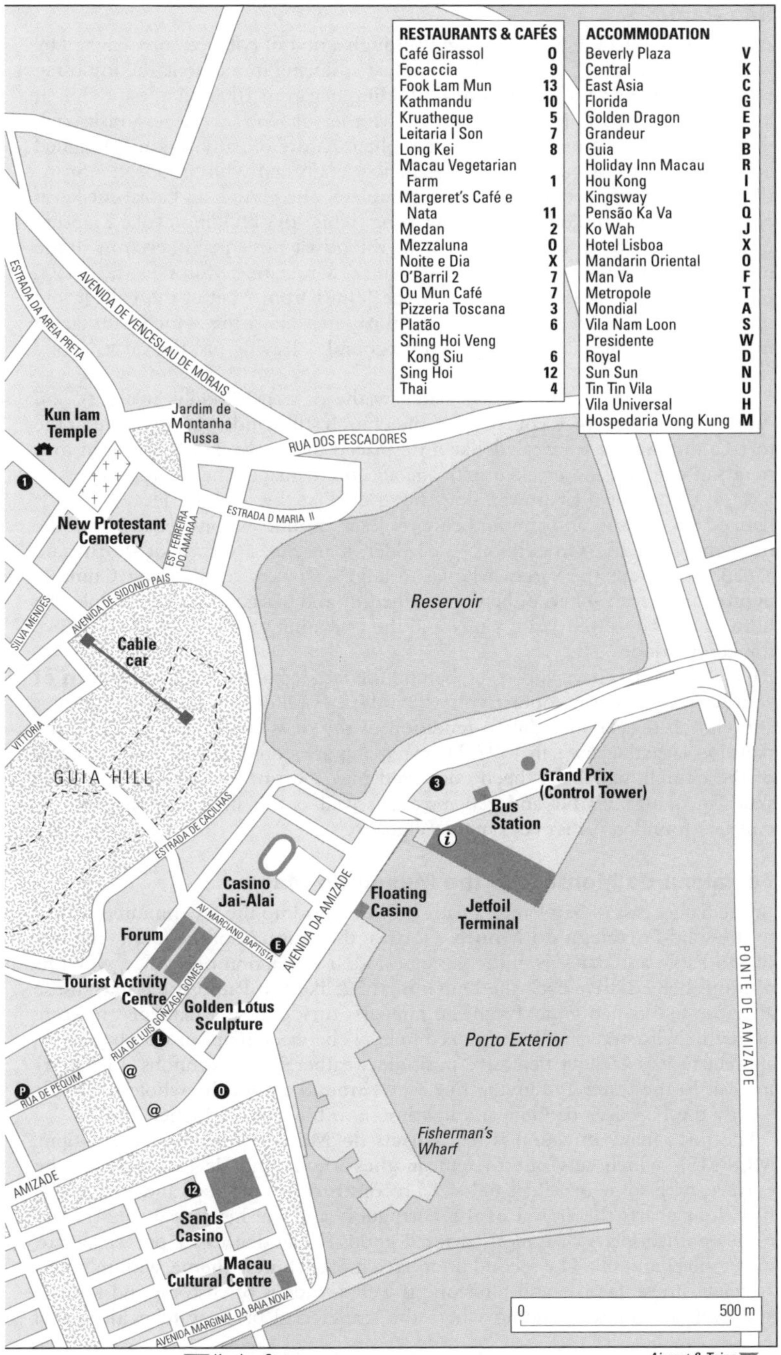

RESTAURANTS & CAFÉS
Café Girassol 0
Focaccia 9
Fook Lam Mun 13
Kathmandu 10
Kruatheque 5
Leitaria I Son 7
Long Kei 8
Macau Vegetarian Farm 1
Margeret's Café e Nata 11
Medan 2
Mezzaluna 0
Noite e Dia X
O'Barril 2 7
Ou Mun Café 7
Pizzeria Toscana 3
Platão 6
Shing Hoi Veng Kong Siu 6
Sing Hoi 12
Thai 4
ACCOMMODATION
Beverly Plaza V
Central K
East Asia C
Florida G
Golden Dragon E
Grandeur P
Guia B
Holiday Inn Macau R
Hou Kong I
Kingsway L
Pensão Ka Va Q
Ko Wah J
Hotel Lisboa X
Mandarin Oriental O
Man Va F
Metropole T
Mondial A
Vila Nam Loon S
Presidente W
Royal D
Sun Sun N
Tin Tin Vila U
Vila Universal H
Hospedaria Vong Kung M
ESTRADA DA AREIA PRETA
AVENIDA DE VENCESLAU DE MORAIS
Kun Iam Temple
Jardim de Montanha Russa
RUA DOS PESCADORES
ESTRADA D MARIA II
New Protestant Cemetery
EST FERREIRA DO AMARAL
AVENIDA DE SIDONIO PAIS
SILVA MENDES
Reservoir
Cable car
VITTORIA
GUIA HILL
Grand Prix (Control Tower)
Bus Station
ESTRADA DE CACILHAS
Casino Jai-Alai
Floating Casino
Jetfoil Terminal
AVENIDA DA AMIZADE
AV MARCIANO BAPTISTA
Forum
Tourist Activity Centre
RUA DE LUIS GONZAGA GOMES
Golden Lotus Sculpture
Porto Exterior
PONTE DE AMIZADE
RUA DE PEQUIM
Fisherman's Wharf
AMIZADE
Sands Casino
Macau Cultural Centre
AVENIDA MARGINAL DA BAIA NOVA
0 500 m
Kun Iam Statue
Airport & Taipa

São Paulo

A short walk north of São Domingos through a nest of cobbled lanes flanked by *pastelaria* (sweet shops), stands Macau's most enduring monument: the imposing facade of the church of **São Paulo**. Building began in 1602 on a Jesuit church here, attached to the Madre de Deus ("Mother of God") college, and its rich design reflected the precocious, cosmopolitan nature of early Macau. Designed by an Italian, it was built largely by Japanese craftsmen who produced a Spanish-style facade that took 25 years to complete. The church and adjacent Jesuit college became a noted centre of learning, while the building evoked rapture in those who saw it: "I have not seen anything that can equal it, even in all the beautiful churches of Italy, except St Peter's" wrote one visitor in the 1630s. However, following the expulsion of the Jesuits from Macau, the college did duty as an army barracks and on a fateful day in 1835, a fire, which had started in the kitchens, swept through the entire complex leaving just the carved stone facade.

Approaching up the impressive wide swathe of steps (floodlit at night), you can just about convince yourself that the church still stands, but on reaching the terrace the **facade** is revealed, like a misplaced theatre backdrop, rising in four tiers and chipped and cracked with age and fire damage. The statues and reliefs have lost none of their power, however: a dove at the top (the Holy Spirit) is flanked by the sun and moon; below is Jesus, around whom reliefs show the implements of the Crucifixion – a ladder, manacles, a crown of thorns and a flail. Below are the Virgin Mary and angels, flowers representing China (a peony) and Japan (chrysanthemum), a griffin and a rigged galleon, while the bottom tier holds four Jesuit saints, and the crowning words "Mater Dei" above the central door.

In what was the nave and crypt, behind the facade, there's now a **museum of sacred art** (daily 9am–6pm; free), which displays religious paintings, sculptures and church regalia, including a rendition of the mass crucifixion of 23 Christians in Nagasaki, Japan, in 1597. Their remains are stored in the former chancel of the church, which has been converted into a **crypt** containing bones and skulls in orange marble and glass boxes, as well as the alleged remains of the college's founder, Father Alexandre Valignano.

Fortaleza do Monte and the Museu de Macau

Immediately east of São Paulo, a path and steps lead up the few hundred metres to the solid **Fortaleza do Monte**, a fortress that was part of the Jesuit complex of São Paulo and dates from the same period. It saw action only once, when its cannons helped drive back the Dutch in 1622; like São Paulo, it fell into disuse after the Jesuits had gone. From the ramparts (made from a hardened mixture of earth, shells, straw and lime, packed in layers between strips of wood) you can appreciate its excellent defensive position, weathered iron cannons still pointing out to the water and giving fine views around almost the whole peninsula – only the Fortaleza da Guia and lighthouse to the east are higher.

The fort's main attraction is the **Museu de Macau** (Tues–Sun 10am–6pm; MOP$15), which sets out to explain the origins and development of the enclave, with some excellent full-sized reconstructions of shops and streets. The first floor charts the arrival of the Portuguese and the heydays of the trading routes with displays of typical bartered goods – wooden casks, porcelainware, spices, silver and silk. The second floor has a more Chinese theme, with religious artefacts, house facades and interiors, as well as videos of customs and festivals and even a Chinese wedding where the scarlet-clad bride watches the ritual

▲ Fortaleza do Monte

burning of all her possessions on her wedding morning. Look too for offbeat items such as the cricket-fighting display, complete with a tiny cricket coffin and grave headstone for expired, prized fighters, along with information about why Chinese babies are wrapped in red, and what the rice dumpling hawker used to cry to advertise his wares. The tour wraps up a bit lamely with a quick look at modern-day Macau and some interactive computer quizzes on the future of the MSAR.

West from São Paulo

There's a fascinating maze of lanes spreading **west from São Paulo** to the seafront, parts of which can have changed little over the last fifty years. It's worth seeking out the unpretentious **Hong Kung Temple**, dedicated to Kwan Tai, god of riches and war, and focus for the extraordinary **Drunken Dragon Festival**, held on the eighth day of the fourth lunar month (April/May). Organized by the Fish Retailers' Association, the festival features opera, religous ceremonies, martial arts performances, and a parade from here to the Porto Interior via all the local fish shops by men carrying large wooden dragon heads who consume vast quantities of spirits. Further on things become more intense as the very old streets degenerate into a noisome wholesale market: wicker baskets full of vegetables and roots, chickens in coops waiting to be killed and plucked, and whole side alleys turned over to different trades – one full of ironmongers, another of street barbers. Along **Rua das Estalagens** and **Rua da Tercena** you'll find smiths beating metal, jade carvers, carpenters working wood and various stores selling joss sticks, wedding dresses, antiques, blackwood furniture, medicines, silk and shoes. **Rua de Cinco de Outubro** is similar, with a remarkable decorated facade of the Farmacia Tai Neng Tong on the left at no. 146. All these streets eventually intersect with Rua do Tarrafeiro, just a short way from Jardim Luís de Camões (see overleaf).

Jardim Luís de Camões and around

From São Paulo, Rua de São Paulo and Rua do Santo António run northwest, past antique furniture shops, to the church of **Santo António**. This is rather plain in appearance, though given that it was wrecked by fire in 1809, 1874 and 1930 it's perhaps surprising that it survives at all. Each St Anthony's Day (June 13) the saint – a military figurehead – is presented with his wages by the president of the Senate, after which his image is paraded around the city to inspect the battlements.

Just beyond here is a square, the Praça Luís de Camões (buses #17 & #18 run past), at the head of which lies the **Jardim Luís de Camões** (Camões Garden; open daily 6am–10pm). This very tropical, laid-back spread of banyans, ferns, fan palms, paved terraces and flowers is always full of people pottering about, exercising, or just playing cards under the trees, and commemorates a sixteenth-century Portuguese poet who is supposed to have visited Macau and written part of his epic *Os Lusíadas* (about Vasco da Gama's voyages) here. There's a bust of Camões, encircled by granite boulders, although there's no real evidence that he ever did come here. The garden was once part of the grounds of the adjacent building, a stylish late-eighteenth-century country villa that once served as the headquarters of the British East India Company in Macau. It now houses the Macau-China Delegation Building.

15 Cemitério Protestante

Established in 1814 on land purchased by the East India Company, **Cemitério Protestante** (Old Protestant Cemetery; daily 8.30am–5.30pm – you may need to knock to get in) houses many of the non-Portuguese traders and visitors who expired in the enclave. For decades Protestants had no set burial place in Macau: the Catholic Portuguese didn't want them cluttering up the city and the Chinese objected if they were interred on ancestral lands. Some of the graves were moved here from various resting places outside the city walls, as the pre-1814 headstones show.

The most famous resident is the artist **George Chinnery** (on the cemetery's upper tier), who spent his life painting much of the local Chinese coast; a plaque on his tomb recounts how he proclaimed the Christian message of Goodwill Towards All Men "by word and by brush". Some of the cemetery's most poignant graves are those belonging to ordinary **seamen** who died nearby. It was a dangerous, uncomfortable time to be a sailor: Samuel Smith "died by a fall from aloft"; the cabin boy of ship's master Athson similarly met his end "through the effects of a fall into the hold"; while poor Oliver Mitchell "died of dysentery". There's also the grave of the missionary Robert Morrison, who translated the Bible into Chinese, and his wife who died in childbirth. For the full rundown of grave inscriptions, the Macau Government Tourist Office (see p.30) sells a fascinating book called *The Protestant Cemeteries of Macau* by Manuel Teixera, which covers both this cemetery and the New Protestant Cemetery over by the Kun Iam Temple to the north of the city.

Museu dos Bombeiros

East of the cemetery along Rua Coelho do Amaral, the **Museu dos Bombeiros** (Fire Department Museum; daily 10am–6pm; free) occupies a yellow sandstone building next to the Kiang Wu hospital. This quirky little museum is housed in the Macau Fire Services headquarters and contains a couple of shiny red and black fire engines, and an enormous collection of fire-fighting tools from Macau and overseas – pumps, hoses, helmets, breathing apparatus, nozzles, ladders, uniforms, radio communication sets and all kinds of fire extinguishers and hydrants.

While the exhibits and captions are clearly aimed at school groups, and are frankly slightly comical, the dramatic news photos of some serious blazes and heroic rescues, and the fire-proof suit made from glass fibre and able to withstand temperatures of over 800°C, are worth a few minutes of your time if you are passing.

Jardim Lou Lim Ieoc and around

Continuing eastwards, you'll first pass **Cemitério São Miguel** (daily 8am–6pm) on Estrado do Cemitério, Macau's largest cemetery and full of both European and Christian Chinese headstones. The street runs into Avenida do Conselheiro Ferreira de Almeida, whose west side is lined with a fine string of colonial mansions housing the **City Library** (Tues–Sun 2–8pm) and the **National Archives**. Just past here and to the left, a high wall encloses the beautiful **Jardim Lou Lim Ieoc** (daily dawn–dusk) a formal Chinese arrangement of pavilions, carp ponds, bamboo groves and frangipani trees where you might catch amateur opera performances on a Sunday. Built in the nineteenth century, it was modelled on the famous classical Chinese gardens of Suzhou, and typically manages to appear much more spacious than it really is. The garden is known locally as Lou Kau, after the Chinese merchant who funded its construction; Lou Lim Ieoc was his son.

Just to the east, on Avenida de Sidonio Pais (at the junction with Rua de Silva Mendes), the granite, Moorish-style **Sun Yat-sen Memorial House** (Wed–Mon 10am–5pm; free) was built by the republican leader's family in the 1930s to house relics and photos. Sun Yat-sen lived in Macau for a few years in the 1890s, practising as a doctor, before developing his revolutionary beliefs, and while there's no massive interest here, you could spend half an hour quite happily in this odd building. There's a Chinese reading room on the ground floor, while upstairs Mrs Sun Yat-sen's former bedroom opens onto a balcony with green twisted pillars. Rooms off here are lined with photocopied manuscripts of less-than-thrilling content ("Dr Sun narrating the beginning of revolutionary activities") and some very poor copies of old photos of Dr Sun and various comrades and committees. The top floor is used for occasional art exhibitions.

Guia Hill and Fortaleza da Guia

The steep ridge east of here is **Guia Hill**, Macau's apex and one-time defence headquarters, and now a landscaped park. The **entrance** is on Avenida de Sidonio Pais through a small botanic garden – housing an aviary and a sad collection of animals in bare steel and concrete cages – from where you can either ascend to the top of Guia Hill along a winding path, or take the **cable car** (Tues–Sun 8am–6pm; MOP$3 return, MOP$2 one-way). Either way, you'll end up on paths to the remains of **Fortaleza da Guia**, a fortress completed in 1638, and originally designed to defend the border with China – though given its extraordinary perch above the whole peninsula it's seen most service as an observation post. The main points of interest here are a network of short, disconnected **tunnels** used in the 1930s to store munitions; and a small seventeenth-century **chapel** within the walls dedicated to Our Lady of Guia, which contains an image of the Virgin that local legend says left the chapel and deflected enemy bullets with her robe during the Dutch attack of 1622. Inside are the recently uncovered original blue and pink frescoes, which combine Chinese elements with Christian religious images. The chapel's other function was to ring its bell to warn of storms, something now taken care of by the fortress's **lighthouse**, built in 1865. The best views from the fortress walls are southeast down over the modern Porto Exterior (cannon up here now threaten the area's casinos), and westwards towards Fortaleza do Monte and the old town.

The redevelopment of Macau

Land reclamation is as big a business in Macau as in Hong Kong; the area of the Macau peninsula alone is already two-and-a-half times bigger than it was 150 years ago. The impetus for this, and the ensuing drive for modernization in the SAR, is Macau's determination not to be left out of the economic boom sweeping the adjacent Pearl River Delta area between Guangzhou and Hong Kong.

Macau's attempts to become a player in the regional infrastructure took off in 1995 with the completion of the **airport**, built at a cost of US$975 million off the east coast of Taipa. To date, however, the airport is running well below an annual capacity of six million passengers, though there are signs that it may be attempting to lure customers away from competition at Hong Kong and the Chinese mainland by repositioning itself as a low-cost gateway to regional hubs such as Bangkok and Singapore. The construction of the airport and a **container port** at Ka Ho on Coloane prompted further development, most notably the reclamation of land westwards from the causeway linking Taipa and Coloane called **Cotai**. There's talk of turning this into a Las Vegas-style casino strip; **Lotus Bridge** here provides a road link for freight goods between Macau's airport and the mainland town of Zhuhai. On the peninsula, the Porto Exterior was developed to include the **Macau Cultural Centre** and (the currently stalled) **Fisherman's Wharf** theme park, while the government got a new Legislative Assembly building, and the southern peninsula's waterfront was enclosed to form two artificial lakes, fringed by a new network of expressways and a further bridge to the mainland. There's even talk of building a surely unnecessary **light rail** network linking the peninsula with Taipa; and of a **bridge to Hong Kong** – an unlikely project, perhaps, but one that developers have declared will be completed by 2010.

One very positive aspect of all this is that this modern development is rising on reclaimed land, and the older parts of town haven't been targeted for wholesale demolition and reconstruction (something all too common on the Chinese mainland). For the moment then, Macau's **Portuguese heritage** – the old buildings, squares, and streets – don't seem to be under an immediate threat, even if all these new projects mean that Macau's atmosphere isn't quite as laid-back as it used to be.

Avenida Da Amizade and the Porto Exterior

The area southeast of Guia Hill is entirely modern, built on land **reclaimed** from the **Porto Exterior**, the Outer Harbour, over the last few decades. The main artery here is **Avenida da Amizade**, a multi-laned carriageway that runs for around 1.5 kilometres northeast from the gaudy *Hotel Lisboa* to the Jetfoil Terminal, where you probably arrived in town from Hong Kong. It's an area aimed at big spenders, thick with upmarket hotels and **casinos** and the setting for the annual **Macau Grand Prix** race (see p.317) – though a couple of museums add a shot of culture too. **Buses** #3, #3A, and #10A run from Avenida Almeida Ribeiro near Largo do Senado, via the *Hotel Lisboa*, and up to the Jetfoil terminal, though not continually along Avenida da Amizade.

Hotel Lisboa & São Francisco barracks

Marking the southern end of Rua da Amizade, the dark orange flanks of the **Hotel Lisboa** are crowned by a multistorey circular drum done up like a wedding cake and lit to extravagant effect at night. No one should miss a venture into the hotel's 24-hour **casinos** – all pseudo-1930s decor and noisy, crowded tables – or a wander through the hotel's gilt and marble surroundings, past the gift shops, Stanley Ho's private art collection, and the ten restaurants and bars inside.

Just north from the *Lisboa*, on Avenida da Praia Grande, stands the area's one old colonial touch: **São Francisco barracks**, painted a deep pink highlighted with white trim (as are all of Macau's military buildings). The public are allowed into the dining room of the **Clube Militar** (see p.310) contained within, but no further. The building itself dates from 1864; before that, on the same site, stood the original São Francisco fortress, which guarded the edge of the old waterfront Praia Grande – giving you some idea of how far land reclamation has changed this part of the city. The fine round tower in the upper level of the ornate gardens behind the barracks was built to honour those from Macau who saw service in World War I.

The Sands and Macau Cultural Centre

Moving up Avenida de Amizade, both sides of road are lined with hotels and casinos, of which the most eye-catching is the gold-plated, US-owned **Sands**, opened in 2003 as Macau's first foreign-operated venture. Completely at odds with the home-grown brand, whose crowds and dim lighting preserve anonymity, the *Sands*' vast lozenge-shaped interior is all Las Vegas slickness, well lit with a live band and a high tier of balcony bars and restaurants from where you can spy down on the action.

Behind the *Sands*, the **Macau Cultural Centre**, on Avenida Xian Xing Hai (buses #8, #12, or #17), sits on the southeast edge of a grid of new streets jutting into the bay. Its highlight is the five-storey **Museum of Art** (Tues–Sun, 10am–7pm; MOP$5) whose galleries contain a display of nineteenth-century paintings of Macau – including pieces by George Chinnery – as well as temporary exhibitions from overseas. The adjacent blue-grey block houses the auditoriums where international music, dance and theatre shows are staged. You can book tickets over the phone on ☎555 555.

A five-minute walk along the waterfront on an artificial island joined to the mainland by a causeway is the captivating **Kun Iam Statue and Ecumenical Centre** (daily except Fri, 10.30am–6pm; free), designed and built by Portuguese artist, Christina Reiria. The twenty-metre bronze sculpture (whose sweeping garments are designed to withstand the strong offshore winds) had a mixed reception from the locals, many of whom feel that it looks more like Mary, mother of Jesus, than the Chinese goddess of mercy. Inside the lotus-shaped dome are a small bookshop, a library, and a display on the story of the statue.

To the Jetfoil Terminal

Across Avenida de Amizade from the *Sands* casino, holidaying mainlanders pose in front of a **Golden Lotus Flower** sculpture – an attempt, perhaps, to rival Hong Kong's Golden Bauhinia – which rises up out of a baldly paved square. Behind here on Rua de Luís Gonzaga Gomes is the **Tourist Activity Centre**, housing two subterranean museums. The **Museu da Grande Prémio** (Grand Prix Museum; daily 10am–6pm; MOP$10) displays vintage and modern racing cars with race videos and information boards. It's a rather dull display, rescued by the opportunity of spending a few minutes strapped into a race simulator experiencing the twists and turns of the Formula 3 circuit (MOP$20). The **Museu do Vinho** (Wine Museum; daily 10am–6pm; MOP$15) charts the history of Portuguese viniculture with maps, peasant costumes, and hundreds of bottles; entry gets you a free sample, and the shop sells some interesting vintages – including much sought-after 1994, considered the twentieth century's finest year for Port.

Back on Avenida de Amizade, the walled-off construction project east of *Sands* casino is **Fisherman's Wharf**, an entertainment complex currently in building limbo but planning to incorporate an adventure park, a forty-metre-high man-made volcano, re-creations of Chinese and European streets, and the usual shopping plazas, restaurants and nightclubs. Moored next to it is the *Macau Palace* casino, better known as the **Floating Casino**, which started life as a floating restaurant in Hong Kong. Despite plenty of gilded screens and dragon carvings, it doesn't have much atmosphere, filled mainly with slot machines (or "Hungry Tigers" as they're known in Chinese). Over the road from here, the old **Jai-Alai Stadium** is now yet another casino, a very downmarket, dingy affair that will possibly live up to your expectations for the seedier side of Macau's gaming industry. Beyond here, the road and a pedestrian overpass bring you to the **Jetfoil Terminal**, outside of which you'll find a **bus terminal** (buses #3, #3A, and #10A will get you back to *Hotel Lisboa* or Largo do Senado) and the **Grand Prix Control Tower** and stands.

The southern peninsula

The hilly, narrow peninsula south of Avenida de Almeida Ribeiro and Largo do Senado was for centuries one of the busiest areas of Macau, faced to the west by its main harbour, to the east by its main promenade, and capped by elegant dwellings and churches. Today it's a mostly quiet, slightly seedy district, but remains an interesting place to roam twisting lanes between quietly mouldering buildings. The two main sights here are **A-Ma Temple**, the most important Chinese place of worship in Macau, and the adjacent **maritime museum**. **Bus** #10A runs from the Jetfoil Terminal, via *Hotel Lisboa* and Avenida de Almeida Ribeiro, down the west side of the southern peninsula to the temple and museum, but elsewhere this is really an area to explore on foot.

The Porto Interior and surrounding streets

The west side of the southern peninsula fronts the **Porto Interior** or Inner Harbour, Macau's main port until the new terminals were built over on the Porto Exterior. Get there by heading off into the warren of backstreets south off Avenida de Almeida Ribeiro, the most interesting of which is **Rua da Feli-**

▲ Rua da Felicidade

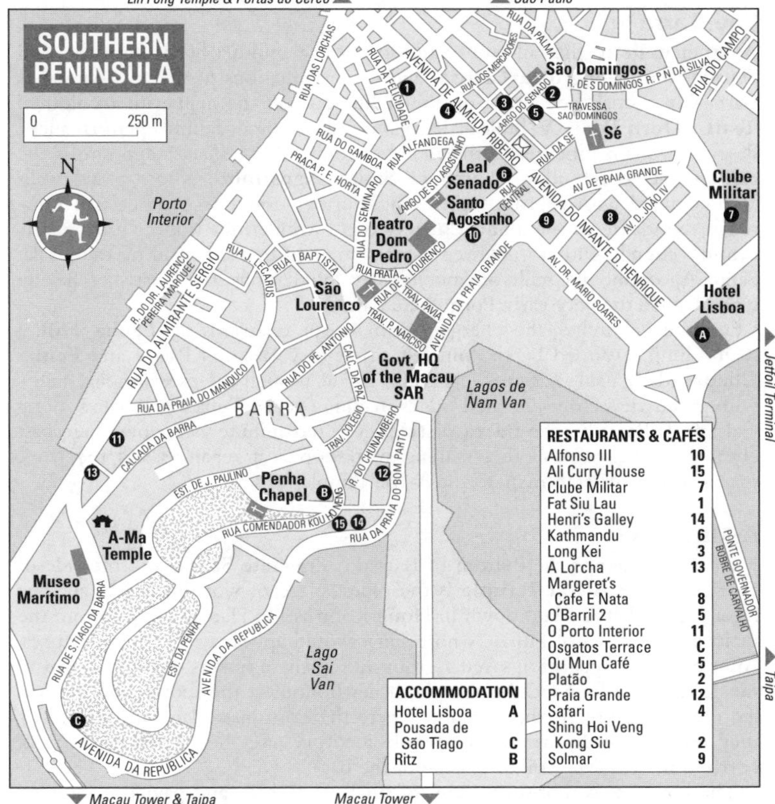

cidade (Happiness Street), once a red-light district of sordid repute but now – even though the prostitutes linger – an endearing run of small guesthouses, *pastelarias* such as **Koi Kei** selling almond biscuits and cured pork, and seafood restaurants. Although the tidy shopfronts have all been whitewashed, and their shutters and big wooden doors carefully restored and painted red, the area was still considered suitably rough to double as old Shanghai when scenes from *Indiana Jones and the Temple of Doom* were filmed here in 1984.

Wander westwards and you'll exit onto **Rua das Lorchas** in the vicinity of Praça Ponte e Horta, an elongated, formerly grand square that is now rather run-down. From here, **Rua do Almirante Sergio**, the main harbour-front drag, runs south for around a kilometre to the A-Ma Temple. There's little of interest to seaward – mostly old wharfs, warehouses, and the well-hidden **China Ferry Terminal** – but the opposite side offers a fascinating twenty-minute walk past a slightly down-at-heel string of small Chinese businesses. The street is arcaded, pillars painted with red Chinese characters advertising each store, including chandlers and fishing-supply shops (selling nets and great steel hawsers), greasy electrical and hardware stores, pawnshops, incense sellers, pedlars with jade ornaments, vegetable sellers and *dai pai dongs*. There's also a small temple at no. 131, while the side streets around conceal a tumbledown world of dark, tatty shops and houses.

The Barra

Another route to the tail-end of the southern peninsula heads from the Leal Senado south along **Rua Central** and its continuations to the area known as Barra. Up a small side street, on the right, you pass the peppermint-coloured **Teatro Dom Pedro V**, built in 1873 and still staging occasional performances, despite its main function as the members-only *Clube Macao*. Opposite is the early nineteenth-century church of **Santo Agostinho**, whose pastel walls are decorated with delicate piped icing. Further down on Rua de São Lourenço, the square-towered **São Lourenço** is a wonderfully tropical nineteenth-century church, with a mildewed exterior framed by palms and fig trees. Like Santo Agostinho it's built on much older foundations, both parishes having existed since the very early Portuguese days.

From the churches, the energetic can detour eastwards up **Penha Hill**, a steep climb rewarded by the nineteenth-century Bishop's Palace and **Penha Chapel** (daily 9am–5.30pm) – peaceful inside, though the exteriors are drab - with grand views south of the bridges snaking over to Taipa. Back below along Calçada da Barra lies the **Barra district**; it's a ten-minute walk down here, past cheap Chinese cafés, clothes-making workshops, car repairers and the work spaces of various craftsmen, to the A-Ma Temple.

A-Ma Temple

Facing the water at the bottom of Rua do Almirante Sergio and the side of Barra Hill, the **A-Ma Temple** is the oldest place of worship in Macau. The legend goes that A-Ma (known in Hong Kong as Tin Hau) was a girl from the mainland province of Fujian, whose spirit would appear to save people at sea. After one such apparition saved a group of Fujianese traders during a storm in the 1370s, they founded this temple in her honour at the spot where she had led them to shore. As this was also where the Portuguese later made landfall, they unintentionally named the whole territory after her ("Macau" being a corruption of A-Ma Kok, the name of the bay).

The complex comprises a series of small stone halls and pavilions jumbled together on the hillside amongst granite boulders, all cluttered with incense spirals and red-draped wooden models of boats and statues of the goddess. Many of these rocks are also carved with symbols of the A-Ma story and poems in flowery Chinese, describing Macau and its religious associations. An array of fish tanks are full of turtles, onto whose shells people try to drop coins for good luck. The busiest time to visit is either around the Chinese New Year or for **A-Ma's festival** (late April/May; the 23rd day of the third moon), when alongside the devotions there's also Cantonese opera in a temporary theatre.

Museu Marítimo

Over the road from the A-Ma temple, in purpose-built premises designed to look like wharf buildings, is Macau's superb **Museu Marítimo** (Maritime Museum; Wed–Mon 10am–5.30pm; MOP$10). Ranged across three storeys is an engaging and well-presented collection relating to local fishing techniques and festivals, Chinese and Portuguese maritime prowess, and boat building. Poke around and you'll discover navigational equipment, a scale model of seventeenth-century Macau, traditional local clothing used by the fishermen, a host of lovingly made models of both Chinese and Portuguese vessels, and even a small collection of boats moored at the pier, including a traditional wooden *lorcha* – used for chasing pirate ships – and a dragon-racing boat. The whole collection is made eminently accessible with the help of explanatory English-language notes, video displays and boat models. Round off your visit with a half-hour motorized **junk ride** (Wed–Mon 10.30am–4.30pm; MOP$10); the Porto Interior route takes you past warehouses, floating homes, dredgers and tugboats in the channel separating Macau from Zhuhai, whilst the Porto Exterior boat chugs east along the new waterfront and under the Ponte Governador Bobre de Carvalho.

Fortaleza da Barra

Keep on past the museum and Rua São Tiago da Barra – a quiet, cobbled street – leads down to the tip of the peninsula and the **Pousada de São Tiago**, one of the nicest hotels in either Hong Kong or Macau, built over the ruins of what was once Macau's most important fortress, the **Fortaleza da Barra**. The fortress, finished in 1629, was designed to protect the entrance to the Porto Interior, a function it achieved by hiding two dozen cannons within its ten-metre-high walls. Over the centuries, it fell into disrepair along with all Macau's other forts, and was rescued in 1976 when it was converted into a *pousada*, or inn. No one will mind if you have a look at the foundations and eighteenth-century chapel inside, and the terrace bar is reasonably priced, and makes a good venue for a drink or a meal overlooking the water (see p.305 for details).

Around the lakes

The *Pousada de São Tiago* sits at the edge of **Lago Sai Van**, the more westerly of the lakes formed by the enclosing of the southern peninsula's eastern side with a causeway. An expressway follows this around the outside edge of the lake to the unintentionally bleak **Porta do Entendimento** ("Gate of Understanding") erected in 1993, where three interlocking black marble fingers, 40m high, supposedly symbolize the "spirit of Macau". Past here, the road continues to the 338-metre-high **Macau Tower**, with an outside walkway at 216 metres (MOP$100) for views as far as Hong Kong's islands on a clear day. Alternatively, you can just make use of the revolving restaurant, a great place for an evening drink with night views of the city. You can get direct from here to the *Hotel Lisboa* or Jetfoil Terminal on bus #32.

Alternatively, instead of following the outside edge of Lago Sai Van, you can walk back to town from *Pousada de São Tiago* along **Avenida da Republica**, a quiet tree-lined esplanade whose modern and colonial-era houses look out over the lake. The road in turn develops into **Avenida da Praia Grande**, once a grand promenade and, in its lower reaches at least, retaining something of that feel, with a further string of trees and European-style mansions culminating in the graceful pink mid-nineteenth century **Palácio do Governo** ("Government House"), now stamped with the five gold-starred emblem of the People's Republic of China. Past here however, you're immediately thrown back into the modern world as the road becomes a highway on the concrete shore of **Lagos de Nam Van**, the Nam Van Lakes, bisected by the main Ponte Governador Bobre de Carvalho. This is the best place to watch the huge **midnight fireworks display** on the first night of the Chinese New Year – conveniently held not to compete with Hong Kong's bigger pyrotechnics show, which is on the third night.

North to the Portas do Cerco

The peninsula's northern end comprises a bland concoction of grey apartment blocks and main roads, though there are a couple of stops worth making on the way north to the **Portas do Cerco** and the Chinese border at Zhuhai. It's not really something to do on foot; take bus #5, which runs from Avenida de Almeida Ribeiro in the city centre, and get off about halfway down Avenida Horta e Costa, from where it's only a short walk north to the Kun Iam Temple.

Kun Iam Temple

Entered through a banyan-planted courtyard, the splendid **Kun Iam Temple** (daily 7am–6pm; free) on Avenida do Coronel Mesquita is one of the most interesting in either Hong Kong or Macau. Dedicated to the Buddhist goddess of mercy (also known as Kwun Yum or Guan Yin), the temple complex is around 400 years old and was the venue for the signing of the first-ever **Sino-American treaty** in 1844. Though the buildings are of the usual heavy stone construction, their roofs are lined with elaborate and colourful porcelain tiles depicting folk tales and historical scenes. Inside the third hall are statues of Kun Iam herself, dressed in Chinese bridal robes and pearls, surrounded by **eighteen Boddhisatvas** (of which Kun Iam was also one), those who had attained the right to enter paradise but chose to stay on earth to help humanity. If you want your fortune told, shake one of the cylinders on the fortune-teller's desk in the main temple until a bamboo sliver falls out, when it's matched with the "correct" fortune hanging behind the desk in return for a few *patacas* – you'll need to find a translator. Another traditional way of acquiring good luck used to be to turn the stone balls in the mouths of the lions on the main steps three times to the left, though both are now fenced off. Directly opposite the temple is an excellent **vegetarian restaurant**, open through the day (see p.312).

Lin Fong Temple and Museu Lin Zexu

Walk back northwest to Avenida do Almirante Lacerda and take the #5 bus as it runs on up past Asia's only **canidrome** (dog track) to the **Lin Fong Temple** (daily 7am–6pm; free) – smaller than Kun Iam's and predominantly Taoist. First established in 1592 to provide overnight accommodation for officials travelling between Macau and Guangzhou, it has a fine nineteenth-century facade and altars dedicated to the god of war, Kuan Kong, and **Lin Zexu**, the official who tried to stamp out the nineteenth-century opium trade by destroying British supplies of the drug (see Contexts, p.325), only to be blamed for precipitating the first Opium War and exiled to China's far northwest. Off the temple's forecourt, **Museu Lin Zexu** (Tues–Sun 9am–5pm; MOP$5) displays an overtly staid collection of documents and period artefacts, though read some of the translations and you'll find some astounding facts. The account books for 1830–1839, for instance, show that the opium trade cost the Chinese treasury between seven and eight million silver pieces annually, amply illustrating why the Chinese court was keen to stop the trade - and why British traders and local Chinese merchants wanted to keep it going.

The Portas do Cerco (Barrier Gate)

Bus #5 from Lin Fong Miu runs through some less edifying parts of the Macau peninsula, primarily apartments and roadworks, before stopping outside the **Portas do Cerco** ("Siege Gate", though referred to in English as the Barrier Gate), which marks the border with China. A gate here has always marked the entrance to Portuguese territory, even when the old city walls were much further south. Once, all you could do was peer through the gate at the other side. These days the original stucco gate has been removed to a small park nearby and replaced with a far less romantic modern terminal building, thronged with queues of people and goods trucks that line up all day in both directions. If you're planning to cross, you'll need to get your China visa in advance – see p.25. The **Sun Yat-sen Memorial Park**, just to the west, sits against the canal that marks the border; there's a statue of the man outside, and an aviary, greenhouse and café inside.

Taipa

In the eighteenth century the island of **TAIPA** (*Tam Zai* in Cantonese)– just to the south of the peninsula – was actually three adjacent islands, whose sheltered harbour was an important anchorage for trading ships unloading their China-bound cargo at the mouth of the Pearl River. Silting of the channels between the islands eventually caused them to merge, providing valuable farming land. With the emergence of Hong Kong and the development of the Macau peninsula, Taipa was left to get on as best it could, and for decades it was a quiet, laid-back sort of place, with little industry – just a couple of fireworks factories – and not much to it. That all changed once it was decided to build the new airport off the island's east coast, and Taipa's centre is now largely a grim network of roads lined with residential and office tower blocks. It's the original village tucked into the south of the island that provides the main attraction these days, with its fine restaurants and colonial houses. Other attractions include the racetrack, the sprawling Pou Tai Un monastery, and a smaller Kun Iam temple with views of the Macau peninsula.

Across the bridges: western Taipa

Three bridges link Macau to Taipa: from east to west these are the four-kilometre-long Ponte de Amizade ("Friendship Bridge"), between the Jetfoil Terminal and eastern Taipa (a route used by the airport bus #AP1); the 2.5km Ponte Governador Bobre de Carvalho (also known in English as the Macau–Taipa Bridge), used by the other Macau-Taipa-Coloane buses; and the brand new Ponte Sai Van ("Sai Van Bridge"), from the southernmost tip of the peninsula to western Taipa.

Once over the central Ponte Governador Bobre de Carvalho, the first bus stop on the island is on a lozenge-shaped roundabout by the *Hyatt Regency* hotel. Uphill overlooking the water from here is the **University of Macau**, just down from which is a small **Kun Iam Temple**, with an image of the goddess of

Buses from Macau to Taipa and Coloane

For Taipa village, take bus #11 from Avenida de Almeida Ribeiro near Largo do Senado; bus #28A from the Jetfoil Terminal; or buses #22 or #33 from the *Hotel Lisboa*. All these drop off at a stop near the unmissable Taipa Stadium, just a short walk from the village. **For Coloane**, you need to catch bus #21 or #21A from the *Hotel Lisboa*; cutting straight across Taipa, these both travel down Coloane's west side to Coloane village, from where the #21A and #26 continue via Cheoc Van Beach through to Hác Sá Beach. If you're already at Taipa village, take bus #15, which runs around Coloane's east side via the *Westin Resort* and Hác Sá Beach, before terminating at Coloane village.

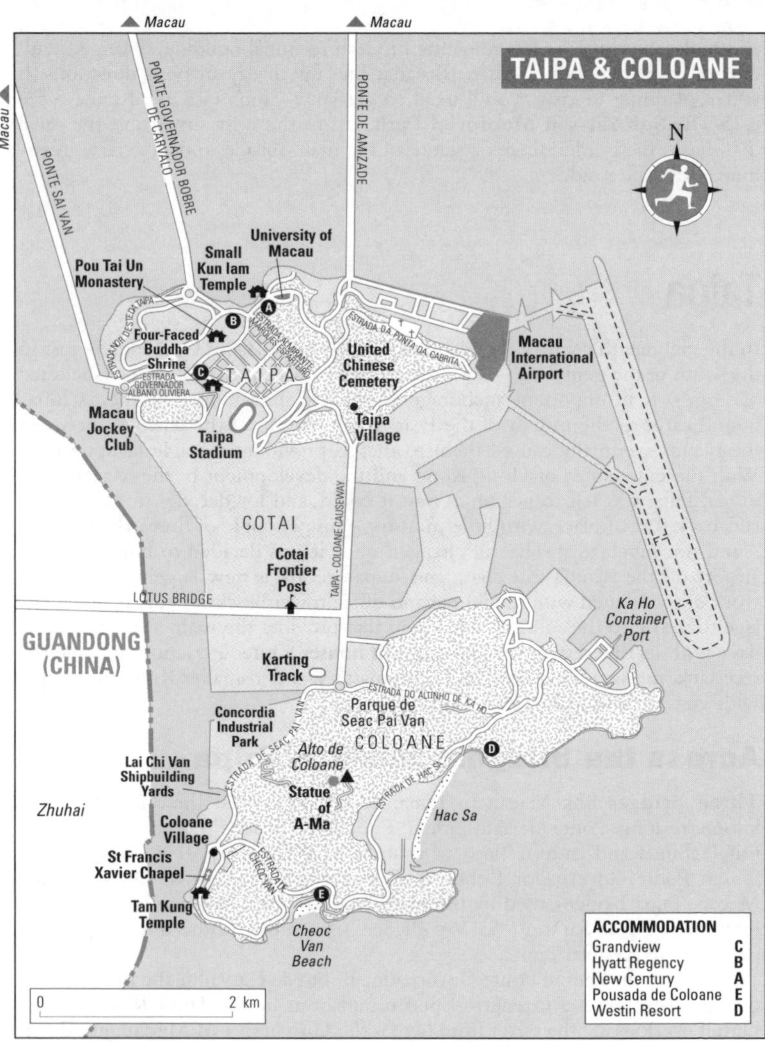

mercy in a pink-tiled altar, where food is offered on tiny red plastic saucers with matching chopsticks. Around 500m west from the roundabout, on Estrada Lou Lim Eoc, is the more interesting **Pou Tai Un Monastery** (daily 8am–9pm; free), the largest temple complex on the island and still expanding. The central part is the three-storey Buddhist Palace, whose ground floor is given over to Kun Iam and sports an unusual statue of the goddess with 42 hands; the middle floor houses reading and meditation rooms for the resident monks; while on the top floor there's a 5.4-metre high bronze Buddha. There's also a **vegetarian restaurant** open at lunchtime.

The next bus stop is the **racecourse**, operated by the Macau Jockey Club, set in an otherwise drab and lifeless part of town. The season runs from September to the end of July and a satellite dish beams the racing to other Asian countries, giving Hong Kong a run for its money. The **Four-Faced Buddha Shrine** outside the stadium is meant to bring luck to the punters.

Taipa village

Taipa's main point of interest is old **TAIPA VILLAGE**, set on what would once have been the island's south coast but now somewhat inland. There are only a few streets to the village, and a wander through them takes in a couple of faded squares and houses in narrow, traffic-free alleys. The many Portuguese and **Macanese restaurants** here are the main reason to visit at any time, though on Sundays (noon–9pm) the streets are packed with handicraft, souvenir and food stalls serving hot snacks, pastries and nougat, while outdoor shows are held in the main square.

You can get off the bus at stops all around the edge of the village, but the account below assumes that you use the northernmost stop, near the **stadium**, which was completely modernized to host the 2005 East Asia Games. From here, you head south past the local indoor produce market down 150m-long **Rua do Cunha**, a narrow pedestrianized street lined with restaurants, *pastelarias*, and shops selling daily necessities. This exits into little **Feira da Carmo**, the village square at whose centre is the covered, colonnaded nineteenth-century marketplace, recently restored; all around are old pastel-coloured homes and more places to eat.

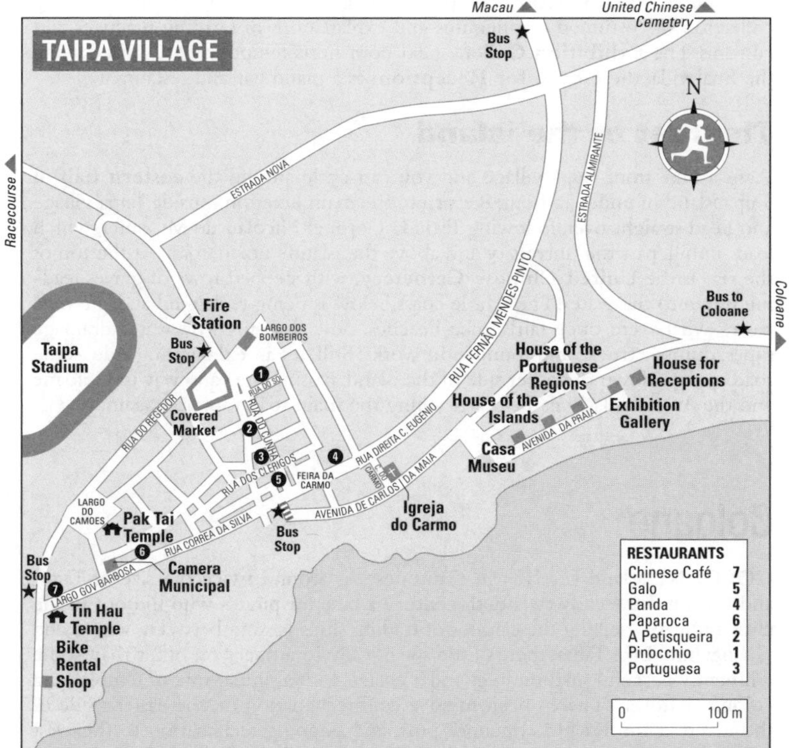

West off the end of Feira da Carmo it's 100m down Rua Correia da Silva, past the peppermint green Municipal Building, to the local **Tin Hau Temple**, a small grey-brick edifice whose doorway is lined with painted red paper. There's also a **bus stop** here, and a cheap Chinese-style café with outdoor tables dealing in noodle dishes, coffee and tea. If you head south to the seafront from the temple you'll find a **bike rental shop**, charging MOP$15 an hour (plus your passport as a deposit). If, however, you take one of the back lanes north, you'll end up by the large **Pak Tai Temple** dedicated to the eponymous god of the north. Inside, there's a carved altar whose figures are echoed in the impressive stone frieze above the entrance.

East from Feira da Carmo on Rua Correia da Silva, look for a flowing set of stairs lined with fig trees; at the top is the 100-year-old **Igreja do Carmo** ("Our Lady of Carmel Church"; daily except Tues 8am–5pm). Below here on Avenida da Praia, are the five early twentieth-century mansions of **Casa Museu** ("Taipa House Museum"; Tues–Sun 10am–6pm; MOP$5, free Sunday), which face south over an egret-infested lagoon to Coloane's container port and power station.

The first building shows off a "typical" Macanese home, the comfortably airy, wooden interior filled with tasteful period wooden furniture, a fully equipped kitchen and assorted chinoiserie and Portuguese-influenced bits and bobs. Next door, the **House of the Islands** displays old photos of Taipa and Coloane detailing their development from tiny fishing settlements to the present, touching also on the rise and fall of the fireworks and shipbuilding industries here. The middle villa, the **House of the Portuguese Regions**, is an unexciting collection of costumed mannequins and explanations of farming practices and customs. The **Exhibition Gallery** next door hosts temporary art shows, while the final villa, the **House for Receptions** is a piano bar and restaurant.

The rest of the island

Rent a bike from Taipa village and you can cycle around the **eastern half** of Taipa island in under an hour. Return to the main junction outside Taipa village and head straight over, following Estrada Coronel Nicolau de Mesquita, which leads uphill, past the university and above the island's north coast. At the top of the rise is the **United Chinese Cemetery**, with stepped rows of graves leading down to the water. The whole coast below is being reclaimed and the road passes what were once fairly nice beaches, now disfigured by water drainage pipes, dumper trucks and foundation works. Still, it's an exhilarating ride as the road swoops down the other side of the island, passing the causeway to Coloane and the Avenida da Praia before reaching the main road junction again.

Coloane

COLOANE island (*Lo Wan* in Cantonese) is around twice the size of Taipa, and was until the early twentieth century a base for pirates who hid out in the cliffs and caves, seizing the cargoes of trading ships passing between Macau and Guangzhou. Like Taipa, there's little specifically to attract you other than some eminently peaceful surroundings and a village with a similar mix of temples and colonial leftovers. There's been massive land reclamation on the eastern side of the island at the Ka Ho container port, and ongoing reclamation to the west of the **causeway** linking Taipa and Coloane (an area called **Cotai**), off which now sprouts an industrial park and a direct bridge west to Zhuhai in China for goods traffic only. Cotai is also earmarked for a new **gaming strip**, which plans to feature an underwater casino by 2009. Despite this, Coloane – dubbed Macau's "green lung" - remains relatively enticing, especially as the island has a couple of good sand **beaches** and the means to waste time gently in some fairly isolated bays and hills.

Parque de Seac Pai Van

On their way around the west coast of the island, buses pass the **Parque de Seac Pai Van** (Tues–Sun 9am–5.45pm; free), with gardens, ponds, pavilions, views out over the water, an aviary and the **Museum of Nature and Agriculture** (Tues–Sun 10am–4pm; free), whose most interesting feature is a display of medicinal herbs. Outdoors, you can clamber around some models of traditional farming equipment. Trails also provide good walking in the park, including one up to the heights of the **Alto de Coloane**, where the twenty-metre-high white marble statue of A-Ma is the tallest of this goddess in the world. To reach the statue, get off the bus at the Mobil petrol station and take the road marked Trilho do Coloane.

Coloane village

In winter most of the buses end their run in **COLOANE VILLAGE**, in a little central square surrounded by shops and cafés; a small covered market stands to one side. Signs point off to the few local attractions down cobbled roads, chickens scratch around the potholes, and a ramshackle air hangs over the low, crumbling Chinese houses, shrines and temples.

Right on the square you'll find *Lord Stowe's Bakery* (see p.309), a must for all lovers of Portuguese custard tarts; otherwise, walk down to the bottom of the square and turn left along an alley of shops which winds around to the tiny, pale-yellow chapel of **St Francis Xavier** (dawn to dusk), set back a few yards from the waterfront. The chapel dates from 1928 and honours the eponymous sixteenth-century missionary who passed through Macau on his way to China and Japan. It reveals its Chinese influences with an unusual painting of Mary and Jesus depicted as a traditional Chinese goddess holding a plump oriental baby. Out front is the **Eduardo Marques Square**, facing China, with a couple of good restaurants hidden under the colonnades either side. By the waterfront, the **monument** with embedded cannons commemorates the repelling of the last pirate attack in Coloane, which took place on July 12–13, 1910.

Further along the waterfront (to the left), past the library, a **Kun Iam Temple** is set back among the houses, though the **Tam Kung Temple** at the end of the road is more interesting, facing China across the narrow channel. The prize piece here is a whalebone shaped into a dragon boat with oarsmen – though the locally caught shark's snout runs it a close second.

Heading the other way from the square, there's a very quiet lane of stone houses facing the waterfront, over which are built corrugated iron and wooden homes painted red, green and blue. Little shrines on the roadside are to Cai Shen, the god of wealth; there's a very Southeast Asian feel to the smell of dried fish, the clacking of mah jong tiles, and red good-luck posters stuck up on doorways. The road terminates 100m on at Largo do Cais, where there's a small police station and a jetty jutting out towards China, beside which a couple of shops sell dried and salted fish. Around the corner is the **Lai Chi Van**

shipyard where wooden planks fashioned from tree trunks lie around waiting to be seasoned while work continues on half-finished boat hulls, all pervaded by the smell of sawdust and grease.

Beaches

Coloane's good **beaches** are all easily reached by bike from the village, or by **bus** – either the #21A, #26A, or #15 (which also continues past the beaches to the *Westin Resort*). Note, however, that swimming is not a good idea, as the water is contaminated by outflows from the heavily industrialized Pearl River Delta towns.

The closest sandy beach to the village is at **Cheoc Van**, just a couple of kilometres east. It's fairly well developed, featuring cafés, the *Pousada de Coloane* (see "Accommodation", p.306) and a swimming pool (daily 8am–9pm, Sun 8am–midnight; MOP$10). A few kilometres further east, however, **Hac Sa** is much the better choice. The grey-black sand beach (*hac sa* means "black sand") is very long and backed by a pine grove, with plenty of picnic places amid the trees, and a campsite. Around the bay, towards the *Westin Resort*, you can rent windsurfers and jet skis (MOP$250 for 30 minutes), while if you don't fancy the sea or sands there's a **sports and recreation complex** behind the beach (Mon–Sat 8am–9pm, Sun 8am–midnight), where a dip in the Olympic-size pool costs MOP$15. On the sands there's a beach bar, as well as a couple of **restaurants** near the bus stop (including the excellent *Fernando's*; see p.311), while at the northeastern end of the beach the upmarket *Westin Resort* complex and golf course sprawl across the headland. Just behind the recreation centre on Estrada de Hac Sa at the **Water Activities Centre** (daily 9am–6pm) you can hire paddle and rowing boats for a quick splash around the small Hác Sá Reservoir (MOP$20 for 20 minutes). There's also a small outdoor café selling sandwiches, soft drinks and beer, and some pleasant walking trails that meander around the surrounding wooded hills.

Places	
Barra	媽閣
Coloane	路環
Lago Sai Van	西灣湖
Lagos de Nam Van	南灣湖
Macau	澳門
Porto Exterior	外港
Porto Interior	內港
Taipa	氹仔
Zhuhai	珠海
Sights	
A-Ma Temple	媽祖閣
Casa Museu	氹仔住宅式博物館
Cemitério Protestante	基督教墳場
Cemetério São Miguel	西洋墳場
Cheoc Van	竹灣
Coloane village	路環市區
Fortaleza da Guia	東望洋山堡壘
Fortaleza do Monte	大炮台
Guia Hill	松山
Hác Sá beach	黑沙海灘

Hong Kung Temple	康公廟
Hotel Lisboa	葡京酒店
Igreja do Carmo	嘉模聖母教堂
Jai-Alai Casino	回力球娛樂場
Jardim Lou Lim Ieoc	盧廉若公園
Jardim Luís de Camões	白鴿巢賈梅士花園
Kun Iam Statue and Ecumenical Centre	觀音像 / 佛教文化中心
Kun Iam Temple	觀音堂
Largo do Senado	議事亭前地
Leal Senado	議事亭
Lin Fong Temple	連峰廟
Macau Cultural Centre	澳門文化中心
Macau Tower	澳門觀光塔
Museu de Macau	澳門博物館
Museu dos Bombeiros	消防博物館
Museu Lin Zexu	林則徐紀館
Museu Maritimo	海事博物館
Pak Tai Temple	北帝廟
Palácio do Governo	鄭家大屋
Parque de Seac Pai Van	石排灣郊野公園
Penha Chapel	主教山教堂
Pousada de São Tiago	聖地牙哥
Pou Tai Un Monastery	菩提禪院
Portas do Cerco	關閘
Racecourse	賽馬常
St Francis Xavier chapel	路環聖方濟各教堂
Santa Casa de Misericórdia	仁慈堂大樓
Santo Antonio	聖安東尼堂
São Domingos	聖母玫瑰堂
São Paulo	大三巴牌坊
Sé	大堂
Sun Yat-sen Memorial House	國父紀念館
Taipa village	氹仔舊城區
Tin Hau Temple	天后古廟
Tourist Activity Centre	旅遊活動中心
University of Macau	澳門大學
Water Activities Centre	水上活動中心
Streets	
Avenida da Amizade	友誼大馬路
Avenida da Republica	民國大馬路
Avenida de Almeida Ribeiro	新馬路
Praia Grande	南灣大馬路
Rua Central	龍嵩正街
Rua da Felicidade	福隆新街
Rua das Estalagens	草堆街
Rua de Cinco de Outubro	十月初五街
Rua do Almirante Sergio	河邊新街
Rua Sul do Mercado de São Domingos	板樟堂街
Transport	
China Ferry terminal	蛇口碼頭
Jetfoil Terminal	港澳碼頭
Macau airport	澳門機場

Macau listings

Macau listings

Accommodation

There's a huge number of places to stay in Macau, and you should always be able to find somewhere to stay outside of peak periods (such as Easter and during the Grand Prix). During major festivals such as Chinese New Year, hotels lose custom to Hong Kong's bright lights and might actually offer discounts.

Prices here are much better value than in Hong Kong – at the bottom end of the market you'll often be able to find a self-contained room for around the same price as a sweatbox Kowloon dormitory bed. Note, however, that **weekend rates** are always around thirty percent higher than midweek. Prices below are for the **cheapest double in high season**, excluding the fifteen-percent tax added by top-end places.

Two things make **booking in advance** advisable: firstly, you'll generally get a discounted rate on mid- to upper-range hotel rooms this way; and weekends and public holidays are always busy with gamblers coming over from Hong Kong, when even the cheaper end of the market may be full. Advance bookings in Hong Kong (not for the cheapest hotels) can be made through most travel agents – see p.272, or try Beng Seng Travel (☎2540 3838) at the Macau Ferry Terminal, Shun Tak Centre, Sheung Wan. You can also try dealing directly with hotels and guesthouses themselves in Macau; many can be persuaded to drop their advertised rates a bit if you call in advance. If you've arrived without a booking, there are **courtesy phones** in the Jetfoil Terminal for the larger hotels.

Guesthouses and hotels

The bulk of Macau's **budget hotels** (called either a *vila*, *hospedaria* or *pensão*) lie around the **central peninsula** between the Porto Interior and Largo do Senado – take buses #3, #3A, or #10A from the Jetfoil Terminal. This is an atmospheric area, full of narrow lanes, cheap restaurants, and street markets, though the atmosphere can be a little sleazy too – hotel lobbies are often adorned with a bevy of prostitutes. Most accommodation here is aimed at weekend gamblers from Hong Kong and China and the rooms – even within a single hotel – can vary between perfectly acceptable and dark, noisy, and grubby. If you find yourself being waved away before you've even reached the reception, it's probably because none of the staff speak English and don't fancy the trouble of booking you in – you'll get around this if you can speak some Chinese (even Mandarin).

You'll have no such problems with **mid-range** and **top-of-the-range** places, some of which offer very good value for money, especially midweek when there may be **discounts** of up to fifty percent available – always check websites for promotional deals. Most upmarket places operate airport shuttle buses, and often casino buses too. The biggest concentration is in **eastern Macau** between the Lagos Nam Van and the Jetfoil Terminal, where many rooms come with good views. There are only a few choices on the **southern peninsula** and the islands of **Taipa** and **Coloane**, and they're all fairly expensive – although the idea of staying at a beach hotel on Coloane is appealing.

East: Lagos Nam Van to the Jetfoil Terminal

The places listed below are marked on the map on pp.230–231.

Beverly Plaza **Av. do Dr Rodrigo Rodrigues 70 ⓣ782288, ⓦwww.beverlyplaza.com.** Just a few doors down from the *Lisboa*, this CTS-run hotel offers 300 good-sized but nondescript rooms, with all the usual facilities – bar a pool and casino. It has its own 24hr coffee shop and offers good midweek deals. MOP$1000

Golden Dragon **Rua de Malaca 199 ⓣ361999, ⓕ361333.** One of Macau's newest upmarket ventures, this mainland-Chinese-run hotel comes with its own casino and is big on opulence and restaurants but a little short on service. MOP$1200, harbour views MOP$1600.

Grandeur **Rua de Pequim 199 ⓣ781233, ⓦwww.hotelgrandeur.com; Hong Kong reservations ⓣ2857 2846.** A CTS-run business hotel with all the trimmings, including a revolving restaurant, sauna, pool, gym and coffee shop. MOP$700

Guia **Estrada do Eng. Trigo 1–5 ⓣ513888, ⓕ559822.** Smart choice with views (if your room's high enough), on the southern fringes of the Guia hill, with an atrium, swish lifts and triple rooms on offer. Decently priced for a three-star hotel, and with a shuttle bus to the *Lisboa* to save you the walk. MOP$450

Holiday Inn Macau **Rua de Pequim 82–86 ⓣ783333, ⓦwww.holiday-inn.com.** Few surprises here – except the low price – with large well-equipped rooms, and an anonymous feel. It has a sauna, bar, pool and casino and a great location surrounded by 24-hour restaurants, supermarkets and a swathe of casinos. MOP$790

Kingsway **Rua de Luis Gonzaga Gomes 230 ⓣ702888, ⓦwww.hotelkingsway.com.mo.** This upmarket spot bristles with facilities – 24hr coffee shop, upmarket casino, sauna and health spa, and well-appointed rooms with views of the city or Taipa. MOP$600

Mandarin Oriental **Av. da Amizade ⓣ567888, ⓦwww.mandarinoriental.com/macau.** Outstanding comforts in a resort tailor-made for families (children's club, poolside restaurant), corporate groups (a team-building climbing wall and trapeze) and the more traditional Macau tourist (casino, popular bar). Guests are pampered with a staff to room ratio of 1:1, and a renowned spa. Although close to the jetfoil it's a fair distance to walk to the old part of town. MOP$2000

Metropole **Av. da Praia Grande 493–501 ⓣ388166, ⓦwww.mctshmi.com.** This well-placed, central hotel is just back from the Praia Grande, and good value if you're looking for rooms with all the trimmings at a lowish cost. It also has a fast food centre, serving *dim sum*, roast meats and *congee* 8am–10.30pm. MOP$530

Mondial **Rua do Antonio Basto 8-10 ⓣ566866, ⓕ514083.** Sixty-four good-sized doubles, and six singles with fridge, air-con, video, TV and telephone. The decor may be old-fashioned and the wallpaper peeling, but the rooms are light, and clean. Take bus #12 from the Jetfoil Terminal. MOP$300

Vila Nam Loon **Rua do Dr Pedro José Lobo 30 ⓣ712573.** Very clean and bright budget hotel; rooms have attached bathrooms but are so small that the beds almost fill them. MOP$230.

Presidente **Av. da Amizade ⓣ553888, ⓦwww.hotelpresident.com.mo.** This ageing tower caters mostly to a business clientele, and is perfectly serviceable if not exactly plush. Harbour views are soon to be blocked by a new hotel going up opposite. MOP$660

Royal **Estrada da Vitoria 2–4 ⓣ552222, ⓦwww.hotelroyal.com.mo.** An ageing but good-value high-rise, close to the Fortaleza da Guia. A ten-minute walk from Senate Square, it's well equipped, with standard and deluxe doubles, suites and a pool. MOP$680

Tin Tin Vila **Rua Do Comandante Mate E Oliveira 17 ⓣ710064.** A few doors down from the Café Nata, this small guesthouse offers cell-like but fairly clean, airy rooms with firm beds, some with their own bathroom and some with shared facilities. Cheap and well positioned, but no English spoken. Air-con use costs an extra $10 per night. MOP$180

The Centre: around the Porto Interior and Largo do Senado

The places listed below are marked on the map on pp.230–231.

Central Av. de Almeida Ribeiro 264 ⓣ373888. One of Macau's oldest hotels, open since 1928, with hundreds of rooms on seven floors. Overall this is a gloomy, elderly place with half-hearted air-con and hot water but the location, friendly staff, en-suite rooms with TV make it fair value for money. MOP$160.

East Asia Rua da Madeira 1 ⓣ922433, ⓦwww.mctshmi.com. In the heart of old Macau, off Rua de C. de Outubro, the East Asia has a lobby full of mainland prostitutes but the serviceable singles, doubles and triples all have air-con, en-suite bathroom and telephone and are reasonably good value for money. MOP$300

Florida Beco Do Pa Ralelo 2 ⓣ923198, ⓕ923199. At night these standard two-star hotel rooms are bathed in pink and red lights from the neon Florida sign, and the lobby is packed with mainland prostitutes. But the rooms are large and clean and the hotel is well located. MOP$250

Hou Kong Travessa das Virtudes 1 ⓣ937555, ⓕ338884. This basic hotel has clean, well-equipped rooms – bathroom, TV, telephone, shampoo and toothbrush – and fairly welcoming service. MOP$330

Pensão Ka Va Calcada de São João 5 ⓣ323063 or 329355. Good budget choice on lane running from the Sé to the upper end of Avenida Praia Grande, with 28 plain rooms with wooden shutters, en-suite bathroom, air-con and TV. Rear rooms are preferable to streetside ones, which can be noisy; a few also prone to damp. MOP$150.

Ko Wah Floor 3 Rua Felicidade 71, ⓣ930755 or 375599. Charming budget place accessed by lift from the cupboard-sized street lobby, with plastic flowers and floral bedspreads offsetting small rooms and elderly furnishings. Check a few rooms out, as some are much better than others. A good budget choice. MOP$180.

Man Va Rua da Felicidade ⓣ388655, ⓕ342179. A brand-new hotel with clean, modern rooms; the bathrooms are spacious and the management helpful, though they don't speak English. Excellent value for money, and worth the slightly higher than usual tag for a guesthouse. MOP$300

Sun Sun Praça Ponte e Horta 14–16 ⓣ939393, ⓕ938822. Smart hotel with the upper floors having a view of the inner harbour, inoffensively furnished rooms with TV and bath, and plenty of marble and wood in the lobby. Bus #3A from the ferry terminal stops just outside. MOP$600

Vila Universal Rua Felicidade 73 ⓣ573247, ⓕ375602. Clean, basic rooms in this elderly guesthouse, priced according to size. MOP$150-190.

Hospedaria Vong Kung Rua das Lorchas 235 ⓣ574016. Macau's cheapest hostel, sole survivor of the days when this street catered to visiting sailors from the port opposite. The dusty mosquito-ridden singles and doubles have fan, sink, membrane-thin walls and wobbly beds; for an extra $5 the friendly owners will heat up a pan of water for you since the shared shower only dispenses cold water. MOP$60.

Southern peninsula

The places listed below are marked on the map on p.289.

Lisboa Av. de Lisboa 2–4 ⓣ577666, ⓦwww.hotelisboa.com. A monstrous orange circular drum (with adjacent annexe) that has roughly 1000 rooms and a bundle of 24hr casinos, shops, bars and restaurants, outdoor pool and sauna – some people never set foot outside the front door. Rooms in the rear block don't have the same atmosphere, but are cheaper than those at the front – all have nice bathrooms and decent furnishings. MOP$850, harbour views MOP$1050

Pousada de São Tiago Av. da República ⓣ378111, ⓦwww.saotiago.com.mo. A gloriously preserved seventeenth-century fortress converted into an upmarket hotel at the foot of the peninsula. Balconied rooms with views cost around 300ptcs extra; there's a swimming pool and terrace bar. You'll need to book well in advance for the weekend. MOP$1600

Ritz Rua do Comendador Kou Ho Neng ⓣ339955, ⓦwww.mctshmi.com. Rather glitzy for a CTS-managed hotel, this 163-room

block has superb views from the terrace and some rooms, plus an indoor pool, billiards room, Jacuzzi and mini-golf among other amenities. It's also the one luxury hotel in Macau likely to have a room at short notice. MOP$980

Taipa

The places listed below are marked on the map on p.294.

Grandview Estrada Governador Albano de Oliveira ⓣ837788, ⓦwww.grandview-hotel.com. Diagonally across from the Jockey Club and Buddha statue, the only real downside of this otherwise excellent business hotel is a location in a soulless part of town, though it perks up on race days. MOP$840

Hyatt Regency Estrada Almirante 2, Marques Esparteiro ⓣ831234, ⓦwww.macau.hyatt.com. Just over the bridge from Macau (all the Taipa buses run past it), it's what you'd expect from the Hyatt chain: smart rooms, casino, landscaped swimming pool, attentive staff and a respected restaurant, the *Macanese Flamingo*. MOP$1200

New Century Av. Padre Tomás Pereira 889 ⓣ831111, ⓦwww.newcenturyhotel-macau.com. Enormous five-star hotel across from the Hyatt, with similar high-class levels of comfort. Views are good, and the 24hr Silver Court dishing up a wide range of Asian food here is also highly recommended. MOP$1200

Coloane

The places listed below are marked on the map on p.294.

Pousada de Coloane Praia de Cheoc Van ⓣ882143, ⓦwww.hotelpcoloane.com.mo. A quirky hotel with 22 rooms, each with their own terrace overlooking the beach tucked into Cheoc Van bay. The rooms on the top floor are enormous with sofa, table and king-sized bed. It's a bit remote as, apart from its own Portuguese restaurant and a stretch of sand, there's not much else here. You'll need to use taxis since it's a steep climb up to the main road to catch a bus and there's no shuttle service. MOP$700

Westin Resort Estrada de Hac Sa ⓣ871111, ⓦwww.westin.com/macau. The *Westin* lies at the far end of *Hác Sá's* narrow beach – a swathe of terraced rooms spread across the hillside. Midweek it's the terrain of corporate groups and fairly quiet, and at the weekend it fills up with Hong Kong families. The hotel offers Macau's only 18-hole golf course, two pools and a Jacuzzi. All the modern, spacious rooms have up-to-date technology, comfortable beds, a terrace and beach or sea views. You're a little stranded once the sun goes down, though Fernando's (see p.311) is just a fifteen-minute walk along the beach and the hotel has three restaurants. MOP$2100

Eating and drinking

Although most of the **food** eaten in Macau is Cantonese, the enclave also enjoys a unique **Macanese cuisine** – a blend of influences from China, Portugal and Portuguese colonies from Brazil to Goa. Sometimes this manifests itself as straightforward imported dishes, such as Portuguese *caldo verde* (cabbage and potato soup), *bacalhau* (dried salted cod), *pudim flán* (crème caramel), or grilled steak, sausages, chicken, or sardines; African-influenced spicy prawns and "African Chicken" (served in a peppery peanut sauce); or *feijoada* from Brazil, an elaborate meal made from meat, beans, sausage and vegetables. However, many cooks cross-fertilize these influences with **Cantonese** ingredients and dishes, creating pigeon, quail, duck and seafood dishes that are ostensibly "Chinese" but unlike anything you'll find elsewhere.

Other Portuguese culinary influences you'll find here are freshly baked **bread** served with meals, and **Portuguese wine** to wash it all down – fine, heavy reds, chilled whites and slightly sparkling *vinho verde*, as well as any number of **ports** and brandies; and you can get decent **coffee** too. In most places, the **menu** is in Portuguese and English as well as Chinese; check the lists overleaf for descriptions of food you don't recognize.

Vegetarians should do well for themselves. Every Portuguese restaurant serves excellent mixed salads; and most places will fry eggs and serve them up with some of the best French fries around. In addition, there are a few Chinese vegetarian eateries in town, too.

Macau also has a reputation for **cakes**, the most famous of which are Portuguese-style **custard tarts**, or *natas*, a light pastry cup filled with set baked custard and then briefly grilled to darken the top. There are also numerous **biscuit shops** – *pastelarias* – in the centre of town on Rua da Felicidade and around São Paulo; you'll find them by the crowds of Hong Kongers busy filling up on presents. Their best products are peanut or sesame toffee, and almond biscuits baked in a mould, but they also sell savouries such as bright red pressed sheets of baked pork.

Finally, if you're after an ice-cream on a hot day, there's only one serious choice: the Italian-style *Lemon Cello* on Travessa Sao Domingos (just off Largo do Senado), where a cone of peach, vanilla, tiramisù or mango sorbet will set you back MOP$15.

People eat out earlier in Macau than in Hong Kong – you should aim to be at the restaurant by 8pm at the latest – and they rarely stay open later than 11–11.30pm. Meals are generally good value, certainly compared to Hong Kong. Soup or salad, a main course, half a bottle of wine and coffee comes to around MOP$200 almost everywhere; dessert and a glass of port adds another MOP$50 – though two courses in most restaurants will fill you to the brim

A Portuguese/Macanese menu reader

Basics and snacks

Arroz – Rice
Batatas fritas – French fries
Legumes – Vegetables
Manteiga – Butter
Omeleta – Omelette
Ovos – Eggs
Pimenta – Pepper
Prego – Steak roll
Sal – Salt
Salada mista – Mixed salad
Sandes – Sandwiches

Meat

Almondegas – Meatballs
Bife – Steak
Chouriço – Spicy sausage
Coelho – Rabbit
Cordoniz – Quail
Costeleta – Chop, cutlet
Dobrada – Tripe
Figado – Liver
Galinha – Chicken
Pombo – Pigeon
Porco – Pork
Salsicha – Sausage

Fish and seafood

Ameijoas – Clams
Bacalhau – Dried, salted cod
Camarões – Shrimp
Carangueijo – Crab
Gambas – Prawns
Linguado – Sole
Lulas – Squid
Meixilhões – Mussels
Pescada – Hake
Sardinhas – Sardines

Soups

Caldo verde – Green cabbage and potato soup, often served with spicy sausage
Sopa álentejana – Garlic and bread soup with a poached egg
Sopa de mariscos – Shellfish soup
Sopa de peixe – Fish soup

Cooking terms

Assado – Roasted
Cozido – Boiled, stewed
Frito – Fried
Grelhado – Grilled
No forno – Baked

Specialities

Camarões – Huge grilled prawns with chillies and peppers
Cataplana – Pressure-cooked seafood with bacon, sausage and peppers (named after the dish in which it's cooked)
Cozido á Portuguesa – Boiled casserole of mixed meats (including things like pig's trotters), rice and vegetables
Galinha á Africana (African chicken) – Chicken baked or grilled with peppers and chillies; either "dry", with spices baked in, or with a thick, spicy sauce
Galinha á Portuguesa – Chicken baked with eggs, potatoes, onion and saffron in a mild, creamy curry sauce
Feijoada – Rich Brazilian stew of beans, pork, sausage and vegetables
Pasteis de bacalhau – Cod fishcakes, deep-fried
Porco á álentejana – Pork and clams in a stew
Pudim flán – Crème caramel
Arroz doce – Portuguese rice pudding

Drinks

Água mineral – Mineral water
Café – Coffee
Chá – Tea
Cerveja – Beer
Sumo de laranja – Orange juice
Vinho – Wine (*tinto* red; *branco*, white)
Vinho do Porto – Port (both red and white)
Vinho verde – Green wine – ie a young wine, slightly sparkling and very refreshing. It can be white, red or rosé in Portugal but in Macau it's usually white

Meals

Almoço – Lunch
Comidas – Meals
Jantar – Dinner
Prato dia/Menu do dia – Dish/menu of the day

since servings are large. Eating Macanese specialities – such as curried crab and grilled prawns – pushes the price up quite a bit. A fifteen-percent service charge is usually included in the bill except in the cheapest places. Be warned that many restaurants, bars and cafés don't take credit cards.

Cafés

You'll find small **cafés** all over Macau, many serving a mixture of local Cantonese food and Portuguese-style snacks – expect to pay around MOP$50 a head for coffee and a cake. Some are known as *Casa de Pasto*, a traditional Portuguese workers' dining room, though in Macau they're usually Chinese in cuisine and atmosphere. For late-night meals and snacks, many hotels have **24-hour coffee shops**, serving bleary-eyed gamblers: the handiest is the one in the *Lisboa*, but there are others in the *Kingsway* and *Beverly Plaza*, too.

Café Girassol **Mandarin Oriental, Av de Amizade. See map on pp.280–281.** High-quality café with lots of choice on the menu, as well as a buffet on most days. Open 24 hours, except on Thursday, when it closes at midnight.

Margeret's Café e Nata **Rua Comandante Mata e Oliveira. See map on p.289.** On a small alley between Av. Dom João IV and Rua P. J. Lobo, just northwest of the *Lisboa*, this Macau institution has street-side benches for munching inexpensive chunky sandwiches, baguettes, home-baked quiches, muffins and some of the best *natas* in town. Also a whole range of iced teas, coffees and fruit juices. Mon–Sat 6.30am–8pm, Sun 10am–7pm.

Lord Stowes Bakery **Coloane Town Square, Coloane.** Although British-owned, this is one of the best places to eat *natas*. The recipe is originally Portuguese, but this bakery claims to use a secret, improved version without animal fat. Buy takeaways from the bakery itself, or sit down for coffee and a light meal at their café around the corner. Daily 7am–5pm.

Leitaria I Son **Largo do Senado 7. See map on pp.280–281.** Look for the neon cow sign. A popular dairy-products café, with an endless variety of inexpensive milk puddings, ice-cream and milkshakes, as well as fried-egg breakfasts and tea with real milk. No English menu. Daily 9am–11pm.

Noite e Dia **Hotel Lisboa, Av. de Lisboa 2–4. See map on pp.280–281.** The *Lisboa's* splendid 24hr coffee shop, serving everything from *dim sum* and breakfast to snacks and meals.

O'Barril 2 **Travessa de S. Domingos 12 (the alleyway running between the Sé and Largo do Senado). See map on p.289.** Solid, satisfying well-cooked snacks, sandwiches and soups. Portions are large and prices cheap. Popular with the Portuguese expat crowd. Mon–Fri noon–11pm, Sat & Sun 10am–11pm.

Osgatos Terrace **Pousada de São Tiago, Av. da República. See map on p.289.** Pricey cheesecakes and cocktails served on the *pousada* terrace along with delicacies such as baked snails with herb butter. Daily 11am–11pm.

Ou Mun Café **Travessa de S. Domingos 12. See map on p.289.** Debatable whether either this or adjacent *O'Barril 2* is the best place in town for an excellent, inexpensive coffee and cake. Tues–Sun 8am–8pm.

Sing Hoi **Ave. Xian Xing Hai, near the Cultural Centre. See map on pp.280–281.** Despite the Chinese name and clientele, this café is one of several in this street that serve good coffee, sandwiches, and Macanese cakes through the day.

Teng Tai Fong **Av. do Dr Rodrigo Rodrigues 118.** An excellent and inexpensive 24hr Taiwanese noodle and dumpling shop with plenty of vegetarian choices just down from the *Beverly Plaza*.

Restaurants

The listings below concentrate on the enclave's excellent Portuguese and Macanese restaurants, but there are other options such as Italian, Indian and Chinese should you tire of this kind of food. Inexpensive wine can be bought in all Macau's restaurants, Portuguese or not.

Macanese and Portuguese

All the places below are marked on the map on p.289.

Alfonso III **Rua Central 11A ☎586272.** Split-level café-restaurant specializing in Portuguese food. Provincial dishes feature, like a mammoth, oily serving of Álentejo pork with clams, drenched in fresh coriander. Check the daily list of specials to see what the mainly Portuguese clientele is eating; expect to pay MOP$40–60 per dish. Daily noon–3pm & 6.30–10.30pm; closed Sundays.

Clube Militar **Av. da Praia Grande 975 ☎714000.** This private club within the São Francisco barracks has a dining room open to the public and offers a grand colonial setting with formal staff and sparkling silver service. The Portuguese food is competent and expensive (around MOP$300 a head for a full dinner), though there's a good-value daily three-course set menu. Alternatively, go for afternoon tea or a drink – they have a large selection of ports. There's a "no sportsware" dress code. Daily noon–3pm & 7–11pm.

Fat Siu Lau **Rua da Felicidade 64 ☎573585.** One of Macau's oldest and most famous restaurants, with pigeon the speciality, best eaten with their excellent French fries. Relaxed atmosphere, but – pigeon apart – not the best food in Macau, whatever the adverts say; around MOP$50 for mains. Daily 11am– midnight.

Henri's Galley **Av. da República 4 ☎556251.** Unexciting decor, but the spicy prawns are renowned as the best in Macau. Alternatively try the roast pigeon, quail or curried crab. The African chicken and *Galinha à Portuguesa* are also terrific at MOP$40 a serving. Go for an indoor window seat, or pavement table with waterfront view. Daily 11am–11pm.

A Lorcha **Rua do Almirante Sergio 289 ☎313193.** Near the Maritime Museum, this attractive wood-beamed restaurant serves outstanding, moderately priced Portuguese food, and is consequently always busy – it's best to reserve in advance for lunch when the Portuguese business community is out in force. There's a large menu of staples, including *serradura,* a spectacular cream and biscuit dessert. 12.30–3.30pm & 7–11.30pm; closed Tues.

O Porto Interior **Rua do Almirante Sergio 259 ☎967770.** Like the nearby *A Lorcha*, this smart, relaxed place excells in mid-priced Portuguese and Macanese fare, served amid a mix of Chinese wooden screens and terracotta tiling. Noon–3pm & 7–11.30pm; closed Tues.

Platão **Travessa Sao Domingos 3 ☎331818.** Set back in a street running between the Sé and Largo do Senado, this lively, pricey restaurant boasts a great sit-out courtyard in front, perfect for a beer. The menu is colonial Portuguese and includes cod soufflé, baked duck rice, and – with advance warning – suckling pig. At least MOP$60 for mains. Tues–Sun noon–11pm.

Praia Grande **Praça Lobo d'Avila, Av. da Praia Grande ☎973022.** One of Macau's best Portuguese restaurants, whose upstairs rooms have a good harbour view. The staff are pleasant and the food is excellent, featuring pan-fried clams with pork, baked onion soup, and grilled codfish. Mains MOP$55 plus. Daily noon–11pm.

Safari **Patio do Cotovelo 14 ☎574313.** A pleasant unpretentious Macanese restaurant with a 1970s feel. Serves inexpensive Portuguese staples and a few French dishes, such as baked snails and onion soup. Their set meals of soup, a main, dessert/coffee for MOP$50 is good value. Daily 11am–11pm.

Solmar **Av. da Praia Grande 512 ☎574391.** Long-established and reliable Macanese restaurant with excellent seafood (including grilled perch and fish soufflé), as well as all the other classics. Prices slightly higher than average. Daily 11am–11pm.

Taipa

All the restaurants below are marked on the map on p.294.

Galo **Rua do Cunha 45 ☎827423.** Decorated in Portuguese country style with the cock (*galo*) – the national emblem of Portugal – much in evidence. The photographic menu sports plenty of boiled meats and pig's trotters, but mainstream dishes include steaks, great grilled squid or crab, and large mixed salads; around MOP$60 a serving. Mon–Fri 10.30am–3.30pm & 5.30–10.30pm, Sat & Sun 10.30am–10.30pm.

Panda **Rua Direita Carlos Eugénio 4–8 ☎827338.** Reasonably priced and with good sardines but it betrays its Chinese influence in the kitchen – unless you order your courses separately, everything comes at once, and not always with good grace. Daily 11am–11pm.

Paparoca Rua Correia da Silva 57-59 ⓣ827636. Blue-tiled walls, and an inexpensive menu which takes in shrimp balls, clam chowder, shrimp *piri-piri*, and Macanese chicken. Daily noon–9pm.

A Petisqueira Rua de S. João 15 ⓣ825354. With its relaxing green interior, this friendly, well-regarded Portuguese restaurant has all the usual favourites including their popular fresh cheese and whole grilled sea bass (the latter MOP$70). Mon–Sat noon–3.30pm & 7pm–11pm, Sun noon–11pm.

Pinocchio Rua do Sol 4 ⓣ827128. Taipa's best-known Macanese restaurant, which is essentially a big brick canteen with an inexpensive menu. Fish cakes, crab and prawns are good, but the crispy roast duck is what it's known for. Daily noon–midnight.

Portugesa Rua do Cunha ⓣ825594. Low-key, good-value family-run place specializing in Macanese staples, including seafood rice, pork and bean stew, rabbit, and roast suckling pig. Daily noon–late.

Coloane

Espaco Off the main village square at Lisboa Rua das Gaivotas 8 ⓣ882226. Welcoming and deservedly popular two-storey restaurant with excellent daily specials and affordable prices – try their flambéed Portuguese sausage. Mon–Fri noon–3pm & 6.30–10pm, and Sat–Sun noon–10.30pm.

Fernando's Hac Sa Beach 9 ⓣ882531. The sign is hidden, but this is very close to the bus stop, at the end of the car park, under the Coca-Cola sign – the nearest to the sea in a small line of cafés. There's a huge barn-like dining room; clams and crab are house specials, the grilled chicken is enormous and succulent. It's an institution with local expats, who fill it on Sundays with their large lunch parties. Slightly pricier than average. Daily noon–10.30pm.

Pousada de Coloane Praia de Cheoc Van ⓣ882143. Reserve a table if you want to eat at this small, mid-priced place, which is deservedly popular for the *cataplana* dishes and other seafood specialities. Wonderful views and quite kitsch inside with disco mirror balls. Daily noon–10.30pm.

Chinese

Café Nga Tim/Chan Chi Mei Largo Eduardo Marques, in front of the Xavier Chapel, Coloane Village. A nice place to sit outside on a warm evening and enjoy a glass of Portuguese wine, while you choose from the mixed bag of Chinese, Macanese and Portuguese dishes. You can also pick from the Chinese seafood menu from the restaurant just behind it, *Chan Chi Mei*, which is run by the same owner. Daily noon—1am.

Fook Lam Mun Av. Dr Mario Soares 259 ⓣ786622. See map on pp.280–281. Next to the *President hotel*, this is the place to come for Cantonese seafood specialities. High prices (although more affordable in the morning and at lunchtime for *dim sum*) but considered one of the best in town. Mon–Fri 11am–3pm & 5.30–11pm, Sat & Sun 8.30am–3pm & 5.30–11pm.

Long Kei Largo do Senado 7B, under the colonnade ⓣ573970. See map on pp.280–281. A huge, inexpensive Cantonese menu, as well as some Western-influenced snacks. Daily 11am–10.30pm.

Shing Hoi Veng Kong Siu Travessa Sao Domingos 1a, at the entrance to the Platao's courtyard. See map on p.289. A clean white-tiled canteen serving inexpensive Shanghaiese stir-fries, dumplings, and meat dishes; you need to get here early or queue outside. No English sign but easy to find. From 6pm Tues–Sun.

Other Asian restaurants

Ali Curry House Av. da Republica 4 ⓣ555865. See map on p.289. An enormous menu of inexpensive mixed Indian and Portuguese dishes with curries made of everything from crabs to mutton. The pleasant green and purple interior is offset by the air-con, which sounds like a rocket taking off. Daily 12.30pm–11.30pm.

Kathmandu Rua Central 8 ⓣ6558574. See map on p.289. Macau's sole Nepali restaurant, this low-key place whips up good naan, curries, kebabs and tandoori dishes at low prices. Closed last Monday of each month.

Kruatheque Rua de Henrique de Macedo ⓣ330448. See map on pp.280–281. Authentic Thai food, which might be too hot for some, with a plethora of fish dishes. A bit pricier than others, but popular with expats in the early hours. You can't miss it, just down from the *Hotel Royal* and hung with dripping fairy lights. Daily 7pm–6am.

Medan **Ave. de Horta e Costa 18 ☎561602. See map on pp.280–281.** Little Indonesian café with canteen decor and great food, including satays, pan-fried fish, *gado-gado*, Pedang beef, and a host of sweet desserts and drinks. Mains from MOP$25. Daily noon–9pm.

Thai **Rua Abreu Nunes 27E ☎552255. See map on pp.280–281.** Thai food in fancy surroundings with portions large enough to defeat most people. Soups are marvellous (especially the mixed seafood) and fish and shellfish are a strong point. Daily noon–3pm & 6pm–1am.

Italian

The places listed below are marked on the map on pp.280–281.

Focaccia **Rua Central 2 ☎331785.** Small Italian takeaway and restaurant, best for pizza, pasta, and focaccia. A little expensive for what you get, but very tasty.

Mezzaluna **Mandarin Oriental, Av. da Amizade ☎567888.** Elegant though expensive Italian cooking in swish surroundings; the wood-fired pizzas are Macau's finest. Tues–Sun 12.30–3pm & 6.30–11pm.

Pizzeria Toscana **Av. da Amizade ☎726637.** Don't be put off by the exterior, as their good-value Italian food is superb, especially the pizzas. Good for breakfast too if you are catching an early ferry. It's out at the Jetfoil Terminal, near the Grand Prix stand. Daily 8.30am–11pm, closed first Tues of every month.

Vegetarian

Macau Vegetarian Farm **Ave. do Cor. Mesquita 11 ☎752824. See map on pp.280–281.** No English sign, but it's the huge place opposite the Kun Iam Temple. Sophisticated Chinese food, which – despite dishes' appearances – is strictly vegetarian, with tofu, gluten, and mushrooms prepared cunningly to resemble meat. The Chinese-only menu is illustrated with photographs, making ordering easy. Main dishes MOP$30-50, with set meals from MOP$60 a head. Daily 11am–9pm.

Pou Tai Un Monastery Vegetarian Restaurant **Pou Tai Un Monastery, Taipa. See map on p.294.** Inexpensive vegetarian canteen inside a temple just behind the *Hyatt*. A tasty range of nuts, fake meats, tofu and glistening braised vegetables. Try the deep-fried walnuts in sweet and sour sauce. Daily 9am–9pm.

Drinking

Macau doesn't have the **bar scene** that there is in Hong Kong, and most drinking is done with meals. There are a few new bars in the chunk of reclaimed land south of Avenida de Amizade, known locally as Lan Kwai Fong, but these mainly cater to a Cantonese clientele, and tend to have deafening dance music, more deafening dice games and arctic air-conditioning. A few, such as the *Macau Jazz Club* are a bit more relaxing, with live music and alfresco seating, plus all the upmarket hotels have their own bars. Macau also lacks any good **nightclubs**, with the few there are tending to be sleazy joints packed with table dancers and call girls. The only two places worth recommending are the club on the sixth floor of the *Fortuna* with its in-house Filipino band, which is popular with expats after 2am, and *Signal Café* on the Macau waterfront, with an in-house DJ spinning club tracks nightly.

Most of Macau's **gay** community heads to Hong Kong for weekend nightlife, but in general gay couples shouldn't face any problem in any of Macau's bars.

Bars

The Embassy Bar **Mandarin Oriental, Av. da Amizade.** One of the better hotel bars and a regular expat haunt. Weekdays 5–9pm and weekends 11am–9pm there's big-screen sporting action. Happy hour 5–7pm.

Macau Jazz Club **The Glasshouse, Macau Waterfront, ☎596014.** Very popular night spot on the harbourside near the new Kun Iam bronze statue. This small joint hosts regular jazz festivals: phone or check their website to see what's on. Live music every Friday and Saturday. Wed-Sun 6pm–2am.

Moonwalker Av. Marginal da Baia Nova, Vista Magnifica Court ⓣ751326. One of the better bars along the seafront, with outdoor seating, live music daily (except Tues) and some Mediterranean food. Daily noon–4am.

Portas do Sol Wine Bar Hotel Lisboa. A brightly lit bar with a good selection of Portuguese wines by the glass. You can also enjoy the live Shanghai band (daily except Mon) playing swing and easy-listening numbers in the adjacent restaurant and join the dancing couples on the floor. Daily 11am–3am.

Signal Café Av. Marginal da Baia Nova, Vista Magnifica Court ⓣ751052. Hip-looking club/bar on the second floor next to the *Moonwalker*, with comfy lounge chairs and plenty of chunky coloured perspex. There's a nightly DJ at the bar, and pool tables. Only gets moving after 1am. Daily 6pm–4am.

▲ Portuguese port

Buying your own food and wine

Apart from the market on Rua Sul do Mercado de São Domingos, where you can buy fruit and veg, there are branches of the **supermarket** Park 'N' Shop at Av. Sidonio Pais 69 and Praça Ponte e Horta 11. Pavilions supermarket on Av. Praia Grande 417–425 (daily 10.30am–9.30pm) just down from the *Metropole* hotel has a wine cellar with bottles for as little as $18. There are also several markets and grocery stores selling snacks, fruit and wine on, and in the back lanes off, Avenida de Almeida Ribeiro.

18

Casinos and other entertainment

Along with eating out, the main entertainment in Macau is **gambling** in various shapes and forms. Most people spend their evenings lurching between Macau's fourteen **casinos** – which is no bad thing in moderation, since a couple of nights is all you need to get around the more interesting venues in which to lose your money. In lots of cases, too, just being a spectator is entertainment enough, whether at a casino or the horse- and dog-racing stadiums (for which, see the next chapter, "Sports and Recreation").

Cultural activities of any kind are thin on the ground, though a couple of annual music and arts festivals do their best to bridge the gap, along with the **Cultural Centre** (see p.316), which hosts regular international film, theatre and ballet performances, as well as free or inexpensive local productions and workshops.

Casinos

With few exceptions, Macau's **casinos** are noisy, frenetic places, nearly always packed, especially at the weekend, with a constant stream of people who leg it off the jetfoil and into the gaming rooms. There's little attempt here to provide any padding to the basic fact of casinos being places to chance your life savings – despite the recent appearance of the US-owned *Sands*, if you're after the gilt and glitter of Las Vegas you're in the wrong town.

Formerly, the vast majority of the **punters** were Hong Kong Chinese who flocked to Macau since there's no legal betting except horse racing in their own territory. Now, mainland Chinese account for seventy percent of casino customers, and an unforseen embarrassment for the Chinese government is that mainland officials have recently been caught gambling away billions of yuan of public funds during holidays in the SAR.

Given that the sole object of the casinos is to take money off ordinary people – amounting to US$500 million a year in Macau – there aren't the **dress restrictions** you might expect. **Cameras**, however, aren't allowed in any of the casinos; **passports** have to be shown at the door; and if you've got a bag you'll have to check it in, noting down the serial numbers of any valuable items on a pad provided.

The games

There are an astounding number of **games** on offer in any of Macau's casinos. Many are familiar: you'll need no coaching to work the **one-armed bandits** or slot machines (called "hungry tigers" locally), which take either Hong Kong dollars or patacas and pay out accordingly. Many of the card games are also the ones you would expect, like **baccarat** and **blackjack**.

However, local variations and peculiarly **Chinese games** can make a casino trip more interesting. For more advice, ask at the tourist information centres where you can buy the *A-O-A Macau Gambling Guide*, which details all the games, rules and odds. **Boule** is like roulette but with a larger ball and fewer numbers (25) to bet on. **Pai kao** is Chinese dominoes and is utterly confusing for novices. **Fan tan** is easier to grasp, involving a cup being scooped through a pile of buttons which are then counted out in groups of four, bets being laid on how many are left at the end of the count – about as exciting as it sounds. In **dai-siu** ("big-small" in Cantonese) you bet on the value of three dice, either having a small (3–9) or big (10–18) value – this is probably the easiest to pick up if you're new to the games. In all the games, the **minimum bet** is usually MOP$100 (MOP$200 on blackjack), though some of the games played in the VIP rooms have minimum bets of MOP$3000 or more.

The most powerful force behind Macau's gambling industry has traditionally been the Sociedade de Turismo e Diversões de Macau (STDM), which owns most of the **casinos**, the turbojet service between Hong Kong and Macau and a handful of luxury hotels including the *Lisboa*.

Most of the casinos are located in a strip between the Jetfoil terminal and Avenida do Doutor Mario Soares. Each has its own character and variety of games. To get in, visitors officially need to be (or look) 18; there's no entry fee. All the casinos are open 24 hours a day.

Casino Jai-Alai Porto Exterior by the Jetfoil Terminal. One of the SAR's more downmarket dens, with all-night table action in a stadium that used to host jai-alai games.

Casino Kam Pek Av. de Amizade. Known also as the Chinese Casino on account of the mainly Chinese card and dice games played here. Very popular and very intense.

Casino Macau Palace Porto Exterior, Av. de Amizade. Otherwise known as the Floating Casino, housed in a new two-decked vessel and – despite opulent red and gold decor – a surprisingly uninteresting place.

Kingsway Rua de Luis Gonzaga Gomes. Fairly flash and not terribly interesting unless you've come to risk your all – there are very high minimum stakes here.

Lisboa At the Hotel Lisboa, Av. da Amizade. The biggest casino in Macau, a four-level extravaganza featuring every game possible. There are enough comings-and-goings here to entertain you without losing a cent. Bars, restaurants and shops are all within chip-flicking distance.

New Century Taipa. Calls itself a "Las Vegas" style casino because of the free paper cups of hot tea and snacks given out to punters. Actually fairly downmarket.

Sands Av. da Amizade. The first and currently only foreign-owned casino in town, appropriately enough with gold-tinted glass facade and unusually bright and spacious.

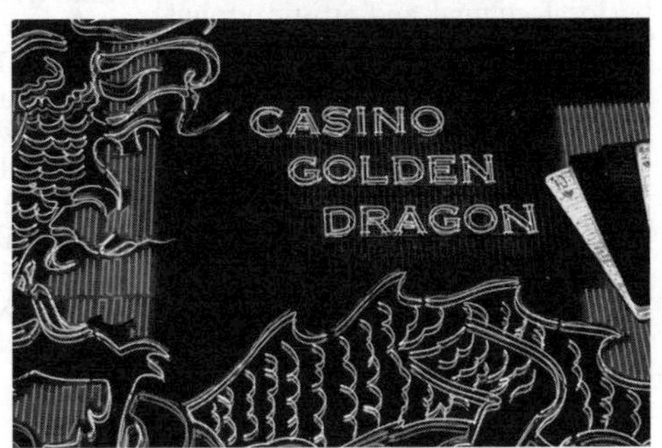

▲ One of Macau's ever-growing clutch of casinos

Hyatt Regency Estrada Almirante 2, Taipa. One of the smaller casinos. Very select and for high-rollers only.

Mandarin Oriental Av. da Amizade. Upmarket hotel casino. Still no Las Vegas, but you'll need decent clothes to play the small range of games.

Arts and culture

You'll find listings of the month's **concerts and exhibitions** in the newspaper, *Macau Talk* and the newsletter *What's On*, both of which are free and can be picked up in main MGTOs (see p.30), and some hotel lobbies. Hong Kong's *South China Morning Post* also runs a Macau listing in its weekly *24/7* magazine, free with the Friday edition of the newspaper. The main **venues** for art exhibitions, concerts, international ballet and theatre include the **Macau Cultural Centre** (Ⓣ555 555, Ⓦwww.ccm.gov.mo/en/index.asp,), which incorporates the **Macau Museum of Art**, on the chunk of reclaimed land nearest the Jetfoil Terminal; the gallery in the **Leal Senado**, which puts on temporary art displays; the **University of Macau** (Ⓣ831622) on Taipa, whose auditorium is used for concerts; and – more rarely – the **Jardim Lou Lim Ieoc**, by the Sun Yatsen Memorial Home, which also hosts recitals and concerts. Other occasional concerts are given in a couple of the central churches (like São Lourenço), the **Teatro Dom Pedro**, and the **Macau Forum** on Avenida Marciano Baptista (Ⓣ702986), which sometimes hosts rock gigs. Tickets for events in Macau are usually cheaper than in Hong Kong.

Annual arts festivals

Annual arts events worth catching include the **International Music Festival**, in October, when Chinese and Western orchestras and performers put on theatre, opera and classical music at all the above venues over a two- or three-week period, and the annual **Macau International Jazz Festival** in May, organized by the Macau Jazz Club, with concerts held in the Cultural Centre. There's also the two-week-long **Macau Arts Festival**, usually held in March, which features events and performances by local cultural and artistic groups. Check Ⓦwww.icm.gov.mo for more information on all these events.

Every autumn Macau hosts an international **fireworks festival**, with teams competing to produce the biggest and brightest bangs over the Praia Grande and Lagos Nam Van. The festival usually lasts several weeks around November, with different competitors putting on displays each weekend, before a grand final between the best two. Check dates with the MGTO.

Chinese Opera

The Macau Cultural Centre is the venue for regular travelling shows put on by mainland operatic troupes – contact the centre or check *Macau Talk* for details. Tickets are MOP$100-300.

Cinema

The **Cineteatro Macau**, Rua de Santa Clara (Ⓣ572050), near the junction with Rua do Campo, has three screens; there should usually be something in English. Tickets are MOP$30. There's also a **UA** cinema (Ⓣ712622) at the Jai-Alai Stadium, near the Jetfoil Terminal, which shows a few English-language films. The Macau Cultural Centre also has a small cinema, which hosts an annual **animation festival** and shows art-house releases from the mainland and Taiwan.

19

Sports and recreation

Apart from horse and dog racing, Macau's biggest sporting draw is the annual **Macau Grand Prix** (usually in November), which takes place on the enclave's streets. Accommodation and transport are mobbed over this weekend, and you'll need to book well in advance if you want to see it.

There are various other recreational **sports** on offer, too, from squash to horse riding, though most people will probably be content with a swim at one of the beaches on Coloane.

Spectator sports

Most **spectator sports** take place either at the **Forum** (Av. Marciano Baptista, near the Jetfoil Terminal ⓣ702986) – which hosts things like volleyball, table tennis and indoor athletics meetings – or the **Taipa Stadium**, a 20,000-seater next to the racecourse, for soccer and track and field events. Major events are listed in *Macau Talk* and *Macau What's On*; or look for posters around the city.

Macau Grand Prix

Held on the third weekend in November, the **Macau Grand Prix** is a Formula 3 event (plus a motorbike race). **Tickets** in the stand run to around MOP$800 for two days' racing and are available from the MGTO or from overseas tourist representatives. Check the MGTO's website (ⓦwww.macautourism.gov.mo) for more information. Be sure to book well in advance.

Horseracing

Horseracing in Macau is as popular as in Hong Kong. The Macau Jockey Club hosts regular meets at the racecourse on Taipa several days a week from September to June (beginning at 12.35pm), and night races from June to August (beginning at around 7pm). Entrance to the ground and first floor stands is free, the second floor costs $20, and the minimum bet is $10. Contact the Macau Jockey Club (ⓣ820868, ⓦwww.macauhorse.com) for exact times and dates of races. The buses to Taipa (#11, #22, #28A or #33) from close to the *Hotel Lisboa* all return via the racecourse.

Greyhound racing

Asia's only **greyhound racing** track is at the Yat Yuen Canidrome in Avenida General Castelo Branco, very close to the Lin Fong Temple; bus #5 from Avenida de Almeida Ribeiro, and buses #23 and #25 from outside the *Hotel Lisboa*, go right past it. The races are held on Monday, Thursday, Saturday and Sunday from

8pm until 12.20am, providing the weather is good. Entrance is MOP$10 which includes a MOP$10 bet (the minimum). You'll pay MOP$40 to get inside the Club VIP room with its bar and ringside view. Phone ☎333399 for more details.

Participatory sports

The list of participatory sports include **squash** and **tennis**, which you can play at the *Hyatt Regency* (☎831234), the *Mandarin Oriental* (☎567888) and the *Westin Resort* (☎871111) for around MOP$90 a session. Otherwise, head for the *Hotel Lisboa* (☎377666), whose labyrinthine twists and turns conceal a **swimming pool** open to the public and a **snooker and billiards** room. There's also a swimming pool at Cheoc Van beach (p.298) on Coloane, while Hác Sá beach (p.289), also on Coloane, has a **recreation centre** (Mon–Sat 8am–9pm, Sun 8am–midnight) with a pool (MOP$15), roller-skating, mini-golf, children's playground and tennis courts. You can rent **windsurfing** equipment and **jet skis** further along the beach towards the *Westin Resort*, while the Macau Golf and Country Club runs a members-only championship **golf** course, just behind the *Westin* on the southeast tip of Coloane island, which *Westin Resort* guests can use at certain times. Paddle- and **rowing boats** can be hired at the Water Activities Centre (see p.298) on Estrada de Hác Sá inland, behind the recreation centre.

Walking/jogging trails crisscross the land around the Guia Fortress, the most popular being a 1700-metre trail reached from the lower car park, just up the hill from the *Guia Hotel*. There are also signposted walking trails on Coloane: the Trilho de Coloane and Trilho Nordeste de Coloane – the latter, a six-kilometre walk that begins and ends near Ká Ho beach, is the more accessible.

At the end of November the **Macau Marathon** clogs up the enclave's streets, the course running from Macau to Taipa and Coloane. Finally, the Macau **Horse-Riding** School, on Estrada de Cheoc Van 2H, Coloane (☎882303; Tues–Sun; around MOP$200/hr), takes proficient riders around the hill trails on Coloane.

Directory

Airport and airlines Macau International Airport (Ⓣ861111, Ⓦwww.macau-airport.gov.mo). Airlines include: Air Macau (Ⓦwww.airmacau.com.mo) to Beijing, Haikou, Nanjing, Guilin, Chengdu, Shanghai, Xiamen, Kunming, Kaohsiung, Taipei and Manila; EVA Airways (Ⓦwww.evaair.com) to Taipei and Kaohsiung; Tiger Airways (Ⓦwww.tigerairways.com) to Singapore; and Air Asia (Ⓦwww.airasia.com) to Kuala Lumpur and Bangkok. East Asia Airlines (Ⓣ727288) run the Hong Kong helicopter service.

Antiques and handicrafts There are dozens of "antique" shops selling reproduction wooden Chinese screens, chests, vanity cases and furniture on Rua de São Paulo leading up to the church ruins. Branching off just before the steps up to the ruins, shops on Rua do Santo António stock Chinese costumes, porcelain, scrolls, sculptures and more furniture. Asian Artifacts (Rua dos Negociantes 25, Coloane Village) sells imported Chinese furniture and a range of Southeast Asian crafts including Cambodian silverware, Tibetan chests and Thai weaves. A few doors down at no. 3A, Taiwan Melody is a tea shop and handicraft store selling Taiwanese goods including garish glass and clay oddments and traditional fabrics. All shops are generally open daily 10am–7pm.

Banks and exchange Banks are generally open Mon–Fri 9am–5pm, Sat 9am–noon, though a bank in the arcade of the *Hotel Lisboa* keeps much longer hours than this. Most banks change travellers' cheques; ATMs can provide either MOP$ or HK$ as requested. The main clutch of banks (all with ATMs) is around the junction of Av. de Almeida Ribeiro and Av. da Praia Grande in central Macau, including Banco Nacional Ultramarino (Av. de Almeida Ribeiro 2); Banco Comercial de Macau (Av. da Praia Grande 22; and Av. Sidónio Pais 69A); Bank of China (Av. Dr. Mario Soares; and in *Hotel Lisboa*); Standard Chartered Bank (Av. do Infante D. Henrique 60–64); and HSBC (Av. da Praia Grande 639; and Av. Horta e Costa 122–124), which gives cash advances on Visa. The large hotels will also change money, at a price, and there are also licensed moneychangers (*casas de cambio*), including one at the Jetfoil Terminal and a 24hr service in the *Hotel Lisboa* – as always, shop around for the best rates. There are also banks on both Taipa and Coloane.

Bookshops The only bookshop in Macau with any selection in English (though most of its stock is in Portuguese or Chinese) is the excellent Livrari Portuguesa, Rua de São Domingos 18–22 (off Largo do Senado), which has titles on local history, cooking, culture and politics.

Bike rental On Taipa, you can rent bikes either from the *Hyatt Regency* hotel, or from a stall in Taipa village (see p.296). In Coloane, the bike rental shop is at the bottom of Coloane village's main square, towards the water. They cost around MOP$10–12 an hour, depending on the bike, or MOP$50 a day. Note that if you want a bike for Coloane it's better to rent one there than ride over the causeway from Taipa.

Car and motorbike rental Prices for all vehicles rise at weekends; remember to drive on the left. Avis at the *Mandarin Oriental* and Jetfoil Terminal (Ⓣ336789, Ⓦwww.avis.com.mo) rent cars from MOP$700 for 24hr, and mokes from MOP$450; rates include vehicle and third-party insurance. You need to be at least 21, to have held a driving licence for two years

and have an international driving licence. 110cc Honda motorbikes can also be rented for around MOP$350 for 24hr from New Spot on Rua de Londres just north of the Cultural Centre (☎750880). You'll need to put down a MOP$3000 deposit, but you can use your own national driving licence.

Departure tax Usually included in the price of tickets, this is MOP$18 by sea, MOP$80 for air destinations within China and MOP$130 to fly elsewhere. Transit passengers who stay less than 24hr are exempt. There is no departure tax if you leave by land.

Doctors Go to the hospital casualty departments (see below) or look in the telephone directory Yellow Pages under "Médicos".

Drinking water It comes straight from China and is perfectly safe to drink. It doesn't always taste wonderful, though, and you might be happier with bottled water, sold in shops everywhere.

Electricity Most of Macau's electricity is supplied at 220V, although some buildings in the older parts of the city still use power at 110V. Plugs are the small three round-pin type.

Emergencies Call ☎999. For the police call ☎919. Other numbers include fire brigade ☎572222 and ambulance ☎577199.

Hospitals There are 24hr casualty departments at Centro Hospitalar Conde São Januário, Calç. Visconde São Januário ☎313731 (English-speaking), and Hospital Kiang Wu, Est. Coelho do Amaral ☎371333 (mostly Chinese-speaking).

Internet Net bars are few and far between in Macau, though there are a couple off Av. Amizade, including *Net Home* and *Tin Ha* (see map on pp.280–281, for locations), which charge around MOP$10 per hour. Otherwise, the UNESCO Centre on Alameda Dr. Carlos d'Assumpcão has six computers in its library on the second floor (daily except Tues noon–8pm; MOP$10 per hour): the entrance is a small glass door on the southeast side of the building. In addition, most of the upmarket hotels have business centres with pricey Internet access.

Newspapers The *Macau Post* is the SAR's single English-language paper, giving a desperately thin round-up of international headlines. You can also buy Hong Kong's newspapers in Macau, as well as imported copies of foreign newspapers, from the newspaper stands along the central *avenidas*.

Pharmacies Farmácia Popular, Largo do Leal Senado 16 ☎573739; Farmácia Tsan Heng, Av. de Almeida Ribeiro 215 ☎572888; Farmácia Lap Kei, Calç. do Gaio 3D ☎590042; Farmácia Nova Cidade, Av. Barbosa, Centro Comercial ☎235812. Each takes it in turn to open for 24hr; details posted on the doors in Chinese and Portuguese. In addition there are two branches of the Hong Kong pharmacy chain Watson's, one in Largo do Senado next to the MGTO, and one on Rua de Santa Clara near the junction with Rua do Campo.

Police The main police station is at Av. Dr Rodrigo Rodrigues ☎573333.

Taxis To order a taxi, call ☎519519 or ☎3988800.

Television You can pick up Hong Kong's television stations in Macau, as well as some from mainland China; there's also a local station, Teledifusão de Macau (TdM), whose programmes are mostly in Cantonese and Portuguese, though a few are in English.

Time Macau is eight hours ahead of GMT, thirteen hours ahead of New York, sixteen hours ahead of Los Angeles, and two hours behind Sydney.

Vaccination centre At Direcção dos Serviços de Saúde (Health Dept), Av. Conselheiro Ferreira de Almeida 89 ☎569011.

Contexts

Contexts

Hong Kong: a history

To Western eyes, the history of Hong Kong starts with the colonial adventurers and merchants who began settling on the fringes of southeast China in the middle of the sixteenth century. The Portuguese arrived in Macau in 1557; almost three hundred years later, the British seized Hong Kong Island. However, the whole region has a long, if not greatly distinguished, history of its own that is thoroughly Chinese – an identity that can only be strengthened now that both Hong Kong and Macau are under Chinese rule once more.

Early times

Archeological finds point to settlements around Hong Kong dating back six thousand years, and while there's little hard evidence, it's accepted that the archipelago off the southeastern coast of China was inhabited in these very early times by fishermen and farmers. There was no great living to be made: then, as now, it was a largely mountainous region, difficult to cultivate and with trying, tropical weather, and though the sea was rich in fish, the islands formed a base for bands of marauding pirates.

Later, though far from the Imperial throne in Xian, the land became a firm part of the great Chinese Empire, which was unified in 221 BC. Throughout the series of ruling dynasties that dominated the next 1500 years of Chinese history, the area around Hong Kong was governed – after a fashion – by a magistrate who reported to a provincial viceroy in Guangdong.

The local population was made up of several **races**, including the Cantonese, who were the most powerful and divided into clans; the Hakka people, a peripatetic grouping who had come down from the north; and the Tankas, who lived mostly on the water in boats. Villages were clan-based, self-contained and fortified with thick walls, and the inhabitants owned and worked their nearby ancestral lands. The elders maintained temples and ancestral halls within the villages, and daily life followed something of an ordained pattern, with activities and ceremonies mapped out by a geomancer, who interpreted social and religious ideas through a series of laws known as **feng shui**, or "wind and water".

This village-based life continued uneventfully for centuries, the small population of the peninsula and islands mostly untroubled by events elsewhere in the empire. Recorded history made its mark only in the thirteenth century AD, when a boy-emperor of the **Song Dynasty** was forced to flee to the peninsula of Kowloon in order to escape the Mongols who were driving south. They cornered him in 1279 and he was killed, the last of his dynasty. The Mongol victory caused a great movement of local tribes in southern China, and general lawlessness and unrest followed, characterized by continuing pirate activity based on Lantau Island.

Trade and the Chinese

The Chinese Empire, however, had begun to engineer links with the Western world that were to bring Hong Kong into the historical mainstream. Although the empire considered itself self-sufficient and superior to other lands, there had been **trade** between China and the outside world for centuries: the Romans dressed in Chinese silks, whilst Central Asia introduced glassware, cloth and horses into the country. However, trade goods were often described as "tribute" from other nations, and foreign merchants were not allowed to settle within the borders of the empire or learn the Chinese language, and were generally treated with disdain by Chinese officials.

This relationship changed slightly in the sixteenth century, when **Portuguese** traders were given a toehold at **Macau**, a tiny peninsula 60km west of Hong Kong. To the Chinese, it was a concession of limited importance: the Portuguese were confined to the very edge of the empire, far from any real power or influence, and when the same concessions were given to other Western nations in the eighteenth century, the Chinese saw those in the same light. But Western nations viewed things altogether differently. Allowed to establish trading operations in **Canton** (Guangzhou) from 1714 onwards, many Europeans saw this as a first step to opening up China itself, and by the turn of the nineteenth century the Dutch, Americans and French had joined the British in Canton, hoping to profit from the undoubtedly massive resources at hand.

For the time being, however, foreign traders in Canton had to restrict themselves to the peculiar dictates of the Chinese rulers. Their **warehouses** (called "factories") were limited to space outside the city walls on the waterfront, where they also had to live. All their operations were supervised, and their trade conducted through a selected group of Chinese merchants, who formed a guild known as a **Cohong**. In the summer, foreigners had to leave for Portuguese Macau, where most of them kept houses and, often, their families. Under these circumstances, foreign merchants somehow prospered and trade thrived. The British East India Company was only one of the firms involved, seeing their Chinese enterprises as an extension of the worldwide trade network they had built up on the back of the British victory over Napoleon and their mastery of the seas.

The opium trade

The problem that soon became apparent was that trade took place on terms eminently favourable to the Chinese. Foreigners had to pay for Chinese tea and silk in silver, while the Chinese wanted little that the Westerners had. The breakthrough was the emergence of the trade in **opium**, in demand in China but illegal and consequently little grown. The Portuguese had been smuggling it into Macau from their Indian territories for years, and as it became clear that this was the one product that could reverse the trade imbalance, others followed suit. Most energetic were the British, who began to channel opium – "foreign mud" as the Chinese called it – from Bengal to Canton, where it was sold to Chinese merchants and officials. Encouraged by the British government, traders such as **William Jardine** and **James Matheson**, both Scottish Calvinists who had no qualms about making fortunes from a Chinese reliance on drugs, were soon importing forty thousand chests of opium (worth some eight million weights of silver) annually into China by 1837.

Eventually, the scale of this new trade imbalance came to the attention of the Chinese emperor in Peking (Beijing), who also began to show concern for the adverse effect that opium was having on the health of his population. In 1839, the emperor appointed the upstanding governor of Hunan province, **Lin Zexu**, to go to Canton to end the import of opium – something he'd achieved fairly spectacularly, by brute force, in his own province. Once in Canton, Lin blockaded the Europeans inside their warehouses until they handed over the 20,000 chests of opium in their possession, and then – unopposed by the British chief superintendent of trade, **Captain Charles Elliot** – publicly destroyed them. Furious at this treatment, the foreign traders retreated to Macau, where – after Lin reminded the Portuguese of their official neutrality – their humiliation was compounded when they were refused permission to establish a new base.

The First Opium War

If it was Governor Lin's intention to end the opium trade and cut the British down to size, then he miscalculated disastrously. There was actually **opposition** to the trade in Britain, particularly among the ranks of the Whigs, but the Chinese destruction of British property – not to mention the potential danger to British personnel – fanned a mood of aggressive expansionism in London, championed by the foreign secretary, Lord Palmerston. Merchants like Jardine and Matheson had long been urging the government to promote British free trade in China, demanding gunboats if necessary to open up the Chinese Empire. Lord Napier, the first superintendent of trade in China, had been given precisely those instructions by the government, but on trying to press British claims in the region, Canton had been closed to him and his frigates forced to retreat, a humiliation that Palmerston had not forgotten.

Palmerston therefore ordered an **expeditionary fleet** comprising four thousand men from India, which arrived off Hong Kong in June 1840 with the express purpose of demanding compensation for the lost opium chests, obtaining an apology from the Chinese, and – most importantly – acquiring a base on the Chinese coast, which could be used like Portuguese Macau to open up the country for free trade. Several ports up and down the Chinese coast had been suggested by traders over the years, including Canton itself, and the expedition was authorized to grab what it could. The British fleet soon achieved its military objectives: it attacked the forts guarding Canton, while other ships sailed north, blockading and firing on ports and cities right the way up the Chinese coast. When part of the fleet reached the Yangtze River, approaching Peking itself, the Chinese were forced to negotiate.

Governor Lin was dispensed with by the emperor, who appointed a new official, Kishen, to deal with the British fleet. The fighting stopped and the British withdrew to the Pearl River to negotiate, but after six weeks of stalling by the Chinese, the fleet once again sailed on Canton and knocked out its forts. Kishen capitulated and Elliot **seized Hong Kong Island**, planting the British flag there on January 26, 1841.

Fighting began again soon after, when in August 1841 Elliot was replaced by Sir Henry Pottinger, who was determined to gain more than just Hong Kong Island. The fleet sailed north, taking ports as they went, that were later recognized as free-trade "Treaty Ports" by the subsequent **Treaty of Nanking** in 1842, which halted the fighting. In this way, Shanghai, Amoy (Xiamen), Fuzhou, Canton and others were opened up for trade; the Chinese were forced to pay an indemnity to the British, but most important of all, the treaty ceded Hong Kong Island to Britain in perpetuity.

The new colony

Not everyone was thrilled with Britain's new imperial acquisition. The small island was called Hong Kong by the British, after the Cantonese name (*Heung Gong*), or "Fragrant Harbour". But aside from the excellent anchorage it afforded to the British fleet, Palmerston for one saw Elliot's action as a lost opportunity to gain further parts of China for Britain. It was a move that cost Elliot his job, while at home Queen Victoria was not amused by the apparent uselessness of her new out-of-the-way colony. Nevertheless, the ownership of Hong Kong – which formally became a British Crown Colony in 1843 – gave a proper base for the opium trade, which became ever more profitable. By 1850 Britain was exporting 52,000 chests of opium a year to China through the colony.

Sir Henry Pottinger became the colony's first **governor**, a constitution was drawn up, and from 1844 onwards, a Legislative Council (later known as **LEGCO**) and a separate Executive Council were convened – though the governor retained a veto in all matters. In the British colonial fashion, government departments were created, the law administered and public works commissioned. Initially though, the colony remained a backwater, since the British were still ensconced at Canton and most Chinese trade went through the other Treaty Ports. The population of around fifteen thousand was mostly made up of local Chinese, scores of whom were attracted by the commercial opportunities they thought would follow; many sold land rights (that often they didn't own in the first place) to the newly arrived British, who began to build permanent houses and trading depots.

The first buildings to go up were around Possession Point, in today's Western district, and included offices, warehouses (called "**godowns**") and eventually European-style housing. This area was abandoned to the Chinese when the first colonists discovered it to be malarial and mistakenly moved to Happy Valley – which turned out to be even more badly affected. Gradually though, sanitation was improved: Happy Valley was drained and turned into a racecourse; summer houses were built on The Peak; and a small but thriving town began to emerge called **Victoria**, on the site of today's Central. The number of Europeans living there was still comparatively small – just a few hundred in the mid-1840s – but they existed within a rigid colonial framework, segregated from the Chinese by early governors and buoyed by new colonial styles and comforts. Streets and settlements were named after Queen Victoria and her ministers: St John's Cathedral was opened in 1849; Government House finished in 1855; the first path up The Peak cut in 1859; and the Zoological and Botanical Gardens laid out in 1864. As Hong Kong began to come into its own as a trading port, the British merchants who lived there started to have more say in how the colony was run, and in 1850, two merchants were appointed to the Legislative Council.

The Second Opium War and colonial growth

Relations between Britain and China remained strained throughout the early life of the colony, flaring up again in 1856 when the Chinese authorities, ostensibly looking for pirates, boarded and arrested a Hong Kong-registered schooner, the *Arrow*. With London always looking for an excuse for further intervention in China, this incident gave Britain the chance to despatch another fleet up the Pearl River to besiege Canton – instigating a series of events sometimes known as the **Second Opium War**. Joined by the French, the British continued the fighting for two years, and in 1858 an Anglo-French fleet captured more northern possessions. The proposed **Treaty of Tientsin** (Tianjin) gave foreigners the right to diplomatic representation in Peking, something that Palmerston and the traders saw as crucial to the future success of their enterprise. But with the Chinese refusing to ratify the treaty, the Anglo-French forces moved on Peking, occupying the capital in order to force Chinese concessions.

This second, more protracted series of military engagements finally ended in 1860 with the signing of the so-called **Convention of Peking**, which ceded more important territory to the British. The southern part of the Kowloon peninsula – as far north as Boundary Street – and the small Stonecutters Island were handed over in perpetuity, increasing the British territory to over ninety square kilometres. This enabled the British to establish control over the fairly lawless village that had grown up on the peninsula at Tsim Sha Tsui, while the fine Victoria Harbour could now be more easily protected from both sides. Almost as a by-product of the agreement, the opium trade was legalized, too.

The period immediately after was one of **rapid growth**. With a more secure base, the colony's commercial trade increased and Hong Kong became a stop for ships en route to other Far Eastern ports. They could easily be repaired and refitted in the colony, which began to sustain an important shipping industry of its own. As a result of the increased business, the **Hongkong and Shanghai Bank** was set up in 1864 and allowed to issue banknotes, later building the first of its famous office buildings. The large foreign trading companies, the **hongs**, established themselves in the colony: Jardine-Matheson was already there, but it was followed in the 1860s by Swire, which had started life as a shipping firm in Shanghai. The town of Victoria spread east and west along the harbour around its new City Hall, taking on all the trappings of a flourishing colonial town, a world away from the rather down-at-heel settlement of twenty years earlier. One of the major changes was in the size of the **population**: in a pattern that was to repeat many times in the future, turmoil in mainland China (on this occasion, the Taiping Uprising), saw swarms of **refugees** crossing the border, and by 1865 there were around 150,000 people in the colony. With Hong Kong soon handling roughly a third of China's foreign trade, the colony began to adopt the role it assumes today – as a broker in people and goods.

By **the 1880s**, Hong Kong's transformation was complete. Although the vast majority of the Chinese population were poor workers, the beginnings of today's meritocracy were apparent, as small numbers of Chinese businessmen and traders flourished. One enlightened governor, **Sir John Pope Hennessy**, advocated a change in attitude towards the Chinese that didn't go down at all well: he appointed Chinese people to government jobs, the judicial system, and even the Legislative Council. It was an inevitable move, but one that was resisted by the colonialists, who banned the Chinese from living in the plusher areas of Victoria and on The Peak.

1898: the leasing of the New Territories

Following Japan's victory in the **Sino-Japanese War** (1894–95), China became subject to some final land concessions. Russia, France and Germany had all pressed claims on Chinese territory in return for limiting Japanese demands after the war, and Britain followed suit by demanding a substantial lease on the land on the Kowloon peninsula, north of Boundary Street. Agreement was reached on an area stretching across from Mirs Bay in the east to Deep Bay in the west, including the water and islands in between, and this territory was **leased** from China for 99 years, from July 1, 1898. These **New Territories** became the legal focus for the return of Hong Kong to China in 1997, as they eventually became so vital to the functioning of the colony that it could never have survived as a viable entity without them; the British authorities had thus unwittingly provided a date for the abolition of what subsequently became one of their most dynamic colonies.

The colony of Hong Kong was now made up of just under 1100 square kilometres of islands, peninsula and water, but there was an indigenous Chinese population of around a hundred thousand in the newly acquired territory that resisted the change. Many villagers feared that their ancestral grounds would be disturbed and their traditional life interfered with, and local meetings were called in order to form militias to resist the British. There were clashes at **Tai Po** in April 1899, though British troops soon took control of the main roads and strategic points. Resistance in the New Territories eventually fizzled out and civil administration was established, but the villagers retained their distrust of the authorities. One further problem caused by the leasing agreement was the anomalous position of **Kowloon Walled City**, beyond the original Boundary Street – a mainly Chinese garrison that had evolved into an unpleasant slum by 1898. The leasing agreement didn't include the Walled City, and China continued to claim jurisdiction over it, hastening its degeneration over the years into an anarchic crime-ridden settlement and a flashpoint between the two sets of authorities.

The years to World War II

By the turn of the **twentieth century** the population of Hong Kong had increased to around a quarter of a million (with more pouring in after the fall of the Manchu Dynasty in China in 1911); the colony's trade showed an equally impressive performance, finally moving away from opium – which still accounted for nearly half of the Hong Kong government's finances in 1890. In 1907 Britain agreed to **end the opium trade**, and imports were cut over a ten-year period – though all that happened was that the cultivation of poppies shifted from India to China, and continued under the protection of local Chinese warlords. Opium smoking was not made illegal in Hong Kong until 1946, and three years later in China.

Alongside the trade and manufacturing booms came other improvements and developments: the **Kowloon Railway**, through the New Territories to the border, was opened in 1910 (and extended to Canton by the Chinese in 1912); the **University of Hong Kong** was founded in 1911; **land reclamation** in Victoria had begun; and the **Supreme Court** building was erected in the first decade of the new century (and still stands today, in Central, as the LEGCO building).

Despite this activity, movements outside the colony's control were soon to have their effect, and the years following World War I saw a distinct economic shift away from Hong Kong. Shanghai overtook it in the 1920s as China's foremost trading city, and Hong Kong lost its pre-eminence for the next thirty years. Most of Hong Kong's Chinese were desperately poor and there had been the occasional riot over the years, culminating in 1926 in the total **economic boycott** of the colony, organized and led by the Chinese nationalists (the Kuomintang), based in Canton. There was no trade, few services and – more importantly – no food imports from China, a state of affairs that lasted for several months and did untold damage to manufacturing and commercial activity. Expatriate volunteers had to keep things going as best they could, while the strike leaders in Hong Kong encouraged many Chinese people to leave the colony so as to press home their demands: a shorter working day; less discrimination against the local Chinese population; and a reduction in rent.

The strike didn't last, but the colony's confidence had been badly dented. Although business picked up again, new worries emerged in the 1930s as the **Japanese occupied southern China**. Hundreds of thousands of people fled into the colony, almost doubling the population, and many saw the eventual occupation of Hong Kong itself as inevitable.

Japanese occupation 1941–1945

The Japanese had been advancing across China from the north since 1933, seizing Manchuria and Beijing before establishing troops in Canton in 1939 – an advance that had temporarily halted the civil war then raging in China. What was clear was that any further move to take Hong Kong was bound to succeed: the colony only had a small defensive force of a few battalions and a couple of ships, and couldn't hope to resist the Japanese army.

Some thought that the Japanese wouldn't attack, and certainly, although Hong Kong had been prepared mentally for war since 1939, there was a feeling that old commercial links with the Japanese would save the colony. However, when the Japanese occupied Indochina, the colony's defences were immediately strengthened. A line of pillboxes and guns was established across the New Territories, the so-called Gin Drinkers Line, which it was hoped would delay any advancing army long enough for Kowloon to be evacuated and Hong Kong Island to be turned into a fortress from which the resistance could be directed.

On December 8, 1941 the **Japanese** army invaded, overran the border from Canton, bombed the airport and swept through the New Territories' defences. They took Kowloon within six days, the British forces retreating to Hong Kong Island where they were shelled and bombed from the other side of the harbour.

The Japanese then moved across to the island, split the defence forces in hard fighting and finished them off. The **British surrender** came on Christmas Day, the first time a British Crown Colony had ever been surrendered to enemy forces. Casualties amounted to around six thousand military and civilian deaths, with nine thousand more men captured. The soldiers were held in prisoner-of-war camps in Kowloon – although some officers were held elsewhere, including camps in Japan itself – while those British civilians who had not previously been evacuated to Australia were interned in Stanley Prison on the island.

It was a dark time for the people of Hong Kong, who faced a Japanese army out of control. Although some Chinese civilians collaborated, many others helped the European and Allied prisoners by smuggling in food and medicines, and helping to organize escapes. It wasn't necessarily a show of support for the British, but an indication of the loyalty most Hong Kong Chinese felt towards China, who had suffered even worse under the Japanese. **Atrocities** faced the Allied prisoners too: during the short campaign, the Japanese had murdered – sometimes after raping – hospital staff, patients and prisoners, and in prison, beatings, executions for escape attempts and torture were commonplace. Life in Stanley meant disease and malnutrition, and being a civilian was no guarantee of safety: in 1943, seven people were beheaded on the beach for possessing a radio.

The Japanese meanwhile sent a military governor to Hong Kong to supervise the **occupation**, but found the colony to be much less use to them than they had imagined. It wasn't incorporated into the Japanese-run parts of China, and apart from changing the names of buildings and organizations – and adding a few Japanese architectural touches to Government House – nothing fruitful came of their time there. The New Territories became a battleground for bandits, various factions of the Chinese defenders and the Japanese invaders. Towns and villages emptied as many of the local Chinese were forcibly repatriated to the mainland, food and supplies were run down, and the cities on either side of the harbour were bombed out. As the Japanese gradually lost the battle elsewhere, Hong Kong became more and more of an irrelevance to them, and when the **Japanese surrendered to the Allies** in August 1945, colonial government re-established itself surprisingly quickly.

Postwar reconstruction: the 1950s and 1960s

The immediate task in Hong Kong was to rebuild both buildings and commerce, something the colony undertook with remarkable energy. This was, however, achieved at a price, and Hong Kong lost out on the **democratic reforms** that were sweeping the rest of the world. There had been suggestions that the colony become a free-trading "international" state after the war, or that it be handed back to China, but quick thinking by the imprisoned British leaders – who declared themselves the acting government on Japan's surrender – ensured that Hong Kong remained a British colony. Liberal measures designed to introduce at least some democratic reforms into the running of the colony were treated with disdain by the population, which was interested only in getting its business back on its feet.

The boost the economy needed came in 1949–50, during which time the renewed civil war on the mainland ended with the **communists** coming to power in China. China's former nationalist Kuomintang government fled to **Taiwan**, and those of their followers who were unable to leave with them poured over the border to Hong Kong. These new migrants, many from Shanghai, set up businesses and provided the manufacturing base from which the colony could expand. By 1951, the population had grown to around two and a half million, and Hong Kong had moved from being a mere entrepôt to become an industrial centre. New, lucrative industries – directly attributable to the recent refugees – included textiles and construction. A further incentive for a change in emphasis in the colony came with the American embargo on Chinese goods sold through Hong Kong during the **Korean War**, so that the territory was forced into manufacturing goods as a means of economic survival.

The new immigrants unleashed problems for the colony however, not least the fact that there was nowhere for them to live. **Squatter settlements** mushroomed, and faced with a private housing sector that couldn't build new homes fast enough, the government established approved squatters' areas throughout the territory. In addition, virtually all of the new immigrants were ardently anti-communist, and they took every opportunity during the 1950s to unsettle the relationship between Hong Kong and China. This resulted in **riots** in the colony between communists and nationalists, pointing the way towards future conflict. In an attempt to solve the problem, thousands of ex-Kuomintang soldiers and their families were forcibly moved to the village of Rennies Mill, on Hong Kong Island, which until its redevelopment just before the handover remained a bastion of nationalist support.

This uneasy link with China was exploited by both sides throughout the 1960s, each action emphasizing Hong Kong's odd position as both a British colony and a part of China, prey to the whims and fortunes of the Chinese leadership. In 1962, the point was made by the Chinese government in the so-called **trial run**, which allowed (and encouraged) upwards of sixty thousand people to leave China for Hong Kong. The border was flooded, and though the British authorities were determined to keep such an influx out, there was little they could do in the face of blatant provocation from the Chinese army, which was directing the flow of people.

Far more serious events soon overtook the colony, however, as the **Cultural Revolution** gained momentum on the mainland. This movement had begun in 1964 as a student protest against China's academic institutions' "old ways of thinking", but had escalated into an attempt to completely demolish traditional Chinese society. The result was near anarchy across China, as the movement's **Red Guard** assaulted academics, burned books and desecrated temples and ancient monuments: tens of thousands of people were ostracized, imprisoned, or simply murdered. Inevitably, the effects spilled over into the colony where pro-Red Guard factions fanned serious rioting through 1966–67, which saw Government House besieged, Europeans attacked in the streets, strikes, a bomb attack on Hong Kong Island, and a virulent anti-British poster campaign. However, it became clear that there was little support from the mainland for these local agitators – indeed, Mao was keen to avoid destabilizing the colony, as it was an important source of revenue – and the protests fizzled out by late 1967.

The 1970s: social problems

As the Cultural Revolution petered out on the mainland in the early 1970s, Hong Kong's relationship with its neighbour improved dramatically. Trade between the two increased, Chinese investment in Hong Kong became substantial – in Chinese-owned banks, hotels, businesses and shops – and Hong Kong was a ready market for Chinese food products. This shift in relationship was recognized in the mid-1970s, when the word "colony" was expunged from all official British titles in Hong Kong: in came the concept of Hong Kong as a "territory", which sounded much better to Chinese ears.

However, these improvements were offset by a number of social problems that still trouble Hong Kong today. The **population** continued to grow, bolstered by the ever-increasing number of immigrants from China. There had been a housing shortage since the end of World War II, creating the huge, slum-like squatter towns that clogged up the colony; the mid-1970s also saw 65,000 **Vietnamese boat people** – fleeing their country after the North Vietnamese victory over America – trying to enter Hong Kong. All this led to the development of **New Towns**, the first of which, Tuen Mun, opened in 1973 as the prototype of the concrete-towerblock cities that now sprawl across the New Territories, housing more than four million people and making the Hong Kong government the world's largest landlord. Roughly half the population lives in public housing, although one reason for this is the fact that the government owns all the land in Hong Kong and carefully controls how many new plot leases reach the market every year. This has enabled property developers to ensure incredibly high prices, something that has made buying even the smallest flat well beyond the means of many. For more on the development of the New Towns, see the box on p.124.

The other major problem during this period was that of **crime and corruption**, behind much of which were various Mafia-like **Triad** organizations. Established as anti-dynastic secret societies in seventeenth-century China, they moved into Hong Kong early in the colony's history, where they were able to organize among the new immigrants, splitting up into separate societies with their own elaborate initiation rites and ceremonies. Through the 1960s, their activities were accompanied by an increase in **official and police corruption** – a state of affairs only partly redeemed by the setting up in 1974 of the **Independent Commission Against Corruption**.

The 1980s

Meanwhile, 1997 – and the expiration of Britain's 99-year lease over the New Territories – was fast approaching. It was clear by this time that the New Territories and the rest of Hong Kong (though technically owned in perpetuity by Britain) had become an indivisible entity, and there was no choice but to hand over the entire package to China when the lease expired. The question was only what Britain was going to get from the deal – it had, after all, invested vast wealth and time in Hong Kong, and would be losing one of the world's great financial centres.

The moves towards finding a solution began in 1982, with a trip to Beijing by the British prime minister Margaret Thatcher. After an initial bout of aggressive posturing, both sides pragmatically agreed that their aim was the "prosperity and stability" of a future Hong Kong. The **Sino-British Joint Declaration** was signed in September 1984, with Britain agreeing to hand back the entire territory to China in 1997. In return, Hong Kong would continue with the same legal and capitalistic system for at least the next fifty years, becoming a **Special Administrative Region** (SAR) of China, in which it would have virtual autonomy from Beijing – a concept the Chinese leader Deng Xiaoping famously described as "one country, two systems".

After the signing, however, critics pointed out that with virtually no democratic institutions in Hong Kong, the Chinese would effectively be able to do what they liked after 1997: only the economic sense of maintaining Hong Kong's wealth-producing status would limit their actions. Confidence in China's future goodwill remained low even after the publication in 1988 of the **Basic Law**, a constitutional framework confirming the preservation of Hong Kong's capitalist system, along with freedoms of travel, speech, and the right to strike. There were also disturbingly vague references to clampdowns on "subversion" post-1997, which did nothing to relieve the concerns of Hong Kong's embryonic but growing **democratic movement**.

The worst pessimist would hardly have predicted the events of 1989, however. On June 4, after student-dominated pro-democracy demonstrations in China, Deng Xiaoping sent the tanks into **Tiananmen Square** in Beijing to crush the protest – an act that killed hundreds, possibly thousands, of people. The Hong Kong population's worst fears that Britain had sold them out to a murderous regime seemed confirmed: with the People's Liberation Army due to be stationed on Hong Kong territory after 1997, nobody doubted that critics of Chinese authoritarian rule would be violently suppressed, whatever the Basic Law said. Successive rallies in Hong Kong brought up to a million people out onto the streets to protest that without democratic institutions in place before 1997, the territory and its people would be entirely at the mercy of Beijing's whims.

The early 1990s

At the turn of the decade Hong Kong's **economy** was booming: the territory ranked eighth in the world league of trading nations; it was the busiest container port in the world; it had the third largest foreign exchange reserves; and was the fourth largest source of foreign direct investment in the world. Its economic growth averaged eight percent a year for more than a decade, and its citizens enjoyed virtually full employment and a GDP per capita of more than US$25,000 – higher than the United Kingdom and not far below that of the United States. In addition, more than half of all China's exports passed through Hong Kong, while the territory itself accounted for well over fifty percent of foreign investment in China – a formidable record for a place that had been founded just a century earlier.

However, despite Hong Kong's long association with Britain, the population had few of the **rights and privileges** that people in Britain enjoyed and expected, especially regarding the **right of abode** in the UK should the situation in Hong Kong deteriorate after the handover to China. It was argued that most people wanted to stay in Hong Kong and that, if forced to leave, wouldn't come to Britain anyway, the most popular destinations for Hong Kong Chinese emigrants being Canada and Australia. But **a British passport** – which would accompany right of abode in the UK – would give the residents of Hong Kong security, and thus lend the territory some stability.

The British government, however, balked at the spectre of a potential five million people flooding into Britain, and instead offered passports and space in Britain to just 225,000 of the territory's elite. This pleased nobody: neither the majority of the Hong Kong population; the UK voters who opposed letting any Hong Kong Chinese settle in Britain; nor the Chinese government, who argued that as Hong Kong would be Chinese after 1997, citizens would not be entitled to leave or enter the territory on "foreign" passports. This of course conveniently ignored those Hong Kongers not of ethnic Chinese origin, such as Indians or Filipinos. China, meanwhile, published the **final draft of the Basic Law** – which included Beijing's right to declare martial law, and cancelled the promise of eventual universal suffrage.

All this confirmed to the Hong Kong people that the British government had no interest in their post-handover welfare, and that the future under Chinese rule looked bleak. Their response was to found fledgling **political organizations**, including the left-wing Democratic Party and conservative, business-led Liberal Democratic Federation. The territory's **first direct elections** in September 1991 saw the Democratic Party winning sixteen of the eighteen seats on the sixty-seat Legislative Council (LEGCO) that were up for grabs (the twenty-one other candidates were appointed by the governor and interest groups). The pro-China candidates failed to win a single seat, making it clear to Beijing that Hong Kong people were dissatisfied with the Basic Law.

The approach of the handover

Into this volatile situation stepped **Chris Patten**, Hong Kong's 28th – and last – governor. Any thoughts that he would sit idly by until 1997 disappeared when he proposed **widening the voter franchise** by lowering the voting age from 21 to 18, increasing the number of indirectly elected council members and creating extra "functional constituencies". This would give the vote to 2.7 million Hong Kong people – as opposed to the two hundred thousand voters allowed by the previous system – a move that infuriated Beijing as contravening the terms of the 1984 Joint Declaration. China vowed to renege on commercial agreements signed by the Hong Kong government without its consent as soon as the colony was returned to its control in 1997 – something that threatened the future of the new Chek Lap Kok Airport and sent wobbles through the financial markets.

Elections in September 1995 marked the first time that each of LEGCO's sixty seats was contested and brought gains for the Democratic Party, which could, for the first time, count on the support of almost half of LEGCO's members. The main pro-Beijing grouping came a distant second, and Beijing announced that it would not recognize the sitting LEGCO. This was a major blow for Hong Kong's democracy activists, who had hoped that legislators elected in 1995 would see out their terms after the handover. Clearly, the Chinese government had no intention of allowing itself to be confronted by a robust democratic legislature that would turn the recovery of its prize into a political fiasco played out on worldwide television.

It's hard not to be cynical about Britain's behaviour in bestowing democracy at the very moment that it made no difference to itself, yet would cause maximum discomfort for the territory's new rulers. Nor did it help the population of Hong Kong: Beijing's counterstrike to Patten's scheming reduced the potential for post-handover democratic reforms even further, by creating a "provisional legislature" made up of compliant politicians and a **chief executive** appointed by Beijing, who would assume the governor's role in the new Special Administrative Region.

Post-handover

After the build-up, however, the **handover** was something of an anticlimax. The British sailed away on HMS *Britannia*, Beijing carried out its threat to disband the elected LEGCO and reduce the enfranchised population, and **Tung Chee-hwa**, a shipping billionaire, became the first chief executive of the Hong Kong SAR. But his highly unpopular tenure was doomed from the start: within days, the **Asian Financial Crisis** had begun, causing a recession and soaring unemployment as stock and property values crashed. Added to this were the recurrent outbreaks of **bird flu**, involving huge slaughter of chickens amid fears that humans might also contract the potentially deadly virus. Meanwhile, Tung stood unopposed for a second term in 2002, despite his inability to propose or see through any effective policy, alter the public's perception of increased government **corruption**, or improve a continuously sluggish economy – not helped by Shanghai's rising star as a place to do business. And the worst was yet come. Previous fears of bird flu soon proved nothing next to the global panic wrought by southern China's **SARS outbreak** of 2003 – some 299 people died and Hong Kong's tourist industry collapsed. Meanwhile, each June 4 (the anniversary of the Tiananmen Square crackdown) saw about half a million people turn out to **demonstrate** against Tung – and by extension, China's rule over the SAR.

It was these public displays of dissatisfaction that most annoyed the powers in Beijing, who wanted Hong Kong to showcase the benefits of the "One Country, Two Systems" approach to **Taiwan** – which, now that Hong Kong and Macau have been reclaimed, remains the last hurdle to China being reunited under one government. In December 2004, Tung was openly chastised by the Chinese leader Hu Jintao, and in March 2005 he **stood down** mid-term to be replaced as chief executive by career civil servant **Donald Tsang**. Despite being a product of the colonial administration (he was even knighted in 1997), Tsang has promoted ties with the mainland post-handover, and is seen as a neutral character, capable of providing a period of stability and so regaining both investor and public confidence in Hong Kong in the face of the above setbacks.

Macau: a history

When the **Portuguese** arrived off the southern Chinese coast at the turn of the sixteenth century, they were looking for trading opportunities to add to their string of successes in India and the Malay peninsula. In particular, they were hoping to break the Venetian monopoly of the Far Eastern spice trade, something that had seemed possible since the seizure of the Malay port of Malacca in 1510. Three years later, the Portuguese explorer Jorges Álvares opened up trade with China; and in 1542 Portugal established further trading links with Japan. Looking for a base from where they could coordinate their regional interests, the Portuguese persuaded Chinese officials to let them rent a remote peninsula of land at the very foot of the Qing empire known as A-Ma-Kok or A-Ma Gao, transliterated by the settlers as "Macau".

Through the sixteenth and early seventeenth centuries, the new city of Macau thrived on trade and Christian **missionary activity**, pioneered in China and Japan by the **Jesuits**. It was their funding that established Macau's great Baroque churches, though from 1612 onwards the authorities were also forced to build fortifications on the city's hills to ward off attacks from a new regional power, the **Dutch**. Despite failing to capture Macau, the Dutch otherwise successfully destroyed Portugal's commercial interests in Southeast Asia by taking over Indonesia's wealthy spice trade from the Spanish, managing to get the Jesuits expelled from Japan in 1639, and finally occupying Malacca in 1641. With its trading links cut, Macau floundered and – despite a respite during the early nineteenth century, when other nations used Macau as a springboard for their ambitions in southern China – the **founding of Hong Kong** as a free port in 1841 sealed Macau's position as a backwater.

Not that the Portuguese took all this lying down. A new governor, João Ferreira do Amaral, arrived in 1846 and annexed the neighbouring island of Taipa, expelled the Chinese customs officials from Macau, built new roads and, in 1847, licensed **gambling** in an effort to garner some income for the territory. After much wrangling, the Chinese decided that they could do without this troublesome corner of their country, and **ceded sovereignty** of Macau to Portugal in 1887.

As with Hong Kong, Macau's **population** increased rapidly through the twentieth century, especially following the Japanese invasion of China in the 1930s and after the Communist victory in 1949. But it was the 1974 **revolution in Portugal** that caused most change in the territory, as Lisbon's new left-wing government began to disentangle itself from former colonial possessions, offering to withdraw unilaterally from Macau. Yet the mainland refused to take the territory back: the gambling and organized crime that was Macau's lifeblood would only be an embarrassment to the Communist government had they left it alone, yet cleaning it up would have killed a golden goose – after all, half of Macau's GDP and seventy percent of its government revenue (around half a billion US dollars annually) comes from gambling.

However, by the time China accepted the return of the colony – as the **Macau Special Administrative Region** (MSAR) – in December 1999, the mainland had become more ideologically flexible. A pre-handover spree of violence by Triad gangs was dealt with, then the monopoly on casino licences – previously held by local billionaire **Dr Stanley Ho** – was ended in 2002, opening up this lucrative market. Response has been swift, and there are currently **fourteen**

casinos in the territory, including the *Sands*, Macau's first foreign-owned venture. Tourism has increased alongside and the long-torpid economy has heated up to the point that, in 2004, the Chinese government used Macau's pace of change to shame Hong Kong's leaders into kick-starting their own sluggish economy – unimaginable at any time during the last century.

Officially, the **1983 Basic Law** means that Macau – like Hong Kong – will keep its capitalist structure intact for at least fifty years under the "one country, two systems model", with members of the executive council, legislative council and other key government posts now filled by Chinese permanent residents of the MSAR. In practice, though, Macau has always been far more under China's influence than Hong Kong. Local liberals and pro-democracy activists are in the minority and on the defensive, concerned that the enclave is rapidly losing its Portuguese heritage under the new system. The conservatives, for their part, talk of the need for "convergence" with China if Macau is to continue to be economically viable. And indeed, the MSAR looks determined to forge ever closer **economic ties with China**, as marked by some huge infrastructure projects that include new highways and rail lines linking it to cities in the adjacent mainland province of Guangdong (and, it is rumoured, a bridge to Hong Kong). Macau is also keen to be a major player in any move to create a Pearl River Delta economy, binding it further to Hong Kong and Guangdong in a super-regional partnership.

Religion

Most major religions are represented in Hong Kong and Macau, though it's the three main Chinese ones – Taoism, Confucianism and Buddhism – that are of most interest to visitors. You'll come across temples and shrines everywhere, while many of the public holidays are connected with a particular religious occasion. There's a pragmatic flexibility within the Chinese belief system that often baffles outsiders – temples often share Buddhist and Taoist shrines, for instance – and the picture is also overlaid by the contemporary importance of superstition and ancestor worship.

The religions

The main belief system, **Taoism**, probably dates back in some form to prehistoric times, though it only became organised as a religion in response to the appearance of Buddhism in China around the first century AD. A philosophical movement, Taoism advocates that people follow the *Tao* or "The Way", which leads to an understanding of the natural order of things. This search for truth has often expressed itself in Taoism by way of superstition on the part of its devotees, who engage in fortune-telling and other similar activities. The Taoist gods are mainly legendary figures, with specific powers – protective or otherwise – that you can generally determine from their form as warriors, statesmen, or scholars. Taoist temples are generally very colourful, hosting the rowdiest of the annual festivals.

Gods and Goddesses

You'll find further information about the following deities throughout the text, usually under the entry for the main temple at which they're worshipped.

A-Ma see Tin Hau below.
Che Kung Protector against floods and plagues
Choi Sin God of wealth.
Hung Sheng (or Hung Hsing) Patron god of fishermen.
Kuan Ti (or Kuan Yue) The red-faced god of war and healing; a warrior.
Kuan Yin (or Kwun Yum/Kuan Yam/Kun Iam) Buddhist goddess of mercy.
Lu Pan Builders' god.
Man Cheong Protector of Civil Servants
Pak Tai God of order and protection; the name means "Emperor of the North".
Pao Kung God of justice.
Shing Wong A city god, responsible for those living in certain areas.
Sui Tsing Pak A god who cures illness; also known as the "Pacifying General".
Tai Sui A series of sixty different gods, each related to a year in the Chinese calendar.
Tam Kung Also a patron deity of fishermen.
Tin Hau Goddess of the sea, and one of the most popular deities, unsurprising in a land where fishing has always been important; known as A-Ma in Macau.
Wong Tai Sin A god who cures illness and brings good fortune.

Confucianism is also a philosophy, first espoused by Confucius (or Kong Fu Zi), who died around 500 BC. The product of a feudal age, Confucianism demanded that children respect their parents, parents respect their ancestors, and everybody respect the nation's rulers: in short, be happy with your lot, and don't question your superiors. Confucius' ideas were slow to catch on – he spent his life orbiting between patrons, failing to get his views established in law – but they became popular after his death, and despite many attempts to cleanse his ideas from the national psyche (China's first emperor ordered a purge of Confucian values around 220 BC, as did Chairman Mao in the 1960s), they have come to permeate every aspect of Chinese life.

Also represented in Hong Kong and, to a lesser extent, Macau, is **Buddhism**, which was originally brought from India to China in the first century AD. It recognizes that there is suffering in the world, which can be relieved only by attaining a state of personal enlightenment, *nirvana*, or extinction, at which point you will find true bliss. Buddhist temples are relaxed places, less common and less bright than Taoist, but often built in beautiful, out-of-the-way places and with resident monks and nuns.

Inside a temple: the deities

The majority of the temples described in the text are Taoist, and what goes on inside is fairly similar everywhere. Most temples are **open** from the early morning until the early evening and people go in when they like, to make offerings or to pray; there are no set prayer and service times.

The **roofs** of Taoist temples are usually decorated with colourful porcelain figures from Chinese legend, while inside you'll find stalls selling joss sticks, and slow-burning **incense** spirals that hang from the ceiling. In most temples there's a stall or special room for **fortune-telling**, most commonly achieved by shaking sticks in a cylinder until one falls out: the number on the stick corresponds to a piece of fortune paper, which has to be paid for and interpreted by a fortune-teller at a stall. Go with a Chinese speaker if you want to try this, or visit Hong Kong's massive Wong Tai Sin temple in Kowloon (see p.117), where fortune-telling takes place on a much more elaborate scale: here you'll find lots of long-established fortune tellers, as well as palmists and phrenologists, who are used to foreign tourists, and lots of explanatory notes.

Obviously, coinciding with one of the main religious **festivals** (see pp.237–241, or Basics, p.45) is an invigorating experience, and this is when you'll see the various temples at their best: lavishly decorated and full of people. There'll be dances, Chinese opera displays, plenty of noise and a series of **offerings** left in the temples – food, and paper goods, which are burned as offerings to the dead.

Books

There's no shortage of books written about Hong Kong and Macau, many of which you can get in the two territories (see pp.247 and 319 for bookshop addresses). What there is a lack of – certainly in translation – is books about both territories written by Chinese authors. In the reviews below, the UK publisher is listed first, followed by the publisher in the US – unless the title is available in one country only, in which case we've specified the country; o/p signifies out of print; UP signifies University Press.

Hong Kong

History and politics

Anthony B. Chan *Li Ka-Shing* (Oxford UP China, HK). An interesting biography of Hong Kong's most successful and powerful entrepreneur.

Austin Coates *Myself a Mandarin* (Oxford UP East Asia, UK). Light-hearted account of the author's time as a magistrate in the colonial administration during the 1950s. For more from the prolific Coates, see under "Macau" on p.343.

Maurice Collis *Foreign Mud* (Faber, o/p). Useful coverage of the opening up of China to trade and of the Opium Wars.

Jonathon Dimbleby *The Last Governor* (Little Brown & Co, UK & US). An insider's account of the battle for democracy between the last British governor and the Chinese government, with a dash of Whitehall treachery thrown in. Colourful portraits of many of Hong Kong's leading figures.

E. J. Eitel *Europe in China* (Oxford UP China, o/p). First published in 1895, this is an out-and-out colonial history of early Hong Kong – lively, biased and interesting.

Jean Gittins *Stanley: Behind Barbed Wire* (HK UP). Well-written and moving eyewitness account of time spent behind bars at Stanley Prison during the internment of civilians by the Japanese in World War II.

Christopher Patten *East and West* (Random House, UK & US). An elegant account from the last British governor of his controversial term in office up to the 1997 handover, and a thoughtful assessment of where the Asian "miracle" went wrong.

Steve Tsang *A Modern History of Hong Kong 1841–1997* (IB Tauris, UK). Thorough account of Hong Kong's history up until the handover – though written with hindsight in 2002 – including a Chinese perspective.

Athur Waley *The Opium War Through Chinese Eyes* (Routledge, o/p). Rare insight into the Chinese side of the conflict, from official papers edited and translated by a noted China scholar.

Frank Welsh *A History of Hong Kong* (HarperCollins, UK). Well-written and accessible Brit-centric account of the colony up until the pre-handover shenanegins.

Travel, architecture, reference and contemporary life

Martin Booth *Gweilo: Memories of a Hong Kong Childhood* (Doubleday/Bantam). Well-observed and humourous account of a Westerner growing up in Hong Kong during the 1950s.

Frederick Dannen and Barry Long *Hong Kong Babylon* (Faber, UK & US, o/p). Subtitled "An Insider's Guide to the Hollywood of the East", this pacey book gets to grips with every facet of the Hong Kong movie scene, from plot summaries to interviews with stuntmen.

Susanna Hoe *The Private Life of Old Hong Kong* (Oxford UP East Asia, UK & US). A history of the lives of Western women in Hong Kong from 1841 to 1941, re-created from contemporary letters and diaries. A fine book, and telling of the hitherto neglected contribution of a whole range of people who had a hand in shaping modern Hong Kong.

Ken Hom *Fragrant Harbour Taste: The New Chinese Cooking of Hong Kong* (Bantam Press/Simon & Schuster). Details modern Hong Kong cooking as dished up in some of the swankier designer restaurants, which culls its influences from all over Asia, as well as the West.

Hong Kong (Hong Kong Government Press, HK). The Hong Kong government's official yearbook, published annually, and a detailed – if uncritical – mass of photos, statistics, essays and information.

Vittorio Magnago Lampugnani (ed) *Hong Kong Architecture: The Aesthetics of Destiny* (Prestel, UK). Beautifully produced, large-format account of Hong Kong's most important and innovative architectural projects, with fine colour pictures and sketches and an informative background history.

John and Kirsten Miller (eds) *Hong Kong* (Chronicle Books, UK). Compendium of extracts from novels and travelogues based in Hong Kong, encompassing all the usual suspects: Somerset Maugham, Jan Morris et al.

Jan Morris *Hong Kong: Epilogue to an Empire* (Penguin/Vintage). A slightly dated view of Hong Kong – historical, contemporary and future – dealt with in typical Morris fashion, which means an engaging mix of anecdote, solid research, acute observation and lively opinion.

Peter Moss *Skylines* (FormAsia, HK). The history of Hong Kong as seen through its changing architecture. Fabulous colour shots of Hong Kong's architecture running the gamut from the famous bank buildings, through churches and temples to the Big Buddha. Both formats, a large coffee-table size and a small pocket-book version, include the detailed story behind each building.

Madelaine H. Tang et al *Historical Walks: Hong Kong Island* (The Guidebook Company, HK). An invaluable little book detailing five walks through parts of Hong Kong Island, with clear maps and directions.

Nury Vittachi *North Wind: What the Hong Kong Media Doesn't Want You to Know* (Chameleon Press, HK). Hong Kong's offbeat and whacky journalist departs from his usual madcap accounts of Asian tales to write this exposé of the Hong Kong media, detailing the constraints placed on the SAR's freedom of expression from big business and Beijing.

Kate Whitehead *Hong Kong Murders* (Oxford UP, UK & US). A local journalist's account of fourteen homicides, covering the work of a serial killer, Triad brutality and a kidnapping gone awry. A coherent effort to make some sense of Hong Kong's hidden violence.

Fiction

John Burdett *The Last Six Million Seconds* (Coronet, UK). Fast-paced cops-and-commissars thriller involving stolen nuclear fuel, Triad gangsters and headless corpses. Written with reeking authenticity from the girlie bars of Mongkok to the bloody roast beef at the Hong Kong Club.

James Clavell *Tai-Pan* (Coronet/Dell), *Noble House* (Coronet/Dell). Big, thick bodice-rippers set respectively at the founding of the territory and in the 1960s, and dealing with the same one-dimensional pirates and businessmen. Unwittingly verging on parody in places.

John Le Carré *The Honourable Schoolboy* (Coronet/Bantam). Taut George Smiley novel, with spooks and moles chasing each other across Hong Kong and the Far East. Accurate and enthusiastic reflections on the territory, and the usual sharp eye trained on the intelligence world.

Richard Mason *The World of Suzie Wong* (Pegasus, UK). Classic 1950s romance between a down-and-out American author and a Wan Chai prostitute. Well told and touching, loosely based on the author's own experiences.

Somerset Maugham *The Painted Veil* (Mandarin/Viking Penguin). First published in 1925, this colonial story of love, betrayal and revenge unfolds in Hong Kong before moving on to cholera-ravaged mainland China.

Timothy Mo *An Insular Possession* (Pan/Random House, o/p). A splendid novel, re-creating the nineteenth-century foundation of Hong Kong, taking in the trading ports of Macau and Canton along the way. Mo's ear and eye for detail can also be glimpsed in *The Monkey King* (Vintage/Doubleday, o/p), his entertaining first novel about the conflicts and manoeuvrings of family life in postwar Hong Kong, and his filmed novel *Sour Sweet* (Vintage/Random House, o/p) – an endearing tale of an immigrant Hong Kong family setting up business in 1960s London.

Paul Theroux *Kowloon Tong* (Penguin/Houghton Mifflin). A wicked caricature of a bumbling British expat in the final days of colonial rule involving a thrilling plot mix of unscrupulous mainland businessmen, local whores and an obsessed mother. A fast-paced if harsh portrait of Hong Kong's final colonial days.

Nury Vittachi *The Feng Shui Detective* (Chameleon Press, HK). Whodunnit with a twist – C.F. Wong, the detective of the title, solves crimes using geomancy. Heaps of cultural background, and solid enough to win critical acclaim in Hong Kong itself.

Xu Xi *Unwalled City* (Chameleon Press, HK). A modern, slightly fluffy novel that whisks through the tangled lives of the central characters, including a young Canto-pop singer, up to the 1997 handover. Xu Xi, a native Hong Konger, has also penned *Chinese Walls* (Chameleon Press) and *History's Fiction – Stories from the City of Hong Kong* (Chameleon Press), useful for their insight into the Chinese view of contemporary Hong Kong.

Language texts

English-Cantonese Dictionary (Chinese UP, HK). This uses Yale romanization to represent Cantonese. The best of the few Cantonese dictionaries in print.

Virginia Yip and Stephen Matthews *Basic Cantonese* (Routledge, UK & US). The best choice if you want to learn Cantonese, this precise and rather dry language text has no nonsense or graphics. There's also a grammar companion text. Both teach the spoken language and avoid the complex characters used in Hong Kong.

Macau

C. R. Boxer *Seventeenth Century Macau* (Heinemann US, o/p). Interesting survey of documents, engravings, inscriptions and maps of Macau culled from the years either side of the restoration of the Portuguese monarchy in 1640. An academic study, but accessible enough for some informative titbits about the enclave.

Daniel Carney *Macau* (Corgi/Kensington). Improbable characterization in a Clavell-like thriller set in the enclave.

Austin Coates *Macao and the British* (Oxford UP East Asia, UK), *A Macao Narrative* (Oxford UP East Asia, UK), *City of Broken Promises* (Oxford UP East Asia, UK). Coates has written widely about the Far East, where he was Assistant Colonial Secretary in Hong Kong in the 1950s. *Macao and the British* follows the early years of Anglo-Chinese relations and underlines the importance of the Portuguese enclave as a staging post for other traders. *A Macao Narrative* is a short but more specific account of Macau's history up to the mid-1970s; *City of Broken Promises* is an entertaining historical novel set in Macau in the late eighteenth century.

Cesar Guillen-Nunez *Macau* (Oxford UP, UK & US). Decent, slim hardback history of Macau, worth a look for the insights it offers into the churches, buildings and gardens of the city.

Cecilia Jorge *Macanese Cooking* (Associação Promotora da Instrução dos Macaenses). Seemingly unavailable outside of Macau, this excellent cookbook includes many classic Macanese dishes, as well as a comprehensive history of the style (though strangely, *natas* are omitted).

Books about China

David Bonavia *The Chinese* (Penguin, UK & US). Excellent introduction to the Chinese – their lives, aspirations, politics and problems.

Tim Glissold *Mr China* (Constable and Robinson, UK). A cautionary tale about doing business in China: the author ended up $400 million in debt and with a heart condition. Essential reading for all budding entrepreneurs.

Christopher Hibbert *The Dragon Wakes: China and the West 1793–1911* (Penguin/Viking Penguin). Superbly entertaining account of the opening up of China to Western trade and influence. Hibbert leaves you in no doubt about the cultural misunderstandings that bedevilled early missions to China – or about the morally dubious acquisition of Hong Kong and the other Treaty Ports by Western powers.

Jonathan Spence *The Search for Modern China* (W.W. Norton, US). From the pen of the distinguished Yale University historian and scholar of Chinese culture, this comprehensive, impartial and wise book is the definitive single-volume account of the violent sweep of Chinese history from the decline of the emperors to the twilight years of Deng Xiaoping.

Frances Wood *No Dogs and Not Many Chinese* (John Murray, UK). Historical snapshot of the Treaty Ports and the life lived within them – entertaining and instructive.

Arthur Waley *Three Ways of Thought in Ancient China* (Routledge/Stanford University Press). Translated extracts from the writings of three of the early philosophers – Zhuang Zi, Mencius and Han Feizi. A useful introduction.

Astrology: the Chinese calendar and horoscopes

Most people are interested to find out what sign they are in the Chinese **zodiac system**, particularly since – like the Western system – each person is supposed to have characteristics similar to those of the sign that relates to their birthdate. True Chinese astrologers, however, eschew the use of the animal symbols in isolation to analyse a person's life, seeing the zodiac signs as mere entertainment.

There are twelve signs in the Chinese zodiac, corresponding with one of twelve animals, whose characteristics you'll find listed below. These **animal signs** have existed in Chinese folk tradition since the sixth century BC, though it wasn't until the third century BC that they were incorporated into a formal study of astrology and astronomy, based around the device of the lunar calendar. Quite why animals emerged as the vehicle for Chinese horoscopy is unclear: one story has it that the animals used are the twelve that appeared before the command of Buddha, who named the years in the order in which the animals arrived. Another says that the Jade Emperor held a race to determine the fastest animals. The first twelve to cross a chosen river would be picked to represent the twelve earthly branches that make up the cyclical order of years in the lunar calendar.

Each **lunar year** (which starts in late January/early February) is represented by one of the twelve animal symbols. Your sign depends on the year you were born – check the calendar chart below – rather than the month as in the Western system, but beyond that the idea is the same: born under the sign of a particular animal, you will have certain characteristics, ideal partners, lucky and unlucky days. The details below will tell you the basic facts about your character and personality; the animals always appear in the same order, so that if you know the current year's animal you can always work out which one is to influence the following Chinese New Year.

Calendar chart

Date Of Birth	Animal	Date Of Birth	Animal
30.1.1930 – 16.2.1931	Horse	13.2.1945 – 1.2.1946	Rooster
17.2.1931 – 5.2.1932	Goat	2.2.1946 – 21.1.1947	Dog
6.2.1932 – 25.1.1933	Monkey	22.1.1947 – 9.2.1948	Pig
26.1.1933 – 13.2.1934	Rooster	10.2.1948 – 28.1.1949	Rat
14.2.1934 – 3.2.1935	Dog	29.1.1949 – 16.2.1950	Ox
4.2.1935 – 23.1.1936	Pig	17.2.1950 – 5.2.1951	Tiger
24.1.1936 – 10.2.1937	Rat	6.2.1951 – 26.1.1952	Rabbit
11.2.1937 – 30.1.1938	Ox	27.1.1952 – 13.2.1953	Dragon
31.1.1938 – 18.2.1939	Tiger	14.2.1953 – 2.2.1954	Snake
19.2.1939 – 7.2.1940	Rabbit	3.2.1954 – 23.1.1955	Horse
8.2.1940 – 26.1.1941	Dragon	24.1.1955 – 11.2.1956	Goat
27.1.1941 – 14.2.1942	Snake	12.2.1956 – 30.1.1957	Monkey
15.2.1942 – 4.2.1943	Horse	31.1.1957 – 17.2.1958	Rooster
5.2.1943 – 24.1.1944	Goat	18.2.1958 – 7.2.1959	Dog
25.1.1944 – 12.2.1945	Monkey	8.2.1959 – 27.1.1960	Pig

28.1.1960 – 14.2.1961	Rat	20.2.1985 – 8.2.1986	Ox
15.2.1961 – 4.2.1962	Ox	9.2.1986 – 28.1.1987	Tiger
5.2.1962 – 24.1.1963	Tiger	29.1.1987 – 16.2.1988	Rabbit
25.1.1963 – 12.2.1964	Rabbit	17.2.1988 – 5.2.1989	Dragon
13.2.1964 – 1.2.1965	Dragon	6.2.1989 – 26.1.1990	Snake
2.2.1965 – 20.1.1966	Snake	27.1.1990 – 14.2.1991	Horse
21.1.1966 – 8.2.1967	Horse	15.2.1991 – 3.2.1992	Goat
9.2.1967 – 29.1.1968	Goat	4.2.1992 – 22.1.1993	Monkey
30.1.1968 – 16.2.1969	Monkey	23.1.1993 – 9.2.1994	Rooster
17.2.1969 – 5.2.1970	Rooster	10.2.1994 – 30.1.1995	Dog
6.2.1970 – 26.1.1971	Dog	31.1.1995 – 18.2.1996	Pig
27.1.1971 – 14.2.1972	Pig	19.2.1996 – 6.2.1997	Rat
15.2.1972 – 2.2.1973	Rat	7.2.1997 – 27.1.1998	Ox
3.2.1973 – 22.1.1974	Ox	28.1.1998 – 15.2.1999	Tiger
23.1.1974 – 10.2.1975	Tiger	16.2.1999–4.2.2000	Rabbit
11.2.1975 – 30.1.1976	Rabbit	5.2.2000–23.1.2001	Dragon
31.1.1976 – 17.2.1977	Dragon	24.1.2001–11.2.2002	Snake
18.2.1977 – 6.2.1978	Snake	12.2.2002-31.1.2003	Horse
7.2.1978 – 27.1.1979	Horse	1.2.2003-21.1.2004	Goat
28.1.1979 – 15.2.1980	Goat	25.1.2004-8.2.2005	Monkey
16.2.1980 – 4.2.1981	Monkey	9.2.2005-28.1.2006	Rooster
5.2.1981 – 24.1.1982	Rooster	29.1.2006-17.2.2007	Dog
25.1.1982 – 12.2.1983	Dog	18.2.2007-6.2.2008	Pig
13.2.1983 – 1.2.1984	Pig	7.2.2008-25.1.2009	Rat
2.2.1984 – 19.2.1985	Rat	16.1.2009-13.2.2010	Ox

The Rat **Characteristics** Usually generous, intelligent and hard-working, but can be petty and idle; has lots of friends, but few close ones; may be successful, likes challenges and is good at business, but is insecure; generally diplomatic; tends to get into emotional entanglements. **Partners** Best suited to Dragon, Monkey and Ox; doesn't get on with Horse and Goat.

The Ox **Characteristics** Healthy; obstinate; independent; usually calm and cool, but can get stroppy at times; shy and conservative; likes the outdoors and old-fashioned things; always finishes a task. **Partners** Best suited to Snake, Rat or Rooster; doesn't get on with Tiger, Goat or Monkey.

The Tiger **Characteristics** Adventurous; creative and idealistic; confident and enthusiastic; can be diplomatic and practical; fearless and forward, aiming at impossible goals, though a realist with a forceful personality. **Partners** Best suited to Horse for marriage; gets on with Dragon, Pig and Dog; avoid Snake, Monkey and Ox.

The Rabbit **Characteristics** Peace-loving; sociable but quiet; devoted to family and friends; timid but can be good at business; needs reassurance and affection to avoid being upset; can be vain; long-lived. **Partners** Best suited to Pig, Dog and Goat; not friendly with Tiger and Rooster.

The Dragon **Characteristics** Strong, commanding, a leader; popular, athletic; bright, chivalrous and idealistic, though not always consistent; likely to be a believer in equality. **Partners** Best suited to Snake, Rat, Monkey, Tiger and Rooster; avoid Dog.

The Snake **Characteristics** Charming, but possessive and selfish; private and secretive; strange sense of humour; mysterious and inquisitive; ruthless; likes the nice things in life; a thoughtful person, but superstitious. **Partners** Best suited for marriage to Dragon, Rooster and Ox; avoid Snake, Pig and Tiger.

The Horse **Characteristics** Nice appearance and deft; ambitious and quick-witted; favours bold colours; popular, with a sense of humour; gracious and gentle; can be good at business; fickle and emotional. **Partners** Best suited to Tiger, Dog and Goat; doesn't get on with Rabbit and Rat.

The Goat **Characteristics** A charmer and a lucky person who likes money; unpunctual and hesitant; too fond of complaining; interested in the supernatural. **Partners** Best suited to Horse, Pig and Rabbit; avoid Ox and Dog.

The Monkey **Characteristics** Very intelligent and sharp, an opportunist; daring and confident, but unstable and egoistic; entertaining and very attractive to others; inventive; a sense of humour, but with little respect for reputations. **Partners** Best suited to Dragon and Rat; doesn't get on with Tiger and Ox.

The Rooster **Characteristics** Frank and reckless, and can be tactless; free with advice; punctual and a hard worker; imaginative to the point of dreaming; likes to be noticed; emotional. **Partners** Best suited to Snake, Dragon and Ox; doesn't get on with Pig and Rabbit.

The Dog **Characteristics** Alert, watchful and defensive; can be generous and is patient; very responsible and has good organizational skills; spiritual, home-loving and non-materialistic. **Partners** Best suited to Rabbit, Pig, Tiger and Horse; avoid Dragon and Goat.

The Pig **Characteristics** Honest; vulnerable and not good at business, but still materialistic and ambitious; outgoing and outspoken, but naive; kind and helpful to the point of being taken advantage of; calm and genial. **Partners** Best suited to Dog, Goat, Tiger and Rabbit; avoid Snake and Rooster.

Language

Language

Language

The language spoken by the overwhelming majority of Hong Kong and Macau's population is Cantonese, a southern Chinese dialect used in the province of Guangdong – and one spoken by millions of Chinese emigrants throughout the world. Unfortunately, Cantonese is a difficult language for Westerners to learn: it's tonal, meaning that the specific tone with which a word is spoken affects its meaning. Cantonese has nine tones, a huge number even by Chinese standards (Mandarin, the mainland's primary dialect, has just four tones). However, this is most of a problem when uttering individual words; set phrases provide their own context and you may be surprised how far your attempts at communication are understood, despite bad pronunciation.

Written Chinese is, in some ways, more accessible to the newcomer. Chinese characters embody meanings rather than pronunciation, so it's not necessary to learn to speak Chinese in order to read it. However, unlike the 26 letters of the Roman alphabet, there are an estimated 10,000 Chinese characters, although relatively few are used in daily life – you need around 2500 to read a newspaper, for example. While this will be beyond the scope of a short stay, with a little curiosity you might learn to recognize enough to get the gist of dishes on a menu.

Most visitors get by without speaking or reading a word of Chinese. Hong Kong is officially **bilingual** in Cantonese and English, and all signs, public transport and utility notices and street names are supposed to be written in both scripts. Many of the people you'll have dealings with in Central, Tsim Sha Tsui and most other tourist destinations should speak at least some English, although it may be hard going, particularly in taxis, restaurants and on the telephone.

To help out, we've provided a basic guide to pronouncing some everyday words and phrases in Cantonese. However, because the romanized versions don't convey the tone, you may find that people don't understand you. We've also provided Chinese characters for some of the most useful signs (see p.351) and place names (see box at the end of each chapter), as well as a menu reader to help you choose and order *dim sum* (see p.204). If you're having problems making yourself understood, simply show the waiter/taxi driver/passer-by the relevant Chinese character in the book.

Cantonese words and phrases

Pronunciation

oy as in **boy**
ai as in **fine**
i as in **see**
er as in **urn**
o as in **pot**
ow as in **now**
oe as in **oh**
or as in **law**

Countries

Hong Kong	**herng gong**	Britain	**ying gwok**
China	**chung gwok**	America	**may gwok**

Meeting someone

Good morning	joe sun
Hello/how are you?	lay hoe ma
Thank you/excuse me	m goy
Goodnight	joe tow
Goodbye	joy geen
I'm sorry	doy m joot
What is your name?	lay gew mut yeh meng?
My name is...	ngor gew...
I am English	ngor hai ying gwok yan
I am American	ngor hai may gwok yan
I am a student	ngor hai hok sarng
What time is it?	ching mun, gay dim ah?
Can you speak English?	lay sik m sik gong ying man?
I'm sorry, I can't speak Cantonese	doy m joot, ngor m sik gong gong dong wa
I don't understand	ngor m ming bat

Asking directions

Where is this place? (while pointing to the place name or map)	ching mun, leedi day fong hai been do ah?
Where is the train station?	for chair tsam hai been do ah?
Where is the bus stop?	ba-see tsam hai been doe ah?
Where is the ferry pier?	ma-tow hai been doe ah?
Train	for chair
Bus	ba-see
Ferry	do lun schoon
Taxi	dik-see
Airport	fay gay cherng
Hotel	jow deem
Hostel	loy gwun
Restaurant	charn teng
Campsite	loe ying ying day
Toilets	chee saw
Where is the toilet?	chee saw hai been doe ah?
Police	ging chat
I want to go to...	ngor serng hoy....

Shopping

1	yat
2	yee
3	saam
4	say
5	mm
6	lok
7	chat
8	bat
9	gow (to rhyme with "how")
10	sap
11	sap yat
12	sap yee
20	yee sap
30	saam sap
100	yat bat
1000	yat cheen
How much is it?	ching mun, gay daw cheen?
Do you have any...	lay yow mo...
Too expensive!	Tai gwei le!
I don't have any money	Ngor mo cheen
Can you make it cheaper?	Peng dee, dat mm dat ah?
Do you have any change?	Lay yow mo sarn zee?

Eating

I'm vegetarian	ngor sik chai
It's delicious!	ho may doe!
Bill, please!	m goy, mai dan!
Do you have an English menu?	lay yow mo ying man chan pie, m goy?
Do you serve beer?	leedo yow mo bair tsow yum ah, m goy?
Yes, we have	yow ah!
No, we don't have	mo ah!

Some signs

Entrance	入口	No smoking	請勿吸菸
Exit	出口	Danger	危險
Toilets	廁所	Customs	關稅
Gentlemen	男廁	Bus	公共汽車
Ladies	女廁	Ferry	渡船
Open	營業中	Train	火車
Closed	休業	Airport	飛機場
Arrivals	到達	Police	警察
Departures	出發	Restaurant	飯店
Closed for holidays	休假	Hotel	賓館
Out of order	出故障	Campsite	野營位置
Drinking/mineral water	礦泉水	Beach	海灘
		No swimming	禁止游泳

Note that the number two changes when asking for two of something **lerng wei** (a table for two) or stating something other than counting **lerng mun** (two dollars).

Language in Macau

Roughly 96 percent of the population of Macau is Chinese, with the remainder consisting of those of Portuguese descent, a large Philippine expat community and other ethnic minorities. Macau's two official languages are **Portuguese** and **Cantonese**, though in reality – other than the street and office signs – Portuguese is little used. A few Portuguese words are given below to help decipher signs and maps, though you won't need much Portuguese to get around; you may find the menu reader on p.204 useful, however. Although taught in schools, English is patchily spoken and understood – a few words of Cantonese will always help smooth the way.

Some useful Portuguese words

Alfandega	Customs	**Hospedaria**	Guesthouse
Avenida	Avenue	**Jardim**	Garden
Baia	Bay	**Largo**	Square
Beco	Alley	**Lavabos**	Toilets
Bilheteira	Ticket office	**Mercado**	Market
Calçada	Alley	**Museu**	Museum
Correios	Post office	**Pensão**	Guesthouse
Edificio	Building	**Ponte**	Bridge
Estrada	Road	**Pousada**	Inn/Hotel
Farmácia	Pharmacy	**Praça**	Square
Farol	Lighthouse	**Praia**	Beach
Fortaleza	Fortress	**Rua**	Street

Sé	Cathedral	Vila	Guesthouse
Travessa	Lane		

Glossary of words and terms

Lots of strange words have entered the vocabulary of Hong Kong and Macau people, Chinese and Westerners alike, and you'll come across most of them during your time here. Some are derivations of Cantonese words, adapted by successive generations of European settlers; others come from the different foreign and colonial languages represented in Hong Kong and Macau from Chinese dialects to Anglo-Indian words. For words and terms specifically to do with Chinese food, see the chapter on "Eating", p.194.

Amah Female housekeeper/servant, nowadays typically from the Philippines.
Ancestral hall Main room or hall in a temple complex where the ancestral records are kept, and where devotions take place.
Aye Ayes Illegal immigrants.
Cha chan teng A cheap indoor restaurant serving basic noodles, rice and European-inspired dishes such as toast and spaghetti.
Cheongsam Chinese dress with a high collar and long slits up the sides.
Chop A personal seal or stamp of authority; also used by the illiterate instead of signatures.
Dai pai dong Street stall or modest café selling snacks and food.
Expat Expatriate; a foreign worker living in Hong Kong.
Feng shui Literally "wind and water", the Chinese art of geomancy.
Godown Warehouse.
Gweilo Literally "ghost man"; used by the Cantonese for all Westerners, male and female (also *gweipor* "ghost woman", *gwei mui* "ghost girl" and *gwei tsa*, "ghost boy"); originally derogatory, but now in accepted use.
Hong Major company.
Junk Large flat-bottomed boat with a high deck and an overhanging stern; once distinguished by their trademark sails, all Hong Kong's junks nowadays are engine-powered.
Kaido A small ferry, or a boat used as a ferry; a sampan (also *kaito*).
Mah jong A Chinese gambling game with similar rules to Bridge, played with tiles by four people on a green-baize table.
Miu The Cantonese word for temple.
Nullah Gully, ravine, or narrow waterway.
Praya The Portuguese word for waterfront promenade (in occasional use).
Sampan Small flat-bottomed boat.
Shroff Cashier.
Tai chi Martial arts exercise.
Taipan Boss of a major company.
Tai tai Literally means "wife", but often used to describe rich ladies who lunch and shop.
Wai A walled village.

Abbreviations

AEL Airport Express.
CE Chief Executive.
EXCO Executive Council.
HKTB Hong Kong Tourism Board.
KCR Kowloon–Canton Railway.
LEGCO Legislative Council.
LR Light Rail.
MTR Mass Transit Railway.
SAR Special Administrative Region.

Small print and
Index

A Rough Guide to Rough Guides

Published in 1982, the first Rough Guide – to Greece – was a student scheme that became a publishing phenomenon. Mark Ellingham, a recent graduate in English from Bristol University, had been travelling in Greece the previous summer and couldn't find the right guidebook. With a small group of friends he wrote his own guide, combining a highly contemporary, journalistic style with a thoroughly practical approach to travellers' needs.

The immediate success of the book spawned a series that rapidly covered dozens of destinations. And, in addition to impecunious backpackers, Rough Guides soon acquired a much broader and older readership that relished the guides' wit and inquisitiveness as much as their enthusiastic, critical approach and value-for-money ethos.

These days, Rough Guides include recommendations from shoestring to luxury and cover more than 200 destinations around the globe, including almost every country in the Americas and Europe, more than half of Africa and most of Asia and Australasia. Our ever-growing team of authors and photographers is spread all over the world, particularly in Europe, the USA and Australia.

In the early 1990s, Rough Guides branched out of travel, with the publication of Rough Guides to World Music, Classical Music and the Internet. All three have become benchmark titles in their fields, spearheading the publication of a wide range of books under the Rough Guide name.

Including the travel series, Rough Guides now number more than 350 titles, covering: phrasebooks, waterproof maps, music guides from Opera to Heavy Metal, reference works as diverse as Conspiracy Theories and Shakespeare, and popular culture books from iPods to Poker. Rough Guides also produce a series of more than 120 World Music CDs in partnership with World Music Network.

Visit www.roughguides.com to see our latest publications.

Rough Guide travel images are available for commercial licensing at www.roughguidespictures.com

Rough Guide credits

Text editor: Keith Drew
Layout: Diana Jarvis, Dan May
Cartography: Rajesh Chhibber
Picture editor: Mark Thomas
Production: Katherine Owers
Proofreader: David Price
Cover design: Chloë Roberts
Photographer: Karen Trist

Editorial: **London** Kate Berens, Claire Saunders, Geoff Howard, Ruth Blackmore, Polly Thomas, Richard Lim, Clifton Wilkinson, Alison Murchie, Karoline Densley, Andy Turner, Ella O'Donnell, Edward Aves, Nikki Birrell, Helen Marsden, Alice Park, Sarah Eno, Joe Staines, Duncan Clark, Peter Buckley, Matthew Milton, Tracy Hopkins; **New York** Andrew Rosenberg, Richard Koss, Steven Horak, AnneLise Sorensen, Amy Hegarty, Hunter Slaton, April Isaacs
Design & Pictures: **London** Simon Bracken, Jj Luck, Harriet Mills; **Delhi** Madhulita Mohapatra, Umesh Aggarwal, Ajay Verma, Jessica Subramanian, Amit Verma, Ankur Guha
Production: Julia Bovis, Sophie Hewat
Cartography: **London** Maxine Repath, Ed Wright, Katie Lloyd-Jones; **Delhi** Manish Chandra, Jai Prakash Mishra, Ashutosh Bharti, Rajesh Mishra, Animesh Pathak, Jasbir Sandhu, Karobi Gogoi
Online: **New York** Jennifer Gold, Suzanne Welles, Kristin Mingrone; **Delhi** Manik Chauhan, Narender Kumar, Shekhar Jha, Rakesh Kumar, Chhandita Chakravarty
Marketing & Publicity: **London** Richard Trillo, Niki Hanmer, David Wearn, Demelza Dallow, Louise Maher; **New York** Geoff Colquitt, Megan Kennedy, Katy Ball; **Delhi** Reem Khokhar
Custom publishing and foreign rights: Philippa Hopkins
Manager India: Punita Singh
Series editor: Mark Ellingham
Reference Director: Andrew Lockett
PA to Managing and Publishing Directors: Megan McIntyre
Publishing Director: Martin Dunford
Managing Director: Kevin Fitzgerald

Publishing information

This fifth edition published April 2006 by **Rough Guides Ltd**,
80 Strand, London WC2R 0RL
345 Hudson St, 4th Floor,
New York, NY 10014, USA
14 Local Shopping Centre, Panchsheel Park,
New Delhi 110017, India
Distributed by the Penguin Group
Penguin Books Ltd,
80 Strand, London WC2R 0RL
Penguin Putnam, Inc.
375 Hudson Street, NY 10014, USA
Penguin Group (Australia)
250 Camberwell Road, Camberwell
Victoria 3124, Australia
Penguin Books Canada Ltd,
10 Alcorn Avenue, Toronto, Ontario,
Canada M4V 1E4
Penguin Group (New Zealand)
Cnr Rosedale and Airborne Roads
Albany, Auckland, New Zealand

Typeset in Bembo and Helvetica to an original design by Henry Iles.

Printed and bound in China

© Jules Brown 2006

No part of this book may be reproduced in any form without permission from the publisher except for the quotation of brief passages in reviews.

368pp includes index

A catalogue record for this book is available from the British Library

ISBN 10: 1-84353-534-3
ISBN 13: 781843535348

The publishers and authors have done their best to ensure the accuracy and currency of all the information in **The Rough Guide to Hong Kong**, however, they can accept no responsibility for any loss, injury, or inconvenience sustained by any traveller as a result of information or advice contained in the guide.

1 3 5 7 9 8 6 4 2

Help us update

We've gone to a lot of effort to ensure that the 5th edition of **The Rough Guide to Hong Kong** is accurate and up to date. However, things change – places get "discovered", opening hours are notoriously fickle, restaurants and rooms raise prices or lower standards. If you feel we've got it wrong or left something out, we'd like to know, and if you can remember the address, the price, the time, the phone number, so much the better.

We'll credit all contributions, and send a copy of the next edition (or any other Rough Guide if you prefer) for the best letters. Everyone who writes to us and isn't already a subscriber will receive a copy of our full-colour thrice-yearly newsletter. Please mark letters: "**Rough Guide Hong Kong Update**" and send to: Rough Guides, 80 Strand, London WC2R 0RL, or Rough Guides, 4th Floor, 345 Hudson St, New York, NY 10014. Or send an email to **mail@roughguides.com**

Have your questions answered and tell others about your trip at **www.roughguides.atinfopop.com**

Acknowledgements

David Leffman would like to thank: Narrell, Deng "CS" Changcheng, Kong Kuo, Wu Ming, Miranda Ma and Jakka.

Readers' letters

Thanks to all the readers who have taken the time to write in with comments and suggestions (and apologies if we've inadvertently omitted or misspelt anyone's name):

Stephen Anderson, Mandi Brooker, Brian Brooks, Matthew Dyke, Paul Goodwin, O Boen Ho & Esther Putman, Michael Kelly, Charles Stuart, K. Tan, Mike Tunstall, Allan Tyrer, Jane Watkins, Ross Williams, Jacqueline Wood, Colleen Yuen.

Photo credits

All photos © Rough Guides except the following:

Cover
Front picture: Big Buddha © Getty
Back picture: Kowloon © Getty

Introduction
Tai Long Wan beach © Robert Harding Picture Library/Alamy

Things not to miss
02 Rock climber © Alamy
03 Buddha statues © Doug Houghton/Alamy
08 Pink Dolphin © Hong Kong Dolphinwatch Limited
10 Cantonese opera performer © A. Parada/Alamy
13 Sharp Peak, Sai Kung Country Park © Ron Yue/Alamy
14 Wong Tai Sin Temple, Kowloon © Jon Bower
15 São Paulo, Macau © Ian Masterton/Alamy
23 Horseracing, Happy Valley © Sean David Baylis/Alamy

Architecture colour section
Traditional Hong Kong tenement © Ian Masterton/Alamy

Black and white photos
p.128 Hong Kong suburbs © Pat Behnke/Alamy
p.148 Sai Kung Town © JG Photography/Alamy
p.240 Dragon Boat race, Aberdeen Harbour © Jon Arnold Images/Alamy
p.259 Bruce Lee in *Fist of Fury* © Bettman/Corbis

Index

Map entries are in colour.

I

J

K

L

M

T

U

V

W

Y

Z

Map symbols

maps are listed in the full index using coloured text

Major road
Minor road
Tunnel
Path
Railway
Ferry route
River
Special admin. region boundary
Tram route
Point of interest
Mountain peak
Rocks
Caves
Gardens
Statue
Internet
Monastery
Temple
Mountain refuge
Museum
Bridge
MTR station

Mosque
Synagogue
Hotel
Restaurant
Airport
Bus/taxi stop
Immigration post
Church (regional map)
Cable car
Tourist information
Airbus stop
Post office
Stadium
Building
Market
Church (town map)
Beach
Cemetery
Park
Reclaimed land
Marshland

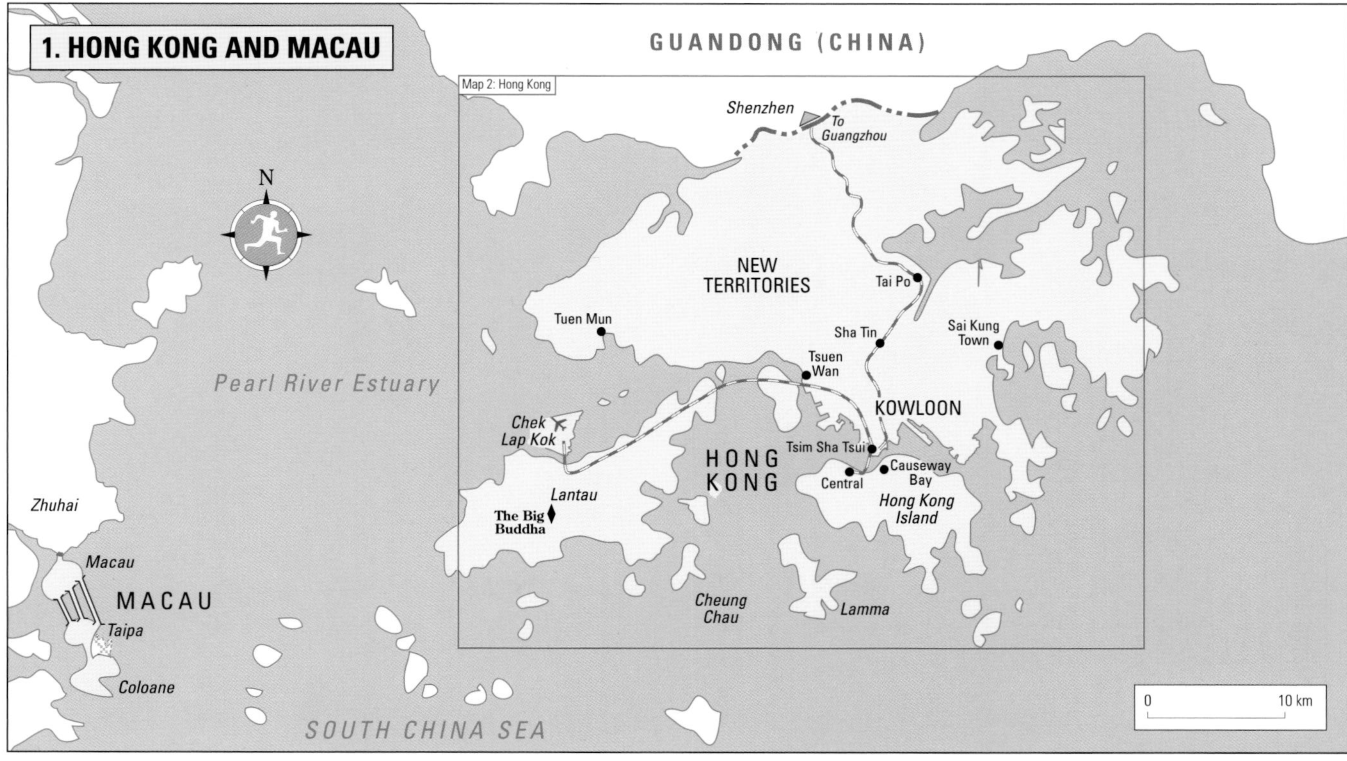
1. HONG KONG AND MACAU
GUANDONG (CHINA)
Map 2: Hong Kong
Shenzhen
To Guangzhou
N
NEW TERRITORIES
Tai Po
Tuen Mun
Sha Tin
Sai Kung Town
Tsuen Wan
Pearl River Estuary
KOWLOON
Chek Lap Kok
Tsim Sha Tsui
HONG KONG
Causeway Bay
Central
Lantau
Hong Kong Island
The Big Buddha
Zhuhai
Macau
MACAU
Cheung Chau
Lamma
Taipa
Coloane
0
10 km
SOUTH CHINA SEA

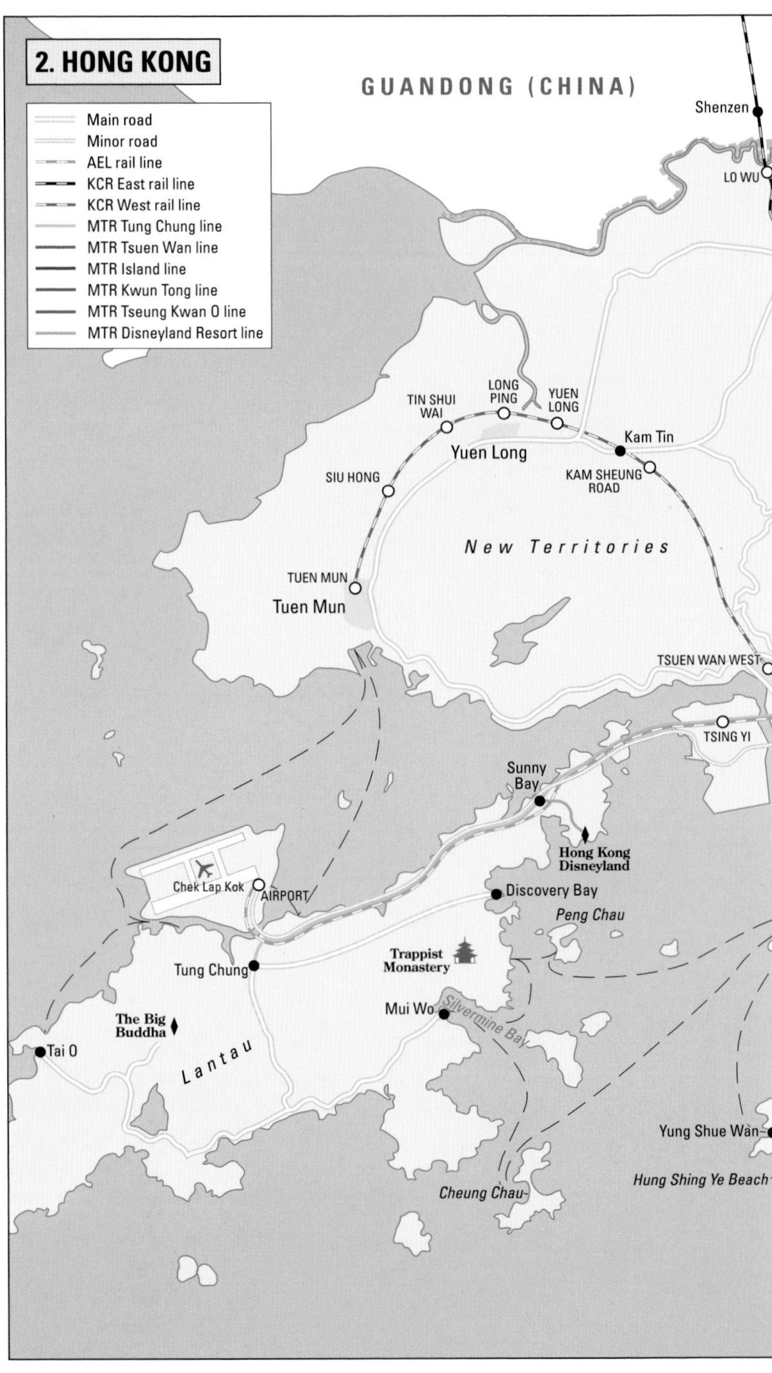
2. HONG KONG
Main road
Minor road
AEL rail line
KCR East rail line
KCR West rail line
MTR Tung Chung line
MTR Tsuen Wan line
MTR Island line
MTR Kwun Tong line
MTR Tseung Kwan O line
MTR Disneyland Resort line
GUANDONG (CHINA)
Shenzen
LO WU
LONG PING
TIN SHUI WAI
YUEN LONG
Kam Tin
Yuen Long
SIU HONG
KAM SHEUNG ROAD
New Territories
TUEN MUN
Tuen Mun
TSUEN WAN WEST
TSING YI
Sunny Bay
Hong Kong Disneyland
Chek Lap Kok
AIRPORT
Discovery Bay
Peng Chau
Trappist Monastery
Tung Chung
Mui Wo
Silvermine Bay
The Big Buddha
Tai O
Lantau
Yung Shue Wan
Hung Shing Ye Beach
Cheung Chau

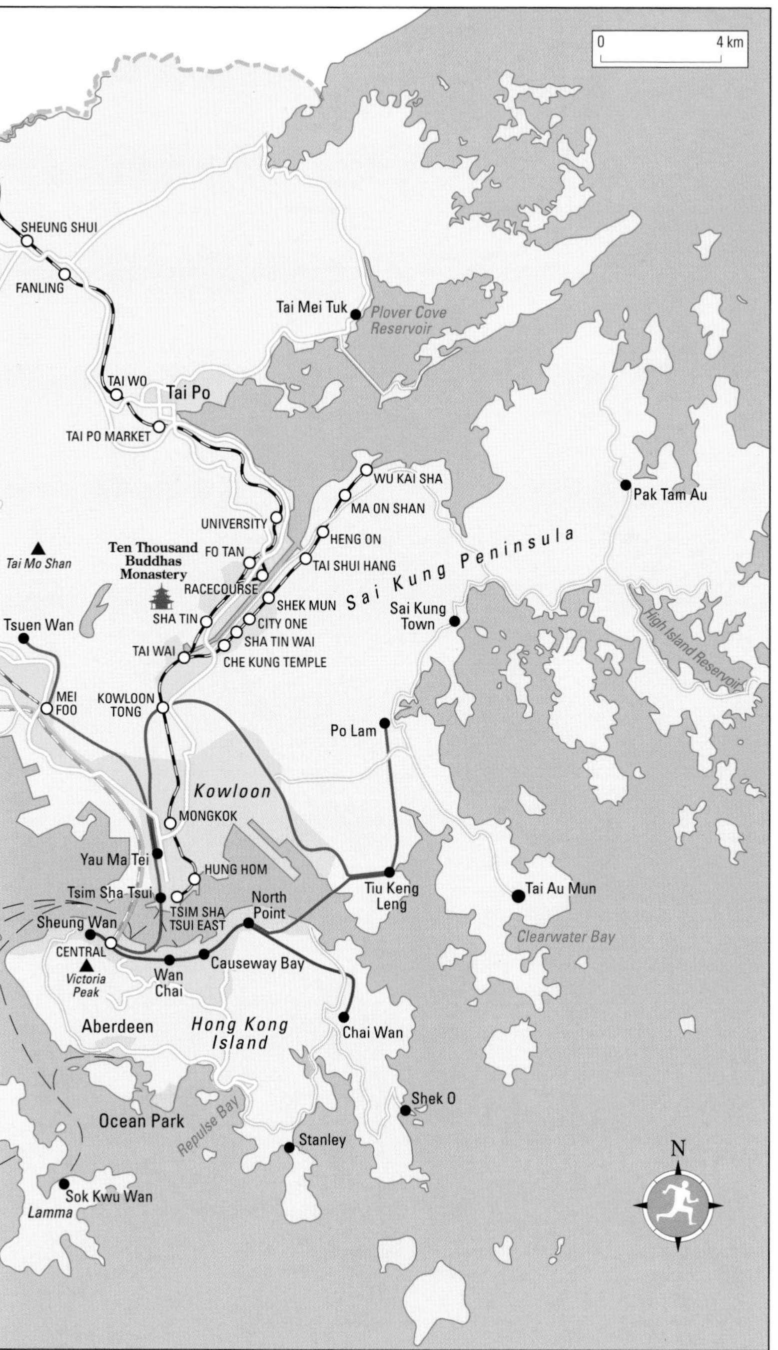

0
4 km
SHEUNG SHUI
FANLING
Tai Mei Tuk
Plover Cove Reservoir
TAI WO
Tai Po
TAI PO MARKET
WU KAI SHA
MA ON SHAN
Pak Tam Au
UNIVERSITY
HENG ON
Ten Thousand Buddhas Monastery
FO TAN
TAI SHUI HANG
Sai Kung Peninsula
Tai Mo Shan
RACECOURSE
SHEK MUN
Sai Kung Town
SHA TIN
CITY ONE
High Island Reservoir
Tsuen Wan
SHA TIN WAI
TAI WAI
CHE KUNG TEMPLE
MEI FOO
KOWLOON TONG
Po Lam
Kowloon
MONGKOK
Yau Ma Tei
HUNG HOM
Tiu Keng Leng
Tai Au Mun
Tsim Sha Tsui
TSIM SHA TSUI EAST
North Point
Sheung Wan
CENTRAL
Clearwater Bay
Causeway Bay
Victoria Peak
Wan Chai
Aberdeen
Hong Kong Island
Chai Wan
Shek O
Ocean Park
Repulse Bay
Stanley
N
Sok Kwu Wan
Lamma

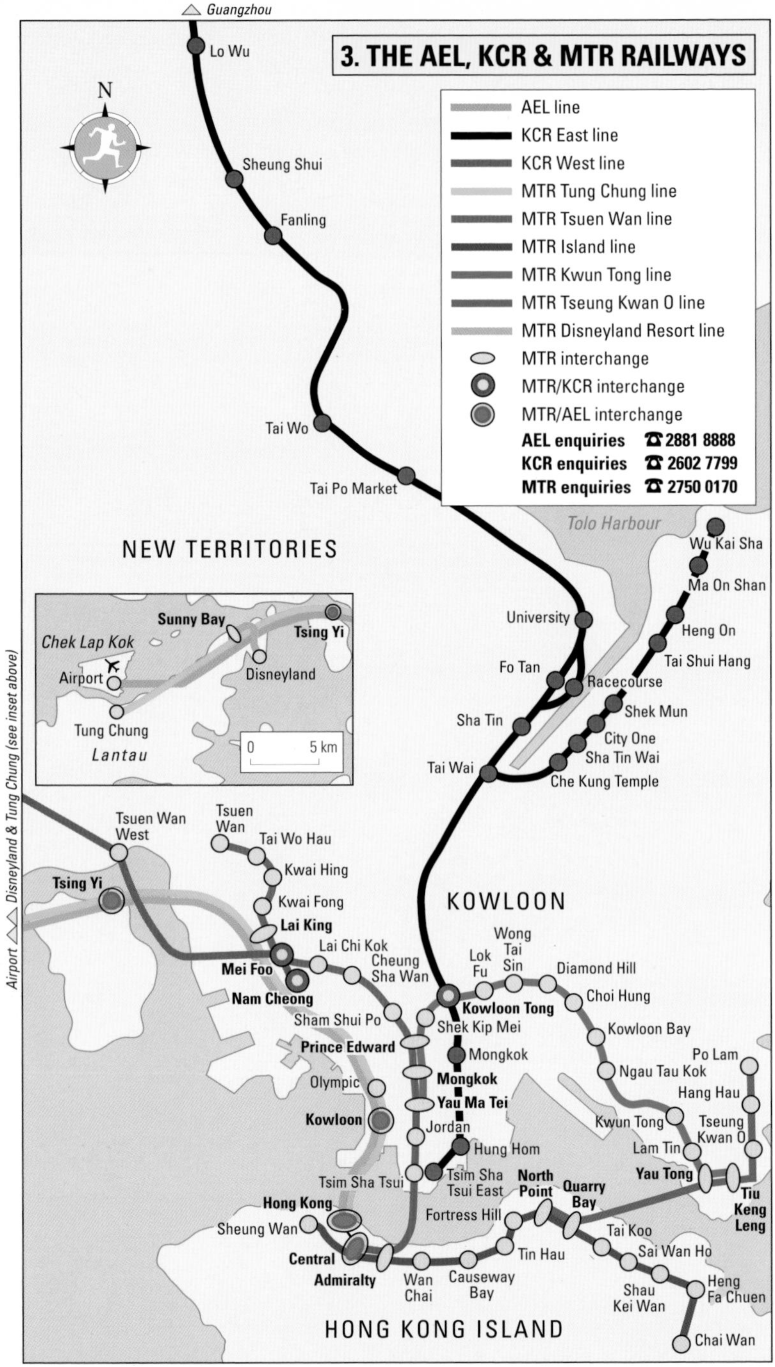

Guangzhou

3. THE AEL, KCR & MTR RAILWAYS

N

- AEL line
- KCR East line
- KCR West line
- MTR Tung Chung line
- MTR Tsuen Wan line
- MTR Island line
- MTR Kwun Tong line
- MTR Tseung Kwan O line
- MTR Disneyland Resort line
- MTR interchange
- MTR/KCR interchange
- MTR/AEL interchange

AEL enquiries ☎ 2881 8888
KCR enquiries ☎ 2602 7799
MTR enquiries ☎ 2750 0170

Lo Wu
Sheung Shui
Fanling
Tai Wo
Tai Po Market
Tolo Harbour
NEW TERRITORIES
Wu Kai Sha
Ma On Shan
University
Heng On
Tai Shui Hang
Fo Tan
Racecourse
Shek Mun
Sha Tin
City One
Sha Tin Wai
Tai Wai
Che Kung Temple

Sunny Bay
Tsing Yi
Chek Lap Kok
Airport
Disneyland
Tung Chung
Lantau
0 5 km

Airport Disneyland & Tung Chung (see inset above)

Tsuen Wan West
Tsuen Wan
Tai Wo Hau
Kwai Hing
Tsing Yi
Kwai Fong
KOWLOON
Lai King
Wong Tai Sin
Lai Chi Kok
Lok Fu
Diamond Hill
Mei Foo
Cheung Sha Wan
Nam Cheong
Kowloon Tong
Choi Hung
Sham Shui Po
Shek Kip Mei
Kowloon Bay
Prince Edward
Mongkok
Po Lam
Ngau Tau Kok
Olympic
Mongkok
Hang Hau
Yau Ma Tei
Kowloon
Kwun Tong
Tseung Kwan O
Jordan
Hung Hom
Lam Tin
Tsim Sha Tsui
Tsim Sha Tsui East
North Point
Quarry Bay
Yau Tong
Tiu Keng Leng
Hong Kong
Fortress Hill
Sheung Wan
Tai Koo
Tin Hau
Sai Wan Ho
Central
Admiralty
Wan Chai
Causeway Bay
Shau Kei Wan
Heng Fa Chuen
HONG KONG ISLAND
Chai Wan

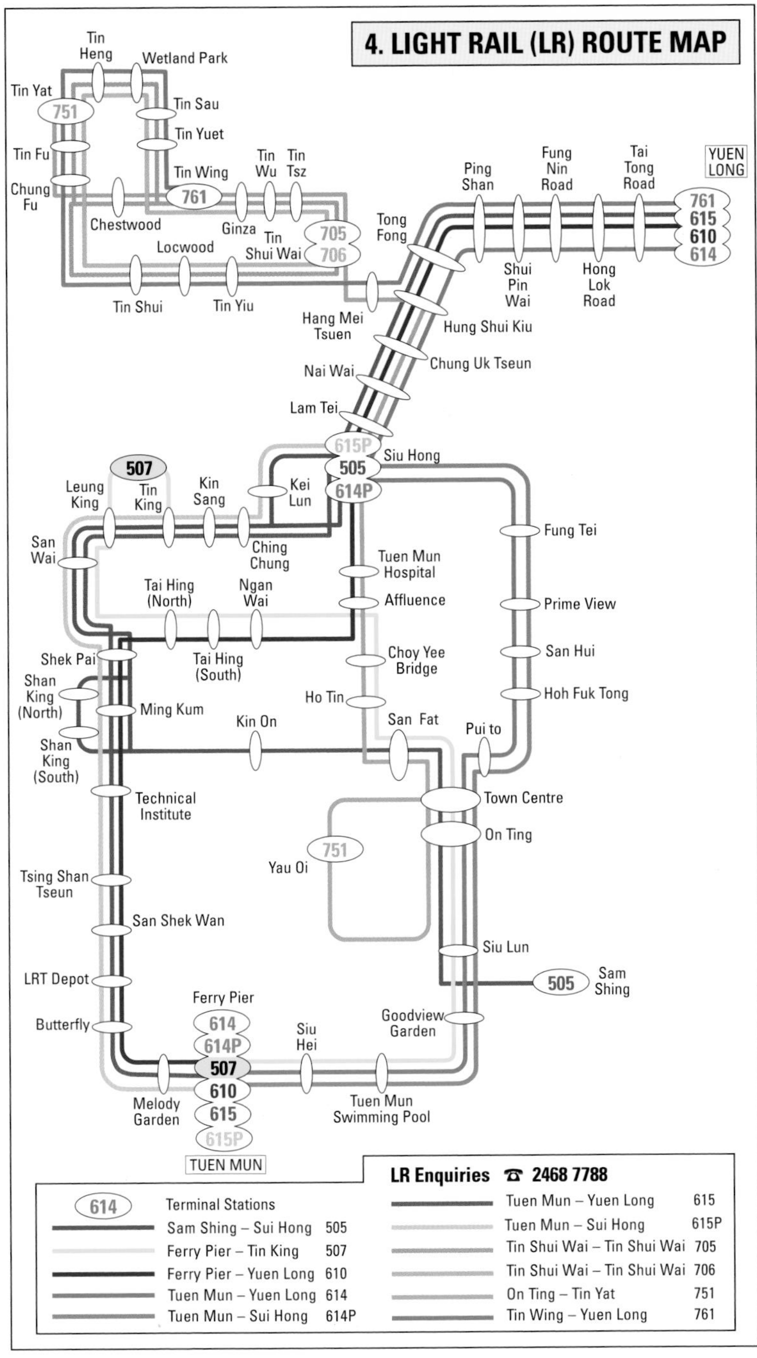

4. LIGHT RAIL (LR) ROUTE MAP
Tin Heng
Wetland Park
Tin Yat
751
Tin Sau
Tin Yuet
Tin Fu
Tin Wing
761
Tin Wu
Tin Tsz
Chung Fu
Chestwood
Ginza
Tin Shui Wai
705
706
Locwood
Tin Shui
Tin Yiu
Tong Fong
Ping Shan
Fung Nin Road
Tai Tong Road
YUEN LONG
761
615
610
614
Shui Pin Wai
Hong Lok Road
Hang Mei Tsuen
Hung Shui Kiu
Chung Uk Tseun
Nai Wai
Lam Tei
615P
505
614P
Siu Hong
507
Leung King
Tin King
Kin Sang
Kei Lun
San Wai
Ching Chung
Fung Tei
Tuen Mun Hospital
Affluence
Tai Hing (North)
Ngan Wai
Prime View
Shek Pai
Tai Hing (South)
Choy Yee Bridge
San Hui
Shan King (North)
Ming Kum
Ho Tin
Hoh Fuk Tong
Kin On
San Fat
Pui to
Shan King (South)
Technical Institute
Town Centre
On Ting
751
Yau Oi
Tsing Shan Tseun
San Shek Wan
Siu Lun
LRT Depot
505
Sam Shing
Ferry Pier
Butterfly
614
614P
507
610
615
615P
Siu Hei
Goodview Garden
Melody Garden
Tuen Mun Swimming Pool
TUEN MUN
LR Enquiries ☎ 2468 7788
614 Terminal Stations
Sam Shing – Sui Hong 505
Ferry Pier – Tin King 507
Ferry Pier – Yuen Long 610
Tuen Mun – Yuen Long 614
Tuen Mun – Sui Hong 614P
Tuen Mun – Yuen Long 615
Tuen Mun – Sui Hong 615P
Tin Shui Wai – Tin Shui Wai 705
Tin Shui Wai – Tin Shui Wai 706
On Ting – Tin Yat 751
Tin Wing – Yuen Long 761

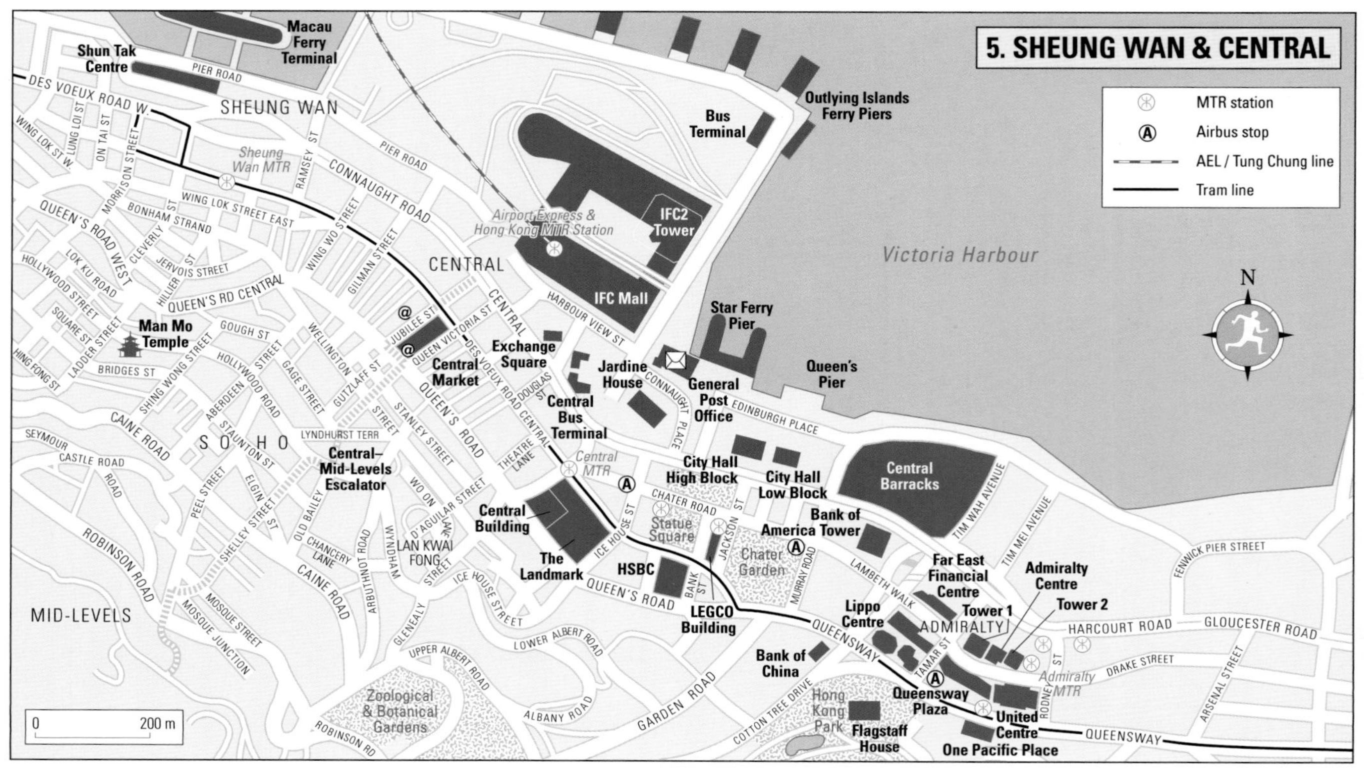

5. SHEUNG WAN & CENTRAL
MTR station
Airbus stop
AEL / Tung Chung line
Tram line
N
Victoria Harbour
Macau Ferry Terminal
Shun Tak Centre
PIER ROAD
DES VOEUX ROAD W.
SHEUNG WAN
Sheung Wan MTR
Outlying Islands Ferry Piers
Bus Terminal
Airport Express & Hong Kong MTR Station
IFC2 Tower
IFC Mall
Star Ferry Pier
Queen's Pier
General Post Office
Jardine House
Exchange Square
Central Market
Central Bus Terminal
Central MTR
CENTRAL
City Hall High Block
City Hall Low Block
Central Barracks
Bank of America Tower
Statue Square
Chater Garden
Central Building
The Landmark
HSBC
LEGCO Building
Far East Financial Centre
Admiralty Centre
Tower 1
Tower 2
ADMIRALTY
Admiralty MTR
Lippo Centre
Bank of China
Queensway Plaza
United Centre
One Pacific Place
Flagstaff House
Hong Kong Park
Zoological & Botanical Gardens
Man Mo Temple
SOHO
Central–Mid-Levels Escalator
LAN KWAI FONG
MID-LEVELS
WING LOK ST W.
LUNG LOI ST
ON TAI ST
MORRISON STREET
WING LOK STREET EAST
BONHAM STRAND
QUEEN'S ROAD WEST
CLEVERLY ST
JERVOIS STREET
HILLIER ST
QUEEN'S RD CENTRAL
LOK KU ROAD
HOLLYWOOD STREET
SQUARE ST
LADDER STREET
HING FONG ST
BRIDGES ST
SHING WONG STREET
GOUGH ST
ABERDEEN STREET
HOLLYWOOD ROAD
GAGE STREET
WELLINGTON STREET
GUTZLAFF ST
JUBILEE ST
QUEEN VICTORIA ST
DES VOEUX ROAD CENTRAL
QUEEN'S ROAD
STANLEY STREET
LYNDHURST TERR
CAINE ROAD
SEYMOUR
CASTLE ROAD
STAUNTON ST
ELGIN ST
PEEL STREET
SHELLEY STREET
OLD BAILEY
CHANCERY LANE
ARBUTHNOT ROAD
WYNDHAM
WO ON LANE
D'AGUILAR STREET
THEATRE LANE
ROBINSON ROAD
MOSQUE STREET
MOSQUE JUNCTION
GLENEALY
UPPER ALBERT ROAD
LOWER ALBERT ROAD
ICE HOUSE STREET
ICE HOUSE ST
ALBANY ROAD
GARDEN ROAD
ROBINSON RD
COTTON TREE DRIVE
RAMSEY ST
CONNAUGHT ROAD
WING WO STREET
GILMAN STREET
CENTRAL
HARBOUR VIEW ST
DOUGLAS ST
CONNAUGHT PLACE
EDINBURGH PLACE
CHATER ROAD
JACKSON ST
BANK ST
MURRAY ROAD
LAMBETH WALK
TIM WAH AVENUE
TIM MEI AVENUE
FENWICK PIER STREET
HARCOURT ROAD
GLOUCESTER ROAD
DRAKE STREET
ARSENAL STREET
TAMAR ST
RODNEY ST
QUEENSWAY
0
200 m

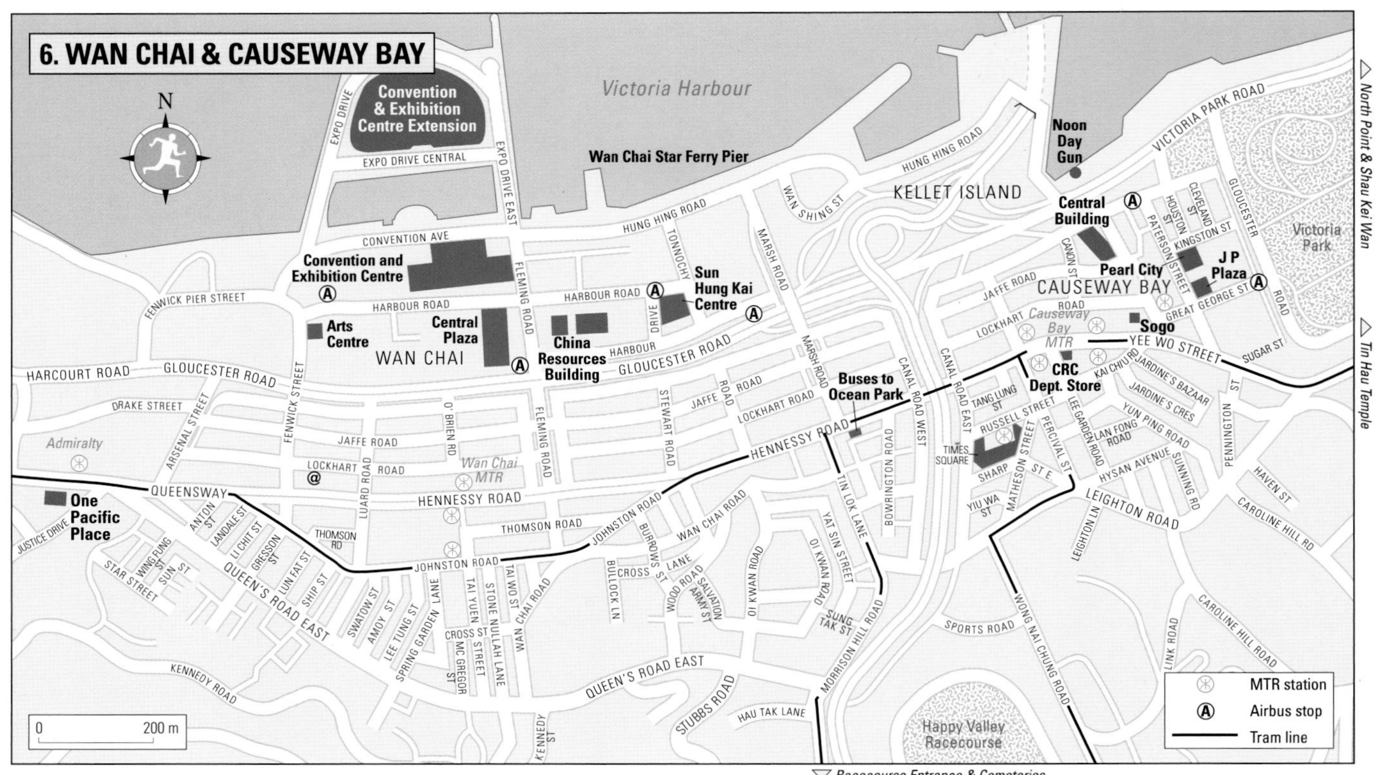
6. WAN CHAI & CAUSEWAY BAY
N
North Point & Shau Kei Wan
Tin Hau Temple
Racecourse Entrance & Cemeteries
Victoria Harbour
Convention & Exhibition Centre Extension
Wan Chai Star Ferry Pier
Noon Day Gun
KELLET ISLAND
Central Building
Pearl City
J P Plaza
Victoria Park
CAUSEWAY BAY
Causeway Bay MTR
Sogo
CRC Dept. Store
Times Square
Convention and Exhibition Centre
Sun Hung Kai Centre
Central Plaza
China Resources Building
Arts Centre
WAN CHAI
Wan Chai MTR
Buses to Ocean Park
Admiralty
One Pacific Place
Happy Valley Racecourse
EXPO DRIVE
EXPO DRIVE CENTRAL
EXPO DRIVE EAST
CONVENTION AVE
HUNG HING ROAD
FENWICK PIER STREET
HARBOUR ROAD
HARBOUR DRIVE
FLEMING ROAD
TONNOCHY
MARSH ROAD
WAN SHING ST
VICTORIA PARK ROAD
GLOUCESTER ROAD
HOUSTON ST
CLEVELAND ST
KINGSTON ST
PATERSON STREET
CANON ST
GREAT GEORGE ST
SUGAR ST
JAFFE ROAD
LOCKHART ROAD
YEE WO STREET
KAI CHIU RD
JARDINE'S BAZAAR
JARDINE'S CRES
YUN PING ROAD
LAN FONG ROAD
LEE GARDEN ROAD
HYSAN AVENUE
SUNNING RD
PENNINGTON ST
HAVEN ST
CAROLINE HILL RD
CAROLINE HILL ROAD
LINK ROAD
LEIGHTON ROAD
LEIGHTON LN
WONG NAI CHUNG ROAD
SPORTS ROAD
CANAL ROAD EAST
CANAL ROAD WEST
TANG LUNG ST
RUSSELL STREET
PERCIVAL ST
SHARP ST E
MATHESON STREET
YIU WA ST
BOWRINGTON ROAD
TIN LOK LANE
HENNESSY ROAD
YAT SIN STREET
OI KWAN ROAD
SUNG TAK ST
MORRISON HILL ROAD
HAU TAK LANE
STUBBS ROAD
QUEEN'S ROAD EAST
WAN CHAI ROAD
SALVATION ARMY ST
WOOD ROAD
CROSS LANE
BURROWS ST
BULLOCK LN
JOHNSTON ROAD
THOMSON ROAD
STEWART ROAD
KENNEDY ST
TAI WO ST
STONE NULLAH LANE
TAI YUEN STREET
CROSS ST
MC GREGOR ST
SPRING GARDEN LANE
LEE TUNG ST
AMOY ST
SWATOW ST
SHIP ST
LUN FAT ST
GRESSON ST
LI CHIT ST
LANDALE ST
ANTON ST
SUN ST
WING FUNG ST
STAR STREET
KENNEDY ROAD
QUEENSWAY
JUSTICE DRIVE
HARCOURT ROAD
DRAKE STREET
ARSENAL STREET
FENWICK STREET
O' BRIEN RD
LUARD ROAD
THOMSON RD
MTR station
Airbus stop
Tram line
0
200 m

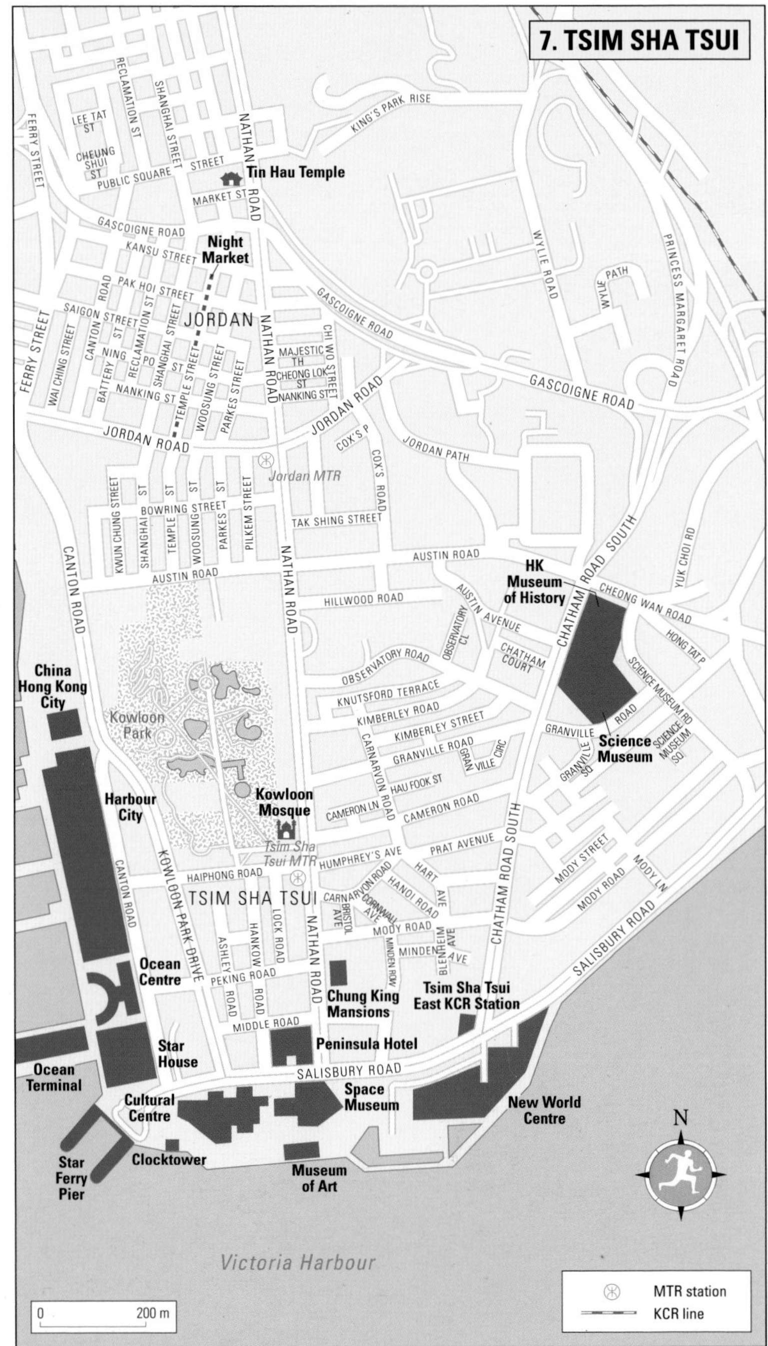
7. TSIM SHA TSUI
Tin Hau Temple
Night Market
JORDAN
Jordan MTR
HK Museum of History
Science Museum
Kowloon Park
Kowloon Mosque
Tsim Sha Tsui MTR
China Hong Kong City
Harbour City
TSIM SHA TSUI
Ocean Centre
Chung King Mansions
Tsim Sha Tsui East KCR Station
Star House
Peninsula Hotel
Ocean Terminal
Cultural Centre
Space Museum
New World Centre
Star Ferry Pier
Clocktower
Museum of Art
Victoria Harbour
Hung Hom KCR Station
Tsim ShaTsui East Ferry Pier
N
MTR station
KCR line
0
200 m
NATHAN ROAD
CANTON ROAD
SALISBURY ROAD
CHATHAM ROAD SOUTH
GASCOIGNE ROAD
JORDAN ROAD
AUSTIN ROAD
KOWLOON PARK DRIVE
HAIPHONG ROAD
PEKING ROAD
MIDDLE ROAD
FERRY STREET
KING'S PARK RISE
WYLIE ROAD
PRINCESS MARGARET ROAD
CHEONG WAN ROAD
GRANVILLE ROAD
MODY ROAD
CAMERON ROAD